Historical and Genealogical Miscellany

You are holding a reproduction of an original work that is in the public domain in the United States of America, and possibly other countries. You may freely copy and distribute this work as no entity (individual or corporate) has a copyright on the body of the work. This book may contain prior copyright references, and library stamps (as most of these works were scanned from library copies). These have been scanned and retained as part of the historical artifact.

This book may have occasional imperfections such as missing or blurred pages, poor pictures, errant marks, etc. that were either part of the original artifact, or were introduced by the scanning process. We believe this work is culturally important, and despite the imperfections, have elected to bring it back into print as part of our continuing commitment to the preservation of printed works worldwide. We appreciate your understanding of the imperfections in the preservation process, and hope you enjoy this valuable book.

HISTORICAL

AND

GENEALOGICAL MISCELLANY

Early Settlers of New Jersey and their Descendants

JOHN E. STILLWELL, M.D.

VOL. IV

NEW YORK
1916

ABBREVIATIONS

Account, Accounting, acct.
Acknowledged, Acknowledgment, ackn.
Adjuster, adjust.
Administered, Administration, admn.
Administrator, Administratrix, admr , admrx.
Affidavit, affi
Affirmation, Affirmed, affirm
Against, agnst
Agreement, agrmt
Allegiance, alleg
Appointed, Appointment, appnt
Application, appli
Appraised, Appraiser, appr.
Arbitration, Arbitrator, arb
Assembly, assemb
Assessment, Assessor, assess.
Assistant, asst
Attestation, attest.
Attorney, atty
Authority, author.

Baptised, Baptism, bp
Biographical, Biography, biog
Births, Born, b
Bondsman, bondsm
Boundary, bndry
Brother, bro
Brother-in-law, bro law
Buried, bur
Buyer, buy

Captain, capt
Census, cen
Certificate, Certified, cert.
Children, Children's chn , chns
Church, ch
Clerk, clk.
Collector, coll.
Commission, Commissioned, comm.
Commissioner, commr.
Committee, comtee.
Company, co
Complainant, compt
Constable, const.
Conveyance, Conveyancer, convey.
Corrected, Correction, cor.
County, co.
Creditor, cred.

Daughter, dau
Daughter-in-law,dau. law
Debtor, detr
Deceased, decd
Declaration, declr
Defendant, deft
Deposes, Deposition, depn.
Deputy, depy.
Died, d
Divided, Division, div.

Emigrant, Emigrate, emig
Employer, employ.
Epitaph, epi
Esquire, esq
Estate, est.
Exchanged, exch
Executor, Executorship, Executrix, exr., exrx.

Father, fa
Father-in-law, fa law.

Genealogist, Genealogy, geneal.
General, gen , genl.
Gentleman, gent
God-mother, godmo.
Government, Governor, gov.
Grand-daughter, granddau.
Grandfather, grandfa
Grandmother, grandmo
Grandson, grands
Great, g
Guardian, Guardianship, guard.

History, Historian, hist.
Husband, husb.

Indictment, indict
Informant, inform
Interest, int
Intestate, intest.
Inventory, invt.

Judgment, judgmt.
Juror, jur.
Justice, just

Legacy, Legatee, leg.
Lieutenant, lieut.

ABBREVIATIONS

Magistrate, magist.
Marriage, Married, md
Marriage License, m.l
Master, mast
Member, memb.
Mentioned, ment
Merchant, mer.
Mortgage, Mortgagee, Mortgagor, mort.
Messenger, mess
Mother, mo
Mother-in-law, mo law

Nephew, neph

Obituary, obit.
Origin, Original, orig
Overseer, ovsr.

Paid, pd
Patent, Patentee, pat
Petition, Petitioner, pet.
Plaintiff, pltf.
Portrait, Portraits, port , ports
President, pres
Prisoner, prison.
Proprietor, Propriety, propri
Proved, pr
Purchase, Purchased, Purchaser, prchs.

Qualified, Qualify, qual

Receipt, recpt.
Received, Receiver, recd
Record, Recorded, Recorder, rec
Reference, ref
Regiment, reg
Register, regist.
Removal, remov.

Request, req
Residence, res.
Resignation, Resigned, resgn

Secretary, secry.
Seller, sell
Servant, servt
Settled, Settlement, Settler, set.
Signature, Signed, sig
Sheriff, shrf
Sine prole (without issue), s p.
Sister, sis
Sister-in-law, sis.-law.
Society, soc
Soldier, sol.
Son, s
Son-in-law, s law
Step-father, step-fa
Step-mother, step-mo.
Step-son, step-s
Surrogate, surro.
Survey, Surveyor, survey

Testator, Testatrix, testa
Testimony, test.
Tombstone, tombs
Town, twn
Treasurer, treas
Trustee, trust

Unmarried, unmd

Vestryman, vestrym.

Widow, Widower, wid , widr.
Wife, w.
Witness, wit.

Yeoman, yeom

CONTENTS

	PAGES
Morford of Monmouth County	1- 13
Morris of Monmouth County	14- 70
Mott of New York and New Jersey	71-110c
Mount of Monmouth County	111-146
Murphy of Monmouth County	147-150
Ogborne of Monmouth County (See Addendum)	151-169
Potter of Monmouth County	170-175
Salter of Monmouth County	176-213
Salter of New Hampshire	213-218
Seabrook of Monmouth County	219-260
Seabrook of South Carolina	260-264
Seabrook of Edisto Island	264-276
Seabrook of Maryland	276-277
Shepherd of Monmouth County	278-288
Spicer of New York and New Jersey	289-294
Stout of Monmouth County	295-360
Line of John Stout	306-317
Line of Richard Stout	317-324
Probable Descendants of Richard Stout, 3	324-325
Line of Mary Stout (Bowne)	325-326
Line of James Stout	326-328
Line of Alice Stout (Throckmorton)	328-329
Line of Peter Stout	329-330
Line of Sarah Stout (Pike)	330-331
Line of Jonathan Stout	331-345
Line of Benjamin Stout	345-347
Line of David Stout	347-360
Miscellaneous Items	360-374
Addenda and Errata	375-383

MORFORD

OF

MONMOUTH COUNTY

1 THOMAS MORFORD and JOHN MORFORD, 2, came from England, and settled at Colt's Neck, Middletown, Monmouth County, N J   Earlier or later, they were seated at the bridge crossing, between Red Bank and Middletown, on the present farm of the Coopers, in Middletown township * Here, in the orchard, is a plowed-over graveyard, and adjacent, a stone wall, against which are three tombstones, lifted from their original positions, one leaning and two lying on the ground, representing all that remains of the original Morford Burying-ground   The tombstones of Thomas Morford, 3, and Jarret Morford, 9, and an indecipherable one, alone remain

1670 Thomas Morfort's lands are referred to in Thomas Herbert's Proprietary deed
1672, Sept 4 He recorded his cattle-mark.
1676 He had one hundred and twenty acres granted to him
1677 He received one hundred and thirteen acres.
1677 Thomas Morford was of Shoal Harbor, Monmouth County, N J
1695, March 27 Thomas Morford was a Grand Juror

1695, Dec 5 Thomas Morford made his will, which was proved Mch 24, 1695, i e , 1696, between which dates he died   From his will we learn that he had a wife, Susannah, (probably Susannah Leonard), whom he appointed his sole executrix, and the following sons and daughters

    Thomas Morford, not twenty-one years of age
    John Morford, not twenty-one years of age.
    Catharine Morford, not eighteen years of age
    Sarah Morford, not eighteen years of age
    Susannah Morford, not yet eighteen years of age
    Johanna Morford, not yet eighteen years of age

Issue

3 Thomas Morford
4 John Morford

---

*In 1687, the road was laid out and ran "Beginning at Thomas Morford's, on Navesink River, going along as the way now goes to the Middletown road by John Stout's Bridge "

    Book A B C of Deeds, Freehold, N J

5 Catharine Morford
6 Sarah Morford
7 Susannah Morford
8 Johanna Morford, baptized Nov 17, 1734

2 JOHN MORFORD. His relation to Thomas Morford, 1, I have not seen stated, but I presume that they were brothers

1676 He was granted one hundred and twenty acres of land.

1676, May 4 He recorded his earmark

1677, June 26 He was granted one hundred and thirty acres of land

1695-6 He was a Grand Juror, in Monmouth County

1699, Aug 31 He was one of the Jurors who met the coroner "upon Sandy Hook ye day above said, and went and went to ye body of a deadman, which we judged had died aboard a ship and shoved overboard"

3 THOMAS MORFORD, son of Thomas Morford, 1, died, Apr. 12, 1750, aged 58 years, 2 months and 10 days, hence born 1692 He married, first, Mary, daughter of Jarrat and Lydia Wall. She was single, in 1711, the date of her father's will, but must shortly have married, as her eldest son was Jarrat Morford, born 1714

"1713-14 coming" Thomas Morford, yeoman, deeded land to John Wilson, Gent.

1736 Thomas Morford, of Shrewsbury, Esq, and Hannah, his wife, sold land to John French, of Shrewsbury Thomas Stillwell was a witness

1747, May 20 Will of Thomas Morford, yeoman, of Middletown, proved June 2, 1750, mentioned
Wife, Hannah
Son, John, received his Shoal Harbor lands
Son, Jarrat, received land
Son, Thomas, received £150
Daughter Mary, of age
Daughter, Sarah ⎫
Daughter, Hannah ⎬ not yet eighteen years of age
Daughter, Catharine ⎭
Son, Joseph

Issue

9 Jarrat Morford born May 28, 1714; died, June 1, 1761, aged 46 years, 7 months and 3 days
10 John Morford

Thomas Morford married, second, Sarah, daughter of Jeremiah Stillwell, Esq, of Middletown

Issue

11 Thomas Morford
12 Mary Morford, she was of age, in 1747, as per her father's will; hence born prior to 1726

Thomas Morford married, third, Hannah, daughter of Jonathan Burdge. She was baptized, at Christ Church, Shrewsbury, N J, 10 br, 25, 1738

Issue

13 Sarah Morford
14 Catharine Morford

15 Hannah Morford, baptized, at Christ Church, Shrewsbury, N. J., Nov 17, 1734
16 Joseph Morford, born 1738.

5 CATHARINE MORFORD, daughter of Thomas Morford, 1, married, first, Edward Taylor, son of Edward Taylor, The Immigrant, second, probably John Ashton

9 JARRAT MORFORD, son of Thomas Morford, 3, was born May 28, 1714, died, June 1, 1761, aged 46 years, 7 months and 3 days He married Rebecca daughter of Edward Taylor She was baptized, June 18 1748, in the river, near her dwelling

1745 He resided in Shrewsbury, and as Jarrat Morford, was an Overseer

1746 As Gerard Morford, he was an Overseer. Town Poor Book, Shrewsbury, N J

1760, Feb "Fifteenth" Will of Jarrett Morford, of the Township of Shrewfbury, Monmouth County, yeoman, proved, Sept 5, 1761, by witness, George Taylor, and Nov 7, 1761, by witness, William Price, mentioned

"well beloved wife, Rebeckah Morford", real and personal estate so long as she remains a widow If she marries, the choice of beds, and furniture belonging thereto, also a riding horse and new saddle, 2 cows and calves, negro wench *beas*, and 10 sheep, and £25

If his wife marries or dies, his plantation is to be equally given to "my two sons, Thomas, haveing the upper part & Gorge haveing the lower part," "wheare I now leaf "

Son, Thomas, also received "£50 more than *Gorge*, to make up the buildings equal betwixt them "
Executors "well beloued wif, Rebeckah Morford, and well beloued brother, Job Throck Morton "
Witnesses George Taylor, William Price and Nathaniel Taylor
He signed his name in full to the will

1761, Sept 5 Qualification of executors, Rebeckah Morford and Job Throckmorton

1761, July 3 Inventory of Jarratt Morford, of Shrewfbury, County of Monmouth, yeoman, taken by Rebeckah Morford, executrix, and Job Throckmorton, executor, of Freehold, and appraised by Mr Samuel Scott and Mr Martin Vandyke, [sig Martain Vandyk], both of the township of Shrewfbury Amount £495-14-9

Issue

17 Thomas Morford, born 10 mo , 10, 1743, died 5 mo , 4, 1818
18 George Taylor Morford, baptized, July 28, 1765, an adult, Christ Church, Shrewsbury.

10 JOHN MORFORD, son of Thomas Morford, 3, died in 1764 He married Margaret, daughter of Richard Morris, of the twenty children family, prior to 8 mo , 10, 1739

1759 John Morford was taxed, in Shrewsbury, for £1-8-5½

1764, Mch 14 Margaret, widow of John Morford, late of Shrewsbury, N J , renounced administration upon his estate, in favor of her son, Jarrat Morford, and David Knott On the 16th, they qualified, with Philip Cooper, the bond amounting to £600 They were all residents of Shrewsbury Margaret, widow of John Morford, made her mark

1764, May 1 Inventory of John Morford, of the Township of Shrewsbury, Taken by David Knott and Jarratt Morford, administrators, and appraised by John Williams, Daniel Seabrooks and John Hance

Items
"To one Silver Tankard"   £6-0-0
"2 negro children Abraham & Hannah"   £25 and £15
                                               Total amount £149-8-4

"Sence Discovered an Award in hands of Mr Stocton, attorney, against Jerimiah Tolmon, of Seventy od pounds   "

1765, Mch 16. An inventory of the personal estate of John Morford, was filed, by Jarrat Morford and his mother, and amounted to £469-8-4

Issue

19 Jarrat Morford

11 THOMAS MORFORD, son of Thomas Morford, 3, married Easter or Hester Bowne, of Monmouth County, by license dated Apr 20, 1752

Issue

20 William Morford, of Chanceville, Monmouth County, N J
21 Thomas Morford
22 Garret Morford
23 Daughter   , married a Johnson, says Mrs Shepherd.

Mrs Shepherd further says, that Thomas Morford, 11, was born in the Eldridge house, near Joseph Field's farm, and that he married Hester Bowne, of the Highlands, known as Riceville, Navesink or Witch Hollow

12 MARY MORFORD, daughter of Thomas Morford, 3, was born May 22, 1723, and died, Apr 19, 1790, aged 66 years, 10 months and 28 days She married, by license dated Apr 4, 1743, Job, son of Joseph Throckmorton, born 12 mo , 10, 1720, died, Feb 2, 1765, aged 44 years, 1 month and 23 days They are both buried in Topanemus Burying-ground See Throckmorton Family

13 SARAH MORFORD, daughter of Thomas Morford, 3.
On the Christ Church, Shrewsbury, Register, appears the following entry
Sarah, daughter of Mr. Morford, died July 14, 1748

I am inclined to believe that this is Sarah Morford, 13, yet it is possible that it is Sarah Morford, 6

14 CATHARINE MORFORD, daughter of Thomas Morford, 3, married Charles Gordon, Esq

Issue

Hannah Gordon, married Judge Jehu Patterson
Mary Gordon; married James P Allen, and had

Issue

Capt Robert Allen
Charles G Allen

16 JOSEPH MORFORD, son of Thomas Morford, 3, was baptized, at Christ Church, Shrewsbury, June 18, 1738, buried in Tennent Churchyard, with a tombstone, which reads died, Aug 20, 1765, aged 27 years, 8 months and 5 days He married, Sarah, daughter of William Vankirk, by license dated Feb 6, 1761.

1767, Mch 5 Joseph Morford died, leaving three children, William, Lydia and Hannah, "not yet 14 years of age " Sarah Morford, his widow, petitioned that Dr Nathaniel Scudder, of Lower Freehold, be appointed their guardian

1774, Apr. 30 William Perrine and Mathias Rue, of Monmouth County, signed a bond, of £200, in a guardianship matter, wherein it is set forth that William Perrine married Sarah Morford, mother of William Morford, "not 14 years of age."

1765, Aug "Sixteenth" Will of Joseph Morford, of Township of Freehold, Monmouth County, "Being Sick in Body"; proved by witnesses, Peter Schenck, Richard Hults and James Robinson, Aug 21, 1765, mentioned

Lands and movable estate, real and personal, except "what my Father in law, William Vancurck, did give to my Well beloved wife Sarah & those things for my s^d wife to have again," to be sold and divided into four parts

"Unto my well beloved wife, Sarah," one part

The other three parts, at interest, for the three children, Lidia, William and [blank], equally, as they become of age, "the boy," at twenty-one years, and the "girls," at eighteen years, or at the time of marriage

The children to be well brought up and have a good "Education," and such expense to come out of each child's portion

Wife, Sarah, "shall keep my two Daughters," or put them out, as she thinks proper

Son, William, to learn a trade, which the executors shall choose for him

Executors John Forman and John Vancurck

Witnesses Peter Schenck, Richard Hulft, [his mark] and James Robinson.

He signed his will "JOS MORFORD"

1765, Aug 21 Qualification of executors, John Forman and John Vankirk

1765, Sept "Second" Inventory of Joseph Morford, appraised by Tho Leonard, William Wikoff and Michael Henderfon, and Jo^n Forman, executor, amounted to £391-7-3 Bonds, etc, £551-3-8 One item was "A Silver Tancard" £6-0-0

Issue

24 William Morford
25 Lydia Morford
26 Hannah Morford, baptized Sept 15, 1765

17 THOMAS MORFORD, son of Jarrat Morford, 9, married, first, Sarah, daughter of Joseph Taylor, by license dated Jan 21, 1765

1775, May 27 Thomas Morford was a member of the Patriotic Committee, Shrewsbury, N. J.

1816, Dec 6 Thomas Morford, Senior, of Shrewsbury, made his will, proved June 4, 1818, and mentioned — wife, Esther, son, Garret, his mother now living, son, Thomas Morford, son, George's portion in trust to son Garret; grandson, Thomas Morford, son of George, granddaughter, Caroline Morford, grandson, Wardell Morford, and such other children as my son George may have at his decease, grandchildren, George Mount, Edward Mount, Horatio Mount, sons of Sarah and Joseph Mount, on condition that they pay to their sisters, Rebecca and Hannah, "my granddaughters", my daughter, Sarah Mount, wife of Joseph my daughter, Hannah Perrine, and her son, Thomas Morford Perrine, not twenty-one

Issue

27 George Taylor Morford, born 1778, died 1827.

Thomas Morford married, second, in 1768, Esther, daughter of Josiah Holmes She died, Aug 9, 1823, aged 85 years.

Issue

28 Garret Morford, of Red Bank, N J, born 1781, died 1865
29 Thomas Morford, born 1776, died 1856

30 Samuel Morford
31 Hannah Morford, baptized 1771, married Mr. Perrine
   Issue
   Thomas Morford Perrine
32 Sarah Morford

20 WILLIAM MORFORD, son of Thomas Morford, 11, was born 1764, married, in 1788, Lydia Stout,* born 1768 She was the daughter of Mary Stout, widow, who died in 1806 † He had an eldest son, John Morford, as per the will of Mary Stout, in 1805-6. He was a weaver, in Chanceville, N J He was also a farmer at New Monmouth, N J

1826, Nov 24 William Morford made his will, which was proved Mch 22, 1828

Issue

33 John Morford, eldest son, deceased prior to 1826, as per will of his father
34 William Morford, Esq
35 Capt. Thomas Morford
36 Charles Morford
37 Sarah Morford, married James Grover Taylor
38 Mary Morford, died, Mch 23, 1875, in her 75th year, married Walter C Parsons, who died, June 17, 1859, aged 64 years.
39 Elias Morford
40 Lydia Morford, married John G Taylor, she being his third wife She was married prior to 1826
41 Lucy Ann Morford, born June 24, 1809, married, Dec. 18, 1833, James, son of John G Taylor.
42 Joseph Morford, authority of Mrs Silas Shepherd

27 GEORGE TAYLOR MORFORD, son of Thomas Morford, 17, was born Feb 3, 1778, died Oct 20, 1827, married Maria Wardell, sister of Benjamin Wardell, of Long Branch, and Robert Wardell, of New York City. She was born Oct 20, 1781, died Mch 7, 1853.

Issue

43 Thomas Morford, of Red Bank, born Mch 6, 1804, died Dec 24, 1872.
44 Joseph Wardell Morford born Mch. 11, 1806, died Jan 29, 1849, married Jane Van Dorn
45 John A Morford, of Long Branch, married Sarah A Conover
46 Caroline Morford, born 1802, died 1850, married, first, Charles W Little, born 1802, died Jan 20, 1827, second, Mch 13, 1831, John Githens, born 1801, died 1873

   Issue
   Lurania S. Little, born Dec 17, 1826
   Mary W Githens, born 1834, died 1854
   Joseph Githens, baptized 1851
   Sarah Githens, baptized 1851
47 Jane Dodge Morford
48 Julia Ann Morford, baptized 1837; married, Jan. 17, 1844, Jacob Corlies Parker,

*Mrs Shepherd said that Lydia Stout had a half sister, Molly
†Mary Stout was born Mary Taylor, and was the wife of John Stout

born Nov 17, 1816, died Aug 25 1855.
49 Jarret Morford, of Bridgeport, Conn , married . . .
50 Charlotte A Morford, born Dec 6, 1808, died May 4, 1848, married George Klotts

28 GARRET MORFORD, son of Thomas Morford, 17, was born May 3, 1781, died Sept 21, 1865 He resided in Red Bank, N J , and received, by his father's will, property at the age of twenty-five years and one month, and the balance of the estate at the age of thirty-four years He married, Apr 2, 1818, Catharine C White, daughter of Timothy White and Hannah, daughter of Richard Crawford, whose will was dated 1781 She was born Feb 28, 1798, and died Jan 14, 1869
1856, Feb 28 Will of Garret Morford proved Oct 4, 1865

Issue

51 Hannah White Morford, born May 2, 1819, died Dec 6, 1894, married, Dec 31, 1840, James McCausland born June 9, 1807, died May 25, 1844 She was his second wife
52 Elizabeth Holmes Morford, born Jan 9, 1826, died Oct 31, 1834
53 Hester Ann Morford, called "Annie," born 3 mo , 24, 1828, died Mch 5, 1868, married William H Grant, born Dec 24, 1820, died Nov 3, 1897
54 Thomas Morford, buried Mch 24, 1827.
55 Samuel W Morford, born Mch 12, 1836, married, December, 1869, Mary Ruth, daughter of George and Eliza Ovens, born 1849, died Feb 8, 1903 He was a coal merchant of Red Bank, N J
56 Henry Hobart Morford, born July 23, 1837, died Mch 15, 1855.
57 Thomas Finch Morford, born Mch 12, 1838, died 1888

29 THOMAS MORFORD, Jr , son of Thomas Morford, 17, was born 1776, died 1854, married Rebecca West, born 1782, died 1858

Issue

58 Dr. John Morford, born, in Shrewsbury, 1803, graduated from the University of New York, licentiate of Monmouth County Medical Society, April, 1824, and became a member of said society in 1826 From 1825, he practiced at Squan, N J., where he died, Dec 15, 1838, aged 35, 7, 25, buried in the old Presbyterian Churchyard at Manasquan He was a popular physician and an esteemed citizen He married Eliza, daughter of Col Abraham Osborn She married, 2nd, Dr Robert Laird and died, Sept 22, 1884, aged 71, 6, 14 Dr Laird died Apr 22, 1903
59 Rebecca Morford, born Jan 25, 1822, died Oct 8, 1891, married, Feb 28, 1843, Robert Drummond, born Aug 28, 1808, died Sept 1, 1882.
60 George Morford, died, in 1825, aged 19 years
61 James Morford, died, in 1825, aged 17 years
62 Meribah West Morford, born 1814, died 1892, married, in 1836, Jacob Van Winkle, born 1805, died 1876
63 Emeline Morford, married, Nov 19, 1823, Samuel L Pyle
64 Austin Wing Morford, born 1808, married, Nov 28, 1833, Mary Osborn, born Dec 23, 1810, died Apr 14, 1872
65 Alexander Morford, baptized, Jan 4, 1814, in Shrewsbury, N J.

HISTORICAL MISCELLANY

32 SARAH MORFORD, daughter of Thomas Morford, 17, married Joseph Mount
Issue
66 George Mount
67 Edward Mount
68 Horatio Mount
69 Rebecca Mount
70 Hannah Mount

34 WILLIAM MORFORD, son of William Morford, 20, was born Sept 23, 1796; married, first, Elizabeth Willett, who was born Feb 14, 1794 She died Jan. 31, 1835. He died, Apr. 28, 1868, in his 72nd year He was a merchant, in Chanceville, N J.

Issue
71 James Morford, born 1819
72 Henry Morford, born 1823, died August, 1881.
73 Elizabeth Morford, born 1830, married, Jan. 1, 1854, Benjamin Frost.
74 Margaret Morford, born 1832, died 1837.

William Morford married, second, October, 1836, Joanna, daughter of Nicholas and Mary Johnson She was born Sept 6, 1804, and died Apr 8, 1872.

Issue
75 Margaret Morford, born 1840
76 George Morford, born Oct 18, 1844, died May 10, 1903

35 CAPT THOMAS MORFORD, son of William Morford, 20, married, first, Lydia, daughter of Samuel and Ann Tilton, May 27, 1829, second, Caroline, daughter of William and Mary (Chadwick) Cook, born circ 1820 His first wife, Lydia, died, Feb. 2, 1845, aged 37 years, 5 months and 16 days His second wife, Caroline Cook, was born Aug 6, 1819, and died Jan 19, 1897 He died, Dec 31, 1862, aged 57 years, 9 months, and 9 days. Fairview Cemetery

Issue by first wife
77 William Morford, married Hortense Gregory
78 Martha Ann Morford, of New Monmouth, N. J
79 Sarah Morford, married, Dec. 1, 1852, James H Frost, of Brooklyn, N Y
80 Thomas T Morford, of Chicago, Ill , and Buffalo, N Y , married
81 Kate Morford, married, Nov. 25, 1860, William Story.
82 Albert Morford, married Anne Spader. He was born Feb 15, 1844, and died Feb 11, 1909 His wife was born Nov 2, 1843, and died Apr 18, 1876
83 Adelaide Morford; married, first, Dec. 18, 1867, Benjamin Frost, second, Mr. Spader.

Issue by second wife
84 James Morford, of Red Bank, N J , a cornetist
85 Emily Morford; married W A Truax

36 CAPT CHARLES MORFORD, son of William Morford, 20, was the seventh son and was born, Mch 25, 1807, in Middletown, N. J. With his brothers, William and Thomas Morford, he carried on a lumber business He was an enterprising and successful business man He married, Sept. 25, 1832, Susan, daughter of Daniel and Margaret Herbert He moved from

his New Monmouth residence, which he left to his son, to property, which, in 1890, was held by his family, on the Main Street, in Middletown, N J He died June 7, 1874. See Ellis' History of Monmouth County. His wife, Susan, was born Aug. 25, 1810, and died Dec 25, 1885

Issue

86 John Morford, born July 2, 1833; died Jan 8, 1905.
87 Caroline Morford, born 1836'; died 1907, married William Wurdemann
88 Almira Morford, married, Feb 5, 1863, David S. Wyckoff
89 Lydia M Morford, married, Apr 2, 1863, Samuel T Hendrickson
90 Margaret H Morford
91 Charles H Morford, married Laura M. Worthley

39 DEACON ELIAS MORFORD, son of William Morford, 20, married Fanny, daughter of Grover Taylor. He was born July 6, 1811, and died Aug 7, 1877 His wife was born July 5, 1808, and died May 13, 1866

Issue

92 Lydia Morford; died single
93 Mary Morford, died single
94 William E Morford, married Emma L Pike
95 Elizabeth Morford
96 Lydia F. Morford

43 THOMAS MORFORD, son of George Taylor Morford, 27, was born Mch 6, 1804, died Dec 24, 1872, married Hannah Voorhees, born Aug 27, 1812, died Aug 21, 1882 He was of Red Bank, N J.

Issue

97 Voorhees Morford
98 Minnie Morford, born 1856.
99 Frances Morford, born 1850, died 1872

44 JOSEPH WARDELL MORFORD, son of George Taylor Morford, 27, was born Mch 11, 1806, died Jan 29, 1849, married Jane Van Dorn

Issue

100 George Morford
101 Charlotte Morford, born 1840, died 1842.
102 Emily Morford
103 Sarah Morford
104 John Morford
105 Walter Morford
106 Thomas Morford

45 JOHN A MORFORD, son of George Taylor Morford, 27, was born Nov 5, 1810, died May 4, 1882, married, Jan. 6, 1836, Sarah Ann, daughter of Tylee and Maria (Schenck) Conover, born 1814 He was a resident of Long Branch, N. J.

Issue

107 Georgiana Morford, died young.
108 Maria N Morford, married, Jan 10, 1856, Abraham T. Vandervere

109 Elizabeth A. Morford, born 1842; married, Oct 26, 1869, Joseph E., son of Joseph L. and Caroline Hance, born 1837.
110 Tylee Conover Morford, married, Feb 20, 1867, Annie E, daughter of John and Lucy Harrington

"Mrs Sarah Conover Morford, widow of John A Morford, for half a century a resident of Long Branch, died Tuesday, [Sept 6, 1910], in the home of her daughter, Mrs Joseph E. Hance, at New Britain, Conn , in her ninety-seventh year She was born near Red Bank, N J, in 1813 She was the oldest original Long Branch resident, having been a month older than Mr Brittain Woolley, who will celebrate his ninety-seventh birthday next November "
N Y Herald.

47 JANE DODGE MORFORD, daughter of George Taylor Morford, 27, was born Dec 25, 1812, died June 12, 1876, married, Mch. 22, 1837, Robert White Parker, born 1814

49 JARRET MORFORD, son of George Taylor Morford, 27, resided in Bridgeport, Conn He married .

Issue

111 George Taylor
112 Essie Taylor, married Mr. Knapp

55 SAMUEL WHITE MORFORD, son of Garret Morford, 28, was born Mch 12, 1836, married, December, 1869, Mary Ruth, daughter of George and Eliza Ovens, born 1849, died Feb 8, 1903

SAMUEL W MORFORD

Samuel W Morford died yesterday at his home, in Red Bank, N J, aged seventy-three years He had been commodore of the North Shrewsbury River Ice Yacht Club ever since it was organized, nearly thirty years ago, and owned one of the first ice racing boats ever tried on the river there About twenty years ago he was Mayor of the town and for a long time had been a director of the First National Bank He was in the coal business A son and two daughters survive him   N. Y. Herald, Oct. 27, 1909

Issue

113 Alice Morford
114 Anna J Morford, born 1872, married, May 3, 1905, Walter French
115 Jarrat Morford, born 1873
116 Nellie R Morford, born 1877, died young

57 THOMAS FINCH MORFORD, son of Garret Morford, 28, was born Mch 12, 1838, died 1888. He married, Jan 16, 1855, Elizabeth C Wilbur, born 1832 He was a coal merchant, of Red Bank, N J.

Issue

117 Jane A Morford, born 1858.
118 Catharine W. Morford, born 1860
119 Laura M Morford, born 1862, married Frederick D. Wykoff.
120 Henry W Morford, born 1867, married Miss Patterson
121 Annie G Morford

64 AUSTIN WING MORFORD, son of Thomas Morford, Jr, 29, was born 1808, married, Nov 28, 1833, Mary Osborn, born Dec 23, 1810; died Apr 14, 1872.

MORFORD OF MONMOUTH COUNTY

Issue

122 Jane Osborn Morford, born 1834, married, Dec. 12, 1853, Edwin Lassee Weeks, born 1818
123 Mary Lavinia Morford, born Oct. 1, 1836 died July 21, 1852
124 Rachel West Morford, born June, 1837
125 Abraham Osborn Morford, baptized Apr 20, 1847
126 Thomas Perine Morford
127 Harriet B Morford, married Mr Knight
128 Julia Adelaide Morford, born October, 1841, married Mr Miller

76 GEORGE MORFORD, son of William Morford, 34, was born Oct 18, 1844, died May 10 or 19, 1903, married, 11 mo , 20, 1867, Emeline, daughter of Jacob H and Hannah Masker, of Newark, N J He was "an active business man in Monmouth County " See Ellis' History of Monmouth County

Issue

129 William Morford, born July 3, 1869
130 George Morford, born July 11, 1874, died 1875
131 Alice Morford, born Aug 19, 1877
132 Harry Morford, born Aug 19, 1881

82 ALEXANDER or ALBERT MORFORD, son of Capt Thomas Morford, 35, married Anne Spader

Issue

133 Daughter   , married James C Hendrickson

86 JOHN MORFORD, son of Capt Charles Morford, 36, was born July 2, 1833, died Jan 8, 1905, married Zilpha Maria, daughter of William Brown, born Mch 5, 1835, died Apr 23, 1905

Issue

134 Edward C Morford
135 William B Morford
136 Rita Morford
136a John Morford, born Dec 6, 1860, died July 26, 1889
136b Carrie Morford, died, Dec 2, 1878, aged 19 years, 7 months, and 11 days

91 CHARLES H MORFORD, son of Capt Charles Morford, 36, married Laura M Worthley

Issue

137 Abbott Morford

94 WILLIAM F MORFORD, son of Elias Morford, 39, married Emma L Pike

Issue

138 Fanny T Morford
139 Alfrida Morford
139a Charles Morford

110 TYLEE CONOVER MORFORD, son of John A Morford, 45, married, Feb 20, 1867, Annie E , daughter of John and Lucy Harrington

Issue
140 Lucy Morford, married Charles Blakely
141 Sarah Morford
142 Harold Morford

MISCELLANEOUS NOTES

In 1878, Miss Morford, of Lynchburg, Va., wrote that her grandfather, (and she was then very aged), was Zebulon Morford, "who was the first one in the country"; that he settled at Cranbury, N J His sons, Stephen and Zebulon, settled at Princeton, and his son, John, at Middletown, N. J This family was not of kin to the Morfords, of Middletown. It is possible she is right, but it is more likely they are an offshoot of the Monmouth County family Miss Morford was a daughter of Stephen Morford of Princeton

1739, Apr 17, O. S. Will of Henry Leonard, proved Feb 11, 1739, O S, stated that he was of Shrewsbury, Gent, and mentioned
Wife, Lydia
Daughter, Mary Leonard, not twenty-seven years of age.
Daughter, Sarah Leonard
Daughter, Susannah Leonard
Daughter, Parthenia Cook
Daughter, Margaret Leonard
Daughter, Elizabeth Leonard [She was, apparently, only daughter by wife, Lydia.]
Executors Brother, Samuel Leonard, *brother-in-law, Thomas Morford*, and sons, Samuel and Thomas Leonard.

1772, July 24 At Burlington, N J, Joseph Barber, of Pennsylvania, and Elizabeth Morford, of New Jersey, were married

1775, Mch 2 Henry Barber and Rachel Morford were married.
St Mary's Church Record, Burlington, N J

1777, July 1 John Morford took the Oath of Allegiance, in Bucks County, Pa.

1779, Nov 5 Geames Bound married Hester Morford Reformed Church, Freehold, N. J.

1784. Thomas Morford, Overseer.   Shrewsbury Town Poor Record.

The following Monmouth County Morfords were in the Revolutionary War.
John Morford, in Capt John Walton's Troop Light Dragoons
John Morford, in Capt Kenneth Hankinson's Company, First Regiment.
Noah Morford, in Capt Kenneth Hankinson's Company, First Regiment
Joseph Morford, supposed to have died on a prison ship, a brother of William Morford.
It is a family tradition that he was captured and died on the prison ship, in Wallabout Bay, New York, and that he died of starvation Provisions were sent to him by his relatives and friends, but each time they were directed to "J M," and there being another prisoner whose name was Jos Morris, of Port Monmouth, N J, they were all given to him.
Stephen Morford
Daniel Morford

James H Morford, of Monmouth County, N J, born 1850, married, Dec 13, 1875, Anna S Elliot, born 1855

Issue

Robert Morford, born 1878

Edward H Morford, of Monmouth County, N. J , married, Oct 26, 1898, Ella V Peckham, of Germantown, Pa.

The name, Morford, in old records, is also spelled Maurfoot and Morfoot

1786, Aug 12. John Morfort and his wife, Mary Forman, were members of the Yellow Meeting House congregation

1815, Sept 25 Will of John Morford, of Freehold, proved Sept. 1, 1817, mentioned·
Wife, Mary
Kinswoman, Melinda, daughter of James Lloyd
Friend, David Parine, who had been kind to him in sickness and health

John Morford died, Aug 5, 1817, aged 66 years, 9 months and 23 [25?] days
Mary, wife of John Morford, died, Oct 21, 1815, aged 62 years, 5 months and 9 days
Baptist Burying-ground, Freehold, N J.

MORRIS

OF

MONMOUTH COUNTY

The early history of the Morris Family, of Monmouth County, N J, is so interwoven with the early history of the Morris•Family, of Westchester County N. Y, that the two are followed from necessity

The Morris Family rose in Monmouthshire, Wales, about the middle of the 15th Century In 1635, they were seized of the estates of Tintern, Denham and Ponterry, then occupied by Lewis, William and Richard, sons of William Morris, of Tintern

1   WILLIAM MORRIS, of Tintern, married
    Issue
    2 Col Lewis Morris, born 1601, died 1691.
    3 William Morris, born 1612
    4 Mary Morris, born 1614
    5 Capt Richard Morris, born 1616, died 1672
    6 Thomas Morris. perhaps

2   COL LEWIS MORRIS, son of William Morris, 1, was born in 1601, and succeeded, upon the demise of his father, to the estate of Tintern, in Monmouthshire, Wales During the Civil War, in England, he espoused the cause of Parliament and raised a troop of horse, in punishment for which, when defeated by the Royal hosts of Charles I, his estates were confiscated, but with the decapitation of this monarch and the elevation of Oliver Cromwell to the Protectorate, he was indemnified for his losses.

In 1654, he was sent by Cromwell to the Spanish West Indies to make himself master of those seas, and was aided in this undertaking by his nephew, Capt John Morris, (son of his brother, William Morris), who had emigrated, some years before, to Barbadoes

In 1655, the Protector sent Capt Lewis Morris a Colonel's commission and instructions to join his forces, with those of Admirals Penn and Venable, in an attack on Hispaniola, (Haiti), and to land his troops according to his own discretion, but the assault failed, owing, to non-compliance with his directions Before joining this expedition. O'Callaghan says "'he prized himself at so high a rate,' that he demanded a present of one hundred thousand weight of sugar to pay his debts, before he would consent to accompany the fleet " He finally, however, did go and was present at the reduction fo Jamaica, after which he returned to Barbadoes

MORRIS OF MONMOUTH COUNTY

The Restoration occurred in 1660, and Col Lewis Morris deemed it expedient to remain at Barbadoes, upon the estate he had bought some time before

In 1663, he acquired, with others, the adjacent Island of St Lucia

At Barbadoes, he became an opulent merchant and planter, and a Member of the Council At his seat, near Bridgetown, he entertained George Fox, in 1671, whose religious beliefs he had accepted As a Friend, he signed the address to the Governor and Legislature, protesting against the ill-treatment of the Quakers, and refused to pay church dues and minister's money and to furnish men and horses for the Militia and was, consequently, fined a large amount in pounds of sugar He, apparently, continued in membership with this Society till his death, in 1691, for he left legacies to be paid, annually, to the Shrewsbury, N J, and New York City Friends' Meetings, to be raised, respectively, from his estates at Tinton and Harlem

In 1673, Col Morris came to New York City, in response to a letter announcing the death of his brother

New York, 29th Oct, 1672

Worthy Sir,—

Since my reception of yours by Wm Shackerly, no opportunity of conveyance to you hath presented from hence till this present Although by the way of Boston, I suppose you would sooner receive the sad tidings of your brother's decease, in whom as you have lost an only brother so have I a dear friend, I shall not insist upon many particulars relating thereto, our general letters arriving to you herewith I hope sufficiently inform you, yet I cannot but reflect upon the transitory condition of poor mortals, when I frequently call to mind in how little time God hath been pleased to break a family, in taking away the heads thereof, first, a virtuous young woman in the prime of life, and then a man full of strength and vigor, inured to hardships, of whom there is remaining but one poor blossom, of whom yet there may be great hope with your kind friendship, for it is a lovely, healthy child, and was well at Harlem, where it is at nurse, and I went to see it yesterday I was also at the plantation on the other side, when there was some public correction of two or three negroes, and breaking the necks of a mutiny among the white men by Mr Gibbs, and through his vigilance it is now in good order The crime of the negroes is reported to be so natural to them, which was both stealing and receiving stolen goods

The Governor presents you his kind respects and service
Col Lewis Morris,
At the Island of Barbadoes

Worthy sir,
Your most dutiful
Humble servant,
MATTHIAS NICOLL

Bolton's Westchester, Vol II, p 287

The brother thus alluded to by Matthias Nicoll, was Capt Richard Morris, a merchant, of New York City, recently arrived from Barbadoes, who resided on a plantation just over the Harlem River This he had purchased in conjunction with his brother, Lewis Morris, who owned a two-thirds part thereof.

Lewis Morris' arrival was opportune, for the Dutch had recently captured the Province of New York, and the estate left by his brother, Capt Richard Morris, was in jeopardy, and to some degree had already been violated, while his, Lewis Morris,' individual estate had been confiscated, by proclamation, Sept 20, 1673 Walter Webley, with good intent and the interest of a relative, had removed some of the effects to Shrewsbury, N J, where resided Lewis Morris, a young kinsman, to whom Col Lewis Morris was well disposed This younger scion of the family was among the first purchasers of Navesinks, and his obligations were guaranteed by Col Lewis Morris

"Mor he pays for Young Lewes Moriss A. 330 at 13^s 9^d pr. an from 1670 = 11 00 00"

To distinguish the two, Col Morris was called "the Elder," Sr, Esq, and Colonel, while the younger man, during the lifetime of the Colonel, was called Lewis Morris, Jr, which gave way, upon the demise of the Colonel, to Lewis Morris, of Passage Point

1681, Aug 2 Lewis Morris, Jr, was confirmed in three hundred acres of land and meadow, as a "First purchaser of Navesinks" The land was located at Middletown.

To this kinsman's home, apparently, Webley and Colonel Morris both went, in order to get a survey of the situation Colonel Morris soon acquiesced in the moderate demands of the Dutch and went about getting his tangled affairs in shape.

Free Pass for Walter Webly

"Whereas I am informed that Walter Webly still scruples to come hither, through fear that he should be molested, on account of the effects which he hath removed hence, for the benefit of the orphan child of the late Richard Morris, therefore have I thought proper, on the request to me made in his behalf, to grant to said Walter Webly again free conduct and passport, and at the same time to make known that it was never intended to seize the effects of said child, but only those belonging in lawful propriety to Col Lewis Morris   A COLVE "

Dated Fort Willem Hendrick, 26th 7ber, 1673

"On request made on behalf of Col Lewis Morris, pass and repass is granted to him to come into this government, on condition that he attempt nothing to its prejudice during his sojourn
Dated Fort Willem Hendrick, 29th of September, 1673   ANTHONY COLVF "

1673, Sept 1 The curators of the estate left by the deceased, Richard Morris and Walter Webley are summoned before The Worshipful Orphan Masters and notified to administer and report thereon as soon as possible

Upon the accession of the Dutch, the recently appointed guardians of the estate and heir of Richard Morris, viz, Messrs Nicoll, Delavall, Steenwyck, Berry and Gibbs, were superceded in office by Col Lewis Morris, who, by a series of efforts, brought order out of chaos

"The Governor-General having read and considered the petition of Lewis Morris, requesting in substance the guardianship of the minor child of his deceased brother, Richard Morris, and of his estate, without any exception, to be managed and administered for the behoof of said orphan child, further to enjoy the same privileges as are granted and allowed to the neighboring Colonies of New England and Virginia, &c IT IS ORDERED. The Petitioner is allowed to have the guardianship of the surviving orphan child of his deceased brother, the late Richard Morris, and granted such power to take into his keeping all goods, effects, negroes and servants, as belonged in lawful property to the said Richard Morris at his decease, on condition that he pay therefrom the deceased's funeral expenses, but he shall, first of all, deliver in here a correct inventory of the property left by the deceased, to be recorded in the Orphan Chamber, which being done, the necessary letters of administration shall then be issued to him What regards the Petitioner's request to import into this government some necessaries for advantage and maintenance of said orphan and estate, the petition is allowed, provided it be done with such ships as are already here or will be permitted, and on paying such customs and public duties as are paid by other inhabitants Regarding the request that he may have such privileges as are granted to New England and Virginia by the Proclamation, dated [blank] last, the petition is refused and denied, being an inhabitant of Barbadoes, which consequently cannot be considered with the neighboring Colonies of New England and Virginia Moreover, the Petitioner shall be at liberty to show where any property belonging to the plantation is lying, and then order will be given for its restitution to the right owner And finally, the Petitioner is allowed to employ such substitutes and servants as in case of his living or dying, shall from time to time, with advice of the Orphan Chamber here, be deemed necessary for the greatest advantage of the orphan, on condition that the Petitioner and his agents shall remain bound at all times to afford said Orphan Chamber due account, proof and balance of their administration
Dated Fort Willem Hendrick, this 11th of October, 1673 "

New York Colonial Manuscripts, Vol II, p 631-632

"On the petition of Lewis Morris, requesting that he may have a grant of the plantation of his late brother, Richard Morris, for the benefit of his orphan child, with the cattle and other dependencies thereof, together with the guardianship of said child, &c IT IS ORDERED That the Petitioner be allowed the requested Bouwery, buildings and materials thereon, for the benefit of the minor orphan child, on a valuation made by impartial arbitrators, in like manner the Petitioner shall be at liberty to appropriate, without any order all the chattels which he can attach that have been removed from the Bouwery, on condition that they be brought to the Bouwery and inventory thereof delivered in, and whereas, since the surrender of the place, divers articles have been removed hence by Walter Webly, it is herewith ordered that said goods be returned to the plantation for the benefit of the child, when the Petitioner shall be granted letters of guardianship, the government will appropriate on account, the fat cattle, such as oxen, cows and hogs, on condition of being responsible for the payment of the orphan's share

Dated Fort Willem Hendrick, this 17th October, 1673."

New York Colonial Manuscripts, Vol II, p 637

1673, Oct 19 "Messrs Francis Rombouts and Gabriel Minvielle are this day, by order of the Governor, authorized to appraise the goods received by Egidius Luyck from the houses of Captain Lavall and Walter Webly, agreeably to delivered inventory, and to render a report thereof"

"Whereas, it has been found that the two-third parts of the estate left by the late Richard Morris belong in real propriety to his brother, Colonel Lewis Morris, a resident of the Island of Barbadoes in the Caribbees, whose estate by the Proclamation dated the 20th of September last, is confiscated for the behoof of the government, and it being therefore necessary that in addition to the guardians and tutors of the aforenamed Richard Morris' surviving orphan child, some one be commissioned on the part of the government to regulate said estate Therefore have I resolved to commission and qualify Balthazar Bayard to that end, as he is hereby commissioned and qualified to assume the said estate for the two-third parts thereof which belong to the government, with said guardians, by name Messrs John Lawrence, Stephanus van Cortlant and Walter Webly, for the one-third part thereof inherited by them, to adjust and settle the debts and credits, to sell the remaining personal property, and thereof to deliver in to the Secretary's office pertinent account and balance, when order shall be issued what further disposition shall be made therein

Dated Fort Willem Hendrick, this 1st November, 1673."

New York Colonial Manuscripts, Vol II, p 650–651.

"To the Honble Anthony Colve, Governor-General of New Netherland
Right Honble Sir

Whereas, departing on your pass from New Orange to Oysterbay, and so to New Haven, I have recovered there some of the missing estate belonging to my nephew's plantation within your jurisdiction, I therefore humbly request you to be pleased to grant me a pass to enable me to bring said property which belongs to my nephew, who is one of your subjects, with the sloop belonging to my cousin's plantation, known by the name of Bronck's land, or to New Orange, or to Oysterbay, or to Silvester's Island, my affairs being such, your compliance herewith will oblige me to be and remain,

Your Honor's faithful friend,
In the name and at the request of
LEWIS MORRIS"

ORDERED The Petitioner is allowed to come hither in person, and to bring all such goods as lawfully belong to the late Richard Morris' orphan child, also said orphan's boat

This 30th 9^{ber}, 1673
By order of the Governor-General
of New Netherland
(Signed) N BAYARD, Secretary"

New York Colonial Manuscripts, Vol II, p 664

"Whereas John Lawrence and Stephanus van Cortlant, guardians of the surviving orphan child of Richard Morris, dec^d, excuse themselves from regulating the estate for the behoof of the general creditors, therefore the Governor-General of New Netherland hath resolved, on behalf of said creditors, to commission and appoint, for that purpose, Messrs Dirck van Clyff and Walter Webly, who are hereby recommended, with Balthazar Bayard, the already appointed Commissioner, to aid in regulating, in the speediest manner, the estate of the abovenamed Richard Morris, and to report the result to the Governor

Done Fort Willem Hendrick, this 28th February, 1674."

New York Colonial Manuscripts, Vol II, p 691

1675 Complaint of Gabriel Minville, of New York, attorney for Lewis du Bois, of Esopus, against Lewis Morris, for the unlawful detention of a negro and negress, belonging to said Du Bois

Answer of Gabriel Minville, attorney for Lewis du Bois, to the complaint of Lewis Morris The suit was protracted till 1680

Col Lewis Morris must have been favorably impressed with the country in and around

Shrewsbury, N J , during his brief sojourn there, in 1673, for he shortly secured grants of land amounting to upwards of six thousand acres One portion of his holdings, lying at Shrewsbury, N J, between Swimming River and Falls River, containing 3840 acres of land, was confirmed to him, Oct 25, 1676 He called this locality *Tintern*, after his Welch home, and speedily took up a residence thereon and set about developing the iron mines on the premises, which Spicer and Grover had started a short while before This district still is known as Tinton Colonel Morris was also instrumental in giving the name of Monmouth to the county that now carries that name He resided here many years, but finally withdrew to his plantation "over against the town of Haerlem, commonly called Bronck's land " This property was part of the tract of five hundred acres that he bought with his brother, Richard Morris, augmented by fourteen hundred and twenty acres more, the whole being confirmed to him, by patent from Gov Andross, Mch 25, 1676 His title he perfected by an Indian confirmation dated Feb 7, 1684

1682-3. Lewis Morris sought from the Council, a patent, for the land that he had lately bought of Samuel Leonard and Leonard Hunt

1685. Lewis Morris, of Shrewsbury, received a power of attorney from Richard Richardson, of Barbadoes, to collect debts in New Jersey, New York and New England.

1685, July 26 Col Lewis Morris, of Tinton Manor, merchant, received a patent, for one thousand acres of land, on the South side of Monmouth River, alias Allawayes Creek, etc , in exchange for one thousand acres of land, on the Delaware River, granted Sept 15, 1681

1689, Apr 23 Lewis Morris, commonly called Colonel Morris, of New York, deeded to William Bickley, of the same place, one thousand acres of land, granted to him, by the executors of John Fenwick, July 26, 1685, lying on the South side of Monmouth River

1690 He was called Lewis Morris, of Tinton, when he received a patent, of three hundred and forty acres of land, in Middletown

Advancing years, and the care of a large estate, failed to keep Colonel Morris aloof from public life

In 1681-2, he was elected a Representative to the Assembly, from Shrewsbury, but his place became void, by reason of his appointment, February, 1682, as a Member of Deputy-Governor Thomas Rudyard's [New Jersey] Council, which he held during 1682 and 1683 As a Member of the Council, he was one of the Judges of the Quorum, for Essex, Middlesex, Monmouth and Bergen Counties

From 1683 to 1686, he was a Member of Governor Dongan's [New York] Council

1686, September Court of Sessions, held at Middletown Lewis Morris, who had been arrested, was brought before the Court to answer concerning an informaćon brought in about the death of a Negro woman named Francke, the s^d Morris did appear with a habeas corpus from the Governor Gawen Lawrie to be removed to the next Court of common right, to be holden at Amboy Perth, etc

Col Lewis Morris married twice   Bolton, Vol II, p 290

"Before leaving Barbadoes, Lewis Morris had, unfortunately, married a woman of low extraction and bad conduct, whom he brought with him to America During Morris' last illness, this woman destroyed all the family papers she could lay her hands on and so remodeled his will, as to leave herself, and one Bickley, her accomplice, the whole personal estate, with negroes and silver The fraud, however, was so evident, that, when young Lewis came of age, some years after his uncle's death, the Legislature gave him possession of the estate, as his uncle's heir-at-law "   New York Genealogical and Biographical Record

If the record of birth given to Col Lewis Morris is correct, he was about ninety years of age when his will was drawn, and perhaps, impressionable to undue influence, but there is such strong evidence of his affection for his wife, and generous provision for many friends, vigorously and lucidly expressed, that it seems difficult to reconcile the treachery attributed to his wife

Further, he sets forth, at length, a sufficient number of grievances to account for his estrangement from his nephew, Lewis Morris There was some irregularity in the execution of the will and several erasures, which suggests that the testator may have meant to revise it, but I think it doubtful Be that as it may, it was successfully probated, and, as Colonel Morris' wife had, in the meantime, died, between Feb 7, 1690 and May 8, 1691, letters of administration were granted to Lewis Morris, his nephew and next of kin

1690 "this seventh day of this twelfth month, called February" Will of Col Lewis Morris, commonly called Colonel Morris, of New York, made at "my plantation over against Harlem, in the province of New York," ' to prevent all discords and variances", proved May 8 and 15, 1691, mentioned

"Whereas I formerly intended to have made my nephew, Lewis Morris, son of my deceased brother, Richard Morris, my sole executor, his many and great miscarryages and disobedience toward me and my wife, and his causeless absenting himself from my house, and adhering to and advizeing with those of bad life and conversation, contrary to my directions and example unto him, and for other reasons best known to myselfe, I doe make and ordaine my dearly beloved wife, Mary Morris sole executrix of this my last will and testament," and

To the meeting of Friends, at Shrewsbury, in Monmouth Co , five pounds current money of New York, per annum, forever, to be paid out of his plantation, at Tinton ironworks, to be paid on 25th March yearly

To Thomas Webley, of Shrewsbury, two hundred and fifty acres on the westermost part of his two thousand acres, lying between Swimming River and Hop River, Monmouth Co ,—he paying quit rent one half penny, sterling, per acre

To Lewis Morris, of Shrewsbury, one of his best mares in the woods, and £20, New York currency

To his nephew, Lewis Morris, son of his brother, Richard Morris, as soon as he attains the age of twenty-one, the residue of the estate, i e his plantation and iron works, at Tinton, with all lands, etc , etc , all his negroes on that plantation, *cattel*, horse, kinde, swine, and all other creatures, all houschold goods, utensils etc , bills, bonds, patents, books of account, debts belonging to ye place, all profits, etc , also one flat handled spoon, one small tankard, one salt cellar, one small sugar box, all of silver, one small cabinet sealed up,— wherein is four pearl necklaces, three or four jewels set in gold and several other things of value, one negro woman named Bess,—which formentioned plate, cabinett, and negro woman, were his brothers—unto which he adds all the children of said woman, Bess, except one that is otherwise disposed of , 1 dozen silver spoons, one large tankard, one large tumbler, one small tumbler, and one porringer all of silver, all of which last mentioned things he gives to his nephew in lieu of some things that are lost and supposed to be embezzled by Walter Webley, also £20, in silver, current at New York, and ten guineys, the whole given with this restriction and limitation, that he shall quietly and peaceably acquiess and submit himself, wholly and absolutely, unto every thing mentioned in the will and shall make no opposition against the same, but to his power shall perform and fulfill all things whatsoever that on his part I have hereby enjoyned unto him, otherwise, it is my final determination and result, that if my said nephew, Lewis Morris, his heirs, etc , on any pretence or right from his rather aforesaid, whether by partnerships with me or purchase, or any way else, shall, at any time hereafter, either by himself, or any other person or persons claiming from, for by or under him or them, by any manner of way or means whatsoever make any demand or pretend any right, etc , to any part of the estate that now doth or may hereafter belong to me, more than I have by these presents entitled unto him, and in such case, I do hereby make void all and every part of what I have hereinbefore given unto my said nephew, Lewis Morris

In case of any disturbance by my said nephew, concerning the premises hereby otherwise bequeathed, and that my said dearly beloved wife, Mary Morris, her heirs, etc , shall thenceforth and then immediately enter into possession, etc , and enjoy all the before recited premises legacys, etc , given or to be given to my said nephew, Lewis Morris, if he or any, under pretence of him, shall at any time molest my said wife, her heirs, etc , in her or their peaceable enjoyment of whatsoever estate, etc , that is or shall be herein and hereby given unto her or them, etc , *only giveing unto him*, and I doe hereby give unto my said nephew, Lewis Morris, the sum of ten pounds, current money of New York, to be paid unto him by my said executrix, etc , in case of any such disturbance or molestation as aforesaid

Unto my honored friend, William Penn, my negro man Yaff, provided the said Penn shall come to dwell in America, otherwise the said Yaff is to serve my said wife, equally, with other negroes

Unto William Bickley one negro girl named Maria

Unto Wm Richardson one negro boy named Jack

Unto Sam'l Palmer one negro girl named Buckey

Unto my negro man Toney, the cooper, the sum of 40 shillings a yeare, during his life, besides his usual accommodation

Unto my negro woman Nell her freedom and liberty to goe att large wheresoever she shall please after the decease of my said wife

These last two bequests on condition that the said negroes shall be obedient and respectful to his wife

Unto John Adams, of Flushing, the sum of five pounds, which is due to me on his obligation

Unto my said nephew, Lewis Morris, all my land and meadows att Mattinicot, on Long Island, together will all the profits and privileges thereof, etc., together with one-half of all my pewter and one-half of all my house linen for bedding and tabling that is on my plantation over against Harlem, and all my printed books, except such as my said wife shall please to reserve unto herselfe

The above legacies are given under the same provisions relating to the earlier bequests to his nephew, Lewis Morris

Unto ye meeting of Friends, in the province of New York, the sum of six pounds, per annum, to be paid out of my plantation over against Harlem aforesaid, in the said province, etc., and on every 25th of the month called March, yearly and every year, forever

The remainder of my estate and plantation, both real and personal, where I now inhabitt over against Harlem aforesaid, I give unto my dearly beloved wife, Mary Morris, her heirs, etc., the lands thereof, containing about two thousand acres, etc., together with all houses, barns, etc., woods, negroes of all kinds, cattell, swine, sheep, horse, kinde, and all other creatures and improvements whatsoever, also all goods, household stuff and utensils, money, plate, and everything else moveable, etc., within doors, etc., that now is, or hereafter shall be in my possession, etc., except what is here otherwise disposed of

Unto my said dearly beloved wife all that my houses, land in New York city, situate over against the bridge, unto all appurtenances, profits and advantages whatsoever thereunto belonging, with all deeds, pattents, writings, bills, bonds, obligations, and all things else whatsoever, named and unnamed, belonging

Unto John Bowne, of Flushing, one negro girl named Abba, is att old Thomas Hunts

Unto Miles Foster one servicible negro boy, such as my dearly beloved wife shall appoint

Unto Richard Jones, merchant, of New York, one negro boy or negro girl, such as my dearly beloved wife shall appoint

Unto William Bickley and my nephew, Lewis Morris, all my right, etc., in and to the ship Friends' Adventure, as also of all my part of her profits and advantages, by freight or otherwise, to each of them the equal alike part

Unto my said nephew, my gold seale and my negroman Yeabba, and whereas, I have bequeathed unto my said nephew, Lewis Morris, all my estate at the ironworks, at Tinton, with this expression, viz., (as soon as he shall attaine to the age of 21 years), etc., I doe now revoake ye said expression as to time, giving unto him full power and authority to enter into and possess the said estate, etc., immediately after my decease, etc., all the rest of my plate and money, silver and gold, I give unto my dearly beloved wife

I appoint my trusty ffriends, Richard Jones and Miles ffoster, of New York, John Bowne, of fflushing, Wm Richardson, of Westchester County, Richard Hartshorne and John Hance, of the County of Monmouth, and Wm Bickley, of Westchester County, aforesaid, to be my executors in trust, and overseers, etc., and in regard to the remoteness of their abodes from one another, I do order that any three of them may act as they shall find needfull, provided Wm Richardson, Wm Bickley, or Richard Hartshorne be of that number, and for want of a 3d persons in the County of Monmouth, Richard Hartshorne and John Hance may act there as they shall find cause, or may choose a 3d person to act, etc

Witnesses Johannis Vermilje, Jan Tibout, Lamueert Zoches, Davied Lillies, and mark of Susannah Roberts, and Wm Bickley Bolton's Westchester, Vol. II, pp 290-293

"The last will and testament of Colonel Lewis Morris having been exhibited, and the six witnesses severally appearing before me, two of them only, to wit, David Lylly and Susanah Robert were able to give oath in due form of law, that the said will was signed, sealed, and published to be the last will of said Lewis Morris, and the executrix being dead, and there appearing several razures, and all the witnesses having declared that they knew nothing of the said razures except Wm Bickley who declared he knew of them and wrote the will, but knew not for what end the said razures were made And the said will remaining not proved nor executed, the said two witnesses David Lylly and Susanah Roberts were accordingly sworne, and administration granted to Lewis Morris, next of kin of the said Colonel Lewis Morris

Dated May 8, 1691

H SLAUGHTER"

New York Wills, Lib 3-4, p 197

The inventory of his estate amounted to £4071

Issue

7 Miss Morris, married John Walters, and probably died without issue "At the attack upon Chepstow Castle, which was defended by Sir Nicholas Kemish, the king's general, Lewis Morris was the second in command After an obstinate resistance, the garrison was reduced by cutting off the supply of water which ran through the estate of Pearcefield, then owned by Col Morris' son-in-law, John Walters, and setting fire to the castle From this circumstance, the family assumed as their crest a castle in flames, with the following motto, 'tandem vincitur'—*at length he is conquered* " Bolton's Westchester, Vol II, p 285

3 WILLIAM MORRIS, son of William Morris, 1, was born in 1612 He was seated at Denham, and upon the breaking out of the Rebellion, he actively sided with the Parliamentary party When defeated, he considered it discreet to cross the ocean until the storm had blown over, but was lost at sea

Issue

8 John Morris

4 MARY MORRIS, daughter of William Morris, 1, was born in 1614

It is stated that she married Walter Webley Of this I have no proof, but have ascertained the following facts about Walter Webley, who may have been confused with a reputed husband of Mary Morris

Walter Webley was a resident of New York City, or of the region just over the Harlem River, likely on property adjoining Capt Richard Morris, in 1673, when the Dutch subjugated this province His active interest in caring for the effects of Capt Richard Morris' infant child, and the estates of Capt Richard and Col Lewis Morris, portions of which he took to Shrewsbury, N J., to place beyond the reach of the Dutch invaders, brought him into direct conflict with that authority. Col Lewis Morris made peace for him however

"On the urgent request of Col Lewis Morris, Walter Webly is allowed to retain his residence within this government, on previously taking the oath of allegiance.
Dated Fort Willem Hendrick, this 19th of October, 1673 "

He, however, shortly violated his parole and was fined in consequence thereof

"Feb 1, 1674
The Fiscal, Pltff
against
Walter Webley, Deft

The Pltff alleges that the Deft hath been contrary to the Proclamation of the 12th Xber last, in the enemy's country and brought letters thence hither, concludes therefor that the Deft shall be condemned in the fine according to the placard, &c

Deft answers that he hath pursuant to the Proclamation, delivered the letters into the Secretary's office and says, he hath had before this a pass to go in search of his uncle Morris, which he claims he can again do, on said pass, &c

The Governor-General and Council having heard the Fiscal's demand and Deft's excuse condemn the Deft for the reasons aforesaid, in a fine of eight Beavers, with costs

Note—'Tis ordered that the above Beavers shall be applied one-half to the Fiscals and the other half to the Church "

The preceding suit establishes the relationship of Walter Webley to Col Lewis Morris, he was a nephew and not the brother-in-law, as has been stated heretofore Further corroboration of Walter Webley's residence and relationship lies, in the application of Lewis Morris to transport his nephew's goods, and the order, issued, in pursuance thereof, Nov 30,

1673, wherein he alludes to his *cousin's plantation, in Bronck's land* The use of the term cousin, for nephew, was general in the phraseology of that day

When Col Morris, in 1674, returned to Barbadoes to wind up his business in that island, he appointed Walter Webley his attorney

1674 Walter Webley was the agent of Lewis Morris, for a grant of land

1675 Judgment of the Mayor's Court, of New York, for plaintiff, in the case of Walter Webley, trustee of the estate of Richard Morris, plaintiff, and Peter Aldrix, defendant, for the recovery of a negro woman

1679 Walter Webley was a witness, to a will, in Westchester County, N. Y

What became of this Walter Webley, I do not know, but he may have been living, in 1691, when his uncle, Col. Morris, spoke disparagingly of him in his will, alluding to his retaining various silver pieces These may be some of the things that he took, eighteen years before, to secrete them from the Dutch, and if so, it proves Col Morris had a singularly retentive memory and unforgiving disposition

"unto wch I add the Children of the said Negro Bess, (Except one that is otherwise Disposed of), and One Dozen of Silver Spoons, One Large Tankard, one Large Tumbler, One Small Tumbler, and one Porringer, all of Silver, all of which last Mentioned things added, I give and bequeath unto my Said Nephew, Lewis Morris, in Lieu of Some things that are Left and supposed to be embezelled by Walter Webley " Will of Col Morris

The relation of the preceding Walter Webley to the following Thomas Webley, I conceive to be a brother, for Walter Webley is the established nephew of Col Morris, and Thomas Webley, in his will of 1698, solicits the kind intervention of his "christian kinsman, Lewis Morris," [the Governor], in his settlement of his affairs

1684 Thomas Webley, of Shrewsbury, was a Debtor

1684 Thomas Webley, of Fenwick's Colony, was a witness

1685 and 1687 Thomas Webley, of Shrewsbury, was a witness

1687. Thomas Webley, of Shrewsbury, was a bondsman.

William West, of Shrewsbury, called Thomas Webley "my loving and trusty brother."

1687 Thomas Webley was a witness

1687 and 1688 Thomas Webley, of Shrewsbury, was an appraiser

1688 Thomas Webley succeeded Robert Hamilton, as Clerk of the Court, and Recorder, of Monmouth County

In 1691, he was willed two hundred and fifty acres of land, at Tinton, by Col Lewis Morris

In 1694, Thomas Webley deposes that he is "thirty ffour Yeares or thereabouts" of age.

1700 Thomas Webley, of Monmouth County, was a Grand Juror

1701, Oct 25 Thomas Webley, of East Jersey, Gentleman, attorney for James Wasse, of London, "chyrurginon," sold three hundred acres of land, near a branch of Morris' River, called Quiahocking, to Jonathan Beere, of Salem Town, gentleman

At a Court of Sessions, held at Shrewsbury, the Third Tuesday in October, 1700

"Thomas Webley having spoke several contemptuous and reproachful words in the Court, and having otherwise misbehaved himself in the presence of the Court, the Court therefore order that said Thomas Webley doe immediately pay the sum of five shillings for the use of the poor, or be put by the constable in the stocks for the space of two hours "

Thomas Webley paid the said five shillings for the use aforesaid

1698-9, Jan 10 Will of Thomas Webley, of Shrewsbury, yeoman; proved Mch 29, 1703, mentioned

Wife, Audria
Daughters, Catharine
      Ann
        Mary
Only son, John

His estate in Wales, inherited from his father, an estate coming from his uncle, Edward Webley, land at Shark River or Squancum, and lands at Barnigat Beach Personal property, including books His Christian kinsman, Lewis Morris, is asked to try and obtain something for "my Indian Wright at Croswicksum" No executor is named

Witnesses William Woolley, John Tilton, Johanna Grant or Gaunt and Abiah Edwards

1702-3, Mch 9 Inventory of the personal estate of Thomas Webley was made by Nicholas Brown and William West, included a negro boy, and amounted to £40-0-0

He married Audrey, daughter of Bartholomew and Catharine (Almy) West, and was lost at sea on a voyage to London

In 1687, Audrey Webley was a witness

1705 His wife, Audrey Webley, was a witness to a Shrewsbury marriage

It was probably she who was a witness, as late as 1732, to another marriage, at Shrewsbury

Thomas Webley stood high in favor with Col Lewis Morris who gave him lands, in Monmouth County, in his will

"unto Thomas Webley, of Shrewsbury, aforesaid, Two Hundred and fifty Acres of Land, to be Laid out att his Charges, on the Westermost Parte of my Two Thousand Acres y^t Lyes between Swimming River & Hop River," etc

Issue, supposed, of Mary Morris Webley

Walter Webley
Thomas Webley

These two brothers, Walter Webley and Thomas Webley, had an uncle, Edward Webley, so called in the will of Thomas Webley He was a resident of Monmouth County, and probably died without issue

1686, Feb. 14 Edward Webley bought lands, of the Indians, at Crosswicks, Monmouth County

1686 Edward Webley sold lands, in Monmouth County, to Thomas Webley

Thomas Webley, by his wife, Audrey West, had

Issue, as per his will

John Webley, married Elizabeth (Woolley?)
Catharine Webley, married Philip Edwards
Ann Webley, married Richard Chambers
Mary Webley

Of these children, John Webley received, in 1698, from Governor Lewis Morris, and his wife, Dame Isabella, of Shrewsbury, sole heir of his uncle, Col Lewis Morris, certain lands, in the deed to which he was spoken of as, a son of his kinsman, Thomas Webley

John Webley resided at Shrewsbury, where he was a witness, to marriages, in 1720 and 1721, and in 1715, the same, with Ann Chambers

The following data concerning the Webleys has been accumulated, but it needs more research to disclose, with certainty, the relationship of the individuals

BAPTISMS—CHRIST CHURCH, SHREWSBURY, N. J

1747, May 9 Audrey Webley, aged 23¼ years, [born 1724]
Ann Webley, aged 18½ years; [born 1728].
Catharine Webley, aged 21¼ years, [born 1726]

1747, May 24 Audrey, daughter of John Webley, aged 23 years, [born 1724]
Catharine, daughter of John Webley, aged 22 years, [born 1725]
Mary, daughter of John Webley, aged 20 years, [born 1727]

1747, Nov 21 Thomas and Elizabeth Webley had daughter, Sarah, baptized, aged — weeks

1748, May 8 Margaret, daughter of John Webley, was baptized
Mary, daughter of John Webley, was baptized.

BURIALS AND DEATHS—CHRIST CHURCH, SHREWSBURY, N J

1749 Mrs Webley, wife of Thomas, was buried, March 6
1762 Elizabeth Webley died, aged 67 years, [born 1695]
1775 John Webley died, aged 82 years, [born 1693]
1789 Ann Webley died, aged 61 years, [born 1728].

1742. Margaret Webley was a witness, to a marriage, in Shrewsbury.

1692, May 12 Mary Webley married to Joseph West, by Peter Tilton
Witnesses Nicholas Browne, his mark
Mary Williams
Audrey Webley
John West
Thos. Webley

MARRIAGE LICENSES

1740, Dec 13 Audrey Webley and Joseph West, both of Monmouth County
1748-9, Mch 24 Catharine Webley, of Shrewsbury, and Peter Slocum
1756, July 27 John Webley and Elizabeth Wardell, both of Shrewsbury
1757, Jan 23 William Smith and Margaret Webley had a license to marry
1759, Nov 17 Mary Webley and Jonathan Slocum, both of Shrewsbury.
1765, Oct 1 Sarah Webley and Daniel Taber, both of Shrewsbury.

MARRIAGES, CHRIST CHURCH, SHREWSBURY

1749, June 27 Peter Slokom and Catharine Webley, both of Shrewsbury, by license

5 CAPT RICHARD MORRIS, son of William Morris, 1, was born in 1616 He, apparently, accompanied his brother, Lewis Morris, to the Barbadoes, where he settled, and by his marriage to Miss Pole, of that island, largely increased his wealth He was appointed Captain, in the regiment commanded by his brother, Col Lewis Morris

In 1670, he settled in New York and engaged in mercantile life His residence was in that portion of Westchester County, later created into the Manor of Morrisania This land he bought in conjunction with his brother, Col. Lewis Morris

He died in 1672, and his wife, Sarah, some time earlier, leaving an infant about six months old The changing of the government from English to Dutch and back again, occasioned some confusion in the guardianship of the infant and settlement of his father's estate·

1672, September "Whereas Captain Richard Morris, of this city, merchant, died intestate, leaving a considerable estate behind him, and whereas his brother, Colonel Lewis Morris, hath a great interest for the protection of the estate, it is judged requisite that some extraordinary care should be taken," and in consequence, Gov L Andross appointed Mr Matthias Nicoll, Mayor of the city, Capt Thos Delavall and Capt

Cornelius Steenwych, of the Council of His Royal Highness' Government, Capt John Berry and Mr Thos Gibbs, to be administrators

1672, July 26 Capt Richard Morris, merchant, of New York City, had a grant of one thousand acres of land, on the Delaware River, over against New Castle, from Philip Carteret.

Issue

9 Lewis Morris, known as Governor Morris, born Oct 15, 1671; died 1746

6 THOMAS MORRIS, supposed son of William Morris, 1

The degree of kinship, of Thomas Morris to Lewis Morris, has never been positively proved but he was, evidently, upon the same plane of descent from a common ancestor This is established by a careful study of dates, appearing under Lewis Morris his son, 10 From these I deduce that Thomas Morris was born about 1630, and was, of necessity, either a brother or a cousin of Col Lewis Morris He probably never came to this country

The original William Morris of Tintern, had four sons, Lewis, William, *Thomas* and Richard   Bolton,* 2nd edition, Vol 2, p 455

Hotten in his Original List of Persons of Quality, 1600–1700, gives

Births Parish St Michael's, Barbadoes, 6 Feb , 1678, Dorothy and Thomasine, daughters of Capt Thomas Morris and Sarah, his wife

Thomas Morris is also mentioned in a census of St Michael's Parish, with wife and three children These allusions may be to Thomas Morris, 6, but I deem it doubtful.

Issue

10 Lewis Morris, of Passage Point, Shrewsbury, N J , born about 1655, died 1695

8 JOHN MORRIS, son of William Morris, 3, received a Captain's commission in 1651

In 1688, he was drowned, and his body, found under the walls of Deal Castle, was buried with military honors His descendants are still numerous in the Barbadoes.   Bolton

Issue

11 John Morris
12 William Morris
13 Lewis Morris
14 Richard Morris

9 GOV LEWIS MORRIS, son of Capt Richard Morris, 5, the "one poor blossom of whom yet there may be great hope," was born Oct 15, 1671, and died in 1746

The anticipations of greatness, expressed by Mr Nicoll, were quickly realized, when Lewis Morris, merged from an unruly youth, into a Judge of the Sessions, at the age of twenty years

1690, '92, '95, '96, '97, 1700, '01, '03, '04 He was a Judge of the Court of Sessions, sitting, alternately, at Middletown and Shrewsbury, N J , and with him, on the same bench, sat, also as a justice, his kinsman, Lewis Morris, of Passage Point, for many years and until his death

In 1700, he was President of the Court of Sessions.

About 1694, friction arose between the two Justices Morris, on the one hand, and their neighbors on the other, which culminated in law suits

1694 The Grand Jury indicted Lewis Morris, of Tinton Manor, for fencing in the highway, and a little later, again indicted him for "stopping and fencing in ye highway that goes to Freehold and Middletown"

---

*Bolton, drew from a manuscript history of the family, written by Valentine Morris, of England a descendant of an elder brother of Captain Richard Morris This Valentine Morris was born in 1727

Called upon to take cognizance of this indictment, it was an awkward situation for his judicial associates, and they hedged for time, by diplomatically directing a process for his appearance, at the next Court The finale of this attempt to restrain Morris was as audacious as it was amusing

Thomas Gordon was appointed by the Court, King's attorney, and when the case of Morris was called "the King's Attorney demanded a Fee of any one that would employ him to plead to the indictment   There was no one that would prosecute the said Morris, so that the presentment was quasht "

But the fight was not over At the Court of Sessions and Common Pleas, held at Shrewsbury, the 26th and 27th days of September, 1698, Lewis Morris, of Tinton Manor, was again presented by the Grand Jury, for fencing in the highway, between Tinton Falls and Swimming River Bridge, and still again, for a like offence, was he indicted, Sept 12, 1699 This persistent opposition to the encroachments of Lewis Morris brought about a mutual dislike and hatred, which found further expression when, in 1700 and 1701, in the Quit Rent fight, the people defied the Justices, who were impotent in office, and whose Sheriff was restrained by the people, from levying on goods, and whose Constables were powerless to arrest The greatest scene in this drama, perhaps, was the seizure of Governor Hamilton, Justices Lewis Morris, Samuel Leonard, Jedediah Allen and Samuel Dennis, the King's Attorney-General and Secretary, Clerk of the Court, and the under Sheriff, who were holding a Court of Sessions, at Middletown, Mch 25, 1701, by about one hundred persons, who "kept them under guard, close prisoners, from Tuesday, the 25th of March, till the Saturday following, being the 29th of the same month, and then released them "

Apparently this attack and incarceration had been premeditated for some time

1700, July 30   the Ambition & folly of Morris being known to the people of Monmoth they sent to advise with their neighborring Countys Middlesex & Essex what was best & most convenient to be done who generaly advised to secure themselves & oppose Morris & the rest that assert & would endeavour to set up Col Hamiltons arbitrary & illegal power & withall have promised assistance if ocation requires   we feare what may be [the] event of these things   you know how hot headed Morris & Leonard are & itt may be feared their pride & mallis may cause great trouble if not prevented   It is the general resolution of the Country that if they make future disturbance to apprehend Hamilton Morris & Leonard & secure them ontill his Majesties pleasure shall be known concerning them   Letter to Jeremiah Basse

1711 Lewis Morris was appointed Second Judge, of the Supreme Court

1715 He was appointed Chief-Justice of New York, and so remained for the succeeding eighteen years

Lewis Morris must have possessed, naturally, a fine, legal mind, for though not bred to the law, he continued to rise in judicial prominence, until he attained the greatest heights of distinction. Even his opponents conceded his ability, but his rulings were not infrequently partisan, and he carried this bias in favor of his friends to the end of his career

"At the time of the preparation and filing of the Bill in Chancery, Lewis Morris was Governor of the Province   He had long been conversant with the matters in litigation and was deeply interested in the issue of this most important case—holding a large part of his property in New Jersey by Proprietary rights, Gov Morris had presumed without, as was alleged, due authority, to erect a Court of Chancery, and to exercise the prerogatives of Chancellor   Could the Bill in question have been, with its Answer, submitted to his adjudication, the plaintiffs would, undoubtedly, have obtained just such a decision as they desired   But this favorable prospect was blighted by the decease of the Governor in May, 1746 "   Hatfield's History of Elizabeth, N. J

Aside from his judicial positions, Lewis Morris held other high office. He was, frequently, a Member of the New York and New Jersey Assemblies, as also a member of various Governors' Councils

1693, '94, '95 He was a member of Governor Hamilton's Council, New Jersey

1697, '98, '99. He was a Member of the House of Deputies, New Jersey

1698, Apr 7. Jeremiah Basse superseded Hamilton, as Governor, by a Commission, dated July 15, 1697. When he had occupied this position thirteen months, friction arose between himself and Morris, which prompted the latter to raise a question as to the sufficiency of his commission.

For some cause, which I am now unable to state, Lewis Morris, May 10, 1699, demanded that Governor Basse and Council should sign a blank writ against Obadiah Holmes, Sheriff of Monmouth County, but the Governor and Council were unanimously of the opinion that it ought not to be signed during the sessions of the Court, not remembering any such practice in this Province, and knowing the said Holmes "to be a Sufficient man & easy to be come at, any time"

The Governor and Council then ordered Lewis Morris and George Willocks to be brought before them and to give security for their appearance at the Court of Common Right, and to be of good behaviour, otherwise a mittimus to be issued "to convey them to Goal till they Should find Security," which Mr Morris desired an hour or two to consider

When Mr Morris was notified, that £300, security, was called for, he refused, and said he would not give it, especially for the good behaviour as by no overt act had he in any way given occasion to them to suspect it

Events now followed thick and fast At the Court of Common Right, held, at Perth Amboy, May 11, 1698, at which sat Basse, and his Council

"Lewis Morris, Esqr, came into open Court & demanded by what authority they Kept Court, the Court declared by the Kings Authority He denyed & being asked who was dissatisfied besides himself, he said one & all, the Court Commanding the sd Morris to be taken into Custodie, Coll Richard Townley, Andrew Hampton, both of Elizabeth Towne, with three or four more cryed out one & all, & he, the sd Lewis Morris, said he would fain see who darst lay hold on him, & when a Constable, by order of the Court, layd hold on him he, in the face of the Court, resisted"

For this, he was committed for contempt of Court There must have been a short but tempestuous scene before Morris was lodged in Woodbridge jail, for,

1698, May 12 'Matt Moore aged 31 years or there abouts maketh Oath that he was in Court & see Lewis Morris affront the Govern^r & upon which the Govern^r ordred him to withdraw but would not & still gave the Governour very Saucy Language upon which he ordred the Constables to arrest the sd Lewis Morris, but he the sd Lewis Morris withstood the sd Constables & would not suffer them to come nigh him, upon which the sd Constables commanded me to lay hands upon him which I went to take hold on him, he made some resistance, & did endeavour to draw his Hanger, but I being quick prevented him"

And several others made similar affidavits

Concurrently with this event, Lewis Morris was elected to serve in the General Assembly, for the town of Perth Amboy, and on the 15th of May, the Sheriff, of the County of Middlesex, made his return This was a moral reinforcement of Morris, and his associate, Willocks, who were promptly rescued, by their friends, who battened in the jail with a heavy plank No sooner were they free, than they returned to the attack Basse had, temporarily, installed in his place, Capt Andrew Bowne, and to him and the Council, Willocks and Morris addressed the following letter, which was delivered by Mrs Willocks, May 16th

S^{rs}

We are now able (God be thanked) to treat with you any way you think fitt if you had valued either your own or the welfare of the Government your procedures had been more calm Your day is not yet out, & it is in your power to follow the things that make for peace, & if you do not, at your door lye the consequence, our friends will not suffer us to be putt upon, farewell

GEO WILLOCKS   LEWIS MORRIS

When Jeremiah Basse was replaced, as Governor, by his predecessor, Hamilton, Lewis Morris was again returned to the Council

1700 Lewis Morris was President of Governor Hamilton's Council

1700, July 23 Col Hamilton hath put Mr Morris into Commission of his Council & Justice believing him to be the onely man that can make the province Submit to him as Governor & itt is saide Morris hath given out that he will carrie his point in makeing the people submit to Coll Hamiltons Government or he will embrue the province in Blood . . . In this posture things stand in this County & we beleive Including the Scotch that throughoutt the province theare is six to one against owneing Col Hamilton Governor and almost all biterly against Morris, whome they looked uppon as the first man as Indead he was that opposed Government, &c Signed Andrew Bowne, Rich Hartshorne one of ye Council

1701 He was a Member of Governor Hamilton's Council.

1701. Lewis Morris was active, in the behalf of the Proprietors, who desired to surrender their rights of government to the Crown, and "In behalfe of all ye Proprietors Residing in East Jersie," signed the memorial to that effect.

1702 Lewis Morris was in London, suggesting the surrender of New Jersey to the Crown, and so impressed the Lords of Trade, that they suggested to the Secretary of State, that the Queen should appoint him temporary governor, but nothing came of it, as it was decided to consolidate New York and New Jersey under one government For his endeavors in England, Governor Hamilton gave him a grant of land.

1703 Lewis Morris was a Member of Lord Cornbury's Council.

1703 Lewis Morris was the head of the Scotch party, who, by reason of a Scotch governor, Hamilton, "carryed it with a high hand ag^t the rest of the Inhabitants "

1705 Lord Cornbury wrote that Lewis Morris "does give his tongue too great a liberty "

1705. Again did Lewis Morris offend Lord Cornbury, who suspended him from the Council, and wrote "he will always obstruct the Queen's service, and indeed he has so intirely given himself up to the Interest of the Proprietors, that he can see with no other eyes but theirs." But, apparently, Lewis Morris was too valuable a man to be continuously suspended, for, in 1707, Lord Cornbury was commanded, by the Lords of Trade, to restore Lewis Morris to the Council, upon his submission.

1707. Lewis Morris wrote, at considerable length, to the Secretary of State, in England. a full account of the Condition of the Province of New Jersey, wherein he scored his enemies and paraded his own loyalty.

1707, June 28, Philadelphia Col Robert Quary, writing to the Lords of Trade, said·

"Mr. Jennings & Coll Morris, with the assistance of two or three others, was very hard at work in hatching the most scandalous paper, that I ever saw in my life;" and further on said that Col Lewis Morris, "at the mouth of them all, told his Lordship, that the Queen's order & instructions did not concern or affect them," i e the New Jersey Assembly.

1708. Lewis Morris was proposed by Lord Lovelace for membership in his council, to which he was appointed

1709. Lewis Morris was the subject of complaints, in letters of great length, written by Lord Lovelace, accusing him of changing his principles, and turning from party to party, as served his interests, and, as Lord Cornbury had said of him, he was possessed of "neither good Principles nor morals."

1709. He was suspended by Lieut -Governor Ingoldsby from the Council, but was reinstated by the Lords of Trade, who stated that he had been removed for insufficient reasons

1709, April The Lieutenant-Governor and Council of New Jersey, viz., Richard Ingoldsby, William Sandford, Dan Coxe, Robert Quary, William Pinhorne, Richard Townley and Roger Mompesson, addressed Governor Lovelace, at New York, at considerable length, upon the great disorder prevailing throughout the Province, wherein they impeached him for want of tact and force, and attribute much of the existing state of affairs to Lewis Morris Alluding to the Assembly, they say

"Their Resolutions of not raising any money for the Support of the Governm^t. nor of making or repairing jayles, a work of so absolute a necessity, But finding them so throwly Guided & Driven by Mr Morris and Saml Jennings whose mischevous tempers this poor Country hath for many years past groaned under, we thought it our duty in Conscience to testifie to her Sacred Majestie our dislike and abhorrence of the Same "

"and that we conceived those disturbances to be wholly owing the uneasie and disloyall Principles of Two men in that Assembly, Mr Lewis Morris and Mr Saml Jennings a Quaker, never known to be consistent with themselves, Men to whom all the factions and confusions in the Government for many years are wholly owing."

"As to Mr Morris the whole County where he lived namely the County of Monmouth are witness to his troublesome temper, whereby he was a perfect torment to his neighbours, those who know him best have most reason of complaint, And since he came to write man hath been Eminently concerned if not Principall in all the Rebellions & Disorders that have been in this Province, as may appear by his own hand writing"

"there is hardly a County in the Eastern Division wherein he did not succeed to stirr them to dangerous and notorious Riotts and Rebellions, but only the County of Bergen where he did not faile for doing mischiefe for want of good-will, But that the Dutch People therein were wiser, and treated him with that Contempt his Evill Designs Required, ffor his old and Present Confederate the Nonjuror Willocks and He made a Journey (or Voyage) into that County to Infuse the same notions of Rebellion ags^t Governm^t as they had preached at Elisabeth Town, with better success But all they got of that People was They did not understand oversetting of Governm^t and pulling Magistrates Judges and Justices from the Bench, It was a werke they had no liking to, and so closed their Resolutions among themselves, that they would not have to do with the Spiker-maker, That was the very term of Contempt (being Dutchmen) they used towards Morris grounded upon the Iron works his Unkle left him"

"But after the Red-hott Letters of Mr Morris Especially that to the Governm^t which is wrote with that Pride and venom that Bedlam would scarce afford a man mad enough to sett a Governm^t at such Defiance and treat Gentlemen with that contempt, and his and Willocks their Short Epistle aforesaid brought into the Councill by Mrs Willocks whilst the Assembly was sitting, and Morris and Willocks aboard a Sloop turning it in the Bay before the Town, Firing Guns as by way of Defiance to the Governm^t and the Record of com'on right in all which Morris was personally contriver and actor of the Disorders as also the Records of those Dangerous Riots in Essex County (after Morris^s Inconsistencies had made him Almanzor like change Parties) carried on by the same Principles and the same men that Morris had stirred up into Rebellion where a Body of about seventy horse came Purposely to destroy the Courts, Pulled the Magistrates of the Bench, tore their Cloaths from their Backs, Striking and abusing them with the greatest Billinsgate Language they could find as appears by the Record of the Court of Sessions at Newark A Place where Morris himself in Person with most of the same men had used a Court much at the same Rate but a little before So that his affording them Precepts and Examples the last Rebellion (tho he was not Present) may Justly be laid at his Door. As also that other Ryott of forcing the Keys of the Jail of the County of Essex from the High Sheriff, and abusing his Person, and setting Criminals at liberty, being no more than was done by the same men, (as appears by the Records of the Court of Com'on Right) but a little before in Middlesex County, for Mr Morris when with a Beam of an house they Batterd Woodbridge Jail to Pieces and set him and his Seditious Companion Willocks at liberty Who were there committed for Severall High Crimes and Misdemeanours as appears by the Presentm^t of the Grand Jury".

. "And we have Just reason to say that the Disturbances of this Province seems to be owing wholly to those two men vizt Lewis Morris and Saml Jennings, their naturall tempers and the constant business of their lives was to be always in Broiles, always in Contention, *Humanum est Errare, sed Diabolic'n perseverare,* Those mens Extravagances are a large field, But after an Instance or two more of Morris's Inconsistencies shall desist"

"Have but patience till the year 1700 and you will find him quite another man wonderfully changed in less than two years time, Then you shall find him accept of Comissions from the Proprietors Governm^t, and declaring that he would go through with them, and if any man resisted he would spill his Blood or he should Spill his, for he made no Scruple of Conscience, and would go through with the office he had accepted from ye Governm^t though the Streets ran with Blood"

"It is apparent what opinion his old friends had of him. Even those whom he led into the former Violences against Government, who broke Jayls to release him His own words are these vizt 'It was your complaint I had left you in the lurch like a villain, deceived you, ingaged you in a Business and left you in the middle of it, That if I came to your Town you would tear me to pieces and more Expressions of this nature you said ' So that we think he has proved his Inconsistences himself under his own hand plain Enough, without any need of our Paraphrase or Explanation, and upon the whole matter The Question lies only here whither he was Guilty of Rebellion in the Year 1698 or in the year 1700"

1710. Lewis Morris, having taken up a permanent residence on his Morrisania plantation, was sent, as a Deputy, from Westchester County, to the New York Assembly, to which he was returned until 1728

1710 Governor Hunter wrote the Lords of Trade that Lewis Morris had been expelled from the New York Assembly, for pressing the reconsideration "with some warm expressions," of a motion to levy for the Governor's yearly expenses twenty-five hundred ounces of plate, "which they interpreted to be falsely and scandalously vilifying the honour of their house " Nevertheless Lewis Morris had the confidence of his constituents, for he was promptly returned to the Assembly As a reward for his defence in the Assembly, Governor Hunter appointed Lewis Morris, Chief-Justice, of New York, in 1715

1711 Lewis Morris wrote a lengthy letter to John Chamberlayne, Esq , defending Governor Hunter from an attack, on the part of the Clergy, for not removing a dissenting minister from the parsonage at Jamaica, and installing the Rev Mr Poyer therein

1712, June 2 Jacob Henderson, Missionary, of Dover Hundred, in Pennsylvania, writing, concerning the state of the Church of England, in New York and New Jersey, stated that "ye Quakers or other Dissenters, " had "at their head one Coll Lewis Morris, a profess'd Church man, but a man of noe manner of principles or credit, a man who calls the service of the Church of England Pageantry, who has joyned in endeavours to settle a conventicle in the City of New York and whose practice it is to intercept letters, and let such as pleases him pass, and those y^t doe not he destroys as can be fully proved "

This, with a further arraignment of Colonel Morris, with Governor Hunter, provoked an answer, in which the writer said that "a little Helebore might do him, (the Rev Mr Henderson), more good than a reply," and denying these imputations said, "if a mans outward behaviour at home or abroad and in all the duties of his life is a true means of judging of a man all who know anything of Coll Morris will say that he is unexceptionable "

1715, Mch 28 Governor Robert Hunter wrote to the Lords of Trade

"Mr Mompesson our Chief Justice is dead, I have commissionated Lewis Morris, Esqr, in his room for these reasons amongst others, that he is a sencible honest man, and able to live without a salary, which they will most certainly never grant to any in that station, at least sufficient to maintain his Clerk "

Despite the doubt in Governor Hunter's mind, Lewis Morris must have been voted a salary, which was raised in due time and provoked antagonism. For Governor Montgomerie reduced this salary as Chief Justice, which had been enlarged from £130 to £300, upon the ground of increased work, although the true reason was ' that the Chief Justice being a Member of the Assembly in 1715, when the revenue was given, his salary was augmented by the great number of his friends he had then in the House, and for the services he did there" . . "This the people of the province have often complained of since I arrived here," and his salary was cut £50.

Between 1720 and 1728, Lewis Morris lived on apparently amicable terms with the Governor, Burnett, and in similar friendly relations with Burnett's successor, Montgomerie, despite the reduction in his salary But another state of affairs prevailed upon the arrival of Governor Cosby, in 1732 Lewis Morris, as Chief Justice, favorably sustained the claims of Rip Van Dam, President of the Council, between Montgomerie's death and Cosby's coming, for a salary which Cosby desired to cut one half This decision provoked the ill-will and even hatred of Cosby, who addressed him a discourteous letter with personal reflections and innuendoes To this Morris made a dignified reply, but Cosby removed him from office An indignant populace turned against Cosby and supported Morris, whom they shortly returned to the Assembly by an enormous vote and with great rejoicing throughout the city The Zenger case arose from this act, and liberty of the press followed, despite Cosby's efforts to suppress it.

1733, May 3, Burlington Governor Cosby, writing to the Duke of Newcastle, gives his version of the situation in the following letter.

'My Lord,

On my arrival at New York I found Mr Lewis Morris Chief Justice, Mr James Delancey Second Judge and Mr Frederick Phillips the third Judge of the Supreme Court of that province, the two last Men of good

Characters both, as to their understanding and integrity, but the Chief Justice a Man under a general dislike, not only for his want of probity but for his delay of Justice, his excessive pride and his oppression of the people These things, My Lord, I have been obliged to hear without the mention of any one virtue in his behalf I have often expected that he would come to me as others before him thought it their duty to former Governours, from whence I might have an opportunity to tell him of these complaints, but whether it be owing to his pride, his folly, or some unaccountable humour, he has not been once to visit me since I have been here, and I have no reason to think, that any admonition would have the least effect upon him, or if it would, things are come to that pass, that I can no longer suffer him to sitt upon that Bench I will point out a few of his faults, and give an instance to prove each, that Your Grace may see I do not displace without reason And

First, of his partiality Some years ago the dissenters of the parish of Jamaica in this province brought an Ejectment against the Church Ministers for the Church he preached in and was possessed of, when the Tryal came on, the Defendant's Council demured to the Plaintiffs evidence, Morris the Chief Justice desired them to waive the demurer, telling them that if the Jury found for the Plaintiff he would grant the Defendants a new tryal, the Defendants Council were very unwilling to do it, but however knowing the Man and fearing the worst from him if they refused they did consent, and the Jury found for the Plaintiff, the Defendants Council moved the next term (before Judgement) for a new tryall, and urged his promise, he denied at first that he gave any, but when they offered to make oath of it, he said a rash promise ought not to be kept, and never would grant them a new Tryall, whereby they lost their Church, and the Dissenters have ever since had it, its talked and believed to, that he was bribed to it, but as I have had no proof offered me, I have made no inquiry about it, his partiality however is evident

Secondly, his delay of Justice The complaints of this to, are the subjects of every day's discourse, in term time especially, I will single out one instance only, wherein not only his delay but likewise his injustice will appear One Renselaer, brought his Ejectment against another Man, which the Lawyers tell me, is done on a feigned Lease for a term of years The cause proceeded to issue, and a special verdict was found The points of Law were afterwards argued before him at several times by Council on both sides, after this they expected and moved for Judgement, term after term, till the lease whereon the Ejectment was brought was pretty near expiring, then the Pltf moved that we would either give Judgement or enlarge the time of the lease, but he would do neither, so the Lease expired and the Pltf lost the benefit of his suit after a tedious attendance and a vast expence

Thirdly, his oppressing the people, by giving them a great deal of trouble, and puting them to a fruitless expence, both, of time and money, in their attendance on the Courts The constant method he takes in opening and adjourning the Court is thus he adjourns it to eight or nine in the morning, but seldom opens it till twelve, one and two, and sometimes three in the afternoon, tho' the Jurys and others who have business are waiting from the hours adjourned to, not knowing when to expect him, and fearing to be fined if they happen not to be there Irregular hours proceed from several causes, some whereof are his pride in makeing the world wait his leizure and his intemperate drinking in which he often spends whole nights , this he does in term time in the Town of New York In the Circuits it is still more intolerable, for there, these hours of adjournment and sitting are not only like those, but the people who go forty or fifty miles from their habitations, live at much greater expence and loose more time, and sometimes after Jurys have been summoned, witnesses subpened, partys attended, and all the Justices of the Peace and other Officers have gone to the place appointed for holding these Courts, as by ordinance of Morris's own procuring, they are directed and waited their several days in expectation of the Chief Justice, who then alone was to go the Circuits, he has not come to hold the Court I have heard the damage that one County has sustained by one neglect of holding the Circuit Courts, computed at above two hundred pounds To remedy in some measure this grievance, the Assembly have, since my comeing to the Govern^t given the Second Judge a Salary, and now both, the Chief Justice and Second Judge are obliged to go the Circuits or forfeit their Salary Besides, in some of the Northern Countys he has neglected going the Circuit near four years "

In 1734 Lewis Morris went, as an agent, to England to inform the Home Government of the situation, but while treated with distinction, he failed in his mission to secure Cosby's removal, though it was determined that Morris had been removed from the Chief Justiceship on insufficient cause

In 1738 Lewis Morris was appointed Governor of New Jersey The references to this remarkable man in the Documentary Histories of New York and New Jersey are too numerous to further quote *in extenso*, but enough has been given to furnish something of an insight into his strength and his peculiarities

Lewis Morris was a member of the Church of England and much interested in religious matters, which secured him the backing of the church party, in England

1700. Lewis Morris wrote a letter to the Bishop of London, concerning the state of religion in the Jerseys, and paid his respects to his Middletown neighbors, saying, "they are, perhaps, the most ignorant and wicked people in the world Their meetings, on Sundays, are at the Public House, where they get their fill of rum and go to fighting and running of races, which are practices very common all the Province over"

His estimate of the inhabitants elsewhere, was only a little less severe "The youth of the whole Province, are very debauched and very ignorant The Sabbath day seems there to be set apart for rioting and drunkenness In a word, a general ignorance and immorality runs through the youth of the whole Province "

This severe arraignment was, in part, an effort on the side of Lewis Morris, to secure to himself, the appointment of Governor of the Province, by propitiating the Church of England, and, in part. an effort to settle his grievances with the people of Middletown, of whose frequent indictments and contempt he had had such abundant evidence Apparently the poor opinion each had of the other, was reciprocal

Lewis Morris was a Member of the Society for the Propagation of the Gospel in Foreign Parts, and a liberal benefactor and Vestryman, of Trinity Church, in New York City

The politics of his time were a confused jumble and Lewis Morris was, apparently, arrayed first with one contending faction and then with another in a most contradictory manner, suggesting a lack of principle, greed of self-advancement and often personal revenge, but it was a day of strife between the Quaker, the Scot and the Englishman, the Proprietor and the Patentee, and the Governor, Council and Assembly, each of whom, with keen and often dishonorable rivalry, strove for supremacy From the vast amount of their crimination and recrimination it is difficult to arrive at a positive conviction of the merits of the struggle, but I feel that Lewis Morris possessed no lofty sense of rectitude, but did possess a selfish ambition allied closely to the principle of rule or ruin

His autocratic nature and inordinate political ambition were the sources of his troubles and they were unceasing and great. For fifty-six years, the whole range of his political life, he wrangled He was intemperate of speech and action in his youth, but became more dignified and restrained as he advanced in years He possessed great aptitude for public life but under any opposition became irritable and aggressive To his superiors he was often hostile, while to his inferiors he was arrogant and overbearing He maintained his own rights vigorously, but had little respect for those of others He was vain, courageous and independent, which caused him to be arrested for contempt and to be expelled from the Assembly of New Jersey and the Assembly of New York With six out of nine colonial governors he warred, and defended himself by writing vigorous and plausible letters to the Home Government, which must have been sorely tried to discover the truth and adjust their differences

That he possessed a large and intelligent grasp on public affairs and served his employers well is established by the length of his service, and whatever may be said of his public life, his private life was free from blemish and his honesty unquestioned If his peculiarities made him foes, his partisanship made him as many friends Up to his last he was physically and mentally strong, and it was typical of the man that, at the very end of his career, he was still in conflict with the legislative authority, in this instance the New Jersey Assembly. who, practicing tactics similar to his own of former years when in New York, withheld his supplies and salary

In his will he requested that he be buried in Morrisania, in a plain coffin, with no funeral sermon, that no mourning rings or scarfs should be given, or mourning worn, saying "I die when I should die, and no one ought to mourn because I do so, but may mourn to pay the shop keeper for his goods, should they comply with (what I think) the common folly of such an expense "

Lewis Morris heired his father, Richard Morris', estate and the greater part of his uncle, Col Lewis Morris', estate, to which he added by his own efforts, and became one of the most opulent men of his day

From about 1689 to 1708, he resided at Tinton Manor, Shrewsbury, whence he removed to the Manor of Morrisania For some years, at least, he spent a part of his time between these two places but as years went on, he became more identified with his Westchester plantation

In 1738, when New Jersey was separated from New York, he was appointed to the governorship of the former state, and rented a farm, near Trenton, which he called Kingsbury, where he resided during the eight years that he held office, and where he died May 21, 1746

1701 Lewis Morris, of Shrewsbury, and Dame Isabella, his wife, made a conveyance of lands

1701 Lewis Morris, of Tinton Manor, heir of Colonel Morris, made a conveyance of land

1702 Lewis Morris, of Tinton Manor, in consideration of his services, with the Ministers of State, in England, received a deed for six different pieces of land, in various localities, and Lord Cornbury says, his quit rents were rebated

1703 Lewis Morris, of Tinton Manor, leased land from the Proprietors, along the beach, between Manasquan and Shrewsbury River for "the trees for sawing and making pitch, tar," etc

1705 Lewis Morris had "lately taken that farme, [in Westchester], into his hands" . and "was very busy putting his affairs in order there " Making this an excuse, he failed to attend the Council, to which he was summoned by Lord Cornbury, who suspended him for his rudeness, but he apologized through Dr Ennis

1708, Mch 15 Lewis Morris, of Shrewsbury, sold land to Samuel Tilton of Middletown, lying next to John Tilton

Lewis Morris married, in New York City, by license dated Nov 3, 1691, Isabella, daughter of James Graham, the Attorney-General of the Province She must have had a strong influence over him, for, from being an unruly youth, he promptly settled down, and applied himself assiduously to public affairs She was born June 3, 1672/3, and died April 3, 1752

Issue

15 Mary Morris, buried Jan 15, 1746/7, married Capt Vincent Pierce (Pearse), of the Royal Navy, died May 28, 1745, without issue
16 Euphemia Morris, born 1710, died Dec 3, 1756, married Capt Matthew, son of Sir John Norris, died Dec 15, 1738
17 Anne Morris, married Edward Antill, of Ross Hall, Raritan, N. J
18 Elizabeth Morris, born Apr. 3, 1712, married Col Anthony White
19 Margaret Morris, born Mch 13, 1711, married, May 19, 1746, Isaac Willetts died 1774.
20 Arabella Morris, married Nov 30, 1788, James Graham, died June 24, 1767
21 Lewis Morris, born Sept 23, 1698
22 Robert Hunter Morris, named by his father after his friend, the Governor of New York.
23 John Morris, living in 1732
24 James Morris

25
26
27
28 } Children who died young

29 Isabella Morris, married Richard Ashfield.
30 Sarah Morris, born 1695-7, died May 29, 1736, married Michael Kearny, born 1669, died May 7, 1741

10 LEWIS MORRIS, son of Thomas Morris, 6, was born, by deduction, about 1655 He was called "Lewis Morris, Jr ," to distinguish him from Col Lewis Morris, and also "Lewis Morris, of Passage Point," to distinguish him from his kinsman, Governor Lewis Morris, of Tintern Manor, Shrewsbury, N J He was among the early settlers of the Monmouth Tract.

In 1681, he was confirmed in his ownership of three hundred acres of land, at Middletown, as a "First Purchaser of Navesink," from the year 1670

1682-3. He was Sheriff of Monmouth County, and Ensign of a Shrewsbury Company of Militia

1690 to 1695 He was a Justice, of the Court of Sessions, in Monmouth County, as was also, at the same time, Lewis Morris, of Tinton

1689, Apr 15. Col Lewis Morris conveyed to Lewis Morris, son of Thomas Morris, land, that he had acquired, in 1681, by purchase from Simon Cooper, and which was called Norransont or Passage Point. This land is now known as Rumson Neck, near Seabright, New Jersey

1689, June 25 At a Court of Sessions, held at Middletown, on this date, Lewis Morris was among a goodly number of individuals accused of "running of races" and "playing at nyne pins on the Sabbath day "

Lewis Morris, of Passage Point, like his kinsman, whose name he bore, was aggressive, fiery and autocratic, and much embroiled with his neighbors

1694, Dec. 25 The Grand Jury indicted Lewis Morris, of Passage Point, for striking Nicholas Sarah, of Freehold, and the Court issued a summons for him to appear at the next Court of Sessions, to be held, at Middletown, Mch 27, 1695

At this Session, the two Justices Morris sat, and Lewis Morris, of Passage Point, did inform the Court how matters was and submitted himself to the Bench, and was dismist

Sarah was evidently much disgruntled by his failure to punish Morris, and abused Peter Tilton, one of the Justices, for which he was presented by the Grand Jury

1694, Sept 25, 26 and 27 The Grand Jury indicted Lewis Morris, of Passage Point, because he, "with several of his negroes, did feloniously take away the hay of William Shattock."

Apparently he little relished a trial by jurors, independent enough to indict him, a presiding magistrate, so that he removed the case, by habeas corpus, to the Court, at Perth Amboy, while Lewis Morris, of Tintern Manor, became his bondsman

1694, Dec 25 Then Lewis Morris, of Tintern Manor, and Lewis Morris, of Passage Point, by reason of their families were sick, did desire that they might withdraw and go home, which was granted.

Lewis Morris was killed by one of his negroes, in 1694-5, who was hung for the offence

It is ordered by the court that the negroes that are in the goal, for the murdering of Lewis Morris, of Passage Point, shall be conveyed, by the Sheriff, to Perth Amboy, to attend the Court of Common Right, on the second Tuesday, of October next And that a mittimus shall be directed to the Sheriff, of Middlesex, to receive and keep said negroes

Upon his death, his widow applied for and received letters of administration, upon his estate, Apr 1, 1696, which was inventoried, May 26, 1696, and amounted to £146-9-5 She was Elizabeth, the daughter of William and Audrey Almy, of Rhode Island

Some years after Lewis Morris' death, Elizabeth (Almy) Morris married John Leonard, Esq, who died 1711-12, leaving a will dated Feb 28, 1711, proved May 2, 1712, which mentioned.

Wife, Elizabeth, executrix.
Son, John
Son, Henry
Son, Samuel
Son, Christopher
Daughter, Sarah
Daughter, Ann
Stepson, Lewis Morris
Cousin, Henry Leonard, empowered to dispose of the real estate
Witnesses William Lippincott, Francis Borden and Sarah Powell.

Issue

31 Lewis Morris
32 Richard Morris
33 Thomas Morris; supposed
34 John Morris, born 1695, died 1769.
35 Rebecca Morris, married John Chamberlain.
36 Daughter, supposed As Cornelius Tomson, of Freehold, yeoman, in his will, Aug 14, 1727, named a son, Lewis Tomson, and John Morris, (who was the son of Lewis Morris of Passage Point, as proved by his signature), was witness to this will, and testified to its proof, Dec. 21, 1727, I infer the existence of this daughter

11 JOHN MORRIS, son of John Morris, 8, resided at Antigua, and died in 1687, married Grizzle Wallace, of Scotland

Issue

37 Richard Morris
38 William Morris died without issue.
39 John Morris
40 Thomas Morris
41 Valentine Morris

17 ANN MORRIS, daughter of Lewis Morris, 9, was born Apr. 3, 1706, married, June 10, 1739, Edward Antill, 2nd, born June 17, 1701, died Aug 15, 1770

Issue

Sarah Antill, born, Aug 18, 1740, at Piscataqua, Middlesex County, N J., married Lieut.-Colonel John Morris, (54)

18 ELIZABETH MORRIS, daughter of Lewis Morris, 9, born Apr 3, 1712, married, Dec 14, 1741, Col Anthony White, born Oct 28, 1717, died June 19, 1787 Her will was dated Feb 10, 1766, and was proved Aug 30, 1784 His will was dated Feb 14, 1780, and was proved Nov 12, 1787

Col White had a son, Anthony W. White, who had a natural child mentioned in his will and in the wills of his sisters

21 LEWIS MORRIS, son of Governor Lewis Morris, 9, born September 23, 1698, at Tinton, N. J., died at Morrisania, N Y, where he spent the most of his life, July 3, 1762. He married, first, March 17, 1723, Trintie, daughter of Dr Samuel Staats, by Johanna Ryndeis, his wife, of New York city She was born, as per the Bible record, Apl 4, 1697, in New York, and died Mch 11, 1731, aged 36 years, "after a violent illness for Nine Days " He married, second Nov. 3, 1746, at Westchester, Sarah Gouverneur (apparently his first wife's niece), born Oct. 17, 1714, died Jan 14, 1786

He was a member of the Governor's Council at the age of 24, and so remained until removed by the inimical Montgomerie He was Speaker of the New York Assembly from 1737 to 1746, Judge of the Court of Admiralty 1738, and one of the Commissioners to fix the boundary line between New York and New Jersey in 1743.

By the side of his greater father he suffers in comparison, but he was a clever politician, suave, humorous and tenacious, and quick with repartee

He had some of the strange whimsical peculiarities and intolerances that stamped his forbears His son Lewis had been educated at Yale, but his father must have taken some offence at that institution, for when providing in his will for the education of his son Gouverneur, he stated

"My express will and directions are that he be never sent for that purpose to the colony of Connecticut, lest he should imbibe in his youth that low craft and cunning so incident to the people of that country, which is so interwoven in their constitutions that all their art cannot disguise it from the world, tho' many of them under the sanctified Garb of Religion have endeavored to Impose themselves on the World for honest men "

Issue by first wife

42 Mary Morris, born Nov 1, 1724, married, May, 9, 1743, Thomas Lawrence, Jr., of Philadelphia, Pa
43 Lewis Morris, born Apl. 8, 1726, died Jan 22, 1798
44 Staats Long Morris, born Aug 27, 1728
45 Richard Morris, born Aug 15, 1730

Issue by second wife

46 Isabella Morris, born Feb. 3, 1747–8, died Oct 31, 1830, married, Nov. 7, 1762, Isaac Wilkins, died Feb 5, 1830
47 Sarah Morris, born Nov 23, 1749, died Nov. 6, 1781, married, by license dated Sep 15, 1772, Vincent Pearse Ashfield.
48 Gouverneur Morris, born Jan 30, 1752
49 Euphemia Morris, born Sep 30, 1754, died June 2, 1818, married, Feb. 5, 1775, Colonel Samuel Ogden
50 Catherine Morris, born Jan 30, 1757; died, Dec. 1, 1776, aged 19 years, 10 months.

22 GOVERNOR ROBERT HUNTER MORRIS, son of Governor Lewis Morris, 9, was born about the year 1700 When his father became Governor of New Jersey, in 1738, he was appointed Chief Justice of that state and a Member of the Governor's Council. He likewise was, for a time, October, 1754 to August, 1756, Governor of Pennsylvania As Chief Justice of New Jersey, he presided until his death He was a genial, hearty man, possessing popularity. His home was at Tinton near where he died in 1764

Smith, the historian, records his death "He had a cousin, living at Shrewsbury, N J,* who was wife of the clergyman of the parish On the evening of the 27th of January, [1764], there was a dance in the village, at which all the respectable families of the neighborhood were present The Chief Justice led out the clergyman's wife, danced down six couples, and then

*Said to be the present residence of Dr Ehrick Parmly, at Rumson

without a word, or a groan, or a sigh, fell dead on the floor " " Unhappy New Jersey has lost her best ornament "

Some years before his death, Robert Hunter Morris made his will, in which he set forth that he was a resident of Tinton, in New Jersey, "intending on a voyage to Great Britain " He was doubtless then about to start on his mission of advancing the interests of the American Colonies, in England, where he resided some years This instrument, dated Sept 24, 1757, and proved Feb 24, 1764, mentioned:

Niece, Ann Morris, that now lives with me, £500 down, and £20 a year

Nephew, John Morris, an officer in Lasscasses' Regiment, [Lafscellses] £500

My son, Robert Morris, who lately lived with Richd Saltar, and now lives with Mr Dove, a schoolmaster, at or near Gloucester, in West Jersey, a share in a mine, at Rocky Hill, when twenty-one years of age

My daughter Mary Morris, now living with Rev^d Mr Samuel Cook, £2000

To Richard Morris, one-third of a property

To his nephews, Lewis and Robert Morris, his share of the land devised, by his father's will, to himself and his brother, near Mohocks River

"And whereas my said children, and my said nephew and niece, John and Anna Morris are natural children and cannot inherit," etc

To Thomas Lawrence, of Philadelphia, a tract of land above the Highlands

To Sarah Robinson £200, for her goodness to my mother

To Elizabeth Stogdale £300.

Executors good friend, David Ogden, and nephew, Richard Morris, who are instructed to pay his debts and apply his estate to bring up his child

Witnesses Anthony Dennis, Thomas Leming and Hannah Leming

Issue

51 Robert Morris, natural child
52 Mary Morris, natural child, supposed by Elizabeth Stogdale

23 JOHN MORRIS son of Lewis Morris, 9

Neither Governor Lewis Morris nor his wife made mention of sons other than Lewis and Robert Hunter Morris, in their wills, who were named as executors That they failed to do so, is no proof that they had no other sons That they did have, is known beyond dubiety The authority for this John is "My son, Staats Long, was born the 27th day of August, 1728, at a quarter after one in the morning, was christened by Parson Oren, Capt Robert Long and my *brother, John*, godfathers, my sister, Ann, and Elizabeth Schuyler, godmothers "

Bible of Judge Lewis Morris, born 1698. New York Genealogical and Biographical Record, Vol 7, p 17

By exclusion of all other relatives, both on his side as well as his wife's, the "brother, John," must have been John Morris

Then again, Mary Corbett, a sister to the Isabella Graham who married Governor Lewis Morris, appointed, as an executor in her will, "her nephew, John Morris," and he qualified for the position

Physically he must have been a man of enormous size, for it is related that on transferring the coffins in the vault, at Morrisania, to a new one that had been built, one of them broke, and Gouverneur Morris, (115), picking up a huge jaw bone that had fallen to the ground, made the remark "This must have belonged to John Morris, for he was an immense man "

John Morris undoubtedly was the Surrogate, of Monmouth County, in 1733 By inference, I believe him to be the father of the two natural children, mentioned in the will of Governor Robert Hunter Morris, as his niece and nephew

Issue

53 Lieut. John Morris, a natural child.
54 Ann Morris, a natural child

24 JAMES MORRIS, son of Lewis Morris, 9
The authority for this child rests upon the following deed
1717, Apr. 13 George Willocks, of Perth Amboy, and Margaret, his wife, granted to "James Morris and Isabella Morris, one of the sons & of ye Daughters, of Lewis Morris, of Morrisania, in Province of New York, Esqr," for the sum of five shillings from each of them, paid, one hundred and seventy acres, in Woodbridge, Middlesex County, N. J.

29 ISABELLA MORRIS, daughter of Lewis Morris, 9, born 1705, died Apr 25, 1741, married, in 1723, Richard Ashfield, born Dec 16, 1695; died 1742
1695 Richard Ashfield, of New York, merchant, sold lands, in Monmouth County, to William Clark.

Issue

(a) Lewis Morris Ashfield, born Feb 9, 1724 He had a natural daughter, Helene, wife of Richard Clay, by his natural cousin, Ann Morris. Lewis Morris Ashfield married, Feb. 4, 1748, Elizabeth, daughter of John Redford He died, Sep 27, 1769, at Tintern, leaving a will dated Aug 5, 1769, proved Aug. 22, 1770, devising a large estate to his son, Redford Ashfield, and to his daughters, two of whom, (aged 17), were Mary and Euphemia Ashfield His son, Redford Ashfield, resided mostly in Barbadoes, where he died, without issue, at Demarara, in 1786 or 1787, leaving his estate to his sister, Mary Ashfield, who married Col Elisha Lawrence, (son of John, near Allentown, N J), late of Nova Scotia, and died, probably near the close of the Revolutionary War, without issue, and to his other sister, Euphemia Ashfield, who married, Jan 12, 1793, George D Brinkerhoff, of Parcipany, Hanover Township, Morris Co., N. J.
Lewis Morris Ashfield had, in addition to the three children mentioned, a daughter, Elizabeth Ashfield, who married William Wilcocks, of New York, and a daughter, Catharine Ashfield, who married the Rev. Thomas Schrieve, of Long Island, and later of Nova Scotia See p 92, Vol 29, N. Y. Gen. & Biog. Record.

(b) Isabella Ashfield, born May 5, 1732, of Monmouth Co , N J., had a license to marry Samuel Hunt, of Westchester Co , N. Y , Nov 27, 1749.

(c) Vincent P. Ashfield married his cousin, Sarah, daughter of Lewis and Sarah (Gouverneur) Morris, license dated Sep. 15, 1772.

(d) Mary Ashfield, born 1728; died Sep. 19, 1791.

(e) Patience Ashfield ⎫
(f) Richard Ashfield ⎬ as per will, of their grandmother, Isabella Morris, 1747.
(g) Pearce Ashfield ⎭

31 LEWIS MORRIS, son of Lewis Morris, 10, succeeded to Passage Point, which he sold to John Leonard, his step-father, in 1710, and moved to Middletown, N J He was born circ. 1680, married, prior to 1710, Johannah . . . . .

1710 Lewis Morris, yeoman, and wife, Joanna, of Passage Point, in the town of Shrewsbury, deeded land to John Leonard, Esq , of Shrewsbury, his step-father "Whereas Christopher Almy, of Rhode Island, was seized of a certain tract of land and meadow, formerly known by the name of Norramsont, now called Passage point", these lands were acquired, in 1679, from the Proprietors, and passed from Simon Cooper, chirurgeon, in 1681, to Col Lewis Morris, who by his conveyance, Apr 15, 1689, did convey them to Lewis Morris, son of Thomas Morris, as also another tract, in Shrewsbury, purchased by Lewis Morris, son of Thomas Morris, (bought, in 1690, by Lewis Morris from William Shattock), and which descended to this Lewis Morris, as eldest son and heir "to my loving father, Lewis Morris, deceased, son of Thomas " This property was sold, to the aforesaid John Leonard, Esq , for £600

1710, Jan 9 Lewis Morris, of Passage Point, and wife, Johanna, sold land, to John Curlice, at Rumson Neck, which he heired from his "Father, Lewis Morris, son of Thomas Morris "

1716, Apr 21 Lewis Morris and wife, Joanna, conveyed, to Richard Morris, his loving brother, certain property, which "fell to me and descended from my loving father, Lewis Morris, at Hog Neck, in Middletown "

1723 He was a member of the Grand Jury

1733, Mch 26 Lewis Morris, yeoman, mortgaged, to the Commissioners, for £26-13-4, one hundred and fifty acres of land, in Middletown, bounded, in part, by Richard Morris' land William Hartshorne was a witness

1737 Lewis Morris mortgaged land for £20, in Middletown, bounded by Richard Morris

1738 Lewis Morris was a witness to the mortgage made by Thomas Morris, of his lands, in Nutswamp, to the Commissioners

1739 Lewis Morris, Sr , and Lewis Morris, Jr , had lands, bounding a mortgage to the Commissioners, in Nutswamp

1740 Lewis Morris, of Middletown, mortgaged lands on Jumping River James Grover and Lewis Morris, Jr , were on the boundaries

1743 Lewis Morris mortgaged lands in Middletown

1745 Lewis Morris took one of the poor to board Shrewsbury, N J , Town Poor Book

1748, May 30 or 31 Lewis Morris, of Shrewsbury, N J , had a daughter, Mary, baptized, at Christ Church

Issue

55 Lewis Morris, Jr , weaver, of Squankum.
56 Richard Morris , married Joanna Patterson, by license dated July 3, 1749 Joseph Patterson was bondsman, and Robert Patterson, and Elizabeth, his wife, gave their consent
57 Samuel Morris, married Hester Patterson, May 14, 1740
58 Christopher Morris, supposed, married Rebecca Layton.
59 John Morris, weaver. In 1740, he signed a bond He is separated, from other Johns, by his signature. This John Morris also signed the marriage license of Obadiah Layton to Hulden Hemones, Mch 22, 1758, which I believe to be a misspelled name

32 RICHARD MORRIS, son of Lewis Morris, 10, was born not far from 1690

In 1716, he received land from his brother, Lewis Morris

1720, May 9 He had recorded the earmark which belonged formerly to his father, Lewis Morris

1733 He had lands in Nutswamp, Middletown, N J

1737. He had lands in the same locality, when he was on the boundary of such lands

1741, June 19 He married, by license, Mary Porter spinster Joseph Shepherd, cooper, was bondsman The signing of his will, twenty-one years later, proves that all of his children, mentioned as under age, in his will, were by this wife As he left, at his death, in 1763, twenty children, of whom nine were minors, he must have been previously married, once if not twice, to account for the additional eleven children

1762, May 10 Will of Richard Morris, of Middletown, N J, proved May 3, 1763, mentioned
Wife, Mary Morris, £50
Son, William Morris, 10 shillihgs, to bar him as heir
Loving daughters, Phebe ⎫
                Anny ⎬ minors, under eighteen years, each, £50
                Rebecca
                Catharine ⎭
Five sons, Jacob ⎫
         Richard
         Lewis ⎬ each, £50 at the age of twenty-one years
         Robert
         George ⎭
Three daughters, Sarah Burdge ⎫
                Mary Burdge ⎬ each, £20
                Margaret Morford ⎭
Son, James Morris, to receive £50, over the others, if he keeps Henry
Son, Henry, to be kept by son, James
Son, Benjamin, the residue of the estate, on conditions
Nine children Richard ⎫
              Lewis
              Robert
              George
              Anny ⎬ to be maintained out of the estate, by Benjamin, until they are of age
              Phebe
              Rebecca
              Lidia
              Catharine ⎭
Son, John
Nine sons William
          Job
          James
          Joseph
          Jacob
          Richard
          Lewis
          Robert
          George
Executors Son-in-law, Joseph Burdge, of Freehold, and trusty friend, William Crawford, of Middletown
Witnesses David Morris, John Taylor and Benjamin Thorp, by his mark
The testator signed the will

1763 The inventory of the estate of Richard Morris, amounted to £1566-9-1¼
      Items.

Bond due, James and William Morris	£140
Bond due, William and James Morris	£147.
Bond due, Job Morris	£ 22
Bond due, James and William Morris	£ 86
Bond due Richard and David Morris	£109
Bond due, Joseph Morris	£ 10
Bond due, Nicholas Stillwell	£ 28.
Bond due, Thomas Stillwell and Mathias Mount	£ 6-16-9½.
Note due, John Stillwell	£ 1-4-0

      Issue
60 William Morris
61 John Morris

62 James Morris
63 Job Morris
64 Benjamin Morris
65 Joseph Morris
66 Henry Morris
67 Jacob Morris, not twenty-one years of age in 1762.
68 Richard Morris; not twenty-one years of age in 1762
69 Lewis Morris, not twenty-one years of age in 1762.
70 Robert Morris, not twenty-one years of age in 1762
71 George Morris, not twenty-one years of age in 1762
72 Phebe Morris, not eighteen years of age in 1762
73 Lydia Morris, not eighteen years of age in 1762.
74 Annie Morris, not eighteen years of age in 1762 Perhaps married, Job Crawford, in 1766
75 Rebecca Morris, not eighteen years of age in 1762
76 Catharine Morris, not eighteen years of age in 1762 Perhaps married, John Conover, in 1765
77 Sarah Morris, married Joseph Burdge, of Freehold, N J
78 Mary Morris, married, Jonathan Burdge, by license dated Nov 14, 1746, of Middletown
79 Margaret Morris, married John, son of Thomas and Mary (Wall) Morford.

33 THOMAS MORRIS, son of Lewis Morris, 10

1738 Thomas Morris mortgaged his lands, in Nutswamp, to the Commissioners Lewis Morris was a witness

1739 Thomas Morris was a witness, in Middletown, to a mortgage

1744 Thomas Morris mortgaged land

1753, July 3 "Margaret Morris, daughter of John Chasey, and wife of Thomas Morris, weaver, who is & has been absent a considerable time " Samuel Holmes' Account Book.

1798, Mch — Margaret Morris, widow, died Record of Baptist Church, Middletown

34 JOHN MORRIS, son of Lewis Morris, 10, was of Squankum, a place now called Farmingdale He was born June 12, 1695, died Mch 2, 1769, married, Nov 15, 1716, Jacomyntie, daughter of Robert and Frances (Stanley) White, born Apl. 3 (or 13), 1697, died Apl. 28, 1794

1721 John Morris appeared in the Court Records, of Freehold, N J.

1723 John Morris was indicted for taking a false oath, pleaded not guilty

1723-4, Jan 15 At a trial on this date, John Morris was defendant John West "being sworn on This Jury and Proving a Relation of the Defend^{ts}, withdrew by Consent of the Parties " Freehold, N J, Court Records

1739 John Morris, yeoman, was on the bond of Rebecka, widow of John Chamberlain, to administer the estate of her late husband All were of Shrewsbury

1769 John Morris, of Squanquam, in Shrewsbury, died intestate, and administration was granted to John Morris and Elazarus Brewer, of the same place. Inventory amounted to £50.

Issue

80 Elizabeth Morris, born Oct. 29, 1721
81 John Morris, born Sep 29, 1724.

HISTORICAL MISCELLANY

82 Lewis Morris, of Squankum, born July 17, 1726; married Gertrude Montgomery
83 Mary Morris, born Apr 23, 1730
84 Frances Morris, born Feb 15, 1732-3, died Feb 27, 1807
85 Robert Morris, born Mch 8, 1735-6, married Elizabeth, daughter of Thomas Ellison, by license dated Feb 10, 1762, Jaratt Morford being surety.
86 Richard Morris, born May 14, 1739
87 Thomas Morris, born Feb 15, 1741-2; baptized 1758

35 REBECCA MORRIS, daughter of Lewis Morris, 10, married John, son of Henry and Ann (West) Chamberlin He was buried Sep. 2, 1739, and she was appointed administratrix, Nov 27, 1739, with John Morris, yeoman, on the bond

Issue

Philena Chamberlain had a marriage license, dated Jan. 13, 1744-5, to Jediah Stout John Chamberlain was on the bond
John Chamberlain
Lewis Chamberlain, married Lucretia Wolsey
Richard Chamberlain
Henry Chamberlain, born 1725, married and had a daughter, Philena.
Joseph Chamberlain*

40 Thomas Morris, son of John Morris, 11, married Dorothy Sadler
Issue
88 Dorothy Morris; married Col Sadler, of Jamaica, West Indies
89 Margaret Morris
90 Charles Morris, married Miss Masters
91 Thomas Morris, married Dorothy Masters, died without issue

41 VALENTINE MORRIS, son of John Morris, 11, was Lieut.-Colonel in Dalzell's regiment, married, first, in 1704, Elizabeth, daughter and co-heiress of Sir Christopher Keynell She died Feb 15, 1715, and he married, second, in 1720, Elizabeth Wilmott

Issue by first wife
92 Grace Morris, born Mch. 2, 1713.
93 Henrietta Morris, born May 2, 1712, married Edward Horne, of Antigua, West Indies.
94 Elizabeth Morris, born May 19, 1709, married John Fry, of Antigua, West Indies
95 Francis Morris, born July 10, 1706
96 John Morris, born June 13, 1705, died without issue

Issue by second wife
97 Caroline Morris, born Mch 8, 1729.
98 Sarah Morris, born Mch 15, 1723
99 Valentine Morris, born Oct 16, 1727
100 Francis Morris, born Oct 16, 1727

43 LEWIS MORRIS, son of Lewis Morris, 21, was born at Morrisania, N Y., Apl. 8, 1726, where he died Jan 22 1798 He graduated from Yale College at the age of 20, was a

*All five of these brothers removed to Middlesex and Hunterdon Counties

delegate to the Continental Congress in 1775, the same in 1776 to the Congress of the Declaration of Independence, which he signed, was Colonel of the Westchester Co militia, and with his sons served in the War of the Revolution He married, Sep 24, 1749, Mary, daughter of Jacob Walton by Maria, daughter of William Beekman, born February, 1727, died Mch 11, 1794

Issue

    101 Mary Morris, married her cousin Thomas Lawrence, of Philadelphia
    102 Catherine Morris, married Thomas Lawrence upon the death of his first wife
    103 Sarah Morris, died single.
    104 Magdelena [Helen] Morris, married John Rutherford
    105 Lewis Morris, eldest son, married Ann Elliott, of South Carolina
    106 Jacob Morris, married Mary Cox.
    107 William Morris, married Sarah Carpenter, resided at Balston Springs, N Y
    108 Staats Morris, married Catalina Van Braeme
    109 Richard Valentine Morris, married Ann Walton, lived at Saratoga Springs, N Y
    110 James Morris, married Helena Van Courtlandt, lived at Pelham, N Y

His grandchildren were fifty-nine in number

44 STAATS LONG MORRIS, son of Lewis Morris, 21, was born Aug 27, 1728, and died Jan 22, 1798 He removed to England prior to the Revolution, where he purchased a commission in the British Army, and rose to the rank of a General He married, by license dated Mch 25, 1756, Lady Catherine Gordon, daughter of William, second Earl of Aberdeen, and widow of Cosmo George, third Duke of Gordon, born 1719, died 1752. She died Dec 10, 1779, and he married, second, Jane Urquart, born 1749, died Mch 15, 1801

45 RICHARD MORRIS, son of Lewis Morris 21, was born Aug 15, 1730, and died Apl 11, 1810 He married, June 13, 1759, Sarah, daughter of the New York merchant, Henry Ludlow, born Sep 15, 1730, died Oct. 28, 1791. He was one of the framers of the first state constitution, and second Chief Justice of New York.

Issue

    111 Lewis R Morris, known as General Lewis R. Morris He served in his youth in the Revolutionary War Moved to Vermont and represented that state in Congress
    112 Robert Morris, of Fordam, N Y
    113 Mary Morris, married Major William Popham of the Revolutionary War They resided at Scarsdale, N. Y

48 GOUVERNEUR MORRIS, son of Lewis Morris, 21 born Jan 30, 1752; died Nov 6, 1816, married late in life, Dec 25, 1809, Ann Cary Randolph, daughter of Thomas Mann Randolph, of Tuckahoe, Virginia, and of the line of Pocahontas She died May 28, 1837 His birth is recorded in the Family Bible in these words

"The 30th of January about half an hour after one of the Clock in the morning in the year 1754 according to the alteration of the stile by act of Parliament my wife was delivered of a son He was christened the 4th May, 1752, and named Gouverneur, after my wife's father Nicholas Gouverneur and my son Staats were his godfathers, and my sister Antil his godmather Parson Auchmuty* christened him"

*"Parson Auchmuty" was then the Rector of Trinity Church

Gouverneur Morris was Minister to France at the time of the French Revolution, and it was from his pen the final draft of the Constitution is said to have come. He was an intimate friend of Washington, a business partner of Robert Morris, the financier, and a signer of the Declaration of Independence.

Issue
114 Gouverneur Morris

51 ROBERT MORRIS, natural son of Robert Hunter Morris, 22, died, in 1815, in Somerset County, N. J. He was a Chief-Justice of New Jersey.

52 MARY MORRIS, natural daughter of Robert Hunter Morris, 22, married James Boggs, M D

Elizabeth Stogdale, in her will on record at Trenton, mentions her son-in-law, James Boggs, thus proving that she was the mother of Robert Hunter Morris' natural daughter, Mary.

Issue
Elizabeth Boggs
And others

53 COL JOHN MORRIS, natural son of Surrogate John Morris, 23, was baptized in Christ Church, Shrewsbury, Jan 1, 1737, and was mentioned in the will of Governor Robert Hunter Morris, in 1757, as "my nephew, an officer in Lascasses, [Lafscellses], Regiment"

New-York, September 16 On Thursday last arrived here in 9 Weeks from Plymouth, but last in 6 from Madeira, His Majesty's Ship the Mermaid, the Honorable Washington Shirley, Esq, Commander, stationed at Boston, having brought the Honorable ROBERT HUNTER MORRIS, Esq, Lieutenant Governor of the Province of Pennsylvania, and in the afternoon of the same Day His Honour landed in good Health near the Flat-Rock-Battery, in this City, where he was welcomed ashore by a great Number of Gentlemen, and from thence conducted up to the House of the Honourable James Alexander, Esq, in Broad-Street We hear he sets out this Week for Philadelphia

Mr Morris, the Governor's Nephew, likewise arrived in the Mermaid, being appointed Captain of the Independent Company formerly Governor Clinton's, in this Garrison —The N Y Gazette or the Weekly Post Boy, Sept 16, 1754   New Jersey Archives, Vol XIX, p 409-410

1764, Mch. 27. John Morris was a witness to a document, in which Mary Ashfield, of Shrewsbury, sets free a negro, sold to her by the executors of the late Chief-Justice, Robert Hunter Morris.

1768, July 26 John Morris was a resident of Shrewsbury, when he bought twelve hundred and twenty-four acres of land, at Barnegat, for £1145-13-0, from the executors of Robert Hunter Morris

1776, Aug 17 John Morris was commissioned Lieut -Colonel, in 2nd New Jersey Battalion, and was in service until 1780 He formerly served in the 47th Regiment, of the British Line   New Jersey Royalist Volunteers, by William S Stryker, Esq

John Morris was "Colonel in the New Jersey Volunteers. In 1777, he was sent by Sir William Howe to destroy the salt works at Tom's River Bridge, but when informed that the property was private, in part, he declined to comply with his orders"
Sabine's Royalists, Vol II, p. 107

Col John Morris married Sarah Antill, who was born 1740.

Issue
115 John Morris, baptized, in Christ Church, Shrewsbury, Aug. 20, 1772.

116 Sarah Morris, baptized, in Christ Church, Shrewsbury, July 24, 1774
117 Amelia Morris, baptized, in Christ Church, Shrewsbury, Jan 29, 1775

54 ANN MORRIS, natural daughter of John Morris, 23

1775, May 31 Ann Morris, of Shrewsbury, singlewoman, makes "my brother, John Morris, of the same place, my attorney," to recover from the executors of Robert Hunter Morris, what was left to them, in trust, for her, by said Robert Hunter Morris

Issue

118 Helene Morris, a natural daughter of Ann Morris by her cousin, Lewis Morris Ashfield Helene Morris, 118, married Richard Clay

55 LEWIS MORRIS, son of Lewis Morris, 31, is mentioned, in 1739, in conjunction with his father, Lewis Morris, as residing in Middletown, and on the boundaries of property in Nutswamp, Middletown, N J

It was probably he who married, as per Christ Church Records, Apr 2, 1735, Margaret Hildreth, at Tinton

57 SAMUEL MORRIS, son of Lewis Morris, 31

1740, Jan 21. Samuel Morris, cordwainer, and Hester Patterson, spinster, both of Monmouth County, had a license to marry, John Morris, "weaver," being surety on the bond She was a daughter of Robert and Elizabeth Patterson.

1741 Samuel Morris was a witness to the mortgage of William Pattan, to the Commissioners

1743 Samuel Morris mortgaged land, in Middletown, bounded by Lewis Morris' line, Jumping Brook, James Grover, and Ebenezer Applegate

1773, July 17. Samuel Morris bought the farm, at Leedsville, N J., from John Morris, son of Richard Morris, deceased

1775, Aug. 7. Will of Samuel Morris, of Middletown, proved Mch 28, 1780, mentioned Wife, but does not give her name
Daughter, Joanna
Sons, Isaac
    Amariah
    James
    Robert
    Zephaniah
    John
    Elisha

Issue

119 Joanna Morris, married William Taylor, of New York
120 Isaac Morris
121 Amariah Morris, born 1747
122 James Morris, born 1754
123 Robert [P] Morris
124 Zephania Morris
125 John Morris
126 Elisha Morris

58 CHRISTOPHER MORRIS, supposed son of Lewis Morris, 31

1742, May 1 Christopher Morris and Rebecca Layton had a license to marry

1758, October He was taxed, in Upper Freehold, for fifty acres

1766 Christopher Morris became a member of the Upper Freehold Baptist Church, by letter, from the Middletown Baptist Church Catharine Morris and William Vaughn appear in the same list of church members.

1796 Christopher Morris was Moderator

1801, Feb 14. Will of Christopher Morris, proved June 17, 1801, mentioned
Wife, Mary
Daughters, Mary Giberson
          Ann Trout
          Catharine Debow
Several sons, all provided for

Issue

127 Mary Giberson
128 Ann Trout
129 Catharine Debow
130 William Morris, of Piles Grove. He is supposed to have been one of the *sons* mentioned in his father's will, but who are unnamed

60 WILLIAM MORRIS, son of Richard Morris, 32, died May, 1777, was, apparently, the eldest son, but was superseded, as his father's heir, by his brother His lands lay at Shrewsbury

1739, 10, 8mo Elizabeth Brewer, of Shrewsbury, was married to William Morris, of Middletown, at the house of Adam Brewer, in Shrewsbury

1768 William Morris, with James Morris, appears on the Town Poor Book, Shrewsbury, N J

1769 He conveyed land to Richard Morris, and in 1770, with his wife, Elizabeth, he conveyed land to Lewis Morris

In 1770, he resided at Shrewsbury, N J

1776 He mortgaged land for £43

1777, Apr. 7. Will of William Morris, of Shrewsbury; proved Oct 10, 1782, mentioned
Wife, Elizabeth
Grandson, Elihu Morris, son of Adam Morris, deceased
Two youngest sons, Joel and Benjamin Morris, who received the homestead, at Shrewsbury
Brother, Henry Morris
Daughters, Phoebe
          Lydia
          Mary
Sons, William
      Richard
Grandchildren, Elihu
             Joseph
             William
             Elizabeth
Executors William Parker, Jr, Jacob Long and Edward Patterson Cook.
Witnesses Lewis Morris, Thos Smith and Joseph Burdge

Issue

131 Adam Morris
132 Lydia Morris, died Jan 16, 1786, married John Warden.
133 Phebe Morris
134 William Morris

MORRIS OF MONMOUTH COUNTY

135 Mary Morris, married, about 1784, Peter, son of Edward Patterson and Lydia (Chandler) Cook
136 Richard Morris, married Mary .
137 Joel Morris
138 Benjamin Morris

61 JOHN MORRIS, son of Richard Morris, 32.

In the possession of the Morris Family, near Leedsville, N. J., is a deed to their lands from John, son of Richard Morris, deceased, to Samuel Morris, July 17, 1773.

1765, June 23 A John Morris and Elizabeth Woodruf, both of Monmouth County, had a license to marry

1789 A John Morris died and his estate was administered by his wife, Anna

62 JAMES MORRIS, son of Richard Morris, 32, resided at Shrewsbury, N. J.

1753, July 18 James Morris and Leah White, of Monmouth County, had a license to marry She was a daughter of Amos White, of Deal, N J, and Jane Borden, his wife

1768 James Morris was mentioned, with William Morris, in the Town Poor Book, Shrewsbury, N J

1769, Jan 16 Will of James Morris, "low in health", proved Mch 18, 1769, mentioned.
Wife, but name is not given
Son, Amos Morris } minors
Son, Joel White Morris }
Two daughters, not named
Executors His father-in-law, Amos White, and Edward Patterson Cook, of Shrewsbury.
The testator signed his will

Inventory of the personal estate of James Morris, which contained negroes, amounted to £389-4-6

1788, Feb 28 Amos Morris and Lydia his wife, and Joel White Morris, as sons of James Morris, convey various tracts of land in Squancum that had been conveyed to their father, Edward Patterson Cook being witness to the deed

Issue

139 Amos Morris
140 Joel White Morris
141 Daughter
142 Daughter

63 JOB MORRIS, son of Richard Morris, 32

1760, May 17 Job Morris and Mary Ansley, both of Monmouth County, had a license to marry

1786 June 28 Will of Job Morris, proved Aug 25, 1786, mentioned
Wife, Mary
Son, Jeames
Daughter, Silfe [Zilpha?]
Daughter, Mary
Daughter, Lida
Daughter, Rebecca, wife of Hugh Jackson

Issue

143 James Morris, married, first, 3mo, 22, 1786, Ann Jackson, second, 10 mo, 10,

1798, Elizabeth, daughter of David and [Lydia White?] Curtis, born July 31, 1759.*
144 Zilpha Morris
145 Mary Morris
146 Lydia Morris
147 Rebecca Morris, born 10 mo , 10, 1763, died 4, 8, 1806, married Hugh, son of and Mary (Wolcott) Jackson

64 BENJAMIN MORRIS, son of Richard Morris, 32, married, first, Mary Robins, by license dated Dec 2, 1763, second, Hannah

1764, June 27 Had recorded the earmark which was "formerly his Fathers "

1810, Apr. 20 Will of Benjamin Morris, of Freehold, proved Jan 29, 1812, mentioned
Wife, Hannah
Son, Ezekiel Morris
Daughter, Nancy Robins, wife of Ezekiel
Grandson, Benjamin Morris, son of Samuel, not yet twenty-one years of age
Son, Calebe Morris
Son, Elisha Morris
Daughter, Molley
Daughter, ' debory"
Executors Son, Ezekiel Morris, and Joseph Robins
The testator signed the will

Issue

148 Ezekiel Morris
149 Ann Morris, married Ezekiel Robbins
150 Samuel Morris
151 Caleb Morris
152 Elisha Morris
153 Mary Morris
154 Deborah Morris
155 Sarah Morris

1793 Will of Leah Robbins, of Upper Freehold, Monmouth County, N J , proved Apr 13, 1804, mentioned
Sons, Joseph
Zebulon
John
To Sarah, Ann, Mary, Deborah, children of Benjamin and Mary Morris, a legacy
To Sarah, daughter of Nathaniel and Margaret Cook, a legacy
To Ann and Leah Imlay, daughters of Samuel and Meribah Imlay, a legacy
Elizabeth Sexton, daughter of William and Elizabeth Sexton, "being all 8 my grandchildren "
To Friends of Robins' Meeting, £3
Grand-daughter, Ann Robins, wife of Ezekiel
Executor Joel Cheshire

65 JOSEPH MORRIS, son of Richard Morris, 32 He died March, 1763

1755, Aug 2 Joseph Morris and Johannah Hulit, both of Shrewsbury, N J , had a license to marry

*It has thus far proved impossible to verify the statement that it was the daughter of David and Lydia Curtis whom James Morris married

1763, Mch 14 Will of Joseph Morris, of Shrewsbury, N J., proved Apr 2, 1763, mentioned
Wife, Joanna
Son, John Morris
Son, Joseph Morris
Daughter, Mary Morris
He alluded to "whatsoever may be left me by will of my father, Richd Morris "
Brother, Benjamin Morris
Executors His wife, brother Benjamin and brother-in-law, William Huhtt
The testator signed the will

The inventory of the estate of Joseph Morris amounted to £77–3–0

Issue

156 John Morris
157 Mary Morris, born Sept 20, 1758, died July 19, 1807, married, Apr 25, 1781, Benjamin White, by license dated Apr 16, 1781.
158 Joseph Morris
All three baptized, May 5, 1765, at Christ Church, Shrewsbury, N. J
159 William Morris, a posthumous child, very doubtful. If so, said child was baptized, June 8, 1766, at Christ Church, Shrewsbury, N. J, as the child of the Widow Morris

66 HENRY MORRIS, son of Richard Morris, 32, was, probably, non compos, from the terms of his father's will

67 JACOB MORRIS, son of Richard Morris, 32

1732, Feb 14 Daniel Grandin, of Upper Freehold, sold to Jacob Morris, blacksmith, of the same place, land on Doctor's Creek, next to Thomas Williams
1734, May 4 Jacob Morris sold land, at Crosswicks, to Ezekiel Forman
1765, Feb 13 Jacob Morris and Elizabeth Ansley, of Monmouth County, had a license to marry
1766, Feb 14 Will of Jacob Morris, of Shrewsbury, proved Sep 23, 1767, mentioned
Wife, Elizabeth, being with child
Son, Jacob Morris
Executors William Crawford and James Grover, his friends, of Middletown
The testator signed the will

The two executors renounced their executorship and the widow was appointed administratrix, with the will annexed, with William Vankirk, of Freehold, as bondsman
The administratrix made her mark Samuel Leonard was witness

Issue

160 Jacob Morris
161 A posthumous child

68 RICHARD MORRIS, son of Richard Morris, 32, married Abigail

1776 Richard Morris, of Shrewsbury, mortgaged land, at Squan, bounded by William Morris, and which he received, by deed, from William Morris, in 1769
Richard Morris and Benjamin Morris, with Mary and Abigail, their wives, mortgage land, about 1795, as recorded at Freehold, in Liber C, of Mortgages, Folio 203

69 LEWIS MORRIS, son of Richard Morris, 32

1768 To the widow of Lewis Morris, for provision, on account of her lame child £1-6-3
Shrewsbury, N J, Town Poor Book

1776. Lewis Morris, of Shrewsbury, mortgaged land, at Squancom, in Shrewsbury, for £15 bounded by William Morris, Samuel Leonard, etc, which was conveyed to him, by deed, of William and Elizabeth Morris, in 1770

1763, May 30 There was a Lewis Morris, of Monmouth County, and Lidy Hoffmire, who had a license to marry

81 JOHN MORRIS, son of John Morris, 34, was born Sept 29, 1724, died May 22, 1789 It is believed he married Rebecca Cox, for a marriage license was issued, Feb 24, 1763, to John Morris, of Middlesex County, and Rebecca Cox She probably married, second, Mr Chasey, for an old family Bible says "John Morris, the son of Rebecca Chasey, was born Sept 29, 1765" This is about two years and a half after the marriage license of John Morris and Rebecca Cox, and while the Bible does not state that John Morris did marry her, and it may be that Rebecca Chasey was a different person from Rebecca Cox, it nevertheless looks as if Rebecca Cox and Rebecca Chasey were the same person

1744, Nov 3 He was surety on the bond for the marriage license of Remembrance Lippincott, Jr., and Rebekah Knott

1747, Nov 4 He was a witness to the will of William Lippincott, of Shrewsbury, and testified at the probate of the same, Apl 5, 1748

1768, Aug. 22. He was a witness to the will of Adam Brewer, of Squancome

1769 John Morris, Jr, resided at Squankum, and was, with Elazarus Brewer, an executor of his father's estate

There was also a John Morris to whom a marriage license was issued to marry Euphame Brindley, both of Monmouth County, Apr 29, 1763

Issue

162 John Morris, born Sep 29, 1765; buried June 5, 1811

82 LEWIS MORRIS, son of John Morris, 34, was born, in Monmouth County, July 17, 1726, married Gertruydt Montgomery, born, Oct 27, 1741, in New Jersey The date of his birth, as given in his Bible, at Watervliet, Rennsalaer Co, N Y, coincides precisely with that given in the old Family Bible, heretofore quoted, and owned by a descendant living in Plano, Kendall Co, Ill

1768 He resided at Farmingdale, or Squankum, N J

Issue

163 Charles A Morris, born Jan 4, 1764, buried Nov 26, 1842 married Catharine Van Antwerp
164 James Lawrence Morris, born Jan 19, 1766
165 Fanny Morris, born July 1, 1768, died May 21, 1834
166 Lewis Morris, born Feb 22, 1771
167 Robert Morris, born Oct 9, 1773, died Sep 19, 1832, married Elizabeth Monell
168 Ann Morris, born Feb 5, 1776, died May 18, 1834
169 Leah Morris, born Jan 29, 1780, died, unmarried, near Watervliet, Rennsalaer Co, N Y

83 MARY MORRIS, daughter of John Morris, 34, was born Apr 23, 1730, died June 1, 1806 She married, by license dated Dec 7, 1757, Asahel Freeman, probably more correctly called, as appears in the Bible record, Essec Freeman

Issue

Morris Freeman, born Dec 5, 1757
Marssey Freeman, born Nov. 19, 1758
Ledia Freeman, born Jan. 22, 1761
Richard Freeman, born Mch. 2, 1763
Essec Freeman, born Sept. 20, 1764
Anne Freeman, born Aug 3, 1766
James Freeman, born Aug 5, 1770

The Bible also says, that Mary Morris was the mother of Deborah White, born Dec. 22, 1754

84 FRANCES MORRIS, daughter of John Morris, 34, born Feb 15, 1732-3, died Feb 27, 1807, married, by license dated June 25, 1755, Elazerus Brewer, cordwinder, of Shrewsbury, son of Adam and his second wife, Deborah (Allen) Brewer, Samuel Lippincott, yeoman, being surety on the bond Although the date of the license is as given above, yet the old Bible states that "John, son of Elazerus and Frances Brewer, was born Sept. 16, 1754," and this date agrees with the inscription on his tombstone, at Farmingdale. I am inclined to think, therefore, that the license was issued in 1753 Elazerus Brewer was born June 23, 1731, died Mch 31, 1820, aged 88, 9, 8

Issue

John Brewer, born Sep 16, 1754, died Feb 6, 1837, married Constant Hulet, born Jan 26, 1761, died Sep 17, 1845, aged 84, 7, 22
Adam Brewer, born Nov 11, 1757, died May 30, 1775
Aaron Robbins Brewer, of Canada, born Jan. 30, 1760, died Feb 25, 1802, married Elizabeth, daughter of Philip and Margaret Cooper
Mary Brewer, born Mch 6, 1763, died May 25, 1806, married William Matthews, as his first wife
Deborah Brewer, born Mch 15, 1765; died Apl 6, 1836, married Amor, son of Edward Patterson and Lydia (Chandler) Cook, born June 16, 1764, died Feb 14, 1852
George Brewer, born Nov 20, 1770, died Mch 23, 1851, married, first, Rebecca Schenck, second, Aug 3, 1810, Lydia Hulet
Elizabeth Brewer, born Apl 15, 1776, married May 19, 1799, James Van Kirk

105 LEWIS MORRIS, son of Lewis Morris, 43, married Ann Elliott, of South Carolina

Issue

170 Colonel Lewis Morris
171 William Morris
172 George Morris
173 Richard Morris, of Pelham, N Y
174 Jacob Morris
175 Sabina Morris, married Robert Rutherford
176 Mary Morris, married W C Wayne
177 Ann Morris, married Elias Vanderhorst

106 GENERAL JACOB MORRIS, son of Lewis Morris, 43, died, at the age of 88, in 1844. At the early age of nineteen he became a Revolutionary Soldier and served throughout that War, being favorably mentioned by General Charles Lee, on whose staff he served in the Battle of Monmouth, New Jersey, as well as distinguishing himself at Fort Moultrie in 1776. General Jacob Morris married twice, first, during the Revolution, Mary Cox, by whom he had twelve children, most of whom lived to advanced ages. He, Jacob Morris, married, second, when over seventy years old, Miss Pringle.

Lewis Morris, (the father of Jacob Morris), with his brother Richard, received a tract of three thousand acres of land in Montgomery County from the State of New York, as indemnification for loss and damage done to their property by the British occupation of their estate in Morrisania during the Revolution. To this great tract of land, situated in the valley of the Butternuts, Jacob Morris migrated, and established his home on the thousand acre tract which was the portion of his father. Here a manor house was built, at what is now known as Morris, Otsego County, still in the possession of his descendants, and where may be found many family relics in the shape of furniture, etc.

Beautiful miniatures of Jacob Morris and his wife, taken when they were young, are in the possession of Mrs Sidney Webster, a daughter of Hamilton Fish. One of Jacob Morris' daughters, a woman of many graces, married Hamilton Fish, who was Secretary of State under General Grant, and as an evidence of her cleverness it is said that "she left Washington without having made an enemy."

General Jacob Morris was interred in the Cemetery attached to the Morris Memorial Chapel of All Saints, which was erected in 1866, by contributions from various members of the Morris family.

Issue by first wife, (from Bolton, in part)
178 Sarah Morris, married, first, Peter Kean, second, Mr. Baker
179 Catharine Morris, married Mr Prentiss.
180 Mary Morris; married Isaac Cooper, of Cooperstown, brother of J Fenimore Cooper, the writer.
181 Augustus Morris
182 Valentine Morris
183 Jacob Morris } Of Butternuts, Otsego Co., N. Y
184 Richard Morris
185 John Cox Morris
186 Lee Morris
187 Daughter, married Hamilton Fish
188
189

Issue by second wife
190 William Morris, of Butternuts
191 A P Morris

107 WILLIAM MORRIS, son of Lewis Morris, 43, married Miss Sarah Carpenter, and resided at Ballston Spa, N Y

Issue
192 Anne Morris, married A G. Stout.
193 Frances Morris, married Captain Brooks, of the United States Army
194 Maria Morris

195 Caroline Morris
196 Arthur Morris, of New York.
197 James Morris
198 Captain Gouverneur Morris, of the United States Army
199 Major William Morris, of the United States Army
200 Lewis Morris

108 STAATS MORRIS, son of Lewis Morris, 43, married Mrs Roberts, says Bolton, but more probably Catalina Van Braeme

Issue

201 Sarah Morris, married Mr Leonard
202 Louisa Morris, married Norman Squires
203 Frederick Morris, of Batavia, Island of Java
204 Walter Morris, of Albany, Vermont
205 Lewis Nelson Morris, killed, at Monterey, 1846.

109 RICHARD VALENTINE MORRIS, son of Lewis Morris, 43, married Ann Walton, and lived at Saratoga Springs, N Y

Issue

206 Gerard W Morris, of New York
207 Richard V Morris, of New York
208 Henry Morris, of New York

110 JAMES MORRIS, son of Lewis Morris, 43, was the youngest son He married Helena Van Courtlandt, and resided at Pelham, N Y

Issue

209 James Van Courtlandt Morris
210 Augustus Frederick Van Courtlandt Morris
211 Richard Lewis Morris, M D
212 Robert R Morris
213 William H Morris
214 Catharine Morris, married H H Stevens, M. D
215 Mary Morris
216 Helen Morris, married Richard Morris
217 Ann Morris
218 Jane Morris
219 Louisa Morris, married Edward Le Roy
220 Charlotte Morris, married Richard Kemble

114 GOUVERNEUR MORRIS, the only child of Gouverneur Morris, 48, born Feb 9, 1813, was a man of wealth and enterprise, and a gentleman farmer on a large scale In 1842, he married his cousin, Martha Jefferson Cary, of Virginia She died in 1873, and he married, second, in 1876, his cousin, Anna Morris He resided at Pelham, N Y., and died, Aug 20, 1888, aged 75 years,

By his first wife he had ten children, five of whom survived him See article of Anne Cary Morris, in New York Genealogical and Biographical Record, January, 1889

HISTORICAL MISCELLANY

121 AMARIAH MORRIS, son of Samuel Morris, 57, was born in 1747, died, Sept 1, 1807, aged 60 years and 9 months, married Sarah   ., who died, Sept. 10, 1810, aged 57 years and 9 months

Issue

221 Elizabeth Morris, died, Dec 5, 1806, aged 24 years, 9 months and 1 day
222 Garret Morris, baptized May 11, 1775, married, 1794, Mary Suydam
223 Jonathan Morris, married Micah   .
224 Mary Morris, baptized June 20, 1779, married Stoffel Longstreet
225 Hannah Morris, married Thomas White*
226 Sarah Morris

122 JAMES MORRIS, son of Samuel Morris, 57, died, Oct. 27, 1820, aged 66 years, 9 months and 18 days; married Lydia Patterson, (probably a daughter of Robert Patterson), who died, Sept 13, 1844, aged 87 years and 8 days

Issue

227 Robert Morris
228 Samuel Morris, died, unmarried, Jan 20, 1837, aged 51 years and 20 days
229 James Morris, died unmarried.
230 Lydia Morris, married Mr Davis
231 Polly Morris; married Mr Lloyd
232 Joseph Morris, married Deborah Bennet

In the graveyard, on the Morris farm, near Leedsville, N J, from which these epitaphs were copied, is a stone which records
Joseph Morris died, Sept 23, 1826, aged 51 years, 5 months and 14 days
Mary, his wife, died, Jan 1, 1828, aged 43 years, 3 months and 15 days
These I cannot place

123 ROBERT P MORRIS, son of Samuel Morris, 57, born 1734; died 1826, married, first, Jan 9, 1766, Content Dunham Christ Church, Shrewsbury, N. J, Record. He married, second, Mary Cooper

Issue

233 Samuel Morris, born Aug 25 1770, of Farmingdale, N. J.
234 James Morris, of Eatontown, N J, afterwards went West
235 Joseph Morris, removed to Rockbridge, Va

124 ZEPHANIAH MORRIS, son of Samuel Morris, 57, married, Jan 25, 1765, Mary Daws

Issue

236 William Morris, born Feb 1, 1765
237 Isaac Zephaniah Morris, born Aug 11, 1766, died May 31, 1856
238 Mary Morris, born Mch 19, 1770, married William Ryer
239 Ann Morris, born June 7, 1772
240 John Morris, born Dec 5 1774

*Nancy White and Thomas White, children of Thomas White and Joanna Morris, were baptized May 2, 1784
Records of the Reformed Dutch Church, of New York

MORRIS OF MONMOUTH COUNTY

241 Joseph Morris, born Apl 9, 1777, died Sep. 23, 1826
242 Ann Morris, born Oct 19, 1779

130 WILLIAM MORRIS, supposed son of Christopher Morris, 58
1768, Mch 4 A William Morris and Martha Vaughn had a license to marry

1785, Jan 12. Will of William Morris, of Piles Grove, Salem County, proved Feb 15, 1785, mentioned
Wife, Martha [Wain or Vaughn, who afterwards married Mr Greene, family tradition]
Eldest son, Christopher, under age
Youngest son, William
Daughter, Elizabeth
Executors Wife, Martha, son Christopher, and friend, Solomon Smith

Issue

243 Christopher Morris, born 1768
244 Elizabeth Morris, married Mr Ripley
245 [Polly Morris?], not mentioned in the will.
246 William Morris

131 ADAM MORRIS, son of William Morris, 60, married .
Issue
247 Elihu Morris

134 WILLIAM MORRIS, son of William Morris, 60, had
Issue
248 Elizabeth Morris, who married and had three children
249 Rosanna Morris, who married and had one child
250 Ann Morris
251 William Morris, married Mary Van Nort
252 Phebe Morris, who married and had five children
253 James Morris, who married and had two children
254 Joseph Morris, who married and had one child

137 JOEL MORRIS, son of William Morris, 60, married Rebecca Stillwell
Issue
255 Richard Morris, married, first, Mary Van Kirk, second, Alice Van Kirk, widow of Francis Errickson, born Mch 23, 1800, died June 19, 1844.
256 Ann Morris
257 Rachel Morris
258 William Morris
259 Joseph Morris

138 BENJAMIN MORRIS, son of William Morris, 60, born Nov 13, 1760, died Feb 22, 1829, married Abigail   , born Oct 6, 1761, died Jan 15, 1798

Issue

260 Deborah Morris, born Nov 3, 1783
261 Adam Morris, born Jan 23, 1785, married, Mch 9, 1811, Lydia Matthews

262 Sarah Morris, born Nov 6, 1786
263 Lydia Morris, born Aug 17, 1788, died Jan 4, 1790
264 Obediah Morris, born June 5, 1790
265 Ann Morris, born Apl 9, 1793
266 Keturiah Morris, born Feb 23, 1795, married, Aug 16, 1821, Gilbert Miller

150 SAMUEL MORRIS, son of Benjamin Morris, 64, married
Issue
267 Benjamin Morris, not yet of age, Apr 20, 1810, when his grandfather made his will

152 ELISHA MORRIS, son of Benjamin Morris, 64, died 1803, married, first, ., second, Dec 31, 1800, Deborah Burges
1803, Sep 23. Deborah Morris made administratrix on the estate of Elisha Morris, deceased, of Monmouth Co
Issue by first wife
268 Elizabeth Morris, married, Nov 14, 1810, Johnson Van Mater

157 MARY MORRIS, daughter of Joseph Morris, 65, born Sep 20, 1757, died July 19, 1807, married, as his first wife, Apl. 25, 1781, by license dated Apl 16, 1781, Benjamin White, son of George and Anne (Lippincott) White, born Dec 4, 1755, died Nov 7, 1841

Issue
Elizabeth White, born Mch 2, 1781, died Oct 4, 1854, married, Sep 12, 1799, Amos, son of William and Hester (Middleton) Tilton, born Oct 7, 1774, died Sep 3, 1819
Caroline White, born May 30, 1782; died Mch 31, 1798.
John White, born Oct 11, 1783, married Jane Wright
Mary White, born Apr 1, 1785, died Oct 21, 1861, married, June 3, 1803, Thaddeus, son of Hezekiah and Mary (Betts) Whitlock, born Oct 21, 1781
Agnes White, born Nov 20, 1786, died Dec 3, 1786
Joanna White, born Jan 20, 1788, died 1788
Annie White, born Mch 11, 1789, died Sep. 22, 1860
Susannah White, born June 3, 1791, died Oct 3, 1796
Joanna White, born Apr. 13, 1793, died Aug. 11, 1793
Morris White, born May 3, 1794, died Oct 1, 1796
Benjamin Morris White, born July 20, 1797; died June 8, 1817
Joseph Embree White, born Jan 23, 1799, died July 9, 1874, married, May 22, 1834, Sarah White, daughter of Jacob and Rachel (White) Corlies, born June 21, 1797, died Feb 21, 1890
Susan White, born July 11, 1801, died July 12, 1865

164 JAMES LAWRENCE MORRIS, son of Lewis Morris, 82, born, at Farmingdale, N. J, Jan 19, 1766, died, at Manasquan, N J, May 13, 1839, married Abigail, daughter of Thomas and Catherine (Potter) Tilton, died Mch 17, 1850

Issue
269 Amos Tilton Morris, married Elizabeth St Clair Berry.

MORRIS OF MONMOUTH COUNTY

270 Gertrude Ann Morris, born Apl 30, 1802, died Aug 20, 1882, married, first, ... Hampton, second, June 30, 1834, Joseph, son of David Corlies
271 William Morris
272 Middleton Morris, died Nov 16, 1850, aged 38 years
273 Catherine Morris
274 Robert L Morris, born Oct 9, 1804
275 Joseph Morris
276 Charles Morris, (supposed), born 1810, died Nov 24, 1842.

213 WILLIAM H MORRIS, son of James Morris, 110 He resided at Morrisania, New York, and married .

Issue

277 A Newbold Morris, in 1895, of 19 East 64th St , New York City

227 ROBERT MORRIS, son of James Morris, 122, married Charlotte, daughter of James Stillwell They lived near Morrisville, N. J

Issue

278 James I Morris, married ....
279 Robert Morris, married
280 Samuel Decatur Morris, a judge, in Brooklyn, N Y
281 William Henry Morris
282 Mary Elizabeth Morris, married Mr Davis
283 Lydia Jane Morris, married Mr Lawson
284 Margaret Morris, married, June 27, 1857, John Brower.
285 Charlotte Ann Morris, married Mr Brokaw
286 Deborah Patterson Morris, married Mr McClain

232 JOSEPH MORRIS, son of James Morris, 122, married Deborah Bennet

Issue

287 James Henry Morris
288 Warren Morris
289 David Morris
290 Daughter, married Mr. Layton.
291 Elizabeth Morris

233 SAMUEL MORRIS, of Farmingdale, son of Robert P Morris, 123, married Catherine Bennett

Issue

292 Bennett Morris
293 James Morris
294 Joseph Morris
295 Samuel Morris, born Sep 15, 1807
296 Robert Wesley Morris, married, Dec 26, 1843, Rebecca Youmans
297 Adaline Morris, born Feb 16, 1816
298 Robert Morris
299 Lydia Morris, married John Hall

300 Polly, or Mary Morris, born 1799, married Mr Hurley
301 Content Morris, married, Jan 26, 1827, Thomas Sutphen

237 ISAAC ZEPHANIAH MORRIS, son of Zephaniah Morris, 124, born Aug. 11, 1766, died May 31, 1856, aged 89, 9, 21, married, Nov 8, 1792, Anne Brewer, born 1769, died May 3, 1862

Issue

302 Mary Morris, born Mch 4, 1794, died Nov 27, 1870, at Yorkville, Ill , married, Mch 21, 1812, John, son of Amor and Deborah (Brewer) Cook, born Oct 13, 1789, died Sep 21, 1852
303 Lydia Ann Morris, died at Aurora, Ill , married Francis Asbury Emmons
304 Cornelius L Morris, born 1804, died 1885, married Maria Lefferts, born 1806, died 1897
305 Harriet Morris, married George Hay.
306 Elizabeth Morris, married Lawrence Earle

241 JOSEPH MORRIS, son of Zephaniah Morris, 124, born Apr. 9, 1777, died Sep 23, 1826, married, June 16, 1805, Mary Brewer, of Shrewsbury, born Oct 15, 1784, died Jan 1, 1828

Issue

307 Mary Ann Morris, born Nov 23, 1806, died June 10, 1881, married, Jan. 31, 1832, Charles Dennis, son of Francis and Margaret (Parker) Borden, born Jan 19, 1808, died June 14, 1856
308 Joseph Morris, born Feb 6, 1808, married, Jan. 13, 1834, Mary Hendrickson
309 Henry Morris, born Feb 6, 1808
310 Ellen Morris, born Oct 31, 1813, died Apr 25, 1879, married, Jan 20, 1841, Joseph C. Ayres, born Jan 7, 1817, died Jan 14, 1873
311 Eliza J Morris, born Feb 20, 1819; died, Sep 12, 1892, unmarried.
312 Forman Morris, born June 2, 1821, married Margaret . . .
313 William Ryer Morris, born Sep 6, 1824

243 CHRISTOPHER MORRIS, son of William Morris, 130, married, first, Lydia Richmond, second, [Elizabeth Humphreys?]

1819 Will of Christopher Morris, of Salem County, N J , proved Oct 29, 1821, mentioned

Daughters, Martha Peak
          Rachel Borden
          Rebecca
Son, William
Sister, Elizabeth Ripsey
Executors Son, William, and friend, Thos Yarrow

Issue by first wife
314 William Morris
315 Martha Morris, married Mr Peak.
316 Rachel Morris, married Mr Borden
317 Rebecca Morris

MORRIS OF MONMOUTH COUNTY

251 WILLIAM MORRIS, son of William Morris, 134, married Mary Van Nort

Issue

- 318 James S Morris, born May 20, 1812, died May 28, 1885, married Edna Van Kirk, born June 7, 1815, died Sep 30, 1879
- 319 John Morris, married Deborah
- 320 William Joseph Morris, born June 20, 1822, died Oct 13, 1890, married, July 22, 1857, Hester Ann, daughter of Caleb Jewell and Susan Osborn, died Dec. 17, 1906
- 321 Caroline Morris, married Mr Hyde

269 AMOS TILTON MORRIS, son of James L Morris, 164, married Elizabeth St Clair Berry

Issue

- 322 Stuart Fitz Randolph Morris, died unmarried
- 323 Lewis Morris, married Agnes Stewart
- 324 Alexander Morris, married Sarah .
- 325 Charles Edward Morris, married Eliza

272 MIDDLETON MORRIS, son of James Lawrence Morris, 164, died Nov 16, 1850, aged 38 years, married . .

Issue

- 326 William Morris, of Bridgeton N J, married Hannah E, daughter of Josiah and Frances (Cook) Wainright

274 ROBERT L MORRIS, son of James Lawrence Morris, 164, born Oct. 9, 1804, died Apl 4, 1889, married, July 27, 1834, Elizabeth Allen, born Aug 6, 1805, died Jan 2, 1886

Issue

- 327 Thomas T Morris, of Manasquan, N J, born Aug 26, 1845, married, June 26, 1875, Elizabeth, daughter of John B Gifford

276 CHARLES MORRIS, supposed to have been the son of James Lawrence Morris, 164, born 1810, died Nov 24, 1842, married. June 5, 1829, Ann Eliza Holmes, born 1812, died Feb 26, 1904

Issue

- 328 Matilda Morris, married Mr. Tullis, of Camden, N J
- 329 Eleanor Gertrude Morris, born 1829, married Mr Stout
- 330 Catharine Morris, married Mr. Walt
- 331 Jacob Holmes Morris, born 1832, died Oct 4, 1904, married, first,   ., second, Catharine   born 1834
- 332 James Morris, of Manasquan, N. J

295 SAMUEL MORRIS, son of Samuel Morris, 233, born Sep 15, 1807, died May 2, 1889, married, first, 1829, Rhoda C Van Mater, born Nov 27, 1812, died June 6, 1863, second, 1870, Mrs Hannah (Loomis) Lincoln, of Plano, Kendal Co, Ill By his first wife he had ten children

Issue

333 Cornelius V. Morris, born 1832, died Dec 20, 1860
334 Orpha Morris, born Oct. 21, 1836; died Jan. 25, 1862.
335 Samuel B. Morris, born Mch 1, 1840; died May 21, 1862
336 Rhody Ann Morris, born Mch 1, 1840, died May 21, 1862
337 Charles M Morris, married twice.
338 Cyrus H Morris, married .
339 John D. Morris, married . . . .
340 Louise Catherine Morris, born February, 1837, married David, son of Amor and Mary Ann (Page) Cook
341 Elizabeth Morris, married O S Ellithorpe
342 Mary Morris, died about 1862 or 3, married Robert White

296 ROBERT WESLEY MORRIS, son of Samuel Morris, 233, married, Dec 26, 1843, Rebecca Youmans.

Issue

342a John F Morris, born Oct. 12, 1827, married, first, Feb. 14, 1849, Sarah A , daughter of Jeremiah and Sarah (Antonides) Tilton, second, Aug 8, 1853, Mary Elizabeth Tilton, her sister.

Issue by first wife

George Morris, married Annie, daughter of William and Hannah Stout

Issue by second wife

John Henry Morris, married Annie Flitcroft

342b Elizabeth H Morris, married John H., son of Jeremiah and Sarah (Antonides) Tilton, born 1843

297 ADALINE MORRIS, daughter of Samuel Morris, 233, born Feb 16, 1816, died Aug 31, 1891; married, Feb 14, 1835, Daniel, son of Montilion and Lydia (Harris) Woolley, born 1811, died Feb 13, 1897

Issue

George W. Woolley, born Nov 30, 1835, married, first, 1863, Jane, daughter of Amos Pierce, born 1846, second, Mrs Hannah Wardell, died Oct 23, 1900.
John Wesley Woolley, born Sep 18, 1837, died Mch 3, 1908, married Julia A De Groot, died Jan 21, 1904
Charles Henry Woolley, born Dec. 23, 1839, married, first, Janie Bush, second, Oct 26, 1859, Lockie Wood, third, Edith   . , and fourth, Mary Finnegan.
Catherine Maria Woolley, born Dec 16, 1841, married, Apr. 3, 1858, Captain Henry B Sherman, born Nov 28, 1833, died Nov 9, 1906.
Joseph Addison Woolley, born Dec 19, 1843, married, first, Elizabeth Mason, second, Katie Hatfield
Dr Daniel Morris Woolley, born Aug 1, 1850, married Henrietta Wilde
Louis F Woolley, born Jan 2, 1854, died prior to 1886, married Annie Forsyth

301 CONTENT MORRIS, daughter of Samuel Morris, 233, married, Jan 26, 1827, Thomas Sutphen

Issue

Samuel Sutphen, born Mch 31, 1828
Catharine Ann Sutphen, born May 3, 1829
Mary Emily Sutphen, born July 7, 1831.
Sarah Emily Sutphen, born Apr 12, 1833
William Henry Sutphen, born Dec 13, 1835
Melville S Sutphen, born Nov. 10, 1837
Clark Sutphen, born Nov 19, 1839
Adaline Sutphen, born Nov. 6, 1841.
Jane Elizabeth Sutphen, born Feb 13, 1844.
John Wesley Sutphen, born May 28, 1849.

304 CORNELIUS L. MORRIS, son of Isaac Zephaniah Morris, 237, born 1804, died 1885; married Maria Lefferts, born 1806, died 1897.

Issue

343 Henrietta Morris, married, became the first wife of James W Stout, born 1836, died June 4, 1906
344 Adelaide Morris, married, Jan 1, 1873, became the second wife of James W. Stout
345 Charlotte Morris, married Benjamin Theodore, son of Joseph T and Lucy G. (Corlies) White
346 Amanda Morris, married Harrison D White, born May 5, ——
347 Cornelia Morris, married, 1860, James Minton, born 1833, died Feb 13, 1908
348 Emily Morris, married Archibald Minton, died 1906.
349 Julia Morris, married Fred Klawberg
350 Augustus Morris, born 1840, married Gertrude, daughter of Augustus J and Mary (Bennett) White.

308 JOSEPH MORRIS, son of Joseph Morris, 241, born Feb 6, 1808, married, Jan 13, 1834, Mary, or Marcy, daughter of Captain Daniel and Catharina (Bedle) Hendrickson.

Issue

351 Daniel Hendrickson Morris, born 1839, married, first, Dec. 1, 1858, Mary Smith, second, Josephine Smith, born 1849

312 FORMAN MORRIS, son of Joseph Morris, 241, born June 2, 1821, married Margaret . . . , born 1832.

Issue

352 Joseph V Morris, born 1858.
353 Ensley Morris, born 1866

314 WILLIAM MORRIS, son of Christopher Morris, 243, married [Elizabeth Humphreys?]

Issue

354 Josiah Morris, married Margaretta V Rice.
355 William Morris
356 Elizabeth Morris, married Mr. Hull or Hare

357 John Morris, married Mary . . .
358 Emma Jane Morris, married Mr Newell
359 Samuel Morris
360 Amanda Morris, married Mr. Wiley
361 Martha Morris
362 Lydia Morris

351 DANIEL HENDRICKSON MORRIS, son of Joseph Morris, 308, born 1839, married, first, Dec 1, 1858, Mary Smith, second, Josephine Smith, born 1849.

Issue by first wife

363 William Ellsworth Morris, married Anna V., daughter of Garret and Susan J (Wyckoff) Smock.

Issue by second wife

364 Daniel S Morris, born 1874, married, first, . Striker, second, Oct. 17, 1905, Irene Budd

354 JOSIAH MORRIS, son of William Morris, 314, married Margaretta Rice

Issue

365 Josephine Morris
366 Agnes Morris, married Mr Starr
367 William Morris, married Alice Anthony
368 Edwin Morris
369 Bessie Morris
370 Samuel Morris
371 Mary Morris

From Mrs A M Starr, 3928 Locust St., Philadelphia, Pa

MISCELLANEOUS NOTES

A John Morris has to be accounted for, who flourished as early as 1717

Freehold Court Records, Feb 28, 1716/17. Thomas Kearny & Mich. Kearny @ John Morris Case £12

Nov 25, 1719 John Morris on a jury
Nov 27, 1719 John Morris on a jury

From an old paper in the Surrogate's Office

October Term, 1730 John Morris, of Freehold, weaver, bound to John Parker, of Perth Amboy

Another paper July Term, 1734 Pintard Executors vs John Morris, of Freehold, Feb. 3, 1723, at Shrewsbury said John Morris bound in sum ———

1 BENJAMIN MORRIS, who I believe to be either a son of Thomas or Lewis Morris, resided at Nutswamp, Middletown, N J He married, by license dated June 1, 1767, Lydia Crawford, who had previously been licensed to marry, July 30, 1756, Cornelius Compton, who left her widowed, shortly prior to her marriage to Benjamin Morris

Issue

2 Joseph Morris
3 Benjamin Morris
4 Stout Morris
5 Lydia Morris, born Jan 25, 1773, died Nov 23, 1863, married James Frost born Jan 1, 1769, died Mch 23, 1821
6 Esther Morris, married, Oct 27, 1799, Jonathan Stout

2 JOSEPH MORRIS, son of Benjamin Morris, 1, was born in 1770, and served in the War of 1812 He married Patience, daughter of James Herbert She died aged 92 years

Issue

7 Joseph Morris, born 4mo., 25, 1804
8 Benjamin Morris, born 4mo, 6, 1809
9 George Morris
10 Tylee Morris, died young
11 Charles Morris
12 Crawford Morris
13 Lydia Morris, married Ezekiel, son of Jonathan and Mary (Madden) Tilton
14 John Morris, born 1821, died 1853

3 BENJAMIN MORRIS, son of Benjamin Morris, 1, was born in 1768

Issue

15 Charles Morris
16 Benjamin Morris
17
18
19
20

7 JOSEPH MORRIS, son of Joseph Morris, 2, was born 4mo, 25, 1804, died 4mo, 23, 1905, married, first, about 1827, Jane A Wallace, who died Dec 24, 1840, second, in 1849, Caroline M Lamb, born 1814, died 7mo, 26, 1903

Issue

21 Elihu Morris
22 William Wallace Morris, born Feb 18, 1830, died Aug 8, 1905, married, 1853, Mary Elizabeth Bines
23 Joseph Morris
24 George Morris
25 Charles Morris, died young
26 Charles Morris, 2nd, born 1851, married Henrietta . . . , born 1859

Issue

Fred Morris, born 1873
Antoinette Morris, born 1879

27 Antoinette Morris, married Asa T Van Winkle
28 Alida Morris, married Thomas Walling

8 BENJAMIN MORRIS, son of Joseph Morris, 2, was born 4mo , 6, 1809, died 1mo 19, 1904, married, 1836, Julia A Comstock, born 1825; died 1900

Issue

29 Spencer Morris, married, Nov 12, 1863, Mary E. Foster
30 Lewis Morris
31 Lavinia Morris
32 Elizabeth Morris, born 1857
33 Charlotte Morris, died May 5, 1903
34 George W Morris, born 1861
35 Susan Morris; married Joseph Taylor

9 GEORGE MORRIS, son of Joseph Morris, 2, married Eliza Banks
Issue
36 Sarah Morris
37 Mary Morris

11 CHARLES MORRIS, son of Joseph Morris, 2, married Sarah Palmer
Issue
38 Caroline Morris
39 Sarah Morris
40 George Morris

12 CRAWFORD MORRIS, son of Joseph Morris, 2, married Eliza More.
Issue
41 Charles Morris
42 Josephine Morris
43 Mary Morris

13 LYDIA MORRIS, daughter of Joseph Morris, 2, married, as his second wife, Ezekiel, son of Jonathan and Mary (Madden) Tilton

Issue

Lydia Tilton, married, May 6, 1858, William Stout
Benjamin M. Tilton, born 1830, died June 26, 1906, married Margaret Hogarth, born 1853
Sarah Tilton, died May, 1909, married James Christy Hughes
George Morris Tilton, born 1835, died Mch. 9, 1904; married, Nov 9, 1858, Maria A Walling, born 1837

29 SPENCER MORRIS, son of Benjamin Morris, 8, born 1844, married, Nov. 12, 1863, Mary E Foster, born 1846

Issue

44 Jessie Morris, born 1865
45 Caroline Morris, born 1866
46 Lewis Morris, born 1869

47 Julia Morris, born 1873.
48 Rebecca Morris, born 1873

Mrs A H Weatherby, of Trenton, N. J , is the authority for saying that Samuel Morris, possibly a descendant of Lewis Morris, of Passage Point (32), married Mary White, was the father of Samuel Morris, (58), who married Hester Patterson, and grandfather of a John Morris, who was killed in the Revolutionary War She further states that this John Morris and Elizabeth Elmer were the parents of Jacob Morris, who married, Nov 21, 1799, Anne Wolcott, and were the ancestors of the family that is given in the following notes But the late James Steen, Esq , of Eatontown, N J , has given me to understand that the above mentioned Jacob Morris was a natural child, and his authority for so saying was one of the descendants of the family who had tried to trace out his ancestry, only to discover that such was the case

1 JACOB MORRIS died, July 30, 1858, aged eighty years, married, Nov 21, 1799, Anne, daughter of Benjamin and Ann (Lewis) Wolcott, born Jan 22, 1784, died Mch 30, 1860, aged 76, 2, 8

Issue

2 Lydia Morris
3 Deborah Morris, born Oct 9, 1803, died Oct. 29, 1857, married, first, Gilbert, son of Cornelius and Jane (Williamson) Brower, second, Mr Whitmiel
4 Benjamin Morris, born 1806, died May 21, 1868
5 John Morris, born Sep 22, 1807, died Oct 18, 1854
6 William W Morris, born 1818, died Oct 26, 1839
7 Jacob Wolcott Morris, born Jan. 29, 1810, died Oct. 10, 1879
8 Samuel Morris, born April, 1812, died Oct 22, 1878, married Hannah Bennett
9 Ann Morris, married Cyrenius Golden

4 BENJAMIN MORRIS, son of Jacob Morris, 1, born 1806 died May 21, 1868, married, Aug 26, 1829, Margaret Chadwick, born 1799, died Nov 11, 1891

Issue

10 Mary Ann Morris, born July 25, 1830, died Jan 9, 1857, married, Apr 26, 1849, Michael, son of Daniel and Catharine (Scott) Hulett
11 Thomas C Morris, born 1833, died Mch 10, 1889, married Malvina M. . . , born January, 1820, died Feb 4, 1864
12 Jacob Morris, born July 20, 1834, died Jan 12, 1882, married Caroline   , and had

Issue

Sarah Margaret Morris, born 1859, died Sep 3, 1862
13 Sarah Morris

5 JOHN MORRIS, born Sep 22, 1807, died Oct 18, 1854, married Mary, daughter of William and Margaret (Morton) White, born July 19, 1798, died Sep 16, 1886

Issue

14 Margaret A Morris, born July 14, 1832, married, July 18, 1849, Joseph Tallman
15 Jane Elizabeth Morris, born Jan 1, 1835, married Daniel B , son of Benjamin Stillwagon, born 1835

16 Ten Brook Morris, born Sep. 19, 1837; married, Jan 13, 1870, Lydia A Davison, and, second, Sarah . ., born 1840

7 JACOB WOLCOTT MORRIS, son of Jacob Morris, 1, born Jan 29. 1810, died Oct 10, 1879, married, Nov 6, 1830, Maria Wardell, second, Mch. 15, 1854, Elizabeth Louise, daughter of Benjamin Davenport and Caroline (Custis-Moore) Pearce, born Mch. 17, 1836, died Sep 16, 1899

Issue by first wife

17 J Lambert Morris, born 1835, died Nov 9, 1835
18 Lydia Morris, married Charles Bennett
19 Sarah Ann Morris, married Isaac Carter
20 Elizabeth G Morris, born 1839, married, Mch 17, 1859, William Russell Morris, born 1836.

Issue by second wife

21 Jacob Van Derveer Morris, born Feb 21, 1855, died Jan 17, 1871.
22 Benjamin Pearce Morris, of Long Branch, born Sep 10, 1857, married, Sep 6, 1889, Minnie Emmons, and had

Issue

Mildred Morris
Oliver Wolcott Morris
Langdon Emmons Morris
Benjamin P Morris

23 Caroline Estelle Morris, born Mch 9, 1859, married, Oct. 8, 1878, James Monroe Green, of Trenton, N J
24 Myrtilla De Graw Morris, born Mch. 22, 1861, married, Nov 14, 1883, Judge Wilbur Arthur Heisley.
25 Ella Wolcott Morris, born Mch 20, 1865, married, Oct. 31, 1888, Frank Mulgrave Taylor, born Feb 28, 1864, died July, 1902
26 Lillie Adams Morris, born Mch 9, 1868, married, Sep 28, 1892, Edward Randolph Slocum, Jr., born Feb 1, 1869.

8 SAMUEL MORRIS, son of Jacob Morris, 1, born April, 1812, died Oct 22, 1878, married Hannah Bennett

Issue

27 J Treadwell Morris, died 1864
28 Garret Morris, born Jan 12, 1833, died Mch 12, 1864, married Cornelia Price.
29 William Russell Morris, born July 20, 1835, died Mch 1, 1862, married, Mch. 17, 1859, Elizabeth Morris
30 S Corlies Morris, born 1841, married, Dec. 21, 1864, Mary A., daughter of Montilion and Emeline Woolley, born 1842, died Nov 4, 1908, and had

Issue

Chrissie Morris, born 1868
Robert L Morris, born 1874
Martha C Morris, born 1877
Arthur C. Morris

31 John Morris

32 Margaret Emma Morris, married Richard Borden
33 Ann Morris, born Aug 3, 1845, died Aug 27, 1875
34 Hannah Maria Morris, born 1846, died Oct. 23, 1878, married, June 6, 1877, Samuel C Dangler

9 ANN MORRIS, daughter of Jacob Morris, 1, married Cyrenius Golden
Issue
Catharine Golden, born May 17, 1832; died Feb 13, 1842
Charles Golden, died Nov. 14, 1880, married Caroline Fleming.
Deborah Golden, married Joseph Winter
William Golden, married   Winters.
Anne Golden, married Henry Magee
Joseph Golden, born Aug 9, 1852, died Mch. 7, 1854.
Sarah Golden
George Golden, born Jan 10, 1858, died Sep 2, 1858

1829, June 5 Charles Morris married Ann Eliza Holmes and had a son, Jacob Holmes Morris, of Manasquan, born 1832, and died Oct 4, 1904
This Jacob Holmes Morris married twice, his second wife being Catharine   , born about 1834. By his first wife he had a daughter, and by his second wife a daughter and a son, Edward Morris, born about 1863.

The following nine individuals were brothers and sisters
John Morris, born 1824, died Mch. 24, 1904, of Middletown Township
George W. Morris, born 1831, died Jan 8, 1905; of Keansburg, married twice, his widow married Mr Percival
Abraham Morris, of Keyport.
Gerardus C. Morris, born about 1841, married, Dec. 17, 1866, Elizabeth Lufborrow, of New Monmouth
Aaron Morris, born about 1843, married Mary E . . . , of Holmdel
Fanny Morris, of Middletown, married William 1 Stillwell.
Emily Morris, of Asbury Park
Cordelia Morris, married George C Luyster.
Caroline Morris, of Keyport

In Monmouth County there were a number of the name John Morris I believe that I have separated them and placed them under their proper heads
1727-1739 John Morris, of Squankum
1730-1736 John Morris was a Surrogate
1740-1758 John Morris was a weaver
1744-1769 John Morris, son of John, of Squamkum, called John, Jr
———— John Morris was a Lieut -Colonel

Ruthero Morris came from Wales, and settled in Salem County He was a Quaker
1702, 20, 11 mo. Will of Ruthero Morris, of Elssenburgh, Salem County, proved Sep 21, 1704, mentioned·

Wife, Jael, she afterwards married John Lewis
Sons, Joseph
    Lewis
    David
    Joshua
    Jonathan

1733-4, 10 [or 11] mo , 26 Will of David Morris, of Elsinburgh, proved Feb 16, 1733, mentioned
Wife, Jane
Sons, David, not yet eighteen
    John Jeffreys, not of age
Brother, Lewis
Daughter, Jane

1739, 11 mo , 4 Will of Lewis Morris, of Salem County, proved July 18, 1740, mentioned
Wife, Grace
Daughters Sarah, eldest
    Mary
    Grace
    Jane
    Jayl (Jael?)
    Anor
    Rebecca
Sister, Lydia Hart
Brother, David

1743, Nov 12 Administration was granted to John Henderson, chief creditor, upon the estate of Eneas Morris, late of Freehold, with the consent of Mary Morris, widow of Eneas.
Inventory of his estate was taken Nov 19, 1743, by Jas Robinson and Peter Clark, appraisers, and amounted to £22-4-0

1789, Apr 4 Anna Morris, widow of John Morris, deceased, gave bond to administer on his estate, Joseph Tomson being the surety Thomas Morford and William Lippincott appraised his estate at £129-7-8 She afterwards married, prior to Aug 10, 1799, Stephen Fleming

The index of an old account book, which was opened as early as 1730, contains the names of the following members of the Morris family
Morris, Thomas, 40
Morris, Jno , Falls, 83
Morris, John, taylor, 116
Morris, Lewis, 119
Morris, Richard, 129
Morris, Lewis, Jr , 146
Morris, John, Freehold, 225

There are many Morris marriage licenses at Trenton, N J , which I am unable to place and which may not belong to the Monmouth County Family

MONMOUTH COUNTY

1742, May 1   Christopher Morris and Rebecca Layton
1765, Jan 25   Zelphamate Morris and Mary Daws
1767, June 19   Thomas Morris and Elizabeth Chandler
1772, Jan 18   Jacob Morris and Meribah Leming

1749, July 3   Richard Morris, Jr., and Johannah Patterson.
1751, Sept. 14 Mary Morris and John Conrey
1757, Dec 7   Mary Morris and Asahal Freeman
1769, Oct 29   Margaret Morris and John Cox, minor.
1781, Apr 16   Mary Morris and Benjamin White

FROM CHRIST CHURCH RECORD SHREWSBURY, N. J

BAPTISMS

1737, Jan 1   John son of John Morris, of Shrewsbury
1754, Sept 15   Thomas, son of John Morris of Freehold
1758, July 30   Edward, son of John and Mary Morris, of Freehold

MORRIS MARRIAGES RECORDED AT FREEHOLD, MONMOUTH CO N J.

1794, Apr 27.   Garret Morris and Polly Sydam
1796, Jan. 20   Samuel Morris and Rebecca Smith
1796, Dec. 7   George Morris and Nelly Covenhoven
1797, Apr. 17. Rachel Morris, of Middletown, and James Coil, of Freehold
1798, Feb 13   Elisha Morris and Elizabeth Smith.
1799, Oct. 27. Hester Morris and Jonathan Stout
1800, Dec 30   Lewis Morris and Catharine Woolley.
1801, Mch 28.   Elizabeth Morris and John Green
1801, Oct 21   Ann Morris and John Francis
1802, Apr. 10. Elizabeth Morris and Robert Lewis; both of Howell
1802, Dec 25   Isabel Morris and Rev Jacob Reckhow
1803, Mch 24   Valeriah Morris and John Johnson
1803, Oct 22   John Morris and Catharine Lane.
1804, Apr 19.   Robert Morris and Rebecca Jackson
1804, Dec 6   Elizabeth Morris and Joseph Brewer.
1805, June 16. Joseph Morris and Mary Brewer.
1805, Dec 7   James Morris and Susannah Lippincott.
1806, Jan 16   David Morris and Susannah Lamery (Lanery?)
1806, May 8.   Deborah Morris and Jacob Lippincott.
1806, July 3   William Morris and Hannah Gardner
1806, July 12   Sarah Morris and Isaac Herbert; both of Howell
1807, Apr 2   Mary Morris and John Aumack
1808, Feb 12   Rosannah Morris and David Emmons, both of Howell
1808, June 25   Charles Morris and Sarah Patterson
1810, Feb 22   Sarah Morris and Jonathan Cooper, both of Middletown
1810, May 19   Hannah Morris, of Howell, and Wilham Van Schoick, of Lower Freehold
1810, May 26   Elizabeth (Morris or More) and Elias Brower, both of Freehold
1811, Jan 13   Sarah Morris and Samuel Kerr
1811, Mch 9   Adam Morris and Lydia Matthews
1811, Apr. 1   M^s Sarah Morris and James Edwards
1811, Oct. 29   Japhia Morris of Middletown and Lydia Morris.
1812, Mch 21   Mrs Molly Morris and John Cook; both of Shrewsbury
1812, Apr 9   Elizabeth Morris and Forman Throckmorton
1812, Aug. 15. Stephen Morris and Elizabeth Cole

1813, Mch 3   Hannah Morris and James G. Hendrickson.
1813, Mch 22   Ezekiel Morris and Mary Wilson
1814, Jan 22   Peter Morris and Mary Van Cleve
1814, Apr 10   Mary Morris and Elisha Lloyd, both of Middletown.
1814, Sep 9   Sarah Morris and John W Lippincott, both of Howell
1815, Sep 9   Catharine Morris and Thomas Phillips
1815, Nov 9   Stephen Morris and Mary Compton
1816, Jan 30   Sarah Morris and William Woolley
1816, Mch 30. Deborah Morris and Ezekiel Johnston, both of Howell
1816, Apr 14   Charles Morris and Ellen Newkirk
1816, Aug 24   Deborah Morris, of Shrewsbury, and Barney Vantassel, of New York.
1817, Feb 6   Ezekiel Morris and Mary Kirby
1817, Feb 22. George Morris and Jedidah Newmon
1817, Aug 16   Elizabeth Morris and Asia Wilson, both of Shrewsbury
1817, Sep 15   William Morris and Maria Wright, both of Middletown
1817, Nov 29   James Morris and Eliza Randolph.
1819, Mch 2   John Morris and Eliza Reed
1819, Mch 10   Elizabeth Morris and Joseph D. Sutphin
1819, Oct 9   Eleanor Morris and Anthony Smith, both of Middletown.
1820, Feb 3.   James Morris, of Howell, and Hannah Youmans, of Shrewsbury
1820, June 1   Samuel S Morris and Sarah W. Sutphen.
1820, Nov 18   Nancy Morris and Andrew Karr
1820, Dec 14. Matilda Morris and Samuel Esth, both of Shrewsbury.

After this date there is a large number of marriages, down to about 1890, not reproduced here for obvious reasons

For information concerning the Morris Family, see:
The Boundary Line, by Martha Morris Lawrence, Deckertown, N. J , 1895.
Old Times in Old Monmouth
Provincial Courts of New Jersey
East Jersey under the Proprietors
Morris Papers, by Whitehead
Robert Morris' Claim, by James Steen, Esq.
Bolton's History of Westchester County, N Y
The New York Genealogical and Biographical Record for January, 1876, and January, 1889

MOTT

OF

NEW YORK AND NEW JERSEY

The Motts had been seated in the adjoining counties of Essex and Cambridge, England, for several centuries, when two of the name of Adam Mott, one from each county, emigrated to America. Adam Mott, from Cambridge, called the *taylor*, came with his family, to Boston, in 1635, and Adam Mott, from Essex, left some years later and settled in New Amsterdam

It is singular that these two Adam Motts, each with sons, Gershom and Adam, should have lived contemporaneously in the early history of this country, and it would have been confusing had they have resided in the same locality, but, fortunately, they dwelt apart, one in Rhode Island, whose descendants have been traced by Austin, while the other, in whom we are interested, resided, first, in New Amsterdam, and later, on Long Island

From certain affidavits and statements, made at various dates, of little interest in themselves, and from appearing as a witness, it would seem that Adam Mott was a resident of Manhattan, in 1643, 1644, 1645, 1646, 1647 and 1648

1646, Aug. 23. He owned a patent of land of twenty-five morgens size, at Mespath Kill, (Bushwick, L I), but by Jan 7, 1653, he had parted with it, for on that date, Claude Barbier and Anthony Jeroe conveyed this tract of land, with the buildings thereon, to Jacob Steendam

1657, Mch. 17. Adam Mott was one of the "townsmen" for Hempstead

1663-4, Feb. 24 Adam Mott, Capt John Underhill and David Denton signed, for the English settlers, an agreement with the Dutch government.

O'Callaghan's New Netherlands, Vol ii, p 578

1681-2, Mch. 12 Will of Adam Mott, being aged about sixty or thereabouts, very sick, etc., mentioned

Eldest son, Adam, fifty acres in land, yet to be taken up, and five shillings in money
Son, James, two cows, and land
Daughter, Grace, four great pewter platters, and lands
Son, John, meadow and lands
Son, Joseph, lands
Son, Gershom, five cows
Son, Henry, three cows and two heifers
Wife, Elizabeth, and the children he had by her, the house and certain lands in Hempstead, with particular provision for his youngest son, Adam
In the codicil, he mentioned "Henry's three children"

1689 [1690], May 10 It was proved, by the witnesses, before Thomas Hicks, Daniel Whitehead and John Cornwell, magistrates, at the Court of Sessions, Queen's County, Apr 8, 1690, at New York, before Gov Leisler, May 12, 1690, when letters of administration were issued to Elizabeth, the widow of Adam Mott, and again, Sept 20, 1691, to Adam Mott, his son, and still again, before Gov Ingoldsby, at Fort William Henry, Oct 30, 1691, when letters were issued to Elizabeth, his widow, and Adam Mott, his eldest son

ADAM MOTT, THE FIRST, was married three times First, in New Amsterdam, July 28, 1647, as Adam Maet, young man from county Esseck, to Jenne Hulet, young woman, from county Buckingam, (Records Dutch Church, New Amsterdam), second, to   , daughter of William Bowne, of Gravesend, L I, and Middletown, N. J, (Genealogy of the Bowne family in Stillwell's Historical Miscellany), third, to Elizabeth Redman, daughter of Ann Parsons, widow of Mr. Redman, and later wife of John Richbell Elizabeth Redman, wife of Adam Mott, upon the demise of her husband, married Robert Hobbs or Hubs, and was living as late as 1698

    Issue by first wife
2 Adam Mott, baptized, at New Amsterdam, Nov. 14, 1649.
3 James [Jacobus] Mott, baptized, at New Amsterdam, Oct 15, 1651.
4 Grace Mott; married Jonathan Smith, Jr.
5 Henry Mott
6 John Mott
7 Joseph Mott

    Issue by second wife
8 Gershom Mott

    Issue by third wife
9 Richbell Mott, born about 1670.
10 Mary Ann Mott
11 William Mott
12 Adam Mott
13 Charles Mott
14 Elizabeth Mott

In the Census, 1698, of Hempstead, appear in a group Mary Anne Mott, Elizabeth Mott, William Mott, Adam Mott

John Richbell, of Marmaroneck, N Y, had an only brother, Robert Richbell, who resided at Southampton, England, and who became his heir-at-law This Robert Richbell had a son, Edward Richbell, Esq, late of the City of Westminster, who in turn had an eldest son and heir, Edward Richbell, of the Parish of St James, in the County of Middlesex This last mentioned Edward Richbell, on the 8th of Feb, 1722, for £380, released to the Palmer family, as heir to his great-uncle, John Richbell, all his reversionary interests in the Middle Neck, in Marmaroneck, and, on the 12th and 13th of Aug, 1723, he likewise released, for £400, all his reversionary interests in the West Neck, and the remaining Richbell lands, unto Eve, wife of Jacobus Van Cortlandt, and daughter of Frederick Philipse, which lands had been mortgaged, by John Richbell, in his lifetime, with certain reservations

1648 Of John Richbell it is known that he was in Charlestown, Mass, at this time (Savage)

1656, Aug 8 He owed the estate of Robert Gibson, of Boston, Mass, £36, as appears in the Inventory of that person's effects

1657, Sept 18 He made an agreement with Thomas Modiford, of Barbadoes, and William Sharpe, of Southampton, England, merchants, to establish a plantation for the carrying on of trade ' in the southwest ports, of New England, in behalf of himself and of subscribers," who were Modiford and Sharpe.

1660, Sept 5 He went to Oyster Bay, L I, and bought the land now known as Lloyd's Neck, also land at Matinecock, over which he had a controversy with his Oyster Bay neighbors, which was settled in his favor

1661. He appears on the Southampton records as a witness to a mortgage

1661, Sept 23 He bought lands from the Indians, at Marmaroneck, over which he had a controversy with Thomas Revell, but was sustained by Stuyvesant and his Council, who issued him a patent for the same, in May, 1662. Upon the overthrow of the Dutch, he recorded the evidence upon which he based his title, strengthening it by a supplemental Indian deed, dated June 6, 1666, confirming that of 1661, and later received an English patent for the same, dated Oct 16, 1668

1662 He was Constable of Oyster Bay

1664, July 23 He was addressed, at Boston, (where he was probably temporarily), by Robert Carr and Samuel Mavericke, two of the Commissioners of the Duke of York, in the expedition to subjugate the New Netherlands, who instructed him to make haste to his Long Island habitation and acquaint those favorably disposed to his Majestie's service, to be in readiness for their prompt arrival, and, at the same time issuing a warrant for Mr Richbell ' to presse a horse if occasion should bee, hee paying for the hire "

John Richbell, like others of his family, was a merchant   He was a man of superior social position, and commonly addressed as Mr Richbell   His wife, Ann, was the widow Redman and daughter of Margery Parsons, who advanced him goods in the Island of St Christopher, in the West Indies, long before his arrival at Marmaroneck   On the 14th of Nov , 1668, he cancelled this obligation by deeding her the entire East Neck, and she, Mrs Parsons, two days later, conveyed this land to her daughter, Ann, wife of John Richbell, as a token of affection and dutiful behavior   To establish her title to this land more fully, her husband, John Richbell, on the 23rd of April 1669, in consideration of a marriage long since solemnized between them, made a settlement of this land upon her, in a deed of trust to John Ryder   He had apparently no issue

1684, July 26 John Richbell died, and his wife, who had become vested, in fee, by conveyances from her husband and mother, of the entire East Neck, extending back from the Sound twenty miles, conveyed, 1684, Aug 8, to her daughter, Mary, and her husband, Capt James Mott, about thirty acres of this tract

1697, Dec 23 Mrs Richbell conveyed the balance of this estate, inherited from her husband, to Col Caleb Heathcote, for £600

1700, Apr 1 Will of Ann Richbell, of Marmaroneck, "Gentlewoman", proved Feb 19, 1700–01, in which she ordered a "decent and comely" burial for her body, at the discretion of her executors, Col Caleb Heathcote, Mr Richbell Mott and Lieut John Horton, and bequeathed

To her son-in-law, James Mott, £10
To his son, James Mott, Jr , £15
To grand-daughters, Ann Gedney, Mary Williams and Mary Mott, each, £40, and a gold ring
To her daughter, Elizabeth, £80, and her gold ring with an emerald stone in it
To her daughter, Annie, £60, and a gold chain
To the rest of her grandchildren, by my two daughters, Mary and Elizabeth, who are not, however, named, £10
To "my two grand-daughters, Jane and Grace, and my grand-children, James and Adam Mott "

Her daughter, Mary Mott, I infer was dead when she wrote her will in 1700   All her legatees were to be paid before her grandson, Adam Mott, received his portion, "because their necessities are greater "

John Richbell, his wife's mother, and his wife's daughter, Mary Mott, were buried in a field adjoining the house of Lieut James Mott, as appears by an entry in the Town Book, set forth more fully under James Mott, 3   Here too, doubtless, Ann, John Richbell s widow, was also interred

Of her children, it is known that Elizabeth Redman became the third wife of the first Adam Mott, that Mary Redman became the first wife of Lieut James Mott, a son of the first Adam Mott, by his first wife, Jane Hulet, hence it appears that father and son (Adam and James Mott), married sisters, Ann, the third daughter, married John Emerson, of White River, Talbot Co , Md , and was probably the mother of the grand-children Ann Gedney and Mary Williams

2 ADAM MOTT, son of Adam Mott, 1, called "my elder son Adam," was baptized, in the Dutch Church, at New Amsterdam, Nov. 14, 1649, witnesses   Thomas Hall, Olof Stephenszen Van Courtlant and Elsje Muijtiens, [Alice Newton, wife of Capt. Bryan Newton]

1671. Adam Mott, Jr , bought of Edward Titus, a house with three acres of land

1674, Mch. 23 Adam Mott, Jr , was a seaman, sailing on the ketch *Hopewell* from New York to Virginia.

1678. Adam Mott, Jr, of Hempstead, was sued for debt by Gabriel Minviell

As Adam Mott, Jr, of Hempstead, he married, by license dated July 9, 1678, Mary, daughter of Mistress Ann Stillwell, of Gravesend (Original document owned by Dr. J. E Stillwell)

In 1688, he was a defendant in a law suit and was spoken of as Adam Mott, Jr. While in 1694, his father having died, he was spoken of as, Adam Mott, Sr, and the appellation, Jr, was conferred upon his younger half-brother of the same name

1681-2 He was a legatee in the will of his father Adam Mott

1691, Oct 30 Adam Mott, the oldest son, and Elizabeth, the widow of Adam Mott, were appointed administrators, with the will annexed, of the estate of Adam Mott, the First.

1693, Sept 20 Adam Mott sold his interest in the Cow Neck lands to William Nicoll.

1694, Apr. 30 Adam Mott, Sr, of Hempstead released unto Richbell, William, and ye rest of the children of our deceased father, Adam Mott, had by his last wife, Elizabeth, being six children in number. (Jamaica Records)

Mr^r Adam Mott, Mi^s Mott, An Mott, Mary Mott, Adam Mott, Jr, and Nicholis Stilwell appear as one family in the Hempstead Census, 1698, (Geneal. and Biog. Record, p. 57, Jan, 1914.)

1704 He was joined in a deed by his wife Mary

1705 He was a Justice of the Peace, living at Hempstead, whence he wrote to the Secretary asking a marriage license for his daughter Mary

1713, June 15. Adam Mott conveyed to his son, Adam Mott, one half of all his lands lying at Rockaway

1719, Nov 28 Adam Mott and his wife, Mary, joined by his son, Adam Mott, and his wife, Elizabeth, sold their lands in the Neck at Rockaway, to John Mott amounting to 264 acres, with houses, barns, etc

Issue

15 Adam Mott
16 Jane Mott, supposed
17 Ann Mott
18 Mary Mott

There is absolutely no evidence to prove that Daniel Stillwell ever had a wife by the name of Mary Mott, as quoted by *Bergen* on the authority of B M Stilwell's Memoirs of the Stillwell Family.

3 JAMES MOTT, son of Adam Mott, 1, was baptized, in the Dutch Church, New Amsterdam, Oct. 15, 1651, witnesses Brian Nuijting, Carel Verbrugge and Rebecca Cornel. He married, first, by license dated Sept. 5, 1670, Mary Redman, daughter of Ann Parsons Redman Richbell, who probably died before 1700, the date of her mother's will; and second, Elizabeth   , who outlived him.

1679, Feb 18 James Mott, of Hempstead, was arrested, and imprisoned in New York, for selling liquor to the Indians, and on the 21st, he petitioned to be forgiven

1684 Aug. 8. He and his wife, Mary, received about thirty acres of land from her mother, Ann Richbell, lying in the East Neck, Mamaroneck

1690, Feb 10 James Mott was commissioned a Justice, in Westchester County

1700 James Mott, of Mamaroneck was commissioned Captain of a company of foot militia

"I, James Mott do give and grant to Margaret Disbow and her three sons, Henery, John and Benjamin, all belonging to Momoronack, to them and their famylies forever the Liberty of burying their dead, whether Father or Mother, husband or wife, brother or sister, son or daughter, in a certain place of Land Laying near the Salt Meadow, where Mr John Richbell and his wife's Mother and my wife Mary Mott, was buried in my home lot or feild adjoining to my house, written by William palmer, Clerk, of Momoroneck, by order of Capt James Mott " (Vol 1, Town Records, p 71, as quoted by Scharf, in Vol 1, p 861, History of Westchester)

1698. His children, as per Census of this date, were. Grace, James, Phebe, Martha, also Elizabeth

1702 James Mott was a Vestryman of Rye Church

1707, Nov. 23. James Mott died, intestate, and letters of administration were granted to his widow, Elizabeth.

Issue

19 James Mott, born about 1675, named in will of grandmother, 1700, living 1728
20 Mary Mott
Other children, alluded to but not named in will of Ann Richbell

The following references *may* refer to the descendants of James Mott, 3

1717, 9, 3mo James Mott, of Marmaroneck, yeoman, married Jane Burling, of Flushing

1725, Nov 2 James Mott, of Marmaroneck, was appointed administrator of Thomas Killend, late of Boston.

1760 William Mott, of Maroneck, was an executor

The residence and name of Burling suggest that the following individual belongs among the descendants of James Mott, 3

1762, 4, 6mo Will of William Mott, of Marmaroneck, proved Mch 18, 1766, makes strong protest against the use of liquors at funerals, gives one-half of his estate to his wife, Mary, the other half to his children, when of age Executors his wife, Mary, and his brother-in-law, John Townsend, of Marmaroneck

By a codicil, he added Edward Burling, Sr , and Edward Burling, Jr , father and son ,to his executors

5 HENRY MOTT, son of Adam Mott, 1, is alluded to directly in the will of his father, Mch. 12, 1681-2, wherein "Henrys three children" are mentioned He was a resident of Hempstead, where he died, Nov 21, 1680, intestate

1682, Nov 13 Administration was granted to his wife, Hannah His inventory showed a house and seventeen and one-half acres of land New York Wills

Issue

21 Edward Mott, supposed
22 Bridgett Mott; supposed.
23 Elizabeth Mott, supposed

6 JOHN MOTT, son of Adam Mott, 1, was born about 1658,* married Sarah, daughter of Capt John Seaman, of Hempstead, L I He is commonly called "Lieutenant John "

1678-9, Feb. 17. He petitioned for land at Hempstead

1683 He was taxed, and was a freeholder, with seventy acres, in 1685

1696. He was called Lieutenant John

1698. He, and wife, Sarah, appeared in the Hempstead Census

---

*New York Geneal and Biog Record, Vol xi, p 151 Seaman Article

1713-1725 He was called John, Senior.
1727 He was still living
1694 Sarah Mott is mentioned in the will of her father, John Seaman, of Hempstead.
1720 Sarah Mott, witness to a will of Hempstead.
1730-31. John Mott, Jr., was a witness to a will in Hempstead
1734-5 John Mott, his son, was an executor of the will of his uncle, Joseph Mott.
1743 John Mott, witness to will of Benjamin Hicks, of Hempstead

Issue

24 John Mott, Jr
25 James Mott
26 Sarah Mott } From the Census of 1698.
27 Martha Mott
28 Patrick Mott, born after 1698, and mentioned in the will of Richard Seaman, as his cousin, i e nephew.
29 Henry Mott

7 JOSEPH MOTT, son of Adam Mott, 1, made his will Mch. 24, 1734-5; proved Feb. 6, 1735-6 He was of Hempstead, weak, etc , and left to his oldest son, Joseph Mott, £300, the residue of his movable estate, he gave to his children, Joseph, Samuel and Jacob Mott, and Ann, wife of Samuel Cornell, and to the children of his daughter, Jane, wife of Benjamin Seaman. Executors Elias Dorlense and John Mott, son of his brother, John Mott. He was a Vestryman, St. George's Church, 1708-1711. The Hempstead Census, 1698, gives Joseph Mott, Meriam Mott, Meriam Mott, Jeane Mott, Joseph Mott, Samuell Mott.

Issue

30 Joseph Mott
31 Samuel Mott
32 Jacob Mott, born Aug 9, 1714, died Oct. 6, 1805.
33 Ann Mott, married Samuel Cornell.
34 Jane Mott, married Benjamin Seaman, prior to 1710.
35 Meriam Mott. Feb. 8, 1712, Miriam Mott, of Hempstead, married Richard Cornell Parish Church, Jamaica, L. I

8 GERSHOM MOTT, son of Adam Mott, 1, by his second wife, Miss Bowne, daughter of William Bowne, was brought up among his mother's family, in Monmouth County, N J
1684 and 1686 "Gershom moot soon of ye deceased John Bowne sister." (Bowne Papers)
1685 His name appears in the (Freehold) Court Records
1686-7, Feb 16 He recorded his cattle-mark, at Middletown, which later was assigned to his son, James Mott
1697, Nov 30 Gershum Moote, of Middleton, Gentl , was commissioned by Gov. Andrew Hamilton, for one year, High Sheriff, of Monmouth County.
In 1707, 1708, 1709 and in 1710, he was a Member of the Colonial Assembly, from the Eastern Division of New Jersey, when he was expelled because of factional fights, but was returned in 1713
1696, Feb 12 He was licensed to marry Sarah Clayton, who was a daughter of John and Alice Clayton, according to Asher Taylor, Esq About three weeks later they were married by a justice.

These may certify that I Joyned Gershom Mott And Sarah Clayton in ye holy state of mariage this 4th of march 1696 given under my hand

ANDREW BOWNE
J CORAM

Monmouth Co, Entered on ye County Records in Liber C page 145
THO WEBLEY
Cherry Hall Papers

Die Jovis 10 ho: A M 18 Jan^{ru}, 1710
The reasons given by Mr Elisha Lawrance & Mr Gershom Mott why they voted ag^t ye Bill of carrying on ye Expedition against Canada being Read and taken into Consideration the Question was put whether Mr Lawrance and Mr Mott applying to ye Council to have said Reasons Entered and their being entered accordingly in ye Council Books be an arreigning the honour of ye Representative[s] in Body of this Province or not? It was carried in the Affirmative—

Mr Gershom Mott (one of the Representatives of this House) being asked if he would acknowledge his fault in this particular? And he not readily answering to the Same
Ordered that Mr Mott have leave till tomorrow Morning to give his answer—

Die Vendris 9 ho A M 19 Jan^{ru} 1710
Mr Gershom Mott (according to the order of the House last night) gave his answer to ye House (in relation to ye Reasons that he & Mr Lawrence caused to be entered in the Council Books) That he is not Sensible or conscious to himself that he has done this House any Wrong—

Mr Mott refusing to acknowledge his fault or give this House any Satisfaction in this matter the Question was put whether he withdraw while the House consider further of this matter or not? It was carried in the Affirmative—

Ordered That Mr Mott withdraw—

After the Reasons given by Mr Mott and Mr Lawrence had been debated in ye House The Question was put Whether the Preamble and Reasons above-mentioned be a false & Scandalous Representation of the Representative Body of This Province or not? It was carried in the Affirmative—

Mr Mott being called in, the above Vote of the House was read to him, and Mr Speaker asked him, Whether he would acknowledge that he had wronged the then Representative Body of This Province, or not? He answered, No, he did not think that he had wronged them—

Mr Gershom Mott having made a false and Scandalous Representation of the Representative Body of this Province, and persisting in the Same, and refusing to acknowledge his Offence therein the Question was put Whether Mr Mott be expelled this House, or not? It was carried in the Arffimative—

Ordered That Mr Gershom Mott be expelled this House And he is Expelled accordingly—

Ordered, That the Speaker do issue forth his Warrent to the clerk of the Crown to make out a Writ forthwith to Elect and Chuse a Representative for ye County of Monmouth in the room of Mr Gershom Mott who is Expelled this House

A true Copy
WILL BRADFORD Clk
Cherry Hall Papers

Die Veneris 9 ho A M 2^d [? Feb^{ris} 1710
The Secretary laying before this House a Return of ye Sheriff of the County of Monmouth of Mr Mots being chosen a Representative of that County

A Motion was made, That whereas Mr Gershom Mott having been Expelled this House for making a false and Scandalous Representation of the Representative Body of this Province and entering the Same in the Council Books

The Question was put Whether Mr Mott be Capable to Sit in this House as a Representative, till he acknowledge his Offence under his hand, or not? It was carried in the Negative

Resolved, That Mr Gershom Mott is not Capable to Sit in this House till he make an Acknowledgement of his Offence under his hand

A True Coppy Examined
P WILL BRADFORD Clk
Cherry Hall Papers

These Do Certify that Mr William Lawrence Junr Duly Deputed and Sworn for the Intent Hereinafter Mentioned Did Survey for Gershom Mott a Tract of Land Beginning at Bumbo Spring being the upper Corner of Kearney's Land on Lupakitunk Creak and Running up sd Creek * * * to the Lower Corner of sd Mott's Survey made by John Reid late Surveyor General Thence * * * to Kearney's line * * * Containing without allowance Thirty Three Acres Also Another small Tract of Land being an Island of Sedge in Chingaroras Bay * * * Bounded on all Sides by Low water Mark containg five Acres—also Another Tract in the County of Monmouth Beginning at the South West Corner of sd Mott's Fifty Acres granted by Patent * * * to the line of Fifty Acres formerly Robert Holmes Thence North * * * to the rear line of Conascunk * * * Thence up the same to the Nor-East Corner of Kearney's Land * * * Containing without allowance fourty one Acre 10 inch Three Tracts after allowance for high ways are to be & Remain for Seventy Five Acres

Witness my hand at Perth Amboy ye Eighth Day of July, 1717

JAS ALEXANDER Sur Genl

Note the last Survey in this Copy is the first in the Book otherwise it is a True Copy Taken out of the Publick Records in the Secretarys office at Perth Amboy L- C- 2 Pag 181, 182 & Examd &

LAWR SMYTH D Secr

Cherry Hall Papers

From a diary kept by one of his sons, now at Cherry Hall, Matawan, N J, is extracted the following
1728-9 october 5 at home   Wm Mott, Asher Mott, Huldah Mott, Martha Clayton, Rebecca Holsted here

1728-9 october 20 to Fathers   Brethren all at home But John Thomas Potts there Martha Clayton there
1733 Feb 27 John Dosett here to tell me Father sick * * *
     28 to Father
     Mch 1   Father Some thing better
         2   Father easier but Coff more and fever harder about eight a Clock at night taken with a Chilly fit and never spoke but a few words after
         3   Father Speechless and Dyed about — aclock
         4   at Fathers
         5   byryed Father

1730, Feb 15 He made a will, proved Mch 20, [30], 1733, and mentioned.
His plantation bounded by Joseph Dorset and Thos Kearny, also land at Barnegat
Son and heir-at-law, John, £20
Son, James, negroes Jack and Jennie, to be supplied by him if need be
Daughter, Huldah, negro girl Cate, that I have already given her
After legacies are paid, estate to be divided among his five children, William, Gershom, Asher, James and Huldah
James has received the westerly part of his plantation, conditional upon his making a life lease to his father of said plantation
Executors   sons, William, Gershom and James
Witnesses   Joseph Dorsett, Samuel Job, John Dorsett, William Walling

A True Inventory of the Estate of Gershom Mott of Middletown Deceased

To wareing Aparrel	22	08	00
To Five Horses	35	10	00
To Cash	45	00	02
To Three Negroes	118	00	00
To Wheat and Rie on the Ground	46	00	00
To Thirteen Cows	37	18	00
To one Yoak of Oxen	7	10	00
To Nineteen Yongue Cattle	27	16	00
To Fourty one Sheep @ 10s	20	10	00
To Seven Hogs	02	10	00
To Rie	05	10	00
To a Wheat Fan	00	06	00
To Five Pitchforks	00	15	00
To Indian Corn	07	05	00
To a Sled	00	06	00
Cart Plows and Harrow	07	00	00
To a Parcell of Axes Hoes Spad and Chains	02	04	00
Sithes and Cradles	01	03	00
To Coopers Tools	02	12	00

To Carpenters Tools	00	12	00	
To a Beatle and Wedges and Horse Geer	02	03	00	
To a Saddle and Bridle	00	14	00	
To a Grinstone and Hay Knife	00	07	06	
To Tramils Tongs and Fire Sovels	00	18	00	
To a Gun	01	05	00	
To Frying Pans Potts and Cettles and Iron Skellet	01	19	00	
To old pails and Iron Ladel	00	15	00	
To one Half Bufhel	00	01	06	
To Eight Hogsheads of Sider	10	00	00	
To Sundry Sorts of Lumber	04	00	00	
To Flax and Linen Yarn	05	06	09	
To Four Wheals and Two Ridels	01	03	06	
To Three Beds and Furniture	21	05	00	
To Sundry Small Articles	03	01	03	
To Two Sets of Curtains	01	04	00	
To Tabels and chests	02	19	00	
To a Piece of Poplin and Nineteen Chairs	02	03	00	
To a Looking Glafs Glafes and Earthenware	01	04	06	
To Sundries of Iron and Tinn Ware	01	02	00	
To Pewter	05	11	00	
To a Culender Watering Pot	00	10	00	
To Brafs Ware	03	02	00	
To Knives and Forks Loks and Baggs	01	03	00	
To Weights and Scales and Sundry	00	18	00	
To a Warming Pan	00	08	00	
To a stak of Hay	01	02	00	
To Linin And Diaper	08	07	00	
To An Oyster Rake	00	10	00	
To Books	05	10	00	
To Sundry Debts Due to Said Estate	17	19	11	½

£497　10　07　½

A True Inventory of the Movable Estate of Gershom Mott of Middletown Deceas d Taken By Us March 22- 1733-4

        OBEDIAH HOLMES Junr
        JONATN HOLMES Minr
            Cherry Hall Papers

March 8th 1733/4
  Then Received of James Mott executor of the Last will and testament of Gerfhom Mott deceased the sum of seven pounds and ten shillings in full for twenty gallons of wine I sold to the above said James Mott for the burial of his father Gerfhom Mott—I say Received pr me—HUGH HARTSHORNE.
            Cherry Hall Papers

Mr Motts Estate   to   Peter Le Conte Dr—

Feb 26th	To 1 Visit	£0—6—0
	To Hord Gall & Rad Glycyrth at twice	0—3—0
	To Ingredt for a Detergl Tinct	0—6—0
	To Spt Ot	—2—6
March 1st	To Ingredt for an Expector Tinct	0—6—0
	To Hord Gall & Rad Liquer at twice	—3—0
	To 1 Vial of Compound Cordial -r[?]	—8—0
	To Spt Ot	—2—6
	To Sal Vol oleos	—3—0
	To 1 Visit	—6—

            £2—6—0

June 6th 1734
  Received of Mr James Mott the full Contents of the within Accompt, being in full of all Debts, Dues and Demands whatsoever Recd
£2—6—0
                                                  Pr me P Le Conte
                                                          Cherry Hall Papers

The name of Mott is now extinct in Monmouth County, but there are numerous descendants of Gershom Mott now living in Iowa.

Issue (from the Family Bible)
36 John Mott, born Dec 1, 1697.
37 William Mott, born Nov 9, 1699
38 Gershom Mott, born May 15, 1702
39 Asher Mott, born June 27, 1704.
40 James Mott, born Apr. 5, 1707
41 Huldah Mott, born Oct 31, 1709

9 RICHBELL MOTT, son of Adam Mott, 1, lived at Great Neck In 1691, he joined his mother, Elizabeth Hubbs in a release.

1696 [1695], Oct. 14 He had a license to marry Elizabeth, daughter of William and Winifred Thorne. On Hempstead Census, 1698.

1700, May 14 Richbell Mott, of Hampstead, Queen's Co., N Y, yeoman, bought from Johannes Lawrenson, of Maidenhead, Burlington Co., N J., 1050 acres of land above the Falls of Delaware

1700 Mr Richbell Mott was one of the executors of Ann Richbell, of Mamaroneck, gentlewoman, his grandmother

1714 He was one of the executors   , of Hempstead

1734, Sept 22 Will of Richbell Mott, of Hempstead, "being in great weakness of body", proved Dec 3, 1734, mentioned.

Wife, Elizabeth, to receive £20, per annum, and the use of his farm on Great Neck, as also all his personal estate save two negro slaves and an Irish servant boy, David, for whom he makes provision
Son, Edmund, 5 shillings
Son, Richard, a crop of winter wheat, if he assists his mother; also the negro slaves if he pays his mother £8
From the sale of his lands at Madnan's neck, his son, Richard, is to get £50,
Daughter, Elizabeth, £100,
Daughter, Mary, £90,
Daughter, Ann, £50,
Daughter, Jemima, £60,
Daughter, Keziah, £110 and
Daughter, Deborah, £40
The residue of his estate is given to his four grandsons, Richbell, son of Adam Mott, of Staten Island, Richbell, son of Edmund Mott, of Cow Neck, and Richard and Joseph, sons of Joseph Mott, of Cow Neck
Executors sons-in-law, Jonathan Townsend, Esq., of Oyster Bay, Joseph Mott, of Cow Neck, and his friend, Jacob Smith, of Hempstead

1737, Mch 7. Will of Elizabeth Mott, of Hempstead, widow of Richbell Mott, sick and weak, proved Apr 16, 1739, mentioned

Son, Edmond, her wheat, a three year old heifer, all her wearing apparell, except "cloak and a pair of mens stockings"
Grand-daughter, Phebe, daughter of Stephen Wood, £10
Grand-daughter, Jemima Wood, a crape gown, and a cotton and wool petticoat
To Stephen Wood that which he owes her for keeping an old negro wench one and a half years

Daughter, Deborah Mott, the rest of her apparell, a piece of new home spun cloth, and some pewter basin.
Daughter, Keziah, a pewter tankard
Grandson, Daniel Kissam, a pair of gold sleeve buttons
The like to her cousin, Phebe, daughter of Richard Thorne
Cousin, Mary Pudney, widow, all her flax
Grand-daughter, Elizabeth, daughter of Adam Mott, all her "tea tackling"
Grand-daughter, Mary Tredwell, her warming pan
The residue of her estate to her children, Edmond, Richard, Elizabeth, Ann, Mary, Jemima, Keziah and Deborah
Among the witnesses was Phebe Mott

Issue of Richbell Mott

42 Edmond Mott
43 Richbell Mott, born about 1700, died about 1724, probably unmarried.
44 Richard Mott
45 Elizabeth Mott, [married Adam Mott, 15, of Staten Island]
46 Mary Mott, married John Treadwell, will 1740
47 Ann Mott, married Daniel Kissam and Jonathan Townsend.
48 Jemima Mott, [married Stephen Wood.]

Issue

Richard Wood, baptized, June 13, 1731, Dutch Church, Staten Island
49 Keziah Mott, [married Richard Jackson] In 1739, Richard Mott was appointed administrator of Richard Jackson, of Queens County
50 Deborah Mott, married Joseph Mott, of Dutchess Co

11 WILLIAM MOTT, son of Adam Mott, 1, was born, at Hempstead, Jan 20, 1673-4, and died June 30, 1740, married, 12, 2 mo., (April) 1705, Hannah, daughter of John and Grace Ferris, of Westchester She died June 24, 1759

In 1702, he was a resident of Great Neck, called Madnam's Neck, where he had bought lands Mch 5, 1696, and was prominent among the Quakers who were wont to assemble at his house When the sect grew in this locahty to considerable size, a meeting house was ordered built, at Cow Neck, and William Mott was one of the committee chosen to determine its plan and size

He was held in esteem by his fellow townsmen, and not infrequently, held minor town offices.

1715, May 9 Hannah Mott, daughter of John Ferris, of Westchester Town, received a legacy of £20, in the will of her father of this date

1740, 22, 2mo (April) Will of William Mott, of Great Neck, Hempstead, proved June 30, 1744, mentioned
Son, William Mott his housing and lands in Hempstead
Son-in-law, Philip Pell, 10 shillings
Grandchildren, Philip, Hannah and Martha Pell, each 10 shillings, as a token of his love and remembrance, he having given their mother "a good sufficient portion in her life time"
Wife, Hannah, wheat, grain, swine, cows, other cattle, horses, household goods, negroes, table, sheep, warming pan, and the use of one-third of his house and lands
Daughter, Martha, a green side saddle, bedstead and bed, and she to be maintained decently and well until she comes to her understanding and reason again, when, in that event, his son, William is to pay her £250, and to live in the homestead as long as she is single

1756, 14, 4mo Will of Hannah, the widow of William Mott, of Madnan's Neck, Hempstead, far advanced in years and feeling the infirmities of old age coming on me apace, etc, proved Apr 8, 1760, mentioned
Grand-daughter, Hannah, wife of Daniel Stevenson, and
Martha, wife of John Alyn, Jr, each, £5
Daughter, Martha, "under a discomposure of mind," a negress who is to be sold in case she is intractable,

the interest on £100, a side saddle, beds and bedding, and wearing apparell, with succession to the testatrix's son, William Mott, if her daughter does not recover her mind

Son, William Mott, and his children

Executors. Son, William Mott, cousin, Adam Mott, of Cow Neck, and friend, Nathaniel Pearsall, of Cow Neck

Issue

51 Hannah Mott, born 22, 10, 1714, married Philip Pell, 5, 3mo., 1731, of Pelham, who died, 1752, making his brother-in-law, William Mott, one of his executors.

Issue

Philip Pell
Hannah Pell
Martha Pell

52 Elizabeth Mott, born 1, 1, 1706, died 25, 12 mo , 1721, unmarried.
53 William Mott, born Aug. 6, 1709; died Mch 25, 1786
54 Martha Mott, born 18, 19, 1716; non compos

12 ADAM MOTT, son of Adam Mott, 1, and the younger of the two sons of like name, married, 5, 11mo , 1731-2, Phebe, daughter of Richard and Abigail (Powell) Willits, of Jericho, who was born 14, mo , 1699, died, at Cow Neck, 7, 9mo., 1782 She was a minister among the Friends, and traveled as such at home and abroad He was born at Cow Neck, L I , Aug 20, 1680

1724 He was a witness to a will at Hempstead.

1715, Apr 2 He bought from his brother, Richbell Mott, for £269, a tract of land, of about six hundred acres, on Hempstead Harbor, where he built a home, still standing, and used by himself and his descendants for several generations

His widow, Phebe, married, 28, 11mo , 1741, Tristam Dodge.

1738, Sept 3 Will of Adam Mott, of Hempstead, weak of body, proved Feb 28, 1739, mentioned

Sons, Adam and Stephen, his houses and lands at Cow Neck, and throughout Hempstead

Daughter, Elizabeth, when she is eighteen, one-half of his cattle, sheep and swine, and a great table, chest and bed, and £50, when his sons reach the age of twenty-five years

Son, Stephen, lands, to be leased by his executors till he comes of age

Wife, Phebe, movable estate, from which she is to give each of his sons a ridable mare, when they reach seventeen, and £15, when they reach twenty-one

Alluded to his brother, Richbell's children, his brother, William's children, and his brother, Charles' children.

He provided that his children should be taught "English fit for Country business "

He made provision for the sale of his negro man and farm products to pay his debts

Executors Phebe, his wife, Richard Mott, William Mott, Jr , and John Willis, all of Hempstead

Issue

55 Elizabeth Mott, born 31, 5mo , 1733
56 Adam Mott, born 10, 10 mo , 1734
57 Stephen Mott, born 1, 2mo , 1736

13 CHARLES MOTT, son of Adam Mott, 1, born about 1672, was a child by the third wife He resided at Cow Neck, in Hempstead, near the head of the harbor, now Roslyn, where he operated a grist and fulling mill, which he had bought of John Robinson in 1709

1698, Aug 31 Charls Mott, Elzabeth Mott, Charls Mott and Gersham mott were among the residents of Hempstead enumerated in the Census of that year (N Y. Biog. & Geneal Record, p 55, Jan , 1914) He married Elizabeth   , prior to 1695, who predeceased him

In 1714, he was Surveyor of Highways for Cow Neck

1714/5, Mch 4 Charles Mott, of Hempstead, Long Island, gave a power of attorney to his "trusty and loving friend," Gershom Mott, of Middletown, N J , to collect debts, etc Joseph Taylor, a witness.

There was, apparently, a greater affection between Charles and Gershom Mott than the others, for the former was the only one of the brothers who named a son, Gershom

1721 Charles Mott was sued, in New Jersey, and the papers were endorsed "non est"

1740, Feb 10. Will of Charles Mott, of Hempstead, yeoman, weak in body, proved Feb 10, 1740, mentioned

Son, Amos Mott, the homestead and farm whereon testator dwelt, lying near Hempstead Harbor, he to pay his mother £4, per year, also one-half of his undivided lands in Hempstead, and a negro boy

Son, Adam Mott, the other half of the undivided Hempstead lands

Grandson, Joseph Starkins, son of daughter Mary Anne Carroll, £50, to be raised by his executors by the sale of lands, at Kakiat or New Hempstead, in Orange Co , [now Rockland Co]

Daughter, Elizabeth Hunter, a negro girl and to the heir of daughter, Elizabeth Hunter, if a boy, at the age of twenty-one, and if a girl, at the age of eighteen years, £60

Son, Gershom Mott, a negro girl

Son, John Mott, his large bible

Grandson, Joseph Mott, 20 shillings, in full for his claim, as heir-at-law

Residue of his estate to his sons, Gershom, Benjamin, John, Adam and Amos, and to his daughters, Mary Anne Carroll and Elizabeth Hunter

Executors his son, Amos, and his kinsman, William Mott, son of William Mott, of Hempstead, deceased

Issue

58 Adam Mott
59 Amos Mott
60 Mary Ann Carroll [St. George's Church, Hempstead Mariana Mott married, July 23, 1730, Patrick Caryl She had previously married Joseph Starkin]
61 Elizabeth Hunter
62 Gershom Mott
63 John Mott, had a son Benjamin Mott
64 Benjamin Mott
65 Charles Mott; who was probably the eldest son and was deceased, in 1740, when his father failed to mention him in his will, but who is alluded to in the will of his brother, Amos, in 1743, and it is Charles' son, Joseph, who received 20 shillings, in full of his claim as heir-at-law, in the will of his grandfather, Charles Mott, in 1740
66 Jacob Mott

14 ELIZABETH MOTT, daughter of Adam Mott, 1, by his third wife, Elizabeth Redman

1703, Oct. 29 John Okeson, of Freehold, N. J , for £82, sold his interest in an estate which Adam Mott, deceased, late of Hempstead, did give his six youngest children, which he had by his last wife, Elizabeth, unto Richbell Mott, William Mott, Charles Mott and Adam Mott, Jr , all of Hempstead Signed by John Okeson, and by his wife, Elizabeth, by her mark. (Jamaica Records)

15 ADAM MOTT, son of Adam Mott, 2
1698. On the Hempstead, L. I , Census
1713, June 15 Had lands from his father Adam

1719 He was residing at Rockaway, when he joined with his wife and his parents in a conveyance of land

1725, June 15. He bought, from Enoch Stephenson and wife, Katherine, land on Staten Island, lying on the south side of the Fresh Kill, with the house, barns, etc , thereon, which he then held under a lease.

1725 Mr. Adam Mott recorded his cattle-mark on Staten Island.

1728 He was Clerk of Richmond County

1730, Apr 10 Adam Mott, yeoman of Staten Island, Henry Young and Joseph Carman made a deposition concerning a wounded whale cast ashore on Staten Island The kinship of this Adam Mott to the Mott family I have not discovered, but he was probably the individual of that name, who later appeared in Cape May County, N. J. This is the more likely as the Youngs and Carmans were also early settlers in Cape May. The following allusions may refer to this Adam Mott and his relatives

> 1724, Nov 18 Will of Thomas Mott, of Little Egg Harbor, Burlington Co , N J , proved May 16, 1726, in which he styled himself planter and mentioned his wife, Deborah, and children Thomas, John, Henry and Mary Witnesses Jone [Jane] Mott, Adam Mott, Joshua Hunloke
> 1724, Dec 16 An inventory was taken of his personal estate by Adam Mott and Roger Orsborne, which amounted to £81–17–9
> 1731, Feb 20 Jane Mott and Peter Scull, both of Gloucester, had a license to marry
> 1738, Aug 7 John Mott, of Burlington, (N J), and Phebe Cramer had a license to marry.
> 1739, Jan 3– Mary Mott and James Arnold, Burlington, had a license to marry.

1731, Dec 23 Albert Johnson, of Staten Island, made his will, and appointed his two sons, with Adam Mott, executors, and to Elizabeth Mott, *Jr* , he willed a gold diamond ring

1734-5 Adam Mott, Jr , of Staten Island, was appointed executor by Cornelius Winans

1734. Adam Mott, of Staten Island, was an executor of Margaret Le Counte

1734 Adam Mott, of Staten Island, called son-in-law in will of Richbell Mott

1735–6 Adam Mott, of Staten Island, was a witness

1737–9 Adam Mott was a member of the Colonial Assembly, from Richmond County.

1738 He wrote to the Governor asking the appointment of his son Richbell as lieutenant at large of Richmond County Militia

1739 Adam Mott, of Staten Island, was principal creditor, and administrator of Nicholas Stillwell.

1739. Adam Mott, of Staten Island, was a witness

1745, July 11 He and his wife, Elizabeth, sold their home farm of 138 acres, formerly belonging to Richbell Mott, and which had been Adam Mott's, lying at Madnam's Neck, (Hempstead), to John Allyn.

1747, Feb 11 Adam Mott, of Richmond County, for £350, bought several parcels of land in Dover Hundred, lying upon Dover Creek and Dover River, with the houses and farms thereon, as also 180 acres of land called "Willinbrook," in Little Creek Hundred in the same county, from Peter Galloway, and his wife, Elizabeth, of the County of Kent, Delaware

1748, Feb 22 Adam Mott, of Kent County, Del , conveyed to his son, Richbell Mott, of the same place, his lands at Dover, bought in the preceding year from Galloway.

1749, Feb 7. Letters of administration were issued at Dover, Kent County, Del., upon the estate of Adam Mott, deceased, to his son Richbell Mott.

1750, [1749], Mch 8 Administration was granted to Elizabeth Mott, widow, of Richmond County, upon the estate of her husband, Adam Mott, gentleman, deceased, formerly of Richmond County, but since of the Province of Penn A bond of £500 was given by Samuel Stillwell, merchant, of New York City, who was a cousin twice removed of this late Adam Mott

Adam Mott married Elizabeth, daughter of Richbell Mott, 9 After her husband's death she returned to Staten Island, where she made her will, Jan 30, 1777; proved Apr 2, 1778, which mentioned her grandson, Richbell Mott, son of her deceased son Richard, who received £160, when he reaches the age of 22, granddaughter, Elizabeth Seaman, daughter of her daughter Elizabeth, who received miscellaneous goods, balance of her estate to her daughter, Elizabeth, wife of Benjamin Seaman   Executors: friend, John Micheau, and grandson, Richard Seaman Among the witnesses was Benjamin Seaman, jr

Issue
67 Richard Mott
68 Elizabeth Mott; wife of Benjamin Seaman in 1743.
69 Richbell Mott, eldest son, born 1717–18.

16   JANE MOTT, supposed daughter of Adam Mott, 2.

Richard Seaman, youngest son of Capt John Seaman, of Hempstead, Long Island, was born about 1673–5, and died Sept 5, 1749.   He married, about 1693–4, Jane, (probably daughter of Adam Mott)   They had fourteen children, given, collectively, in his will, and in the Records of the Society of Friends, printed in New York Geneal and Biog Record, January, 1873.

Among these children is one by name, *Adam Seaman*, which is suggestive, if not substantiative, of a Mott alliance   Inasmuch as Adam Mott, the supposed father of this Jane, was married, in 1678, to Mary Stillwell, and Richard, the eldest son of Richard Seaman and Jane, his wife, was born 31, 11mo , 1694–5, it crowds the dates somewhat closely, and suggests that Adam Mott, the elder son of the first Adam Mott, may have had an earlier wife than Mary Stillwell, and it is worthy of note, that among the many children that Jane Mott (?) had by Richard Seaman, the characteristic Christian names of the Stillwell family do not appear If we credit Adam Mott (the elder son Adam, of the first Adam Mott), with two wives, there would be no difficulties in the way of these otherwise crowded dates   That Jane, the wife of Richard Seaman, was a Mott is strengthened by the fact that her husband, Richard Seaman, in his will, 1749, appoints, as one of his executors, his "cousin," Patrick Mott

If Jane was the daughter of Adam Mott, then Patrick Mott, as the son of Lieut John Mott, was *her* cousin, and nephew (which in old records is called cousin), to her husband, Richard Seaman, whose sister Sarah, became the wife of this said Lieut John Mott

18   MARY MOTT, daughter of Adam Mott, 2

1705, Mch 5   Under this date there is recorded in the Calendar of English Colonial Manuscripts, in the State Library at Albany, N. Y , a memorandum of a letter written by H. Mott, the Secretary, requesting a marriage license for his daughter, Mary, with Solomon Samans This is an error and should read as follows

hamfted 5 day of March 1705

Mr sacatary sr be pleased to inform yr governor that i have given my consant that this barer Solomon samens shall have my dagter mary pray afist him in gating a lysans for thare marag and i shall be willing to you my wife is allso willing to ye same so i rest your afured friend and servant

A{d} MOTT

This same day a license was granted to Solomon Simmons and Mary Mott to marry   He was probably, nearly doubtless Solomon, son of Solomon, son of the first Capt John Seaman, of Hempstead

21   EDWARD MOTT, supposed son of Henry Mott, 5

1704, June 26   Edmund Mott was one of the witnesses to the will of John Bridges, Chief-Justice of the Province of New York

1704–5, Feb 27   Administration was granted upon the estate of *Edmund* Mott, "of New York, in parts beyond the seas," to Joseph Bentham, S T P , his principal creditor, Bridget

Mott and Elizabeth Mott, his sisters, first renouncing Edmund Mott was, apparently, a bachelor, and died in England New York Geneal and Biog Record, October, 1903.

1708, Feb 28. Edward Mott died intestate, and letters of administration were granted to William Bradford, printer, as principal creditor.   New York Wills

24 JOHN MOTT, JR , son of John Mott, 6, born prior to 1685, of Hempstead, 1735. He was an executor in the will of his uncle, Joseph Mott, 7

I suspect that the John Mott, of Hempstead, who made his will, in 175-, which was proved April, 1751, was John Mott, Jr , son of John Mott, 6   In this will he left to his

Wife, Rebecca, a larger number of household utensils, and maintenance by his son, Micajah Mott
Son, Samuel, two steers
Son, John, carpenter's tools, and one-half of his surveyor's compass and chain
Daughter, Sarah, wife of Benjamin Hulse, a bed, with Dimity curtains
Daughter, Martha, wife of Daniel Carman, an iron pot and a side saddle
Son, Jehu, one-half of his hand saw and one-third of my three-quarter augur, and one-half of my inch augur, etc
Daughter, Rebecca Mott, a feather bed
Daughter, Phebe, wife of Daniel Wright, £5, and a cow
Son, Micajah, part of testator's tools, a riding horse, house, barn and orchard, where the testator lives—between the lands given to his sons, Jehu and Jacob, and lands and meadow at Rockaway
Further reserves on the land given to his son, Micajah, land where his son, John, lies buried, to be used for a burial place for himself, his children and grandchildren

1785, Aug. 21. Micajah Mott, son of John Mott, was married, at Saint George's, Hempstead, to Ann Flowers

Issue

70 Micajah Mott
71 Samuel Mott
72 John Mott
73 Sarah Mott, wife of Benjamin Hulse
74 Martha Mott, wife of Daniel Carman
75 Jehu Mott
76 Rebecca Mott
77 Phebe Mott, wife of Daniel Wright
78 Jacob Mott

25 JAMES MOTT, son of Lieut John Mott, 6; probably born 1685-90. Cattle-mark recorded Sept 30, 1706

1727 Named in his father's deed to Patrick Mott
1743 He was one of the four executors of Benjamin Hicks, of Hempstead

28 PATRICK MOTT, son of Lieut John Mott, 6, born 1698-1701   Received homestead from his father, 1727

1738 He owned land, at Hempstead, and was one of the executors of Richard Gildersleeve.
1748 Benjamin Burleigh, of Hempstead, appointed his wife, Hannah, and his brother-in-law, Patrick Mott, executors of his will
1749 He was appointed an executor in the will of his uncle, Richard Seaman, of Hempstead.

He was a Friend and a much trusted business man, and was executor of wills dated 1753, 1758, 1759, 1760, 1761, 1763, 1765, and witness, at Hempstead, 1749, 1753, 1760, with Deborah Mott   Executor of his brother Henry in 1758.

He died 1775

29 HENRY MOTT, son of John Mott, 6, was born about 1702, died 1767, married Hannah   . He was of Far Rockaway, and a witness at Hempstead, in 1742 In his will, 1767, he mentioned his children:

Issue

79 Adam Mott
80 Hannah Lewes
81 Abigail Foster
82 Henry Mott
83 Sarah
84 Richard Mott
85 Mary
86 John Mott
87 Elizabeth

30 JOSEPH MOTT, of Cow Neck, son of Joseph Mott, 7, was born Mch 1, 1700, was a farmer of Hempstead, 1759, was mentioned in the will of his father-in-law, Richbell Mott, 1734, as the father of two sons Richard and Joseph.

He married, first, Deborah Mott, his cousin, daughter of Richbell Mott, born May 3, 1708, married, second, June 3, 1759, Catharine Baerum, widow.

Issue

88 Richard Mott
89 Joseph Mott

John Tredwell, 1740, appointed Joseph Mott, his brother-in-law, one of his executors.
The following individual may be Joseph Mott
Joseph Mott, of Charlotte Precinct, Dutchess Co., left a will dated Sept 28, 1762, in which he gave land, in Nine Partners, to his sons, Richard and Jacob, and mentioned daughter, Martha, wife of James Valentine, Jone, wife of Timothy Smith, Elizabeth, wife of Samuel Smith, Jemima, wife of John Conon Also his loving brother, Jacob Mott, of Queens County, Long Island

31 SAMUEL MOTT, son of Joseph Mott, 7, was born 1707
1736, Dec. 21 Will of Samuel Mott, of Hempstead, very sick, etc ; proved Mch 26, 1737, mentioned
Wife, Martha, £100, the use of his house and barn, and the use of certain lands, for the education of his children
To his wife and children his personal property, stock and slaves
Executors his wife, Martha, his brother, Joseph Mott, his uncle, Elias Dorlan, his brother, Samuel Cornell, and Jacob Smith
1728, May 27 Samuel Mott and Martha Smith were married, at St George's Church, Hempstead
1734 Samuel Mott was a witness at Hempstead

32 JACOB MOTT, son of Joseph Mott, 7, married, it is said, Kesia Seaman, daughter of Nathaniel Seaman, born 1699, who married Sarah Powell, and certainly Abigail Jackson
1743, Aug 28 Abigail, wife of Jacob Mott, was baptized, at St George's, Hempstead
1742 He was one of the administrators of Jeronimus Johnson, of Queens County
1750 Jacob Mott was a witness at Hempstead
"Abigail Jackson, born Nov 18, 1720, died 1781, married Jacob Mott"
1750, Dec 4. Will of Isaac Johnson, of Jerusalem, in the Town of Hempstead, L I, mentioned.

"my sister, Abigail Mott," to whom he willed £200, and he appointed her husband, Jacob Mott, one of his executors, and their children, Joseph, Isaac, Jerusha Mott, Miriam Mott, and Ruth Mott were among his legatees

Abigail Mott was also the sister of Thomas Jackson, of Hempstead Harbor, who, in his will, Sept 3, 1752, alluded to her as such, and made her a contingent legatee, and appointed Jacob Mott, a brother-in-law, one of his executors.

Issue

90 Joseph Mott, born Oct 18, 1736
91 Samuel Mott, born May 31, 1731, died young
92 Jackson Mott, born Aug. 16, 1740.
93 Isaac Mott, born May 6, 1743, married Nancy Coles.
94 Miriam Mott, born Apr. 30, 1745, died young
95 Ruth Mott, born June 6, 1747, married, Nov 9, 1763, Jordan Lawrence, of Oyster Bay; second, Stephen Coles
96 Samuel I. Mott, born Feb 9, 1753
97 Jacob Mott, born June 30, 1756
98 Miriam Mott, born Sept. 7, 1759, baptized, at St George's, Hempstead, Apr 12, 1761, married Benjamin Birdsall
99 Richard Mott, born May 9, 1761, married Polly Sutton, and, second, Freelove Sutton
100 Joseph Mott, born Aug. 21, 1763, moved to South Carolina
101 Jerusha Mott

36 JOHN MOTT, son of Gershom Mott, 8, born Dec 1, 1697, died 1734, married, Dec. 21, 1731, Charity Lindsley She married, second, David Wheeler

1728 Cleared at Amboy, Sloop Catharine, John Mott, Master, navigated with four men: bound for Boston Cargo, wheat, corn, flour, bread, meal, tongues, etc.

Dec 20, 1731 "to People to envite them to wedinge"
Dec. 21, 1731 "John Mott Married to Charety Lindeley by Budd"

From Mott Diary.

Will of John Mott, of Hanover, dated Nov. 27, 1732, proved Oct 1, 1734, mentioned: Son, Gershom, under age; brother, Gershom Mott, to whom he willed his clothes, wife, Charity, his sawmill, etc Executors wife and brother, Gershom Inventory amounted to £159 14 0

Issue

102 Gershom Mott, married Mary Day. He died soon after his marriage; probably left no issue.

37 WILLIAM MOTT, son of Gershom Mott, 8, born Nov. 9, 1699, died Jan 21, 1760; married Margaret, daughter of William and Catharine (Bowne) Hartshorne

1741, Feb. 26. William Mott, of Hunterdon Co, N. J., yeoman, conveyed to James Mott, of Middletown, Monmouth Co, yeoman, for £30, about one hundred acres of land, in Middletown, bounded by lands of James Walling, Thomas Walling, Thomas Kearney, etc William and James Mott are alluded to as executors of Gershom Mott, deceased, late of Middletown, N J

1742 He was a member of the Provincial Assembly

Issue (from family bible in possession of his descendants in Iowa.)

103 John Mott, born Jan 18, 1734.

104 Sarah Mott, born Aug 10, 1735, [married, by license dated Oct. 4, 1780, William Biles]
105 Gershom Mott, born Nov 18, 1737.
106 Asher Mott, born Feb 17, 1739.

38 GERSHOM MOTT, son of Gershom Mott, 8, was born May 15, 1702, moved to Morris County, N. J., and rose to eminence

1740, July 14 and Sept 16 Gershom Mott was Judge of the Inferior Court of Common Pleas, and Judge of the Court of General Sessions, and Judge of the Superior Court of Common Pleas, Morris County, N J

In the records his name proved a trial to the Clerk, for it is spelled Girshom, Garcham, Garsham, Garshom.

Josiph Mott's name appears about this time, and is doubtless a connection.

1749, July 4 New commissions for judges were issued   Gershom Mott was last mentioned as Judge, Dec 26 1749

1750, Mch. 27 Gershom Mott, surety, on application of Elias Cook to keep a public house in Hanover, Morris County.

1750 Mch 28 Gershom Mott, surety, on application of Isaac Mourison to keep a public house in Paquanack Township

1751, Sept. 18. Lemuel Bowers vs Gershom Mott   Case £200

1751, Dec. 24 Gershom Mott, surety, on application of Timothy Tuttle to keep a public house at Hanover.

1752, Mch 24 Gershom Mott, surety, for Sam^{ll} Smith, on application to keep a public house at Hanover.

1752, July 8 Gershom Mott, one of three arbitrators, in suit of Archilus Young vs Jacob Scott

1757, July 5 Paul Vanderbeak vs Gershom Mott. Debt £60

1757, July 5 Paul Vanderbeak vs Gershom Mott, Junr. Debt £60

1756, Mch 10. Gershom Mott, Jr, surety on the application of Daniel Tuttle to keep a public house

1756, July 6 Gershom Mott, Jr, surety, on the application of Ellis Cook to keep a public house

1756, Sept 29 Gershom Mott, Jr, surety, on the application of Saml Tutthull to keep a public house

1761, Mch. 11, and Mch 10, 1762. Gershom Mott petitioned for a license to keep a public house.

1761, Dec 16 Gershom Mott and Jacob Ford, Esq., executors of David Wheeler, deceased, vs Abel Hathaway, administrator of Jonathan? Hathaway.

1762, July 6 James Jauncey vs Gershom Mott.

1762, December John Ray vs Gershom Mott   Debt, non est, and vice versa

1763, July. Hendrik Ovdenaarde vs Gershom Mott   Debt £100, non est

1764 Benjamin Howel vs Gershom Mott   Case £200, non est

1765, December. Executors of Alex^r Eagles vs Gersohm Mott   Debt £132, non est.

Issue

107 Gershom Mott, Junior.
108 Joseph Mott [?]

39 ASHER MOTT, son of Gershom Mott, 8, born June 27, 1704, died Mch. 5, 1761; married Deborah, daughter of James and Abigail (Hicks) Tallman

Issue
109 Asher Mott, died 1750.
110 Abigail Mott, married, 1763 William Wilson
111 Mary Mott, married 1773, Arthur Howell
112 Huldah Mott, died 1825
113 Sarah Mott

40 JAMES MOTT, son of Gershom Mott, 8, born Apr. 5, 1707, died Feb 11th, 1787, married, first, Mary, daughter of Obadiah and Alice (Ashton) Holmes December, 1734, who died Oct., 1749, married, second, Amey Herbert, by license dated May 8, 1752, who died Oct , 1754 She was the daughter of Safety Borden, of Bordentown and married, first, William Maghee and had by him

James Maghee, born 1728.
Safety Maghee, born 1731.
Catharine Maghee, born 1731 (sic)
William Maghee, born 1738.

She married, second, Daniel Herbert, and third, James Mott

Issue by first wife
114 Sarah Mott
115 Huldah Mott, married Joseph Saltar, of Shrewsbury
116 James Mott, died 1823
107 Gershom Mott
118 John Mott

Asher Taylor gave also "Mary and a daughter, who married Shore Stevens."

Aug 22, 1775   Commission from Provincial Congress
James Mott, Esq , appointed Capt of a Company in 2nd Regiment' Foot in Monmouth Co , whereof David Brearley, Esq , is Colonel   Cherry Hall Papers

James Mott was appointed 2nd Major of Monmouth Militia, October, 1775
Deputy to the Provincial Congress and Council of Safety from Monmouth Co , June, 1776
Resigned his commission in the Militia, 1776

Inventory of Personal Estate of James Mott, of Middletown, Mch 2, 1787, amounted to £932 8 11 and among the items of interest are

2 silver Table spoons	£ 1—2—6
Peter, a negro aged 67	
Phillis, a negro aged 67	
Oliver (man) a negro aged 36	50—0—0
Peter, a negro aged 21	80—0—0
Betty 34	45—0—0
Esther with her child	65—0—0
Negro boy Samuel	15—0—0
Negro boy Isaac	16—0—0

These are to Certyfy that at a certain Munmouth Court which to the best of my memory was laft April term that at the House of Jofeph Morfords and in the Barr Roame Near the foot of the Stares Some Difcoarfe Brock out Betwixt me and James Mott as adminiftrator to the Estate of Jofeph Holmes Def^d to which I mentioned that I underftood Thare was a Judgment againft Uriah Carle at the Sute of Said adminiftrators and that I underftood Said Carl complained of being Ronged I alfo aded that Said Carel would Lay under a

Difadvantage of Coming to Juftice after Judgment went againft Him by His Not Entering a Plea in time or words Nearly to that Porpose

to which Mr Mott Reply'd that He Could Not tell How the matter waf but waf willing Said Carel Should Have Juftice Done Him and that Even after Execution if anything appeared in favour of Said Carel Said Mott would alow it

the above was the Subftance of the Difcoarce as Near as I can Remember which I will at any time Declare under oath if Required

ROB^t CAMPBELL fr

ye 13th February 1766

Cherry Hall Papers

November ye 20 1755

Bordentown

Honoured Father I Send you thefe Line To Let you know my Prefent Circumstances we are all in good health at Prefent Through mercy and hope these may find you in the same—Being the greateft Blesfing we Can Enjoy in this life god grant that we may Implore his goodnefs for so Doing he still Continuing to feed us with his good Creature and Refrefhing us by our natural Sleep in Peace and Quietnefs while our fellow Creatures upon our fronteers about us are suffering the most inhuman Deaths immaginable By our Cruel Lnemies and Savages the Lord Being now about to threaten us with the Sword and Earthquakes which god may grant may be for our good—Dear father not having an opertunity To Converfe with you By word of mouth I muft Conclude to do it by letters and firft of all I pray that god of his infinite mercy and goodnefs would give me a heart to lead a Righteous holy and godly life here in this Prefent world in all my affairs both Spirituall and Temporall and next I humbly afk your Confent To my maching my Self with a Perfon whom I and all my friends Efteems to Bee worthy of me the young woman is William Folwells Daufhter mary that lives at william Pottses it is Like you may not know her at Prefent But when you Do I hope you will own her To be your Ever Loving and Dutifull Daufhtr I hope you will favour me with an anfwer By the first oppertunity the Time is fixed Between us By the Confent of you and other friends that is concern'd in the affair if nothing happens more than we expect the week Before Chriftmas.

So I Conclude with mine and all our friends Tendereft Love and Effections To you and your family

from your Ever Loving and Dutifull Son

SAFETY MEGHEE

P S Please To Remember in Particular my Love to Sifter and kind Respects to huldah and Miss Sally Holmes

Cherry Hall Papers

Letter of Safety Meghee to James Mott, Middletown Point, Aug 31, 1757

Dear father—

"My brother Billy is dead & Buryed yesterday" etc "Our child is poorly & Mrs Borden is very poorly but we are in hopes will recover"

Loving & Dutiful Son
SAFETY MAGHEE

41 HULDAH MOTT, daughter of Gershom Mott, 8, born Oct. 31, 1709 died Sept 4, 1784, married, Dec 7, 1731, Samuel Holmes, born Apr. 17, 1704, O S , died Feb 23, 1760, and had ten children See Holmes Family.

"Jan 13, 1731/2 Huldah Mott Marryed to Samuel Holmes" (From Mott Diary)

42 EDMOND MOTT, son of Richbell Mott, of Hempstead, 9 On Hempstead Census, 1698

1741, 4 6mo [August] Edmond Mott made his will, proved June 13, 1744, and mentioned·
Wife, Catharine, £200, and the use of his estate to bring up his children
Daughter, Margaret, £170, when she is ten years old
Son, Richbell Mott, one-half of his farm, when of age, with its buildings and improvements
The remaining half of his farm to be divided between his sons, Edmond and John, when they arrive at age.

Executors his wife, Catharine, and his esteemed friends and kinsmen, Joseph Mott and William Mott, both of Hempstead

He married Catharine, daughter of Capt. John and Sybil (Ray) Sands, born about 1700
Austin's Rhode Island Dictionary

Issue

119 Margaret Mott
120 Richbell Mott, born 3, 6mo., 1728, died 1758, without male issue
121 Edmond Mott, born 25 8mo., 1730, mariner, married Oct 13, 1753, Deborah Sands, no issue
122 John Mott, born 1, 8mo., 1732   From Westbury, L I , Friends' Records.

Of these children Margaret was a legatee of her grandmother, Elizabeth Mott, in 1737, but was omitted in her father's will, 1741, wherefore she probably died young

Edmond Mott probably died unmarried and non compos

John Mott died, in 1781, leaving a will dated 28, 2 mo., 1773, proved Mch 16, 1781, in which he styled himself as of Cowneck, alluded to his brother, Edmond, as in a delirious and unsettled condition of mind, but who was to receive his estate in the event of his recovery, with remainder to the testator's niece, Margaret, wife of Melancthon Smith   Executors his kinsmen, Richard Sands and Adam Mott, and among the witnesses were Stephen Mott and Elizabeth Mott

44 RICHARD MOTT, son of Richbell Mott, 9, was born about 1710, died 15, 8mo., 1743, married, 26, 1mo., 1741, Sarah, daughter of Thomas and Sarah (Underhill) Pearsall of Hempstead born 6, 11mo., 1714; died 9mo., 1800.   His widow married Richard Alsop in 1747.

1743, 10, 8mo   Will of Richard Mott, of Hempstead, weak and indisposed, proved Oct. 24, 1743, mentioned·

Wife, Sarah, £100, in lieu of dower, and one-third of the remainder of his estate

The other portion of which is ordered put at interest till his son is of age, but should he die during his minority, then his share is to go to Richbell, Edmond and John, sons of my brother, Edmond Mott

Executors   wife, Sarah, his father-in-law, Thomas Pearsall, his brother, Edmund Mott, and his kinsman, Richard Thorne, of Great Neck, Hempstead

Issue

123 James Mott, born 8, 8mo., 1742, married, in 1765, Mary, daughter of Samuel and Ann (Carpenter) Underhill of Oyster Bay

53 WILLIAM MOTT, son of William Mott, 11, died Mch 25, 1786. His wife died November, 1780. He married, 6, 8, 1742, Elizabeth, daughter of Mary Allen, widow of Henry Allen   Mary Allen was of Hempstead, and made her will 1746, proved 1747, and mentioned, among others, her daughter, Elizabeth, wife of William Mott, whom she made one of her executors   Thompson's Long Island Vol ii, p 57, says he married Elizabeth Valentine

1735 William Mott, of Flushing, was a witness

1752 William Mott, of Marmaroneck (?), was one of the executors of John Sutton, of Marmaroneck, he also held lands at Cowneck

1760 William Mott was an executor of Tristam Dodge.

1782, 1, 12mo   Will of William Mott, when he was "far advanced in age", proved Sept. 13, 1786, mentioned

Sons, William, Samuel, John, Richard, Joseph and Benjamin, to whom he bequeathed his estate, and to whom he willed his farm, at Great Neck, etc , they to pay his son, Henry Mott, and his daughter, Elizabeth, wife of David Underhill, and to his daughter, Hannah Mott, amounts equalling their shares   Some of the children were yet minors

Executors   son-in-law, David Underhill, and sons, William, John and Henry Mott.

MOTT OF NEW YORK AND NEW JERSEY 93

Issue

124 William Mott, born Jan. 8, 1743. [8, 1mo., 1743, Westbury Records] Left issue
125 Hannah Mott, born 4, 6, 1744, died 15, 3, 1750. Westbury Records.
126 James Mott, born 29, 6, 1745 Westbury Records
127 Elizabeth Mott, born 5, 2, 1747. Westbury Records Married David Underhill
128 John Mott, born 17, 2, 1749, died 7, 3mo., 1750. Westbury Records
129 Samuel Mott, born 16, 12, 1750 Westbury Records Died Apr 1, 1791, left issue.
130 Hannah Mott, born 18, 4, 1753. Westbury Records
131 John Mott, 2nd., born 24, 6, 1755 Westbury Records Died, without issue, Nov 11, 1823
132 Henry Mott, born 31, 5, [May] 1757 Westbury Records Died, 1840, leaving issue
133 Richard Mott, born 20, 8, 1759 Westbury Records
134 Joseph Mott, born 11, 1, 1762 Left issue
135 Benjamin Mott, born 19, 3, 1765. Left issue

55 ELIZABETH MOTT, daughter of Adam Mott, 12, the younger son, was born 31, 5mo., 1733, died 13, 9mo., 1783, married, 5, 3mo., 1755, John, son of Samuel and Mary (Fry) Willis, a minister among Friends, born 8, 2mo., 1734, died 4, 3mo., 1789 Her children are traced by Mr. T C. Cornell, in "The Mott Ancestry" John Willis resided at Oyster Bay

1757 She received a silver spoon and porringer, in the will of her grandmother, Abigail Willetts.

Issue

Adam Willis, born 1757, 13, 7mo., died 9, 3mo., 1758
Samuel Willis, born 1759, 7, 3mo
Phebe Willis, born 1761, 5, 4mo.

56 ADAM MOTT, son of Adam Mott, 12, the younger son, was born 10, 10mo., 1734; died 18, 12mo., 1790, married, first, 5, 3mo., 1755, Sarah, daughter of Samuel and Mary (Fry) Willis, born 14, 7mo., 1736, died 10, 1mo., 1783; married, second, 5, 1mo., 1785, Abigail, daughter of David Batty, of South Hempstead, born 1733; died 10, 12mo., 1807 T C Cornell
Adam Mott was of Cow Neck

1757. Adam Mott received a silver spoon and a silver porringer, in the will of his grandmother, Abigail Willetts
1758 Adam Mott, of Cow Neck, was an executor of the will of Samuel Pearce
1760 He was executor of the will of Hannah, widow of William Mott
He succeeded to the homestead and the Eastern half of the farm

Issue

136 Elizabeth Mott, born 19, 7mo., 1755, died 10, 4mo., 1782
137 Daughter Mott, born 28, 10, 1758, died 30, 10mo., 1758
138 Lydia Mott, born 24, 11mo., 1759.
139 Adam Mott, born 11, 10mo., 1762.
140 Samuel Mott, born 29, 9mo., 1773.

57 STEPHEN MOTT, son of Adam Mott, 12, the younger son, was born 1, 2mo., 1736, died 11, 11mo., 1813, married, 6, 10mo., 1762, Amy, daughter of Samuel and Mary (Fry) Willis, born 27, 3mo., 1738, died 10, 11mo., 1822

He succeeded to the Western part of the farm where he built a house, occupied to-day by his descendants in the third generation   T. C Cornell

1757 He, like his brother Adam, received a silver spoon and porringer, in the will of his grandmother, Abigail Willetts.

58 ADAM MOTT, son of Charles Mott, 13, born prior to 1716 He resided at Cow Neck and may have married Elizabeth Smith

Issue

141 Jacob Mott; eldest son.
142 Daniel Mott
143 Jonathan Mott
144 Marianah Mott
} living in 1748

59 AMOS MOTT, son of Charles Mott, 13, resided, at Oyster Bay, in 1745-6.

1743 He was a witness at Hempstead

1745-6, Mch 20 He made his will, proved Mch. 29, 1746, in which he mentioned

Brother, Benjamin Mott, to whom he gave all his lands, and in default of his having issue, then to Jacob Mott, eldest son of his brother, Adam Mott

Nephew, Joseph Mott, eldest son of his brother, Charles Mott, five shillings

Brother, Benjamin Mott, the use of his personal estate for life, and after him to Jacob, eldest son of his brother, Adam Mott

Appointed his brother, Adam Mott, and beloved friend, Thomas, son of Samuel Jackson, deceased, executors

62 GERSHOM MOTT, son of Charles Mott, 13, born prior to 1698, of Oyster Bay, 1727, where he sold his farm in 1736, and moved away. Was of New Hempstead, Orange County, N Y

1758, Aug 7. He made his will, proved Mch. 2, 1759, and mentioned:

Eldest son, Solomon Mott, "my gun for his birth right, being my heir at law, and having had his portion before"

Son, Gershom Mott

Daughters, Molly Lott and Elizabeth Clark, each, 5 shillings

Son, Charles Mott, 5 shillings They having had their portions before

Grandson, Gershom, son of Peter and Molly Lott, 5 shillings, when he is twenty-one

Wife, Ruth, one third of his movable estate, with succession thereto, to his son, Benjamin, £14, outright, and £6, yearly

Son, Charles, all the money due him from Absalom Little, of Lewiston, Penn

Son, Benjamin, £20, and his house, lands, and land rights in Orange County, and the residue of his estate

Executors son, Benjamin, and Jacob Halstead

Issue

145 Solomon Mott, of Kingwood, N J
146 Gershom Mott, of Kingwood, N J , and later of Baltimore, where he died 1772.
147 Molly Mott
148 Elizabeth Mott
149 Charles Mott
150 Benjamin Mott

64 BENJAMIN MOTT, son of Charles Mott, 13, was of Oyster Bay.

1748, Sept 20 He made his will, proved Sept 29, 1748, and was, apparently, unmarried, and mentioned

Nephew, Samuel, son of his brother, Charles Mott, deceased, £200
Nephew, Silvanus, the sum of £50
To Daniel, Jonathan, Jacob and Marianah, the four children of his brother, Adam Mott, £50
Nephew, Joseph Mott, son of his brother, Charles Mott, eight shillings
His lands in Orange County to be sold, and the proceeds given to his brother, Adam, and his nephews, Samuel and Silvanus
To Benjamin, son of his brother, John Mott, all his lands, at Cape Fear, North Carolina
To Jacob, son of his brother, Adam Mott, his lands, in Hempstead
To his brother, Adam Mott, his wearing apparell
Nephew, Joseph Starkins, his broad axe and gun
To Jacob, son of his brother, Adam Mott, a bed
Executors his nephews, Samuel and Jacob Mott, and Sylvanus Townsend

65 CHARLES MOTT, son of Charles Mott, 13, born prior to 1696 and had died, probably prior to 1740, when his father failed to mention him in his will, but alluded to one, Joseph Mott, his grandson, who was willed twenty shillings, in full of his claim as heir-at-law.

1743 and 1748 Charles Mott is, however, alluded to in the wills of his brothers, Amos Mott and Benjamin Mott, respectively He married, Deborah Pearsall, prior to 1729, and moved to Kakiat, (New Hempstead), Orange Co, N Y

Issue

151 Joseph Mott, eldest son
152 Samuel Mott
153 Silvanus Mott Silvanus Mott was a witness, at Hempstead, in 1748

66 JACOB MOTT, son of Charles Mott, 13, born 1698–1705, resided at Hempstead, where he made his will Dec 4, 1737, proved Sept 6, 1738, in which he gave all his estate to his loving father, Charles Mott, consisting of lands, at Kakiat, Orange County, and his interest in the schooner, Fortune Executors his father, Charles Mott, and Joseph Mott, Sr Among the witnesses were Adam Mott and Joseph Mott He died without issue.

67 RICHARD MOTT, son of Adam Mott, 15, was born as late as 1728, for he was still a minor, in 1749, the date of his father's decease

1757, Dec 14 Richard Mott, of Kent Co, yeoman, conveyed to John Vining divers pieces of land in Dover

1759, Jan 1 He was a Vestryman of the Parish of St Mary, in Kent Co, when his brother Richbell conveyed land to three trustees, of whom he was one, for local church educational purposes

1763, May 27 He sold to Govey Emerson the 180 acres of land that belonged to his late father, at Willingbrook, in Little Creek Hundred

1766, Dec 17 Jerusha Mott, widow, was granted letters of administration on the estate of Richard Mott, deceased.

Issue

154 Richbell Mott, mentioned in will of his grandmother, Elizabeth Mott, of Staten Island, 1777, as the son of her deceased son Richard Mott, and to whom she gives a legacy when he attains the age of 22 years

69 RICHBELL MOTT, son of Adam Mott, 15 was born 1717–18 He married, Mch 1, 1736, Mary, daughter of Richard Seaman, of Herricks, Hempstead, L I, who, in his will, 1751,

gave this daughter, Mary, wife of Richbell Mott, £100, in trust, the use of a house, land about the house, firewood, the use of two cows, a horse, negro woman, etc "All these she is to have during the time she doth or shall live apart from her husband, Richbell Mott," etc. Richard Seaman likewise devised to his granddaughter, Elizabeth Mott, £20, and £5 to Nathaniel Parsell, or William Mott, for the use of the Monthly Meeting at Westbury In a codicil, made 1752, he gave to his daughter, Mary, in lieu of the house and lot originally devised, the use of the new house he was building and the half acre of land adjoining it, so long as she lives separate from her husband.

1738 Adam Mott suggested to the Governor the position of Lieutenant of Richmond Co Militia, for his son Richbell.

1744, Mch 10 Richbell Mott, gentleman, of Richmond Co, was granted letters of administration upon the estate of Samuel Britton, deceased, of the same place

About 1747, he moved to Kent Co, Delaware, where his father, Adam Mott, conveyed to him lands, Feb 22, 1748, in Little Creek Hundred

1750, Oct 1. Richbell Mott, gentleman, of Kent Co., Delaware, aged 32 years, testified, in Queen's Co, N Y, that he was a bondsman on the license and was present at the marriage of George Manlove, Little Creek Hundred, Kent Co, Delaware, to Mary, daughter of John Treadwell, of Hempstead, performed by Mr Reading, rector of the Parish Church of St. George, in New Castle County, "In the Territories of pensilvany"

1753, Feb 7. Richbell Mott, farmer, of Kent Co, Del, conveyed to Richard Wells part of the land received from his father, Adam Mott, in 1747

1759, Jan 1. Richbell Mott, gentleman of Little Creek Hundred, conveyed for love and good will, to the Church of England and to the Presbyterians for the education of the youth of these denominations, a part of his homestead in Little Creek Hundred, called York

1762, June 10 Letters of administrations were granted upon his estate (his widow Mary having renounced) to Mathew and Sarah Manlove The widow was still living in 1767

Issue

155 Sarah Mott; married Mathew Manlove
156 Elizabeth Mott, wife of Solomon Seaman of Maryland in 1768
157 Richard Mott
158 Seaman Mott

84 RICHARD MOTT, son of Henry Mott, 29, was born about 1735, living 1768.

Issue

159 Elkanah Mott, born 1761, died 1822
160 Richbell Mott, born about 1763, died 1828; lived at Far Rockaway.

88 RICHARD MOTT, son of Joseph Mott, 30, was of Hempstead, and made his will May 5, 1757, proved Apr 18, 1758, in which he gave his estate to his wife, Elizabeth, and made her, with his uncles, Jacob Mott and Richard Thorne, executors.

92 JACKSON MOTT, son of Jacob Mott, 32, was born 1740 He must have married twice

The following must refer to his second marriage

MOTT OF NEW YORK AND NEW JERSEY

Jackson Mott and Gloriana Coles, both of Queen's County, were married, at St George's Church, Hempstead, Jan. 25, 1774

Issue

161 Samuel Mott, baptized, at St George's Church, Hempstead, Oct 22, 1758 "Samuel, son of Jackson, son of Jacob, son of Jacob and Abigail Mott," which must be an error, as one too many Jacobs occur.

93 ISAAC MOTT, son of Jacob Mott, 32, was born May 6, 1743, died Mch. 28, 1780; married Anne Coles, born Aug. 10, 1747; died July 16, 1840

Issue

162 Samuel Coles Mott, born Nov 19, 1766, drowned Oct 30, 1839, married, Mary Leonard, June 25, 1793, who died Nov 22, 1826

*Issue**

Ann Maria Mott, born Aug 15, 1794, married Caleb Willis.
Nathaniel Leonard Mott, born Aug 23, 1796, died May 13, 1822, married Ann Eliza   , born May 14, 1809, died, May 6, 1895, leaving issue.
Jerusha Mott, born June 17, 1798, married Richard Mattocks
Catharine Mott, born Apr 8, 1800; died an infant.
Clementina Mott, born Aug 31, 1801, married Nathaniel Willis
Samuel Leonard Mott, born Aug. 16, 1803, died Mch. 29, 1871, married, Oct. 15, 1838, Lavinia Strebeck, left no issue.
Catharine M Mott, born Oct. 1, 1807, married William Robinson.

163 Jordan Mott, born, at Hempstead Harbor, Feb. 6, 1768, died Jan 8, 1840, married, first, Elizabeth Ellison, Jan. 7, 1793, no issue, married, second, Lavinia Striker, Sept 24, 1801, born May 27, 1782; died Mch 16, 1862

Issue

John Hopper Mott, born Apr. 30, 1803, died, young, unmarried
James Striker Mott, born Aug 29, 1804, died Dec 20, 1867, married Amelia Taylor, left issue.
Samuel Coles Mott, born Aug 7, 1806; died unmarried, 1855
Jordan Mott, born Oct 24, 1808, died 1874, unmarried
Jacob Hopper Mott, born Feb 20, 1810, died May 14, 1861, married Julia M. Soulé, no issue
Garrit Striker Mott, born Dec 7, 1812, died 1869, unmarried.
Matavus Hopper Mott, born Sept 23, 1815; died Jan 9, 1864, married Ruth Ann Schuyler, left issue.

164 Jacob Coles Mott, born Jan 5, 1770, died Apr. 3, 1833, married, Mary Green Smith, Aug 30, 1792, born 1776, died, aged 82 years, in New York City.

Issue

Mary Ann Mott, born 1793, died 7, 29, 1877, married, 1821, Charles Coles Feeks, left issue

---

*For a fuller account of the descendants of Isaac Mott, see pp 61, 62, 63, of the New York Geneal and Biog Record, January, 1905

Isaac Thomas Mott, married   Rose, left issue
Clara Gertrude Mott, married William Dymock, of Maryland, had issue
George Smith Mott, killed, about 1836, in the Seminole War, Fla , unmarried
Charlotte Smith Mott, married Capt. John W. Patterson, left issue
Emeline Laura Mott, married Frederick Mayer, left issue

165 Jerusha Mott, born Feb 5, 1772, married, Rev George Strebeck, Oct 24, 1793, left issue
166 Isaac Mott, born Mch 28, 1780, probably died young

97 JACOB MOTT, son of Jacob Mott, 32, was born June 30, 1756, died Aug 16, 1823, married, Deborah, daughter of Dr William Lawrence, at St. George's Church, Hempstead, Aug. 25, 1776

Jacob Mott moved from Hempstead to New York City, and became prominent. Mott Street was named after him.

From 1804 to 1810, he was Alderman   President of the Board of Alderman and Deputy Mayor of New York City.

Issue

167 William L Mott, born Jan. 16, 1777, married Dorothy Scudder.
168 Richard L Mott, born June 6, 1782, married Elizabeth Deal
169 Jacob L Mott, born Sept 13, 1784, married Hannah, daughter of Peter Riker, of Williamsburgh, by his wife, Mary Kelly   She was born June 16, 1787   They resided at Tarrytown, and he was an eminent preacher among the Friends.
170 Jordan L. Mott, born, at Manhasset, L I , Oct. 12, 1798.
171 Mary Mott, married Ezekiel G. Smith.

103 JOHN MOTT, son of William Mott, 37, married, June 17, 1784, at the age of 50 years, Elinor Johnston, widow of Capt Alexander, of the British Navy

Issue, (from the family bible in possession of his grand-daughter, Eleanor Hines Abel, of Providence, R I)

172 Gershom Mott, born July 12, 1785
173 William Mott, born Mch 29, 1790

John Mott was a guide to Generals Washington and Sullivan Dec. 25, 177–, in the attack upon Trenton

Feb 9, 1776, 1st Lieut. in Capt Patterson's Co , in the Third Battalion, although he may have served earlier

Nov 29, 1776, he was Captain in Fifth Co , Third Battalion, probably part of Maxwell's Brigade

Served at Brandywine, Sept 11, 1777, later at Germantown
Winter of 1777 and 1778, at Valley Forge
June 28, 1778, at the Battle of Monmouth
June 23, 1780, at Springfield
He retired Sept 26, 1780, and the following year was recruiting officer in Hunterdon Co
He was a Whig and an active public man

It is traditionary in the family that he had served in his youth in the British Army before Quebec. At the opening of the Revolutionary War he was living on his farm above Trenton, now the site of the N J Hospital for Insane, and early joined the army He and his wife are buried in the Quaker Burial ground, in Trenton

105 GERSHOM MOTT, son of William Mott, 37, married, May 11, 1773, Anne Godley
1750, June 15   Know all Men by thefe Prefents that I Gershom Mott of the township of Hannover in the County of Morris in the Weftern divition of the Province of New Jersey, Yeoman, am Held and firmly bound unto William Mott of the township of trenton in the County of Hunterdon and province aforesaid, yeoman, in the Sum of two hundred and fourteen pounds * * *   Samuel Holmes a witness

The indebtedness was paid off, in 1760 and 1761, and receipted for by Gershom Mott and John Mott, executors

Issue

174 Sarah Mott, born Mch 1, 1774

106 ASHER MOTT, son of William Mott, 37, married Anne Biles

Issue

175 Mary Mott, born Apr. 3, 1770, married Isaac Chapman
176 William Mott, born Sept 11, 1771
177 John Mott, born Oct 24, 1773, married Lydia Swift
178 Margaret Mott, born Oct 29, 1776, married Alexander Chambers
179 Asher Mott, born Apr. 24, 1778

107 GERSHOM MOTT, JR, son of Gershom Mott, 38, resided in Morris County, N J He married Deborah Carman, by license dated Apr 23, 1751; also given Apr 10, 1750 She died Nov. 19, 1755

Issue

180 John Mott, history unknown
181 Phebe Mott, born Mch 26, 1754, single in 1797

113 SARAH MOTT, daughter of Asher Mott, 39, married, on 1st of 2nd mo., 1770, Samuel Emlen. They had a daughter, Deborah, who died, unmarried, and a daughter, Elizabeth Emlen, who married, Sept. 18, 1800, Philip Syng Physick, who died Dec 15, 1837.

They had a daughter, Susan Physick, who married, 1828, Commodore David Conner, who died, Mch 20, 1856, leaving P S P. Conner, of Philadelphia, Pa

114 SARAH MOTT, daughter of James Mott, 40, married, by license dated June 24, 1752, Joseph Holmes

Issue
Asher Holmes
James M Holmes

115 HULDAH MOTT, daughter of James Mott, 40, married Joseph Saltar, by license dated Oct 22, 1759 He was of Shrewsbury

Issue
Eliza Saltar
Rachel Saltar, married Ephraim Clyne and had eight children
Hannah Saltar

Margaret Saltar
James Salter
Sarah Saltar
Richard Saltar

116 JAMES MOTT, son of James Mott, 40, died 1823.
He was a Member of Congress, and resided about one and a half miles South of Keyport, N J.

To
    Mr James Mott
                Merch^t
                          Wood Bridge
Pr Stage
                                              New York 20th April 1761

Dr James

    I did not till this Instant receive Yours of the 14th Curr^t and had it come to hand in a proper [?]—I should not have been able to have Given my self the pleasure of Enjoying the Company of them I so heartily Long to be with, Business Interfering in such a manner that its Impofsible for me to Promise myself any pleasure without neglecting it, and as money, is one of the material objects we seek after, and an object so Afsentiall necefsary is one of the Greatest Inducements to apply ourselves Closely to businefs—Please to Give my duty to my parents Love to all friends and am Dr Sir in great haste
                                                    Yours
                                                    JOHN TAYLOR
    P S if there's Likelihood of there being there next Sunday if pofsible I will be with them
                                                                               Cherry Hall Papers

To
    Mr James Mott
                        at Shrewsbury
p Capt Price
                                                               New York 6 October 1763

Dear Brother

    I received your letter p Capt Price yesterday & the Shirts which came very seasonable as to fiting they are too short by seven Inches they come just in my breeches   the collars are too tight & I should like the Risbons narrower, with small what do ye call thems & in them
    I'me very glad to hear that you all are mending   I think that the scheme of Mooving to Fathers is what I'me glad to hear and I think is like to be attended with the Least Difficulty of any scheme that could be proposed   Father wrote me word that he and you intended to administer on the estate as you observe there will be the greatest Difficulty in Stillingis accounts   Should be very glad indeed to see you here   I should have come over to have seen you in these melancholy Secumstances but must have Intirely Neglected our Business & as I thought that our friends were there, But Asher Holmes Tells me that Uncle Jonathan's Family have behav'd very unkind   We have this day stopped some Money for you from John Van horne he wont allow all your account & he says the barrels of pork he was not to pay for, we have Likewise stopt some from Aaron Buck
    My love your Self & Sister and the children
                                                        from you affectionate Brother
the Risbons are Two Tight   GERSHOM MOTT
                                                                             Cherry Hall Papers.

Mr James Mott ju^r to Th Henderson
1771   york money
September 9th For a visit and sundry medicine   £2—13—0
                      For your assumption of Tunnis Cornelis Acct   £0—11—0
                                                                                                       £3— 4—0
March 24th 1772 Rec'd the above in full allso of Mr Mott ten shillings on Acct of William Johnson
                                                               TH^o HENDERSON
                                                                                             Cherry Hall Papers

To
    James Mott jun^r Esqr
        at
                Prince   Town
                  East. New Jersey
                          On board Sloop—140 Miles from N. York
                                        14th Sep^t 1776

My dear Brother,
    I arrived at New York the Saturday morning after I parted with you, & found this vessel just on point of sailing & no other there, which induced me to put my baggage on board immediately and then to find a Breakfast But all the Taverns & Coffee Houses were shut up & at last procured two mouthfuls of Beef, price 1/6, a sorry breakfast for a sick man—I cou'd find nobody I wanted Except Mr Hughes, not even our poor little Asher, tho' I had some shirts his Grand Father had sent him Dear little fellow how glad he would have been to have seen me but I could not tarry However I put the shirts into the hands of a Captⁿ Leonard of the same regiment who promised to deliver them The Day before yesterday (this being the 6th day of our passage) I had certain intelligence from the shore, that the Militia thereabouts, & our regiment had marched for Fort Stanwix in consequence of part of Burgoines army being near said Fort Acct^s say 7,000 including Indians so that I don't expect to tarry in Albany but a few hours & therefore take this opportunity to write while its in my power—before I close this I will inform you how to direct me, for I take it for granted you will write to me, when you have opportunity Your letters will be a great comfort to me, while I live for which reason, you won't I hope, neglect me—you'll give my love to Brother, sister and children, & remember me to the Gentlemen I saw with you at prince town—Cousin Joseph in particular also please to inform Mr James Mc Comt [Le Comt?] that I cou'd find no person, to inquire of about the salt-petre kittles he mentioned to me, & that I had not time to write him, from New York, where I staid but three or four hours—as to the affair on long island I can't learn any thing satisfactory about it—May God bless and preserve us, & mercifully grant that we may behold each other again in peace prays your
                                    affectionate brother
Fort Stanwix is about 70 miles this side of Ossego—[Oswego]   GERSHOM MOTT
                                                        Albany 15th Sept^r
    arrived here last night accts from Fort Stanwix now are, that 700 Indians had been seen at Oswego & that a large number besides were on the march to fall on our people You'll please to direct me at Fort Stanwix on the Mohock River, to the care of Mr James Verner in Albany, If by post Mr Verner must be omitted Adieu my Dear [?] Brother
                                      G M   Cherry Hall Papers
    [Another letter containing the substance of the above, written Sept 14-1776, "On board sloop-140 miles from New York" to "Mr James Mott at Middletown, East New Jersey" addressed "My dear Father" and signed "your affectionate son Gershom Mott"]
    Col Asher Holmes
                          Freehold
Pr Flag
                                                                Sandy Hook 22nd June 80
Dr Sir
    my misfortune I suppose you have heard of before this reaches you I would therefore beg of you to Soliced my exchange which can be don in lieu of Richd Reading who was taken, not many days ago, of the Banks afishing, I am obliged to go immediately to New York, which place I very much dread, as I am in an Ill State of health I am promised here that, James Wallen & Jno Wallen would be exchanged for Richd Readings Two Sons who was taken with their father, I hope when you Judge of my * * *[?] That you will use your Interest to have the Exchange Effected and I make not the least doubt of your succeeding
                                  I am Your Humb^l Servt
                                        JAMES MOTT
    N B I am informed if you will promise to Effect this Exchange that I will be immediately admitted to go home   (Cherry Hall Papers)
                                                             Halifax December 9th 1786
D. Sir
    Its with pleasure I inform you that I am allowed as Guardian of your Relation Young Stevenson £270 Sterling, as a first Dividend of Compensation—This sum I suppose to be in the £30 Pr Cents—and tho' it is less than I expected still it will be something handsome for the Young Gentleman, should Government pay the whole reported sum, which I flatter myself it will do—It will be necessary for me to have Young Stevenson in

this County in the course of next Summer, least his remaining in the States, should be a means of precluding him from receiving the income of his Claim—He must be kept at School for some time and bro't up to some businefs   I wish his friends would consult together and give me their Sentiments through you on the Subject I mean respecting what profefsion it would be most proper to bring him up to—you may rely upon my promoting his Interest as much as is in my power and that I shall at all times be attentive to any Instructions or advice you shall be pleased to honor me with relative to my ward—I write you in great haste, & am Sir,
           Your most Obed Servt
            W TAYLOR
James Mott Esq'   (Cherry Hall Papers)
 Trenton
                  Trenton Ap¹ 29 1800
Dear Sir
 I rec'd yours the day before yesterday in which you say you are rather better, This I need not say I am glad of, nor that I am sorry you do not get quite well
 The name of the young man that married my sister Rachel is Ephraim Clyne—
 We are all as well here as usual Mifs Higbee continues ftill at Philad'ª but is expected home fhortly—
 Col Rhea left here on faturday last for monmouth from whence he returned yesterday—Businefs and the situation of his wife, who is very ill, prevented from visiting you, although he was in your neighborhood—
 I put off writing untill this morning being busy yeasterday, and having overslept myself accounts for the fhortnefs of this—
 With love to every body I am sir
           Your Aff't Nephew
            JAMES SALTAR
James Mott Esq   (Cherry Hall Papers)
                Shrewsbury 24 March Free——
        James Mott Esq'
         Wafhington City
             Middletown March 23· 1802
Dear Brother,
 I Received yours of the 6 was forre to hear you was fo ill   I hope ear this you are better   Please to rite as foon as you receve this and let me know how you are   if you get know Better I think you had better com home if you do be able if not Rest a fhured I Shall com to you we all in very good health except granne   She appears to be going fast   Doctor Pitney lade a blister on her fide it has releved the Pain but the shortnefs of breth continus   I expect him hear to day   I did not receve your letter until the fifth of March thare fore did not fend your hors and chase as I was then informed you was not at trenton   wee have got to planing   I have hired Obediah tise but fear I fhant keepe him long   Mr holmes Saes he can get me one   I have been difsepinted in getten clover fead but expect it today   I am told it is not to late to Sow it and will have it done amedetly   my Children at New York is all well anne goynes in love to you
           Your affectinate Sister
            SARAH MOTT
James Mott
 Sarah Mott March 23ᵈ 1802
  Received Sunday 28ᵗʰ
    Anfwered 31ˢᵗ   Cherry Hall Papers.
        James Mott Esq'
         Washington City
             Middletown February 8ᵗʰ 1804
Dear Uncle
 with the blesing of god I am able to write you, to inform you we are tollerable well, I am forry you have been fo ill but ernistly hope you have quite recovered before this we now begin to Count the week for your return, fell very impatient to have you with us I ashure you we mifs you very much, we have had no accounts of Obadiah, lately, the last the owners heard was that thay lay in the downs wateing for a fare wind to fail for batavia, John Bostwick has gon to Charlston on buisnefs for Mr Paul, our friends, I believe is all well at New York, we have not heard from them this fome time the Creck has been froze over this fore weeks it has been extream Cold, this fome time past, but is now quite moderate, Poor Mrs Vanderhoof is in a very poor way, at times quite deprived of her reason, I am told fhe was in the fame way fome years before fhe was married, Mrs Applegate is deceased, the daughter of John Stillwel, she has left tow infents of a few hours old   Mrs Van Marter is also dead, the daughter of huldah Van Marter   Mrs William Crawford is very ill with the quinsey,

the rest of our neighbors is gennerally well, little Sally Mott has been very fick but is now much better, was obliged to give her three Pukes before we Coud get the fleme of her ftummac, Mary gives her love to Uncle Mott, Mother fays fhe will write you by the next Post, I fhould be much pleased to get a letter from you, with love & efteem I am your debter

ANN BOSTWICK

Cherry Hall Papers

117 GERSHOM MOTT, son of James Mott, 40, born 1744, died 1786 He was a Captain in the Revolutionary war.

He married Elizabeth Williams

"I and my children are Safe arriv^d after a Long Disagreeable time 16 I left New York, we had Seven Days pasage," etc. Letter from Elizabeth Mott to her father-in-law, James Mott, 40, Albany, Sept 29,

Elizabeth Hendrickson of Toms River, Township of Shrewsbury, power of attorney to James Mott, Jr , of the same place, to dispose of her sloop "that is or was Lately on the Rocks on Long Island Near the Narrows," dated Nov 5, 1765

She made her mark Witness Gershom Mott

Gerfhoin Mott's receipt.

Received of Afher Holmes one of the adminiftrators of the Eftate of James Holmes late of the City of New York deceafed, the fum of five pounds, on acct of a demand againft said Eftate, which I promife to return if demanded Witnefs my hand

GERſHOM MOTT

Cherry Hall Papers

New York 5 October 1762

Dear Father

I Received your letter Last Sunday Evening & am Glad to hear that you and the Family are well, Brother James Is Getting Better

We Receiv'd the Viniger & Butter, I have got the Deer skins they are a Large price But I think they are good ones There is a Ballance due to you of ten Shillings as you will see by the Inclos'd accompt—Exclusive of the Bill you Sent—

I have not got my Breeches yet they are Dearer than in Philadelphia by Much Sifter Defires that Some of the Family Would get her some cucumbers as Sam Cottrel never Sent the cucumbers [torn] put aboard but brout them here again [torn] damag'd Sifter would have a hundred [torn] they are good only Fifty [torn] We are Sorry you dont confent [torn] Candidate at this time as there is a very fair profpect, Longftreet is a very Unfit Perfon, There is not a man Befides you that is fit and if Longftreet will carry anything I fhure you a great Many More James & I with you Would Confent as there is a Nefcefity of it at this time againft hartshorn you would carry it I [am] certain theres nothing would Make It doubtfull but harshorn's Dropping it and Anderfons standing alone So hoping you Will Excuse our Earneftnefs in an affair We have to Much at heart
I am your affectionate Son

GERſHOM MOTT

P S I Will Send the over plus of the Money after I git the Breeches I want a Surtuit Very Much if you think you could Spare It I Would be very Thankful for It grows Cold Whether and We Nothing to Ware if you could [illegible] it would be a favor [torn] I Shall be very th[torn]

G M.

Cherry Hall Papers

New York 8th Oct 1764

Dear Cousin

I received your favour this morning by the hands of one Simon Pure, Come come this is something like when you confess your fault and Promise amendment But you charge me with being equally faulty with yourself but I will not take notice of this Because its natural for people to like Company if its going to the gallows

Yes yes we can * * * guess what it is that the ladies want without your telling But you can certainly tell us some thing about the creatures I hear Margaret Forman & John Longstreet are going to join Tiblits What say you, Is it so there is another Zankin Cousin come from Newport Mifs Lydia Townsend Miss Wileys niece, She's a sensible genteel pritty little thing as you'd wish to see I did not see Mifs Leconte other wise than along street I had a servant from and returned one as she went past our door, I sitting on the stoop, so that I cant say I did not know she was in town

Most wonderful is the news you write, dreadful astonishing Now I hope he's easy—for its more than he has been this three years   Well, well what shall I say to it, Why I cant say anything ha ha ha and five or six more of them, I should laugh to see them—But why—his flesh and blood as others, are But but what, why ho ho ho Lawful heart Curs   Well great joy to them, So I'll leave them and conclude with my love to Aunt Polly   I hope she's much better in health and all the family and my friend Obadiah—that ornament of virtue I wish you was as good   adieu, Your affectionate friend

GERSHOM MOTT

To
  Mr Asher Holmes
      at
    Scots Chester *   Cherry Hall Papers

    To
      Asher Holmes
          at Scots Chester
            Monmouth County
              East New Jersey

New York 15 June 1765.

My dear Cousin
I think I shall Begin soon to Catehise you if you thus neglect your friend, especially as I understand by the Zankin Girls that you had something of consequence to impart to me, I pray be spedy for you don't know what may be the consequence of such delays   Let it be upon Politics, or what else you ought to send it espress, the Maple Ladies tell me that you shew'd them my letter   I Believe they lie, if not Lydia saw something that has put her in mind of the Matrimonial Peace Maker which I think necessary that she should partake of—Because I think there is some uneasiness in the lower part of her fabrick, so that the * * * Peace Maker's Company would be very sutible

Whether Mr. Tate is to be the Person thats to Commission that office of Concord I cant say—

I have rattled on for a breath hardly knowing what I've wrote for I cant write much for I'm not well—so you must excuse me & I will write you if you'l write soon

I congratulate you on your new sister   I wish it may be for the happiness of you all—

Please to present my love to Aunt Polly, Brothers & self & Remember your affectionate friend & Cousin

GERSHOM MOTT.

To Mr James Mott   Cherry Hall Papers
    at Middletown
        East New Jersey

favoured by ⎫
Mrs Cooper   ⎭   New York 13th June 1776

My dear Father
When I arrived in this City, I pleased myself with the hopes of seeing you a few Days after, but must now bid adieu to those endearing reflections, for Some Weeks at Least, for the following reasons, first, I am ordered by the Major of our Regiment to go to General Schuyler, who is at Fort-George two hundred & twenty miles from hence, to obtain orders, for Drawing inlisting mony from the pay office here, which will take up two or three weeks, or if these orders should be Countermanded which is probable, I Can't Leave Town, as Certain advices are arrived this Day that the enemy may be expected Every hour, & in Eight Days at farthest so that my anxious Wishes Can't be gratified for some time if Ever—This grieves me greatly & the more so, as we have not above Eight Thousand men present I hope my countrymen, will on this trying Occasion Come at the first Call, as now is the important Cricis

I have not heard any news of my Brother since I came here, but am Expecting it every hour

The bearer of this, Mrs Cooper, who Lodges (as She informs me), at the Widow Stillwells our Neighbour, has given me much pleasure, by the character she has given my Father, the people of this House you may Easily imagine, how I felt, When they told me, with how much respect, she mentioned you as one of the Best, the most amiable of men, in this, have I always conforted & prided myself, I can't help feeling an Esteem for her, because she is Capable of Esteeming, the person Dearest to me, of all the World—My love to My Brothers, Sister &c and may we live to see each other again, in peace, prays

Your affectionate son
GERSHOM MOTT

To Mr James Mott   Cherry Hall Papers.

* Scots Chester Burg, now called Edinburg, was near Holmdel   John W Holmes' old place was there

Issue

182 Mary Mott, married Mr. John R. Williams
183 Cornelia Mott

118 JOHN MOTT, son of James Mott, 40, married Sarah Miller, widow of Samuel Cornell. He resided at Middletown Point, N J, and died between 1809 and 1823.

Issue

184 Elijah Mott, married Mary
185 Ann Mott, married Mr. Bostwick
186 Sarah Mott

120 RICHBELL MOTT, son of Edmond Mott, 42, lived at Hempstead, and married, in 1749, Deborah Doughty. Deborah Dodge says Harris

In 1745 and 1758, he was a witness, at Hempstead.

1758, Apr. 28. He made his will at Hempstead, proved June 9, 1758, in which he distributed his estate to

Wife, Deborah, and
Daughters, Margaret and
    Phebe, both under eighteen years, and in the event of their deaths, without issue, his estate was to pass to his
Brothers, Edmond and
    John Mott
Executors wife, Deborah, and his brother, John Mott

Issue

187 Margaret Mott, born Sept 21, 1749, married, in 1772, Melancthon Smith, eminent in the history of New York State. They were the parents of Col. Melancthon Smith, who was the father of Admiral Melancthon Smith.
188 Phebe Mott, born Aug 21, 1751

123 JAMES MOTT, of Premium Point, son of Richard Mott, 44, married Mary Underhill. He was a merchant, in New York City, prior to the Revolution, but retired, when aged thirty-three, with a competency, to Mamaroneck, where, during the War, he and his family were exposed to the dangers and excitements incidental to life in neutral zones His wife died during this exciting period He built a fine two story house, still standing, and operated a tide mill, for many years, which stood hard by.

1759 In the will of his grandfather, Thomas Pearsall, of Hempstead, he is willed a horse, and as he had been put to great charge in bringing up his grandson, James Mott, these expenses are to be deducted from his share

Issue

189 Richard Mott, born 1767.
190 Robert Mott
191 Samuel Mott
192 Ann Mott, born 1768; married, in her seventeenth year, 19, 5mo, 1785, at Mamaroneck, Adam Mott, of Cowneck, Hempstead, son of Adam and Ann Mott   New York Friends' Records.

These boys built a new mill which they operated with success, and exported, with profit, much flour to England while that country was at war with France.

HISTORICAL MISCELLANY

124 WILLIAM MOTT, son of William Mott, 53, was born Jan 8, 1743; married, Dec. 2, 1789, Mary, daughter of William Willis. She died, Aug. 5, 1842, at an advanced age

Issue

193 William Willis Mott, born Feb 28, 1791, died, young, from an accident.
194 James Willis Mott, born June or July 18, 1793, married, first, Abigail, daughter of Walter Jones, second, Lydia, daughter of Obadiah Townsend.
195 Robert Willis Mott, born Oct 10, 1796, married Harriet, daughter of Dr James Cogwell, of New York

Issue

Harriet Mott, married William H Onderdonk

129 SAMUEL MOTT, son of William Mott, 53, was born 1751, died Apr 1, 1791, married, Apr 7, 1784, Sarah Franklin; both of New York Presbyterian Church Records

Issue

196 William F Mott, born 11, 1mo, 1785.
197 Walter Mott, born 4, 12mo, 1786
198 Samuel F Mott, born 7, 2mo, 1789
199 Sarah Mott, born 25, 9mo., 1791.

132 HENRY MOTT, M D, son of William Mott, 53, was born May 31, 1757; died 1840, married, 1784, Jane, daughter of Samuel Way She died in 1840
Dr Henry Mott was an esteemed physician in New York City, whither he had moved from Glen Cove, Long Island
1833, 10, 9mo Will of Henry Mott, M. D ; proved Apr. 17, 1840, gave.
To wife, Jane, his estate, consisting of real estate, furniture, plate, horses, carriages, etc , with the remainder
To their three Daughters, Esther W Mott, Eliza Mott, and Maria, wife of Sette M Hobby
Son, Valentine Mott, M D , stock, books, etc , but less than to his sisters, because of the expenses incident to his education
Executors. appointed from his children, and his nephew, Benjamin A Mott

Issue

200 Valentine Mott, M D , born, at Glen Cove, L I., Aug 20, 1785, died, in New York City, Apr 26, 1865 He was a graduate of Medicine, Columbia College, in 1806, studied, in London and in Edinburgh, became professor of surgery in Columbia College, taught and wrote extensively on surgery, and became the most eminent surgeon of his day
201 Esther W. Mott
202 Eliza Mott
203 Maria Mott; married S M Hobby

157 RICHARD MOTT, son of Richbell Mott, 69, was born about the year 1742 He was a minor in 1762, when letters of administration were granted upon his father's estate.
1767. May 6 Richard Mott, of Queen's Co , N Y , yeoman, eldest son, joined with his mother, Mary Mott, widow and relict of Richbell Mott, in conveying their interest in two tracts of land called York and Willingbrook, in Little Creek Hundred, to Thomas Irons, of Kent Co , Delaware

1779, 12, 8mo Will of Richard Mott, of Herricks, in Hempstead (L. I) gives his estate to his brother, Seaman Mott, to his sister, Sarah Manlove, and to their children Also £4 to the Westbury Friends' Meeting Proved July 28, 1780

158 SEAMAN MOTT, son of Richbell Mott, 69, was probably born about 1744-46

1767, May 14 He bought of James Stevens, for £360, lands on St. Jone's Neck, Kent Co., Del

1768, Feb 24 Seaman Mott, of Little Creek Neck and Hundred, yeoman, sold to Abraham Vamoy, Jr., for £300, his interest in lands called York, formerly his father's

1768, Apr 21 He and his wife, Nancy, of Kent Co., conveyed to Govey Emerson his interest in the York and Willingbrook lands.

1776, July 30 He was a sergeant in Capt Manlove's Delaware battalion.

1785 Simmons Mott on Dover, Delaware, Tax List

He had issue mentioned but not named, in the will of his brother, Richard Mott, which are still unknown.

168 RICHARD L MOTT, son of Jacob Mott, 97, married Elizabeth Deall, who was born Sept. 13, 1785, and died Mch 18, 1812

Issue

204 Jane Nicoll Mott
205 Samuel Deall Mott

170 JORDAN L MOTT, son of Jacob Mott, 97, born 1798, was a well known inventor and founder of the Mott Iron Works He possessed great enterprise and energy, and was a generous contributor to the church He married Mary W Smith, born Sept. 6, 1801, died Dec 24, 1838

Issue

206 Mary J. Mott, married Matthew D Van Doran
207 Jordan L Mott

172 GERSHOM MOTT, son of John Mott, 103, born July 12, 1785, died Oct 14, 1848, married, Apr 11, 1811, Phebe Rose Scudder

He lived at Lamberton, near Trenton, where he was Collector of the Port, from 1828 until his death, in 1848

He was Judge of the Court of Common Pleas, Burlington Co , Oct. 31, 1833, and held the same until his death

He was a deacon of First Baptist Church, Trenton

(For History of his wife's family, see Croley's Ewing Settlers)

Issue, (from family bible in possession of his grand-daughter, Kate A. Mott.)

208 Elinor Mott, born Feb 17, 1812, died May 14, 1835; married Rev W D. Hires
209 John S. Mott, born Jan 22, 1814, died June 13, 1834, married, Oct. 9, 1843, Martha Schenck
210 Mary Mott, born Mch 29, 1817.
211 Sarah Mott, born Mch. 16, 1820, married, Apr. 16, 1862, Samuel S. Hill
212 [General] Gershom Mott, born Apr 7, 1822, died Nov 29, 1884, married, Aug 8, 1849, Elizabeth Smith, who died December, 1895.

HISTORICAL MISCELLANY

213 Phebe Rose Mott, born Aug 4, 1831, died Dec. 26, 1857; married, Sept. 30 1855, Caleb Coleman
214 Morgan Holme Mott, born Mch 19, 1834; died Jan 28, 1894; married, Jan 4, 1869, Mary B Morris.

173 WILLIAM MOTT, son of John Mott, 103, born Mch 9, 1790, married, Aug. 2, 1821, Sarah Edgerton. They moved to Ohio. They became Quakers, many of the children living in 1896.

Issue

215 David M Mott, born Oct 9, 1822
216 Mary Mott, born Feb 17, 1825.
217 James E Mott, born Dec 15, 1826
218 Richard Mott, born Nov. 8, 1828.
219 Gershom Mott, born Nov 29, 1830
220 Asher Mott, born Oct 19, 1832.
221 George Mott, born June 27, 1834
222 Sarah Mott, born Apr 20, 1836.
223 Elinor Mott, born July 9, 1838.
224 William Mott, born May 23, 1841

182 MARY MOTT, daughter of Gershom Mott, 117, married John R. Williams, of Detroit.

Issue, (from Bishop Williams and his brother Lieut Williams)

Ferdinand Williams, born 1806
Theodore Williams, born 1808, married Miss Hall.
Gershom Mott Williams, born 1810; married Emily Strong.
Thomas Williams, born 1815, died 1862. General Thomas Williams was a Major in the Regular Army and served with distinction during the Mexican War He was Brigadier General in the Union Army, and was killed at Baton Rouge, in 1862

Issue

John R Williams, Lieutenant 3rd Artillery, U. S A
Gershom Mott Williams, Bishop, of Marquette
Mary Josepha Williams

Cecelia Williams, born 1815
John Constantine Williams, born 1817
James Mott Williams, born 1819.
Mary Williams, born 1821, married, first, D Smart, second, Capt McKinstry, U. S Navy
John C. Devereaux Williams; married daughter of General McComb, U. S. A.
Elizabeth Williams, born 1812, married John Winder.

189 RICHARD MOTT, son of James Mott, 123, was born 1767, died, at Mamaroneck, in 1857, in his ninetieth year He withdrew from the milling business, conducted jointly with his brothers, and established a mill, producing "Mott's Spool Cotton," known favorably for many years His personal appearance was graceful and his speech pleasing He became a preacher of eminence among the Friends

207 JORDAN L MOTT, son of Jordan L. Mott, 170, was born Nov. 10, 1829 He succeeded his father in business and was interested in city politics He filled the position of Alderman, for a time was Acting Mayor, and was appointed a Member of the Rapid Transit Commission. He married Marianna, daughter of James V Seaman, of Westchester.

Issue

225 Marie Mott, married William M Oliffe, Park Commissioner, New York City, second, Judge McLean
226 Jordan L. Mott, Jr , married Katharine Jerome, daughter of Fay Purdy
227 Augustus W. Mott, unmarried

For a fuller history of the Jordan L Motts, see Scharf's History of Westchester County, N. Y., Vol 1, pp. 830-831.

212 GENERAL GERSHOM MOTT, son of Gershom Mott, 172, was born at Lamberton, educated at Trenton Academy

He was 2nd Lieut in Tenth U S Infantry, Mexican War, and in all the battles from Vera Cruz to the City of Mexico.

He was Collector of the Port, Lamberton, 1849, and for years following

When the Rebellion commenced, he volunteered and was appointed Lieut Col Fifth N J Regiment He was wounded at the Battle of Second Bull Run

1862, May 8 He was promoted to Colonel of Sixth N. J Volunteers

1862, Dec. 4 He was in command of Second Brigade, N J Volunteers, then of Third Brigade, Second Division, Third Army Corps He was wounded at Chancellorsville

In May 1864, in command of Second Division, Third Corps, and later Third Division, Second Corps.

Brevetted Major General, Sept 9, 1864, for taking the enemy's outpost and line and over one hundred men.

He was wounded, Apr 6, 1865, at Amelia Springs.

After peace was restored, he was in command of the Division of Provincial Corps, a member of the Wirtz Commission, one of Committee to investigate difficulties between State of Massachusetts and the Austrian Government, commissioned full Major General, May 26, 1865, and resigned Feb 20, 1866

In 1867, he was tendered and declined the appointment of Colonel of 22nd U S Infantry

He was Treasurer of the State of New Jersey and keeper of New Jersey State Prison for five years under Gov Bedle

He was Major General, in 1873, N J National Guard (by Gov Parker), which he held till his death.

1882, Mch 21 He was a Member of the Riparian Commission (by Gov Ludlow), and held other numerous public and private offices.

He was a Member of the Society of Cincinnati, Loyal Legion, etc.

He married Elizabeth Smith

Issue

228 Kate A Mott, who wrote an interesting article on Major General Gershom Mott, her father, and his ancestry, from which I have taken memoranda for this history of the Mott family.

MISCELLANEOUS NOTES*

1672. Lorus Mott, of Hempstead, "an informer," was prosecuted for too free speech against the officials   N Y Geneal. and Biog. Record, January, 1871, p 11

1724, Oct 5   Hannah Mott married John Darby.   Dutch Church Records, New Amsterdam.

1727. Apr 5   Richard Mott, father, and Richard Mott, son, were baptized   St George's Church, Hempstead

1730, July 23   John Mott married Hannah Youngs.   St. George's Church, Hempstead

1730, Nov. 24   Amy Mott married John Parent, of Oyster Bay   St. George's Church, Hempstead

1748, Sept 21   David, son of Adam Mott, was baptized.   St. George's Church, Hempstead

1751, Nov 17.   Joseph Mott baptized, at Huntington; adult   St. George's Church, Hempstead.

1751, Dec 31   Rebecca Mott baptized, at Huntington, adult   St. George's Church, Hempstead

1755   Ruth Mott, daughter of Thomas Powell, of Oyster Bay, was a legatee in his will

1756, Feb 21   Hannah Mott and Nathaniel Ogden were married, and had Mary Ogden, born July 3, 1770, baptized Sept 16, 1770   Presbyterian Church Record, New York

1755, May 8   Mary, daughter of Joseph and Deborah Mott, was baptized, at Huntington, adult   St George's Church, Hempstead.

1757   Adam Mott was a witness at Hempstead.

1757   John Titus, of Hempstead, mentioned in his will, his daughter, Mary Mott, and named John Mott, of Matinecock, one of his executors.

1757, Jan 23   Martha Mott and Lucas Eldred [Eldert, says marriage license], were married   St George's Church, Hempstead

1758, Sept 17   At Oyster Bay, Joseph Mott, adult, was baptized   St. George's Church, Hempstead.

---

*This genealogy of the Motts is not claimed to be an exhaustive account of the family, but simply an outline. The following works may be consulted, more thoroughly and advantageously, for data concerning the Mott family
(1) Mott Ancestry by Thomas C Cornell, who made an extensive contribution to the Mott genealogy, but who erred in his arrangement of the children of the first Adam Mott, and in his elimination of the daughter, Elizabeth. He particularly follows the lines of Richbell, Adam, William and Charles, sons of Adam Mott, the first, by his wife, Elizabeth Richbell, (2) Descent of Major General Mott, of New Jersey, by Miss Kate A Mott, in the New York Genealogical and Biographical Record, April, 1894, who likewise has made a valuable contribution to the Mott genealogy, but who errs in giving the marriage of the first Gershon Mott to a Bowne, citing Salter's History of Monmouth and Ocean Counties, as authority, (3) Clute's History of Staten Island, which gives a few facts concerning Adam Mott, of the third generation, (4) Bolton's History of Westchester, 1st Edition, which is largely wrong, (5) Thompson's History of Long Island, 1st Edition, Vol II, p 57, which is wrong to an amazing degree, save, perhaps, in the allusions to William Mott and his posterity, (6) New York and New Jersey Wills, Deeds, etc , (7) Records of the Town of Westchester, at the County Court House, White Plains, N Y , for the descendants of Richbell, and, perhaps, James Mott   Also Town Record of Mamaroneck, (8) Records of the Society of Friends, and other data published in the New York Genealogical and Biographical Record, (9) Jacob T Bowne, of Springfield, Mass , who has for many years been actively investigating this family's history, (10) Printed Records of the Town of Hempstead, (11) Austin's Rhode Island Genealogical Dictionary, which gives the descendants of Adam Mott and Nathaniel Mott, of Rhode Island, (12) Thurston Genealogy, which gives accounts of the Rhode Island Motts, (13) Livermore's History of Block Island, which alludes to, apparently, some of the descendants of Nathaniel Mott, of Rhode Island, (14) Scharf's History of Westchester County, N Y , Vol 1, pp 830 and 876, (15) New York and New Jersey Marriage Licenses, (16) Genealogy of The Cornell Family by Rev John Cornell, (17) Manuscript History of the Mott Family by Edward Doubleday Harris, of New York City   The work of Mr Harris is so exact and so exhaustive that had I have known of its existence I would never have printed my notes on the Mott Family   Should his Mott history not be published I understand the manuscript will ultimately pass to the New York Gen & Biog Society   To him I owe most of the interesting data that relates to the children of Adam Mott, 1s

1758, Oct. 22 Isaac and Ruth Mott, adults, were baptized. St George's Church, Hempstead

1759 John Hallet, of Newtown, made his will, in which he mentioned his wife, Sarah, and seven children by name, and appointed his brother, Jacob Mott, and brother-in-law, Jacob Blackwell, executors.

1759. David Bedel, of Hempstead, mentioned in his will, his daughter, Phebe Mott.

1759, June 3. Joseph Mott and Catharine Boorum were married St. George's Church, Hempstead

1759, Oct. — Richard Mott and Jane Pettitt were married St George's Church, Hempstead

1760 Elizabeth Mott was a witness at Hempstead

1760, Feb. 27. Elizabeth Mott, adult, was baptized. St George's Church, Hempstead

1761, Feb 26 Thomas, son of Joseph and Deborah Mott, was baptized St George's Church, Hempstead

1761, Aug —. Jacob Mott and Elizabeth Kissam were married St George's Church, Hempstead

1761, Dec. 11. Will of Joseph Mott, of Rockaway, in Hempstead; proved May 24, 1763, mentioned·

Wife, his estate until the youngest child reaches the age of ten years, she to rear the children; the estate then to be divided into halves, one of which was to go to his wife, the other to his two sons, or if his wife should have another child by him, it was to share equally with its brothers

Upon the death or remarriage of his wife, entire estate to pass to his sons, Benjamin and Joseph, they paying to his

Two daughters, each, £50

Executors his brothers, James and John Mott, and Patrick Mott.

Witness Richard Mott.

1762, Sept 1. Deborah Sans, 4. (Edward, 3, John, 2, and Sybyl Ray, James Sands, 1), wife of Edward Mott, died, aged 26 years. Marriage license of Edmund Mott and Deborah Sands, Oct 13, 1753

1762, Oct. 10 Sarah Mott and James Reyner [Raynor says license] were married St George's Church, Hempstead

1766, June 29 Elizabeth Mott and Philip Platt were married St George's Church Records New York Marriage Licenses say· Philip Smith Platt, June 10, 1766

1766, Dec 28 Adam Mott and Elizabeth Hewlett were married St George's Church, Hempstead

1768, Aug 21 Bridgett Mott and James McComb had Eleazer, baptized Presbyterian Church, New York The New York Marriage Licenses say marriage license Jan 5, 1763

1769, Jan 22 Mary Mott and Daniel Hewlett were married St. George's Church, Hempstead

1769, Nov 22 Deborah Mott and Thomas Hallowood were married St. George's Church, Hempstead

1773, Sept 5 Jonathan Mott and Jane Burtes were married St George's Church, Hempstead

1773, Nov 16 Mary Mott and Jacob Pratt, both of Oyster Bay, were married. St George's Church, Hempstead.

1775, Dec 5 Benjamin Mott and Rachel Wilson, of Oyster Bay, were married St George's Church, Hempstead. New York Marriage Licenses say Benjamin Mott and Rachel Whitson had a license issued Oct 18, 1775

1777, June 15. Ruth Mott and Joseph Carmen were married   St George's Church, Hempstead.

1777, July 3. Miriam Mott and Benjamin Birdsall were married   St George's Church, Hempstead.

1778 Isaac Mott was a private in Capt French's Company, Ulster Co., N Y   He died Sept. 15, 1781.

1778, Oct 5 Samuel Mott and Deborah Denton were married, "by necessity." St George's Church, Hempstead

1779, Feb 12. Samuel Mott and Margaret Keshow, both of Queens, were married   St. George's Church, Hempstead

1779, June 13 Benjamin Mott and Polly Southward were married   St. George's Church, Hempstead

1779, Dec 30 Rebecca Mott and William Timpson, both of Oyster Bay, were married   St George's Church, Hempstead   New York Marriage Licenses say· Rebecca Mott and William Simpson had license Dec 24, 1779

1780, Sept 17 Phebe Mott, of Hempstead, and Joseph Dunbar, of Jamaica, were married   St George's Church, Hempstead

1780, Dec 9 William Mott and Catharine Clows [Clowes] were married   St George's Church, Hempstead

1781, June 10 Rebecca Mott and John Raynor were married   St. George's Church, Hempstead

1782 Jonathan Mott, of New York City, was a Loyalist

1782, Apr 7 Rebecca Mott and Samuel Carpenter were married. St George's Church, Hempstead

1783   Henry Mott, of Dutchess County, N Y., carpenter.

1784 William Mott was a Justice, in Onondaga County, N. Y

1784, Oct 18 Margaret Mott and Samuel Doxee were married   St. George's Church, Hempstead

1786, Feb 26 Samuel Mott and Phebe Gidney were married   St George's Church, Hempstead

1786, Aug 8 Rebecca Mott, of Hempstead, and John Davidson, of Nova Scotia, were married   St George's Church, Hempstead

1786, Dec 18 Adam Mott and Hannah Simmons were married.

1794 Mary, daughter of Jacob Mott, married Aaron·Duryea, who was born 1754   They had Abraham Duryea, born 1794, and Aaron Duryea, born 1797   They were of Hempstead.

1795, Apr. 29 Robert Mott and Lydia Stansbury were married. Presbyterian Church, New York   See p 15, Mott Descendants

1801, Jan 2. Amy Mott and Zebulon Smith were married   St. George's Church, Hempstead

Hannah Mott married James Leverich, who died, in 1811, and his wife at an earlier date, leaving issue. Riker's Newtown, p 353

MOTT OF NEW YORK AND NEW JERSEY

NEW YORK MARRIAGE LICENSES

1737, Nov   4   Adam Mott and Elizabeth Smith
1738, July   5   Martha Mott and John Hicks.
1757, June 30. Thomas Mott and Keziah Brush.
1758, Sept   7. John Mott and Ann Somerendike.
1760, Sept 30   Richard Mott and Jane Perrit
1761, June 18   Herodia Mott and Henry Higbie
1761, Sept 25   Elizabeth Mott and William Doty.
1763, Jan. 26   Kesiah Mott and James Whippo
1763, Mch.   5   James Mott and Catharine Sibly.
1763, Apr   16   Ceeors Mott and Susannah Barnes
1763, Nov   2   Deborah Mott and Ezekiel Cooper
1765, Apr   26   Elizabeth Mott and Benjamin Hicks
1770, Mch   22   John Mott and Margaret Burtis
1771, Mch   5   William Mott and Letitia Leadbetter
1771, Aug   3   John Mott and Martha Sammons, [married, at St George's, Hempstead, Oct 16, 1771, as Martha Sammis]
1773, Nov   11   Mary Mott and Jacob Pratt
1780, Oct   3   Richard Mott and Martha Sutton
1781, Nov. 22. Amelia Mott and John Ryan
1782, Apr   7. Rachel Mott and John Hooton
1782, Sept 10   Elizabeth Mott and John Whitehand
1783, Oct. 30   Joseph Mott and Lida Cyrus

NEW JERSEY MARRIAGE LICENSES

1731, Feb.   20. Jane Mott, Gloucester, and Peter Scull, Gloucester.
1733, May   23   Anna Mott and Julius Ewan, Burlington
1738, Aug   7.   John Mott, Burlington, and Phebe Cramer
1739, Jan.   3.   Mary Mott, and James Arnold, Burlington.
1739, Mch   17   Charity Mott, Morris, and David Wheeler, Morris
1771, Sept. 15. John Mott, Burlington, and Patience Austin, Burlington
1773, Sept   22. Joshua Mott, Hunterdon, and Mary Kitchen, Hunterdon
1781, June   2   Sarah Mott and Joseph Potts, Kingwood

ST GEORGE'S CHURCH, HEMPSTEAD, L I

1734, Dec.   9. Samuel Mott and Hannah Wood, married
1746, Feb   17   Miriam Mott and William Cornell, Jr, married
1750, Nov.   18   Sarah Mott and Stephen Titus, married
1753, Feb   28   Henry Mott and Mary Southward, married
1753, Mch   18   Elizabeth Mott and Samuel Smith, married
1755, Mch.   18   Samuel Mott and Rebecca Mott, married
1756 Nov   14   Jemine Mott and John Cannon, married, license dated Oct 29, 1756
1782, Dec.   31. Rebecca Mott, adult, baptized

MOUNT

OF

MONMOUTH COUNTY

GEORGE MOUNT was born, by deduction, about 1635, and was the first of the name to settle in Monmouth County, where he was one of the "Associates" in the purchase of the Monmouth Tract in 1665-7. He was, doubtless, an Englishman, but I am unaware that there is any knowledge extant concerning his origin or his kinspeople. It has been asserted that George Mount came first to Salem, Mass., about 1636, thence to Gravesend, Long Island, which was settled in 1643-4, and later to Middletown, N. J., which was settled in 1665-7. Assuming that his supposititious birth date, 1635, is correct, this migration seems unlikely, for he would have been very much of a child in 1636, and in need of a parent, and still too young to have been a settler of Gravesend. That he may have come to New Jersey from Rhode Island, which furnished the Monmouth Tract with so many of its early settlers, is most likely, but nothing that I know sheds any light on his personal history previous to his appearing in Middletown, N. J.

In 1672, George Mount's name was *coupled together* with Benjamin Borden in the purchase of lands from the Indians at Middletown, and again, in 1676, the same individuals, George Mount and Benjamin Borden, received patents for lands *adjacent to each other* in Cohansey, West Jersey. This intimate association raised a hope in the minds of some that the maiden name of the wife, or the mother of George Mount, was perhaps Borden, but a study of the wills of Matthew Borden, of Hedcorn, England, and his two emigrating sons, Richard and John, eliminates any such conclusion, and we are forced to decide that the intimate relations of Mount and Borden were based upon friendship and not kinship. Further it might be well here to eliminate another suggestion, that George Mount married a sister of Abigail Grover, wife of Benjamin Borden, but this, too, falls to the ground when an analysis of the known Grover history is made.

Upon his advent in Middletown, George Mount received in the first division of lands, Dec. 30 and 31, 1667, the town lot No. 10, and the outlying lot No. 19.

1688, Apr. 22 George Mount was one of the two Deputies chosen to the General Assembly to be held at Portland Point, and, July 20, 1669, he was re-elected.

He likewise filled the positions of Juryman, Town Overseer and Surveyor.

He is alluded to in deeds as a *blacksmith*, which in those days, meant a worker in iron, and in such an avocation, many of the artists and artisans of mediæval times have created lasting monuments of great beauty. There was little call, however, for a display of much talent, in the early days of Middletown, but we can readily see George Mount fashioning the iron work of the villages, from the scythe and plow to the hinges and latches. Few men could be more valuable than he in such an environment

1688 George Mount was one of the Constituent Members of the Baptist Church of Middletown. Edwards

1698, Apr 13 George Mount conveyed to his son, Richard Mount, one hundred and eighty-five acres of land, in Middletown township, which, in 1710, formed part of the two hundred acres of land which Richard Mount sold to Eden Burrowes, and inasmuch as Richard Mount is not mentioned in his father's will, this land probably represented his interest in his father's estate and the gift cut him off as heir-at-law.

George Mount presumably married about 1660

1702-3, Feb 16 he made his will, proved Aug 31, 1705, and mentioned his wife, Katherine; daughter Katherine, grandsons, Matthias and Thomas, sons of his deceased son, Matthias

1705, Sept. 18 Inventory of George Mount's estate was made by Richard Stout and James Cox, at Middletown, and proved by James Cox, appraiser

Issue
2 Katherine Mount
3 Matthias Mount; died 1694-5; married Mary
4 Richard Mount, married, prior to 1687, Rebecca Wall.

3 MATTHIAS MOUNT, son of George Mount, 1, has a wife Mary, and two sons mentioned in the will of their grandfather as not of age when it was made, Feb 16, 1702-3

I believe Matthias Mount may also have had a daughter Mary, who married her first cousin, because John Mount, son of Richard Mount, 4, had a wife Mary, born in 1694, according to a Bible record, and he named his, apparently eldest, son, Matthias.

Matthias Mount died in the spring of 1695.

1695, Apr. 10 An inventory of his estate was taken by Safty Grover, Francis Harburt, Jarat Wall and Ed (?) Lawrence

"ye 27 of march—Where an order of Cort was made at middletowne, That wee underwritten should aprise the Estate of matThias mount, of midletown, deceecd, now," etc Total £24 11 08.

"Reserved of saifty Grover account of Mathias Mounts deseased on the behalf of Mary Mount widdow of the said Mathias Mount . Dated desember ye 17th 1695 Signed ABIGALL LIPPINCOTT"

"December the 21st, 1695 Then Receved of Mary Mount late widowe to Mathias Mount decased the sume of fortenn shillings to say 9ˢ dew from her husband decased and five shillings for writing his will I say Received by me"
RICHARD HARTSHORNE"

"Rec the 10th of Janʳ, 1694, The Sume of 2s 6d of Georg Mount by the appointmt of Mary Mount for board to make her husbands coffin"
JOHN BROWN

"Rec the 11th of Janr, 1694, the sume of 3s of Richard Mount for digging a grave for Mattheas Mount by me
WILL. PURDANE"

Issue
5 Matthias Mount, born prior to 1692.

NOTE —William Mount, who was brought over to this country in October, 1685, as a "servant," by James Johnston, was a witness to the marriage of John Langford, Oct 30, 1686, to Isabella Bowman, in Burlington, and Jan 8, 1686-7, a witness to the determination of the arbitrators of the West Jersey division line is, apparently, no connection of George Mount

6 Thomas Mount, born prior to 1692
7 Mary Mount, (attributed), born 1694, died 1745, supposed married John Mount, 9

4 RICHARD MOUNT, son of George Mount, 1, was born probably about 1665-6 He resided, first, at Middletown, then at Cranbury

1694, Aug. 8   He recorded his cattle-mark in Middletown

1703, Mch 28   Richard Mount, of Middletown, was alluded to as son and heir to George Mount, of the same place, late deceased   He made his mark to documents

About 1710, Eden, the son of Edward Burrowes, of Jamaica, Long Island, came to Middletown   What occasioned his friendly separation from his kinspeople and the selection of a new place of abode would now be mere speculation, but the fact that he took over *all* the lands of Richard Mount and that he had a daughter Rebecca, whose name conforms to the name Rebecca, the wife of Richard Mount, raises the suspicion that Rachel, the heretofore unidentified wife of Eden Burrowes, *possibly may* have been a daughter of Richard Mount

The deed that conveyed the land from Richard Mount to Eden Burrowes, and which was dated Mch. 13, 1710, and recorded Apr. 24, 1827, recited that Richard Mount was a yeoman, of Middletown, that the consideration was £200, and that the lands were (1) Seventy-six acres in Middletown, on the South side of Mill Brook, thence *** adjoining Thomas Cox *** to South side of Layton's line   Bounded West by Thomas Cox, Southeast and North by land of ye said Layton, (2) a tract of land of one hundred acres, adjoining Safety Grover, (3) a tract of nine acres, at Poplar Field, bounded East by John Smith, South by Mill Run, North by William Layton, West by a small brook, "being ye same which George Mount, ye father of ye said Richard Mount, late purchased of Richard Hartshorne", (4) six acres of meadow at Shoal Harbor, bounded North by Sarah Reape, and South by Richard Hartshorne, (5) nine acres of salt meadow, at Waycake, bounded North by the Bay, West by Richard Gibbins, East by John Bowne   All to be two hundred acres   Witnessed by W Laurie, Benjamin Laurie and William Lawrence, Jr   By this transfer he completely divested himself of his Middletown lands and forthwith removed to Cranbury, Middlesex County

1711, Mch 12   Richard Mount, of Middlesex, yeoman, conveyed to "my son Richard Mount, Jr., of the same place," two hundred acres, at Cranbury, adjoining Thomas Morford, bounded on the West by "land intended for my son George Mount"   Signed by Richard and Rebecca Mount, both by their marks

1717, Mch 23   Richard Mount, of Cranbury, in the city of Perth Amboy, yeoman, and Rebecca, his wife, made a conveyance to Joseph Dennis, cooper

1723, Jan 25   Richard Mount, Sr, of Middlesex, and Rebecca, his wife, for £200, conveyed to Humphrey Mount, yeoman, two hundred acres, on the South side of Cranberry Brook, adjoining Richard Mount, Jr's, land   Witnessed by Matthias Mount, (who acknowledged the same May 15, 1774), and Joseph Britton, first of whom was, doubtless, his son, and the second, in all likelihood, his son-in-law

Richard Mount married, prior to 1687, Rebecca Wall, as appears in the Court Records, of that date, at Freehold, N J, Lib. B, for Garret Wall gave evidence concerning the mare he gave to his sister Rebecca, Richard Mount's wife   See Wall Family

1715   He was Lieutenant on the Muster Roll of this date

Issue

8 Richard Mount, born prior to 1691.
9 John Mount, born prior to 1691
10 George Mount, born prior to 1695
11 Humphrey Mount, born prior to 1699.

12 Matthias Mount, born 1706-7.
12a Ann Mount, supposed

5 MATTHIAS MOUNT, son of Matthias Mount, 3, was born prior to 1694-5, and not of age Feb 16, 1702-3 He received one hundred acres, on Neversand River, in the will of his grandfather, "where I now live," adjoining sixty-five acres left to his brother Thomas He was living in 1739, when he signed his consent to the marriage of his daughter Margaret to James Herbert

· *Issue*

13 Timothy Mount
14 (Daughter) Mount
15 Margaret Mount
16 Joseph Mount
17 George Mount
18 Matthias Mount

6 THOMAS MOUNT, son of Matthias Mount, 3, was born prior to 1694-5, and was not of age Feb 16, 1702-3 He received sixty-five acres, on the Neversand River, as a legacy from his grandfather, adjacent to the land of his brother Matthias, but seems to have settled at Shrewsbury.

Issue

19 Mary Mount, born May 31, 1715; died, Nov. 24, 1800, aged 85, 5, 24; married Joseph Cox, born Aug 18, 1713, died, Apr. 17, 1801, in 88th year

Extract from letter written by Samuel J. Cox to his uncle, Benjamin Cox, March 4, 1867 "Mary Mount, who married Joseph Cox, of Upper Freehold, Monmouth County, N J, was born May 31, 1715, whose father was Thomas Mount, of Shrewsbury Township Joseph Cox, who married Mary Mount, lived not far from Imlaytown Joseph and Mary were my grand-parents I remember them well, being past eleven years old when they died Joseph Cox, from my recollection of him and from all I have ever heard, was a farmer in easy circumstances, of unblemished character, strong mind and highly respected in the community where he lived He was a very old man at my first recollection, of fine, venerable appearance My grand-mother was in no way inferior to him Both of them were remarkably calculated to inspire respect from all who approached them There was scarcely any symptom of childishness about either of them, notwithstand-ing their great age My grandmother was remarkable for her fine form and countenance, even in her old age, and in her earlier years must have been beautiful They occupied one end of their large old house, while my father and his numerous family occupied the other part When I was a little boy I spent many a pleasant hour in their rooms They were very kind to me and were very fond of having me sing hymns to them "

See Cox Family

20 John Mount, born 1717
21 Samuel Mount, moved to New York City
22 James Mount, born 1711, died 1786.

8 RICHARD MOUNT, son of Richard Mount, 4, was born prior to 1691, and died between July 22 and Aug 11, 1777, the dates of his will and probate Like his father, he relocated himself, for, while he was of Middlesex County, Mch 31, 1725, as appears from a deed of that date, in which he styles himself cordwainer, and was joined by Rebecca, his wife, both making their marks, conveying to Stephen Warne, yeoman, the two hundred acres of land, at Cranbury, deeded to him by his father, Richard Mount, Mch 12, 1711, he was, shortly thereafter, a resident of Monmouth County, where he had bought, Feb 4, 1725, from Thomas Humphries, agent and attorney for the heirs of William Dockwra, one thousand acres, on Rocky Brook, beginning at the mouth of Brenthall's Brook, at Millstone River, etc.

1726 Richard Mount, Jr, sold five hundred acres, in Freehold, of the land he had bought from the Dockwra heirs the year preceding, to Joseph Holeman

He is alluded to as cordwainer, distiller and gentleman He apparently married three times first, about 1715-18, Rebecca   , second, supposed, Rachel, daughter of John and Mary Cox, third, Elizabeth Seabrook, born 1711, died Mch 16, 1791, who married, first, Ezekial Forman, born Nov 1, 1706, died Oct 3, 1746, and secondly, Richard Mount. Elizabeth (Seabrook-Forman) Mount's will is on record at Trenton, bearing date May 28, 1784, proved Jan 27, 1792

1728, Apr 9 John Cox, of Freehold, made his will, and appointed his brother, James Cox, Richard Mount, Jr, and William Lawrence, Jr, to divide his real estate, which was done by them, Sept 30, 1728, between his sons John, Joseph and Samuel Cox   Freehold Deeds

1731. Richard Mount was taxed, in Upper Freehold, on four hundred acres.

1736, Mch 8 Richard Mount, Jr, of Upper Freehold, conveyed one hundred and sixty acres, in Upper Freehold Township, to John Morford

1750, Nov 11 Richard Mount, gentleman, of Upper Freehold, conveyed to his son, Thomas Mount, blacksmith, one hundred and ninety-eight acres, in Upper Freehold. Witnesses Michael Mount and Mary Mount

1756, Nov 19 Richard Mount, yeoman, of Upper Freehold, conveyed to Michael Mount, husbandman, of the same place, land, beginning at Rocky Brook, at the lower corner of land formerly granted by said Richard Mount to John Morford, * * * down brook to lands patented to Walter Benthall, thence Easterly to a corner of Thomas Mount's land * * * conveyed to the said Richard Mount by the heirs of William Docwra, deceased   Acknowledged by Richard Mount Feb 1, 1760 Recorded Dec 23, 1805   Freehold Deeds

Part of this land was conveyed by Michael Mount, and his wife Mary, to William Vaughan, gentleman, of Upper Freehold, Apr 1, 1757, who, by his will of Oct 2, 1762, authorized his executors to sell the same, in the event of the remarriage of his wife, Marcy Vaughan, which they did, by deed of Apr 10, 1777, to William Mount, of Upper Freehold. It would further appear that William and Mercy Vahan conveyed, July 5, 1760, to Thomas Mount, a part of the lands conveyed him by Michael Mount, (Mch 31) Apr 1, 1757.

1758 Richard Mount was taxed, in Upper Freehold, on six hundred and ninety acres

Issue

23 Thomas Mount, eldest son
24 Michael Mount, born 1720
25 Ezekial Mount, born 1731
26 Samuel Mount, born 1724, died, Aug 7, 1801, aged 87 years, buried at Hightstown, with his wife, marriage license, with Frances Cook, June 20, 1755, born Sept. 16, 1731, died Sept 16, 1806
27 Rebecca Mount; eldest daughter, married a Bates and died prior to July 22, 1777.
28 Mercy Mount
29 Patience Mount
30 Rachel Mount, died prior to 1777
31 Rebecca Mount, youngest daughter, died 1808

9 JOHN MOUNT,* son of Richard Mount, 4, was born prior to 1691, and resided at Middletown. He died, according to a bible record, Mch 29, 1772, [elsewhere 4, 13, 1772], leaving a will dated Mch 9, 1772, and proved Apr 24, 1772 He left a wife, Mary, born 1694, who died 8, 4, 1745 This wife Mary, because of the date of her birth and the naming of her

(apparently oldest) son, Matthias, is supposed to be his own cousin, and daughter of Matthias Mount, 3

1760, May 23 John Mount, of Middletown, yeoman, conveyed land to James Grover, yeoman, of the same place, in settlement of a dispute, beginning at a point in land that was formerly Safety Grover's, deceased * * * thence to George Mount's line Witnessed by John Stillwell, Joseph Mount, John Anderson, (judge).

Issue

32 Matthias Mount
33 John Mount
34 Katherine Mount, married, by license dated June 13, 1739, Joseph Tilton
35 Phebe Mount, married, by license dated Nov 3, 1739, Silas Tilton
36 Alice Mount, married, by license dated July 23, 1746, John Porter.

10 GEORGE MOUNT, son of Richard Mount, 4, resided at Lower Freehold. His will, signed by his mark, was dated May 15, 1769, proved Apr 2, 1770

He was born prior to 1695, for he was constable for Piscataqua, 1715-16, and a defendant and plaintiff in law suits in 1715-16, 1716 and 1718, as appears in the Middlesex County Records, at New Brunswick

1723, Dec 23 He was of Freehold, when he bought two hundred acres of land in that town, as well as a tract near Cole's Creek, in the same place, from John Estill, of Freehold.

1760, May 23 George Mount had land adjoining some which John Mount, of Middletown, conveyed to James Grover in the settling of a dispute.

He had a wife Sarah.

Issue

37 John Mount
38 Francis Mount
39 Thomas Mount
40 Nanny (Hannah) Mount, married John Wetherell, their second intentions being dated 7mo., 1744. Chesterfield Monthly Meeting She died 1787
41 Rebecca Mount, married Mr. Gaa

11 HUMPHREY MOUNT, son of Richard Mount, 4, was born, probably, not far from 1695.

1723, Jan 25 Richard Mount, Sr , of Middlesex, and Rebecca, his wife, conveyed to Humphrey Mount, yeoman, for £200, two hundred acres, on the South side of Cranberry Brook, adjoining Richard Mount, Jr Witnessed by Joseph Brittain, Matthias Mount, (who acknowledged May 15, 1744), and George Rascarrick

1751 Humphrey Mount bought of Robert Lettis Hooper, land, which, Apr 7, 1755, he sold to Nisbit Mount for £50, and acknowledged the same, Aug 20, 1761, when he called himself of Perth Amboy, yeoman Cranberry, at this date, was spoken of as in the city of Perth Amboy

*While George Mount, 1, made allusion to only two sons of his deceased son, Matthias Mount, 3, viz , Matthias Mount, 5, and Thomas Mount, 6, this would not exclude the existence of another son who need not of necessity have been mentioned and for whom provision would have been made by the law of primogeniture If this is conceded, it might follow that John Mount, 9, called a son of Richard Mount, 4, was a son of Matthias Mount, 3, which has in favor of it the fact that John Mount, 9, called his, apparently eldest son, Matthias

The Bible from which the references to John Mount, 9, and his family are taken, contains the following "Record of old Mount Family Bible, bought by Thomas Mount in 1763 " John Mount was either brother or cousin to Thomas Mount, the owner of the Bible, and it remains to be explained why his family record should appear in a Bible other than his own

1715. He was a private on the Muster Roll

It has been suggested that he married a Britton, as he named a son this name But should his sister, Ann, have been the wife of Joseph Britton, which is likely, it is just as probable that Humphrey's son, Britton, should have been named after his uncle, Joseph Britton

Issue

42 Britton Mount, baptized, June 2, 1731, at Tennent Church
43 Dorcas Mount, baptized, May 5, 1734, at Tennent Church
44 Mary Mount, baptized, June 7, 1736, at Tennent Church
45 William Mount, baptized, May 14, 1739, at Tennent Church *
46 Nisbit Mount

It is likely Humphrey Mount had other children than those given above, for he was established on a farm of two hundred acres, in 1723, and it is practically certain that he was the father of Nisbit Mount, who married, in 1744, Mary Hay That Humphrey Mount married twice is likely, and that one of his wives was a Nisbit, is more than probable The Nisbits or Nesbits were members of the Scotch community that early settled at Freehold

1727 Dorothy Nisbett was one of the witnesses, by her mark, to the will of Alexander Clark, of Freehold

12 MATTHIAS MOUNT, son of Richard Mount, 4, was born 1706-7, and died Apr 7, 1791 He married Anne   . , born 1714-15, died June 23, 1792 They lie buried in Cranbury Yard, between the Humphrey and Matthias Mount mentioned below He was a ruling elder in the First Presbyterian Church, of Cranbury, for nearly fifty years.

Perhaps Matthias Mount married twice

In 1745, he was residing at Freehold, where he bought land from one, Hankins and wife, and moved to Middlesex County

He was a Revolutionary Soldier when over seventy years of age.

1755, Oct. 24 Jediah Stout, of Windsor, yeoman, conveyed land to Matthias Mount, of the same place, yeoman, in presence of Thomas Mount and Stephen Warne.

1756, Mch 10. Will of Frederick Debogh, of Freehold, mentioned wife, Hannah, son, Van Hook Debogh, daughter, Hannah, cut off, and her share left to her daughter, Mary Van Hook, and her grandson, Frederick Brown, daughter Frances and daughter Sarah, unmarried, son, Solomon Executors, his wife Hannah, son, Lawrence Debogh, and *son-in-law, Matthias Mount*

1771, Aug 15. Matthias Mount, as executor, advertised the sale of the property of the late Frederick Debow, in Lower Freehold, about five miles from Monmouth Court House, on Sept 27, 1771

1771, Oct 5 Matthias Mount, of Windsor, Middlesex Co , only surviving executor of Frederick Debogh, late of Freehold, conveyed land to Matthias Rue

1783, Mch 25. Matthias Mount, Sr , and Anne, his wife, sold to their son, Humphrey, for £400, the West end of their plantation, in Windsor township, Middlesex County, amounting to two hundred acres.

The same date Matthias Mount, Sr , and his wife, Anne, conveyed to their son, John, the East end of their plantation, amounting to two hundred and twenty acres

Issue

47 Matthias Mount, born 1734-5.
48 Richard Mount

---

*William Mount may, perhaps, be he who had marriage license with Anna Perrine, Aug 31, 1761 There is also a will, recorded at New Brunswick, N J , Lib A, p 462, which may be his

49 John Mount, born Apr. 12, 1743.
50 Rachel Mount; baptized (1745?), at Tennent Church.
51 Humphrey Mount, born 1745-6
52 Ann Mount, born Feb 11, 1749.
53 Thomas Mount; moved to Virginia
54 Joseph Mount   There may have been a son Joseph in this family, but proof that there was is lacking   It may be that he is added to the list of children solely because there was a Joseph Mount on the subscription list of 1758, together with the names of the brothers, John, Humphrey and Matthias, Jr , and that of Hezekiah Mount

1760, May 23   Joseph Mount was a witness to a deed given by John Mount, of Middletown, and it may be that he was identical with this supposed son of Matthias   Yet there may have been two of the same name one of Middletown and one of Cranbury. He of Middletown, had a license to marry, Mch. 7, 1761, with Anne Stillwell

12a   ANN MOUNT, supposed daughter of Richard Mount, 4, was the Ann Mount who married, Apr 5, 1714-15, in the Dutch Church, in New York City, Joseph Britain   She must, therefore, have been born about 1695 to have been twenty years of age at the time of her marriage, and would, consequently, belong to this generation, as a child of either Matthias or Richard Mount, and a grandchild of George Mount, the First

As Humphrey Mount, 11, names a child Britton, baptized June 2, 1731, and as the name of Joseph Britton appears as a witness on the deed, Jan 25, 1723, from Richard Mount, Sr , 4, of Middlesex, and Rebecca, his wife, to Humphrey Mount, 11, this association of facts and names makes it practically certain that Ann was the daughter of Richard Mount, 4, and wife of Joseph Britton

13   TIMOTHY MOUNT, son of Matthias Mount, 5, was a resident of Middletown   He married "Elizabeth, daughter of Elizabeth White."

1752, Dec 27. He made his will, proved Jan 31, 1753, in which he appointed his friends, Thomas Mount and James Grover, his executors   He left three daughters not twenty-one years of age   Witnesses   James Rice, Samuel Mount and Matthias Mount.

1753, Mch 29   Inventory of Timothy Mount, signed by James Grover and Thomas Mount, as executors, has on it a note that reads "Edward Taylor, Appriser   Garrett Morford the other appraiser dyed before he signed the inventory."

Issue

55 Hannah Mount, had license to marry, Dec. 23, 1756, Cornelius Compton, Jr , who, dying 1757-8 (as per will), she married, second, prior to June 22, 1763, David Stout, who died prior to Aug 13, 1813.
56 Jemima Mount, married, prior to June 22, 1763, Samuel White
57 Elizabeth Mount   She may, perhaps, have married . . . Eldreth, and have been the mother of John Eldrith, who conveyed four and one-half acres of salt meadow, which formerly belonged to Timothy Mount, on Jan 3, 1794, to Job Layton

15   MARGARET MOUNT, daughter of Matthias Mount, 5, had a license to marry, dated Mch 24, 1739-40, with James Herbert, yeoman, both of Middletown, she a spinster and the daughter of Matthias Mount, who gave his consent, Joseph Mount, yeoman, being surety

It was, probably, her husband, James Herbert, whose will is at Trenton, dated Mch 1, 1745-6, proved Oct. '17, 1746, wherein he styles himself of New Brunswick, and mentions his brother, Richard Herbert, wife, Margaret, and three sons, Richard, Daniel and James Herbert

Issue, as per will of James Herbert
Richard Herbert
Daniel Herbert
James Herbert

Margaret Mount married, second, Oct 11, 1749, Matthew Rue.*

Issue

Margaret Rue, baptized Sept. 30, 1750.
Matthias Rue, born Apr 27, 1752, died June 22, 1820, married Phebe, daughter of Joseph Combs, born Aug. 24, 1752, died June 28, 1834
John Rue, born Mch. 20, 1754, died 1844, married, first, Jan 1, 1777, Ann Combs, second, Rebecca Perrine.

Margaret Mount married, third, Nov. 25, 1760, James Dey

16 JOSEPH MOUNT, son of Matthias Mount, 5, married, by license dated Sept. 28, 1741, Alice Van Wickley, with Symen Van Wickley as surety. He was then of Somerset
1752, Dec. 27. He is called "brother," in the will of Timothy Mount
1764, June 22. Administration was granted on his estate to "Frances, widow of Joseph Mount, late of Somerset Co"
1764, July 4 Nicholas Van Wickley and Jacob Suidam were made guardians over Simon and Matthias Mount, "over 14 years of age"

Issue

58 Simon Mount, born 174-; died 1809-10 He was of South Amboy, Middlesex Co., when he made his will Jan 21, 1809; proved Mch 14, 1810; married Anna .. , probably died without issue.
59 Matthias Mount, born 1748, died, 1822, aged 74 years and 24 days, buried in Tennent Churchyard, married, *second*, Mary

---

*Matthew Rue had, by his first wife, Elizabeth (who was buried, at Topanemus, Apr 29, 1748), the following children Joseph Rue married, by license, Dec 2, 1752, Ann Disbrow, both of Middlesex, William Rue married Nellie Conover, Samuel Rue married in New York, Matthew Rue married Catherine Voorhees, James Rue married at South River, Eleanor Rue, Jean Rue baptized Apr 29, 1748, "by his late wife"

Matthew Rue's issue, by his second wife, Margaret Mount, has already been set forth He, Matthew Rue, died Nov 5, 1755, and was buried at Topanemus He, and his first wife, Elizabeth, are the great-grandparents of Nathaniel S Rue, Esq, my father-in law, writes Mrs Mary Holmes Rue, of Cream Ridge, Monmouth Co, N J

Matthias Rue, son of Matthew and Margaret (Mount) Rue, was born Apr 27, 1752, died June 22, 1820, aged sixty years, 1 month and twenty-six days, married Phebe Combs, born Aug 24, 1752, died, June 28, 1834, aged 81 years, 10 months and 4 days *Issue* Samuel Rue died Oct 14, 1808, Matthias Rue, born May 8, 1793, married Elizabeth Potts, John Rue, born Aug 23, 1775, married Mary Cox, Matthew W Rue married Rebecca Ely

Of these children, *Samuel Rue* was the father of Joshua Rue, who died Sept 27, 1808, *Matthias Rue*, by his wife Elizabeth Potts, had Rebecca Rue, who married Enoch Mount and located at Hightstown, and Ellen Rue, who married Matthias (?) , *John Rue*, by his wife, Mary Cox, had Ann Rue, born Aug 14, 1804, died Nov 17, 1840, married William Cotterell, Enoch Rue, born Mch 21, 1807, married Lydia Davison, Phebe Rue married Elias Bergen, *Matthew W Rue*, by his wife, Rebecca Ely, had Mary Rue, born 1809, died 1870, married Matthias, son of Richard and Theodosia (Allen) Mount, born 1816, died 1855, and located near Dutch Neck, and Joseph Rue who married Cornelia Mount, likewise a child of Richard and Theodosia Mount, and removed to Englishtown

Concerning John Rue, son of Matthew and Margaret (Mount) Rue, born 1754 He married Ann Combs and Rebecca Perrine *Issue* Margaret Rue, born 1777, died 1810, married John Brown, Mary Rue born 1779, died 1814, married Peter Conover, Matthew Rue, born 1782, died 1828, married, successively, a Bael, a Smith and a Higgins, John Rue, born 1783, died 1866, married Mrs Meeker, James Rue, born 1783, died 1810, Phebe Rue, born 1786, died 1821, married Henry Davis, Lewis Rue, born 1789, died 1794, Joseph Rue, born 1790, married Mary Bergen, Ann Rue, born 1792, died 1795, Hannah Rue, born 1794, died 1815, Peter Rue, born 1800

60 Ann Mount, born Dec 27, 1746, died Oct 8, 1816, married, July 4, 1773, Nicholas, son of Abraham DuBois, born Mch 5, 1756, died Dec. 5, 1825. He married, second, Apr. 16, 1818, Jane Suydam Buried at Frankfort, Somerset Co., N J

61 Joseph Mount, born about 1750, died 1826, married Mary, daughter of John and Susannah (Burtis) Baylis, born July 9, 1755

17 GEORGE MOUNT, son of Matthias Mount, 5, married Audrey Woolley, by license dated Mch 4, 1748-9, and attached thereto is Feb 20, 1748-9, Hannah Lippincott consents to marriage of her daughter, Adria to George Mount, both of Monmouth This mother-in-law of George Mount was Hannah Cook who married Bartholomew Woolley prior to 1714-15, for in that year they were witnesses to the will of Joseph West Upon the death of her husband, Woolley, she married, 10, 12, 1740, Thomas Lippincott, who left a will dated 1760, and she outliving him, left a will dated Feb 17, 1772, wherein she mentioned her grand-daughter, Margaret Mount.

George Mount, 17, I believe had an earlier wife than Audrey Woolley A comparison of his signatures, on his license to marry Audrey Woolley and on his will, establishes the fact that he married Amy Chambers, by license dated Jan. 18, 1744-5, and that he was also the surety on the marriage license of John Mount, 33, dated Feb 8, 1748

1757, Aug 14 He made his will, proved Apr. 17, 1760, in which he styled himself as of Middletown Thomas Mount qualified as executor at the date of probate, Joseph Mount, May 19, 1760, and John Mount, Jr , Aug 13, 1760. He mentioned his wife, Ordery, and two sons and a daughter without names

Following his demise, his widow, Audery Mount, married, by license dated Mch 27, 1760, John Chasey, with John Mount, 33, as surety.

The name of his daughter is established as Margaret, through the will of her grandmother, Hannah (Cook-Woolley) Lippincott, wherein she is called her grand-daughter Margaret Mount

I suspect the two sons mentioned without names were Timothy Mount, (named after a brother of George), who married Deborah Winter, and Matthias Mount, (named after his paternal grandfather), who married Martha Stillwell

Issue

62 Timothy (?) Mount Timothy Mount was of Howell, and died, leaving a will dated Jan 29, 1802, proved Feb. 12, 1802 He married Deborah Winter and had a daughter, Mary, who married a Covenhoven. See Winter family.

63 Matthias (?) Mount

64 Margaret Mount

18 MATTHIAS MOUNT, son of Matthias Mount, 5, was, by deduction, doubtless the son of Matthias Mount, for in a Bible, in the possession of Timothy M Maxson, Navesink, N J., there is a record that Timothy Mount, 65, was a son of Matthias and Mary Mount, and was born Dec. 19, 1784 And he says that the said Timothy was born in a house on a farm, part of which now comprises Fairview Cemetery. The names, Timothy, Joseph and Margaret, transmitted in this family, and living in Middletown, make it almost absolutely certain that Matthias Mount could have belonged nowhere else than as here placed, and as named after his father

Matthias Mount, 18, married Mary . . . ., widow of Obadiah Stillwell, who died in the Sugar House, 1777 She died July, 1792 She had issue by both of her husbands. By her first husband she had Rebecca Stillwell, who married John Davis, and went West, Elizabeth Stillwell, who married John Chasey, and Martha Stillwell, who married Matthias Mount, who left her in early life

Issue by Matthias Mount

65 Timothy Mount, born Dec 19, 1784
66 Mary Mount, lived as housekeeper, with a Rhinelander, on Bowling Green, New York City, for many years
67 Joseph Mount, born Apr. 12, 1791, died May 25, 1863, married Amelia Goldsmith.

20 JOHN MOUNT, son of Thomas Mount, 6, was born 1717, died Dec 27, 1809, married, by license dated Aug 27, 1754, Elizabeth, daughter of William and Elizabeth (Corlies) Brinley His tombstone stands in Fairview Cemetery, Middletown, N J

1754, Mch 19 I, John Mount, of Shrewsbury, do herewith Quit Claim unto my honoured father-in-law, William Brinley, of said town, Esquire, all right in the following deed that was *gave* to the aforesaid John Mount and John Brinley for this Tract of Land and meadow called Potopeck Neck, bounded on the North by several lots of salt meadow, part on Shrewsbury river and part by Samuel Wardell, West part by a highway and part by Ebenezer Wardell, South by a Branch of said Shrewsbury river, and East by a small creek, and part of Dr Steven Talman Bought September, 1749

1800, Dec 15 John Mount, of Middletown, to Timothy B Mount, of the same place, for $125, to be paid unto my son, Thomas Mount, in the State of New York, and he at the same time to provide a proper support for me during my life, for which consideration, I do convey to the said Timothy B Mount, all my plantation whereon I now dwell, near Navesink, beginning in the creek between myself and Jehu Patterson, thence up the gully to the end thereof, to the land of John Hull, it being a Northerly course, thence nearly West to the Southwest corner of Widow Stillwell's land, thence Southerly down the line of Marcus Headon, Moses Shepherd, Jr, and Thomas Layton, as the line now runs to a gully, thence down the same to the creek to the beginning This property was sold, Mch 31, 1806, by Timothy B Mount, and wife, Mary, for $2,062, to Kourtenous Schenck

Issue

68 Thomas Mount, moved to New York State
69 Becky Mount, born July 16, 1746, married, prior to Jan 29, 1774, Job Layton
70 Betsy Mount, married, first, Matthias Conover, second, Schenck
71 William Mount, born Aug 8, 1750, (Bible says Dec 25, 1750), died Oct. 3, 1804, married, Dec 25, 1782 Rebecca Stevenson, born July 6, 1761, says Bible, died July 23, 1798
72 Timothy B Mount, born 1753, died 3, 25, 1833, married, (record at Mount Holly), Mch 6, 1806, Mary Olden, (though the family always call her Mary Bonham), who died 6, 2. 1834 He had no issue
73 Lydia Mount, born Aug 10, 1760 Sally (Bowne) Crane Bible, Middletown, N. J
74 Margaret Mount, born 1756; died, May 4, 1830, aged 74 years, married, by license dated Aug 21, 1780, George S Woodward, son of Anthony, son of Anthony

There was also a son, John Mount, based upon statements of Becky Mount's granddaughter, Lydia (Wilson) Bowne, but I find no evidence to support it

21 SAMUEL MOUNT, son of Thomas Mount, 6, removed to New York City He married, Apr 15, 1752, Margaret, daughter of Adam (Aaron?) Dobbs This family also settled in New York City

Issue

75 Adam Dobbs Mount, born Sept 10, 1761, died aged 92 years, married, Jan 1, 1784, (Presbyterian Church Records, New York), his cousin, Ann Dobbs, who died aged 87 years.
76 Joseph M Mount, born Jan 15, 1757, died 1802, married, 1786, Mary, daughter of Richard and Theodosia (De Gray) Edwards, born 1767, died 1796.
77 Frances Mount, born 1763.
78 Thomas Mount, born 1764
79 William Mount, born 1773.

22 JAMES MOUNT, son of Thomas Mount, 6, married, by license dated Nov 30, 1757, Patience Price, who was baptized, in Christ Church, Shrewsbury, N J , Dec. 9, 1770

1770, Apr. 21   James Mount, of Shrewsbury, yeoman, and Patience, his wife, give a purchase money mortgage, of £60, on twenty acres of land, adjoining Thomas Morford, to Samuel Breese, late of New York, now of Shrewsbury, gentleman

This family settled in New York City, where Patience Mount, widow, appears in 1840.

Issue

80 Mary Mount, baptized Dec 9, 1770   She is reputed to have married, Mch 18, 1770, Nathaniel Ward, which if so, gives her father an earlier wife
81 Margaret Mount, baptized Dec 9, 1770, buried Sept 27, 1771.
82 Joseph Mount, baptized Dec. 29, 1770
83 Patience Mount, baptized Dec 29, 1770
84 Michael Price Mount, baptized Dec 29, 1770
85 Ann Mount, baptized Dec. 29, 1770, died July, 1837, married, about 1805, Ebenezer Allen Tucker, born May 5, 1783, died about 1818
86 James Mount, born 5, 5, 1765, died 7, -, 1837.
87 Littleton Mount, baptized May 9, 1773   This individual is said to have been a daughter, Letitia, by Samuel Mount Schenck, Esq., on the strength of a letter from Samuel J Cox, Esq , Zanesville, Ohio, Mch 4, 1867   But the child is called *he*, in the record of Christ Church, Shrewsbury, N. J , as well as Littleton.

23 THOMAS MOUNT, son of Richard Mount, 8, resided at Upper Freehold

1777, Apr 17   He made his will; proved Apr 27, 1777, in which he calls himself blacksmith, and mentions his wife, Mary, and sons, Richard, Hezekiah, John, Samuel and William   He gave, by will, to his two sons, Richard and Hezekiah Mount, equally, the tract of land whereon he lately dwelt, and which he had purchased Apr 7, 1771

1795, May 1   Richard Mount, one of the two sons, joined by Lydia, his wife, sold, for £1,794 gold, these lands, which are described as in Windsor, to Samuel Ely, of Windsor township

Issue

88 Richard Mount, born May 18, 1741
89 Hezekiah Mount
90 John Mount
91 Samuel Mount
92 William Mount, born June 11, 1743

24 MICHAEL MOUNT, son of Richard Mount, 8, was born in 1720, died Feb 4, 1805, married Mary, daughter of Ezekial and Elizabeth (Seabrook) Forman, born 1734, died Sept 2, 1809 Both of their wills are recorded at Freehold, N J

1757, Apr 1. Michael Mount, of Upper Freehold, yeoman, and Mary, his wife, son of Richard Mount, conveyed land to William Vaughn, of the same place, gentleman.

1768, Jan. 25. Michael Mount corrected the deed, at which time Vaughn was dead William Vaughn and Mercy, his wife, conveyed this land, July 5, 1760, to Thomas Mount

Issue

93 Michael Mount
94 Elizabeth Mount, born Jan 12, 1756
95 Rebecca Mount
96 Forman Mount

25 EZEKIAL MOUNT, son of Richard Mount, 8, was born in 1731, and died Jan 28, 1773. Administration was granted to his wife, Rebecca Mount, et al., Mch. 9, 1773 She was born in 1734, and died 1796, leaving a will dated Oct 10, 1796, proved Dec 27, 1796, in which she mentioned five daughters, Permelia Vaughn, Rebecca Chamberlain, Elizabeth Ely, Mary Chamberlain and Rachel Chamberlain Her son-in-law, John Chamberlain, was appointed executor

Ezekial Mount and his immediate family, all resided in Upper Freehold, and the farm devised to his sons, James, Jesse, William and Ezekial, by their grandfather, Richard Mount, was sold by them to Ezekial Mount, Jr., Mch 26, 1813

Ezekial Mount, 25, was one of the constituent members of the Yellow Meeting House

Issue

97 James Mount, born 3, 27, 1753
98 Jesse Mount, born 1758
99 William Mount, born May 29, 1762, twin with Elizabeth
100 Ezekial Mount, born May 16, 1767
101 Permelia Mount, born Oct 7, 1755, died Jan 12, 1805, married Samuel Vaughn, born 1750, died Dec. 22, 1837.
102 Rebecca Mount
103 Elizabeth Mount, born May 29, 1762, married George Ely
104 Mary Mount, died, July 5, 1817, aged 53 years, 5 months and 23 days, married Lewis Chamberlain, who died, Mch 23, 1829, aged 66 years, 3 months and 19 days.
105 Rachel Mount, died, Feb 17, 1833, aged 66 years, 9 months and 17 days; married Enoch Chamberlain, who died, Apr 21, 1837, aged 72 years and 1 month.
106 Daughter Mount, married a Job, and went West

26 SAMUEL MOUNT, of Upper Freehold, son of Richard Mount, 8, was born in 1724, died, Aug 7, 1801, aged 77 years, married, by license dated June 20, 1755, Frances, sister to Nathaniel and daughter of Abiel Cook, born Sept 16, 1731, died Sept 16, 1806

1801, May 30 He made his will, proved Sept 7, 1801, on record at Trenton

Issue

107 Richard Mount, mentioned in the will of his grandfather, killed by Indians, in New York State

108 Samuel Mount, born Apr 20, 1759
109 Michael Mount, born June 23, 1768
110 Joseph Mount, born 1757
111 Timothy Mount, killed by Indians, in New York State.
112 Rebecca Mount, married, first, William Potts and had six children, second, Vincent Wainright and had three children.
113 Peggy Mount

28 MERCY MOUNT, daughter of Richard Mount, 8, married William Vaughan, of Upper Freehold, who died, leaving a will dated Oct 2, 1767, proved Oct 28, 1767 He was a resident of Freehold, and named his wife, Massey Vahne, and friends Thomas Morphet, Thomas Farr and Peter Sexton, executors William and Ezekial Mount were two of the witnesses. William Vaughan was a man of good position and wealth

On Apr 10, 1777, these executors, Thomas Morford, of Middlesex Co , Thomas Farr and Peter Sexton, of Upper Freehold, and Marcy Stout, of Hunterdon Co , late Marcy Vaughan, conveyed to William Mount, of Upper Freehold, part of the two hundred acres which Michael Mount purchased of his father, Richard Mount, Nov 19, 1756, and which William Vaughan bought, Apr 1, 1757, and which he ordered disposed of in the event of the remarriage of his wife.

1760, July 5 William Vahan and Mercy, his wife, of Upper Freehold, yeoman, sold land, conveyed to him by Michael Mount, Mch 31, 1757, to Thomas Mount, yeoman Witness Ezekial Mount.

Issue

Samuel Vaughan, remembered in the will of his grandfather, Richard, together with "the rest of her children." Mercy Mount was at that time married to David Stout. Samuel Vaughan was born in 1750, died Dec 22, 1837, married Parmelia Mount, born Oct 7, 1755, died Jan. 12, 1805

29 PATIENCE MOUNT, daughter of Richard Mount, 8, had a license to marry Robert Gordon, dated Dec 18, 1742

1778, Apr. 2 Letters of administration were issued to Patience Gordon, on the estate of her late husband, Robert Gordon, deceased She was referred to in the will of her father, Richard Mount, who likewise alludes to her three daughters

30 RACHEL MOUNT, daughter of Richard Mount, 8, had died prior to the date of her father's will, July 22, 1777 She married Peter Sexton, born 1727, died, Jan. 31, 1813, in his 87th year. Peter Sexton was a brother to James Sexton who married Rachel Mount's sister, Rebecca, and they were sons of William and Anne (Stringham) Sexton Peter Sexton's will is on record at Freehold, and mentions his children and grandchildren

Issue

William Sexton, eldest son.
Richard Sexton, married Phebe Wardell
Samuel Sexton, died 1790–91, married Sarah, daughter of Jacob Woolston, died 1835 They had sons, Jacob W , and Samuel Sexton
James Sexton, died, prior to 1812, leaving a son, Peter.
Ezekial Sexton, born 1768, died Jan 17, 1834, married, first, Elizabeth Van Kleek, second, Henrietta Hayden

Elizabeth Sexton, married an Emley, died, prior to 1812, leaving two sons (These two sons took the name of Sexton), and Joseph

Rachel Sexton, born 1772, married Daniel, son of Daniel and Sarah Sexton, born Feb 28, 1763

Joseph Sexton, born 1773, died Aug. 14, 1823, married Elizabeth Hillman

Thomas Sexton, born Apr. 30, 1775; died Aug. 13, 1834; married, Jan 5, 1797, Mercy Wykoff, died Aug 24, 1838

31 REBECCA MOUNT, daughter of Richard Mount, 8, married, about 1758, James Sexton, born 1728-1732 His will is on record, at Trenton, written Aug 20, 1784, proved Oct 30, 1784 Her will is on record, at Freehold, written June 24, 1806, proved July 28, 1808 From these wills, and those of Patience Sexton, their daughter, who died 1792, and Joseph Cox, of Upper Freehold, who made his will 1786, proved 1801, it appears that they had

Issue

Rachel Sexton, married Eseck, son of Joseph and Mary (Mount) Cox, born Oct. 4 or 14, 1757, died Apr 12, 1815

Patience Sexton, died, 1792, unmarried

Peter Sexton, under 21 years in 1792, married Sarah .

James Sexton, under 21 years in 1792, born about 1773, married, 1800-1802, Deborah, daughter of Samuel and Hannah (Gill) Budd, born Oct 6, 1774, died Apr 9, 1852

Ann Sexton

Rebecca Sexton

32 MATTHIAS MOUNT, son of John Mount, 9, married . .

Issue

113a Joseph Mount [Was he the one who had license to marry Anne Stillwell, of Middletown, Mch 7, 1761?]

113b William Mount, supposed

33 JOHN MOUNT, son of John Mount, 9, died Sept 27, 1779 He married, first, by license dated Feb 8, 1748, Elizabeth Cummings, who died, 12, 4, 1749, after giving birth to a daughter Chloe, second, Mary . , born 1721, died 8, 2, 1808.

He was probably "John Mount, boatman," whose property was confiscated after the Revolution

1772, July 27 John Mount, of Middletown, boatman, and Mary, his wife, for £300, sold one hundred acres of land, at Navesinks, adjoining Safety Grover and George Mount, to Thomas Stevenson, of New York City

Accompanying the marriage license of John Mount and Elizabeth Cummins, on which George Mount was surety, is the following "Feb 8, 1748-9 To the Secretary of Amboy These are to certify that I, William Hodson, am willing and free that Licence should be Granted to John Mount and Elizabeth Cumins Wm Hodson "

Issue by first wife

114 Chloe Mount, born 11, 24, 1749, married, in New York, 8, 21. 1781, James Thearn

Issue by second wife

115 Sarah Mount, born 3, 19, 1751, married a Pintar, [Pintard].
116 Thomas Mount, born 4, 4, 1753, died 8, –, 1770
117 George Mount, born 2, 8, 1757
118 Martha Mount, born 8, 3, 1759, married a Patten, removed to Nassau, N P
119 Mary Mount, born 10, 24, 1761.
120 John Mount, born 8, 22, 1764
121 Matthias Mount, born 11, 21, 1766.

38 FRANCIS MOUNT, son of George Mount, 10, had a license to marry, issued Jan 4, 1758, with Ann Reynolds Upon her death, he married Elizabeth, daughter of Andrew Reed, by license dated Feb 8, 1764

Issue by first wife

122
123

Issue by second wife

124 Ezekial Mount, baptized, at Tennent Church, June 7, 1767, died (1849?)
125 Anne Mount, baptized, at Tennent Church, July 16, 1769
126 Elizabeth Mount, baptized, at Tennent Church, June 5, 1774

42 BRITTON MOUNT, son of Humphrey Mount, 11.

Issue

127 Nesbit Mount, born Nov 11, 1767

46 NESBIT MOUNT, son of Humphrey Mount, 11, had a license to marry Mary Hay, spinster, of Cranbury, with Thom^s Stricklin, surety, Aug 9, 1744.

1755, Apr 7 Humphrey Mount, of Perth Amboy, deeded land to Nisbit Mount, adjoining his own, at a nominal price, which he had bought, in 1751, of Robert Lettis Hooper.

1757, June 25 Nisbit Mount made his will, proved Apr 4, 1760, wherein he calls himself of Cranbury, and refers to "my children not 20." Wife, and John Tomson, executors.

Issue

128 Mary Mount; baptized, at Cranbury, Oct 4, 1747
129 Ann Mount, baptized, at Cranbury, Oct 4, 1747

47 MATTHIAS MOUNT, son of Matthias Mount, 12, died, Dec. 21, 1807, in his 73rd year, buried in Cranbury

1807, Feb 14 He made his will, proved Jan 13, 1808, in which he styled himself as of West Windsor, and mentioned wife, Margaret; sons, John and Elijah, daughter, Hannah, wife of James Barkley, daughter Lydia's three children

He was ruling elder of the Cranbury Presbyterian Church, from Dec 12, 1792, to his death.

Symes' History of Old Tennent, page 452, says he was born 1729, but his tombstone says, plainly, that he died Dec 21, 1807, in the 73rd year of his age, hence born in 1735 or 1736, and not in 1729 Statements have been made that Matthias, a son of Humphrey Mount, was baptized in 1729, in Old Tennent, but no such record as that either in name, date or parentage, can be found there The location of the graves, in Cranbury Yard, shows, almost unmistakably, that this Matthias Mount was a son of Matthias Mount, born 1706, and a brother of Humphrey Mount

Issue

130 John Mount
131 Elijah Mount
132 Hannah Mount, married James Barclay
133 Lydia Mount, born May 31, 1772, died Apr 14, 1798, married, Nov. 17, 1791, William J. Perrine, born 1771, died June 1, 1810

48 RICHARD MOUNT, son of Matthias Mount, 12, was a Revolutionary soldier and ancestor of the Hamilton Square family It was in this locality that his farm lay Tradition says he was married twice, and had an only child by his first wife, Matthias, and left two sons and eight daughters, in 1787, when his son, Matthias Mount, and Joseph Disbrow were made administrators of his estate These same individuals were also made guardians of his children, Mary, Joseph, Rebecca and Catharine, and the question has been raised whether Richard Mount, 48, did not marry a sister or a daughter of Joseph Disbrow, after whom he named a son, Joseph Mount.

Issue

134 Matthias Mount
135 Catharine Mount
136 Mary Mount unmarried, and living, in 1797, in Philadelphia, Pa
137 Joseph Mount, born 1776, died 1859, married Hannah, sister to Ethan Allen, died, 1862, aged 77 years They had a son, Richard Mount, who died, 1872, aged 62 years All buried at Hightstown, N J.
138 Rebecca Mount
139 Elizabeth Mount, married David Cubberly, for his second wife
140 Daughter Mount, married a Parmer [Palmer?]
141 Daughter Mount
142 Daughter Mount
143 Daughter Mount

Of these daughters, it is thought that Rebecca, who married a Warren, is she to whom a marriage license was issued, Feb 2, 1768, with Jacob Warren, of Burlington Co , and that either the Anne Mount, who had a marriage license with Levi Bowker, Oct 16, 1773, or the Ann Mount, who had a marriage license with Samuel Wright Hartshorne, May 8, 1779, may have been the daughter of Richard Mount, 48, and named after his mother.

49 JOHN MOUNT, son of Matthias Mount, 12, was born Apr 12, 1743, baptized, at Old Tennent, June 5, 1743, died 1824. married, first, in 1764, Hannah Freeman, born Mch. 17, 1743, died Aug 10, 1791, married, second, (June 10, 1792?), Anne Toms, born Jan 10, 1754 He was ruling elder in the First Presbyterian Church, at Cranbury, from Oct 14, 1802, until his death, in 1824

He was a Lieutenant in the Revolutionary War

About 1804, he and his son, James, removed to Maidenhead, Hunterdon Co , near Trenton, where they operated mills, woolen, grist and saw, a kiln and a distillery, later known as Hutchinson's Mills

1783, Mch. 25 He received from his parents, Matthias Mount, Sr , and Anne, his wife, two hundred and twenty acres, being the East End of their plantation

1805 John Mount and Anne, his wife, and James Mount and Amey, his wife, of Maidenhead, Hunterdon Co , for £1,650, sold the land, in East Windsor, "to which John Mount hath title by deed of sale from his father, Matthias Mount," dated Mch 25, 1783, to John Chamberlain, of East Windsor.

In 1823, he made his will and mentioned his wife, Ann, son, James, daughter, Hannah, wife of John Mount, and grandson, John Conover, son of his daughter Anna Executors his son, James, and his son-in-law, John Mount.

Issue

144 James (Lawrence) Mount, born 11, 10, 1765.
145 Ann Mount, born May 9, 1771, died July 11, 1791, married . Conover, and had son, John Conover
146 Hannah Mount, born Aug 7, 1780, married, Apr 24, 1800, John Mount, 222, son of Hezekiah and Mary (Patterson) Mount, 89
147 John Mount, born 12, 7, 1786, died 7, 24, 1791

51 HUMPHREY MOUNT, son of Matthias Mount, 12, was born 1745-6, and baptized, at Cranbury, July 13, 1746 "died Sept 22, 1801, in 56th year of his age, an elder in 1st Presbyterian Church of Cranberry," from Dec 12, 1792, till his death Buried, at Cranbury, by the side of "Abigail, his widow, died Jan 27, 1837, in her 83rd year." His wife was Abigail Baylis, born 1754-5 Symes says his death occurred Sept 27, but it was more correctly Sept 22, 1801

Humphrey Mount was a Revolutionary soldier

1783, Mch. 25 Matthias Mount, Sr , and Ann, his wife, conveyed, for £400, to their son, Humphrey, the West End of their plantation, in Windsor township, being two hundred and twenty acres

They both left wills

Issue

148 Mary Mount, born Mch 8, 1773, married, Jan 1, 1800, Elijah Mount, 131, son of Matthias and Margaret Mount
149 John Baylis Mount, born 1781
150 Samuel H Mount, born Oct 18, 1777
151 Daniel Mount, born June 22, 1786
152 Humphrey Mount, born June 13, 1790
153 Anna Mount, born June 18, 1783, married, Oct 15, 1806, John Hulick
154 Matthias Mount, born Mch. 18, 1775 ⎫ Not mentioned in father's will
155 Isaac Mount, born Nov 27, 1788 ⎭

52 ANN MOUNT, daughter of Matthias Mount, 12, died Apr. 8, 1824, married, Nov 12, 1772, William Perrine, of South Amboy, who, in his will, dated May 8, 1820, proved Dec 4, 1820, calls her "Hannah" According to the Cranbury records, she was baptized as Ann, daughter of Matthias Mount, Apr 23, 1749 "Hannah Perrine was born Feb 11, 1749," according to a Bible record in the possession of Howland Perrine, and she is called Hannah, on her tombstone, at Cranbury

William Perrine was a Revolutionary soldier, born 11, 28, 1743, died Nov 25, 1820

Issue

Lydia Perrine, born 1774, died, prior to May 8, 1820, married Thomas Baldwin
Anna Perrine, born 1773, died prior to May 8, 1820, married Israel Baldwin

Dr William Williamson Perrine, born 1793, married Sarah Voorhees, had two daughters, moved to Philadelphia, Pa
Matthias Perrine, born 1775, married Ann Knott
Peter Perrine, born 1777; married Ann Duncan, moved to New York
John Perrine, born 1779, married Betsey Riggs
Margaret Perrine, born 1780, married Major James Cook (Cash)
Rev Humphrey M Perrine, born 1786, a Professor at Princeton College, married Fanny Dodds, and had son, Dr William Perrine
Rebecca Perrine, born 1792, married John McMichael
Daniel Perrine, born 1784, married a Holmes } These two are named in Clayton's History of Middlesex Co.
Hannah Perrine, born 1788

53 THOMAS MOUNT,* son of Matthias Mount, 12, went from New Jersey, presumably about 1768, to Fauquier Co ; later to Shelby Co , Ky , where he died about 1815 He married Mary . , and was "the ancestor of the late Gov. James A. Mount, of Indiana, the late William Sidney Mount, a banker, and Mayor and City Treasurer of New Orleans, and the late Charles Mount, a famous lawyer of Mississippi," wrote Paul W. Mount, Esq

He was a man of large wealth, owning many slaves and much land, which he bequeathed, equally, to his children, by a will, recorded in Shelby Co , Ky. In this instrument, he alludes to

---

Thomas Mount, probably a grandson of Thomas Mount, 53, went, with his brother, Stephen, to Virginia, and from there to Raymond, Miss He died in 1861
    Issue
    William S Mount, of McComb, Miss , died 1882, married Paralee Grayson
        Issue 10 children, all dead but
        William Mount
        Matilda Mount
        Page Mount
        Bettie Mount
        Paralee Mount
    Charles Edwin Mount, of Raymond, Miss , died 1881, married, 1837, Mary Eliza Roberts, died 1873
        Issue
        Mary Mount
        Consande Mount
        Thomas E Mount, born 1843, died 1904
        Pauline Bertha Mount, married   McDougall, of Palestine, La
        Jasper Mount
    Joseph Mount, died, 1850, single, of yellow fever
    Thomas Lafayette Mount, of Baltimore, married Sophie Keener, died 1904
        Issue
        Carroll Mount
        Mary Mount
        Keener Mount
    Martha Mount
    Mary Frances Mount, married   McRoberts

Stephen Mount, probably a grandson of Thomas Mount, 53, went with his brother, Thomas, to Virginia
    Issue
    Mary Tom Mount, of Vicksburg, Miss , married Julius Klein
    Annie Mount, married Julius Bradfield
    Sarah Mount, of Baltimore, Md , married   Anderson
    Daughter Mount, went to Missouri

Atwell Mount, a descendant, perhaps a grandson of Thomas Mount, 53, was born, in Virginia, in 1806, was of Kentucky in 1813, of Indiana in 1828, died 1881 He had twelve children
    Issue
    James Atwell Mount, born, in Indiana, 1843, died 1902, was Governor of the State in 1897, married Kate A Boyd
        Issue

    Rev Harry N Mount, of Indianapolis Presbyterian Church

his plantations in Virginia, and plantations in Kentucky, one of which, in the latter state, amounted to five thousand acres

Issue

156 Matthias Mount, born Mch 11, 1767, died Jan 23, 1848, married, first, Elizabeth Stephenson, born Nov. 6, 1776, died Feb. 16, 1805, married, second, Ann Elliott, born Dec 31, 1778, died Mch 29, 1847
157 John Mount. Went to Kentucky, like his brother, Matthias Mount He remained there and became a large slave holder
158 Elijah Mount
159 Ezekial Mount
160 Hannah Mount, married a Maddon.
161 Polly Mount, married a Barnit
162 Letitia Mount, married Jonathan Swindler
163 Rhoda Mount, married James Beatty
164 William Mount
165 Thomas Mount
166 Amos Mount
167 Jasper Mount

56 JEMIMA MOUNT, daughter of Timothy Mount, 13, married Samuel White, probably the son of Robert and Margaret (Hartshorne) White, because he named one child after Jemima's father, and two others, Robert and Margaret

Issue

Robert White. Administration, on his estate, was granted to Samuel W Trafford, July 30, 1845
Timothy White, married, Mch 9, 1797, Hannah, daughter of Richard and Catharine (Shepherd) Crawford Administration granted, on his estate, to Jarrat Morford, Jan 18, 1842
Margaret White, married, first, Ebenezer Hart, second, a Wardell
Mehitable White, born Aug 27, 1763, died Mch 15, 1849; married, October, 1782, Samuel Trafford, who died June 22, 1806

59 MATTHIAS MOUNT, son of Joseph Mount, 16, was born 1748; died 1822; buried at Tennent Church He resided at Matcheponix, as early as June 1, 1772, when he bought land of Nicholas Van Wickle, and where he and his wife, Mary, sold land, for $5,000, to George Snowhill, in 1811 His Christian name was contracted to Tice, by which name he was commonly called

He was a Revolutionary soldier and a large property holder.

Issue by first wife

168 Joseph Mount, died 1839, married Sophia, daughter of Henry Delatosh Had issue
169 Hugh Taylor Mount, born Jan 9, 1774, died Aug 24, 1857, buried at Tennent Church, married, June 25, 1798, Catharine, daughter of Cornelius Johnson, born Aug 22, 1776, died Feb 25, 1851 Had issue
170 Fanny Mount, married David Larrison

MOUNT OF MONMOUTH COUNTY

Issue by second wife

171 Catherine Mount, not twenty-one, Mch 28, 1803
172 Rebecca Mount

61 JOSEPH MOUNT, son of Joseph Mount, 16, lived near Princeton, N J He was born about 1750, and died 1826, married Mary, daughter of John Baylis, of Kingston, N. J.

Issue

173 John Mount, born May 10, 1777; died Mch 21, 1853, buried at Trenton; married, first, May 12, 1799, Elizabeth, daughter of Alexander and Sarah (Norris) Smith, born 1780, died 1835, second, 11, 3, 1836, Hester Seaman Had issue
174 William Mount, disappeared
175 Margaret Mount, living in 1875, buried at Lambertville, N J ; married Jonathan P Burroughs
176 Mary Mount, died December, 1873, unmarried, buried at Lambertville, N J
177 Anne Mount, married Frederick Cox, lived at Somerville, N J
178 Sarah Mount, died 1868, married, 1808, Gerrit D Stryker, resided at Lambertville, N J.
179 Susan Mount; unmarried
180 Amy Mount, born Dec 20, 1790, married William Webster, and moved to Terre Haute, Ind , and had Frederick Webster and James Webster
181 Euphemia Mount, died, in 1821, in Indiana, unmarried

65 TIMOTHY MOUNT, son of Matthias Mount, 18, was born Dec 19, 1784; died 8, 11, 1863; married Cornelia, daughter of Robert and Catharine Hill, born Jan 3, 1783, died Dec 25, 1865

Issue

182 Mark L Mount, born Apr 13, 1807, died 1891, married Catharine S . Had issue
183 John H Mount, born Dec 29, 1808, married Mary Elizabeth Swan
·184 Joseph E Mount, born Jan 23, 1811, married Elizabeth Ann .
185 Mary Ann Mount, born May 29, 1813
186 Margaret H Mount, born July 17, 1815, died young
187 Margaret Amelia Mount, born Jan 13, 1817, married a Maxson, and had Timothy Maxson, of Navesink, N J
188 William S Mount, born Dec 13, 1819, not named in his father's will
189 Timothy Mount, born Feb 6, 1822
190 Matthias Mount, born Oct 20, 1825, not named in his father's will
191 Cornelia Mount, died, young, at Middletown, Sept 15, 1828

69 REBECCA MOUNT, daughter of John Mount, 20, was born "Wednesday 16 July 1746", married, prior to 1774, Job Layton His will is, at Freehold, dated Aug 31, 1820, proved Jan 26, 1827

Issue

Elizabeth Layton, born Jan 29, 1774, died Aug 7, 1828, married Isaac, son of David and Elizabeth (Davis) Burdge, born Feb 28, 1767, died Mch 22, 1858
Rebecca Layton, born Jan 7, 1776, died Feb 24, 1860, married, Aug 8, 1793, William Wilson, born Jan 5, 1766, died Sept. 15, 1837, buried in Fairview Cemetery, Middletown, N J Her epitaph says died Feb 21, 1860

John Layton born Jan 21, 1772, died Apr 5, 1844, married, Nov 8, 1801, Elizabeth Mersereau.

Job Layton

Euphame Layton, died prior to Aug. 31, 1820; married Joseph Cooper

Sally Layton, born June 1, 1781, died Sept 4, 1859, married, Aug. 16, 1801, Peter Mersereau.

71 WILLIAM MOUNT, son of John Mount, 20, was born Aug 25, 1750, died Oct. 3, 1804; married, Dec 25, 1782, Rebecca, daughter of Edward and Rebecca Stevenson, born July 6, 1761; died July 23, 1798

Guardianship proceedings for Elizabeth and Margaret, daughters of William Mount, over fourteen years of age, by Timothy B Mount, Elizabeth Covenhoven and Lydia Mount, brother and sisters of the deceased   1805, January Term, Monmouth County Orphans' Court.

Issue

192 Timothy B Mount, born Oct 6, 1783, died May 17, 1797.

193 Cornelius S Mount, born Apr 14, 1787; died July 18, 1857, married, Jan. 26, 1809, Eleanor, daughter of Thomas Hankinson, who died Jan 23, 1862. Had issue

194 Rebecca S Mount, born Dec 6, 1789, married, first, Jan 25, 1810, Edward Tilton, who died 1815, second, Sept 25, 1816, Benjamin Cooper.

195 Edward Mount, born May 30, 1792

196 Elizabeth Mount, born May 8, 1793, died Aug. 16, 1831 (tombstone reads: died, May 16, 1831, aged 38, 3, 8), married Richard Corlies, born Nov 18, 1797, died Jan 2, 1879

197 Margaret Mount, born Dec 31, 1795, died Nov. 19, 1872; married James Beadle, born Oct 28, 1797, died Mch 22, 1879

198 Timothy Mount, born May 17, 1797.

74 MARGARET MOUNT, daughter of John Mount, 20, was born, near Middletown, in 1756, and died, at White Hill, in the Delaware, May 4, 1830, married, in 1777, George Woodward, born 1744, died Dec 25, 1817, (aged 73 years), who was a son of the second Anthony Woodward   He was taken to task, 1781, 4, 5mo, for marrying out of meeting, (Chesterfield Monthly Meeting)

Not less than fifteen of her relatives served in the Revolutionary Army Timothy Mount, her brother, was Colonel, and one of Washington's most trusted agents, so serviceable was he, that Congress granted him a large tract of land in Ohio

Tradition relates that he plotted to take General Arnold a prisoner, in New York City, and to carry him, after capture, within the lines of the Continental Army Twice the plans for his seizure were all laid, but a dinner party, on the one occasion, and a severe storm on the other, made them of no avail   (E M Woodward's Contributions to the History of Burlington)

Issue

Lydia Woodward, married William Woodhouse, of Philadelphia

Margaret Woodward, married Jacob Seebohm, of Philadelphia

George Woodward, married Margaret Wynkoop, moved to Montgomery Co, Penn

Rebecca Woodward; married Thomas Field, of Philadelphia

Jesse Woodward, died, at White Hill, N. J, 1830, no issue

Martha Woodward; married Isaac Field
Anthony Woodward, died, June 24, 1817, aged 21 years

76 JOSEPH MOUNT, son of Samuel Mount, 21, was born 1757, and died 1802, married Mary Edwards.

Issue

199 Richard Edwards Mount, born 1786, died 1872, married, in 1813, Maria, daughter of Capt Ware Branson, born 1792, died 1878 He was a Captain in the War of 1812, and, in 1821, Colonel of a New York Militia regiment He possessed great wealth

82 JOSEPH MOUNT, son of James Mount, 22, while baptized, at Christ Church, Shrewsbury, Dec 29, 1770, was born, perhaps, about 1762. He married Sarah, daughter of Thomas Morford, of Shrewsbury, who was born Sept 24, 1768, and died Sept 30, 1823.

Joseph Mount was living, Jan. 30, 1824, when he conveyed land to his son, Horatio, but had died prior to June 6, 1831, when his son, Horatio Mount and wife, Matilda, of Shrewsbury, and Edward Mount, of New York City, conveyed to Joseph King, of Shrewsbury, two-thirds of the land left to them and their brother, George Mount, by Thomas Morford, their grandfather. His residence was in Shrewsbury, on land derived from Thomas Morford, (by will dated Dec 6, 1816), bounded by James and Michael Mount, and which Morford had bought from James Mount, and in which he, Joseph Mount, 82, and his wife, Sarah, had a life interest, with reversion to their sons, who disposed of the same as given above.

Issue

200 Joseph Mount, baptized May 27, 1799.
201 George M Mount, married Mary   .
202 Edward Mount
203 Horatio Mount, married Matilda   .
204 Rebecca Mount
205 Hannah Mount

84 MICHAEL PRICE MOUNT, son of James Mount, 22, resided at Shrewsbury He married, May 10, 1809, Abigail Cooper, baptized June 8, 1823. He was a resident of New York City in 1830.

Issue

206 Alfred W Mount
207 Cynthia Mount; baptized June 8, 1823, married John Lamoin

88 RICHARD MOUNT, son of Thomas Mount, 23, resided on his estate, called Kildare, at Upper Freehold He was born May 18, 1741, died July 12, 1825, married, first, Lydia Dey, born May 10, 1748, died Feb 10, 1804, second, Ann, widow of Peter Job He is named as eldest son, in the will of his grandfather, Richard Mount, July 22, 1777 His own will is on record, at Freehold, written Oct 16, 1824, proved Aug 8, 1825 Richard Mount and his wife, Lydia (Dey), are buried in the Baptist Churchyard, Hightstown

He was a man of considerable means

1795, May 11. He bought from Samuel Mount, for £3,000, "all that certain messuages, farms and plantations, commonly called and known by the name of Kildare, in the counties of Monmouth and Middlesex," amounting to four hundred acres

1798, Feb 15 He added one hundred and twenty-six acres of land, along Millstone Creek, in East Windsor township, to his holdings, for which he paid Nicholas Hooper £500

Issue

208 Thomas R Mount, born Jan 26, 1777, died Jan 4, 1855, married, first, Jan 21, 1802, Margaret Cook (Freehold Records), second, 4, 9, 1809, Margaret Hendrickson
209 Peter Dey Mount, born 3, 28, 1780; died 12, 7, 1842, married, Dec 29, 1803, Margaret, daughter of Matthias and Phebe (Combs) Rue, born Feb 27, 1785; died 9, 6, 1870.
210 William R. Mount ("Killdear"), born 1783, died, Apr 30, 1847, aged 64 years, 2 months and 3 days, buried at Hightstown, married Cornelia Thompson, born 1789, died, Dec. 15, 1852, aged 63 years, 8 months and 23 days, buried at Hightstown
211 Rachel Mount, born Feb 13, 1769, died Mch 11, 1833, married Samuel, son of Samuel and Frances (Cook) Mount, born Apr 30, 1759; died June 18, 1853.
212 Margaret Mount, married a Cox, went West
213 Nancy Mount, born Aug 28, 1778, died 1856, married Samuel Ely.
214 Rebecca Mount, married, Mch 11, 1795, Britton Moore, went West
215 Mary Mount, born 1775, died, Apr 5, 1856, aged 81 years, 2 months and 25 days; buried at Hightstown, married, Feb 3, 1803, Rediord, son of Peter and Ann Job, died, Mch 23, 1850, aged 70 years, 6 months and 18 days Both buried at Hightstown.
216 Lydia Mount, born 1780, died Mch 14, 1810, married, Jan 14, 1801, James Bowne
217 Phebe Mount, married Daniel Dey
218 Euphemia Mount, born 1781, died 1856, married, first, Jan. 6, 1802, James Montgomery Johnson, second, Jan 5, 1832, Judge John Baylies Mount

89 HEZEKIAH MOUNT, son of Thomas Mount, 23, resided at East Windsor

1795, May 1 Richard Mount and Lydia, his wife, of Monmouth Co, for £1,794, gold, sold to Samuel Ely, lands at Windsor, "which lands were purchased by Thomas Mount, father of said Richard, by deed dated Apr 7, 1771, and by said Thomas Mount willed, Apr 7, 1777, unto his two sons, Richard and Hezekiah Mount, to be equally divided between them . . . the place where Richard Mount lately dwelt"

1806, Aug 2 Hezekiah Mount was one of the Trustees of the Baptist Church, in Hightstown, in East Windsor, Middlesex Co

1807, Oct 24 He made his will, proved Dec 14, 1807, in which he mentioned. wife, Mary, and appointed his brother, William Mount, and his son, Thomas, executors Some of his sons were not of age

Issue

219 Thomas Mount, married, Dec. 17, 1801, Rebecca Chamberlain
220 Hezekiah Mount, born 8, 1, 1792, married, 7, 2, 1814, Charity Voorhees, born 1795, died 1837
221 Nehemiah Mount, eldest son, married Ezuba Newall
222 John Mount, born 1780, died, 1876, aged 96 years, married, Apr 24, 1800, Hannah, daughter of John and Hannah (Freeman) Mount, born 1780

223 Samuel Mount, born 1784, died 1873, married Hannah Chamberlain, born Mch 3, 1791, died July 3, 1842
224 William H. Mount, died prior to 4, 2, 1839, married, Sept 16, 1812, Sarah, widow of Vincent Wetherill
225 Jane Mount, married John Chamberlain
226 Richard Mount, married Eliza P . .

Rebecca, Hannah and John Chamberlain were sisters and brother, and children of John Chamberlain and (Rebecca?) Mount.

91 SAMUEL MOUNT, son of Thomas Mount, 23, married Patience . . . . They resided at East Windsor, where, May 7, 1806, he sold two hundred and thirty-six acres of land, for $11,812.50, adjoining land of William Mount, to Wilson Hunt. After this transaction, he went West to Warren Co., Ohio, with most of his family

Issue

227 Thomas Mount, born 10, 23, 1770
228 Mary Mount, born 11, 7, 1772.
229 Ann Mount, born 1, 15, 1775
230 John Mount, born 3, 6, 1777, died, Oct 19, 1820, aged 47 years, 7 months and 12 days, buried at Hightstown, married Rebecca Perrine Dec. 28, 1796
231 Rebecca Mount, born 8, 20, 1779.
232 Amos Mount, born 8, 19, 1782, died 9, 29, 1857, married Nancy Kirby, born 10, 12, 1785, died 1, 2, 1864
233 Rachel Mount, born 3, 5, 1785
234 Patience Mount, born 8, 30, 1788, died 12, 18, 1818
235 Katherine Mount, born 3, 15, 1791; died 3, 26, 1821.
236 Elijah Mount, born 12, 26, 1793, died 4, 15, 1821

92 WILLIAM MOUNT, son of Thomas Mount, 23 Both he and his wife are buried at Hightstown. His tombstone says he died, Mch 11, (Bible says 14), 1818, aged 74 years, 8 months and 3 days, her tombstone says died, Feb 15, 1817, aged 61 years and 2 months. (Bible says she was born Feb 13, 1756) He married, by license dated Nov. 20, 1775, Rebecca, daughter of Thomas and Sarah Cox

1811, Oct. 16 He is mentioned in deeds and calls himself "miller"
1818, Jan 15 He made his will, proved Apr 6, 1818, and styles himself of Upper Freehold

Issue

237 Achsah Mount, born Feb 2, 1782; died Oct 13, 1848; married, Nov 26, 1800, John J Ely, born May 7, 1778, died Jan 11, 1852
238 Mary C Mount, born 1780, married, Jan. 28, 1802, George Ely, went to Ohio
239 Hiram Mount, born Aug 10, 1786, says Bible died, Jan 9, 1847, aged 60 years, 4 months and 30 days, married Margaret, sister to Enos, and daughter of Thomas and Mary (Forman) Allen, born Mch —, 1790, died, Feb. 13, 1865, aged 74 years and 11 months Mary Forman was the daughter of Andrew Forman
240 David Mount, born Feb 3, 1778 Mentioned in Freehold Deeds May 23, 1801
241 Hezekiah Mount, born July 5, 1788, married Catherine, daughter of Taylor Mount Removed to Indiana.

242 Abijah Mount, born Dec 16, 1795, died 1877; married, Feb 6, 1817, Mary Chamberlain, born Feb 27, 1797, died, June (20?), 1881, aged 85 years.
243 Addison Mount, born Apr. 16, 1798, married Hetty, daughter of John Clayton; went to Illinois
244 Sarah Mount, born Jan 15, 1791

93 MICHAEL MOUNT, son of Michael Mount, 24, according to Mrs. Charles P. Britton, 126 West State St., Trenton, married Mary . . .
This Michael Mount must have been he whose land was sold by the Sheriff, October, 1807, and as it was sold to Garrit P. Wikoff, I imagine it was the same Michael Mount on whose estate Garret P. Wyckoff and Gilbert Hendrickson were appointed administrators in 1812

Issue

245 Mary Ann Mount, died single.
246 Hannah Mount, married George Howell, lived in Philadelphia.
247 Jefferson Mount, married Miss Millie . . ; lived in Boston
248 Forman S. Mount, born about 1802, died July, 1860, married Catherine Dennis.

94 ELIZABETH MOUNT, daughter of Michael Mount, 24, was born Jan 12, 1756; died July 24, 1832, married, by license dated May 2, 1771, Jacob Hendrickson, son of Gilbert and Elizabeth (Polhemus) Hendrickson, born Mch 15, 1744, died Aug 15, 1810

Issue

Forman Hendrickson, married Theodosia, daughter of Daniel and Elizabeth (Grover) Hendrickson, born Nov 2, 1795.
Jacob Hendrickson, died Nov 7, 1826, married Sarah Vandeveer, born Jan. 28, 1790, died Dec 3, 1878

95 REBECCA MOUNT, daughter of Michael Mount, 24, married, first, Samuel P Forman, and is called Rebecca Forman in the will of her father, Feb. 1, 1805, but in the will of her mother Mary, 8mo , 19, 1809, she is called Rebecca Rainburgh, and has a son, Michael Forman Her own will, at Freehold, made and probated in 1840, shows that she must have died in that year.
1814, Mch 29 Rebecca Forman, of Upper Freehold, sold to Appollo Meirs, a house left her by the will of her father, Michael Mount (The discrepancy between her surname here and as in her mother's will, is to be looked up)

Issue

Michael Forman; lived at Allentown.
Eleanor Forman; unmarried
Mollie Forman, married Humphrey Mount
    Issue
  Humphrey Mount
  Mollie Mount
Elizabeth Forman, married John Lawrence Hendrickson
Peter Forman, married . , and had issue.

96 FORMAN MOUNT, son of Michael Mount, 24, married Margaret, daughter of Alexander and Ann (Marshall) Edwards, born Apr 18, 1760, died about 1834. He resided, with his wife, at Middletown Point in 1795, and in 1806, at Northern Liberties (Philadelphia).

MOUNT OF MONMOUTH COUNTY

Issue

249 Ann Mount, born 1786, died, Dec 6, 1848, aged 62 years, married Nathaniel Britton, born Dec 16, 1786, died Mch 31, 1833 Both are buried in Presbyterian Churchyard, Allentown
250 Michael Mount, lost at sea, unmarried
251 Margaret Mount, born 1789, died Dec 26, 1833, married Nicholas Britton, born 1791 She is buried at Yellow Meeting House, Allentown
252 Edwards Mount, married Sally   He was appointed sailing master, Jan 28, 1815, and up to 1820, was stationed on Lake Erie He died at his home, near the Navy Yard, Philadelphia, and his wife, later, in Pennsylvania No issue
253 Forman Marshall Mount, born May 4, 1793, died May 14, 1827, married Mary Ann Russell, a very beautiful Englishwoman
254 Mary Mount, born 1787, died Oct 13, 1861, buried in Greenwood Cemetery, Trenton, married John Hughes

97 JAMES MOUNT, son of Ezekiel Mount, 25, was born 1752, died Dec 27, 1786, married Jane, daughter of John and Jane Gaston, born Dec 11, 1758, died Jan 7, 1808 She afterwards married, prior to July, 1791, Lewis Anderson. James Mount was appointed guardian of John and Martha Rue, May 3, 1780, and she administratrix of his estate, Jan 24, 1787

1791, July In the settlement of her accounts as administratrix, she calls herself Jane Anderson, formerly Mount, administratrix, and says James Mount was guardian of Matthias Rue

Issue

255 Ezekiel I. Mount, born 8, 17, 1777; died 1865, married, first, Leah R .   , second, Mch 12, 1814, Margaret Gaston, born 1790, died 1874
256 John Mount, born 7, 24, 1779, married Ann (Scott?)
257 Catherine Mount, born 1784, married, after June 20, 1805, and prior to Feb 8, 1808, Peter, son of John and Mary (LaRue) Perrine, born Mch 3, 1768, died Sept. 6, 1846.
258 Rebecca Mount, born 1786
259 Sexton Mount, born 7, 24, 1781, married, June 4, 1808, Margaret Mount
260   Mount, possibly Jane, a witness to deed, June 20, 1805

98 JESSE MOUNT, son of Ezekiel Mount, 25
1801 Jesse Mount was fined £5, in Upper Freehold.

Issue

261 Jefferson Mount
262 Ezekiel J Mount, born 1809, died 1897, married Emeline L   , born 1815, died 1890, buried at Perrineville
263 Ann or Nancy Mount, married, Jan 5, 1825, Joseph Emley
264 Lydia Mount, married, May 13, 1824, Lewis Allen
265 Rebecca Mount, married Elijah Wall
266 Mary Mount, married Elijah Wall

99 WILLIAM MOUNT, son of Ezekiel Mount, 25, was born May 29, 1762, died July 30, 1825 He was, apparently, the third son of Ezekiel Mount, not of age in his grandfather,

Richard Mount's, will, July 22, 1777, married, Mch. 12, 1795, (Middlesex Records), Catherine Carlisle, who outlived him and was alive Oct. 6 1830

    Issue

267 Jesse Mount, born Nov 12, 1795, died Jan 10, 1839, married, Aug 14, 1824, Sarah S Parker. born Nov 19, 1799 died July 26, 1856
268 Elizabeth Mount, born 1797, died July 7, 1880
269 Enoch Mount (Died Feb 2, 1862?, and buried, at Hightstown?, aged 46 years) One, Enoch Mount, married Rebecca Rue and located at Hightstown See Woodward's History of Mercer Co , p 870
270 Rachel Mount
271 Hannah Mount, born June 18, 1803, died June 5, 1840
272 Richard R Mount, born 12, 27, 1804, died, 7, 29, 1858, aged 53 years, married Mary C   , born 1815, died 1845

    100 EZEKIEL MOUNT, son of Ezekiel Mount, 25, was born May 16, 1767, died, Sept 17, 1849, aged 82 years, 4 months and 1 day, married, first, Helena Downs, born Sept 15, 1772, died, Jan. 4, 1825, aged 52 years, 3 months and 19 days, second, Anne Wright, born Aug 31, 1795, died May 6, 1859. All three are buried at Hightstown

Ezekiel Mount was called "New York" or "York Ezekiel"

1845, Jan 15 He made his will, proved Oct 12, 1849, and called himself of Millstone, and mentioned wife, Ann, sons, Morgan F , and Charles W Mount, not twenty-one; "other children, residing in New York, or elsewhere" Executor Richard Norton

    Issue by first wife

273 James Mount, born Nov 13, 1790, died, Dec 25, 1830, aged 40 years, 1 month and 12 days, buried in Hightstown yard
274 Randolph Mount
275 Sexton Mount
276 George Mount
276a Rebecca Mount, born Aug 23, 1795, died, July 25, 1812, aged 16 years, 11 months and 2 days
277 Foreman Mount
277a Lucy Mount, born Jan 16, 1798, died, July 22, 1812, aged 14 years, 6 months and 6 days
278 Caroline Mount
278a Eleanor Mount, born Feb 5, 1809, died, Apr 7, 1813, aged 4 years, 2 months and 2 days Hightstown Yard

    Issue by second wife

279 Morgan F. Mount
280 Charles W Mount

    102 REBECCA MOUNT, daughter of Ezekiel Mount, 25, was born Sept 28, 1758, died, Mch 26, 1820, aged 61 years, 5 months and 28 days, buried at Hightstown, married John Chamberlain, born 1760, died, July 21, 1835, in 75th year, buried at Hightstown.

    Issue

Ezekiel Chamberlain, died, June 1, 1799, in 7th year, buried at Hightstown
Harriet Chamberlain, youngest daughter, married a Van Nest

Issue
Vincent D. Van Nest
John Chamberlain, married Jane Mount
Rebecca Chamberlain, married, Dec. 17, 1801, Thomas Mount
Hannah Chamberlain, born Mch 3, 1791; died July 3, 1842, married Samuel Mount

103 ELIZABETH MOUNT, daughter of Ezekiel Mount, 25, married George Ely, of East Windsor

1806, June 25 He made his will, recorded at New Brunswick, proved Feb 12, 1808, and mentioned: wife, Elizabeth, sons, Ezekiel Ely and William Ely, neither twenty-one, sons, Richard, Saxton and James, neither seventeen He mentions having given to sons, John and George Enoch Chamberlain was a witness

108 SAMUEL MOUNT, son of Samuel Mount, 26, was born Apr. 20, 1759, died, June 18, 1853, aged 94 years, 1 month and 29 days, married Rachel, daughter of Richard and Lydia (Dey) Mount, born Feb 13, 1769, died, Mch 11, 1833, in 65th year Both buried at Hightstown

1836, Aug 26 In his will at Freehold, proved June 28, 1853, he calls himself of Millstone, and bequeathes a tanyard to his son Aaron

1853, June 20 Renunciation of Aaron Mount

Issue
281 Aaron Mount, born May 6, 1786; married, first, Apr 2, 1814, Lydia Stillwell, second, Dec 24, 1817, Elizabeth Dey
282 Zebulon Mount, born Jan 16, 1800, died Aug 25 1870
283 Samuel Mount, born May 1, 1802, died 1868, married Euphemia   , born 1803, died 1864, both buried at Cranbury
284 Peter Mount, born Mch 9, 1804, died Sept. 7, 1858, buried at Hightstown.
285 Timothy Mount, born June 4, 1793, died young
286 Timothy Mount, of Hightstown, born Nov 30, 1796, died Feb 22, 1845, buried at Hightstown
287 Lydia Mount, born July 4, 1791, married, Feb 12, 1812, John M. Buckalew.
288 Phebe Mount, married John Clayton
289 Mary Ann Mount, born Apr 11, 1806, died July 14, 1882, buried at Maplewood, Freehold, married, May 27, 1829, Henry Schenck, born Jan 24, 1805, died Dec 20, 1891
290 Eleanor Mount, born 1811
291 Richard Mount, born Jan. 31, 1788, married Sarah Dean
292 Foreman Mount, born 1809

109 MICHAEL MOUNT, son of Samuel Mount, 26, was born June 23, 1768, died, July 31, 1831, aged 63 years, 1 month and 8 days He was named, as executor, in his father's will of 1801 He married, Dec 16, 1801, Mercy Vaughan, born 1778, died, July 10, 1861, aged 83 years, 3 months and 20 days Both buried at Hightstown.

1831, Aug 15 Letters of administration were granted on his estate, to Peter C Bergen and *Tomas* Ely.

Issue

293 Michael (Henry?) Mount, married, Apr 2, 1827, Hannah Clayton.
294 Parmelia A Mount, married . . . . . Ely *

110 JOSEPH MOUNT, son of Samuel Mount, 26, was born 1757, died July 27, 1822. He married, prior to Apr. 1, 1799, Theodosia, daughter of John and sister to Ruth Rogers, born 1761.

1822, Aug 13 Administration was granted on his estate to his widow, Theodosia, his son, John, and John Emley Theodosia Mount died Mch 4, 1846, leaving a will, on record at Mount Holly, dated Mch. 24, 1844, proved Mch 27, 1846.

Issue

295 John Mount; married Gertrude, daughter of Thomas and Mary (Wykoff) Sexton.
296 Joseph Mount, of Manasquan, married Sophia   .
297 Rebecca Mount; unmarried. See New Brunswick Wills.
298 Ezekiel Mount; married Ann   . .
299 Hannah Mount; married, June 29, 1826, John Harris.
300 Elizabeth Mount; married Peter Sexton
301 Susan Mount; married Thomas Forman
302 Samuel Mount, died prior to Mch 24, 1844
303 Sarah Mount, married, Apr 2, 1825, Joseph Poinsett

117 GEORGE MOUNT, son of John Mount, 33, was born Feb 8, 1757; died Dec 17, 1832; married Hester Pettinger, born 1765

George Mount, like his father, John Mount, and his brother, John Mount, was a Loyalist, and all three were attainted.

1784, Feb 10 George Mount, late of Middletown, was the son of John Mount, who was attainted The father, [John Mount], was murdered by the Rebels, leaving a widow and a large family of children The Memorialist is his eldest son and heir-at-law His farm was about three miles from Middletown, and near the Shrewsbury River Evidence given by John Mount, (produces conveyances from his elder brother, of all rights, and a letter of attorney), second son of said John Mount, who was shot in September, 1779, says, he, John, now the claimant, is now twenty-two years of age, and lived with his mother until sixteen, when the Americans wanted him to join their army, on which he went off and joined the British Army in 1780 His father, [John Mount], owned two hundred acres, in Middletown, which came to him from his father, his father had owned it thirty-one years. He left a widow, who is now in possession of part of the house He left three sons and three daughters The claimant is the second son, Matthias is the third son, eldest sister, Chloe Thain, is now living in St John, second sister, Sarah Pentar, is in the States, third sister, Oria Mount, is now with her mother Witness Captain Tilton, being sworn, testifies that George is the eldest son, knew second son, John, whom the Americans wanted to serve at the age of sixteen George Mount, eldest son and heir of John Mount, arrived in New Brunswick, in June, 1787, with wife and two children American Loyalists MS., in Lenox Library, New York, Vol 16, p 171

His father was Master of a schooner in the Government's service, died without a will, stayed in New York until the evacuation, his wife was ill, and died about six months afterwards, his mother is living Idem, p 518

1788, Oct 17 George Mount makes affidavit

Issue

304 Matthias Mount, born Jan 26, 1795, died young
305 Matthias Mount, born Mch 1, 1797

---

*Tombstones in Hightstown Baptist Churchyard
Permelia, wife of *John L* Ely, died, July 23, 1850, aged 32 years and 9 months
Martha Rebecca, daughter of *John L* Ely, and Permelia Ely, died, Aug 22, 1853, aged 4 years, 10 months and 22 days

MOUNT OF MONMOUTH COUNTY

306 John Mount, born 3, 3, 1791; died 7, 12, 1839, married Barbara Myers, born 1795, died 1835.
307 George Mount, born 3, 5, 1799, died 183-, married Charlotte . . . . .
Issue
George Bell Mount, born 4, 3, 1822, of Philadelphia
308 James Mount, born 1, 6, 1808.
309 Sarah Mount, born 1, 19, 1786
310 James Mount, born 4, 25, 1788; died young.
311 Elizabeth Mount, born 3, 1, 1793
312 Hester Mount, born 8, 9, 1801, died young.
313 Hester Mount, born 1803
314 Martha Mount, born 10, 25, 1805.

120 JOHN MOUNT, son of John Mount, 33, was born 8, 22, 1764, yet, according to the preceding affidavit, the year of his birth is 1762 Sabine, in his American Loyalists, says, "John Mount went to St John, New Brunswick, at the peace, and was a grantee of that City He removed to Lancaster, in that Province, but died, while at St John, in 1819, aged fifty-seven " This statement would, likewise, make his birth date conform to 1762, but is it likely that Sabine drew his information from the manuscript just quoted

121 MATTHIAS MOUNT, son of John Mount, 33, was born Nov. 21, 1766, died Mch 16, 1809, married Martha . .

Issue
315 Euphemia Mount, died 1878, married Silleck Nichols

127 NESBIT MOUNT, reputed a son of Britton Mount, 42, was born Nov 11, 1767, died, Dec. 7, 1856, aged 89 years and 26 days, buried in Atlantic View Cemetery, Manasquan, married Ann (Nancy) Webb, according to her grandson, Joseph F Mount, born May 13, 1770, died, May 29, 1855, aged 85 years and 11 days

Issue
316 John Mount, born Nov 11, 1790
317 Lucretia Mount, born Mch 24, 1792
318 Umphry Mount, born Sept 14, 1794
319 Brittain Mount, born Aug 14, 1796, died, Apr. 10, 1831, aged 34 years, 7 months, and 27 days, married, Jan 29, 1818, Ann, daughter of Asher and Sarah (Osborn) Curtis, born Nov 4, 1796, died Nov 8, 1881
320 William Mount, born Mch 20, 1799
321 Joseph Mount, born Sept 10, 1801, died, Aug 26, 1874, aged 72 years, 11 month and 15 days, married, first, July 21, 1821, Catherine D Clayton, born July 28, 1800, second, Mch 26, 1845, Charlotte (Curtis) Allen, born Mch 15, 1812, died, Sept 29, 1877, aged 65 years, 6 months and 14 days
322 Zacharias Mount, born July 13, 1806, died, Feb 9, 1836, aged 29 years, 6 months and 26 days, married, Aug 2, 1833, Ann (Curtis) Mount, widow of his brother Brittain, born Nov. 4, 1796, died Nov 8, 1881
323 Elizabeth Mount, born July 1, 1808, married Benjamin Lewis
324 Susannah Mount, born Feb 10, 1811, died Jan 28, 1884, married, Feb 7, 1829, Samuel Hannaway, born May 20. 1806, died Apr 17, 1885

130 JOHN MOUNT, son of Matthias Mount, 47, married Elizabeth . . . .
1808, Feb 26 John Mount, Elijah Mount, and Matthew Rue, executors of Matthias Mount, late of West Windsor, conveyed to Richard Job, for $6,661 50, two hundred and twenty-eight acres

There are several deeds by John Mount, as executor of different estates

Issue

325 Gilbert Snowden Mount, baptized Feb 19, 1792
326 Margaret Chamberlain Mount, born 1794, baptized Apr 20, 1794

131 ELIJAH MOUNT, son of Matthias Mount, 47, is reputed to have married Mary Mount, and he is also accredited with a child, unnamed, by a wife, Lydia Barclay, who was baptized, at Cranbury, Feb 19, 1792

He was a Deacon of the Cranbury congregation, and is marked "Dismissed March 10, 1801."

1808, Feb 26 John Mount, Elijah Mount and Matthew Rue, executors of Matthias Mount, late of West Windsor, conveyed to Richard Job, for $6,661.50, two hundred and twenty-eight acres

He probably removed to Albany, N Y , and is said to have had four children.

1842, July 7 Elijah Mount, of Philadelphia, cabinet maker, and Susan H , his wife, are mentioned in Burlington deeds

Issue

327   Mount, baptized, at Cranbury, Feb. 19, 1792.

134 MATTHIAS MOUNT, son of Richard Mount, 48.

Matthias Mount, in his will, styles himself of Nottingham; commonly he is known as Matthias Mount, "of the Square," i e Hamilton Square, where he had an estate of one thousand acres. He died November, 1837, leaving a will recorded at Mount Holly, N J He married Elizabeth Chambers

"Tradition says he and his father were both in the War of the Revolution, enlisting from Middlesex Co , the original line of which was then only a short distance East of the Mount farm But it is highly probable that the family lived in Middlesex Co , and came to this section at the close of the war " Joseph H West, Esq

Issue

328 Richard C Mount, born 11, 19, 1789, died, July 23, 1864, aged 74 years, 8 months and 4 days, married, 1811, Theodosia Allen, born 1792, died, Aug 13, 1855, aged 63 years, 7 months and 15 days
329 Robert Mount, born 5, 1, 1791, died 10, 29, 1875, married Elizabeth Combs
330 Rebecca Mount, born 8, 2, 1792, married Thomas Combs
331 Samuel Mount, born 12, 6, 1793, died 5, 9, 1871; married, 1819, Rebecca (Combs) Allen, born 1796
332 Matthias Mount, "of the Square," as his father was also called, born 12, 19, 1801; died 5, 4, 1870, married Phebe (Rogers) Hooper
333 Elijah Mount, born 4, 17, 1803, died, 1857, aged 53 years, married Sarah (Schenck) Van Nest, died, 1876, aged 77 years
334 Mary Mount, born 1, 25, 1804, died 1894, married Elisha Jewell, of Penn's Neck.
335 Jane Mount, died young.
336 David Mount, died young

144 JAMES MOUNT, son of John Mount, 49, was born 1765, died 1840, married, first, Amy Combs, second, 10, 2, 1813, Permelia Emmons

1805, Apr 24 John Mount and Ann, his wife, and James Mount and Amey, his wife, of Maidenhead, Hunterdon Co , conveyed to John Chamberlain, of East Windsor, for £1,650, land, in East Windsor, "to which John Mount hath title by deed of sale from his father, Matthias Mount," dated Mar 25, 1783 Middlesex Co Deeds

Issue by first wife

337 John Mount (called Jonathan C), baptized, at Cranbury, Oct 9, 1791, died, 1813, aged 23 years
338 Thomas Cox Mount, born 11, 14, 1794, died, 8, 31, 1838, aged 43 years; married Mary B Hutchinson, born 1801, died 1878
339 David Combs Mount, born June 22, 1799, died 3, 19, 1869, married, first, Hutchinson, a twin sister to Mary B Hutchinson, born 1801, died, 1833, aged 30 years, second, Ann E Embly, died, 1897, aged 83 years
340 Ann Mount, born Apr 30, 1803, married Dr Slack

Issue by second wife

341 John Woodhull Mount, born 1814, died 1877, married, first, 9, 19, 1838, Matilda Veghte, married, second, 6, 3, 1848, Mary E Davis He was of New York City and later of Maryland
342 James Baldwin Mount, born 10, 14, 1815, died, 9, 23, 1837, single
343 Matthias B Mount, born 3, 23, 1817, died 5, 13, 1874, married, 1, 8, 1839, Cornelia Barber He was of New York City
344 George Alexander Mount, born 6, 30, 1820, died 12, 31, 1828
345 Hannah Mount, born 1829, died 1885, married Jesse A Kirk, of Maryland

Issue

Mount Emmons Kirk

149 JUDGE JOHN BAYLIS MOUNT, son of Humphrey Mount, 51, was born 1781, died 1864, married, first, Dec 30, 1801, Hannah Johnes, second, Jan 5, 1832, Effy, daughter of Richard and Lydia (Dey) Mount, and widow of James M Johnson. His children were baptized at Cranbury

Issue all by first wife

346 Daniel Johnes Mount, born Oct 2, 1802, died, 1828, unmarried.
347 Abigail Baylis Mount, born May 5, 1805, died 1896, married, Jan 27, 1831, Col Rescarrick Moore Smith, Treasurer of New Jersey
348 Hannah Mount, born Apr 8, 1809, married, Nov 23, 1830, Peter C Bergen, born 1792, died 1857
349 Stephen Mount
350 Hatty Mount; married . . . Rue.

Issue

Johns Rue, married Ellen (Baylis?)

140 SAMUEL H MOUNT,* son of Humphrey Mount, 51

1838, Feb 19 He made his will, proved Sept 20, 1838, as of Upper Freehold, and mentioned wife, Lucy, daughter, Lydia Ann Reed, and her daughter, Ellen Reed, daughters,

---

*It has been said that Samuel H Mount was a son of William, of the Allentown family, but this is incorrect

Hannah Applegate and Abigail Mount. Executor son, John S. Mount Both Samuel H. Mount and his wife are buried in the Allentown Presbyterian Cemetery

Issue

351 Lydia Ann Mount, married . Reed

Issue

Ellen Reed

352 Hannah Mount, married .. .. Applegate.
353 Abigail Mount
354 John S Mount, born 1812, died, about 1878, aged 66 years, married Abigail B. (Hulick?), died, 1889, aged 70 years Both are buried in Allentown Presbyterian Cemetery

151 DANIEL MOUNT, son of Humphrey Mount, 51, married Eliza P He died without issue.

1814, Dec 1 Daniel Mount, of Upper Freehold, conveyed to John B Mount, of East Windsor, for $2,100, part of land bequeathed to him by the will of the late Humphrey Mount, in East Windsor.

152 HUMPHREY MOUNT, son of Humphrey Mount, 51, was born June 13, 1790, married Millie Forman, daughter of Samuel P and Rebecca (Mount) Forman. If it is he who is buried in Allentown Presbyterian Cemetery, he died, Feb. 9, 1832, aged 40 years.

Issue

355 Humphrey Mount
356 Woodhull Foreman Mount, married Margaretta E. He was of Albany, and then of Philadelphia
357 Thornton Mount, died without issue.
358 Mary Elizabeth Mount

153 ANNA MOUNT, daughter of Humphrey Mount, 51, married, Oct 15, 1806, John Hulick Their children were baptized at Cranbury

Issue

Humphrey Mount Hulick, born July 31, 1807.
Hamilton Hulick, born Aug 1, 1809
Mary Ann Hulick, born Mch 3, 1813
Catherine Amanda Hulick, born July 22, 1815
Abigail Mount Hulick, born Sept. 19, 1818.
Daniel Mount Hulick, born Sept 1, 1821.

156 MATTHIAS MOUNT, son of Thomas Mount, 53, was born Mch 11, 1767, died Jan 23, 1848; married, first, Elizabeth Stephenson, born Jan 16, 1776, died Feb 16, 1805, second, Ann Elliott, born Jan. 23, 1778, died Mch 29, 1847. He removed to Kentucky and later to Indiana.

Issue by first wife

359 Mary Stephenson Mount, born Dec 15, 1791, married Benjamin Van Cleve.
360 Thomas Jolly Mount, born May 18, 1794, died May 30, 1842. He was of Indiana
361 James Mount, born July 11, 1797

362 William Mount, born Jan. 21, 1799, married Mary Still
363 John Mount, born Feb 15, 1802, died Feb 23, 1840, married Nancy Applegate, born Feb 23, 1802, died Apr or Nov 3, 1885 He was of Indiana
364 Stephenson Mount, born June or July 11, 1804, died about 1900 He was of Stony Centre, Iowa

Issue by second wife

365 Robert Elliott Mount, born Sept 4, 1806, married Mary Jones
366 Elizabeth Mount, born Feb 17, 1809, married George Clark
367 Matthias Mount, born Aug 7, 1810, of Indiana
368 Ann Jane Mount, born Feb. 7, 1812, married Hugh Van Cleve
369 Commodore Clayton Mount, born Oct 24, 1813, married Jane Gordon, was of Philadelphia, then Indiana.
370 Martha Mount, born May or June 30, 1818, died Mch 4, 1887, married Gordon Miller
371 Elijah McClure Mount, born May 22, 1820, died about 1906, married Rachel Miller. He was of Little York, Indiana

UNCONNECTED MOUNTS

1 THOMAS MOUNT and Penelope Smith, from New Jersey, settled at East Setauket, Long Island

Issue

2 Thomas S Mount; married Julia Hawkins
3 Judge John Mount

2 THOMAS S MOUNT, son of Thomas Mount, 1, by wife Julia Hawkins, had

Issue

4 Henry S Mount, born 1802, died 1841, married Mary Ford, of Flemington, N J Was an artist of less distinction than his brother, William S Mount
5 Shepherd Alonzo Mount, born 1804, married Elizabeth Elliott.
6 William Sidney Mount, born 1807, died 1868, unmarried—the well known artist
7 Robert Nelson Mount
8 Ruth Mount, married a Seabury.

There was a Moses Mount, of Monmouth County, who married Lydia Bills, in 1739, and died in 1748 He had a son, Moses, who was an aide to General Washington There is little doubt, if any, that this line belongs in George Mount's family, for, to quote Paul W Mount, in the Newark, N J, News, "the late Samuel Mount Schenck, Esq, mentions in his notes on the Mount family, that his mother, both of whose parents were Mounts, and direct descendants of George Mount, referred to Moses Mount, the son, who kept the hotel at Mount's Corner, now West Freehold, as having been a distant relative, but said 'she did not like to acknowledge it, as she did not countenance the business of the hotel.' Pretty hard on Moses, but as he had been an aide of General Washington, we can afford to feel charitable toward him Mr Schenck mentions, also, that this Moses Mount was a lover of fast horses and a great rider of race horses."

"Another old Mount trait, more commendable, perhaps, is found in connection with Nisbet Mount, previously referred to, who donated land in Manasquan, for a house of Public Worship, which, as deed expresses it, 'is to be free for all denominations professing Christians to worship Almighty God therein according to the dictates of their own conscience who are of good standing and moral character' This exhibited a broad-mindedness and tolerant spirit in rather a marked contrast to a unique church edict affecting another Mount, which I found in the Hightstown Baptist Church records It reads 'Richard Mount Excluded from Communion and Church Fellowship for non-attendance and keeping bad company joined the Presbyterians!'"

In printing the Mount genealogy I am content to give the first six generations, as my interest invariably wanes as I recede from the founder of a family and his immediate descendants, then again it becomes the legitimate province of some of the Mount blood to follow the lines to the present time, rather than it should fall to a student of many families I understand that this will be the case, for Mr. Paul W Mount is employing his facile pen to such an end To his contributions to the Newark (N J) News as well as to the communications of Mr J R. Mount, in the same sheet, I am much indebted, and above all would I recognize my obligations to my late esteemed friend, the Rev William White Hance, whose industry was as great as his work was accurate, and who was a helpful friend for many years.

MURPHY

OF

MONMOUTH COUNTY

TIMOTHY MURPHY was born, in Ireland, May 8, 1749, emigrated to America, in 1770, and died, May 8, 1812, aged 63 years He married, in Cohansey, Salem County, N J , in 1777, Mary, daughter of Abraham and Mary (Hartshorne) Garrison * She was born Apr 5, 1754, and died, May 2, 1834, aged 80 years and 27 days. He was a physician, a farmer, a school teacher, a Justice, etc

Shortly after his marriage, he purchased three hundred acres, five miles West of Middletown, at Bethany, where he and his wife lived and died, highly honored and respected in the community. They were pioneers in Methodism, and before that Society was strong enough to build a house of worship, his home was used as a place of worship, and a residence for all ministers

Timothy Murphy, on the outbreak of the Revolutionary War, served in the ranks at the Battle of Monmouth and elsewhere

Issue

2 Anna Murphy
3 William Murphy
4 John Garrison Murphy
5 Mary Murphy
6 Francis Murphy
7 Catharine Murphy, born, Jan 10, 1790, at Bethany, died, Feb 4, 1875, aged 85 years and 25 days, unmarried, at Freehold

---

*Abraham Garrison married Mary Hartshorne, who was born, in Middletown, N J , in 1716 He died in October, 1754, and she married, second, Elias Bailey,† and died, Jan 6, 1796, aged 80 years

Issue

John Garrison, born, at Middletown, Oct 11, 1744
Catharine Garrison, born, at Middletown Nov 28, 1746
Elizabeth Garrison, born, at Middletown, Apr. 14, 1748
Hartshorne Garrison, born, at Middletown May 5, 1750
Abigail Garrison born, at Middletown, May 5, 1753
Mary Garrison, born, at Middletown, Apr 5, 1754

†William, son of Elias Bailey and Mary Hartshorne, widow of Abraham Garrison, was born, in Middletown, Oct 18, 1759

8 Elizabeth Murphy, born Mch. 14, 1792, died, Sept. 20, 1877, aged 85 years, 6 months and 6 days, married Cornelius Walling, born Dec 22, 1769, died Oct 1, 1825 For issue see Walling Family
9 Joseph Murphy

2 ANNA MURPHY, daughter of Timothy Murphy, 1, was born, in Bethany, Middletown, N J , Oct 3, 1778, and died, May 2, 1863, in Brooklyn, N Y She married, first, Joseph Michell, at Bethany, in 1795, second, George Ingraham, of Rhode Island, in 1812, who was born July 8, 1764, and died Mch 6, 1832

Issue by first husband

10 Lauretta Michell, born August, 1796, married Samuel Ingraham, in October, 1816
11 Mary Michell, born Mch 11, 1798, married George Ingraham, Nov 16, 1816; and died Feb 17, 1858

Issue by second husband

12 Timothy Murphy Ingraham, born September, 1813, died December, 1813.
13 Rebecca Ingraham, born Aug 22, 1818, married, May 24, 1836, Crawford C. Smith, of Brooklyn, N Y

3 WILLIAM MURPHY, son of Timothy Murphy, 1, was born, at Bethany, Apr 19, 1780, married Phebe Burge, Dec 25, 1803, and died, Sept 23, 1847, aged 67 years, 5 months and 4 days She was born Apr 14, 1781, and died Sept 21, 1853

Issue

14 Timothy Murphy, born Mch. 13, 1805, died, at Keyport, July 29, 1887, unmarried
15 Richard Garrison Murphy, born Mch 26, 1808, died July 30, 1808.
16 William Murphy, born Nov 12, 1809, died May 2, 1810.
17 Mary Eliza Murphy, born Apr 5, 1817, died Sept 9, 1821.
18 William Murphy, born Mch 29, 1820, died May 19, 1843

4 JOHN GARRISON MURPHY, son of Timothy Murphy, 1, was born, at Bethany, Jan 7, 1783, and died, Feb 11, 1853, in Brooklyn, N Y He married, first, Clarissa Runyon, of Princeton, N J , who was born Aug 15, 1785, and died July 30, 1824, second, Mch 20, 1825, Caroline Applegate, who was born July 8, 1808 His widow married, August, 1854, Elijah Stout, and died Jan 24, 1881

Issue by first wife

19 Henry Cruse Murphy, born, in Brooklyn, N Y , July 3, 1810, died Dec 1, 1882, married, July 29, 1833, Amelia Greenwood, of Haverstraw, N Y , born July 10, 1813
20 Mary Murphy, born June 27, 1812, died young
21 Catharine Murphy, born Apr. 25, 1818, married, first, Horatio C. Riley, Jan 9, 1841 He died Dec 30, 1843 She married, second, Francis B Fitch, Dec 20, 1844, who died Sept 10, 1870 She married, third, Winfield S Mitchell, Feb 19, 1885

Issue by second wife

22 Mary Applegate Murphy, born Dec 12, 1825, married Robert B. Clark
23 John G. Murphy, born Apr 22, 1828, died Jan 2, 1853

MURPHY OF MONMOUTH COUNTY

24 Clarissa Murphy, born Apr 24, 1830, died May 11, 1863, married George H Ford
25 Caroline Amelia Murphy, born Mch 19, 1833, married William S Thorn
26 Francis Asbury Murphy, born Aug 17, 1836, died Sept. 27, 1882.
27 William W Riley Murphy, born Apr 10, 1839, died Jan 26, 1844.

5   MARY MURPHY, daughter of Timothy Murphy, 1, was born, at Bethany, Oct. 2, 1784; married, Oct. 7, 1804, Richard Greenwood, born in 1776, and died Mch 29, 1825

Issue

28 Eliza Booth Greenwood, born Dec 24, 1805
29 Henry Greenwood, born May 13, 1803
30 Adeline Greenwood, born Oct 23, 1808.
31 Mary Hannah Greenwood, born Feb 24, 1810
32 Sophia Greenwood, born Sept 16, 1811
33 Amelia Greenwood, born July 10, 1813, married Henry C Murphy
34 Richard B Greenwood, born Oct 16, 1815
35 William Murphy Greenwood, born Jan. 12, 1819.
36 Benjamin Greenwood, born Nov 20, 1821.
37 Joseph B Greenwood, born Jan. 18, 1824

6   FRANCIS MURPHY, son of Timothy Murphy, 1, was born, at Bethany, Feb. 10, 1788; died Oct. 8, 1866, married Ann Bray, Apr. 18, 1811. She was born Mch 6, 1794, and died Dec. 14, 1870

Issue

38 John Wesley Murphy, born Aug 7, 1812, married Lauretta Chandler.
39 Caroline Knott Murphy, born Nov 7, 1814, married Frank Hatfield.
40 Frances Amelia Murphy, born Sept 20, 1817, died Mch 16, 1885; married John S. Stillwell, who died Sept 30, 1883
41 Timothy Ingraham Murphy, born July 14, 1819, married, first, Catharine Grant, Nov 24, 1841 She was born July 4, 1818, and died, at Keyport, N J, June 2, 1873, married, second, Isabella S Kisner, Aug 22, 1875, born June 12, 1842
42 Ann Ogborne Murphy, born Dec 6, 1821; married Rev Garner Snyder, May 2, 1849, born Feb 27, 1821
43 Catharine Elizabeth Murphy, born Nov 24, 1845, died Oct. 17, 1873, married, first, Aaron Peck, second, William Concklin
44 Mary Hartshorne Murphy, born Nov 5, 1827, died Dec 16, 1828.
45 James Henry Murphy, born June 2, 1830, died Feb 26, 1831
46 Mary Garrison Murphy, born Dec 3, 1831, unmarried.
47 William Spafford Murphy, born Apr. 30, 1834, died Mch 8, 1883, married Mary E Burnham, Aug 5, 1857, born Sept. 29, 1834.
48 Francis Asbury Murphy, born Apr 1, 1837, married, first, Carrie Ward, of Brooklyn, N Y, Nov 1, 1859, born June 20, 1838, and died Nov 4, 1872, married, second, Josephine A Silva, of Brooklyn, N. Y, Apr 30, 1874, born May 1, 1851

9   JUDGE JOSEPH MURPHY, of Freehold, son of Timothy Murphy, 1, was born Jan 1, 1797, died May 6, 1884, married Alice Holmes, Jan 1, 1820, born Aug 2, 1802, and died July 18, 1880.

Issue

49 Timothy Murphy, born Apr. 30, 1821.
50 Holmes W Murphy, born Nov 28, 1822.
51 Louisa S. Murphy, born Dec. 4, 1826.
52 Phebe Murphy, born Oct. 14, 1828; died Oct 17, 1866
53 Catharine Murphy, born July 20, 1830
54 Joseph Garrison Murphy, born Apr. 18, 1834, died Sept 20, 1866
55 Ann Elizabeth Murphy, born July 15, 1838; died Feb. 13, 1879
56 William Henry Murphy, born Apr 11, 1846, died Feb 19, 1850.

OGBORNE

OF

MONMOUTH COUNTY

In the Church of St Olave's, Hart Street, London, England, there is erected a monument to the memory of Sir William Ogborne·

Near this
Place Lyes the Body
of Sr WILLIAM OGBORNE Kn.
who dyed October 13th 1734 aged 72
He was Mafter Carpenter to the
Office of Ordnance 35 Years
Sherriff of this City,
Colonel of the Militia,
An Elder Brother of the Trinity Houfe,
And one of his Majeftry's Juftices &c;
A moft tender Hufband, loving Parent
Sincere & kind Friend, a Man of great
Piety and Vertue, mix'd with much
Candor and Humanity;
Endued with a Noble and
Generous Difpofition,
Always ready to Comfort
and relieve the Poor
and in every Circumftance
of Life worthy Imitation

Alfo the LADY JOYCE
Relict of S^r. Wm OGBORNE K^t
who Departed this Life
Augt. 4th 1744

Malcolm's London, 1807, Vol IV, and Rev Alfred Povah's "The Annals of St Olave's, Hart St., and Allhallows Staining"

Will of Sir William Ogborne, dated Oct. 5, and proved Oct 23, 1734, in which he mentions himself as "Kn^t, Citizen and Carpenter" of Rosemary Lane, Parish of St Mary, White Chapel, County of Middlesex, and makes the following bequests:

The freehold property, in Cheapside and Lawrence Lane, in occupancy, and an empty house adjoining, he gives to his wife Dame Joyce, and also the residence, in Rosemary Lane, during her lifetime, she paying £20, in half-yearly payments, to his Grandson, Ogborne Churchill

Upon his wife's demise, these properties are given to his Grandson, Ogborne Churchill and Grand-daughter, Sarah Churchill, equally In case both die before twenty-one years of age and leave no heirs, then these properties are to be equally divided between St Thomas' Hospital, Southwark, County of Surrey, and The Carpenters' Guild, of London, for the benefit of their poor.

The testator also gave to his wife his coach, his chariot horses, plate, hay, corn, etc. He owned many houses leased to many individuals

To his sister, Mary Bedson, of Tower St, London, widow, he gave the other three messuages in Rosemary Lane, in occupancy These properties at her decease to his Grandson, Ogborne Churchill and Grand-daughter, Sarah Churchill, who were his chief legatees, and in case of no issue to either of the grandchildren, the properties to St Thomas' Hospital and The Carpenters' Guild, as mentioned above

To his wife Joyce one-third of his personal estate, as widow's thirds, and one-third "to my daughter, Mary Churchill," and the remaining one-third to his widow Joyce.

To his Grandson, Richard Churchill, £200, as he, being the eldest son of his father and mother, was amply provided for as heir of his parents in their marriage settlement.

To Walter Coleman, his son-in-law, Woolen Draper, of Black Fryerres, London, £200.

To the Poor of Trinity House, £100

To the Poor Quakers, of Ratcliffe Meeting, £20, to be distributed by his son-in-law, Walter Coleman, and his wife, Dame Joyce

To the Poor of the Carpenters' Guild

To Thomas Ogborne, of Hillingdon, County of Middlesex, Labourer, £10

His widow, Dame Joyce, to pay £1,000, due on purchase of property in Cheapside

Executors Walter Coleman and his wife, Dame Joyce

Witnesses J^{no} Martin, Sam^{ll} Troughton and Hudson Tastolf [or Tastotf].

His widow, Dame Joyce, died about ten years later, and was mentioned in her will as of Greenwich, Kent County, England. She was doubtless a second wife for she mentions none of his legatees, except "Sister Mary Bedson " She willed her estate to her kinspeople, females, by the names of Williams, Clopton and Searles, and the residue of her estate to her nephew, William Singleton, of St Christophers, West Indies She made many bequests of good size to friends and servants

"Mr Deputy Merry of Southwark was educated in this school [i e the Charity School] in grateful remembrance of which he has left to it the reversion of property amounting to 200£ a year after the death of Mr. Ogborn, stationer in Bishopsgate street " "Mr Merry also left to the school the reversion of 4500£ Three per cent Consols after the decease of three persons named in his will and 1000£ South Sea Annuities "
Manning and Bray's History of Surrey, Vol III, p 630

"   Ogbourn, Esq," 1724, was a benefactor of the Guilford Library.
Manning and Bray's History of Surrey, Vol I, p 77

1859, Apr 9 Frederick William Ogborn, who was born on this date, in Bristol, England, has brothers residing in that city, namely Harry, George, Alfred and Edward Ogborn. They are Quakers.

In New Jersey the name was favorably known through the State for many years, especially in the vicinity of Middletown, but now, save in its application to the site of an old homestead, "Annie Ogborne's Corners," on the road between Middletown and Holmdel, it is extinct.

In 1900, even this name is lost, for to this locality the name on the sign-board and in Ellis' History has been corrupted to Ogden.

The Ogbornes were socially a prominent family, but, with few exceptions, held no political positions. Through the female side of the house have descended the late Amos R. Manning, Esq., of the Supreme Court of Alabama, the Hon. Edward Scudder, of the Supreme Court of New Jersey; Prof. John Stillwell Schenck, of Princeton College; the Drs. Stillwell, of New York City; Ex-Governor Bedle, of New Jersey; the Taylors, of Middletown, N. J., and others.

John Ogborne and Samuel Ogborne were early settlers in Burlington County, N. J.

1 JOHN OGBORNE

1684, 6, 11mo. John Ogbourne bought of Joseph Blowers, for £110, a house recently erected, in Burlington, and one hundred and fifty acres.

1685. John Ogborne recorded his cattle-mark, at Burlington.

1686, 3, 6mo. He, then residing at Burlington, sold the above property to Walter Humphary, of Burlington, Carpenter, for £110.

1691, 2, 4mo. John Ogbourne, yeoman, of Burlington County, bought one hundred and fifty acres, in the First Division of lands, from Charles Reade, of the town of Burlington.

1694. John Ogborne located three hundred acres of land at Oneamickon, in Springfield, which he sold, in 1697, to Eleazor Fenton.

1699, Apr 20. John Ogborne, of Burlington County, carpenter, bought, for £31, from Thomas Kendall, bricklayer, of Burlington County, a lot, in Burlington, on the High Street.

1699, Apr 29. Thomas Kendall, of Burlington, for £31, sold to John Ogborne, of Burlington, a lot on High Street.

1701. He was Town Clerk, of Burlington.

1707, Apr 4. Thomas Kendall, of Burlington, sold, for £100, to John Ogborne, of Springfield, carpenter, property on High Street, in Burlington, near the Market House.

1711, May 3. Richard Ridgway, of Springfield, for £100, sold to John Ogborne, of Springfield, yeoman, one hundred and fifty acres, in the township called Mattacopeny.

1716, Nov. 19. Will of John Ogborne, of Springfield, proved Mch 28, 1720, mentioned
Wife, but no name is given, "now in England."
Daughter, Sarah, "now in England."
Daughter-in-law, Anna, wife of John Hocton [Stockton?]
Grandson, John Ogborn
Grand-daughter, Hannah
Francis Roe, widdow, a bequest
Grand-daughters, Sarah and Anna, daughters of his deceased son, John Ogborne
    Elizabeth, Mary and Hannah, daughters of his deceased son, William Ogborne

1719–20, Mch 15. The inventory of the personal estate of John Ogborne, taken this date, amounted to £178-6-7½.

Issue

2 John Ogborne

3 William Ogborne
4 Sarah Ogborne

2 JOHN OGBORNE, son of John Ogborne, 1, died, at Burlington, intestate, leaving a widow, Ann, who applied for administration on his estate, which was granted Feb 14 [22], 1713–14 He was an innholder, and the inventory of his personal estate amounted to £310-17-4.

1704, Jan. 8. James Wild, of Burlington, sold, for £55, a lot on High Street, to John Ogborne, Jr, of Burlington County

1694, Jan 22 John Ogborne, Jr, of Mansfield, near Burlington, bought for £20, of George Hutchinson, of Burlington County, three hundred acres of land.

1709, June 8 A petition from Ann Kendall and John Ogburn, Jr, of this date, praying leave to sell land was considered at various times by the New Jersey Assembly, and, Dec. 29, 1709, after "reading and examining of severall deeds, accounts and other writings, the sd Committee . resolved that they did not think fitt to take any farther cognizance of the sd petition"

John Ogbourn died, Jan 31, 1713–14, aged 41 years.
St. Mary's Churchyard, Burlington, N J
His widow married John Hocton or Stockton

Issue, as per his father's will.
5 Sarah Ogborne
6 Anna Ogborne

3 WILLIAM OGBORNE, son of John Ogborne, 1, married, in 1698, Mary Cole, by license dated Nov 17, 1698

"William Ogborne married Mary Cole, at house of Daniel Leeds, at Springfield, Nov. 17, 1698, by Justice Daniel Leeds," and in presence of many witnesses, whose names are not given. Apparently this marriage was in open court

1695 William Ogborne, of Burlington County, bought one hundred acres, for £12, from John Snape

1696 William Ogbourne was a witness.

1700, 3 of 5 mo. William Ogborne was a witness to the marriage of Samuel Lippincott, of Burlington, to Ann Hulett, of Shrewsbury, at the Shrewsbury Meeting House

1708–9, Jan 18 Will of William Ogborne, proved Apr. 8, 1714, mentioned
Wife, Mary
Father, John
Son, John Ogborne, a minor
Daughters, Elizabeth
Mary
Hannah
Executors his father, John Ogborne, his wife, and Samuel Lippincott

William Ogbourn died, Feb. 17, 1713, aged 43 years
St. Mary's Churchyard, Burlington, N. J.
The inventory of his personal estate amounted to £296-7-6.

Issue
7 Elizabeth Ogborne, of Burlington, married, John, son of Joseph Pancoast, 6 mo., 1724

OGBORNE OF MONMOUTH COUNTY

    8 Mary Ogborne; married, Joseph, son of William Pancoast, of Mansfield, 8 mo , 14, 1731   Burlington Quaker Records.
    9 Hannah Ogborne
  10 John Ogborne

    6 ANNA OGBORNE, daughter of John Ogborne, 2.

Ann, daughter of John Ogborne, Jr , had a license issued June 25, 1728, to marry Jobe Lippincott.

Jobe Lippincott died, May 31, 1759, aged 51 years.   St. Mary's Churchyard, Burlington, N J
Ann, his wife, died, Apr. 15, 1791, aged 85 years   St Mary's Churchyard, Burlington, N J

        Issue

  11 Joseph Lippincott; died, in 1752, aged 8 years.
                                St. Mary's Churchyard, Burlington, N J

   10 JOHN OGBORNE, son of William Ogborne, 3

John Ogborn, of Burlington County, married Sarah, daughter of Caleb Shreve, at Chesterfield Meeting, 1, 19, 1723–4.   Chesterfield Meeting Records

"John Ogborn, 12, 3, 172-, had a certificate to marry in Chesterfield Meeting."
                                                         Burlington Meeting Records.

    1718, 27, 6 mo. John Shinn sold to John Ogborne, Jr., both of Springfield, for £28, three hundred acres of land in Springfield.

    1745, Jan 8 John Ogborne, carpenter, of Burlington County, sold to James Wilde, for £155, land, on the Highway, in Burlington City.

        Issue, attributed·

As the descendants of John Ogborne, bearing his name, became extinct, except in the person of John Ogborne, 10, I am disposed to credit him, John Ogborne, 10, with the following children

        12 Caleb Ogborne   See his issue under Miscellaneous Notes
        13 John Ogborne, married Hannah Warner
        14 Sarah Ogborne, married, by license dated Oct 18, 1769, John Warner, of Middlesex Co.
        15 Joseph Ogborne   It was probably he who was a witness to the will of John Quicksall, Jr., of Nottingham, Sept. 6, 1783, and probably it was also he who was taxed, in Upper Freehold, in 1790–91, for a house and lot, one and a half acres of land and one cow

   13 JOHN OGBORNE, son of John Ogborne, 10, is probably he who was buried in old Crosswicks Methodist Churchyard

John Ogborne died, Oct. 15, 1814, in his 69th year   Hannah Ogborne, his widow, died, Feb 13, 1832, in her 84th year.

John Ogborne, of Burlington, was licensed to marry Hannah Warner, Mch 23, 1769

        Issue

      16 Letitia Ogborne, buried adjacent to and in line with her parents   Letitia, widow of Aaron Stewards, died, Sept 13, 1850, in her 81st year   She was the second wife of Aaron, son of John and Martha (Robins) Steward

1 SAMUEL OGBORNE was also a resident of Burlington, and contemporary with John Ogborne, and no doubt of kin

1685, 3 mo., 29 Jane Ogbourne was present at the birth of Ann, the daughter of Thomas and Hester Butcher   Register of Burlington Monthly Meeting.

1686, 3, 9 Samuel and Jane Ogborne, Sarah Harvie, and others, were witnesses to the marriage of William Atkinson and Elizabeth Curtis   Burlington Quaker Records

1693, Aug 9 William Fryley, of Burlington, carpenter, sold to Samuel Ogbourne, of the same place, carpenter, for £13, one-fifth part of an acre, lying on the High Street, in Burlington, bounded by Christof Weatherill on the West, etc., etc., being part of the town lot late belonging to George Hutcheson

1695, Mch 26 John Harwood, of Springfield, Burlington County, yeoman, sold to Jane Ogborne, widow, of the town of Burlington, for £80, a house and ninety acres, which was previously sold by her husband, Samuel Ogborne, to said Harwood, lying near Matoropan Bridge, South of Maple Creek, and North of the Great Swamp.

1695, June 8 Jane, the widow of the aforesaid Samuel Ogbourne, sold, as executrix, the preceding purchase of 1693, fronting on High Street, with forty-six feet front and one hundred and twenty-one feet, ten inches in depth, with stone, wood, timber and other materials, which Samuel Ogborne had gotten together, intending to build on the said site, for £52, to Lyonell Britton, of Philadelphia   She made her mark to the deed.

1697 May 27. Jane Ogborne, of Springfield, Burlington County, widow, sold lands to Richard Ridgway, of the same place.

1694, Nov 7 Will of Samuel Ogborne, of Burlington, sick, etc., proved Dec. 8, 1694, mentioned
"dearly beloved wife, Jane "
He gave £5 to each of his children, at the discretion of his executrix, if so much remains when they are brought up
Executor   wife, Jane   His brother-in-law, Peter Harvey, trustee and assistant
The will was written and signed by the testator, and was a fine specimen of caligraphy

Daniel Leeds, of Burlington, Gent., and William Atkinson, of Burlington, yeoman, went on her bond   She made her mark

1694, 21, 9br The inventory of his personal estate, of this date, amounted to £127-11-7.

Jane, daughter of Thomas and Jane Curtis and wife of Samuel Ogborne, was born, at Bugbrook, Northampton, England, 2mo., 11, 1661
Records of Northampton Monthly Meeting

Jean Curtis, the widow of Samuel Ogborne, must have been an attractive woman, for, upon her husband's demise, she married, second, John Hampton, of Freehold, and after his death, became the wife of Nathaniel Fitz-Randolph, of Woodbridge, N J, and he dying, she married, fourth, John Sharp, of Gloucester, whom she outlived

Issue

2 Samuel Ogborne
3 Mary Ogborne, married, in 1707, in Evesham Meeting, John Engle; married, in 1727, Jonas Cattell, married, in 1732, Thomas French   By John Engle, she had
Issue
Robert Engle
Jane Engle, married Mr. Turner

John Engle
Mary Engle, married Mr Lippincott,
Hannah Engle, married Mr Lippincott

4 Sarah Ogborne, permission granted Edmond Kinsey and Sarah Ogborne to marry, 21, 8, 1708   Friends' Records, Plainfield, N. J.

Issue

Samuel Kinsey
David Kinsey
Mary Kinsey, married Mr. Fell
Elizabeth Kinsey; married Mr. Smith.
John Kinsey
Joseph Kinsey
Sarah Kinsey; married Mr. Smith
Benjamin Kinsey
Jonathan Kinsey

By her second marriage, to John Hampton, Jane Curtis had

Issue

Joseph Hampton; died in 1767; married Mary Canby,

Issue

Sarah Hampton, married Mr Wilson
John Hampton
Benjamin Hampton
Jane Hampton, unmarried.
Joseph Hampton
David Hampton
Mary Hampton, married Mr Stokes.

John Hampton married, first, Janet . . . . .; second, Martha Brown, by whom he had most of his children.

1702 He died at Freehold, Monmouth County

1702, Jan 23 Will of John Hampton, proved Feb 26, 1702, mentioned
Wife, Jane, [his third wife], and her children before "our marriage," Sarah and Mary Ogborne, to whom he left a legacy
Daughter, Janet Ray, and her children.
Daughter, Elizabeth Hampton
Daughter, Lydia Hampton
Sons, John Hampton
     David Hampton
     Andrew Hampton
     Jonathan Hampton
     Noah Hampton
     Joseph Hampton, a son by his wife, Jane
Executors wife, Jane, and Robert Ray

1698, May 12. John Hamton, of Freehold, and wife Jane, sold a house, in Burlington, late in the tenure of Samuel Ogborne, former husband of Jane Hampton, to John Borradaill, of Burlington

By her third marriage, to Nathaniel Fitz-Randolph, Jane Curtis had

Issue

Benjamin Fitz-Randolph, born 10, 23, 1707.

Nathaniel Fitzrandolph, of Woodbridge, and Jane Hampton, of Freehold, were married 4mo., 12, 1706. Records of Shrewsbury, N. J., Monthly Meeting.
John and Grace Kinsey, who was a Fitz-Randolph, were among the witnesses

1713, "fift day of ye third month Commonly Called may." Will of Nathaniell fitz-Randolph, of woodbridge, Co of midelsex, planter, "am att the writing hearof of a found perfect disposing Minde"; proved by John Kinfey, a witness, May 12, 1714, mentioned:

"to my Grandfon Isaac fitz Randolph ye ten pounds that is in my fon famuell fitz Randolph hands and ye Interest of ye money that wafs and is part of it due to me from my fd fon and also the Interest of money that wafs Due to me from Jofeph fitz Randolph my fon"

"to my youngest fon Benjamin fitz Randolph the twenty-two accers and one half be it more or lefs of land that I had of my fhare ot ve last diuision in Raway Neck and also my free hold that Belongs to my land and me out of ye lands yett in Comon in woodbride ... with the appurtenances thereunto Belonging and ye free hold aforefaid To him ye faid Benjamin fitz Randolph his heirs ... always prouided . that in Case my faid fon Benjamin fhould Die before he ariues to the age of twenty-one years that then faid land and freehold fhall be fold and ye price of it to be Diuided Betwenn the furuiuors of my fons and my Grandfon the sd Isaac fitz Randolph fhare . like Equaly also to my faid fon Benjamin thirty pounds out of my moueable Eftate to be putt out to Interest within fourteen months after my Deceas by my Executrix and trustees ... untill my fon Comes to twenty one years . . prouided alwayes . that in Cafe my fon Benjamin Dies afore he ariues to ye age of twenty-one that then y[e] fd thirty pounds with ye Interest shall be Equaly Diuided between ye furuiuors of my wife and Sons . and grandson Isaac fitz Randolph". ...

"I gue . the fheep that is att John Nokes to Be Equaly Diuided Between my faid fon Benjamin and my fon In law Joseph Hamton and Thomas Nessmith fhare ... alike"..

"to my welbeloued wife all things of what Kinde quanntity quality or Value whatfoever which belongs or appertaines To my personall or moueable Efstate for her ... and her heirs for her owen Confortable maintainenanc and maintenance and fcooling wafhing & Clothing of my faid fon Benjamin fitz Randolph During his minority"

Executor. "my faid wife to be my whole and fole Executrix."
Overseers "my well Efteemed freinds, John Laing and John Kinfey, and my fon famuell fitz-Randolph" "and by Councell help Execute this my laft will ."
Witnesses. John Laing, William Laing, Edward ffitz-Randolph and John Kinsey
The testator made his mark to the will

1714, May 12 Declaration of "Jean, the widdow & Executrix of . . . Nathaniel fitz randolph," before Thomas Gordon, Surrogate.
Recorded in Lib. I, continued, p 483, Trenton, N J

1715, 2mo., 15 At a monthly meeting, at Woodbridge, of this date, Jane Fitzrandolph requested a certificate of removal for herself, her son-in-law, Edmond Kinsey, and his wife, to Falls Monthly Meeting Minutes of Woodbridge Monthly Meeting

1715, 8mo., 5 At a monthly meeting, at Falls, of this date, Edmond Kinsey, wife, and mother-in-law, produced a certificate of removal from Woodbridge Monthly Meeting
Minutes of Falls Monthly Meeting, Bucks County, Pa

1719, 8mo., 7 At a monthly meeting, at Falls, of this date, Jane Fitzrandolph was granted a certificate of removal Minutes of Falls Monthly Meeting.

John Sharp, of Evesham, Burlington County, and Jane Fitzrandle, widow, were married 10 mo., 20, 1719 Records of Haddonfield Monthly Meeting.

1725, 3mo., 17. Will of John Sharp, of Evesham, Burlington County; proved Mch. 29, 1727, mentioned
Wife, Jane
Sons, William
  John
  Thomas
  Samuel

Former wife, Elizabeth Green, [i e his second wife]
Daughters, Elizabeth Sharp
    Sarah Sharp
    Hannah Adams

1729, "8th day of ye 6th month called August." Will of Jane Sharp, of Buckingham, in ye County of Bucks and province of Pensilvania, widow, proved Dec 13, 1731, mentioned.
"to my son Samuel Ogburn the sum of 8 pounds proclamation money"
"to my son Joseph Hampton 12 pound"
"to my son in law Edmond Kinsey 5 pounds"
"to my son in law Jonas Ketle 5 pound."
"to my son Benjamin Fitzrandle twenty pound and also one bed and 2 pair of sheets 2 pillows and 2 pairs of pillow cases 1 diper table cloth 3 blankets one bird eyed coverlidd one silver spoon one great Bible one great looking glass one pair iron doggs"
"to my Grand daughter Jane engle a great pewter dish"
"to my daughter Mary Ketle 25 pound"
"to my daughter Sarah Kinsey 25 pound."
"after my legacies is payd if any money remains let it be given to my two daughters and Jo Hampton"
"to my daughter Mary's three daughters and to my daughter's Sarah's three daughters and to my son Joseph Hampton's one daughter (who are all now living) 7 pound in Siluer and Gold, twenty shillings apeace each"
"to Mary Kinsey and Elizabeth Kinsey each of them one trunck"
"all my horse and mares be sold or valued and the value of them to pay all charges to my executors that may accrue to them by funeral expenses or any otherwise whatsoever upon my account and . after legacys and other charges are all payd if any thing remains of value I hereby give . . it to Edmond Kinsey, but if it should so happen that my estate shall fall short of paying my legacyes and all charges then . all Legtees shall abate their proportion according to their shares"
"I give . my executors . forty shillings apiece."
Executors "my son in law Edmond Kinsey and Joseph Fell"
Witnesses John Hill and Elizabeth Fell
The testator made her mark to the will

1731, 28th of Xber The inventory of her personal estate was exhibited, which was made 18th day of the Ninth Month, 1731, by John Hill and John Walton, and amounted to £118-10-9.

  2 SAMUEL OGBORNE, son of Samuel Ogborne, 1, was born Dec. 25, 1684, and died Apr 25, 1768 He married Abigail. . , who died Dec. 3, 1760

1712, July 29 He purchased of Hendrick Gulick and wife, Katharine, one hundred and twenty acres, in Middletown, and in the deed is mentioned as "of Hopewell, in Burlington County, N J., wheelwright." The consideration was £185, and the witnesses were John Bray, Joseph Ashton and William Lawrence, Jr.

1713, 1st Tuesday in June Samuel Ogburn was fined £0-13-4, with others, for default in serving on the Grand Jury Court of Quarter Sessions, Shrewsbury. Freehold Records

1713. Nov. 5 He was a resident of Middletown, and bought three acres of land at Shoal Harbor, for £5, from John Smith, of Middletown

In 1715, having become identified with the town, he was chosen an Overseer of the Poor, and from this date onward, he was an active man, his name frequently occurring in the records as an office holder.

1721 and 1722. Samuel Ogborn was on the Grand Jury

In 1739, possibly earlier, he was a Justice of the Peace, a position he occupied as late as 1756.

1761. Samuel Ogborn appeared on the Assessment List of Middletown.

Their family Bible, and a will made, in 1751, by Samuel Ogborne, which was revoked, are now in the possession of Dr J E Stillwell, New York City, and another will, which was probated, of later date, both enumerating the same children and devising a considerable estate

Issue

    5 Mary Ogborne, born June 10, 1711.
    6 Samuel Ogborne, born Dec 26, 1712.
    7 John Ogborne, born Dec 12, 1714
    8 Sarah Ogborne, born Feb 12, 1715
    9 Abigail Ogborne, born Oct 13, 1718
   10 Elizabeth Ogborne, born Dec 23, 1720.

5 MARY OGBORNE, daughter of Samuel Ogborne, 2, was born June 10, 1711, and died Dec. 30, 1772 She married Edward Taylor, a large land holder and merchant in Middletown, who was the son of George, and grandson of Edward Taylor, the Emigrant He was born Aug. 20, 1712, and died Jan. 18, 1783

Issue

    Col George Taylor, born Jan. 29, 1733
    Samuel Taylor, born Nov. 28, 1735, died young
    Eleanor Taylor, born Dec 27, 1737; married Fenwick Lyell.
    John Taylor, born Mch 25, 1740.
    Joseph Taylor, born Aug. 26, 1742

7 JOHN OGBORNE, son of Samuel Ogborne, 2, was born Dec 12, 1714, married Mary, daughter of Gershom and Elizabeth (Grover) Stillwell, who was born Apr. 2, 1718.

1760, Aug. 25 John Ogborne died.

1760 Letters of administration were granted Mary, widow of John Ogborne, of Monmouth County.

1760, Nov 4 Bond for £300, of Mary Ogborne, widow and administratrix of John Ogborne, was signed by John Stillwell, Jr , of Middletown, yeoman She and her bondsman made fine signatures

1760, Nov 15 The inventory of the personal estate of John Ogborne, deceased, late of Middletown, was made by Joseph Golden and William Crawford, appraisers, and amounted to £196–10–2.

1761, May 25 Mary Ogborne, widow and administratrix, filed the inventory of her deceased husband

1765, Oct 8 Mary Ogborne, wife of John Ogborne, died

1765 Letters of administration were granted to William Applegate, on the estate of Mary Ogborne, late of Middletown, a relative, who lately died intestate

1765, Oct 12 Bond for £400 was signed by Wm Applegate and Edward Taylor, both of Middletown, yeoman, for the administering of her estate

1765, Oct 15 The inventory of the personal estate of Mary Ogborne, of Middletown, deceased, was exhibited, signed by William Applegate, as administrator, and Richard Crawford and Joseph Golden, appraisers, and amounted to £104–15–0. Elsewhere the amount is given as about £150.

1766, Oct 2 The above inventory was filed Among the items appears "6 silver spoons and 6 silver teaspoons £4–10–0"

> *Issue*
> 11 Samuel Ogborne, born 1740, died, Jan. 3, 1816, aged 75 years, 11 months and 25 days
> 12 William Ogborne; died about 1822.
> 13 Mary Ogborne, born 1742, died, Jan. 9, 1820, aged 77 years, 9 months and 19 days
> 14 Sarah Ogborne, born 1745; died, Oct 28, 1817, aged 72 years, 8 months and 14 days
> 15 Hannah Ogborne
> 16 Anne Ogborne
> 17 Elizabeth Ogborne, born Apr 3, 1738

8 SARAH OGBORNE, daughter of Samuel Ogborne, 2, was born Feb 12, 1715, married Obadiah Holmes, by license dated Nov 2, 1747 He was the son of Obadiah, who was a son of Jonathan, who was a son of the Rev Obadiah Holmes, of Rhode Island He died in 1752 She died Oct 20, 1774

> *Issue*
> Huldah Holmes, married Chryneonce Van Mater
> > *Issue*
> > Lloyd Van Mater, married Miss Longstreet Henry H. Longstreet, of Holmdel, has Ogborne silver.
> Rhoda Holmes, married Capt John Schanck, moved to Ohio
> Obadiah Holmes

9 ABIGAIL OGBORNE, daughter of Samuel Ogborne, 2, was born Oct. 13, 1718, married Edward Taylor, of Freehold, by license dated Oct 17, 1757 He was the son of William Taylor, who was the son of Edward Taylor, the Emigrant They had no issue She died Sept 3, 1770, and he married, second, Susan Erickson He was called Edward Taylor, "the stutterer" His mother was Hannah, daughter, probably, of James Grover.

10 ELIZABETH OGBORNE, daughter of Samuel Ogborne, 2, was born Dec 23, 1720 She was single, in 1760, as per her father's will, but subsequently married Humphrey Wall, by license dated Mch 6, 1765, son of Garret and grandson of Garret Wall, the Emigrant Humphrey Wall was murdered in Burlington County and "Old Si" was hung for it
In the Wall Burying-ground, Middletown, are two stones with the following inscriptions
Humphrey Wall died, April 11, 1795, aged 74 years, 9 months and 28 days
Elizabeth, wife of Humphrey Wall, died, March 26, 1800, aged 79 years, 3 months and 3 days

11 SAMUEL OGBORNE, son of John Ogborne, 7, was born Jan 9, 1740, and died, Jan 3, 1816, aged 75 years, 11 months and 25 days He married, by license dated Jan 5, 1765, Ann, daughter of Guisbert van Brackle and Rachel Brittain, a woman possessed of many admirable qualities, who was born May 8, 1744, and died, Dec 21, 1831, aged 87 years, 7 months and 13 days They resided in and were buried in the town of Holmdel
The names of their children and grandchildren were obtained from their wills, recorded at Freehold, and from papers, in the possession of Miss Dorset, of Matawan, a sister of Governor Bedle's mother, the record of most of their births Miss Dorset has likewise an old Delft bowl, some silver, which has been melted over, and a large cedar chest, which had

belonged to some of the first Ogbornes Perhaps all of these things were bought at the vendue of his aunt Abigail's effects, following her demise

1805 May 20 He purchased land from the Trustees of the Baptist Church, of Middletown, probably the present site of Ogborne's Corners

1806, May 9 He sold this and other property, extending from his location to Richard Crawford's Corner, and land at Tinton, for $1143 , to Matthias W. Covenhoven

Issue

18 John Ogborne, born Dec 15, 1771
19 Mary Ogborne, born Oct 9, 1766
20 Rachel Ogborne, born Nov. 5, 1774
21 Ann Ogborne, born Mch 23, 1778
22 Sarah Ogborne, born Apr. 15, 1784.
23 Rhoda Ogborne, born Jan. 28, 1765

The following grandchildren were mentioned in the wills of their grandparents, Samuel and Ann (Van Brackle) Ogborne, also their three sons-in-law, Peter Schenck, James Bray and Joseph Dorset, who were nominated as executors

Ichabod Ogborne
Mary and Amelia Bray
Louette and Catharine Bray
Ann Murphy
Ann Schanck
Ann Applegate
Ann Dorset

Be it Remembered that I Gifbert Van brocle on this twenty thurd Day of february in the Year of Our Lord one Thoufand Seven hundred and fourty three foure Do Bind My Self By Promife Unto John Dorfett and James Mott Executers of the Laft Will * * * of Samuel Dorfett Deceaft for the Love Good Will and affection that I Bare to My Wife Rachel and to her tow Children Elizabeth Dorfitt and Mary Dorfett and in confideration of a legafy Left to My Wife Rachel By her Deceafed hufband Samuel Dorfett that I will take into My Special Care Said elifabeth Dorfett and Mary Dorfett to Edicate and Bring up at My own Care and Coft Without Any further Demand on the Eftate of Said Deceafed Samuel Dorfett

in Witnefs Whareof I Set My hand

In the Prefents of   GIFBERT VAN BRACKLE
ABRAHAM SMITH
JOHN WALL   Cherry Hall Papers

Know all Men By thefe Prefents that We Samuel Ogborne And Anne Ogborne Wife of Said Samuel Ogborne and Daughter of Gifebert Van brocle Deceaft Bothe of the townfhip of Middletown and County of Monmouth and Colliny of Newierfey are held and firmly Bound Unto Steven Van brockle and James Mott Executers of Gifebert Van brockle Deceaft * * * * Dated this fifth Day of May in the Sixth Year of his majefties Reign And In the Year of Ower lord * * * * * 1766 * * *

Signed Sealed and Delivered   SAMUEL OGBORNE
In Prefens of   ANNA OGBORNE
JONATHAN PEAIRS
RACHEL PEAIRS   Cherry Hall Papers

Know all Men By thefe Prefents that we Rachel Van brocle And Samuel Ogborne Juner Bothe of the townfhip of Middletown and County of Monmouth And Colliny of New Jerfey are held And firmly Bound unto Steven Van brockel and James Mott Executors of Gifbert Van brockel Deceaft In the Juft and full Sum of Eighty Six Pounds Mony at Fight Shillings the Ounce to Be Paid Unto the Said Steven Vanbrockel and James Mott * * *

Dated this Twenty nine Day of October in the Sixth Year of the Reign of Ower Soveran king Gorge the third And in the Yeare of Ower lord * * * One thoufand Seven hundred and Sixty Six, 1766

The Condition of the above written obligation I[s] Such that Whareas the Above Named Steven Vanbrocle and James Mott hath Payed Unto the Above Named Rachel Vanbockel Daughter of the Above named Gifbert Van brockel the Sum of fourty three Pounds Mony at Eight Shillings the Ounce Being full half of all the Estate of Gifbert van brockel Deceaft In the hands of Said Steven Vanbrockel and James Mott
Signed Sealed and Delivered
In the Prefents of
RACHEL PEARS
MARY VANDER HOEF

RACHEL VANBRAKEL
SAMUEL OGBORNE, JR
Cherry Hall Papers

12 WILLIAM OGBORNE, son of John Ogborne, 7, married Rebecca Perine, of Freehold He resided, first, at Middletown, where he and his wife, June 6, 1784, sold property to Anthony Layton, and in later years, at Freehold

1779, Apr 9 He transferred the property which his grandfather, Samuel Ogborne, had purchased, in 1712 and 1715, and another piece, bought of Joseph Golden, in 1720, and which he devised to his grandsons, Samuel and William Ogborne, to his brother, Samuel Ogborne. He died about 1822 He was a private in Lieutenant Barnes Smock's Troop of Light Dragoons, Monmouth County, during the Revolutionary War

Issue

24 Henry Ogborne, who had one son and one daughter
25 Sarah Ogborne, married Jacob Niverson She died, in 1879, aged 88 years They had seven children
26 William Ogborne, married Rhoda Martin
27 Samuel Ogborne, died aged about five years
28 Elizabeth Ogborne, died unmarried
29 Lydia Ogborne, married Abraham Tunis, of Tinton Falls She died about 1850.

Issue

John Tunis
Several daughters

30 Harriet Ogborne, the youngest, married John Harris She was living in 1879 Among her children is Mrs Eliza Bishop, widow of Capt Bishop, of Keyport, N J
31 Susan Ogborne, died young.
32 John Ogborne [?]

13 MARY OGBORNE, daughter of John Ogborne, 7, was born in March, 1742, and died, Jan 9, 1820, aged 77 years, 9 months and 19 days She married, by license dated Oct 19, 1761, Joseph Stillwell, Esq , son of John and Mercy (Burrowes) Stillwell, of Nutswamp, who was born Sept 28, 1739, and died Mch 8, 1805

Issue

Major John Stillwell, born Sept 19, 1762
Dr William Stillwell, born Jan 6, 1768
Joseph Stillwell, born Sept 17, 1765
Mary Stillwell, born Feb 12, 1766
Ann Stillwell, born Sept 13, 1778

14 SARAH OGBORNE, daughter of John Ogborne, 7, married William Stillwell, son of Thomas, son of Thomas and Alice (Throckmorton) Stillwell She died, Oct 28 1817, aged 72 years, 8 months and 14 days They resided in Nutswamp

Issue

William Stillwell, "Lame Billy," married Miss Patterson.
Thomas Stillwell [?]
Sarah Stillwell, married Mr. Patterson.

    Issue

    Katy Patterson
    Rebecca Patterson
    Stillwell Patterson

Rhoda Stillwell, married James Brannon
Martha Stillwell, married Joseph Cooper, of Nutswamp, whose first wife was Euphame Layton

15 HANNAH OGBORNE, daughter of John Ogborne, 7, married, first, Mr Maxin, second, David Thorp

    Issue

Anne Maxin; married Daniel Smith. They had twelve or thirteen children.

    Issue

Eldest son, married Deborah, daughter of Maj. John Stillwell.

    Issue

Daughter, married Sidney McClain
Daughter, married Mr Daly, of New York.
Mary Thorp, married William Taylor.

    Issue

Hannah Taylor, married Sylvanus C. Bedell.
Jane Thorp, married Asher Stillwell. For their issue, see Stillwell Genealogy.

17 ELIZABETH OGBORNE, daughter of John Ogborne, 7, married William Applegate, Mch 9, 1758.

    Issue

Richard Applegate; married a daughter of John Stillwell, of Garrat's Hill.
Mary Applegate, married Mr Hoff.
et al

18 JOHN OGBORNE, son of Samuel Ogborne, 11, probably married Ida . . , and had a daughter, Rhoda, and one other child. He died, July 18, 1847, in his 76th year, and was buried in Holmdel, N J

Asher Taylor, Esq, said John Ogborne died without issue

19 MARY (POLLY) OGBORNE, daughter of Samuel Ogborne, 11, married, first, Samuel Bray, second, Stout Holmes, who was born July 24, 1756, and died, Jan. 27, 1817, aged 60 years and 8 months He lies buried in Holmdel, N. J She married, third, Major John Stillwell She died, Sept 21, 1831, aged 64 years, 11 months and 18 days, and lies buried in the Holmdel Baptist Churchyard, under the name of Holmes. She was the second wife of Major John Stillwell about two years

I have spoken with several who were present at her third marriage, the Applegates, Dorsets and others She lived with Joseph, son of Major John Stillwell, for a while, but finally went to

Freehold, where she died and was buried. She was a cousin of her husband, Major John Stillwell.

Issue by first husband

Samuel Bray
Rachel Bray
Mary Bray
Ann Bray

Issue by second husband

Alice Holmes, married Judge Murphy, of Freehold.
Lydia Holmes, married William Wyckoff, of near Keyport, N. J.

20 RACHEL OGBORNE, daughter of Samuel Ogborne, 11, married, first, James Bray, who died, Sept 1, 1810, aged 37 years, 11 months and 29 days. Bray "cleared out", it is said he was poisoned. She married, second, Mr. Bent. By him she probably had one child. Mr Bent disappeared. She died, Feb 20, 1855, aged 80 years, 3 months and 15 days. Her portrait is in the possession of George W. Bell, Esq., of Matawan.
Rachel Ogborne had a daughter, Lauretta, who married, first, Mr Harris, second, Mr Bell.

Issue

Ann Bray; eldest; married Mr Murphy. She was a lovely old lady and brought up her brothers and sisters.
Catharine Winter Bray, died, July 29, 1837, aged 36 years, 7 months and 3 days
David Bray
Samuel Ogborne Bray, died, Nov. 10, 1802, aged 5 years and 14 days
Samuel Ogborne Bray; died, Mch 27, 1872, aged 69 years, 4 months and 20 days
   He married Elizabeth   , who died, Apr 2, 1858, aged 48 years and 20 days

21 ANN OGBORNE, daughter of Samuel Ogborne, 11, had a son, Ichabod, who died, Dec 21, 1841, aged 44 years and 5 days. She lived, and died, at Ogborne's Corners, Oct 16, 1847, aged 69 years, 6 months and 23 days.

22 SALLY OGBORNE, daughter of Samuel Ogborne, 11, married, first, Joseph Dorset, of Matawan. She married, second, Oliver Sprouls, and died, May 24, 1858, aged 74 years, 1 month and 9 days.

Issue

Ann Dorset
Hannah Dorset
Joseph Dorset

23 RHODA OGBORNE, daughter of Samuel Ogborne, 11, married Peter Schanck. She died, Aug 21, 1848, aged 83 years, 1 month and 24 days. Her husband died, June 6, 1837, aged 71 years and 10 days.

Issue

Rhoda Schenck, died, Jan. 28, 1821, aged 20 years, 5 months and 4 days
Sarah Schenck; died, Dec 22, 1823, aged 27 years and 20 days
John P Schenck, died, Feb. 10, 1863, aged 57 years, 6 months and 23 days

26 WILLIAM OGBORNE, son of William Ogborne, 12, was born Apr. 7, 1787, and died, Dec 26, 1851, aged 62, 8, 19 He married, first, Rhoda Martin, born Sept 16, 1789, who died, July   , 1820, in her 31st year. He married, second, Rachel   ., born May 8, 1799, died Sept 20, 1873. He was a resident of Upper Freehold. William Ogborne and his two wives are buried in the Baptist Churchyard, Hightstown, N J

1810, May 7 With his wife, Rhoda, he conveyed property to Joshua Barker.
1819 With the same wife, he conveyed property to Hiram Mount

Issue

33 Mary Ogborne, born July 12, 1806
34 Hannah Ogborne, born Oct 9, 1807
35 Robert Jones Ogborne, born May 10, 1810.
36 Elizabeth Ogborne, born Nov 13, 1812
37 Sarah Ann Ogborne, born Dec 10, 1815
38 Lydia Ogborne, born Oct 13, 1816, living, in 1878, at 1225 Shackamaxon St, Philadelphia, Pa , married Mr. Way.
39 Rhoda Ogborne, born Sept 28, 1818
40 William Ogborne, born Mch 21, 1820
41 Mary B Ogborne, born Nov 8, 1825
42 Rachel Ogborne, born Feb 16, 1827; living in 1878
43 Henry Ogborne, born Aug 13, 1828.
44 Archibald R Ogborne, born Apr 27, 1830, living in 1878
45 Mary Elizabeth Ogborne, born June 14, 1834.
46 Emmaline Ogborne, born Jan 8, 1836
47 Ezekiel Ogborne, born May 30, 1837.
48 Rebecca R Ogborne, born Sept 21, 1839
49 Henry C Ogborne, born Oct 3, 1844

35 ROBERT JONES OGBORNE, son of William Ogborne, 26, was born May 10, 1810, married Elizabeth Neal. They resided at Hightstown, N J, where they had ten children born, four of whom died in infancy

Issue

50 Rev Willard N Ogborne, of Smith's Landing, N. J., in 1878.
51 Abner R Ogborne, married Emma L., daughter of Col. James and Sarah (Scroggy) Burk
52 Rebecca Ogborne, married Enoch Dey

Issue

Elmer E. Dey
Viola Dey
Mary E. Dey

53 Samuel M Ogborne
54 Lydia M Ogborne, married Ernest W McIlvaine

Issue

Ernest W McIlvaine

55 Joanna Ogborne; married Joseph Ketchum

Issue

Hannah Ketchum

42 RACHEL OGBORNE, daughter of William Ogborne, 26, married John R. Ely. She was living, in 1878, at Harlington or Harlingen, N J, and corresponded with me, supplying the preceding transcript of the Family Bible, in the possession, at one time, of her mother.

50 REV. WILLARD N. OGBORNE, son of Robert J Ogborne, 35, died prior to 1907 He married, first, Phebe Seely, and second, Olivia Van Duyn.

Issue by first wife
56 Willard Ogborne

Issue by second wife
57 Gertrude Ogborne
58 Harold Ogborne

51 ABNER R OGBORNE, son of Robert J Ogborne, 35, married Emma L, daughter of Col James and Sarah (Scroggy) Burk, Scotch people.

Issue
59 Sarah Elizabeth Ogborne
60 Robert J Ogborne, of New York City
61 Le Roy Ogborne

53 SAMUEL M. OGBORNE, son of Robert J Ogborne, 35, married Addie Springer
Issue
62 Isaac Ogborne

MISCELLANEOUS NOTES

The name Ogborne has been variously spelled Ogborn, Ogbourne and Ogburn

There was a noted English engraver of this name in 1788

Mrs. William Van Tine, the Tunis family, at Eatontown, N. J, and John Walton, of Tom's River, N J, could give additional information about the Monmouth County Ogbornes

1721, Dec 18 Letters of guardianship were granted to William Ogborn, as guardian of his sister, Mary Ogborn, by William Burnet, Esq., the Governor.

1841, 4 mo, 18 Ann Ogborn died aged about 82 years   Quaker Records, Burlington, N J.
1729, Sept. 11. Anne Ogburn, of Burlington, licensed to marry Benjamin Butterworth

The similarity of the names Osborn and Ogborn occasions confusion and creates doubt as to certain individuals

1754. Samuel Osborn, of Shrewsbury, made his will. In it he mentioned his eldest daughter, Alice Longstreet

1759 The estate of William Osburn, of Shrewsbury, was inventoried, and among the appraisers was Samuel Osburn.   The deceased left a large estate

1765 The inventory of the estate of Ann Ogborn, widow, deceased, so written inside, is endorsed "Inventory of Ann Osborne, of Monmouth Co Filed 1765," and amounted to about £50, and included:

"to a silver tankard, Two silver spoons £10–0–0"

Samuel Longstreet appeared as an executor, and Thomas Bell and Samuel Ogborn, as appraisers I feel certain that she was an Osborn and not an Ogborne

1 CALEB OGBORN, son of . . . . .
   Issue
   2 Caleb Ogborn, of Mount Holly, N. J.

2 CALEB OGBORN, son of Caleb Ogborn, 1, of Mount Holly, N J, married Ann, daughter of Joseph Parker

1773, July 9. Perhaps it was he who was a witness to the will of Thomas Woodward, of Upper Freehold, N J, at this date

1778 and 1779 Caleb Ogborn was on Friends' Service.

   Issue
   3 Joseph P Ogborn, born Mch 10, 1785
   4 Daniel Ogborn, born May 27, 1786
   5 Samuel Ogborn, born Mch 14, 1788.
   6 William Ogborn, born Feb 12, 1790
   7 Phebe Ogborn, born Nov 30, 1791, married Benjamin Parker.
   8 Eliza or Elizabeth Ogborn, born June 15, 1793, married Samuel Fenton
   9 Fothergill Ogborn, born June 14, 1795, married Sarah Wills Owen
   10 Stephen Ogborn, born Jan 14, 1797
   11 Caleb Ogborn, born Feb 6, 1799

5 SAMUEL OGBORN, son of Caleb Ogborn, 2, was born Mch 14, 1788, and married Esther, daughter of Isaac and Rebecca Andrews, born Nov 11, 1784 They were married in 1811. Esther Andrews' sister, Betsy, also married an Ogborn Samuel Ogborn left New Jersey and settled in Waynesville, O, some time before 1823 Later, he moved to near Washington, twelve miles West of Richmond, Wayne County, Ind., where he died July 13, 1838 His wife, Esther, died about 1864

   Issue
   12 Joseph Ogborn, born Feb 9, 1812
   13 Mary Ogborn, born Sept 9, 1814.
   14 Allen W. Ogborn } born Aug 25, 1816 } twins.
   15 Edwin F Ogborn
   16 Evan A. Ogborn, born Mch 20, 1819
   17 Lydia Ogborn, born Jan 3, 1821
   18 Ezra E. Ogborn, born Nov 25, 1823
   19 Ann Ogborn, born Oct 2, 1825
   20 Joel E Ogborn, born Mch 16, 1828. He was living in 1900, the last of his family, at New Sharon, Iowa He married Martha . . Her mother's youngest brother, Jacob Cooper, lives in New Brunswick, N J, and is connected with the college there He has five children living in 1900, one, a daughter, is a missionary in China.

9 FOTHERGILL OGBORN, son of Caleb Ogborn, 2, married Sarah Wills Owen

Issue

21 Elizabeth Ogborn, married Mr Phillips, living, in Westchester, Penn , in 1900, aged about sixty-five years
22 Morris Ogborn, of Philadelphia, Pa , a merchant.
23 Emma Ogborn, married Mr Jones.
24 Brothers

18 EZRA E OGBORN, son of Samuel Ogborn, 5, was born, Nov. 25, 1823, in Waynesville, Warren County, O , his parents having formerly lived in New Jersey, probably at Little Egg Harbor He married, Aug 25, 1847, in Wayne County, Ind , Mary Ann, daughter of the Rev. Rany and Margaret Gillam, born Dec 13, 1829

Issue

25 C. H Ogborn
Twelve other children, six of whom are now living, in 1900

The foregoing line is compiled from information contained in the letter of C H Ogborn, Esq , of Kingman, Kansas, dated July 26, 1900, to the Rev W. N. Ogborn, of Hammonton, N J , and some additions of my own

Mr Ogborn further states

"There is a tradition in the family that the Ogborns were formerly very wealthy potters, in Wales, and drifted from there into England, from whence they were driven, being Quakers, by the persecutions of those good people and that they settled in New Jersey, in 1684 Of this, except that they really were Quakers, I do not know

If this information proves of interest to you I could give you considerable of information in regard to the younger branches of the family

I presume all the Ogborns in America are related though a great many generations removed

There is one branch of the family spelling their name—'*Ogburn,*' which settled, in the Southern states, long, long ago, coming from England

Do you know anything of the Ogborns prior to their coming to America?

There are two places named in the Universal Postal Union Directory called 'Ogbourne'—I believe in England—I can find them for you Perhaps these places were named for some ancient ancestor of ours "

POTTER

OF

MONMOUTH COUNTY

1 THOMAS POTTER came from Rhode Island and settled in Monmouth County, N. J He died 10th of 12 mo, 1703 He married, first, Ann   , who died, in Shrewsbury, 1st of 2 mo, 1694, second, Sarah Bickley,* widow of Mr Lawrence, by Justice John Hance, 1 mo, 29, 1695, she married, third, Henry Graves, who died prior to 1720

In 1670, Thomas Potter had five hundred and fifty-two acres.

1670-71, Mch 10 Thomas Potter, of Shrewsbury, bought Anthony Page's towne share of land, in Middletown, being lot number 12, and reconveyed it to Page, Nov 28, 1671

1672, Nov 27 Nicholas David sold to Thomas Potter two shares, at Potapeck

1676, Oct 21 Thomas Potter, of Deale, in Shrewsbury, husbandman, sold to Therlaugh Swiney and Francis Jeffry, of Deale, land, which he had recently purchased of the Indians

1677 He held two hundred and forty and five hundred acres of land and meadow, "Being one of the Patentees"

In 1679, he held one thousand and fifty-two acres.

1681, Jan 10 Thomas Potter paid quit-rents on three parcels of land, "due 1670," at Deal, near Shrewsbury, N J.

1684, 21, 11mo Thomas Potter signed by his mark, the inventory of Thomas White, carpenter, late of Shrewsbury, N J

In 1686, Thomas Potter and John Tucker paid quit-rents on one thousand acres of land

In 1688, Thomas Potter paid quit-rents on lands, in Shrewsbury, N J

1692, Mch 20 John Starkee [Tucker?], of Monmouth County, and Mary, his wife, in the name and behalf of Mary Channelhouse, late of the same place, to Thomas Potter, for £70 Mary Channelhouse was the daughter of Adam Channelhouse, deceased. Both Starkee and his wife made their marks to the deed

---

*1695, 29, 1mo Thomas Potter and Sarah Lawrence, both of Shrewsbury, N J, were married by John Hance Witnesses
  Thos Cooke   Abram Bickley
  Wm West   Susannah Bickley
  Elisha Allen   Margaret West
  Richd Chambers   Elizabeth Cook

1691 William Bickley, merchant, of New York, bought land of Restore Lippincott, of Shrewsbury
1696 William Bickley, shopkeeper of New York, with Susannah Bickley, for £125, paid by Thomas Potter, of Shrewsbury husbandman, sold to Abraham Bickley, of Burlington, land, in Shrewsbury
1696 Abraham Bickley of Burlington, conveyed this to

John Starkey, for £15, payable to Thomas Potter, gave a deed, to be confirmed by Mary. Chanelhouse, at the age of twenty-one.

1694, Dec 1 Thomas Potter, of Shrewsbury, appoints, as his agent, "my loving son-in-law and loving friend John Woolley," of the same place, yeoman

1700, Sept 11 Thomas Potter made a deposition, concerning the boundary of land, in Shrewsbury, in which he declared himself to be "aged about seaventie years," hence born about 1630

Thomas Potter moved from Shrewsbury to Freehold, N J

1702, Nov. 2 Will of Thomas Potter, proved Nov 1, 1704, mentioned
Wife, Sarah, and created her sole executrix.
Sons, Ephraim
      Thomas
Daughters, Susannah
        Elizabeth
        Mercy Woolley

1703-4, Feb 24 In an inventory of his personal estate, he is spoken of as yeoman, late of Shrewsbury, which was taken by John Williams and George Curleis, and amounted to £198-03-00.

1709, Nov. 2. John Williams, aged upwards of three score years, and George Curleis, near fifty, both of Shrewsbury, testified to the accuracy of the above inventory, before Justice Samuel Dennis

1709, Dec 19 Sarah Potter, widow and executrix, of Thomas Potter, in a conveyance to Thomas White, mentioned "her loving father, William Bickley, late of New York, deceased"

        Issue by first wife
2 Mercy Potter, married John Woolley.
3 Mary Potter, born, at Newport, R I , July, 1664, according to Austin She was born in Rhode Island, as per Shrewsbury Quaker Record, but the date is obliterated I consider Mercy Potter, 2, and Mary Potter, 3, the same person, inasmuch as this Mary Potter married John Woolley, and Mercy (Potter) Woolley, calling herself Mercy Woolley in an affidavit, was called by her father in his will Mary Woolley. It is well, however, to read the footnote on page 130, Vol. III, in conjunction with this assertion
4 Ephraim Potter

        Issue by second wife
5 Thomas Potter
6 Susannah Potter
7 Elizabeth Potter

4 EPHRAIM POTTER, son of Thomas Potter, 1, married, first, Sarah, daughter of Abraham Brown, who was born, in Shrewsbury, 20 of 5mo , 1669. She died 6, 9mo , 1715 He then married, second, Mary Chambers, widow of Nicholas Brown, and daughter of John and Mary Chambers He died 11 month, 1717

Ephraim Potter was born, at Shrewsbury, as per the Quaker Records, 24, 6mo , —— [the year is obliterated]

1704, Mch 1 Ephraim Potter, of Shrewsbury, planter, bought of Nicholas Wainwright, of Shrewsbury, and wife, Mary, for £60, land, in Shrewsbury, that Nicholas Wainwright had bought from Edward Woolley Feb 1, 1700

1716, Oct 31 Ephraim Potter, of Shrewsbury, was a party to a tripartite agreement, of this date, by which he, and "Mary Brown, widow of Nicholas, who is about to marry the said Ephraim Potter," convey to Richard Chambers, Esq, brother of Mary Brown, all her property received from the late Nicholas Brown, her husband, as per his will written Feb. 21, 1711 The said Richard Chambers to hold the same, in trust, for the said Mary Brown, and to be returned or distributed at her option. This was an antenuptial contract made to secure her rights and to put her in position to transmit her estate to her daughter Mary.

          EPHRAIM POTTER [his mark.]
          MARY BROWN
          RICHARD CHAMBERS.

1716, Dec. 25 Will of Ephraim Potter, a resident of Shrewsbury, sick, etc., proved Apr. 15, 1717, mentioned

Loving wife, Mary Potter, for whom he made liberal provision during her widowhood, giving her the use of certain rooms in his house, the use of one-half of the orchard, firewood, cattle, horse, etc, and all the goods she brought with her that were formerly Nicholas Brown's

Son, Ephraim Potter, "a pair of Worsted combs, now in his own possession"
Daughter, Ann Potter, received 5 shillings
Daughter, Marcy Jackson, received 5 shillings
Son, John Potter, £20, when he arrives at the age of twenty-one
Daughter, Martha Potter, received 40 shillings
Daughter, Catharine Potter, received 5 shillings
Daughter, Leah Potter, received 5 shillings
Son, Abram Potter, a two year old heifer.
Daughter, Preserve Potter, received 5 shillings
Son, Joseph Potter, £5, when he arrives at the age of twenty-one
Son, Nicholas Potter, received the plantation, lands and improvements thereon, if he pays the debt still owing on the same, and the legacies mentioned in the will In the event of Nicholas Potter refusing so to do, the estate is to be sold and other provisions are made

Executors Richard Chambers, Jno Lippincott, Jr, and William Woolley, son of John Woolley
The testator signed the will by his mark

An inventory of his estate was taken by Jeremiah Stillwell and Gabriel Steele, and amounted to £74-9-6

Items:
Wearing "apparrell"   £6-0-0
Cattle, hogs, etc   42-0-0
One silver spoon, etc   1-0-0

1707, Apr. 19 Nicholas Brown, of Shrewsbury, conveyed to Alexander Innes, clerk, John Reid and Thomas Bell, in trust for his intended wife, Mary Chambers, one hundred and forty acres of land.

In 1712, Nicholas Brown having died, Mary Brown, his widow, intending to marry Ephraim Potter, conveyed these lands in trust for herself, to her brother, Richard Chambers.

1716, Oct. 31. Richard Chambers, upon the death of Ephraim Potter, husband of his sister, Mary, released these lands to her, Mary Potter.

1729, Jan 24 Mary Chambers, now married to her third husband, William Exceen, joined by her husband, William Exceen, and her daughter, Mary Brown, made a conveyance of these lands, as conveyed to her and her daughter, Mary Brown, in the will of her former husband, Nicholas Brown, to William Woolley, of Shrewsbury

         Perth Amboy and Trenton, N J, Deeds

Issue by first wife
8 Thomas Potter, born, in Shrewsbury, 18, 12mo., 1689, living in 1716.

9 Marcy Potter, born, in Shrewsbury, 8, 12mo , 1690, married Hugh Jackson, she was living in 1716
10 Ann Potter, born, in Shrewsbury, 1, 2mo , 1693, living in 1716
11 Ephraim Potter, born, in Shrewsbury, 30, 9mo , 1694, married Miss Woodmansie, living in 1716.
12 Nicholas Potter, born, in Shrewsbury, 19, 7mo , 1697, living in 1716
13 Martha Potter, born, in Shrewsbury, 22, 6mo , 1699, living in 1716
14 John Potter, born, in Shrewsbury, 24, 1mo., 1700–01, living in 1716
15 Catharine Potter, born, in Shrewsbury, 23, 7mo , 1702, died Mch 16, 1762; married Peter Knott, born 1681; died Feb 15, 1770
16 Abraham Potter, born, in Shrewsbury, 1, 2mo , 1704, living in 1716.
17 Amos Potter, born, in Shrewsbury, 23, 8mo , 1705, died 9, 1mo , 1705–6.
18 Preserve Potter, born 22, 12mo , 1706, died 1747
19 Leah Potter, born, in Shrewsbury, 6, 1mo , 1707, living in 1716
20 Joseph Potter, born, in Shrewsbury, 8, 6mo , 1709-10, married, first, 6, 12mo , 1736, Rebekah Champlice, second, 12, 2mo. [or 2, 12mo.], 1753, Abigail, daughter of Peter and Lydia (Bills) Tilton, born 7, 2mo [or 22, 7mo.], 1723.

8 THOMAS POTTER, son of Ephraim Potter, 4

1712, 4th Tuesday in February. County Court of Sessions, Shrewsbury, N J

In an indictment "for Killing of Six small hoggs on ye land of ye s^d Alfree," Indian Peter, a servant of Alfree, Thomas Potter and Thomas Alfere, Alfree or Affere, were bound in their recognizance   Court Records, Freehold, N J

9 MARCY POTTER, daughter of Ephraim Potter, 4, was born 8, 12mo , 1690, and was living in 1716

Marcy Potter had married prior to Dec 25, 1716, as per her father's will, in which she is mentioned as "Marcy Jackson."

1729, Dec 13 Nicholas Potter, of Shrewsbury, quit-claimed his interests to his loving brother-in-law, Hugh Jackson, in land, lying in Shrewsbury

10 ANN POTTER, daughter of Ephraim Potter, 4

1712, 4th Tuesday in February County Court of Sessions, Shrewsbury, N J

Bill against "Robert Edmonds for gitting a bastard Child on ye body of Anne Potter & they brought it in "

Child "Cald Nicholas Lately borne of Anne Potter in June last," apprentice to Cornelious Lain, by consent of Robert Edmonds, until he attains the age of twenty-one years
                 Court Records, Freehold, N J

11 EPHRAIM POTTER, son of Ephraim Potter, 4.

It is probably Ephraim Potter, 11, who is referred to in the following will

1733, Sept 22 Will of Thomas Woodmansee, of Shrewsbury, yeoman, proved June 11, 1737, mentioned
    Wife, but not named
    Son, Thomas, received 5 shillings
    Son, John, received £5
    Son, David, received £5
    Son, Gabriel, received £5

Daughter, Sarah, received £4
Daughter, Elizabeth, received £4
Daughter, Hannah, received £4
Daughter, Margaret, received £4.
"to my son-in-law," Ephraim Potter, 1 shilling
Daughter, Leadea, received £4
Daughter, Abigail, received £4
Daughter, Ann, received £4
The testator directed that his plantatiom, in Shrewsbury, and his interest in lands, in or near New London, in New England, to be disposed of by his executors
Executors   his wife, and Jno Littel and George Williams, both of Shrewsbury
Witnesses   Richard Higgins, John Woodmansee and David Woodmansee
The testator signed his name to the will

12   NICHOLAS POTTER, son of Ephraim Potter, 4, was born, in Shrewsbury, 19, 7mo., 1697

1729, Dec 13. He was living in Shrewsbury, when he made a conveyance of his interests, in lands, in that town, to his brother-in-law, Hugh Jackson, who had married his sister, Mercy Potter

18   PRESERVE POTTER, son of Ephraim Potter, 4, died in 1747-8

1742, July 22   He married, by license, Catherine Cunningham

1746, "Twenteth Eight" of June. Will of Prefarue Potter, of Shrewsbury, Monmouth County, Labourer, proved Jan 27, 1747/8, mentioned.
Katharine, his "Dearly beloued wife," received her wearing apparel and 7 shillings
"Dutifull and well beloued Son, Thomas, ⅔ of rite to take up land, which I bought of Robert Savage."
"Dutiful and well beloued Daughter, Hannah," a bed, etc.
"beloued Son, Robert, 5 shillings"
"beloued Daughter, Deborah, £5"
The remainder of the estate to be equally divided between his son, Thomas, and daughter, Hannah
"beloued Brother's, Jofeph Potter's son, Jacob," residuary legatee
Executors   "Loueing Brother Jofeph Potter & my trofty frind, Jofeph Patterson
Witnesses   William Newbray, his mark, Jon Herring and Hen Herbert.
The testator signed his name in full to the will

Joseph Potter qualified as executor, by affirmation, being one of the people "Call'd Quakers"

1747/8, Mch 17   Jofeph Patterfon renounced his executorship of Prefarve Potter's will
1747 '8, 15 day of 11mo   The inventory of "preferue potter" was taken by "John Williams, Cordwinder, and Joseph potter," and amounted to £39-07-06.

Issue

21 Thomas Potter
22 Hannah Potter
23 Robert Potter
24 Deborah Potter

20   JOSEPH POTTER, son of Ephraim Potter, 4, is named, as an executor, in the will of his brother, Preserve Potter, 18, and therein is stated to have a son, Jacob, in 1746.

Issue

25 Jacob Potter

MISCELLANEOUS NOTES

There were Potters residing in Woodbridge, N J

George, Robert and Nathaniel Potter were early settlers in Rhode Island

1693, Sept 18 Richard Potter had a license to marry Katharine Reay   New York Wills

1697, Nov 8 Marmaduke Potter married Mary Bingla.

No date "Hannah Potter deceased in the county of Monmouth "
Quaker Records, Shrewsbury, N J

1707, 3rd of 5th mo   Will of William Bickley, shopkeeper, of New York, proved Nov 20, 1707, mentioned

Two daughters, Sarah Potter, widow, and Elizabeth Brown, 20s, each, in full of all claims upon his estate grandson, William Cook, £20, if he serves the remainder of his indentured time, to the testator, to each of his grandchildren and his son-in-law, Nicholas Brown, each, 12s , to his daughters-in-law a piece of gold of 12s value, to various friends, viz Thomas Ives and his wife, Susanah, Dr John Rodman, Hugh Cowperthwaite, and Samuel Bowne, of Flushing, and to George Curtis [Curlis?], John Lipincott, Sr , and William Worth, of Shrewsbury, in New Jersey, each, a legacy, and to his son, Abraham Bickley, of Philadelphia, the balance of his estate, whom he enjoins "to be helpful and assistant to his helpless sister, Sarah Potter, during her widowhood '

William Bickley was a prominent Quaker of New York City

FROM THE SHREWSBURY, N. J., POOR BOOK

1743 Jos Potter took one of the town poor
1743 Nicholas Potter took "Blind Nick," one of the town poor
1758 Jos Potter mentioned
1772 Nicholas and Ephraim Potter were of the town poor
1781. Ephraim Potter and his mother were of the town poor.
1785 David Potter mentioned

1758, 2, 2mo Lydia Potter, daughter of Joseph and Abigail, was born

1765, Oct 31 Will of William Potter, of Shrewsbury, yeoman, proved Nov 25, 1766, mentioned

Ann, "once the wife of John Soper," "£5 and £5, yearly, till £35 are paid and no more." "she having been very wicked to me & Distructive to my Interests "

Daughter, Susanna Dickeson, and her husband, John Dickeson, "for good reasons to myself well known," 5 shillings

Son, Samuel Potter, who is to pay the legacies, £10 He had four children who received £109

Daughter, Ann Cowperthwaite, wife of John Cowperthwaite, £20, and to her children, £109, equally between them when they arrive at the age of eighteen years

Grandson, William Potter Brock, £200, when eighteen years of age, and to the two daughters of "my daughter, Mary Brock," £50, when aged eighteen

The testator signed his name to the will

The inventory of his estate amounted to £423-18-3

Burbridge Brock and Mary, his wife, were sworn at Burlington, N J He made his mark— a hatchet.

1750, Apr 12 John Chambers and Charity Potter had marriage license granted
1763, Feb 4 Ephraim Potter and Abe Edwards had marriage license granted

SALTER

OF

MONMOUTH COUNTY

The Salter family may justly lay claim to considerable antiquity In the reign of Henry VI, temp 1423, there lived one, William Salter, who was possessed of good estate and whose ancestors had resided at and were the Lords, for over two hundred years, of a manor called Bokenhamis, in England

Walter Salter lived in the time of Richard III, temp 1482 At the upper end of the South aisle, in the church of Tottengen, in the County of Norfolk, there is erected to himself and lady, a tablet with the following inscription

"Orate pro animabus
Walter Salter et Alice uxoris ejus
Et pro quibus tenentus."

"Pray for the souls of Walter Salter
And Alice his wife, and for the
Souls of all that belong to them"

1524 Henry Salter was one of the Sheriffs of Norwich, England

1600 Henry Baldwin, in his will, mentions his wife, Alice, his daughter, Mary Baldwin, who married Richard Salter, and had children, and his daughter, Agnes Baldwin, who was baptized 1579   Baldwin Genealogy, p 988.

1598, Jan 30 Mary, the daughter of Henry Baldwin, married, at Aston Clinton, County of Berks, England, Richard Salter

In 1622, Alice Baldwin left £10 to "my daughter, Mary Salter", 40 shillings to each of her seven grandchildren, and created Richard Salter and Richard Baldwin, executors

1632, Feb 18 Richard Baldwin, in his will of this date, left £10 to his sister, Mary Salter, and a like amount to each of her four children, Mary Salter, John Salter, Sarah Salter and David Salter.

1669, Apr. 11 David Salter, the last named, made his will on this date, creating his wife sole legatee.

1618 William Salter was a resident of Devon, England.

1655 John Salter was Mayor, of Norwich, England

1663 The charter of the said city of Norwich was renewed by Charles II, and John Salter was one of the twenty-four Aldermen, who were appointed

He died, the 20th of Nov, 1669, aged 77 years, and was buried in the church of St Andrew.

1670 Bridget, the wife of Matthew Salter, died, Dec 31, aged 42 years She was interred in the church of St Ethelred, and from her tomb is copied the following quaint epitaph.

> "Tho' dead, yet dear,
> Tho' dead, yet dear to me,
> Dead is her body,
> Dear her memorie"

It is doubtless from some of the foregoing persons that the Salters in this country are descended If Mrs Bridget Salter, last above mentioned, was, as is positively asserted, the mother of twenty-two children, it was no wonder that some of them wanted to leave

1734 The Rev Samuel Salter was Archdeacon, of Norfolk, also Prebendary, of Norfolk; Rector, of Bramerton [?]. and Curate of the Parishes of St George and St Andrew, in the same city, England.

In England, at the present day, the name is still met with, especially in the vicinity of Norfolk and Devon.

In America there are several distinct families of the name whose arrivals date back to the latter part of the Seventeenth Century In what degree of relationship, if any, their progenitors stood, it is now impossible to ascertain.

The descendants of John Salter, who came from Exeter, Devonshire, England, and settled at Odiorne's Point, New Hampshire, and the descendants of Richard Salter, the early settler in Monmouth County, N. J, have been the most prominent in point of numbers, as well as the most conspicuous in social and political life.

A family of the name, residing in North Carolina, during the Revolutionary War, contributed a commissary to the army, and two members to the Provincial Congress Robert Salter, from Pitt County, 1775, Edward Salter, from Pitt County, and William Salter, from Bladen County, delegates to the Provincial Congress, 1774, in North Carolina.

See Wheeler's Historical Sketches of North Carolina

Another, residing in New York City, during the post-revolutionary period, was engaged in mercantile pursuits, and was represented by Abraham Salter, who was born in New York City, about 1785. In 1830, he was a merchant doing business in Pearl St, New York City He had a son, Albert, who married, and was the father of George W. Salter and W H Salter, both attorneys-at-law; the former employed in the War Department, at Washington, the latter, practicing in New York City

In this family there is a tradition that, in olden times, they intermarried with the Dutch, and that the first-comer came from Strasburg, and that some of the descendants, now living in Paris, have changed the spelling of the name to "Saltaire."

Thomas Salter, of New York City, who had a license to marry Mary O'Neil, granted Mch. 2, 1756, *may* be a connection of this family.

In 1878, while the Rev. William Salter, of Burlington, Iowa, was traveling in Colorado, he met the Rev Charles C. Salter, who stated that his grandfather came to this country in 1794, from Tiverton, Devonshire, England

In Rhode Island, Sampson Salter was admitted a Freeman, the 20th of 3rd month, 1638, while in the Massachusetts Bay Colony, Will Salter was admitted to a similar position, May 26, 1636

The latter individual was born in 1607, was the keeper of the Boston jail, and, being able to write a good hand, frequently subscribed his name to the wills and documents of his fellow-townsmen   He died, Aug. 10, 1675, and was interred in the King's Chapel-yard. His will made his wife, Mary, his executrix, and alluded to a son, John, "who has gone away, but if he returns he shall have five acres of land." This son, John, was born 1651. He returned and claimed his legacy, and it is recorded that he disposed of it, in person, in 1679, when he was married and settled

John and Henry Salter were enlisted, as soldiers, in King Philip's War

Henry and Hannah Salter had a son, Richard, baptized in October, 1673

                       Savage's New England Genealogical Dictionary

John Salter, aged eighty years, was married, Oct 9, 1720, by Rev. Thos Foxcraft, of Boston, to Abigail Durrant, which would make him born about 1640, and exclude him as the son of William, if the birth date of William's son, John, is correctly given as 1651

Thomas Salter, of Boston, died, Aug 2, 1748, aged 62 years, buried in Woburn Burying-ground

Capt Thos Salter, of Port Royall, captured a Spanish vessel   He resided at Jamaica, and was Commander of a private man-of-war   See proceedings of the Court of Admiralty about the Ship Cedar and ye Privateer, after their return from the French port, in Accadie

In 1711, John Salter was a private, in the Governor's Company, New York

1762, Aug 10 James Salter was a private, in the pay of the Province of New York, at Fort Ontario

Joseph Salter was a private, in the Company of Militia, at Katskill, Coxhakki and Pothook.

                       Report of the State Historian, New York

1754, Dec 24 Samuel Walter vs Peter Solter

1765, March John Psalter was Constable, of Hanover, N J

1767, September Ravaud Kearney vs David Ogden, Jr , Lawrence Salter, et al

1779, Sept 28 John Salter petitioned for a license to keep a public house, granted.

1781, March Widow Phebe Salter produced a certificate, as being the widow of Benjamin Salter, who died in the service of the United States, and asked for half pay

1791, September John Saltar sued Conrad Hopler, of Morris County, N J, for £450, debt, and trespass   Evidence, a promissory note dated, Apr 12, 1790, at Newark, Essex County, for £250   He took judgment   Morris County Court Records

The following were privates, from New Jersey, in the Revolutionary War:

Benjamin Salter, of Morris County, killed in 1779   Henry Salter, of Somerset County. John Salter, Sr , and John Salter, Jr., of Burlington County.   John P. Salter, Sr , and John P Salter, Jr   See Stryker

1675, July 9. Henry Salter, with his wife, Anna, obtained a patent of ten thousand acres, in *his* Colony, wherein he is described as, of the Parish of St Buttolph, without Bishopsgate, London, silkman   The wording, "in his Colony," implies an existing residence here

In 1677, both he and his wife had a Proprietary right

In June, 1679, he had died, for reference is made, in a survey, to land in the ranges of Monmouth River, adjoining Henry Salter, deceased   His residence and estate was largely in Salem County, and he was described as, merchant, of West Jersey   Upon his demise, his widow took up a residence in Tacony, Pa , now part of the City of Philadelphia, and dealt extensively in lands These she obtained, in part, from her husband, who owned ½ of 1/6 of the 1st Tenth of West Jersey, also a part of the 2nd Tenth Her sales and purchases of lands in Burlington, and Salem Counties, N J, as taken from the Trenton Records, roughly computed, amount to about four thousand acres, and she dealt, as well, in dwellings, mortgages and cattle

The New Jersey records further allude to her ownership of four hundred acres in Pennsylvania, and the Bucks County, Pa, records, speaking of her, in May, 1684, as of New Castle, Pa, refer to a sale, by her, of one hundred acres, to Morgan De Wett Doubtless additional evidence of her holdings could be found in the Philadelphia Records She is as frequenty called, Anna, as Hannah Salter She was living in 1687, for, April 1, of that year, she sold one thousand acres of land, in Salem County, and was joined in the conveyance by her son, John Salter, but had died prior to Dec 31, 1689, for then her executors confirmed this sale They continued, for some time after her demise, to sell her lands

The New Jersey family, which solely interests us, became, very early, distinguished in the history of the State, and for a long time remained prominent Today, however, none can be found within its borders, and in Freehold, and its vicinity, where once they clustered and were powerful, they can hardly be traced

The tradition, current in the family, states that shortly after the accession of Charles II to the English throne, (probably in 1664), three of the younger sons of the family, endowed with a handsome property, came to this country They landed at or near Boston, where one remained, while the other two moved thence to the State of New Jersey Of these, one settled in Salem County, and died without issue, leaving a considerable estate to his widow, Hannah, who, upon her decease, left this property, situated in and about Philadelphia and New Jersey, equally divided among her own and her husband's relatives

RICHARD SALTAR, the youngest of the three, became the founder of the branch we are about to follow

From some caprice, he changed the spelling of his name from *Salter* to *Saltar*, which some of his descendants still use, though many have lapsed into using the original orthography The names of the other two brothers and their parentage, are unknown

The statement that Richard Saltar, of New Jersey, came from Devonshire is an assumption, and the use of arms, as they appear in Salter's History of Ocean County, was the outcome of a strange chance, which threw an old law book in a second-hand shop, in Beekman St, New York City, in the way of James Steen, Esq, of Eatontown, N J, who purchased it On its inside cover appears the signature "Richd Saltar," and a book plate containing arms Thus it found its way to Monmouth County, and unknown to Edwin Salter during his life, was utilized, subsequently, by his publisher, as a frontispiece. Of such misleading material is history often made

The earliest date of Richard Saltar's appearance in Monmouth County, that I have found, is 1687 It is probable, however, that his settlement there antedated it by some years, for he is found, at that time, as a prominent and influential personage among his fellow-townsmen, a position he could attain only by a long and tried association

1695 Richard Saltar was elected a Member of the House of Deputies

1696-7, Jan 11 He owned land at Wickatunck, a locality beyond Matawan, to which he may have removed, for in a deed of land at this place, dated Aug 18, 1698, he is alluded to as, "Richard Salter having become a neighbor in place of Dr Cox "

HISTORICAL MISCELLANY

In 1697, Richard Saltar was residing at Freehold, N. J It was in the vicinity of Upper Freehold that his estates mainly lay, and his family lived As late as 1793, Saltar's Dam, on the main brook, in Freehold, is alluded to.

1697 Richard Saltar, of Freehold, was spoken of as, "King's Attorney."

1700 Some time prior to this date, he was in possession of the Baker Tract, at Upper Freehold, purchased from George Willocks, upon which he built the mills, at Imlaystown This land passed to his son, Richard Salter, Jr., who sold the mill tract, in 1727, to Peter Salter, Jr.   Ellis' History of Monmouth County, p 617

1701, Mch 25 He was a witness to a commission issued in London by William Dockwra to Charles Goodman, of Perth Amboy, to be Deputy Secretary and Register, by which we can infer that he kept up an intimate relation with the old country

1701, Mch 25 Wm Dockwra, of London, gave Richard Salter a power of attorney, as land agent, and invested him with additional powers, Mch 31, following

1701, Mch 26 Being in London, he must have conferred with those interested in New Jersey, for Thos Cooper, of London, merchant, gave him a power of attorney to collect debts, wherein he is mentioned as of Freehold, planter.

1701, Mch 26 Thos Cooper, of London, gave a power of attorney to Richard Salter, of Freehold, and Richard Hartshorne, of Middletown, as land agents.

1702. "Letters of Attorney" were given to Richard Saltar, of Freehold, by Caleb Plumstead and William Dockwra

1704 He was a Member of the Second Assembly.

1704 Richard Saltar was a Captain, in the Provincial Service, from Freehold.
                State Historian's Report, Colonial Series, New York, Vol II, p. 482.

1704, Feb. 28. He was a Justice and Judge of Monmouth County, and was alluded to as such, Dec 11, 1704, 1705, 1707, 1722, 1723, 1724 and 1728
                                Minutes of Assembly and Freehold Court Records.

1706-7. Richard and Sarah Saltar, of Freehold, sold land to Jacob Van Dorn. Both signed.

1708. Richard Saltar and wife, Sarah, conveyed lands

1716, July 27 Richard Saltar, Gentleman, and wife Sarah, of Freehold, made two conveyances of land, at Freehold, to Richard Jewel. Both Saltar and his wife signed Thomas Saltar was a witness.

1709-10, "ninth day of June," 8th of Queen Anne "Capt Richard Salter, of the township of Freehold, county of Monmouth, Esq , to Ghertie Romain, Widdow of Stophel Romine, Deceased, of the township of Freehold, conveyed land."

For £450, said Salter sold "two hundred acres of land, more or less, in the County of Monmouth Beginning at a ftake ftanding in the line Between Sd Salter's & Thomas Boel's land   and is one of the Corners of John Vankirk's land . . . . to another branch of hop brook to a maple tree marked, Standing by ye old Dam Formerly made to flow the Swamp   to the Mouth of a fmall Run which comes out of Elexander Nipper's land . . as Johanus courten Vanvorus' Line Runs till it comes to Alexander Nipper's land   . till it comes within fifteen chaines of the Jntended Highway Spoken of in Said Salter's Deed   . from Clement Plumsted, ... to another ftake Standing Jn Thomas Bole's line   . . along Thomas Boel's line " Bounded "North Eaft by Thomas Boel's Land & South East & South by John Vankirk & Johanus Corten Vanvorus; weft & North weft by Alexander Nipper and fd Salter's Land, Intended for yͤ uſe of yͤ *Prisbyterion Miniſt———,*" under the yearly *Preiſe* or Quitrent of three pence, to be paid to the Lords Proprietors

    Witnesses Wᴹ Lawrence   Richard Salter
                    Obadiah Bowne   Sarah Saltar
                    John O Keson

Acknowledged by Wᴹ Lawrence and John Okeſon, "two of yͤ ſubſcribing evidences," on oath, before John Reid, 2ᵈ of June, 1714.

1711 He was a Member of the Assembly for the Eastern Division of New Jersey

Richard Saltar was a man of marked ability, of high social standing, and a lawyer by education Through his talents, and the influence he may have acquired by his marriage, he attained, and was able to hold, a leading position in the community. He was in sympathy with the Middletown Patentees and their successors, and took a spirited part in opposing the encroachments of the Proprietary Party As counsel for the people, in which capacity he seems to have been employed, he championed their rights both within and without the halls of the Assembly, though he needed not the stimulus of identity of interests to defend so just a cause While acting in his professional capacity, he, and Capt. John Bowne, undertook to raise money to defend the Patentee rights before Lord Cornbury, then Governor of the Province. This provoked the ill will of the Proprietors, who charged them with committing felony, crime, etc Capt Bowne, who was a Member of the House of Representatives, was brought up for discipline, but proving obdurate, was expelled Lord Cornbury was also notified of their displeasure in a lengthy phillipic, which provoked a rejoinder, in which he took occasion to comment upon the illegality of this removal, and to deny the accusation that the money, thus raised, had been conveyed to him for the purpose of dissolving the Assembly, that the people might escape payment of the Proprietors' quit-rents. The impeachments were subsequently proven to be false, and resulted merely from the intense party feeling then existing. Saltar and Bowne represented the people, and were sustained by them in all their acts, despite the criminations of the Proprietary Party.

To estimate the character and services of Richard Saltar, at this distant date, is a difficult matter We, who are in sympathy with the people, see him as a man, great in his day, in that locality—as one who, by his deed as well as word, served to mould the events of his time, and as one of those who have stood out, in all ages, as fearless and resolute advocates of individual rights Viewed from the standpoint of the Proprietary Party, he appears as, "a factious and seditious person," given to false representation and desirous of evading, as well as assisting others to evade, their just obligations According to our own individual convictions will these opinions prevail

The dates of Richard Saltar's birth and decease are not known, but the latter occurred subsequently to 1728, for, at this date, he was still an acting Judge in his County

He married Sarah, daughter of Capt John Bowne, by Lydia Holmes, his wife She was born, at Gravesend, L I, Nov. 27, 1669, and was living as late as 1714, the date of her brother, John Bowne's will, in which she and several of her children, are mentioned as devisees

This brother, John Bowne, between the date of his will, in 1714, and the date of its probate, in 1716, recognizing his approaching end, made a deed of trust, which largely distributed his estate, and mentioned many of his kinspeople, among others, the Salters

1715/16, Feb 5 John Bowne, of Middletown, merchant, gave a bond of £5260, at eight shillings the ounce, to William Lawrence, Sr , and Richard Hartshorne in trust, for the use of said John Bowne's wife, Frances, and John Bowne, Anne Bowne and Lydia Bowne, son and daughters of Obadiah Bowne, and Richard Saltar, William Saltar, Ebenezer Saltar, James Saltar, Deborah Saltar, and Oliver Saltar, children of Capt

Richard Saltar, and Margaret Hartshorne, Richard Hartshorne and William Hartshorne, children of William Hartshorne, and Thomas Taylor, James Bowne and Samuel Willet, their executors, administrators and assigns

To Frances Bowne there was to be paid, yearly, £45, during her life, at the dwelling of said Richard Hartshorne or William Lawrence

To John Bowne, son of Obadiah Bowne, there was to be paid £400, when he reached the age of twenty-one years

To Anne and Lydia Bowne there was to be paid £200, each, when they reached the age of eighteen years

To Richard Saltar, William Saltar, Ebenezer Saltar, Deborah Saltar, James Saltar and Oliver Saltar, there was to be paid £125, each, when the boys reached the age of twenty-one years, and the girl the age of eighteen years

To Richard Hartshorne, Margaret Hartshorne and William Hartshorne, there was to be paid £150, each, when the boys reached the age of twenty-one years, and the girl the age of eighteen years

Thomas Taylor, James Bowne and Samuel Willet were to be discharged from all debts

Witnesses Joseph Dennis and John Saltar

Freehold Deeds, Lib G, p 101.

1713 Sarah Saltar was a member of the Baptist Church, of Middletown

Issue

2 Thomas Saltar
3 John Saltar
4 Hannah Saltar
5 Richard Saltar
6 William Saltar
7 Ebenezer Saltar
8 James Saltar
9 Deborah Saltar
10 Oliver Saltar

Still others appear, in the Freehold Records, who must be the issue of Richard Saltar, or his children

1713 First Tuesday in June Nicholas Salter, defendant, in a suit brought by John Mills to recover a debt of £12 Plaintiff ordered to give bail to pay costs within thirty days, or be nonsuited, defendant to plead thirty days before next Court of Judgment

Record of Common Pleas, Freehold, Monmouth County, N J

In 1715, Nicholas Salter was still living in Freehold, and owned land adjoining John Salter

1719, February. Samuel Saltar was a party to a suit in Monmouth County, N J.

1720, Aug 5 Margaret Salter, a supposed grand-daughter of Richard Saltar, 1, was born. Mrs Levi Holbrook, of New York City, a lady conspicuous in genealogical and historical circles, descends from Margaret Salter, born 1720, died June 16, 1799, married William Dey, or Dye, Sr, of Monmouth County, N J, born July 6, 1718, died Sept. 6, 1784. They lived on a fine farm near Hightstown, N J

There is some reason to believe that Margaret Salter, born 1720, was a Crawford, rather than a Salter

1725 James Grover, Elizabeth Forman and Mary Saltar, being severally called on their recognizances, appeared to give evidence to the jury

1726 William Everingham vs Mary Saltar Suit for debt £40

1728 Samuel Saltar brought before the Court for breaking jail

Freehold Court Records

1727 Peter Saltar, Jr, bought of Richard Saltar, Jr, land lying at Upper Freehold.
Ellis' History of Monmouth County, p 617

1733, June 4 Peter Salter and Rebecca Mount were married at Christ Church, Philadelphia, Pa.

1743 Sarah Salter married Nathan Allen, of Monmouth County, N. J
1748 . . Salter married Ann Rockhill, widow, shortly after 1748
From Mr Howard Deacon, of Philadelphia, Pa

2 THOMAS SALTAR, son of Richard Saltar, 1, died in early manhood, during the lifetime of his father He was of age in, or before, 1716, as appears by the will of his uncle, John Bowne He dwelt at Freehold, and I have found but very few allusions to him

1716–17, Mch 5 Thomas Saltar, yeoman, of Freehold, bought of Thomas Parker, Sr., of Freehold, merchant, two hundred acres, more or less, lying at Crosswicks, bounded by Richard Borden, Philip Smith, Doctor's Creek, "the Mill Dam he bought from William Purdy," etc, including all buildings, orchards, fields, etc, and appurtenances belonging to the mill and the farm The conveyance was signed by Thomas Parker and Mary Parker, his wife, by their marks, and witnessed by John Saltar, *Jonothon* Robins and George Parker The deed was recorded in 1739, when *Jonothon* Robins acknowledged witnessing the same, before John Campbell, Esq, one of the Judges for Monmouth County

1719, August He was a Petit Juryman

1722, June 13. Will of Thomas Saltar, proved Apr 25, 1723, mentioned
Wife, Rachel
Father, Richard Saltar, his executor
Daughter, Hannah Saltar
Daughter, Deborah Saltar
Son, Richard Saltar
Trenton Wills, Lib II, p 248

1725. Richard Saltar, Esq, executor of Thomas Saltar, was sued by Cornelius Van Horne, for a debt of £60 Freehold Court Records

1731, June 29. Thomas Saltar, of Freehold, and Rachel, his wife, for £50, sold lands, at Freehold, to James Ashton, Esq, and Elisha Lawrence, Gent., both of Freehold Rachel, the wife, made her mark Witnesses John Saltar, Richard Borden, Thomas Smith

Issue
11 Hannah Saltar ⎫
12 Deborah Saltar ⎬ not traced
13 Richard Saltar ⎭

3 JOHN SALTAR, son of Richard Saltar, 1, was born Oct 22, 1694, as deduced from his tombstone, standing in the Yellow Meeting House graveyard, at Cream Ridge, Monmouth County, N J, which states
John Saltar died, Aug. 29, 1723, aged 28 years, 10 months, and 7 days

In 1714, he is alluded to as, a minor, in the will of his uncle, John Bowne, but in 1716, when that instrument was probated, he had passed his minority, and received property with other devisees

1716–1717 He was a witness to a conveyance from Thomas Parker to his brother, Thomas Saltar, and was probably then residing at Freehold, where he dwelt to the date of his decease

1719, November He was a Petit Juryman

1721 John Saltar was frequently sued by one, Gomez, and others, and was "non est," in a number of the suits.

1723 He was spoken of as Mr John Saltar   Freehold Court Records.

1723, May 4 Will of John Saltar, of Freehold; proved Oct. 1, 1723, mentioned·
Daughter, Lucy Saltar
Daughter, Elizabeth Saltar } all under the age of eighteen years
Daughter, Sarah Saltar
Daughter, Lydia Saltar
Wife, Elizabeth, appointed sole executrix and guardian of his children

Trenton Wills, Lib. II, p 254

His personal estate amounted to £722-8-0, and included nine negroes valued at £300-15-0.

John Saltar married Elizabeth, daughter of Elisha Lawrence   She died in 1741

1728, Oct 8 Will of Elizabeth Saltar, of Freehold, widow, and sick
She devised lands situated in New Jersey and Pennsylvania, and orders others to be sold, "near the house that I dwell in, at the Iron Works," excepting fifty acres, "near the end of my husband's plantation", one hundred acres of land "that my father gave me," and mentioned
Daughter, Sarah
Daughter, Lucy
Daughter, Lidey } all under age and unmarried
Daughter, Elizabeth
Daughter, Mary
Executors   friends and brothers, Elisha Lawrence, John Lawrence, John Emley and Richard Salter, Jr
Witnesses   Robert Lawrence, Ebezar [Ebenezer] Saltar and James Tapscott

Elizabeth Saltar left an estate that was inventoried at £722-8-0.

Issue

14 Lucy Saltar
15 Elizabeth Saltar
16 Sarah Saltar
17 Lydia Saltar
18 Mary Saltar

4 HANNAH SALTAR, daughter of Richard Saltar, 1, married Mordecai Lincoln, who was born April 24, 1686

*Mordecai Lincoln, the son of Mordecai Lincoln, a blacksmith, accompanied or followed by his brother, Abraham, both young men, left Scituate, Mass., early in 1700, where they had spent twenty years, more or less, of their youth, and traveled to New Jersey   Here they located in Monmouth County, and after a residence of some years, moved on to Pennsylvania, then an inviting field for the venturesome settler, where Mordecai died at Amity, Philadelphia County, in 1736, and Abraham, at Springfield, Chester County, Pa, in 1745.

*Samuel Lincoln emigrated from England to Massachusetts, where he resided at Hingham   He married, about 1648-50, Martha   , by whom he had born, between 1650 and 1673, the following
Issue
Samuel Lincoln
Daniel Lincoln
Mordecai Lincoln
Mordecai Lincoln, 2nd
Thomas Lincoln
Thomas Lincoln, 2nd
Mary Lincoln
Sarah Lincoln
Sarah Lincoln, 2nd   (*Footnote continued on page 185*)

MORDECAI LINCOLN'S marriage to HANNAH SALTAR, and perhaps her death also, occurred before the year 1714, as appears from the will of her uncle, John Bowne, the settlement of whose estate was only accomplished with considerable friction between his legatees. Obadiah Bowne, one of his administrators, brought numerous actions against the said legatees, among which were suits against Mordecai Lincoln in 1716, 1717, 1719 and 1720

1721, Nov. 30. Mordecai Lincoln reversed this legal status, and became plaintiff in a suit against John Lining, for a debt of £11-9-0. Defendant was non est.

1720, Feb. 2. Richard Saltar, of Freehold, conveyed to Mordecai Lincon, of the same place, for the sum of £152.

"all those Tracts of Land and Meadow on Machaponix River & gravell Brook in the County of Middlesex, the first Tract Is bounded on said Machaponix River on ye South by ye Pine Brook East by the Land now or late of Willm Estill on ye West, and by Land unsurveyed on ye North Also all that Tract Bounded Westerly by Gravill Brook Southerly by the Land of William Estill from ye mouth of Long Medow Run Easterly & Northerly by land unsurveyed Also all ye Long Medow upon ye s^d Long Meadow Run Bounded West by ye Last mentioned Tract of land and all round ye other side by upland unsurveyed In all Containing four hundred acres more or less," etc, the title to which Saltar had, by deed of sale, dated Nov 7, 1717, from John Reid, Esq. Witnesses Thomas Cox and R Saltar, Junr

1727, Apr. 5. Richard Saltar, Junr, appeared before John Anderson, Esq, and acknowledged that he was a subscribing witness to the above instrument

At what date he removed to Pennsylvania, I have no knowledge, but he was a resident of Chester County, Pa, in 1726, and earlier, probably by some years

1735, Feb 22. Mordecai Lincon made his will, proved June 7, 1736, in which he mentioned
Wife, Mary
Son, Mordecai Lincon
Son, Thomas Lincon
Daughter, Hannah Lincon
Daughter, Mary Lincon
Son, John Lincon
Daughter, Ann Lincon
Daughter, Sarah Lincon
A prospective child, which proved to be a boy, and was named Abraham

   Rebecca Lincoln
   Martha Lincoln
Mordecai Lincoln, son of Samuel Lincoln, 1, married
     Issue
    Mordecai Lincoln, born Apr 24, 1686
    Abraham Lincoln, born Jan 13, 1689

These two sons were the pioneers of this family in Monmouth County, where they were in evidence as early as 1714, but they had, probably, arrived there some years before this date, and left there in 1721-22, to take up a residence in Pennsylvania

Mordecai Lincoln, son of Mordecai Lincoln, was born Apr 24, 1686 He married, as set forth above, prior to 1714, Hannah, daughter of Richard Saltar, who died, according to the late William H Egle, Esq, the Pennsylvania Historian, "Feb 4, 1717, in East Jersey"

Abraham Lincoln, son of Mordecai Lincoln, was born Jan 13, 1689 He settled in Monmouth County, N J, where, Apr 3, 1730, calling himself blacksmith, of that place, he sold land to Thomas Williams, which he had received from Safety Borden, by deed dated Feb 11, 1722 Freehold Records He made his will at Springfield, Chester County, Pa, in 1745, which mentioned

     Issue
    John Lincoln
    Jacob Lincoln
    Isaac Lincoln
    Mordecai Lincoln, "being absent from the Province," and perhaps he who is referred to as Mordecai Lincoln, of Taunton, mentioned in Dean's History of Scituate
    Rebecca Lincoln } who received a plantation in Springfield and two houses in Philadelphia
    Sarah Lincoln

1770, June 9 Abraham Lincoln married (no name) Records of Augusta Co, Va, beginning 1749
William F Reed, Esq, of 915 F Street, N E, Washington, D C, has a full account of William Tallman's descendants
In 1883, Samuel Shackford, of Winnetka, Ill, addressed me, concerning the Salter genealogy, stating he was a descendant of Samuel Lincoln, and had been asked, as he had made researches into the Lincoln genealogy, by Isaac N Arnold, of Chicago, who was rewriting the Life of Abraham Lincoln, to contribute the chapter on Abraham Lincoln's ancestry

Contributions to Lincoln genealogy in the way of memoranda, appear in the New York Genealogical and Biographical Record, for April and July, 1872, and in Old Times in Monmouth County, N J

Mordecai's widow, Mary, it is said by the Pennsylvania Lincolns, remarried

The above will of Mordecai Lincon, establishes the fact that he had a later wife than Hannah Saltar, by the name of Mary, and there is nothing to disprove the fact, that I know of, that he might have had a still earlier wife than Hannah Saltar, except his youth.

There is no positive knowledge of the descent of the children from these respective wives, and there is some clash in the traditions given concerning them And I feel quite sure that the children are not enumerated in the will in the order of their birth

However, that Mordecai Lincon's eldest son and heir was John Lincon, there can be no doubt

1748, Nov 8 John Lincon, of the Township of Carnarvin, in the County of Lancaster and Province of 'Penselvania," weaver, the son and heir of Mordecai Lincon, deceased, sold to William Dye, of the County of Middlesex, yeoman, for the sum of £200, that tract of land, lying in the County of Middlesex

"Beginning where the land formerly Walter Benthals crosses Cranbury brook from thence along said Benthals land towards the Post Road to the Land formerly Robert Burnets and from thence along said Burnets line," etc, containing three hundred acres

1750, May 24 John Lincon, party to the above written instrument, acknowledged the execution of the same, before Andrew Johnston, one of His Majestie's Council for the Province of New Jersey.

Charles Carleton Coffin, in his Life of Abraham Lincoln, says "John, son of Mordecai, was born, in Massachusetts, by a first wife" Also that Ann and Hannah Lincoln were daughters by a second wife On the other hand, David J Lincoln, of Birdsboro, deceased, stated that John Lincoln was a full brother to Ann Lincoln, and she a daughter of Mordecai Lincoln by Hannah Saltar Here is direct contradiction, and if the first authority cited is correct, then Mordecai Lincoln had three wives, the second of whom was Hannah Saltar.

The descent of John Lincon and the other children may be conjectured from the disposal of the lands of Mordecai Lincon:

To John, he conveyed the tract of three hundred acres that he, John, sold, in 1748, to William Dye

To two of his daughters, he deeded one hundred acres, and to the other two daughters, one hundred acres, which he had bought, in 1726, when of Chester County, Pa, from Richard Saltar ·

The land he owned in Pennsylvania was bequeathed to his sons, Thomas, Mordecai and Abraham

It would seem from this partition of his estate that John Lincon, and his four sisters, inheriting all the New Jersey lands, were children by the wife, Hannah Saltar, while the other three children were by the wife Mary

Issue

19 John Lincoln
20 Hannah Lincoln, married Joseph Millard
21 Mary Lincoln, married, first, Mr. Morris, second, Francis Yarnell, Jr In 1769, Francis Yarnell, his wife, Mary, and brother-in-law, Joseph Millard, were living in Pennsylvania
22 Ann Lincoln, born Mch. 8, 1725, married, in Pennsylvania, William Tallman, son of Benjamin and Patience (Durfee) Tallman, son of Peter Tallman, of Rhode Island He was born, in Rhode Island, Mch 25, 1720, and died, in Virginia, Feb 13, 1791 Issue. Benjamin Tallman, born Jan 9, 1745, mar-

ried Dinah Boone, cousin of Daniel Boone, and daughter of Benjamin and Susannah Boone She was born May 10, 1749. Their descendant, Miss M J. Roe, 6901 Harvard Ave , Chicago, Ill , has studied the Lincoln and Tallman families

23 Sarah Lincoln
24 Mordecai Lincoln, born 1730
25 Thomas Lincoln
26 Abraham Lincoln, born 1735-6, died 1806
26ᵃ "Debora Lincon", died, May 3, 1720, aged 3 years and 6 months Tombstone very rudely cut, and of poor quality, like a field stone, in the Graveyard on the Robbins' farm, (wherein all the other stones are relatively modern), about a mile beyond Cox's Corners, near Imlaystown, Monmouth Co , N J

5 RICHARD SALTAR, son of Richard Saltar, 1, was born, probably, in 1699, and became a prominent personage in his State.

1717, May Richard Saltar, was a witness, in court, which may refer to his father
1720, Nov 22 Richard Saltar was foreman of the Grand Jury, which, however, may mean his father
1724 Richard Saltar, Jr , was mentioned in a suit.   Freehold Court Records
1733, Mch. 6 Richard Saltar mortgaged lands to the Commissioners of the Loan Office, lying in Upper Freehold, for £26-13-4
1734, June 8 He again mortgaged to the Commissioners of the Loan Office, for £25, land amounting to three hundred acres, in Upper Freehold, bounded by Robᵗ Imlay, James Tapscott, and land "late John Saltar's "
1744, 1745, 1746 and 1748 Richard Saltar was a Justice Shrewsbury Town Poor Records
1745 Gov. Lewis Morris recommended him for a seat in the Council
1746 He was designated one of those who were to give orders for firing the beacon lights, on the Navesink Highlands, to indicate the approach of French cruisers
1748. He was suggested, by Ferdinand John Paris, to fill the place of John Hamilton, the lately deceased President of the Council, and was endorsed for it by James Alexander, as a "man of good understanding " He, soon thereafter, was appointed and filled the position until 1762, the date of his decease
1754, Mch 29 Judge Morris tendered his resignation and suggested Mr Saltar as the best man for the succession, being "a man of good understanding and fortune, a firm friend to the government, and will act in that station with honor to himself, and justice to the public "
1754, May 2 He was Commissioned an Associate Judge of the Supreme Court
1761 He was recommissioned by Gov Hardy
During the years 1749 to 1762, he was a Commissioner to buy lands, to make Indian treaties and to do other public work

He resided, for awhile, in Trenton, as also, for a time, in Allentown He likewise built a large, substantial house on Black Point, West of the Navesink River, near the place now called Seabright Finally he settled in Nottingham, Burlington County, West Jersey, as appears from a deed, dated Dec 18, 1761, in which he conveys the farm, upon which he dwells, consisting of seven hundred and two acres, bounded by the River Delaware, Isaac Watson's line, etc , with the houses, buildings, orchards, woods, etc , to Joseph, John and Lawrence Saltar, yeomen, of the same place The deed was signed by Richard Saltar, who was joined in the conveyance by his wife, Anne Saltar The witnesses were Thomas Saltar and Susannah Saltar
Trenton Records, Lib Y , p 344

1762, Feb. 11. Richard Saltar made his will, which is recorded at Trenton, proved Nov. 17, 1762, in which he alluded to his wife as still living, but no name is given, and mentioned:
"I have already given to my three sons Joseph, John and Lawrence, the plantation on which I now live" Daughter, Elizabeth Saltar

"My grandson, Richard Saltar, son of my son, Elisha Saltar, and my nephew, Thomas Saltar..., who I beg and desire to undertake the friendly office of giving their advice and order in the premises"

In 1768, John, Joseph and Lawrence Saltar are alluded to as children of Richard Saltar, Esq., dec⁴, all of Nottingham, Burlington County, N J, Gentlemen, and associated with them is Huldah [Mott], wife of the said Joseph Saltar, and Rachel [Rhese], wife of John Saltar
Trenton Deeds.

He was spoken of as Richard Saltar, Jr., as late as 1728, proving that his father, Richard, the first-comer, was still alive

He married, June 23, 1721, Hannah, daughter of Elisha and Lucy (Stout) Lawrence She was born 1696

Issue

27 Richard Saltar, born 1725, died, 1745
28 Joseph Saltar
29 John Saltar
30 Lawrence Saltar
31 Elisha Saltar
32 Elizabeth Saltar
33 Sarah Saltar
34 Lucy Saltar
35 Catharine Saltar, died in infancy
36 Susan Saltar

The late Miss Frances Saltar, a granddaughter of Richard Saltar, 5, supplied me with a list of his children, which gave no Susan, but did give two sons, William and James. It is fair to believe that she would know her own uncles and aunts and that her version would be correct She likewise wrote that Richard Saltar had eleven children.

6 WILLIAM SALTAR, son of Richard Salter, 1
1724, Mch 3 William Saltar was a witness in Court
In 1725, William Saltar was sued for a debt of £11
In 1726, William Saltar was sued again   Court Records, Freehold, N J

7 EBENEZER SALTAR, son of Richard Saltar, 1
He had, apparently, a dual residence, Freehold and Staten Island, as he appears in both places about the same time.

1724 He was residing on Staten Island and was married

1724, Mch. 3 Ebenezer Saltar was a witness in Court.
1726 Ebenezer Saltar was a juryman, in Monmouth County   Freehold Court Records

1731/2, Mch 1. Ebenezer, Rebeckah and Hannah Saltar were members of the Middletown, N J, Baptist Church

1732, Dec 16 Ebenezer Saltar, of Upper Freehold, Monmouth County, N J, yeoman, for £900, conveyed to Edward Taylor, Jr, and John Taylor, yeomen, sons of Edward Taylor, of Shrewsbury, N J, land that he, Saltar, had obtained by deed of sale from the Commissioners of the Loan Office, for the County of Monmouth

Situated in Upper Freehold containing two hundred acres, and land that he, Saltar, had bought from Elisha Lawrence, of Upper Freehold, Apr 3, 1732, which adjoined the preceding tract, containing one hundred and eighty and a half acres, bounded by land of Richard Saltar, being the Easterly corner of that tract he purchased of his father, Richard Saltar, Senr, with the mills, now called Imlay's Mills, and by the lands of Moses Robins, Robert Lawrence, James Cox, John Lawrence, and southeasterly by land formerly John Saltar's, deceased The deed was signed by Ebenezer Saltar and Rebecca Saltar

1733, May 11 Ebenezer Saltar, yeoman, of Staten Island, conveyed to John Van Voorhies, a piece of land lying in "Old Town," for £1,100

1734-5 He was a witness to the will of Martha de Bonrepos, of Staten Island

1736. He was a witness to the will of Nathaniel Brittain, of Staten Island

1738, May 25 He transferred another piece of property, on Staten Island, for £1,100, to John Garretsons, of the township of Aquackenon, N J In the deed it is stipulated that the purchaser need not travel more than ten miles from his house to pay the installments The instrument was signed by both Ebenezer Saltar and his wife Rebecca.

1743. Ebenezer Saltar was a witness to the will of Elizabeth Saltar, of Freehold

1749. Ebenezer Saltar took an oath in a Court matter.

New Jersey Archives, Vol VII, p. 455.

Ebenezer Saltar married Rebecca, daughter of John and Rebecca (Throckmorton) Stillwell, of Staten Island

In 1757, he was probably dead, and she was living The petition of John Corson, concerning the administration of the estate of John Stillwell, recited that Rebecca "resided the best part of the time in the western part of Monmouth county"

Rebecca Saltar married, after Ebenezer's death, James Cox, of Monmouth County, who died in 1750 The place of her interment is unknown As she outlived her last husband, she probably withdrew to her Stillwell or Saltar kindred

Issue

37 Manassah Saltar
38 Daniel Saltar
39 Alice Saltar
40 Thomas Saltar
41 Elezar Saltar

There is considerable uncertainty in my own mind as to the correctness of the list of children attributed to Ebenezer Saltar.

Of Manassah and Daniel Saltar, I feel certain The descendants of Daniel Saltar, know, for a certainty, his parentage, and he named one of his children, Ebenezer Manassah Saltar was always Daniel's reputed brother The other three children, assigned to Ebenezer Salter, are purely upon assumptions set forth under their respective names

8 JAMES SALTAR, son of Richard Saltar, 1, appeared as a witness, with Ebenezer Saltar, and others, to a quitclaim deed from Rebecca Stillwell and John Coward, son of Patience Lake, deceased, heirs of Joseph Throckmorton, deceased, to Susannah, wife of Barnes Johnson, of Middletown, N J, dated Oct 8, 1726

14 LUCY SALTAR, daughter of John Saltar, 3, was under the age of eighteen years, in 1728 She married, August 1739, James Johnson, as per St Mary's Church Record, Burlington, N J

Issue

42 Mary Johnson; married Joseph Ogden
43 Elizabeth Johnson, married Mr Jimmerson

15 ELIZABETH SALTAR, daughter of John Saltar, 3, married John Shaw, by license dated Feb 28, 1739-40 He then resided in Upper Freehold, N. J , but, Sept 18, 1756, he was a resident of Burlington, N. J , when he became bondsman for William Stillwell, who was licensed to marry Catharine Knott, (not Mott) John Shaw was designated, Gentleman, and "Inn holder," "At the Sign of the Blue Anchor."

Elizabeth Saltar died July 22, 1770, and was buried the following day, at Burlington, N J

John Shaw died intestate, and letters of administration were granted, June 2, 1776, to John Shaw and Ellis Wright

Issue

John Shaw
Mary Shaw, married, Oct 20, 1768, James Sterling She died, Apr 19, 1785, aged 36 years, buried in St. Mary's Churchyard, Burlington, N J
Ann Shaw, married, October, 1776, Ellis Wright

16 SARAH SALTAR, daughter of John Saltar, 3, was under eighteen years of age in 1728 She married Thomas Lowrie

Issue

44 James Lowrie, died young.
45 William Lowrie, died young
46 Lucy Lowrie, married Samuel Abbott

17 LYDIA SALTAR, daughter of John Saltar, 3, married, Mch 10, 1737, elsewhere Mch. 10, 1740, Richard Douglass, of Monmouth County. who died in 1782.

*Issue**

47 Richard Douglass
48 John Saltar Douglass
49 Sarah Douglass, of Bordentown, N J
50 Charles Douglass, of Bordentown, N J
51 Lydia Douglass, as appears from the will of Thomas Saltar, of Philadelphia County, who mentioned his "cousins," as follows
"To my cousin, Richard Douglass, £100,
"To his sister Lydia, £50,
"To his brother, John, £25,
"To his sister, Sarah, £25 "
Thomas Saltar's Will, 1790, Philadelphia Records, Book U., p 513.

1782, June 5 Administration upon the estate of Richard Douglass late of the County of Middlesex, deceased, was granted to John Saltar Douglass Trenton Wills, Lib 24, p. 72

1716 Thomas Douglass was named in a bond of John Saltar The original paper was in the possession of James S Crawford, Esq., Middletown, N. J , deceased.

18 MARY SALTAR, daughter of John Saltar, 3, married Moses Ogden

---
*All as per Douglass Genealogy, 1879, p 447

19 JOHN LINCOLN, son of Mordecai Lincoln and HANNAH SALTAR, 4, went from New Jersey to Pennsylvania with his father, Mordecai

In 1758, he was taxed at Uniontown, Fayette County, Pa., and subsequently removed, with some of his neighbors, to Rockingham County, Va., while it was a portion of Augusta County, Rockingham County having been organized in 1779

Issue

52 John Lincoln
53 Thomas Lincoln
54 Abraham Lincoln, went to Kentucky
55 Isaac Lincoln, residing on the Watauga, near where Virginia, North Carolina and Tennessee meet
56 Jacob Lincoln

John Lincoln, 19, was the ancestor of Abraham Lincoln, President of the United States, through his son Abraham, who had a son, Thomas, the father of the President.

26 ABRAHAM LINCOLN was a posthumous child of Mordecai Lincoln and HANNAH SALTAR, 4, and was born 1735-6. He died 1806

1752 He was taxed, at Exeter, on his estate.
He was a Member of the Colonial Assembly.
1782, 1783, 1784 and 1785. He was the Representative of Berks County, in the Assembly
He married Ann, cousin of Daniel Boone, the pioneer
He had a grandson, living, in 1883, at Birdsboro, Pa., who published several erroneous letters in Berks County newspapers.

28 JOSEPH SALTAR, son of Richard Saltar, 5, was another prominent member of the family

1759 He was taxed in Shrewsbury, N J, £5-4-7½
1760 He resided at Shrewsbury, N. J., where he was an Overseer. Town Poor Records.
1767 Joseph Saltar, Esq., was a member of a Court, held in Monmouth County, in July of this year
1768 He resided at Nottingham, Burlington County, N J
About 1770, he founded the celebrated Atsion iron furnace
1775, Oct 25 He was Lieutenant-Colonel, of the Second Regiment, Monmouth County Militia, which he resigned on this date
1775. He was a Member of the New Jersey Provincial Congress in June and August of this year.
1777 He was imprisoned, in Burlington County jail, from April to October, of this year, by order of the Council of Safety, but no charge of disloyalty or other reason is assigned It has been thought that some Quakerish influence of his second wife, Huldah Mott, might have been the cause of his withdrawal from active service, and thereby been the means of casting suspicion upon him.
1797 He is alluded to as Joseph Saltar, of Atsion works
In 1805, he again resided in Shrewsbury, N. J

"Joseph Salter my uncle died, 8 mo., 28, 1820, aged 88 years"
From the Bible of Mr Asher Holmes, Wickatunk, N J

He married, first, Sally, daughter of Samuel Holmes She was born Sept 19, 1734, and died in 1757

"Sarah Salter departed this life January 14, 1757, Daughter of Samuel and . . [worn] Holmes" From the Bible of Mr Asher Holmes, Wickatunk, N J.

He married, second, 10 mo , 25, 1759, Huldah Mott, who died Dec 6, 1778, whereupon he married, third, 9 mo., 10, 1779, Rachel Robinson, née Hartshorne

New York, Febr. 20th, 1768

Mr James Mott,
  Sir

I Recd yours of the 16th Inft whare you Inform me of the moneys Mr Solter has Due to him I never Doughted his Abelety to pay his Debts all I Say Is that Mr Salter Built house and Barn with my money, when he knew I wanted it & then wrighs to me, that he cannot, even pay the Entrist, you Likewise tel me, Mr Solter Is to have the Money by the first of May, I will stay tel then for my money, befour I put my In sute, I must tel you, that It will be a very Difagreeable task for me to do aney thing that Looks like Ill Nature, but force put Is the Case, I am Sir

Your Most Humble Sarv^t
THO^s RANDALL   Cherry Hall Papers.

His will is on record at Freehold, N J , Lib B., p. 207.

Issue by first wife
57 William Saltar

Issue by second wife
58 Sarah Saltar, born 4mo , 13, 1761.
59 Richard Saltar, 10 mo , 30, 1762
60 Elizabeth Saltar, born 9 mo., 11, 1764.
61 Margaret Saltar, born 2 mo , 20, 1766
62 James Saltar, born 7 mo , 30, 1767.
63 Margaret Saltar, born 4 mo , 6, 1769.
64 Hannah Saltar, born 12 mo , 7, 1770
65 John Saltar, born 11 mo., 12, 1772.
66 Rachel Saltar, born 12 mo , 11, 1773.
67 Phebe Saltar, born 8 mo , 23, 1776

He had no issue by his third wife.

29 JOHN SALTAR, son of Richard Saltar, 5, was born Nov 17, 1733.
1759 He was taxed in Shrewsbury, N. J., £1-16-8
In 1761 and 1768, he resided in Nottingham, Burlington County, N. J ; later at Oxford, Philadelphia County, Pa , and finally in Northern Liberties, Philadelphia County, Pa.
In 1765, John Saltar, with other Citizens or Landholders, signed for a Municipal Government, for Northern Liberties, Philadelphia County, Pa
1769, Mch 5 John Saltar, merchant, of Northern Liberties, is mentioned in a land transaction
1770 John Saltar and Rebecca, his wife, of Northern Liberties.
Philadelphia Deed Book, E 7, p. 29, 159.
1780. John Saltar, of the Township of Oxford County, of Phila., Gentleman, and Elizabeth, his wife, are mentioned.
1784, Mch 1. John Saltar, residing in the City of Philadelphia, Gentleman, and Elizabeth, his wife, convey land to Thomas Cuthbert
1785 John Saltar, of the City of Philadelphia, merchant.
1795 John Saltar and wife, Elizabeth, of Oxford, Pa
1805 John Saltar, of Oxford Township, Pa.

1808, Sept. 27 Will of John Saltar, of Philadelphia County, Pa, mentioned
Wife, Elizabeth, "all on my farm in Philadelphia County"
Daughter, Margaret
Daughter, Maria
Daughter, Lucy
Son, John
Son, George
Son, Francis
He alluded to lands, in New Jersey, that he owns

1810, July   . Codicil
Son, George deceased
Grandson, Lynford Lardner, executor in the place of his son, George Saltar, deceased, with testator's wife, Elizabeth, and son, John   Philadelphia Wills, Book 3, p 352

He married, first, in 1765, Rachel Rheese, who died in 1770 He married, second, in 1774, Elizabeth Gordon, daughter of Thomas Gordon,* by his wife, Janet, daughter of David Mudie.

Issue by first wife
68 Margaret Saltar

Issue by second wife
69 Maria Saltar
70 Lucy Saltar
71 Lawrence Saltar, died, unmarried, at the age of twenty-two years.
72 John Saltar
73 George Saltar, died, unmarried, at the age of twenty-two
74 Frances Saltar, my correspondent, in 1879
75 Gordon Saltar, died in childhood

30 LAWRENCE SALTAR, son of Richard Saltar, 5
1768 He was a resident of Nottingham, Burlington County, West Jersey
1780 He resided in Evesham, Burlington County, N J He was dubbed, "Iron-master," and had wife, Dorothy It appears she was a daughter of Thomas Gordon, Gentleman, late of Oxford, Pa, deceased, who left a will dated June 30, 1769, which conveyed his estate to his daughters.
Mary Gordon, [Rebecca Gordon?]
Dorothy, wife of Lawrence Saltar
Elizabeth, wife of John Saltar
Rebecca, wife of William McMurtrie, merchant, [Ann McMurtrie?]
Son, Thomas Gordon
Frances, wife of Enoch Edwards, physician
Son, George Gordon

While his will was dated 1769, the deed which contained the foregoing allusions to his children was dated 1785, and it was probably during this period that some of his children, single when the will was made, married.   Philadelphia Deeds, Book D 13, p 2

1805. Lawrence Saltar was a resident of Shrewsbury, N J

---

*Thomas Gordon was a shipping merchant, of Philadelphia, trading with the West Indies He had children, Elizabeth and Thomas The descendants of the latter reside in Philadelphia Among his grandchildren was Miss Gordon who at the advanced age of 82 years, was living, a few years ago The parents of Thomas Gordon, first mentioned, were Alexander Gordon, of Edinburgh, Scotland, and Miss Hobart of the Bishop's family of that name The wife of Thomas Gordon, first mentioned was Mary Bembridge, née Clark, a daughter of Mr Clark, by Miss Shewell, a cousin to the wife of Benjamin West Miss Coleman has letters referring to this connection

There was seemingly another Lawrence Saltar contemporary with the one we have mentioned, who occasions much confusion. It has been claimed that Richard Saltar left two sons by the name of Lawrence, but a careful scrutiny of his will and records does not sustain any such assertion.

Miss Frances Saltar wrote "Concerning this uncle there is the record of his marriage to Dorothy Gordon, but no notice of a previous marriage. Among some old letters written by Elizabeth Gordon, wife of John Saltar, I find one to a friend, dated Dec 3rd, 1769, and quote from it these words. 'Dolly was married last Thursday'; then follows a list of guests and an account of the wedding festivities, quaint and amusing. There is nothing to indicate that Dolly was the second wife."

Lawrence Saltar, who married Dolly Gordon, left no issue.

1783, Oct 25 John Saltar and Thomas Saltar, of Philadelphia, and John Lawrence, of Burlington, and Sarah Saltar, widow of Lawrence Saltar, administrators of Lawrence Saltar. Trenton Administrations, Lib. 25, p. 78.

1785, August Will of Sarah Saltar, of Philadelphia, widow of Lawrence Saltar, late of New Jersey, Gentleman, deceased, proved Feb. 3, 1786, bequeathed
To Women's Monthly Meeting of Friends, Philadelphia, £10
To sister, Deborah Howard's children, a legacy
To father, John Howard

The Lawrence Saltar, who complicates matters by appearing here, married Mary Tremaine. What his relation may be to Lawrence Saltar, the son of Richard Saltar, I have not determined.

31 ELISHA SALTAR, son of Richard Saltar, 5, was born 1727, and died in 1756. He had a son mentioned in his father's will, as

76 "Richard, son of my son Elisha, deceased."

32 ELIZABETH SALTAR, daughter of Richard Saltar, 5, was born 1739. She married, first, Esek Hartshorne, second, Thomas Ustick.

Issue

77 Richard Saltar Hartshorne, married Hannah Stevens
78 William Hartshorne, married Jane Ustick
79 Ezekiel Hartshorne, married Susan Treat
80 Elizabeth Hartshorne, married Tylee Williams
81 Hannah Hartshorne, married, first, Thomas Ustick; second, Jacob Corlies She died in 1869

33 SARAH SALTAR, daughter of Richard Saltar, 5, married Robert Hartshorne

Issue

82 William Hartshorne, married Sarah Lawrence.
83 Elizabeth Hartshorne; married Robert Bowne
84 Richard Hartshorne, married Susan Ustick
85 Sally Hartshorne, married William Ustick

34 LUCY SALTAR, daughter of Richard Saltar, 5, married John Hartshorne

Issue

86 Lawrence Hartshorne, married, first, E Ustick, second, Abigail Tremaine
87 Hannah Hartshorne, married Thomas Eddy
88 John Hartshorne, married, first, E Field, second, Hannah Hopkins

36 SUSAN SALTAR, daughter of Richard Saltar, 5, married Henry Scott.

Issue

89 Henry Scott
90 Eliza Scott
91 Charles Scott
92 Anne Scott

37 MANASSAH SALTAR, son of Ebenezer Saltar, 7, was an eminent New York merchant. He resided in that city, at the corner of Broadway and Cortlandt St He married Catharine Wright, who after his demise, bought Governor Ogden's place, in Elizabethtown, N J, where her son, Thomas, and her grandson, Commodore William D Saltar, subsequently lived His license to marry Catharine Wright is dated Jan 6, 1764

His wife and issue, are mentioned in his will, written Jan 19, 1798, proved May 27, 1799. All three survived him In this instrument, he expresses himself strongly against Robert McMenomy, who it appears married his daughter Eliza, for his unkind treatment of his wife and her family That he could in no way control any part of her legacy, he leaves it in charge of his worthy friend, the Rev. Benjamin Moore, assistant minister of Trinity Church, and his son, Thomas Saltar.

Issue

93 Thomas Saltar
94 Eliza Saltar

38 DANIEL SALTER, son of Ebenezer Saltar, 7, is said to have been born in New Jersey, and inferentially about 1738. His remains lie in "the Ryerson Churchyard." He lived on Staten Island, at Black Horse, about the center of the County, where he owned much land, and was, at one time, Collector During the Revolutionary period, he resided on the Island, and was an object of suspicion to both Whig and Tory When the British came to the Island, they billeted themselves upon him and made way with most of his movable property His sympathy, though possibly then disguised, was with the American party, as is abundantly proven by subsequent developments Both he and his brother Manassah, were constantly in contact with the British, and to avoid imprisonment and confiscation of their property, tried to remain neutral By old residenters, he was thought to have been the only one of the name upon the Island In a list of the officers of the first Court, on Staten Island, under the Republican Government, 1784, he appears as one of the Constables

In 1786, he gave to John Mersereau a bond for £50, both being of Staten Island

1788, Apr 1 He took a bond from Richard Merrell,* yeoman, both of the County of

---

*Daniel Salter was financially ruined by going security, says tradition, for the Collector of Staten Island, presumably Richard Merrill, or Morrell, who gave his bond, for £200, to Daniel Salter, April 1, 1788 The Black Horse property, in his day, had a lien on it, which was subsequently removed About 1847 a purchase of land was made there by Capt George Malcolm, subject to claims by heirs of Daniel Salter The proof to establish the claim was given to his son, Amos Salter, who would not engage in a law suit Amos Salter gave the papers to Paul Salter, the son of John Salter, who probably did nothing, as he returned a bond, since lost, in 1857, to Amos Salter

Richmond, N Y, for £200, to guarantee the payment of £100 to be paid in one year. Witnesses A Ryertz and John Salter In the bond Daniel Salter is designated as "Innholder."*

Subsequent to this date, he removed to Bergen County, N J, which then included Hudson County. Here he held the position of Deputy and then Acting-Sheriff of the County, under Sheriff Westervelt, who had become incapable

He married, first, Miss Ellis (?), second, Patience Heaggy or Hedden, of Mornstown, N J, third, the widow Van Houton, the sister of Capt. Berry, fourth Miss

Issue by first wife
95 John Salter
96 Ebenezer Salter
97 Daniel Salter
98 Richard Salter

Issue by second wife
99 William Salter
100 Amos Salter
101 Joseph Salter

By his third and fourth wives he had no issue

Daniel Salter and his descendants, by accident or intent, reverted to the original way of spelling the name, *Salter* instead of *Saltar*

39 ALICE SALTAR, supposed daughter of Ebenezer Saltar, 7, married James Lisk, of Staten Island, by license dated Aug 16, 1757. It was signed by James and John Lisk, and James Reed, as bondsmen With the exception of the last, who was of Perth Amboy, all were of Staten Island

40 THOMAS SALTAR, supposed son of Ebenezer Saltar, 7

About 1879, when I commenced to compile the Salter notes, which were shortly after published in the files of the Monmouth Democrat, Freehold, N J, and which afterward were reissued in pamphlet form, I had no knowledge of certain children, since discovered, belonging to Richard Saltar, the First Because of this I was disposed, by an eliminative process, to attribute certain children to Ebenezer Saltar, who now I would be disposed to classify as descendants of Richard Saltar, the First, through unknown lines. Of these, Alice, Thomas and Elezar Saltar are instances

In the will of Richard Saltar, 5, is mentioned "my nephew Thomas"; hence a grandson of Richard Saltar, the First.

The name Thomas, occurs in, and I may say is restricted to, the line of Ebenezer Saltar, hence the inference that he is a son of this individual The nephew Thomas, that Richard Saltar alludes to, I think is, without doubt, Thomas Saltar, the opulent merchant, of Philadelphia, who died in 1790 Against this supposition is the fact that the sisters to whom he bequeathed his estate, and who likewise would be children of Ebenezer Saltar, are not, from any knowledge I possess, his issue, but the lack of my knowledge is so great that it would not warrant their exclusion

1731, May 31 James Ashton and Elisha Lawrence, of Freehold, send greeting Whereas Thomas Saltar, of Freehold, by deed of this date, gave twenty-five acres of land, lying in Freehold, to them, they do declare the same a trust for "the Society of People called Baptists."

*The original is now 1882 in the possession of Smith Salter, Esq, Forked River, N J

41 ELEZAR SALTAR, supposed son of Ebenezer Saltar, 7 Possibly this name is correct, but it suggests itself to me that an error has occurred in copying, and that it should be Ebenezer instead

The name appears as a witness to the will of Elizabeth, widow of John Saltar, which was written 1728 and proved 1741

Elezar Saltar is placed among the children of Ebenezer Saltar, merely because of the supposed similarity of names

54 ABRAHAM LINCOLN, son of John Lincoln, 19, went to Kentucky, in 1782, where he was killed, by an Indian, in 1784, who in turn was shot and killed by Abraham's eldest son, Mordecai, a lad of fourteen years, who had been concealed behind a log and who picked up his father's gun

He married Mary, daughter of Robert and Sarah (Rachael) Shipley, and her sister, Nancy Shipley, married Joseph Hanks This last mentioned pair had a daughter, Nancy Hanks, who married her first cousin, Thomas Lincoln, son of Abraham Lincoln, 54

Issue

    Thomas Lincoln, died, Jan 17, 1851, in Cole Co., Ill, where he had resided twenty years He married, first, Nancy Hanks, who died Oct 5, 1818, second, Dec 2, 1819, Sarah Bush, widow of Daniel Johnson She was born Dec 13, 1788.

    Issue

    Abraham Lincoln President of the United States, an only son, who, in 1854, was of Springfield aged forty-five, and had three children, the eldest of whom was eleven years of age His wife was born and raised in Kentucky He was born Feb 12, 1809

    Mordecai Lincoln, born 1770, died, 1831-2, in Hancock County, Ill, whither he had recently removed from Kentucky with his children.

    Josiah Lincoln, living, or dead, in 1854 He had lived on the Big Blue River, Hancock Co, Ind.

    Mary Lincoln

    Nancy Lincoln, born Feb. 10, 1807.

57 WILLIAM SALTAR, son of Joseph Saltar, 28, as appears in the will of his sister, Hannah, written in 1854, had one son, Joseph, a legatee in her will

He married Sarah, daughter of Thomas and (Rachel Hartshorne) Robinson Her mother, Rachel, upon the death of her husband, Thomas Robinson, married Joseph Saltar

In 1796, William Saltar, with John Hartshorne, bought lands of Josiah Foster, in Gloucester County, N J

William Saltar moved to Utica, N Y, where he was an officer in the branch of the U S Bank. In 1796, the condition of the Indians was so unsatisfactory that Joseph Saltar, 28, though advanced in years at this time, was, with others, appointed to attend to the lands assigned to them, etc.

In 1801, the Indians wishing to sell their lands and move to New Stockbridge, near Oneida Lake, William Saltar, William Stockton and Enoch Evans, were appointed Commissioners to sell their lands

In 1802, William Saltar had resigned and another person occupied his place.

Issue

102 Joseph Saltar, residing in Buffalo, N Y, in 1882, has a daughter
103 Miss Saltar; married Mr Mappie, Mappa or Mapps

104 James Saltar; died, at Trenton, N J, under tragic circumstances He was State Treasurer. He was probably the person who wrote a letter, from Trenton, N J, Dec. 28, 1802, to James Mott, at Washington, D. C

105 Miss Saltar

58 SARAH SALTAR, daughter of Joseph Saltar, 28, resided in Shrewsbury, N J, where she died Sept. 29, 1840 Her tombstone, in Christ Churchyard, gives her birth as Apr 13, 1761

1839, Mch 29. Will of Sarah Saltar, proved Jan 27, 1841, mentioned
Sister, Elizabeth Saltar
Sister, Hannah Saltar
Sister, Margaret Saltar
Sister-in-law, widow of her brother, Richard
Nieces, Huldah Price and Mary L Saltar, daughters of her brother, Richard
Joseph Saltar, son of her brother, William Saltar
Jane, daughter of John and Sarah Mappa
Elizabeth Mappa
Nephews, Joseph Saltar and Nathan J Saltar, sons of her brother, Richard
Niece, Rebecca S, wife of Joseph B Shinn
Niece, Frances S Cline
Nephews, Charles, Richard S, and Jesse E Cline

59 RICHARD SALTAR, son of Joseph Saltar, 28 He was deceased prior to 1839, when his widow was alluded to, in the will of his sister, Sarah Saltar She was Elizabeth Jackson, to whom he was married Nov 18, 1815

He resided at Red Bank, N J, or in its vicinity

In 1816-17, Richard Saltar, Jr, was living in Shrewsbury, N J.

In 1818, he was temporarily residing at Tom's River, N. J. He may have been interested with his sisters in the property known as Ballantrail, in this town, which some time later they conveyed to Garret Irons

Issue

106 Huldah Saltar, married Mr Price, prior to 1841
107 Mary L Saltar
108 Joseph Saltar
109 Nathan Jackson Saltar

60 ELIZABETH SALTAR, daughter of Joseph Saltar, 28, resided at Shrewsbury, N J, where she died Apr 21, 1846 Her tombstone, in Christ Churchyard, gives her birth as Sept. 11, 1764

1841, May 26 Will of Elizabeth Saltar, proved Oct 29, 1850, mentioned
Niece, Mary Saltar, daughter of her brother, Richard
Niece, Huldah Price
Niece, Frances S Cline
Niece, Rebecca, wife of Joseph B Shinn

Elizabeth Saltar and her sisters, Sarah, Margaret and Hannah, maiden ladies, resided with their uncle, James Mott, during his lifetime, and after his decease, they kept house in Shrewsbury, N J All four are buried in the Episcopal Churchyard, in Shrewsbury, N J., adjacent to each other

63 MARGARET SALTAR, daughter of Joseph Saltar, 28, is interred in the Episcopal Churchyard, in Shrewsbury, N J, with tombstone record

Margaret Saltar born Apr 9, 1769, died Aug 21, 1860

64 HANNAH SALTAR, daughter of Joseph Saltar, 28, resided at Shrewsbury, N. J, where she died Aug 12, 1855. Her remains were interred in Christ Churchyard, in that village, and her tombstone gives her birth as Dec. 7, 1770

1854, Jan 18. Will of Hannah Saltar, proved Dec 5, 1860, mentioned
Sister, Margaret Saltar
Sister, Elizabeth Saltar
Brother, William Saltar
Children of her brother, Richard Saltar, viz .
                  Mary Saltar
                  Huldah Price
                  Joseph Saltar
                  Nathan Jackson Saltar
Joseph Saltar, son of her brother, William
Niece, Frances S Kline
Niece, Rebecca Shinn
Elizabeth and John Mapps
Executor   Edmund T Williams

66   RACHEL SALTAR, daughter of Joseph Saltar, 28, married Mr. Cline, of Atsion
Issue
110   Joseph Cline
111   Fanny Cline, who lived with her aunts at Shrewsbury, N. J.
111ª   Rebecca Cline, married Joseph B Shinn, moved West

68   MARGARET SALTAR, daughter of John Saltar, 29, married John Lardner   He died in 1825, and she, in May, 1833 or 1834   They resided at Tacony, outside of Philadelphia, Pa
Issue
112   Lynford Lardner
113   Elizabeth Lardner
114   Richard Lardner
115   Penn Lardner
116   John Lardner
117   Lawrence Saltar Lardner
118   James Lawrence Lardner
119   Henry Lardner
120   Edward Lardner
121   Alexander Lardner

69   MARIA SALTAR, daughter of John Saltar, 29, married, Nov 11, 1795, Kearney Wharton, of Philadelphia, who was born about 1765, and died Jan. 4, 1848   The Wharton family history appears in Keith's Provincial Councillors of Pennsylvania, Philadelphia, 1883
Issue
122   Thomas L Wharton, born 1799
123   John Wharton; died, about 1833, unmarried
124   Lloyd Wharton
125   Elizabeth Wharton
126   George Wharton, died unmarried.
127   James Wharton, residing in Philadelphia, 1882

72 JOHN SALTAR, son of John Saltar, 29, lived at Tacony, Pa., where he married Margaret, daughter of Samuel Howell, Esq

Issue

128 Lawrence Saltar, died, October, 1832, in his twenty-first year
129 John Saltar, of Tacony, Pa
130 Annie E Saltar

74 FRANCES SALTAR, daughter of John Saltar, 29, was born about 1790, and died, unmarried, Sept 20, 1880, at Pemberton, N. J.
It was through the courtesy of this most estimable lady that I obtained much of the information embodied in this manuscript.

93 THOMAS SALTAR, son of Manassah Saltar, 37, was born Nov 4, 1764, and died Apr 6, 1853 He married, first, July 24, 1785, Charlotte, daughter of Jonathan Dayton, born Sept 20, 1766, died May 11, 1802 He married, second, Oct 28, 1802, Abby, daughter of the Hon Abraham Clarke, one of the signers of the Declaration of Independence She died, Oct 25, 1811, aged thirty-eight years He married, third, July 18, 1812, Susan Henrietta, daughter of Matthias Williamson, an eminent member of the New Jersey bar She died, July 19, 1866, aged eighty-nine years

Issue by first wife

131 Thomas Beston Saltar, born Aug 21, 1786, died Aug. 27, 1789
132 Charles Wright Saltar, born Sept 21, 1787, died young
133 Charlotte Dayton Saltar, born Nov 23, 1790, died Feb 21, 1870
134 Thomas Barton Saltar, born Oct 27, 1792, died Nov 6, 1850
135 William Dayton Saltar, born Aug 23, 1794, died Jan 3, 1869.
136 Jonathan Dayton Saltar, born June 9, 1796, died Mch 3, 1797
137 John L Youngsberg Saltar, born Aug 26, 1798, died Apr 20, 1800
138 Catharine Maria Saltar, born July 28, 1800, died Sept 19, 1861.
139 Jonathan Steel Saltar, born May 9, 1802, died Jan. 11, 1837

Issue by second wife

140 George Wright Saltar, born February 1804, died June 17, 1805.
141 Louisa Abby Wright Saltar, born Mch 14, 1805; living in 1879

Issue by third wife

142 Matthias Williamson Saltar, born Aug 3, 1813; died Sept 6, 1857.
143 Frederick Henry Beesley Saltar, born Feb 18, 1815
144 Susan Henrietta Saltar ⎫ twins ⎧ living in 1879
145 Maria Louise Saltar   ⎭   ⎩ born Sunday, Apr. 7, 1816.
146 Harrietta Saltar, born June 10, 1817, died Feb 28, 1818
147 Harrietta Matilda Spencer Saltar, born Dec. 15, 1821; living in 1879.

94 ELIZA SALTAR, daughter of Manassah Saltar, 37, married Robert McMenomy, a clerk in her father's store, who successfully aspired to her hand
In the latter part of his life he kept an auction store in Chatham St., New York City.

Issue

148 Mary Catharine McMenomy

SALTER OF MONMOUTH COUNTY

149 Eliza Loskiel Bernardo McMenomy, married John Cronly, and was deceased, in 1879, without issue
150 Lavinia Louise McMenomy

95 JOHN SALTER, son of Daniel Salter, 38, married Mary Latourette?

Issue

151 Paul Salter
152 Mary Salter
153 Daniel Salter
154 Rev David B Salter

96 EBENEZER SALTER, son of Daniel Salter, 38, married Sally . , and died, on Staten Island, leaving a son, who was lost from a vessel, in New York Bay, when seventeen or eighteen years of age.

97 DANIEL SALTER, son of Daniel Salter, 38, married Miss Stormes? He lived, in Reade St , New York City, about the year 1797, but subsequently removed it is supposed up the North River, where he died, probably leaving a son, viz.

155 John Salter

98 RICHARD SALTER, son of Daniel Salter, 38, died at Pompton, N J It is not known whether he left issue

99 WILLIAM SALTER, son of Daniel Salter, 38, was born about 1786 or 1787, and died probably in 1826 He moved to Yorktown, Va., became a Presbyterian minister and preached at Madison, then called Battle Hill

Issue

156 Miss Salter, married Dr Nelson, of Yorktown, Va
157 Gawen Lane Corbin Salter, born about 1821, of Richmond, Va

100 AMOS SALTER, son of Daniel Salter, 38, was born Jan. 7, 1789. He married, first, Sarah Frazier, born Dec. 15, 1791 He married, second, Amy Latourette, who died, in 1841, without issue. He married, third, Alice Walton, of Philadelphia, Pa

Issue by first wife

158 Uriah Salter, born Jan 8, 1809
159 Warren Salter, born about 1810, died aged eleven months
160 Elizabeth Salter
161 Emeline Salter
162 Silas Hedden Salter
163 Smith Salter
164 Sarah Salter, born Aug 9, 1821, unmarried, in 1879, living at Forked River, N J
165 Edwin Salter
166 Rachel Matilda Salter

Issue by third wife

167 Charles Burleigh Salter, born about 1842, died, at Leonardville, N J , in 1910
168 Samuel Dexter Salter, died leaving one son.

169 Ann Eliza Salter, of Salterville, married Anthony Vanzee
170 Wesley Fountain Salter, married Miss . .
171 Julia Salter, married Washington Warden, of Forked River, N J.

101 JOSEPH SALTER, son of Daniel Salter, 38, married Miss Walker He died in Yorktown, Va., and probably left no issue.

102 JOSEPH SALTAR, son of William Saltar, 57, was residing, in Buffalo, N Y, in 1882.

1890, May 3 The following paragraph appeared in a New York paper, which I think must refer to him " Joseph Saltar, said to have been the oldest inhabitant of Buffalo, in point of years, is dead, aged ninety-four. He went to Buffalo, in 1829, as teller of a branch of the United States Bank. For many years he was cashier of the Buffalo Custom House "

122 THOMAS L. WHARTON, son of MARIA (SALTAR) Wharton, 69, married Sarah Ann Smith, of Philadelphia, Pa.

Issue

172 Lucy Wharton, married Joseph W. Drexel, of New York; banker

Issue

Catharine Drexel
Bessie Drexel
Lucy Drexel
Josephine Drexel

173 Fanny Wharton, married Guy V Henry, U S A He was a Civil War veteran, and subsequently an officer in the regular army, rising by his great valor to the position of Brigadier-General. He was popularly known as "Fighting Guy," and bore numerous scars telling of hairbreadth escapes from the Indians and other enemies He died, in 1899, from illness contracted in the Spanish-American War Mrs Henry died in 1873

124 LLOYD WHARTON, son of MARIA (SALTAR) Wharton, 69, changed his name upon inheriting the Bickley estates, from Wharton to Bickley He married Margaret A, daughter of Samuel Howell, of Tacony, Pa.

Issue

174 Lloyd W Bickley, married Hannah, daughter of Daniel Miller
175 Robert Bickley, married Agnes Singer, of Philadelphia, Pa
176 Abraham W Bickley, married Laura Vail, of New York
177 Howell Bickley, married Miriam, daugther of Thomas Scott, of Philadelphia, Pa

125 ELIZABETH WHARTON, daughter of MARIA (SALTAR) Wharton, 69, married Thomas Morris, of Reading, Pa She died May, 1877

Issue

178 Wharton Morris
179 Maria Morris, married D J B Brooke, of Reading, Pa

129 JOHN SALTAR, son of John Saltar, 72, married, first, Ellen Gilmore, second, Miss

Issue by first wife
180 Frances Saltar; died young
181 John Saltar

Issue by second wife
182 Margaret Saltar

130 ANNIE E. SALTAR, daughter of John Saltar, 72, married Dr. J. P. Coleman, of Pemberton, N J

Issue
183 Sallie Pearson Coleman
184 Annie Saltar Coleman
185 James Pearson Coleman

Mrs. Coleman, and her daughter, Miss Annie S Coleman, aided in making this sketch much more complete than it otherwise could have been, by kindly supplying considerable information concerning their branch of the family

133 CHARLOTTE DAYTON SALTAR, daughter of Thomas Saltar, 93, was born Nov 23, 1790, married William D. Williamson.

Issue
186 William Saltar Williamson ⎫
187 Henrietta Louise Williamson ⎬ All deceased in 1882.
188 Charlotte Dayton Williamson ⎭

134 THOMAS BARTON SALTAR, son of Thomas Saltar, 93, was born Oct. 27, 1792, died Nov 6, 1850 He was a Surgeon in the U. S Navy

1850, Jan 3 Will of Thomas Barton Saltar, proved Dec. 30, 1850, mentioned himself as "now stationed at New York," and referred to his sisters, Charlotte and Catharine, and suggested that, at an early date, they should make their wills He appointed his cousin, Jonathan Dayton Hull, of New York City, and Dr. Charles Davis, of Elizabethtown, N J, executors   New York City Wills, Lib 101, p. 28

He probably never married and left no issue

135 WILLIAM DAYTON SALTAR, son of Thomas Saltar, 93, born Aug 23, 1794, died Jan 3, 1869. He was a Commodore in the U S Navy, and served with marked distinction He married Margaret Armstrong

Issue
189 George T Elliott Saltar ⎫
190 Meta Armstrong Saltar ⎬ All deceased in 1882
191 Emily Hewson Saltar   ⎭

143 FREDERICK HENRY BEESLEY SALTAR, son of Thomas Saltar, 93, was born Feb 18, 1815 He graduated in Philadelphia, Pa , about 1838, and soon after went West, where he practiced medicine, at Montezuma, Iowa, until his decease, Feb 1, 1882 He married Caroline Wells

His widow, several of his children, and grandchildren survived him.

Issue
192 Thomas Saltar
193 Caroline Saltar
194 Henry Saltar, deceased, in 1879.
195 Frederick Saltar, deceased, in 1879.
196 Charles Atkinson Saltar
197 Louisa Saltar, deceased, in 1879

144 SUSAN HENRIETTA SALTAR, daughter of Thomas Saltar, 93, married Col. George W Wallace, U S A   Mrs Wallace was living, in 1882, in New York.

Issue
198 William Wallace
199 Thomas Wallace
200 Lizzie Wallace

145 MARIA LOUISA SALTAR, daughter of Thomas Saltar, 93, married Col. William E Prince, U S A   She died Aug. 11, 1864

Issue
201 Annie Coolidge Prince
202 Gertrude Prince
203 Louise Gordon Prince
204 Susan Lyman Prince, married, Romulus R. Colgate, Aug 31, 1882

147 HARRIETTA MATILDA SPENCER SALTAR, daughter of Thomas Saltar, 93, was born Dec 15, 1821; married Elisha R Codwise

Issue
205 Edward Bertie Codwise
206 Louisa Saltar Codwise, born Nov. 11, 1850.

148 MARY CATHARINE McMENOMY, daughter of Robert McMenomy and ELIZA SALTAR, 94, married Thomas Bell   She was deceased in 1879

Issue
207 Rosa Bell, married Samuel Brevoort, of New York, by whom she had three sons and one daughter, Mary Brevoort

150 LAVINIA LOUISE McMENOMY, daughter of Robert McMenomy and ELIZA SALTAR, 94, married Laurent Allien

Issue
208 Miss Allien, married Earle Douglass, of New York

151 PAUL SALTER, son of John Salter, 95, was born about 1788   He located in Ocean County, N. J , with his brother, the Rev David B. Salter, between 1810 and 1818, but removed, in 1833, probably to Salterville, Hudson County, N J., and later to Henderson County, Ill , about 1840 to 1850, where he died, about 1870, leaving numerous descendants   He married Betsey Cubberly.

Issue

209 John Salter
210 Thomas Salter
211 Paul Salter
212 David Salter, died in the late Civil War
213 Susan Salter
214 Mary Ann Salter
215 Sarah Salter

152 MARY SALTER, daughter of John Salter, 95, was born in 1792, married Lorenzo Jaquins, of Jersey City, N J, who was at one time Sheriff of Bergen County, N. J.

No issue.

153 DANIEL SALTER, son of John Salter, 95, was born about 1795: married Mary Cook, of Athens, N Y.

Issue

216 William Salter

154 REV DAVID B SALTER, son of John Salter, 95, was born May 5, 1798 About 1818, he lived in that part of Monmouth County, N J., now called Ocean County, whence he removed, in 1833, to Salterville, Hudson County, N. J., of which place he was still a resident in 1878

In 1817, he married Abigail Parker, a cousin of the Hon Joel Parker, of New Jersey Upon her demise, he married a daughter of Sylvester Hutchinson, of Hightstown, N J, who, with his brother, Robert, were famous, as preachers, among the Methodists of New Jersey.

1817, July 2 In the Staten Island records, of this date, there appears a transfer of property from the Rev. David B. Salter, of Dover, Monmouth County, N J, to Paul Latourette, Sr, of Paulus Hook, N J, but formerly of Northfield, S. I

Issue by first wife

217 Anthony Parker Salter, born about 1818
218 John Salter, born about 1823
219 Daniel Salter, born about 1825.
220 Paul D. Salter, born about 1828.

158 URIAH SALTER, son of Amos Salter, 100, was born Jan 8, 1809.

In 1879, he was living, in New York, and had a family of several daughters and one son, by name

221 George W. Salter

160 ELIZABETH SALTER, daughter of Amos Salter, 100, was born Jan 3, 1812 She married Capt Jacob Conover Williams, of Forked River, N J She was living, in 1879, and had a family of three sons and one daughter

161 EMELINE SALTER, daughter of Amos Salter, 100, was born Nov 12, 1814, and died Mch 2, 1859 She married Capt David Stout Parker, of Forked River, N J, and had a daughter

222 Sarah Elizabeth Parker, married John Calvin Bowers

162 SILAS HEDDEN SALTER, son of Amos Salter, 100, was born May 25, 1816, and died Aug. 9, 1851 He married Alice Woodbury

Issue
223 Elizabeth Salter, married Christopher Van Riper
224 George W. A Salter

163 SMITH SALTER, son of Amos Salter, 100, was born June 23, 1818, and was living in 1879 He married, first, Mary Stryker, second, Sarah King

Issue by first wife
225 Edwin Salter, killed at the battle of Pittsburgh Landing
226 Eliza Salter, married, and moved to Illinois

Issue by second wife
227 Joseph Salter, born 1860.

165 HON EDWIN SALTER, son of Amos Salter, 100, was born Feb 6, 1824

Mr. Salter from early life until the date of his demise, was actively engaged in politics For many years he largely shaped the political course of Ocean County, N J , which he represented, for several terms, in the State Legislature, commencing in 1856 In 1859, he was chosen Speaker of the House, and had it not been for his retiring disposition and excessive modesty, he would have been crowded into more important places In later life, he was employed in the Auditor's Division of the Treasury Department, at Washington In the discharge of his duties, he was able and active In speech, he was terse, direct and logical, rather than eloquent. In all his dealings with his fellow man, he was upright and downright, yet urbane beyond common, and punctiliously punctual He was an ardent student of history, local and general, and a member of several historical bodies He contributed to them and to the newspapers, innumerable articles on history and genealogy, and was at the date of his death, preparing an history of Ocean County, N. J., which was produced in its skeleton form, as a posthumous work To him is due great credit as a pioneer in this line of research He awakened in many a feeling of family pride, whereby was rescued traditions and facts from oblivion Much of his material was prepared distant from the scenes about which he wrote, and from the records and individuals which could best supply him with information, yet his articles for the press were replete with interest to the general reader, as well as to the historian and genealogist He was sincerely mourned by a large circle of friends

He married, Mch 6, 1853, Margaret J Bodine, of Staten Island, who was born in February, 1830

Issue
228 George William Salter, born Dec. 30, 1853, died, Mch 27, 1880, while serving as Paymaster's Clerk, in the U S N , at Rio de Janeiro, Brazil.

An only son, an upright man, his loss was greatly deplored and found expression in many tributes appearing in public print which his father gathered and published in pamphlet form, "In Memoriam"

166 RACHEL SALTER, daughter of Amos Salter, 100, was born June 22, 1826; married, first, Capt. George Malcolm, of Forked River, N J , second, George Vreeland She died in 1873

Issue by first wife
229 Washington Irving Malcolm, deceased about 1863
230 Edwin Malcolm
231 Leslie Malcolm
232 Frederick Malcolm
233 Horatio Malcolm
234 Matilda Malcolm
235 Ida Malcolm

No issue by the second marriage

181 JOHN SALTAR, son of John Saltar, 129, married Miss Sallie Pearson, daughter of Dr J Pearson Coleman, of Pemberton, N J

Issue
236 Joseph Coleman Saltar

205 EDWARD BERTIE CODWISE, son of HARRIETTA MATILDA SPENCER (SALTAR) Codwise, 147, was born May 9, 1849 He married, Emma Snyder, Mch 28, 1872

Issue
237 Harrietta Frances Codwise, born Jan 21, 1874.
238 Henry Rogers Codwise, born Mch 13, 1877

Mr. Edward B Codwise, in 1881, resided at Rosendale, Ulster County, N. Y. He supplied me with much of the information I possess concerning the descendants of Manassah Saltar

217 ANTHONY PARKER SALTER, son of Rev David B Salter, 154, was born about 1818, married Clarissa McDonald.

Issue
239 Daniel Salter
240 Thomas Salter
Other children

218 JOHN SALTER, son of Rev David B Salter, 154, was born about 1823, died about 1848 He married, about 1847, Mary Grant

No issue.

219 DANIEL SALTER, son of Rev David B Salter, 154, was born about 1825, married, about 1850, Catharine Ann, daughter of Jos J Ely

Issue
Jos Ely Salter, M D, born Apr. 24, 1859, died Feb 25, 1896, buried at East Windsor, Monmouth County, N. J

220 PAUL D. SALTER, son of Rev David B Salter, 154, was born about 1828, moved to Henderson County, Ill, with his uncle, Paul, where he married and raised a family
He has served two terms in the Illinois Legislature.

MISCELLANEOUS NOTES

In arranging genealogical material it is not uncommon to find a number of descendants who cannot be united to the parent stem It is likewise not uncommon to find pedigrees, of the same family, differing very considerably, even indeed to the extent of being irreconcilable

In a letter from Col I S. Buckalew, of Jamesburg, N J, dated Mch. 15, 1882, he stated, in response to a query, that his notes, concerning his Salter ancestry, yielded the following information

1 JOHN SALTER, born about 1735, was killed, while "loading a log," about 1775   He married "Epenetus, daughter of Thomas Gordon and Janet, daughter of David Mudie"
Whitehead's History of East Jersey, p 47.

Issue
2 Thomas Salter
3 Jacob Salter
4 John Salter
5 Margaret Salter
6 Ann Salter
7 Catharine Salter
8 Epenetus Salter, a posthumous child.

2 THOMAS SALTER, son of John Salter, 1, married Jane Sutphen.

Issue
9 Ann Salter
10 Charity Salter, married Peter Stults, of Cranbury, N. J   Had issue
11 Hezekiah Salter
12 John Salter
13 Epenetus Salter
14 Jane Salter
15 Catharine Salter
16 Arthur Salter

They moved to Hamilton County, Ohio, about 1810, accompanied by all their children, except Ann and Charity

9 ANN SALTER, daughter of Thomas Salter, 2, married Isaac G. Snedeker, of Cranbury, N J

Issue
17 Gertrude Snedeker
18 Garret I Snedeker
19 Thomas Salter Snedeker
20 Margaret Chambers Snedeker, married, Dec 12, 1829, James Buckelew, and had, among other children, Col I S Buckelew, of (Camden), Jamesburg, N J

After careful examination and correspondence, I still fail to connect John Salter, 1, with the parent stock, though it would seem as if he might be identified with John Salter, son of Richard   But a glance at the two sets of children belonging to these individuals, would exclude any such thought, even if direct assurances were wanting from the descendants of John Salter, that no such descendants, as are ascribed to John Salter, had ever been heard of

Probable Descendants of Ebenezer Saltar

—— SALTAR, probably Ebenezer, had issue, mentioned in the will of Thos Saltar, of Philadelphia, Pa., viz.

2 Thomas Saltar
3 Meribah Saltar
4 Mary Saltar
5 Sarah Saltar
6 Hannah Saltar
7 John Cox, a stepson.

2 THOMAS SALTAR, son of Ebenezer Saltar (?), is mentioned in the will of Richard Saltar, 1762, as "my nephew."   He early resided in Freehold   He wrote a fine signature and his name appears frequently as a witness to many of the mortgages made by the Loan Commissioners, at Freehold, and it may be that he was employed in that office

1748, Mch 25 Robert Hankison mortgaged twenty-eight acres, in Upper Freehold, being the plantation of Thos Taylor, dec^d Thomas Saltar was a witness to the transaction

After some years, Thomas Saltar moved to Northern Liberties, Philadelphia County, Pa , and became an opulent merchant   He married Susannah, daughter of Caspar and Eve Ulrich, of Philadelphia, as is set forth in a quit-claim deed, dated May 10, 1763, between Eve Ulrich, of Philadelphia, widow, and relict of Caspar Ulrich, dec^d, of Philadelphia, and Thomas Saltar and Susannah, his wife, a daughter of the said Caspar and Eve, and Philip Ulrich, of Philadelphia, baker, a son of the same   In the deed, it appeared that Caspar Ulrich left a will bearing date Nov 22, 1751   Philadelphia Deeds, H 18, p. 183

Susannah Ulrich was the widow of Thomas Rutter, of Philadelphia, and is so alluded to in her father's will   Her marriage to Thomas Saltar occurred, at Christ Church, Philadelphia, Dec 23, 1758, and she has been erroneously called Susannah Butler   Upon the death of his wife, Susannah, Thomas Saltar married Sarah Stewart, a widow with four children

In 1765, he was among the Citizens or Landholders who signed for a Municipal Government for Northern Liberties, Philadelphia County, Pa

1772 and 1779 Thomas Saltar was joined by his wife, Susannah, frequently, in deeds

In 1790, in a deed of land, in Upper Freehold, the "land now or late Thomas Saltar's," is alluded to, near Doctor's Creek, Burlington Path, Daniel Grandin's land, Job Throckmorton's land, and others

1790 His death occurred, and his large estate was distributed, by will, among his kinspeople as he, himself, was childless.   As it throws light upon the family, and is, itself, an interesting document, a synopsis of it follows

1785, Oct 4 Will of Thomas Saltar, of Northern Liberties, City of Philadelphia, merchant, proved June 7, 1790, mentioned

Executors my nephew, Thomas Britton, and good friends, Peter Knight, Charles Wharton and Richard Whitehead

My step-brother, John Cox, now living in North Carolina, all my wearing apparel to be forwarded to him.

To my executors my dwelling house, household goods, furniture, plate and all the rents and profits of my other lands, etc., to hold during the life of my beloved wife, Susanna Saltar, for support of said wife

All those persons now of my family to continue and dwell in my said dwelling house; to live there and be supported, except only my brother-in-law, Thomas Leaming, who must "cloathe himself"

If the said rents and incomes be more than sufficient for support of my said wife and family to pay and distribute the overplus annually, to and among my two sisters, Mary Leaming and Meribah Robbins, (now living in New Jersey), and such of their daughters and sons in need thereof

To my niece, Sarah Williamson

My executors to sell my lands

To my nephew, John Britton, £50, after death of my wife Susanna, the son of my late sister, Hannah Britton

To my nephew, Thomas Britton, son of my late sister, Hannah Britton, all my said dwelling house and lot, now in tenure of Manuel Lyre, Esq., together with the water lot wharf, stores and all my other possessions situate, between Callowhill St., and Poole's Bridge, in the Northern Liberties, City of Philadelphia, to hold to him, charged with the payment of £1,750, payable to his sister, Sarah Williamson, in four yearly payments The like sum to his sister, Rebecca Fleeson, with interest in gold or silver money, in case of death to her children

An annuity of fifty Spanish milled silver dollars to my negro boy Tom

Unto my said niece, Sarah Williamson and in case of her death, to her children, £1,750, gold or silver money with interest

After decease of my said wife, I give to my sister, Mary Leaming, [Liming], an annuity of £100 To each of her six children, John, Thomas, Ephraim, Hannah, Lucy and Ossa, £300 To her said son, John, his heirs and assigns, the lots of land, whereon he now dwells, in Upper Freehold, Monmouth County, N J, containing thirty-seven acres

After the decease of my wife, to my said brother, John Cox, lands and tenements in North Carolina To each of his ten children, Aaron, Paul, Elijah, Elisha, Rebecca, Mary, Rachel, Anne, Elizabeth and Susanna, £100, apiece

After the death of my wife, to my sister, Sarah Leaming, now living with me, an annuity of £100 After her decease, to her three daughters, Meribah, Rebecca and Sarah, £300, each, and to her son, Isaiah, now in Carolina, £200

After the decease of my wife, to my sister, Meribah Robbins, wife of Joseph Robbins, annuity of £100 After her decease to her five sons, Jacob, Thomas, John, Ezekial and Samuel, £300, each, and to her three married daughters, Priscilla, Sarah and Susannah, £300, each, and to her daughter, Rebecca, now living with me, £350

After the decease of my wife, to my niece, Rachel Woolman, (wife of Asher Woolman), £300

After the decease of my wife, to my cousin, Richard Douglass, £100 To his sister, Lydia, £50, to his brother, John, £25, and to his sister, Sarah, £25

After the decease of my wife, to Mary Chancellor, who now lives with me and attends on my wife, £200.

To Jane Brown, wife of John Brown, joiner, £25

To my good friend, Richard Whitehead, £100

After the decease of my wife, plate, bedding, household and kitchen furniture, to be divided among Sarah Williamson, Rebecca Fleeson, Rebecca Robins and Mary Robins

A great part of my estate lays in public securities which fluctuate

Signed
THOMAS SALTAR

1790, May 21   Codicil

I, Thomas Saltar, reconsidering my last Will and Testament For as much, as it has pleased Almighty God to take out of this life my wife, Susanna, and as I have since intermarried, I give to my present beloved wife, Sarah, all the plate and household furniture which she brought me, also one-third part of all my other plate, etc., and she shall have the choice

Executors said wife, Sarah, and nephew, Thomas Britton

Revokes bequest of £50, to my nephew, John Britton, and gives him 5 shillings and no more.

To nephew, John Leaming, premises in New Jersey, whereon my sister, Meribah, now dwells

Revokes bequest made to Thomas Britton of my dwelling house, bank and water lots, divides them into three equal parts for Thomas Britton and his sisters, Sarah Williamson and Rebecca Fleeson

To my beloved wife, Sarah, an annuity of £300

To sister, Meribah Robins, the tract of land and premises, in New Jersey, whereon she and her husband now dwell, after her decease to be sold, etc

Confirms the bequest or devise of land, in Upper Freehold, to John, son of his sister, Mary Leaming, whereon he dwells

To my wife's four children, John, Sarah, Helen and Charles Stewart, £150, apiece

Philadelphia Wills, Lib U, p 513

His estate was inventoried at $115,000

Mrs John Scollay, [Anne Lane Scollay, of 4014 Spruce St, Philadelphia, Pa], says that the widow of Thomas Saltar married Thomas Brittain

3 MERIBAH SALTAR, daughter of Ebenezer Saltar (?), married Joseph Robbins
In 1785, she was living in New Jersey

Issue

8 Jacob Robbins
9 Thomas Robbins
10 John Robbins
11 Ezekial Robbins
12 Samuel Robbins
13 Priscilla Robbins, married in 17—
14 Sarah Robbins, married in 17—
15 Susannah Robbins, married in 17—
16 Rebecca Robbins
17 Isaiah Robbins ⎫ as given by Mr Howard Deacon
18 Mary Robbins ⎭

4 MARY SALTAR, daughter of Ebenezer Saltar (?), married Mr Leaming
In 1785, she was living in New Jersey

1740, Nov 4 There was a Mary Cox and John Liming who had a marriage license issued in New Jersey If she is identical with Thomas Saltar's sister, she was born Cox, and was his step-sister and not a Saltar

Issue

19 John Leaming, a resident of Upper Freehold, N J
20 Thomas Leaming
21 Ephraim Leaming
22 Hannah Leaming
23 Lucy Leaming
24 Ossa Leaming

5 SARAH SALTAR, daughter of Ebenezer Saltar (?), married Thomas Leaming They resided with her brother, Thomas Saltar

Issue

25 Meribah Leaming
26 Rebecca Leaming
27 Sarah Leaming
28 Isaiah Leaming, a resident in Carolina, in 1785.

6 HANNAH SALTAR, daughter of Ebenezer Saltar (?), married Richard Britton.

"Hannah Saltar was wife to Richard Britton, late of Monmouth County, N J" Manuscript Records, First Baptist Church, Philadelphia, not Marriage Records, but Registry of Members admitted to said church wherein it was stated   Tho⁵ Allen Glenn

In 1733, Hannah Salter, wife of Richard Britton, was a member of the Middletown Baptist Church, with her parents, Ebenezer and Rebecca (Stillwell) Salter   Their names are mentioned in the original Middletown Baptist Church Record Book

1762, October She was transferred to Pennypack Baptist Church, Lower Dublin, Pa, by letter, from Middletown.   Pennypack Baptist Church Records

1771 Hannah Britton is mentioned as a member of the Montgomery County Baptist Church   Morgan Edward's History of the Baptists.

Issue

29 Thomas Britton
30 John Britton, born, July 21, 1737, in Monmouth County, East Jersey.
31 Sarah Britton, married Jesse Williamson, prior to 1785
32 Rebecca Britton, married, Thomas Fleeson, "at the house of Thomas Saltar," 27 January, 1774   First Baptist Church Marriage Book, Philadelphia, at Historical Society, p 40

7 JOHN COX, son of James Cox (?) He is spoken of as a step-brother, in the will of Thomas Saltar, 1785, and was then a resident of North Carolina. He had ten children, as enumerated in Thomas Saltar's will

33 Aaron Cox
34 Paul Cox
35 Elijah Cox
36 Rebecca Cox
37 Mary Cox
38 Rachel Cox
39 Anne Cox
40 Elizabeth Cox
41 Susanna Cox
42 Elisha Cox

29 THOMAS BRITTON, son of Richard Britton and HANNAH SALTAR, 6, was a resident of Philadelphia, and an executor and extensive devisee in the will of his uncle, Thomas Saltar 1785-1790

Thomas Britton was one of the Citizens or Landholders, who petitioned for a Municipal Government for Northern Liberties, Philadelphia County, Pa

Mrs Scollay says he was born, in 1739, and married, in 1763, Catharine Forbes, and perhaps later, Sarah Saltar

30 JOHN BRITTON, son of Richard Britton and HANNAH SALTAR, 6, was born, in Monmouth County, N J., July 21 1737 He early moved to Pennsylvania, where he was living in 1785-1790, as he is mentioned as a devisee in the will of his uncle, Thoˢ Saltar   At the latter date, 1790, his bequest of £50, was revoked, he seemingly having displeased his uncle, who cut it to 5 shillings

He married, Apr 1, 1767, (Christ Church, Philadelphia), Elenor, daughter of Thomas and Ann (Bartholomew) Waters, born, in Montgomery County, Pa, Apr 25, 1748

They had fourteen children, all born in Northern Liberties, Philadelphia County, Pa, save one, who was born in Montgomery County See Baptismal Register, First Baptist Church, Philadelphia, p 13 Also "Forde and Hansell Ancestry"

In 1765, John Britton was one of the Citizens or Landholders who signed for a Municipal Government for Northern Liberties, Philadelphia County, Pa

Westcott's History of Philadelphia, p 261

1777, Apr 19 John Britton, of Philadelphia, Pa, bought land from Peter Imlay, Jr, and wife

1779, May 27 John Britton, of the Northern Liberties of Philadelphia, Pa, lumber merchant, bought, for £20,000, New Jersey money, from Peter Imlay, yeoman, and his wife, Euphemia, of Upper Freehold, Monmouth County, N J, a plantation, in Upper Freehold, bounded by Wilkins' line, Doctor's Creek, Grover's line, Jeremiah Stillwell's corner, old forge pond, Robert Imlay's land, dec^d, John Imlay's indenture granted 1758, Peter Covenhoven's, Richard Lloyd's, Richard Britton's and Daniel and Cornelius Hendrickson's lands

1779, June He bought land in the same locality from William, Rachel and Oke Hendrickson

1790, Sept 7 He was still a resident of Philadelphia and bought again, land in this locality, from Matthias Van Horn and Catharine, his wife

1816, Mch 7 Will of John Britton, proved Mch 15, 1816, in which he set forth that he was John Britton, Senior, of the Northern Liberties of the City of Philadelphia, being advanced in years, and mentioned

Son, John Britton
Son, William Britton
Son-in-law, George Budd
Friend, Charles Biddle
} executors.

Daughter, Mary, deceased
Daughter, Susan Budd
Daughter, Sarah Forde
Son, Benjamin Britton, deceased
Daughter, Eleanor DeWees, [married, Dec 10, 1805, William De Wees], (Christ Church, Philadelphia)
Son, Saltar Britton
Daughter, Rebecca Hellings

Signed JOHN BRITTON

He was a lumber merchant residing, in 1796, at 259 N Front St Philadelphia

Stephen's Directory

SALTER

OF

NEW HAMPSHIRE

JOHN SALTER, born, probably, in the neighborhood of 1672, came from the vicinity of Exeter, England, first to the Isle of Shoals, where he was, in 1724, and thence to Odiorne's Point, where he dwelt upon an island, in Portsmouth harbor, N H, bearing his name He probably brought his wife from England He was commonly called Capt John Salter, and was the owner of sailing vessels, and his descendants for several generations followed in his footsteps as mariners He owned a farm at Rye, N. H , of thirty acres, which he willed to his grandson, Alexander Salter He was a man of courage, public spirit and of considerable affluence.

By his first wife, Martha   , he had issue, and by his second wife, Amy   . . . ., he probably had none.

1752, May 12 Will of John Salter, proved, at Exeter, N H , in 1755, set forth that he was a resident of Rye, [the township in which Odiorne's Point still remains], styled himself, "Gent ," and further mentioned

Wife, Amy, who receives £25, and many small bequests
Son, Richard Salter
Son, Titus Salter
Grandson, John Randall
Daughter, Mary Mace
Daughter, Elizabeth Ruby
Daughter, Charity Leach
Daughter, Margery Hall
Daughter, Martha Sanborn
Daughter, Sarah Sloper
John Salter ⎫
Alexander Salter ⎬ children of his deceased son, Alexander Salter
Mary Salter ⎪
Lucy Salter ⎭
Elizabeth Salter, widow of his deceased son, Alexander Salter
Executors Wife, Amy, and his son, Titus Salter

Issue by first wife
2 Richard Salter, born Mch 14, 1709
3 Titus Salter, born October, 1722, died Sept 20, 1798.
4 Alexander Salter
5 John Salter, baptized, in North Church, Oct 4, 1730, died young.
6 Mary Salter, married Mr Mace
7 Elizabeth Salter, married Mr Ruby
8 Charity Salter, married Mr Leach.
9 Margery Salter, married Mr Hall
10 Martha Salter, married, June, 1740, Ebenezer Sanborn, who was born July 25, 1712
11 Sarah Salter, married Mr Sloper.
12 Daughter   , married Mr. Randall

2 RICHARD SALTER, son of John Salter, 1, was born 1709; died, at Halifax, N. S , Apr 10, 1768 He married, Oct 8, 1731, Elizabeth Odiorne, born Feb 21, 1709; died, on Salter's Island, September, 1748

Issue
13 Elizabeth Salter, born July 6, 1732, died 1772, married Richard Mills
14 John Salter, born 1735, died an infant
15 Mehitable Salter, born 1738, married, first, 1759, Israel Tibbits, and second, John Moulton
16 John Salter, born Nov 14, 1740
17 Titus Salter
18 William Salter; single, Captain of a vessel, in 1768
19 Richard Salter, married, first, Elizabeth Ayres, and second, Elizabeth Tuesdall

SALTER OF NEW HAMPSHIRE

3 CAPT TITUS SALTER, son of John Salter, 1, served, with distinction, in the Revolutionary War, as a Captain of Militia, as also as a Captain of a frigate, during the same period At the close of the war, in 1783, he received from the General Assembly, a vote of thanks for his services He was a man of considerable activity, originality and enterprise He served, as an executor, under his father's will. He married, July 11, 1745, Elizabeth Bickford.

Issue

20 John Salter
21 Ann Salter; married, Samuel Bowles.
22 Mary Salter, born, 1761, married, Dec 2, 1788, William Emery, of Sanford, Mass She died, May 2, 1842, aged 81 years Her grandson, Titus Salter Emery, in January, 1890, resided at 138 South 4th St, Philadelphia, Pa
23 Titus Salter, married, June 24, 1804, Nancy Salter

4 ALEXANDER SALTER, son of John Salter, 1, married Elizabeth   . He died, during his father's lifetime, leaving surviving, his wife and four children His descendants may still be found at Rye, N H

1746, July 2 Alexander Saltar was on the Muster Roll of Capt Francis Locke's Company, at Fort William and Mary

Issue

24 John Saltar
25 Alexander Salter
26 Mary Salter
27 Lucy Salter

16 CAPT JOHN SALTER, son of Richard Salter, 2, was born 1740, died Sept 28, 1814 He was commonly called, John Salter, mariner He built a house, in Portsmouth, N H, which to this day is occupied by his descendants He married, first, Dec 13, 1762, Dorothy Bickford, born May 13, 1740, and who died Mch 18, 1776, whereupon he married, second, Apr. 14, 1778, Elizabeth March, of Greenland, born June 26, 1745 Upon her demise, he married, third, Nov. 1, 1781, Jane Frost, born Mch 7, 1757, died Dec 10, 1837

Issue by second wife
28 Joseph March Salter born Apr 18, 1781, died 1837

Issue by third wife
29 Dorothy Salter, born 1782, died 1853, married John Frost.
30 Elizabeth Salter, born 1784; died 1808, married William Henry Wilkins.
31 William Frost Salter, born Jan 23 or 25, 1787, died Sept 25, 1849
32 John Salter, born 1788, died 1858.
33 Maria Jane Salter, born 1790, married Hon Samuel Cushman.
34 Benjamin Salter, born Apr 6, 1792, died, Sept. 8, 1858, in New York City
35 Sarah Ann Salter, born 1794, died, single, in 1876

17 TITUS SALTER, son of Richard Salter, 2, married . . . . .
Issue
36 Titus Salter

19 CAPT RICHARD SALTER, son of Richard Salter, 2, married, first, Elizabeth Ayres, who died, July 25, 1805, aged 54, second, Elizabeth Tuesdall, who died, June 17, 1836, aged 82 Capt. Salter died prior to his last wife. He commanded the Letter of Marque brig called the Scorpion

Issue

Three Elizabeths
Two Johns } died infants.

37 Richard Salter
38 Perkins Salter
39 Thomas Salter
40 Joseph Salter
41 Nancy Salter, born 1778; married her second cousin, Titus Salter, 23.

23 JOHN SALTER, son of Capt Titus Salter, 3, married Abigail Ayers, October, 1778 He was appointed Second Lieutenant, of the privateer, General Sullivan, Nov. 17, 1778. He died in 1794

Issue

42 Henry Salter

23 TITUS SALTER, son of Capt. Titus Salter, 3, married, June 24, 1804, Nancy, daughter of Capt Richard Salter, 19.

Issue

43 Ann Salter, married C S. Toppan
44 Mary Salter; married J. M. Tredick.
45 Charlotte Salter
46 Henry Salter

24 JOHN SALTER, son of Alexander Salter, 4, was probably he who was on the pay roll of Col John Langdon's Light Horse Volunteer Company, in the expedition to Rhode Island, August, 1778

25 ALEXANDER SALTER, son of Alexander Salter, 4, was mustered, in Capt. Jos Parson's Company of Minute Men. Nov. 22, 1775 In 1785, he signed the petition for a bridge at New Castle, N H , and on Dec. 18, 1797, a like petition for a bridge at Sagamore

28 JOSEPH MARCH SALTER, son of John Salter, 16, was born 1781, died October, 1837. married, Mch 3, 1806, Sarah Frost

Issue

47 Joseph Salter, of the U S Navy, died in Columbus, Miss

31 WILLIAM FROST SALTER, son of John Salter, 16, was born 1787; died Sept. 25, 1849, married, Sept 30, 1817, Mary Ewen, born July 15, 1787, died Apr 2, 1851 They were both born in Portsmouth, N H , and died in New York City

Issue

48 Rev William Salter, of Burlington, Iowa, born, Nov 17, 1821, in Brooklyn, N. Y

SALTER OF NEW HAMPSHIRE

    49 Benjamin Salter, born, at Portsmouth, N H , 1818.
    50 Mary Salter
    51 Francis Salter
    52 Charles Salter

  32 JOHN SALTER, son of John Salter, 16, was born July 5, 1788, died Jan. 10, 1858, married Sarah Tibbits

  34 BENJAMIN SALTER, son of John Salter, 16, was born, in Portsmouth, N. H , Apr. 6, 1762; died, in New York City, Sept 8, 1858, married, Harriet Chase Tibbits, Aug 23, 1821, who died, in New York City, Nov 1, 1872.

      Issue
    53 Mary Salter, married Richard G. Porter.
    54 Jane Salter, married Samuel W. Thomas.
    55 George H. C. Salter
    56 Caroline Salter; married Marcelo M Delgado
    57 William T. Salter
    58 Harriet Salter, married J Freeman Howard
    59 Albert Salter

  36 TITUS SALTER, son of Titus Salter, 17, married Abigail Frost.
      Issue
    60 John Lake Salter; married four times.

  42 HENRY SALTER, son of John Salter, 20, married ...
      Issue
    61 John E Salter, who died, at Portsmouth, N H , about 1879

  46 HENRY SALTER, son of Titus Salter, 23, married
      Issue
    62 Thomas P. Salter

  49 BENJAMIN SALTER, son of William Frost Salter, 31, was born, at Portsmouth, N H , Sept 4, 1818, died, at Paterson, N. J., Oct. 3, 1873; married, Nov 25, 1846, Eleanor Bolton

      Issue
    63 Ella Bolton Salter, born June 4, 1852
    64 Edwin Ewen Salter, born Mch 17, 1855.

  55 DR GEORGE H. COLTON SALTER, son of Benjamin Salter, 34, was of China, in 1878, married Mary E Keeler.
      Issue
    65 Wesley Bray Salter
    66 Jasper Colton Salter
    67 Mabel C. Salter

57 WILLIAM T SALTER, son of Benjamin Salter, 34, married Georgianna Harrison
   Issue
   68 May Florence Salter; died 1886.

59 ALBERT SALTER, son of Benjamin Salter, 34, married Frances Philbrook.
   Issue
   69 Huldah Jenness Salter

The preceding outline of the New Hampshire family has been drawn from a book of fifty-eight pages, written by Mr W T. Salter, of New York City, and printed, in 1900, by John Highlands, of 16 North Eleventh St, Philadelphia, Pa, entitled, "John Salter, Mariner," containing illustrations, and brief histories of the Salter, Pepperell, Frost, Colton and Tibbit families, as well as from an "In Memoriam, of Benjamin Salter," printed by his brother, the Rev. William Salter

SEABROOK

OF

MONMOUTH COUNTY

The surname of Seabrook is so rare, both in England and America, that a suppositive kinship might be claimed very plausibly for all bearing the name

The references to them, in England, are not numerous, and no account of them appears in any of the Heralds' Visitations, that I have seen, though they were granted arms

Seabrook Arms   Argent, a lion passant gules, in chief, a cross crosslet fitcheé sable
Crest, a hand erect holding a cross crosslet fitcheé, in pale gules.

Another arms, given by the same authority, Burke, is. Argent, three roses sable.

The former arms are and were used by the South Carolina Seabrooks, and an impression, from a seal ring bearing them, was given to me about 1880

THOMAS SEABROOK, an Englishman, and the progenitor of the New Jersey family, was settled at Mineford Island, now known as City Island, lying off Pelham Neck, Westchester County, New York, Aug 29, 1664, at which date he purchased, of John Seaman, of Hempstead, in the North Riding of Yorkshire, (Long Island, New York), one hundred and twenty acres of land, situated on the North Neck, in Hempstead, commonly called Mattgairisons Neck, the lot being on the East side of said neck, and known as Number 41, thither he removed

1664, Aug 29

Know All Men, etc , that I, John Seaman, now dwelling in Hempstead, in North Riding, in New York Shire, on Long Island, have sold and do sell, etc , unto Thomas Seabrooke, now dwelling on Mineford Island, in New York Shire, a certain allottment of land, at the North Neck, belonging to the foresaid Hempstead, commonly called Mattsgairisons Neck, being at first laid out to me, the foresaid John Seaman, being in the East Side of the said neck, and in number 41, and containing in quantity, one hundred and twenty acres, more or less, etc , for a valuable sum of money in hand paid, etc
                Queens County Records, Jamaica, N Y , Lib C , p 318

1670 Feb 2   He sued Cornelius Mott, his Hempstead townsman, for debt, which the Court decided in his favor, and awarded him, in addition, 15 shillings damages
                Hempstead, L I., Town Records, Lib B

In 1673, he was enumerated in the census of Hempstead, as an inhabitant
                New York Documentary History, Vol I, p 658

1672, Oct 30 Roger Townsend sold to Morgan Bedient, his house and orchard, situated in the town of Westchester, Westchester County, N.Y., for a similar house and land in the same place.

1672, Nov 27 Morgan Bedient sold his recently acquired property from Roger Townsend, to Thomas Seabrooke, of Westchester, and with it, one acre and a half of fresh meadow Recorded in the "Office of Records, at ffort James, in New Yorke, the 27th day of November, 1672"*

After he had removed to the town of Westchester, and in the year 1675, he was assessed for 2 horses, 6 cows, three "3 year old," three "1 year old," 2 swine, 5 [acres of] land and 12 [acres of] meadow   New York Colonial History, Vol 13, p 488

He died, at Westchester, the 17th December, 1675, as appears by the following.

The Testimony of John Clarke, of Westchester, concerning Tho Seabrooke, Aged about 29 years

This Deponent saith, That when there was an Alarme of Indyans being at Castle Hill, Loaden with Ammunicoñ, last Summer, this deponent was then a Sojourner, in the House of Thomas Seabrooke, was commanded, (among others), to go to Capt Osborne's House, And at his going away, hee, the said Thomas Seabrooke, tooke his wife, (the now p^rsent widdow Seabrooke), by the hand in the Doore, as hee was going out, and said, wife I am going out, I know not but I may bee Knockt on the head, If I never come againe, I give all that I have to thee, (meaning his wife), And furthur said to this Deponent, Pray take notice what I say, and furthur Saith not   Sworn before me
May 15, 1676.   JOHN PELL

The Testimony of Penelope Cooke, aged about ffifty yeares, concerning Tho Seabrooke.

This Deponent saith, That Thomas Seabrooke, of Westchester, the late Husband of the Widdow Seabrooke, being some time last winter at Consider Woods, hee did declare that hee was going over to Long Island, and then at the same time did say, that when soever hee did dye, hee would make his wife, full and whole Executor, and give all to her, his wife, and no Body else should have anything to do wth any thing hee had, but his wife, and furthur Saith not

         Sworne before mee
Westchester, May the 15th, 1676   JOHN PELL

Thomas Seabrooke dyed, at Westchester, the 17th of December, 1675
An Inventory of the Estate of the dec'd
One House and Home Lott
Nine Acres of Land in the ffield
Twelve Acres Meadow
Two Mares, two Colts, 2 yea^{rs} old
Two young Colts
five Cowes, two three yeare olds
Two Steeres, two yeare old
Three Yearlings, 5 Calves
Three Swine
One ffeather Bedd
ffive Blanketts, 2 Sheetes
One Iron Pott
Three Gunns
At the desire of the Widdow, this Estate Prized by
the Constable and two Overseers

	£	s.	d.
The whole Accomodacoñs prised at	90	00	—
Two Mares, and two 2 yea^{re} old Colts	09	00	—
Two young Colts	01	10	—
ffive Cowes, two three yea^{rs} olds	26	00	—
Two Steeres, two yea^{rs} old	05	00	—

*The original of this paper was found at the Seabrook Homestead, at the Bay Shore, Middletown, N J, and is now in the possession of Dr J E Stillwell, of New York City

SEABROOK OF MONMOUTH COUNTY

Three yearlings, five Calves	07 00 —
Three Swine	03 00 —
The feather none of Tho Seabrookes nor two Blanketts	
Three Blanketts	01 04 —
One Sheet	00 12 —
One Iron Pott	00 10 —
Three Guns	02 10 —

This Estate, prised as above
Witnesse our hands
EDWARD WALTERS
THO MOLLENNEX
NICHOLAS BALLY

New York Wills, Vol 1, pp 240, 241 and 242

The wife of Thomas Seabrook brought to him, one feather bed and two blankets, probably a wedding present from her parents

Sometime following his demise, and prior to 1688, she married Thomas Whitlock, as appears by the following deeds

Know all Men by these p^rsents that I, Roger Townsend of West=Chester, & Mary, my wife, being at present possest of a certaine House and Orchard, situate in the said Towne of Westchester, (the which is now in the tenure and Occupačon of Philip Minton), have, for a valuable Consideration, or y^e Conveyance of another House and Land, unto me in lieu thereof, Bargained, sold, assigned, & set over, unto Morgan Beadient, of the said Towne, Singleman, his Heyres and Assignes, all my Right, Title, & Interest to the said House and Orchard, scituate in Westchester aforesaid, Hee, the said Morgan Beadient, having by virtue of these p^rsents full power and lawfull Authority (after ye expiračon of two compleat yeares from the 10th day of June last past, or before if the said Philip Minton shall resigne up the same sooner) to enter into possession of the premisses, & of every part & parcell thereof, and the same to have, hold, use, occupy, possess, & enjoy unto the sole, proper use, behoofe, & Benefitt of him the said Morgan Beadient his Heyres & Assignes forever, against any Clayme, Title, or p^rtence of any person or persons whatsoever, by, from, or under mee my Heyres or Assignes, or by any of their Ord^{rs} or Appointm^t

IN TESTIMONY whereof, I have hereunto sett my Hand & Seale, at New Yorke, this 30th day of Octob^r, 1672

Sealed & Delivered in ye p^rsence   the T marke of   the R marke of
of RICH CHARLTON
JO CLARKE   MARY [?] [wax seal] TOWNSEND   ROGER [wax seal] TOWNSEND

Mem^{dm} That before ye Signing & Sealing of these p^rsents It is agreed upon by & betwixt ye partyes within menčoned that Roger Townsend reserves to himselfe all Priveledges & Appertenances belonging to his House, not herein sold & made over to the within written, Morgan Beadient, yet not thereby intending to abridge or cutt short ye said Morgan of what is herein sold & dispos'd of

Entered in the Office of Records, at ffort James, in New Yorke, the 27th of November, 1672
MATTHIAS NICOLLS, SECR

Know all whome this may concirne that I, Morgan Bedient, of Westchester, doe, by these p^rsents, assigne and make over unto Thomas Seabrooke, of Westchester aforesaid, All my Right, title and intrest of this within Mentioned House and Orchard, specified in this Bill of Sayle, on the other side, as Alsoe, all my Right, title and intrest of One Acre and halfe of fresh Meaddow, being Number 6, lying to the Eastward of Longe Neck, in the boundes of Westchester aforesaid, from me, my heires, Executors and Assignes, unto him, the said Thomas Seabrooke, his heires, Executors and assignes for ever, to possess and enjoy, as his owne proper right, with out let or Molestation from mee, the said Morgan Bedient, or any other claiming right, title or intrest under mee, my heires, Executors or assignes, alsoe to ffree and discharge Thomas Seabrooke, his heires, Executors & assignes, from an Obligation made to pay him yearly, One hogshead of Sydar, I doe, by these p^rsents, Acquitt & discharge the said Tho Seabrooke thereof

In testimony Whereof, I have hereunto put my hand this 25th of Novemb^r, 1673
Witness p^rsent   his mark
   his marke   MORGAN X BEDIENT
EPHRAIM X ALDRIX
fFRANCIS ffRENCH

The paper is endorsed   Roger Townsend his Bill of Sale to Morgan Beadient

Know all men by these presents that I, Thomas Bedient, of Westchester, in the County of Westchester, yeoman, have Remissed, Released, and forever quit Claimed, and by these presents do, ffor me my heires, Executors & Administrators, Remise, release, and forever quitt Claime vnto Thomas Wittclock aforesaid, his heires, Executors & Administrators, all and all manner of Actions, Cause and Causes of Actions, suites, Bills, Bonds, Writeings, Obleigations, Debts, Dues, Dutyes, Accompts, Sume & Sumes of monney, Judgements, Executions, Extents, Quarrells, Contreversies, Tresspasses, Damages and Demaunds, whatsoever, both in Law and Equety, or other wise howsoever, which against the said Thomas Wittclock I Ever had, now have and which I my heires, Executors, and Administrators shall or may have Claime, Challings or demaind, ffor or by Reason or meanes of any matter, Cause or thinge, ffrom the Beginng of the world vnto the Day of the Date of these presents, as wittness my hand and seale this twenty second day of May, in the fourth yeare of his Majties Reigne, Annoqe Domj 1688

Signed Sealed and   THOMS BEDENTE* [His seal]
Delivered in presents of
NATHANIELL VNDERHILL
JOSEPH LEE

The endorsement on the back of the paper is as follows Thomas Bedient's Release to Thomas Wittclock

From the preceding data, we conclude that Thomas Seabrook bought, in November, 1672, the house and land of Morgan Bedient, in the town of Westchester Shortly after this transaction, both Bedient and Seabrook died, and the property being still unpaid for, Bedient's brother, Thomas, who had succeeded to his estate, brought an action against Thomas Whitlock to enforce the completion of the contract Evidently Whitlock had become liable, as the husband of Seabrook's widow, for Seabrook's debts, as she carried to him all her late husband's estate.

In 1688, the action was discontinued and a release was signed by Thomas Bedient

The two Bedients, Morgan and Thomas, were sons of Morgan Bedient, as appears from the following memorandum:

"Morgan, Son of Morgan Bedient, of Staynes,† in England, was born June 25 1651, And Thomas Bedient, Son of ye foresaid Morgan, was born July 22 1654, wc to Oath was made before mr Henry Clark & Leiut Smith, of Hadley, by Lawrence Carter & Mary Bedient, Mother of ye sd two Sons " From Hadley Records

1686, Sept. 3 Morgan Bedient was sued, at Court of Sessions, at Westchester, by Mr John Inians

Mary Barnard, wife of Morgan Bedient, Sr, apparently married Roger Townsend, of Westchester, who made his will May 7, 1674, proved Apr 15, 1675, in which he mentioned his wife, Mary, who received his estate, excepting bequests to his overseers, Capt William Lawrence and Mr Richard Cornell, and to his three sons, Mordecay, Thomas and John Bedient, who received £10, each

Thomas Bedient, son of Morgan and Mary (Barnard) Bedient, died, at Westchester, intestate, for Mary, his wife, applied for letters of administration May 7, 1698 Before moving to Westchester, he resided at Fairfield, Conn

Thomas Whitlock was a prominent man in the early settlement of Gravesend, Long Island. He had friends among the English and foes among the Dutch, by reason of his efforts to overthrow Dutch rule in the Gravesend village, and in abetting the general discontent and uprising He was a Monmouth County Patentee in 1664, and was one of those, who, in a sloop, prospected, some time previous to this date, the lands which the English later conveyed in

---

*The seal, apparently, is three lions' heads affronté on a fess, and in the chief, apparently, a bird

†Staynes or Staines, is near London Mary, the wife of Morgan Bedient, Sr, was a sister of John Barnard, of Cambridge, who came, probably, in the "Francis," from Ipswich, in 1634, aged 36 years, and his wife, Mary, aged 38 years He was, perhaps, the Freeman, Mch 1 1635, removed in 1636 to Hartford, thence to Hadley, in 1659, or soon after He died in 1664, leaving no children He left a good estate and left his kinsman, Francis Bedient, his executor, giving much to Morgan and Thomas Bedient, sons of his sister, Mary, then living in England, who came over to enjoy it His widow, Mary, died next year, and she gave much of her estate to Daniel and William Stacy, of Barnham, near Malden, in the County of Essex, her brothers, and £10, to bring up Thomas, son of Francis Bedient, to school This legacy was well bestowed, for the father was poor and the son worthy Savage

the Monmouth Patent, but which the Dutch nipped in the bud by threatening measures After breaking soil in Middletown, he became a resident of Westchester, where he married, for his second wife, Mary, the widow of Thomas Seabrook His first wife was Susannah Stock, by whom he had his issue His career is too extended to follow here, but it is written in full in the genealogy of his family.

Some time after his marriage to his second wife, he removed to Shoal Harbor, on the Bay Shore, (now Port Monmouth) Middletown, Monmouth County, N. J., where he erected the house which, for many years, has been the Seabrook Homestead

What issue Thomas Seabrook, the First, had it is impossible, at this date, to tell, other than a son

It would appear that when Thomas Whitlock removed to Middletown, the infant child, or children, of Mary Seabrook, were taken to their stepfather's house

Upon his coming of age, there was a controversy between the eldest son of Thomas Seabrook and Thomas Whitlock

"Whereas there is a Twenty ffifve pound priviledge of Comonage belonging to the Orphant of Thomas Seabrook, late freeholder of this Town, Deceased, and the said Priviledge being in Possession of Thomas Whitlock, Wee, the Trustees, do declare that the said twenty-five pound privilege do belong to the orphant of Thomas Seabrook & no wise intended for the said Thomas Whitlock." Westchester Town Records, Vol II, p 38

It is evident that the orphan of Seabrook succeeded to some of his estate and doubtless had more by gift from his mother

1696, June 10 Thomas Whitlock, of Middletown, Carpenter, sold to Daniel Seabrook, "my son-in-law," of Middletown, planter, for the sum of £80, his property at Shoal Harbor, consisting of two hundred and two acres, which Whitlock received as follows

1676, Jan 10 By patent from the Proprietors, twenty acres of upland and six acres of meadow
1689, Mch 26 By purchase from John Bowne.
1691, Feb. 20 By purchase from Garrat Wall
1693, Sept 11 By purchase from John Pearce
Thomas Whitlock signed by his mark T W Freehold Records, Lib E, p 307

"The orphant" of Thomas Seabrook was, doubtless, Daniel Seabrook

He was born about 1665–1670 Thomas Seabrook had also a son, James Seabrook, who must have been born between 1671–1675, always provided he is not the son of Daniel Seabrook

Issue

2 Daniel Seabrook
3 James Seabrook, perhaps the son of Daniel Seabrook, 2, or the son of Thomas Seabrook, 1
3ª Ann Seabrook, married, first, Andrew Bowne; second, Rev John Bray

2 DANIEL SEABROOK, son of Thomas Seabrook, 1, was born about, or somewhat earlier than, 1670 Of this individual I know nothing beyond the facts recited above Whether he married or left issue, or even when he died is unknown The farm that he purchased from Thomas Whitlock, at the Bay Shore, was, in 1717, in the possession of James Seabrook As the owner of such an estate and house, it is more than likely, yes, even certain, that Daniel Seabrook was married How the property passed from him to James Seabrook is unsolved If he was the father of James Seabrook, he was probably born nearer 1660 than 1670, and it seems that he must have been such, as it is the only way to account for the title of the homestead being vested in James Seabrook

1688, Nov. 9 Daniel Seabrook was a witness to the sale of lands made by Thomas Whitlock to John Ruckman, Jr., in Middletown, N J

1696, June 10 Thomas Whitlock, of Middletown, carpenter, for £80, sold to "Daniel Seabrook, my son-in-law," of Middletown, planter, two hundred and two acres of land, at Shoal Harbor, Middletown.

3 JAMES SEABROOK, perhaps the son of Daniel Seabrook, 2, or Thomas Seabrook, 1, married Hannah, daughter of Joseph Grover and Hannah Lawrence She was born not far from 1690 Elizabeth Grover, her sister, was born in 1685 Hannah (Grover) Seabrook died about 1745 Daniel Seabrook, in that year, was her heir James Seabrook died about or after 1745.

1700. He was a witness in court

1701. He signed the petition from East Jersey, asking for a suitable governor.
New Jersey Archives, Vol II

1704, Apr. 28. He recorded his cattle-mark, in Middletown.

1710, 1723 and 1725. He was a Juryman

1711 and 1719. He bought land.

1712 He was one of the Overseers of Highways, for Middletown.
Court of Sessions Book, 1712

1712, June 28. He bought one acre of meadow from Thomas Stillwell, at Shoal Harbor, and one other acre elsewhere, for £4

1712–1731 He was a member of the Baptist Church, Middletown, and, in 1735, was excommunicated

1716 He was debtor to the estate of John Bowne, merchant, to the amount of £14-15-03
March 11th 1722 /

Mr George Taylor please to pay to Mr William Taylor of ffreehold in the County of Monmouth in the Eastern Division of New Jersey the sume of Thirty pounds Eighteen Shillings, and Six pence farthing Current Silver money of New York at 8^s p oz it being his proportional dividend pertaining to him out of the Estate of his brother John Taylor late of Middleton deceased, and his receipt shall be yor discharge As Wittness my hand the day and year above written /
JAMES SEABROOK

1725 He was an Overseer of the Poor, Middletown.

1727 He accounted with his successors, the Overseers of the Poor, of Middletown

1730, Aug 15 James Seabrook, of Middletown, N. J., yeoman, sold to Daniel Seabrook, of the same place, for £800, the land whereon his dwelling, at "Shole harbor," stood, including six or more tracts of land and meadow, in and about Shoal Harbor, amounting to three hundred acres:

Return of the Middle part of Seabrook's Shoal Harbor Plantation, surveyed by Wm Lawrence, Jr, for James Seabrook, having right, as appears on the margin a tract of land containing, after allowance for highways, 65 5/6 acres, bounded on the S by a tract of land of 175 acres, belonging to said James Seabrook and formerly belonging to Gerrit Wall, & on the N by a tract of land of 20 acres, belonging to said James Seabrook, on ye E by ye edge of the Meadow on Compton's creek, on the W. by the edge of the meadow on John Reves' [?] creek, which is certified the 8 day of July, 1717
JAMES ALEXANDER
Sur General

'On the margin] "Turner's Proprietie ye 20th thereof held by James Grover 1st & 2^d Division being taken up at date hereof ye Adition 125 acres which fell to ye six daughters of Joseph Grover, one of which, James Seabrook has married & James Grover has bought 3 of 8 shares of ye other sisters out of which 3 shares he has sold James Seabrook 45 acres. 65 5/6 acres remains to be taken up by James Grover 17 3/6 by each of 2 sisters 20 5/6 In all 59 1/6 acres"

SEABROOK OF MONMOUTH COUNTY

1730, Aug 18. James Seabrook, of Middletown, yeoman, sold to Daniel Seabrook, of the same place, for £200, such cattle, horses, hogs and every other creature, and also the household stuff, as bedding, iron, brass, pewter, stone and wooden wares, with all ye plows, carts, tackles, and also all "my movable estate &c, in or about the houses, lands & tenements whereon I now inhabit and dwell, situated at Shole Harbor, in Middletown." Signed James Seabrook He then probably removed to the vicinity of Freehold

1731 He was Overseer of the Highways

1737, Mch 19 James Seabrook and George Taylor were sued by William Smith for a bill of £40 "The Body of James Seabrook Is Taken and in Coftody But ye Body of George Taylor Is not To be found in my bailwick"

1739, Mch 24. A writ to the Sheriff of Monmouth County is endorsed "unable to find Seabrook"

1744. James Seabrook vs Andrew Hinman for debt Middlesex County Court Records, Clerk's office, New Brunswick, N J

1745, Feb 7. James Seabrook, yeoman, of Middletown, sold to Daniel Seabrook, of Shrewsbury, yeoman, that parcel of land left, in 1688, by the will of Joseph Grover, to his daughter, Hannah, for the sum of £15

Issue, supposed
4 Daniel Seabrook, oldest son and heir
5 Hannah Seabrook, born 1706, married, first, Cornelius Van Horn, second, Benjamin Drake.
6 Thomas Seabrook, drowned about 1740.
7 Rebecca Seabrook, married James Fitz-randolph
8 Elizabeth Seabrook, born, 1711, died March 16, 1791, married, first, Ezekial Forman, second, Richard Mount See Mount family.
9 Son ....., married Eleanor McDowell, who was born 1713

4 DANIEL SEABROOK, eldest son and heir of James Seabrook, 3, married Mary, daughter of Nicholas Brown, by his third wife, Mary, daughter of John and Mary Chambers, whom he had married in 1707 By her, Mary Chambers, he had his only child, Mary Brown, born, in Shrewsbury, Aug 25, 1710

From the Family Bible owned by Dr J E Stillwell
Hannah Seabrook Daughter of Daniel and Mary Seabrook born in Midletown Octor 21 1734 about 1 Oclock in the morning being Monday
Ther Second Child Thomas born in Midletown on Monday Febry 16th 1735/6 about two oclock morning
Daniel there Third Child born July 10th 1737 being the Sabbath Day about 9 oclock att night
Nicholas Brown Seabrook There fourth child born May 25th 1739 being Fryday the sun being about ½ an hour high att night
James there Fifth child Born Novbr 14th 1740 being Fryday about 2 hours before Day
There Son James Departed this Life for abetter The 3d Day Janry 1741/2 being the Lords Day about 3 Oclock in the Afternoon aged 1 year 1 month and 20 Days The Lord prepare us all for so Great & happy a Change
James, Son of Daniel & Mary Seabrook was born in Shrewsbury on Tuesday the Fourth Day of January aboutt one a clock Morning 1742/3
James Seabrook Departed this Life on the 16th of Febry 1743/4 aged 1 year one Month and twelve Days
John Son of Daniel and Mary Seabrook there Sixth son was born in Shrewsbury on Septr 4th 1744 aboutt 10 of the Clock att night on Tuesday
Mary Daughter of Daniel & Mary Seabrook was Born in Shrewsbury on the 20th Day of May Being Wednesday about 1 O clock Morning

James the Seventh and Last Son of Daniel and Mary Seabrook was born in Middletown on the twenty fifth Day of November 1749

In addition to the preceding entries, the following likewise appear

Mary Brown, Daughter of Nicolas & Mary Brown, Born in Shrewsbury august 25th 1710
Mary Chambers born March 8th, 1711
Elizabeth Exceen born August 31st 1715
Mary Exceen Born May 4th 1717
John Exceen Born December 4th, 1719
William Exceen Born April 9th, 1721
Isabella Little Daughter of Thos & Mary Little Born December 22d 1730 being Tuesday about 8 oclock
Hannah Chambers, Daughter of Thos Chambers Born December 22d 1723
Sarah, Daughter of Godfery & Elizabeth Swat Born att Midletown Novbr 17th 1740 about ½ hour after 5 oclock on Munday Morning and I wish her as good a father In Law as myself

[This last remark, as it appears in different writing, was evidently added at a subsequent date.]

Daniel Seabrook died March 23, 1749/50. Mary, his wife, died in April, 1750, aged about 40 years.

1728 Daniel Seabrook bought from his uncle, James Grover, land.

1730, Aug 15 He bought the house and all the lands, at Shoal Harbor, from his father, James Seabrook, for £800

1730, Aug 18 He purchased from James Seabrook, his father, for £200, such cattle, horses, hogs & every other creature, and also all the household stuff, as bedding, iron, brass, pewter, stone & wooden wares, with all ye plows, carts & tacklen, and also all "my moveable estate &c, in or about the houses, lands & tenements, whereon I, James Seabrook, now inhabit and dwell, situated, at Shoal Habor, in Middletown."

1733 He was a member of the Baptist Church, at Middletown.

1734, '35, '36 He was an Overseer of the Poor, Middletown.

1735, Dec 9 He recorded an Estray, in Middletown

1738 He signed a bond

1738, May 13 Daniel Seabrook sued James Wilson for trespass

Supreme Court Files, Trenton, N J.

1738, Sept 12 He bought of James Rochead, of New York, merchant, and one of the Proprietors of the Eastern Division of New Jersey, for 42 shillings, proclamation money, four acres of unappropriated land, yet to be located

1739, Feb 11, Joseph Dorsett, Roelef Schenck and Richard Saltar were arbitrators in a dispute concerning the ownership of meadow land, at Shoal Harbor, between Johannas Smock and Daniel Seabrook They determined the bounds of the disputants' property

1739, Feb 20 Daniel Seabrook, yeoman, of Middletown, for a money consideration, released and quit-claimed to Johannas Smock, a two acre lot, at Shoal Harbor This was probably the result of the arbitration

1740, Mch 26 Beriah Goddard, of Dartmouth, in the County of Bristol, and Province of Massachusetts Bay, in New England, agreed with Daniel Seabrook, of Middletown, in New Jersey, that in case any land belonging to Stephen West, of Dartmouth, in New England, aforesaid, should upon just and legal inquiry be found to lie within the bounds of the Indian purchase, bearing date July 25, 1689, of Nicholas Brown, late of Shrewsbury, that he should pay the purchase money for the land, etc

1740, Aug 30 Daniel Seabrook, yeoman, and wife Mary, sole heir of her father, Nicholas Brown, late of Shrewsbury, for £140, at 8 shillings per ounce, sold to John Chambers, yeoman, of Shrewsbury, N J, all that tract of land & meadow, in the town of Shrewsbury, lying on the N side of Shark River, being part of a tract of land patented by Nich Brown, July 20, 1688, Also 50 acres of land, near the head of one of the branches of the Manasquan River, in Shrewsbury, lying in the Barrens & including the half of the bogg where Wm West & Wm

Woolley mowed their hay, etc., etc , the same being conveyed to the said Nicholas Brown by deed from Gawin Drummond, the 25th of July, 1693

In 1741, he brought suit

1741, Oct 1. Daniel Seabrook and wife Mary, of Shrewsbury, for £20, sold to John Forman, of Freehold, blacksmith, Proprietary rights, acquired by Nicholas Brown from Robert Turner, in 1685 Daniel Seabrook acquired title through his wife, Mary, daughter of Nicholas Brown   Perth Amboy Records

In 1742, he was of Shrewsbury, and bought land from .. . Forman.

In 1742, he was a witness to the will of Richard Stillwell, of Shrewsbury

In 1745, he was heir to his mother, deceased

1745, Feb 7 Daniel Seabrook, of Shrewsbury, yeoman, bought of James Seabrook, of Middletown, that parcel of land left, in 1688, by will of Joseph Grover, to his daughter, Hannah, for the sum of £15

1746 He was a witness to the will of Mercy Stillwell, of Shrewsbury

1748 He recorded an Estray, at Middletown, Nov 24, and again, Dec 30

1748/9, Jan. 5 He gave a bond to Samuel Ogborne, for £36, payable Mch 6, 1748/9

1749, Mch 23 Will of Daniel Seabrook, of Middletown, N J, yeoman, mentioned "eldest son, Thomas," who received £5, at the age of twenty-one years

"My two well beloved sons, Daniel and Nicholas," to share, equally, his plantation, at Shoal Harbor, upon condition that they pay certain legacies, as follows

"my well beloved daughter, Hannah Seabrook," £100

"my well beloved son, John Seabrook," £200, and one-half of his lands, at Shrewsbury

"my well beloved son, James Seabrook," £200, and the other half of his lands, at Shrewsbury

"my well beloved daughter, Mary Seabrook," £100

Executors friends, Edward Taylor and Jos Stillwell

This will, for unknown reasons, was not signed, and he died shortly thereafter, intestate, and his chosen executors, Edward Taylor and Jos Stillwell, were appointed administrators The will singularly omits mention of his wife and bequeathes only £5 to his son, Thomas

1750, May 2 Letters of administration were granted to Jos Stillwell and Edward Taylor, of Monmouth County, on the estate of Daniel Seabrook. The bond was for £800, and James Pew, bondsman Skelton Johnson and James Mott were witnesses

A True and Perfect Invitary of the Goods and Chattels Rights and Credits of Daniel Seabrook, of Middletown, in the County of Monmouth, Deceased, Apprized by Samuel Ogborne and James Grover, Jun, and James Pew this 12th Day of May, 1750, as follows

	£	s	d
to wearing Apparrel and Cash,	51	5	11
to 7 two year Old horse and Mair Colts,	22.	10	00
to a young Sorril Mair with white face,	12	00	00
to a young black horse,	11	00	00
to 4 Mairs and a Colt,	27.	00	00
to an Old Stalyon and 3 horses,	13	00	00
to 4 yearling Colts and 1 old horse,	9	00	00
to 16 Cows and Heffers with Calves,	40	00	00
to 5 Cows without Calves,	11	00	00
to 7 three yr old Steers,	14	00	00
to 2 two yr old Steers and bull,	3	15	00
to 13 yearling Cattle	9	15	00
to 23 two yr old Cattle,	27	10	00
to 10 Cows with 4 Calves,	29	00	00
to 10 young Cattle,	14	00	00
to 5 hoggs and Sow with piggs,	4	4	00

to an Iron bound Waggon,	12	00	00
to an old Cart and Wheels,	00	15	00
to 2 Ploughs and 2 Corn Harrows,	2	7	00.
to an Oyster Rake,	00	18	00
to Sundry Empty Casks,	1.	4	00
to a tub with Pork,	2	00	00.
to Sundry Axes and hoes, 1 old Spade,	1	4	6.
to an Iron Crow, with other Old Iron,	00	7	00
to a fish Gig and Spear, an old Sword, and Sythe,	00	3	00
to a Small plough Shear,	00	4	00
to wheat in Casks,	1.	15.	00
to old forks and Sundries,	00	3	00
to a fish Nett,	00	15	00
to 2 old Saddles and bridles,	1	00.	00
to 3 Churns 18/, to an old Side Saddle, 25/,	2.	3.	00.
to tallow, Cheese Rack, Leather, and Lumb^r,	1	00	00
to a Grinstone, tubs, a ½ bushel, with Sundries,	00	10.	6.
to bed Steads and Cords,	00	11.	00.
to Murrin Skins,	00	6	00
to Gears, Yoke, Lines, and Clevisses,	1	4	00
to augers, a han Saw, and Sundry tooles,	00	12.	00.
to a warming pan and p^r of Stilyards,	00	17	00
to 2 Guns 40s, and a Meel troughf 7/,	2	7.	00
to Iron Potts and Kittles, with an old brass Kittle,	1	10.	00
to 2 trammels, tongs, Shovel and Grid Iron,	00.	17	00
to Pewter baysons, Platters, Plates, Porringers, tankerd, Quart, and Spoons,	1	18.	00
to a Chavin Dish, pepper Mill, with Sundries,	00	10	00
to a frying Pan, Shott Mold, Spoon Mold, button Mold, with Lumber,	00	13	00
to bottles and Sheep Shears,	00	3.	5
to Chairs and table	1	12	00
to a bed, bolster, Pillows, Coverled bed stead, and Cord,	3	00	00
to a bed, bolster, 2 Sheets and a Coverled,	2	15	00
to a bed, bolster, and a Pillow, a blanket, and bed Quilt,	2	5	00
to a Small bed, a Rug, and a Sheet,	1	5	00
to a bed curtins, bolster, a Pillow, sheets, a Coverled, a bed Stead,	5	00	00.
to a trundle bed Stead, a bed bolster, Pillows, a Sheet, and a Coverled,	2	15	00.
to 4 Gammons, a flitch of bacon, and smoak beef,	2	00	00
to an old Cradle 1/, to tea Cups, with Sundries 6/,	00	7	00
to a Reel, old Casks, Earthen Potts, Candle Sticks,	00	5.	00
to Iron Rodds,	00	4	00
to a Cubbord, and Looking Glass,	4	10	00
to a pair of hand Irons, with 2 Tables,	00	16	00
to white Lead, and Spannish brown,	00.	3.	6
to Sundry books and a *hatchel*,	00	11	00.
to a toe Sheet, a woolen blanket, with Sundries,	1	00	00
to a Negroe Man,	50	00	00
to a Negroe Girl,	20	00	00
to a Servant boy,	15	00	00.
to a ½ bushel, and Lumber in the barn,	00	4	00
to an old Cart and Wheels 18/, to 2 hoggs 28/,	2	6	00
to a Syder Mill and press bottom,	00	10.	00.
to Empty Casks and Lumber in the Milk Room,	00	10	00
to an Iron Pott,	00	3	00
to an old Spade, an old Ax, with old Iron,	00	8	00
to Old Pewter and wooden trenchers 6/,	00	6	00

SEABROOK OF MONMOUTH COUNTY

	£	s	d
to an old Saddle and old table, and Kealers,	00	7	6
to old Tuggs, [Juggs?]	00	1	6
to a bed, bed Stead, Bolster and Pillow with bedden,	3	5	00
to 53 pound of Swingled flax, at 9^d p pound,	1	19	9
to books and Old Chairs,	00	5	6
to a Quilting frame, and Sundries,	00	3	6
to a pan, a Spitt, a trammel, and Joiners Plow,	00	15	00
to a Shayes, not finished, with Quilers, and Sundry things thereunto belonging,	10	00	00
to 182½ bushels of Indian Corn, at 2/ p bush,	18	5	00
to 17 bushels of Rye, at 2/ p bushel,	1	14	00
to wheat and Rye on the Ground,	9	6	00
to a bond from Willson Hunt for 9$^£$ proclamation,	9	00	00
to a bond from Benjamen Drake for 9$^£$ proclamation,	9	00	00
to a Note of hand from William Whitehead for,	4	16	00
to Sundry book Debts,	16	10	9
to a Chest with Sundries,	00	12	00
to a Steel trap, a hammer, with Sundries,	1	0	7
to 22 hides sold for,	14	9	11
	£558	7	10

by us, JOSEPH STILWELL } Administrators
EDWARD TAYLOR }
SAMUEL OGBORNE
JAMES GROVER, JUNER
his
JAMES × PEW
mark

[This Inventory is endorsed as filed 23 Feb, 1750—1 e 1750/1]

"ACCO^T OF ADMIN^N OF DANIEL SEABROOK'S ESTATE."

D^r

May ye 1st, 1751 Joseph Stilwell and Edward Taylor, D^r. to the Estate of Daniel Seabrook Deceaced as appears p Invitary

May the 1st, 1751 Per Contra C^r £558-7-10

by Cash Paid by Joseph Stilwell and Edward Taylor Administrators to the Estate of Daniel Seabrook of Middletown, Deceased, as follows

	£	s	d
to the Charge of Administring Jersey Money at 8/ p oz	3	0	10
to Sundries in Sicknefs and funeral Charges	14	9	8
to paid Doctor Stephan Talman in part of his bill	24	1	0
to paid Mrs Mary Walton in full of one bond and in part of another in York money £202 17s Advance to make Jersey money at 8/ the ounce £15-12s Added	218	9	0
to paid Benjamin Drake which was due to his wife	8	7	0
to paid John Lippincott in part of his Demand	12	2	0
to paid Sam^{ll} Ogborne	41	8	4½
to paid George Taylor	25	0	0
to paid Richard Crawford in part of his bond	35	0	0
to paid John Hire, vandue Master, for selling, and to Liquor for the vendue	6	11	9
to paid the appraiser	1	7	6
to paid three women nurses for their attendance,	4	6	3
to paid William Weakfeild for his attendance, forty one Days at 3/ p day	6	3	0
to paid James Pew	4	19	4½

to charge for time and expense in selling receiving and paying with the charge of writing	30—	0—	0.
to paid James Toy and Mary Morris for work done	1—	3—	6
to paid the widow Walton on bond £42 York money advance to make Jersey money £ s d	45—	4—	7
to paid William Wooley 3 4 7	2—	16—	0
	[£484—	9—	10]

Errors Excepted p us

JOSEPH STILLWELL.
EDWARD TAYLOR

March 13, 1749 50

	Daniel Seabrook To Edward Taylor Dr.	£	s	d
14th	to a ½ Gallon of Rum	0	02	06
	to 2 Gallons of Molasses 2/4 p Gall	0	04.	08
10th	to a Gallon of Rum	0	03.	00
	to 6 pound of Sugar 9 d p pd	0	04	06
19	to a ½ Gallon of Rum 2/6 to 4 Handerchiefs 5/	0	07.	06
22	to a ½ Gallon of Rum 2/6, to a Cotten Cap 2/4	0	04	10
24	the Estate Dr			
	to a ½ qr of Hundred Sugar	0	09	00
	to 7 Gallons of Rum at 4/10 P Gall	1	13	10
31	to a ½ Gallon of Rum	0	02	06
April 2, 1750	to 3 pound of Sugar 9d P pound	0	02	03
1750 13	to a ½ Gallon of Rum	0	02	06
17	to 3 Gallons of Rum 5/ Pr. Gall	0.	15	00
	to 3¾ yds Linnen 4/6 p yd 16/10 ½, to thread 3 d	0	17	01½
24	to a Gallon of Rum	0	05	00
	to 5 yds and ½ qr of Linnen 4/6 p yd	1	03	03¾
25	to 5 Gallons of Rum 4, 10 p Gall	1·	04	02
		8	03	5¾
	Added 20d to the pound to make York Money Jersey money	0·	13·	07
	to paid John Wall for a barrel of Sydar	0	14 ·	00
	to paid John Carman for a Cofin for a Girl	0·	10	00
	to paid John Webleys 2 Daughters Nursing in Sickness	2.	14	03
	to David Allin on Acct of Wm Whitlock and Himself for making 2 Coffins and Screws	1	10.	00
	to paid James Pew for bords and Necessaries for Cofins	0	16	00
	to paid John Wardell for Sundries in Sickness	0	18	07
	to paid Humphrey Wady for Sundries	0	09	10
	to paid Richd Burdge for Rum in Shrewsbury at the Grave	0	06	10
	to paid James Joy and John Webly for Digging 3 Graves	1	01·	00
	to paid Hannah Vandevanter for Nursing in Sickness	1·	12	00
	to paid Wm Weakfield for Nursing and attendance in Sickness 41 days at 3/ P Day	6·	03·	00
	to writing a Will	0	6	00
		25	18·	6¼
	from the Book of Seabrook afairs	590	12·	11½
		59	2	4
		675·	13·	09¾
		624·	2·	7
		51.	11	2¾

SEABROOK OF MONMOUTH COUNTY

May 1st 1751

Debts due from the Estate of Daniel Seabrook, Deceased, discharged by Joseph Stilwell and Edward Taylor Administrators

as follows·	£	s	d
To Cash paid at the Office and Expence in Administring	3	00	10
To Edward Taylors Own Acct for Sundries in Sickness and funeral Charges			
To paid Docter Stephen Talman in part of his bill	24	01	00
To paid Docter Richd Stilwell	14	07	02½
To paid Mrs Mary Walton in full of One bond York Money	112	17	00
Added Upon Account of the above bond 20^d to the pnd to make Jersey Money	9	08	01
To Cash paid at 2 Sundry times on another bond to Mrs Walton as per her Acct taken by Thos Seabrook, York Money	132	00	00
Added as above to make Jersey Money 20^d to the pound	11	00	00
To Cash paid upon a bond Given to Hannah Seabrook, the Wife of Benjamin Drake	8	7	00
To 1 bond Discharged Given to Richard Crawford	59	10	6
To 1 bond taken up Given to Geo Taylor whereon was due	25·	2	11
To 1 bond Given to Isabel Little taken up £ s d	137	18	4
To 1 bond p^d Jo^s Smyth and his attorney 23 6 10, proc made Light	27	4	7½
To paid the Apprisers	1	7	6
To paid the Vandue Master for Selling and Liq^r for Vandue	6.	11	9
	590	12	10½

Errors Excepted

May ye 1st 1751

Paid by Joseph Stilwell and Edward Taylor Administrators to the Estate of Daniel Seabrook, of Middletown, Deceased, as follows

	£	s	d
to Charge of administering Jersey Money at 8/ P. oz	3	00	10
to Sundries in Sickness and funeral Charges	14	9	8
to paid Docter Stephen Talman in part of his bill	24	1	00
to paid Mrs Mary Walton of New York in full of one bond and in part of another £202 17s York money Advance £15 12 to make it 8/ the Ounce	218	9	00
to paid of a bond given to Hannah Seabrook wife of Benjamin Drake whereon was Due	8	7.	00
to paid John Lippincott	12	2	00
to paid Sam^{ll} Ogborne	41	8	4½
to paid George Taylors bond	25	2	11
to paid Richd Crawford in part of his bond	35	00	00
to paid John Hire Vandue Master for Selling and to Liq^r for the Vandue	6	11	9
to paid the Apprisers	1	7	6
to paid three Weoman Nurses for their Attendance	4	6	3
to paid Wm Weakfield for his attendance 41 Days at 3/ p Day	6	3	00
to paid James Pew	4	19	4½
to Charge for time and Expence in Selling, Receiving paying and writing	30	00	00
	435	8	8
to paid James Joy and Mary Morris for work Done	1	3	6

1750, Mch 29 Will of Mary Seabrook, of Middletown, in the County of Monmouth, New Jersey, "being Sick and Weak in body", proved, May 2, 1750, by witnesses, James Mott and Skelton Johnson, and by executors, Joseph Stilwell and Edward Taylor, mentioned

"all my Lands and Meadows which is Lyeing and being in Shrewsbury Should be Rented Out by my Executors untill my two Sons Daniel and Nicholas Seabrook Shall Arive to the Age of twenty One years the Rents Should be Disposed of in bringing up my Children and Schooling," the remainder to be divided among all her children Also that her children be put out to trades, "of their own Choice," at a suitable age.

"my well beloved Son Thomas Seabrook the Sum of five pounds Money at Eight Shillings p Ounce to be paid by my Executors out of my Estate when my Said Son Shall Arrive to the years of twenty four to Cut him of as Heir at Law"

Estate to be sold "when My two Sons Daniel and Nicholas Shall be of Age and the Money to be Equally Divided amongst the four Sons Namely 1st Daniel, Secondly Nicholas, thirdly John and fourthly James Excepting the Sum of Two Hundred Pounds Money at 8/ p ounce" One Hundred Pounds to be first paid my well beloved Daughter Hannah Money at 8/ p ounce and the Other One Hundred Pounds I . . Give my well beloved Daughter Mary"

"if any of my abovesaid Children Should Die without Heirs then that part which Should be paid them to be Equally Divided amongst the Living Thomas Excepted"

Executors "my beloved *friend* Joseph Stillwell and Edward Taylor both of Middletown"
Witnesses James Mott, Skelton Johnson, Elizabeth forman and Judah Comton
The testator signed her name in full to the will

A bitter feeling existed between the Seabrooks and Taylors Edward Taylor died before the estate of Mary Seabrook was settled and his executors had difficulty in the accounting.

1769, Jan. 25. Edward Taylor, executor of Mary Seabrook, deceased, to David Knott. Joseph Stillwell, deceased, of Middletown, with Edward Taylor, of the same place, were executors of Mary Seabrook, of Middletown, and, as such, disposed of her estate as directed, but overlooked, as they are informed by David Knott, of Shrewsbury, a small gore or gusset of land, where the Presbyterian Church stands, at Shark River, bounded by David Knott, Joseph Cook, Easterly by the highway from Shrewsbury town to Manasquan, by Peter Knott's land and by the land of Mary Stillwell, deceased, which, at the request of Daniel Seabrook, one of the children and heir of Mary Seabrook, "who undertook to sell and discount a sum agreed for with the said David Knott, for two shares of said right of land, if any there be, the one his own, the other his brother, Nicholas Seabrook's, which the said Daniel claimed a right to by virtue of a power of attorney from said Nicholas . . and further, at the request of Thos Seabrook, who being the eldest son and heir-at-law of Mary Seabrook, and whereas Gawin Drummon, brother-in-law to the said David Knott, makes a demand of said Thomas Seabrook, as heir," etc , "to the value of twelve pounds, on account of a deficiency of land sold by Nicholas Brown, father of the said Mary Seabrook, to Gawin Drummond, grandfather of the present Gawin Drummon, now for the aforesaid consideration, I, Edward Taylor, do hereby release," etc

Daniel Seabrook and his wife, Mary Brown, had the following

Issue

10 Hannah Seabrook, born 1734
11 Thomas Seabrook, born 1735-6
12 Daniel Seabrook, born 1737.
13 Nicholas B Seabrook, born 1739
14 James Seabrook, born 1740
15 James Seabrook, born 1742-3
16 John Seabrook, born 1744
17 Mary Seabrook, born ——
18 James Seabrook, born 1749

5 HANNAH SEABROOK, daughter of James Seabrook, 3, married, first, by license dated Mch 15, 1730, Capt Cornelius Van Horn,* second, Benjamin Drake She "was born ye 15 day of November in year 1706"

*Will of Alexander Clark, dated Aug 2-, 1727, of Freehold, yeoman, with wife, Sarah, and children, William, Richard, John, Benjamin, Mary and Elisabeth appointing wife, her brother Cornelius Van Horn, and William Lawrence, Jr, of Middletown, as his executors This will had as witnesses John Reed, Thomas Kinnan, Dorothy [+] Nisbett, and Willm Lawrence, Junr

Issue

19 Mary Van Horn, born April 12, 1733.
20 Cornelius Van Horn, born May 4, 1737
21 Abraham Van Horn, born Aug. 28, 1738
22 James Van Horn, born April 3, 1740.
23 John Van Horn, born May 3, 1742.
24 Daniel Van Horn, born May 2, 1743

Mr M A De L Van Horn, attorney-at-law, 721 Walnut St, Philadelphia, Penn, is her descendant, and published in a genealogical journal, "Our Ancestors," an account of the Van Horn Family. There were but few issues of the journal, when it died. From it, and personal correspondence, the accompanying notes are taken

Abraham Van Horn, his brother, Capt Cornelius, and half-sister, Lena, came from the Province of New York and settled in Monmouth County, N J, prior to 1724

Abraham Van Horn married Anna Covenhoven about 1724-25, and afterward moved to Whitehouse, Hunterdon County, N. J, and, about 1737, his brother, Capt Cornelius, followed him

Burt Van Horn, of Lockport, N Y, owns the original family Bible, "James Van Horn his great Bible given to him by his mother, Hannah Drake, before she died 1788" "The James Van Horn is my grandfather and Hannah Drake my great-grandmother," writes Burt Van Horne She, Hannah Drake, who died 1788, was born May 8, 1749, and was the daughter of Benjamin and Hannah Drake.

The Seabrook notes are also in this Bible

6 THOMAS SEABROOK, son of James Seabrook, 3.

In 1726, he was plaintiff in a suit in Monmouth County
In 1734, he was a member of the Baptist Church, at Middletown, N J
In 1738, Thomas Seabrook signed a bill of lading

1739, May 2 John Webb, probably a sea captain, accounted with Thomas Seabrook, and owed him £24-8-3.

"N B The acct ment not adjusted is the Voyage of the said Brigantine Orange from New York to Ireland, thence to Cadiz to Cape Devards Islands and home made in the year 1738
JNO WEBB"

Middlesex Warrant issued to Sheriff to take Thomas Fowler, of the Citty of Perth Amboy, Marriner, into custody to produce him before the Lord, the King, at the Citty of Burlington, on the first Tuesday of November, to answer Thomas Seabrook of a plea of trespass, as also a bill of said Seabrook against Thomas Fowler for converting and disposing of Four pipes of Wine, valued at £100 proc
Fenw'k Lyell, atty   xxvIII August, M D CCXXX VIIII [1739]

Writ to Sheriff of County of Middlesex, to produce Thomas Seabrook Marriner, before court, at City of Burlington on second tuefday in May next, to answer unto Pontius Stelle of a plea of trespass, and also to the bill for £106
Robert Hunter Morris, Esqr, Chief Juftice, at City of Perth Amboy, 24th Mch, 12th of George II, [1739].
Burnett, Cl'k   Mc Evers, atty
To James Hooper [or Hoops]   Supreme Court Files, Trenton, N J

1740, Feb 1, Newport, R. I. Capt Thos Seabrook, Master of the Brigg Orange, of Perth Amboy, arrived here the 27th of Jan., past from London, in 12 weeks passage, &c, &c
New Jersey Archives, Vol XII, 1st Series

1740, Feb. 18 His ship left New York for Perth Amboy
                                    New Jersey Archives, Vol. XII, p. 12

Rhode-Island, March 28 We are informed that about Three Weeks ago, a Sloop from the Jersey's bound to Rhode-Island, Dehart Commander, was overset by a hard Gale of Wind in Long-Island Sound, his Sails being frose so that he could not lower them, and having no Ax on board could not cut down the Mast. They had nine Men on board, eight of them perished in the Seas, amongst whom was one Capt Thomas Seabrook, and his Mate Godfrey Sweet, who were Passengers, and the Person whose Life is saved is froze to that Degree that it is feared his Legs must be cut off   *The Boston Weekly Post-Boy, March 31, 1740*

New York, March 18 We hear from *Mount Misery*, on the North Side of *Long Island*, that the *Johanna*, Capt *James De Hart*, belonging to *New Brunswick*, was cast away there on Tuesday last. She went from here on Monday, the Sloop and Cargo is mostly lost, and also the Hands and Passengers, amongst whom was Capt *Seabrook*, they were Nine in Number, one whereof escaped, with frost-nipt Hands and Legs
                                    The Boston Evening Post, March 31, 1740

It is possible the newspaper statements, concerning Thomas Seabrook's death, may be an error, for I find among my memoranda, Thomas Seabrook signed a receipt in 1742, and he may have been living, in 1751, as would appear from the following item, yet, it is possible this last reference may be to his nephew, Thomas Seabrook, born in 1735, and sixteen years of age when this transaction occurred, a somewhat early period in life to entrust a money matter to

May 1st 1751, Debts due from the Estate of Daniel Seabrook, Deceased
"To Cash paid at 2 Sundry times on another bond to Mrs Walton as per her Acct taken by Thos Seabrook York Money £132 0.0"

Mary Stillwell, daughter of John Stillwell, of Staten Island, son of Richard Stillwell, was single, in 1724, as per her father's will, but she was the widow, Mary Seabrook, in 1748, as per her brother, Richard's will   She was the wife of Daniel Corsen, November, 1757, who was born about 1714, and who died Jan 26, 1761   She was living as late as 1766, when she was nominated, an executrix, in the will of Christian Corsen, her father-in-law   She, apparently, had no children by her husband, Mr Seabrook

I have often thought that Mary Stillwell was the wife of Thomas Seabrook, and certainly do not believe she was the wife of a Daniel Seabrook, as set forth in B. M. Stillwell's Memoirs, and in Bergen's Kings County Settlers, quoting from the same

7 REBECCA SEABROOK, daughter of James Seabrook, 3, married, between 1725-1740, Isaac Fitz-Randolph, who was born 1701

Upon the death of Rebecca Seabrook, her husband, Isaac Fitz-Randolph married, second, Hannah Lee

Issue by first wife
25 James Fitz-Randolph, married Deliverance Coward. They were the parents of Hannah Fitz-Randolph, who married William, son of Stoffel and Abigail (Woolley) Longstreet   William and Hannah (Fitz-Randolph) Longstreet were the parents of A B Longstreet
26 Daniel Fitz-Randolph, married Margaret Stewart.
27 Benjamin Fitz-Randolph, married Anna Brombich
28 Stephen Fitz-Randolph
29 Isaac Fitz-Randolph
30 Huldah Fitz-Randolph, married Mr. Combs
31 Rebecca Fitz-Randolph
32 Rhoda Fitz-Randolph; married Moses Robins.
33 Ruth Fitz-Randolph, married Esek Robins

Issue by second wife

34 Elizabeth Fitz-Randolph

Rebecca Seabrook and Isaac Fitz-Randolph were the great-grandparents of the late Judge Longstreet and of Gen James Longstreet Edward Mayes, Esq , a distinguished lawyer of Jackson, Miss , who married a grand-daughter of Judge Longstreet, and daughter of the late Justice Lamar, of the U S Supreme Court, wrote from Oxford, Miss , in 1890

"I am engaged in preparing a biographical work on a prominent branch of the Longstreet family " "Hon A B Lonsgtreet, author of 'Georgia Scenes,' and one of our most esteemed men, is a great-grandson of Rebecca Seabrook " "The confederate Gen'l James Longstreet is descended from the same parties but is one degree further removed "

8 ELIZABETH SEABROOK, daughter of James Seabrook, 3, was born 1711, died Mch 16, 1791, married Ezekiel Forman, born Nov 1, 1706, died, Oct 3, 1746, in which year his will was made She married, second, Richard Mount, born prior to 1691, died between July 22 and Aug. 11, 1777, the dates of his will and probate

1746, Sept 30 Will of Ezekial Forman, of Upper Freehold; proved Oct 22, 1746, mentioned·

His executors to pay his debts, then his "mortgages in the loan office " They were empowered to sell the plantation which he bought of "Richd Brittain or portion of the Homestead farm lying on the north side of the Brook" as they deem best

They to keep a farm until his eldest son, Saml, comes of age, and that his wife and children will dwell on the farm, she to "enjoy a handsome and comfortable maintainance and my children good education, " etc

To wife, Elizabeth, the interest of £200, yearly, during her widowhood, with right to dispose of it to her children at death In the event of remarriage, she is to receive £60

His estate to be divided into 17 shares, of which 10 shares are to be divided equally between his sons, Samuel, Thomas and Aaron, and 7 shares to be divided among his daughters, Mary, Hannah and Elizabeth In the event of his wife giving birth to another child, the boys and girls to contribute one share each, [two in all], from their share of the estate, for said child

Executors "dearly beloved wife Elizabeth, his brother, Jon^n Forman, brother-in-law, Daniel Seabrook, and trusty friend, Elisha Lawrence

Witnesses James Tapscott, Wm Maddock, John Chasey, [his mark], and George Danser

Elisha Lawrence refused to act as executor, the others qualified.

The will was well drawn   Lib D , of Wills, p 241, Trenton, N J

Issue

35 Dr. Aaron Forman, settled in Hunterdon County, N J , married Ann, daughter of John and Sarah (Lawrence) Emley His great-grand-daughter is Mrs John Moses, of Trenton, N J
36 Samuel Forman*
37 Thomas Forman§†
38 Ezekial Forman, posthumous child ‡
39 Mary Forman
40 Hannah Forman
41 Elizabeth Forman

---

*Samuel Forman remained in Monmouth County, N J , and married Helena Denyse

§Thomas Forman married his second cousin, Jane Throckmorton, born 1750 They moved to Kentucky, in 1789, where they became wealthy and influential

Issue
Mary Forman, married Mr Alexander
Ezekial Forman, married Dolly Wood

Issue
Thomas Seabrook Forman, born, in Madison County, Ky , Nov 9, 1808, died, in Louisville, Ky , June 24, 1849

(*Footnotes continued on page 236*)

9 .... SEABROOK, son of James Seabrook, 3, married Eleanor McDowell, of Shrewsbury She was born in 1713. The authority for this marriage is James Steen, Esq., of Eatontown, N. J. It is well to note here that Andrew McDowell married a daughter of Daniel and Mary Seabrook in the next generation.

The following reference is to one of the name, but it may not refer to the McDowells, of Shrewsbury

April 9, 1719
Wm Leveridge Sr., Vintor, formerly of Albany, N Y, deceased, feltmaker, lived at Richmond County, N Y, and also at Perth Amboy, N J He had children, viz
    Wm Leveridge and Mary, his wife.
    Hannah Leveridge
    Temperance Leveridge, wife of Wm Van Urden
    Margaret Leveridge, wife of Alexander Mack Dowall, Mariner, of Somerset County
There is some confusion in this transcript, probably from Perth Amboy Records, as to the occupations and residences of Wm Leveridge

11 THOMAS SEABROOK, son of Daniel Seabrook, 4, died, Feb. 22, 1805, [Stillwell Bible says Mch 1], aged 67 years, 11 months and 25 days, married Martha Tallman, who died July 14, 1828

    1761 Thomas Seabrook was assessed, in Middletown, £0-14-5, and £2-4-3
    1765 Thomas Seabrook was Overseer of Highways, Middletown, N. J.
    1767 Mr. Thomas Seabrook was an Overseer of the Poor, Middletown, N J
    1769 He was Commissioner and Arbitrator for the town
    1771 He was a Commissioner.
    1789, '90, '91, '92, and '93 He was a Commissioner of Appeals
    1799 Major Thomas Seabrook was Moderator and Judge of Elections.
    1801 He was Commissioner of Appeals, Moderator, Judge of Elections and Assessor
    1802 He was Judge of Elections
    1803 He was Presiding Officer of the Town Meeting and Judge of Elections
He was Major of First Regiment, Monmouth County.

†Mrs Isaac Weatherby, of Trenton, N J, is a great-grand-daughter of Thomas Forman
‡From the Autobiography of Charles Biddle—Vice president of the Supreme Executive Council, of Pennsylvania, 1745-1821, [1883]
After having been a prisoner, & exchanged, Captain Biddle was en route, through New Jersey—when the following passage occurs
"When we came near the tavern at Woodbridge —I heard a very stout man that was walking the piazza, say—in a loud voice—'I'll be d——d——if any man shall search Captain Biddle's baggage'—Looking at him, —I found it was *Ezekiel Furman* —an old friend that served his time to a merchant at Philadelphia —With Furman, I had been acquainted when boys—& in our boyish expeditions,—he always headed us —(It was not *General* E Furman—him, I did not know) Although I had nothing to be taken,—I was very glad to see Furman & to find him the same honest fellow he had ever been —Some of those in the wagon ahead of us—had told him I was in the wagon coming up,—& he waited to see me —If the people here had any intention of searching us,—they could not have done it —Furman was brave, as he was stout & had several friends—& none in the wagon would have suffered a search without resistance I was very sorry to hear from Furman, that he had been unfortunate, & much more so—to hear since, that his misfortunes had made him intemperate
He married a Miss Wikoff of a respectable family —Taking leave of this good fellow—we arrived safe in Philadelphia "
                                                                                       p 166
In August this year, [1812], I went to Long Branch —At Edentown—near the Branch, I heard that my old friend—Captain Furman—lived there, (the person who was at Woodbridge—& swore that none of my luggage should be searched —When I came a prisoner from New York)—When he came to the tavern, I knew him immediately—although it was upwards of *thirty-one* years since we had met —He did not know me—but when I told him who it was, that was conversing with him, he was greatly rejoiced to see me —Agreeably to his promise he came the next day to the Branch to see me —He is a very hale, hearty man—& rode down on a race horse, which he mounted & managed with great ease —He has a large respectable family —Upon some disgust he joined the British Army & being taken in arms—would have suffered an ignominious death, but for his relation General Furman—& some powerful friends —He told me that after the war—he lived near Frankford, & a report of some of his friends —that he could beat any man in America, had occasioned him many severe battles It appeared to me, that few men,—now—could beat him
He has a small pension from the British government to which government he is warmly attached—and has as much hatred to the French as man in America "

1776, Apr. 5 Return of pay and subsistences due Captain Henry Waddle's Company of Grenadiers, in 1st battalion N Jersey Militia, commanded by Major Thomas Seabrook, from the time they began their march Original in New Jersey Historical Society, Newark, N. J.

1776, Nov. 27. Lieut-Colonel in Col. Read's Battalion, State Troops

1776, Nov 28 Lieut-Colonel in First Regiment, Monmouth County.

1777, June 6 Lieut-Colonel in First Regiment, Monmouth County, resigned Apr 18, 1778.

1779, '80 and '81 He was a Member of the General Assembly from Monmouth County, also a member of many local patriotic committees—one that demanded retaliation for the murder of Capt Huddy, and also signed the General Articles of Retaliation, in 1778.

Barber and Howe, p 372

To
  Thomas Sebrook Esq' at Trenton or any other of the represfentives for the County of Monmouth

Freehold September 26- 1780

To the Honoribel the Legiflature of the State of New Jerfey

Whereas in and by an act of the general affembly of the Said State pafed in the Month of June in the year of our Lord one thoufand and Seven hundred and Seventy Seven The Subfcriber together with three other Citizens of the County of Monmouth wheare appointed commitioners for takeing Charge of the forfited Eftates in the County of Monmouth And wheareas the Subfcriber hath faithfully Served in the said office from the said appointment till this Time, but finding the execution of the Said office attending with so many difficulties and Inconveniencies that he cannot confiftant with his own honor or conveniency continue in the Said office any longer beg Leave to refign the Said office and do accordingly refign the Said office and pray that this refignation may be accepted by your honoribel Houfe

from your humbel Servent
JACOB WIKOFF

The old house, (built by Thomas Whitlock in all probability), had a cannon ball shot through a clap board in the roof, during the Revolutionary War, which they can still show.

When the Hessians visited and plundered it, they left, setting it on fire after cutting the well ropes, but a negress, too aged to flee with the others, was smoked out of her hiding place, and with good presence of mind extinguished the commencing blaze, by overturning the wash tubs, which had been set with the clothes to soak On another occasion, the silver was saved by hurriedly throwing it behind the asparagus bush which filled the big chimney place I have one of these spoons which was the property of Dr Stephen Tallman, and another is with the Hill family at Mt Pleasant, Iowa Another piece, a silver tankard, was seized and put in the capacious hanging pocket, on the person of the Major's daughter, Patty (Vandevere), who courageously followed up the Hessians, constantly protesting against the theft of the beds, mirrors, etc , and the lid of the tankard giving an occasional click, kept her mother in a constant fright for fear of its discovery The house itself was saved by the understanding that the day it burned, so would the Taylor [Tory] house in Middletown village

The following account of one of the depredations is in my possession

Thomas Seabrook was Robed June the 16th 1777 By George Taylor, Late Colo¹ & others the following things, Vis- -

	£	s	d
To 10 hames seposed to way 20 lb Each - - at 1/6	15	0	0
To 1 Hogsed Cyder of the first Qullety Seposed to Contain 3½ barels at 40/ p' barel	7	0	0
To my wifes Sues & hir Silver buckels	2	15	0
To 1 Shurt 30/ to 2 pare Stokens 20/	2	10	0
To 1 pare mens Sues & walking Cane	1	0	0
To 1 Shift 1 hankerchef & 1 aporn	1	8	0
To 1 lamb & 1 weather	1	15	0
To 1 pare Shepe Shers	0	8	0
	£31	16	0

May 21ˢᵗ I was not at home until the evening when it was told by my father Edward Taylor had been cutting some of his shore fence. I went soon after & counted the rails & post cut & found 22 rails, splices cut & 9 post cut & split

May 25, '99 my father sent for me to come to the house & informed me that James Kelsey told him that Edward Taylor was cutting our fence again & told me to tell sᵈ Taylor to not make unnecessary waste I went in company with James Kelsey & when we came to the fence Edward Taylor was by the cut fence with his axe in his hand. Upon our coming to him a conversation began between me & said Taylor about the fence & land. I told Taylor it was poor business. Taylor acknowledged he had cut 20 or 30 Pannel & he would be damned if it was put up again, he the sᵈ Taylor would cut down as much or more & that he had money enough, could have as much money as he could carry & that he would spend the last six pence. at the last cutting fence I found 44 cedar rails cut in two & 28 splices cut of & 23 posts cut & split

1786 Thomas Seabrook sued James Holmes for a bill of £170

1786, May 20 Wᵐ Livingston, Governor, appointed Thomas Seabrook, Guardian of Jacob, son of Jacob Covenhoven, late of Monmouth County.

Tombstones in Fairview Cemetery, Middletown, N J

Maj. Thoˢ Seabrook died, Feb 22, 1805, aged 67 years, 11 months and 25 days

Martha Seabrook, his wife, died, July 14, 1828, aged 89 years and 2 months

These stones originally stood in a lot just East of the lane leading from the Highway, in Middletown village, to the residence of the late Charles I Hendrickson, Esq, and about one hundred and fifty feet from his front door. They were removed by the Hendricksons, which was the cause of a disturbance between the two families. The location of this cemetery raises the question whether this may not have been one of the homestead sites of the Seabrooks

1800, Mch 25 Will of Thomas Seabrook, of Middletown, Monmouth County, N. J; proved by the only surviving executor, Thomas Seabrook, Mch 19, 1805, mentioned

"to my beloved Wife, Martha Seabrook, all my plate, the use of the Northeast room & the choice of one rume up stars to Dwell in during her Widowhood, also a chest of Drawers, two of the best beds, with a set of curtains, two Bolsturs, fore pillurs, six linning shets, Eaight wollen blancets and three Coverleds, two bedsteads, all of the first choice, six of the best chears, shovel & tongs, the brase handirons, the choice of two looking Glafses, two of the best tables, one Tea Kettle & all the Tea Tacklen & half the puter & one half of the Table linning & towells & a Negro woman to wate on hir when she is wanted, and a Hansome, Decent Living found her as longe as she remanes my Widow or continues to live with my son Thomas, But if my said wife should chuse to quit the house where we now live, I give hir in lue of hir two Rumes & Bord, . . . a Negrow wench caled Esabel & Exclusive of all other gifts sixty dollars a year to be paid her, yearly, by my Executors, which shall be in Liew of her Doury or power of thirds"

"to my son, Stephen Seabrook, all that tract of Land and Meadow whereon he now dwells, formerly Thomas Thorn's, also forty-two Acres & seventy-six hundrets of an Acre of Pine land, lying in the Township of Dover, , also the one half of my Preportion or Right of Propriete, also one half of the Cedar Swamp or swamp formerly Anthony Dennis's, also all my part of the Ore resarved by my Father & Mother in Brown's bog"

"to my Daughter, Martha Vanderveer, & my Daughter, Hannah Stillwell, the sum of Five hundred dollars, each, to be paid out of my Estate, in four Equal payments, the first payment in one year after my Decease and the Remandur Early"

"to my grand daughter, Catherine Crawford, the sum of Fifteen dollurs over & above what I have already Given hir Mother, to be paid hir when she arrives at the age of Eaighteen"

"to my son, Thomas Seabrook, all the plantation whereon I now Dwell, at Shoulharbur, with all the meadow lots thaireunto belonging, Also the place formerly Jonathan Stout's, lying at Mounten hill, the Equel Half of all my propriety Rights, the one Equal Half of all my Cedar swamps, formerly Anthony Dennes's, also fifty-six Acres of pine land, laying in Dover & to the Southard of the pine land given to my son, Stephen ,

Also One hundred and forty-three Acres of pine land, laying in the above township & tow the Westerd of Stephen Seabrook's (one hundred acres) , also one acre at Muskets Cove landing, Also all my Negros (Except as matturs may be surcumstanced with a Gift or lent of one wench to my wife) and also all the Remaining part of my Estate namely my Household furniture, all my Stock of Every Kind, my vessel, all my Farming Utensels And in Kace my Wife, Martha Seabrook, should take the thirds of my land, according to law, . . . all that of my Estate heretofore Given to my s^d Wife, unto my son, Thomas Seabrook, and all Lagefes to be stopt during the time my wife holds hir thirds & after hir deth or giving up hir [share] of my landed property, the lagetees to be paid theair Lageses in the same Rotation"

Executors son, Thomas Seabrook, and Aaron Longstreet
Witnesses Cornelia Dennis, Nicholas Willson and Benjamin Bennet
Recorded in Book A of Wills, p 76, Freehold, N J

1815, July 1 Will of Martha Seabrook, of Middletown, County of Monmouth, N J, no date of proof, mentioned.

"to my grand daughter, Julia Stillwell, my best bed field bedstead and set of curtains, with the following articles of beding, one of the best coverlids, four [of] the best sheets, two pair of the best pillow cases, also the following articles of my wareing Apparel six of my best Gowns, two Dimety petticoats and four of my best petticoats, six of my best handkerchiefs, eight pair of the best Stockings, four Silk Shawls, two Cotten Shawls, six of the best shifts, sattin cloak and tipet, also my Tea tackling, Shovel and Tongs, And Irons, Table, two large silver spoons and Trunck"

"to my grand daughters, Mariah Seabrook and Anne Seabrook, (Daughters of my son, Stephen), all the Remainder of my wareing Apparel, to be Divided, equal, between them"

"to my grand daughter, Mary Seabrook, (the daughter of my son, Thomas), my Looking Glass"

"to my grand daughter, Martha Seabrook, (Daughter of my son, Thomas), my Chest of Drawers"

"to my son, Stephen Seabrook, my other bed and beding, together with all the Remainder of my estate"

Executor Friend, James Frost

No witnesses' names appear, neither does the will appear to have been signed

1818, Oct 24 Will of Martha Seabrook, of Middletown, County of Monmouth, N J, no date of proof, mentioned

"unto my son, Stephen Seabrook, the equal half of the money that I may have on hand or that may be due to me at the time of my Decease, Also my Cloth cloak"

"Unto my son, Thomas SeaBrook, I give nothing he having nearly all the Estate of Thomas SeaBrook, Dec^d"

"Unto my Daughter, Hannah, the other equal half of the money that I may have on hand or that may be due to me at the time of my Decease, also one Bed and all my Bedding, excepting only such articles as will be hereafter specified in the bequest to Julia Stillwell Two Silver Table Spoons, all my Tea Spoons and a Satin Cloak"

"Unto my Grand daughter, Julia Stillwell, . my best Bed, Bolster & Pillows, Field Bedsted—curtains and Bed Quilt and to choose from among my bedding, two coverlids, five Woolin Blankets, Six Linen Sheets and three pair of Pillow Cases, also from among my wearing apparel, a Double Gown, and to choose four frocks, four Petticoats, Six shifts & eight pair [of] Stockings, Also the Chest of Drawers, a Wooden chest and a silver Table Spoon"

"Unto Martha, the daughter of Thomas SeaBrook, my trunk'

"Unto Delia Ann Stillwell a Silver table Spoon"

"Unto Mariah Ann, the Daughter of Stephen SeaBrook, my tables, crockery-ware, tongs & shovel, andiron"

"All my wearing apparel and other property not already dispos^d of unto my three granddaughters, and to be equally divided between them, that is to Maria SeaBrook & Ann SeaBrook, daughters of Stephen Seabrook, and Delia Ann Stillwell, the daughter of Hannah Stillwell"

Executors James Frost, Esqr, and John Patterson, Esq
Witnesses Benjamin R Robson and John S Conger
The testator signed this will in full

Issue

42 Stephen Seabrook, born, probably, between 1759 and 1764
43 Thomas Seabrook, born 1771
44 Hannah Seabrook, born 1772
45 Mary Seabrook
46 Martha Seabrook

12 DANIEL SEABROOK, son of Daniel Seabrook, 4, had a license to marry Mary, daughter of John and Mercy [Mary?] (Longstreet) Little, June 21, 1759. She was born Apr 5, 1739, and died between 1800 and 1805. He followed his brother, Nicholas Brown Seabrook, to Portsmouth, Va., when he sold his land in Middletown, Monmouth County, N J, to his brother, Thomas Seabrook, May 1, 1767. He remained at Portsmouth until after the birth of his youngest child, James, when he removed to North Carolina, where he seems to have settled in Hyde County, as his sons were living on Smith's Creek and News River, near Germanton, in 1823. He died before his youngest son, James, was nine years of age. Upon the death of her father, John Little, which occurred shortly before Feb 4, 1785, Mary (Little) Seabrook returned to Shrewsbury, Monmouth County, N. J., for her share of his property, bringing with her, her two youngest children, Elizabeth and James. She died while at Shrewsbury, and these two children were brought up by their uncle, Major Theophilus Little.

1761 Daniel Seabrook was assessed, in Middletown, £0-7-6 and £1-6-1.

1763, May 13 Middletown. Note of Daniel Seabrook, for £407 15 0, to Thomas Seabrook, "Lite Jersey Money," at 8/ per ounce, with lawful interest until paid. Witnesses William Crawford and Nicholas Brown Seabrook.

1764 Daniel Seabrook was assessed for the Poor Rate, at Shrewsbury, £0-15-22.

1765, May 1, [April] Daniel Seabrook, of Middletown, sold to Peter Knott, of Shrewsbury, for £260, proc. money, the plantation whereon he was living, supposed to contain two hundred and twenty acres, excepting & reserving out of the same, forty acres at the South end of the tract adjoining Dr Jaquish.

1767, May 1. Middletown, N J. Daniel Seabrook sold to Thomas Seabrook, of the same place, for the sum of £2-10-0 sterling, that piece of ground, in Middletown, lying to the westward of Willson's burying ground, being within the lot of land at present Belonging to Richd Jaquish, &c, &c.

1767, May 16 Daniel Seabrook, yeoman, of Shrewsbury, was sued by Thomas Seabrook for a note of £815-10-0, given May 5, 1764, at Freehold, to secure a debt of £407-15-0, payable at the end of one year. Judgment was taken in Court, at the City of Burlington, by Thomas Seabrook, and the money was to be delivered by the Sheriff to the Court, at the City of Amboy.

1767, Nov 10 Daniel Seabrook was sued for a bill of £129, by Thomas Stevens.

In 1782, he is mentioned in his brother's letter.

In 1794, he and his wife were living.

Letter from Thomas Seabrook, of Smith's Creek, North Carolina, to his brother,[*1] James Seabrook, of Lambertville, N J. Post-marked "Germanton, July 16, 1823. Postage 25 cts."

The original, from which this is copied, is in possession of the daughter of James, Miss Elizabeth Seabrook, of Lambertville, N. J.

"Smiths Creek, July the 11th 1823

Dear Brother this is in answer to yours of the 25th of August 1820 wich is the last Letter of yours that I have not answered the causes of wich was maney, at first ill health and maney others followed in—that you Complain (and verrey Justly) of my not being Regular in my correspondence to you thear is several reasons you ought to consider—you are not stationary but moving from place to place and no knowing whear to find you—I could say as Dane Swift said to Lord Bolingbroke it is not writing to you but at you Continue my Dear James to write and that often. Remember you are the younger & that I was your nurs, you have had Children and have nurst them and can form an idea of the tender feeling and attachment these Little Offices beget Independant of the tyse of Bloud, which I think between you and me is as strong as between aney Brothers, my ill health and Perplexitys in buisnefs if the Sole cause of not writing oftener, write to me

---

[*1] Miss Elizabeth Seabrook, daughter of James, says her father, in 1823, was living in a small house on his father-in-law's (John Lambert), farm, whence he removed to Lambertville, N J, Apr 1, 1824, and where she, (Miss Seabrook), was born Apr 30, 1824. John Lambert's farm was in Amwell Township, Hunterdon County, N J, about three miles back of Lambertville.

as Long as I live & when I die I shall give orders for you to be informed of that event—of my Self and famely my helth is verry precarious—at this time I am allmost Confined to the House of that most Dangerous the Liver Complaint but I flatter Myself that I am geting better the fever has Abated & the pain has Allmost but I am Verging to an old man   I have the Rumatics most all the time and deefness which is a verry unsosial Complaint espesially for me that is so fonde of convers with my fellow man   I had my Ears hurt 15 or 20 years Since by the Bursting of a gun which causes the deefnefs but it is not so bad but I can hear when aney one raises thear Voice a Little above the comon tone—My Wifes helth is Rather wors than mine   She has had Risings in her head and Runing from her nose Seven or Eight years and for more than two years past has been afflicted with inflamatry Sore Eyes occtioned by the Risings in her head as we believe—as no aplication that we can find by Applying to the best Medical Ade we have has yet Given Relef

Betsey Herron my Wife's daughter was married Last January two years to a worthy man by the name of Nathan Jennett—but Lost him in five months to a day from thear marriage—and no child—but he was a Widower and had a Daughter of ten years old   Betsey and her Daughter-in-law now both Lives with me   Betsey is Tolerable helthy at this time

James Seabrook is a Stout young man and not Married and Lives with us   I see by yours to Daniel Seabrook that he has informed you of his mothers deth (but that I had done some time agoe) & his Fathers Marriage   you seem to be a Little surprised at Brother Daniels marrying at his time of Life, what will you think when you hear he has a child & married an old woman that had been Married twise before to young men and never had a child before   Brother Daniel lives on News River & Quite Remote from me   he had three of his sons with and about him—Abner—Esau & Benj [?] his son John Lives in this County & his Daughter Ann & is married & had 3 Living Children   she married a man by the name of William Swindle— you say to Daniel (and I know it is ment for me from what you say before) that you and your wife is going in August to Shrewsbury & Shole harber to see ower Relations thear—when you return write me & write me particular of ower Friends & Relations thear   I should like to hear something of Ben Jackson and Uncle Thops*¹ & his famely the Last you have said of him is that he had Lost his wife & Lived with his son Tobias   uncle Connelly & famely*² I wish to hear from—your Last information says Aunt was Dead & he has married to or three years & his Dauter was married & Lived in Great Stile but did not say if theay had children or not & what his two sons are doing—in yours of the 17th of Jany 1818 you say that Mr James Rinds only son and only child now Living is in the Pensilvania Hospital in a state of mental derangement—let me know is this the only Surviving Grand Child of Uncle Nicholas Seabrooks*³—the Last knowledge I have of Cousin John Seabrook*⁴ he had an incresing famely   Remember me to Aunt Hanah*⁵ & to Sister Merriam *⁶   I remain you[r] Eaver loving Brother

THO⁵ SEABROOK

P S   If you go to Shole harber perhaps you can hear from Doctor Stillwell & Cosen Hanah—theay had but one child when I was in New Jersey & that a Daughter

Direct to me & Daniel Seabrook both N° Carolina—Hyde County Germanton—Adieu—T S

P S   in your Letter to Daniel you are mistaken in the age of Brother Daniel—Ower Parents was married one some [same] day (21st) of June 1759   Brother Daniel was born the 12th of June 1760   John Seabrook the 28th of Feby 1762   Nicholas B Seabrook the 25th Decbr 1764   Myself January the 27th 1767—and Andrew the 24th Feby 1769   Elizabeth the 20th of Feby 1771 [This is corrected in a later list]   yourself as you have stated on the 24th of Oct 1775   Ower Sister Polley being so young I neavr had aney account of her Birth—She was between John and Nicholas   again Adieu T S''

The following record, evidently sent by Thomas Seabrook, (born 1767), at a later date than his 1823 letter is indorsed·

"Date of the marriage of my Father and Mother, and the ages of their children "   Then in James Seabrook's handwriting

"Sent to me, James Seabrook, by my Brother Thomas from North Carolina "

"Daniel Seabrook Senr and Mary Little was married June 21, 1759

Daniel Seabrook Junr was born June 12th 1760

---

*¹ "Uncle Thops" was his mother s brother Theophilus Little, of Monmouth County, who settled at Eaglesmere, Pa , about 1810

*² "Uncle Connelly" was Col John Connelly, of Philadelphia, who married his mother's sister, Ann Little

*³ "Uncle Nicholas Seabrook" was Nicholas Brown Seabrook, of Virginia

*⁴ "Cousin John Seabrook" son of the above Nicholas

*⁵ "Aunt Hanah" his mother's sister Hannah Little who married, first, Major Benjamin Dennis, of Monmouth County and, second, John Lambert, (his second wife)   She was the mother of *⁶ Merriam Lambert, wife of James Seabrook   James and Merriam were first cousins

John Seabrook was born February 28th 1762
Mary Seabrook was born Nov'r 17th 1763
Nicholas Seabrook was born Decem'r 25th 1764
Thomas Seabrook was born Janu'ry 27th 1767
Andrew McD Seabrook was born Febru'y 22d 1769
Elizabeth Seabrook was born Febru'y 12th 1773
James Seabrook was born October 24th 1775"

Of the children of Daniel Seabrook and Mary Little, save James, not much is known

The other children remained in North Carolina, and the only knowledge we have of them is that "One son went to sea and never was heard from", "another son had a daughter, Mrs Herbert, who was a nurse in New York about 1840 or 45"; and the information given in the preceding letter

Issue

47 Daniel Seabrook, born June 12, 1760
48 John Seabrook, born Feb. 28, 1762
49 Mary Seabrook, born Nov 17, 1763.
50 Nicholas B Seabrook, born Dec 25, 1764
51 Thomas Seabrook, born Jan. 27 1767.
52 Andrew McDowall Seabrook, born Feb 22, 1769   I have a receipt signed by him in Monmouth County N. J., in 1798.
53 Elizabeth Seabrook, born Feb 12, 1773, married, in Monmouth County, and had a daughter   Rebecca . . . . ., who married Mr Davidson
54 James Seabrook, born Oct. 24, 1775

13   NICHOLAS BROWN SEABROOK, son of Daniel Seabrook, 4, was born, at Middletown, N J, May 25, 1739, O S ; died, at Richmond, Va, June 28, 1790, married, Dec 19, 1761, by license dated Dec 15, 1761, in New York City, Mary Dutchess, born, Oct 30, 1742, at Phillipse Manor, N. Y.

1763   He removed to Portsmouth, Va

1770, Oct 4   Nicholas Brown Seabrook, for £325, bought land, in Henrico County, Va., from Jacob Valentine

Numerous sales of property and leases, by Nicholas Brown Seabrook, are recorded in the records of Henrico County.

1771, December   He removed to Norfolk, Va.

1775, September   He was driven from Norfolk, by the British fleet, under John, Earl of Dunmore, and removed to Richmond.

1779, December   He removed to his plantation in Hanover County.

1782, Feb. 7   Nicholas Brown Seabrook, of Virginia, gave to his brother, Major Thomas Seabrook, of Middletown, N. J , a power of attorney.

Letter from Nicholas B. Seabrook, of Virginia, to Major Thomas Seabrook, of New Jersey:
Dear Brother,
Your favours of October & Decembor Last duly came to hand, & I Should have answered them Sooner, but did not know whome to direct to the care of in Prince Town, not knowing the Name of any man there, & You live so fur of the Post Office, that you never apply for, nor git a Letter, unless by axident, I wonder you never sent me some mans Name to Direct to, but by axident I found one, I shall direct to his care untill you can find some fitter way to git your letters, I am Vary glad to hear you are all well, & also wish you a Great deal of joy at my Cousin Patseys marrage, give our Loves, to her & her husband   I am glad of Your Popurality for two Reasins Viz   it is a sine you are Worthey, & the next is, that Inables you to Prossecute the Wrascall Taylor the more   I rejoice with you on the Capture of Corn-Wallis & hope ere long we Shall Injoy a

Peace, I have wrote Brother Daniel, desiring him to Send you a power & his act & have Inclosed You my Power Edward Taylor must owe me my Proportion of the Rents of the Shrewsbury Plantation, as I naver Received anything from him, Indeed I naver Received my Legacee from him   Some time ago I wrote you that I had Suffered by the depresiateing of the money, & had Quit Trade & Bought Lands & Negroes & Turnd Farmor, Now by the Mooving of the Seat of Goverment to Richmond, where I have Five half acre Lotts of Ground & my Plantation of 727 acres of Land Leying 11 miles from the Town, it has more than doubled its Value, & made ample amens for the Losses of Depreseation, my Istate is worth about Eight Thosend Pounds Sterling, & is Vary Capable of Improt as I have Ground anough in Town to build 12 more housis, & I am going to See again to Import Meterals, & Fix my Son in Europe to finish his Education, I find I am more in want of money than Avir I was, as I have twelve houses to build, my Wife & Children joines me in Love to you & Family   I remain your Loving brother
NICHs B SEABROOK

Richmond, February 15, 1782

Mrs Dr Studdiford, of Lambertville, N. J., owns portraits of Nicholas B Seabrook, and his wife, and miniatures of them are owned by Dr J E Stillwell of New York City

SEABROOK FAMILY REGISTER, VIRGINIA

Nicolas Brown Seabrook was born, at Middletown, in the State of New Jersey, May the 25th, 1739, old style, the son of James Seabrook,* whose progenitors came from England, and settled in Connecticut, about the time King Charles the 2nd was restored to the Crown of England, as our ancestors were opposed to Monarchical Governments, and had rendered themselves obnoxious to the King's party, they found it expedient to emigrate to New England, as above   The history of Connecticut makes mention of the family
Nicolas B Seabrook was married to Mary Dutchess, in the City of New York, December the 19th, 1761, she was born, at Philips Mannor, State of New York, October the 30th, 1742   In August, 1763, they removed to Portsmouth, Virginia, where they had a daughter born, March 11th, 1764, & named Mary, who died when aged 17 months
John Seabrook, a graduate of Princeton, son of the above, was born also, at Portsmouth, on the 17th day of February, 1768   Molly Seabrook was born the 22nd October, 1770, and died, at Portsmouth, aged 4 weeks—Removed to Norfolk, in December, 1771—Sally was born there on the 18th of October, 1773—Nicholas B Seabrook was driven from Norfolk by the British fleet, commanded by John, Earl of Dunmore, at the commencement of the American Revolution, and removed to Richmond, at the falls of the James River, in September, 1775, where Polly Seabrook was born on the 28th February, 1777   N B S removed to his plantation in Hanover County, in December, 1779—Betsy Seabrook was born there July 15th, 1780, and died of the measles, at Richmond, Oct 2nd, 1783—Nicholas B Seabrook, Jr was born, at Dungaroon, in Hanover, [Co] Sept 11, 1782—
The above record by N. B Seabrook, Senr

Nicholas B Seabrook, Senr, died, at Richmond, June 28th, 1790   Mary Seabrook, his widow, and her children, John, Sally, Polly, and Brown removed to the plantation, at Hanover, of John, soon after the death of N B Seabrook, Senr, but lived, in Richmond, during the year 1791   Nicholas B Seabrook, Junr, while going to school to Harris and McCray, in Richmond was inoculated for the small-pox at Mr John Cunliff's, and died thereof on the 13th of Feby, 1794
Sally Seabrook was married to James Rind, attorney-at-law, Nov 3, 1794, at Dungaroon, in Hanover County   N B Rind, their first child, was born March 13th, 1796   Maria Dutchess Rind was born the 28th, Jany, 1798   Betsy Rind was born in May, 1802 & died in May, 1803
James and Sally Rind, left Richmond for the Hot Springs about the first of July, 1803, for the benefit of his health, but he died before he reached the Springs, at the New Store, (Mr Fosset's), on the 4th of August, 1803, & Sally, his wife, survived him but a few weeks   She died at John McClung's, on the south side of the Warm Springs, Octr the 8th, 1803, and James & Sarah Rind were buried at Staunton
Polly Seabrook was married to Bartholomew Trueheart at the same time & place that her sister Sally was married to James Rind, Nov 13th, 1794, and died at James Rinds, in Richmond, May 11th, 1796, while her husband was in Kentucky
John Seabrook was married to Ann Sydnor, October 18th, 1793, which Ann was the daughter of William & Ann Sydnor, of Hanover County, Virginia   She was born the 6th of October, 1775

---

*Nicholas Brown Seabrook was the son of Daniel Seabrook, all statements to the contrary notwithstanding   It seems incomprehensible that if this record was written by N B Seabrook Sr, that he should not have known the given name of his own father   The statement that the family appeared in Connecticut history was made also by my own grandmother, Hannah Seabrook, the wife of Dr William Stillwell, and had its origin, doubtless, from the application of the names of Lord Say and Seal and Lord Brooke, after whom Saybrook, Conn, was named   J E Stillwell

1 Nicholas Brown Seabrook first child of John & Ann was born, Aug 10th, 1799, at Dungaroon, Hanover County.

2 Edward Sydnor Seabrook was born on Monday morning, the first day of December, in the year of our Lord Eighteen hundred (1800), at Dungaroon, also

3 Betsy was born the Eleventh day of Feby, (Thursday morning), Eighteen hundred and two, at Dungaroon, 1802

4 John Blair was born the twenty-first of March, in the Year of our Lord, Eighteen hundred and three, at Dungaroon & died on Tuesday, the 4th September, 1804, Eighteen hundred and four, at Dungaroon John and Ann Seabrook removed to Richmond, in September, 1803

5 William was born, in Richmond, the 28th July Eighteen Hundred and four, & died there August 12th, same year

6 Sally was born, in Richmond, the first day of August Eighteen hundred and five, & died, at Oakwell, in Hanover [Co], Octr 8th, 1806

John and Ann Seabrook removed from Richmond to Oakwell in Hanover [Co], Jany 22nd, 1806, & went to the Hot Springs the first of June following & returned the 12th Septr, 1806

7 Polly was born, at Oakwell, the 29th (twenty-ninth) day of January, Eighteen hundred & seven, 1807.

8 Sally Ann was born at Oakwell, the first day of Novr, in the afternoon Eighteen hundred and Eight, 1808

John & Ann Seabrook removed from Oakwell, in Hanover [Co], to Hardbargain house, in Richmond, in December, 1808

On the 17th of May, 1809, Edward S Seabrook fell into a well of water, in the absence of his parents, and was providentially saved from drowning by a servant named Easter

On the 20th June, 1809, Nicholas B Seabrook, venturing too far into the river, (without the knowledge of his parents), was swept away by the current, & when quite spent and exhausted was rescued from inevitable death, by the providential interposition of Captain Richard Denny, who at the imminent hazard of his own life, rushed into the torrent to save a stranger

In the months of June and July my eldest daughter Betsy & Docia a black girl, were dangerously afflicted with the nervous inflammatory fever

9 John was born, in Richmond, on Saturday morning, the Eighteenth day of Feby, 1810, Eighteen hundred and ten & departed this life in Nov, 1810

10 William Henry was born on Thursday, the twenty-eighth day of November, Eighteen hundred and Eleven, 1811

11 John Benjamin Thompson was born on the fourth day of September, in the Year of our Lord Eighteen hundred and thirteen, about one oclock in the morning

Nicholas Brown Seabrook, in a juvenile trial of strength with his cousin N B S Rind, was thrown with violence on the pavement & received a contusion on his head

About the 15th November, 1813, John B Thompson being left with his little black nurse Betty, she in order to quiet him gave him a rag baby to suck, the greater part of which he swallowed, together with a quantity of paper and a pin which were in it, from which he was providentially delivered, in a natural way, in the course of 24 hours

12 Camilla Tyrrell was born at six o'clock in the Morning Friday, the twenty-third day of June, Eighteen hundred and fifteen (23rd June, 1815) on Richmond Hill.

The Children of John & Ann Seabrook were baptized, To wit —N Brown, Edward S, Betsy, John Blair, Wm & Sally were baptised by the Rev John D Blair in my own house Polly was baptised by the Rev Thomas Hughes at house Oakwell Sally Ann and John were baptised by the Rev John D Blair on Church Hill at home William Henry, John B T, & Camilla Tyrrell were baptised at Church, in the Mason's Hall, Richmond, by the Rev John H Rice

Ann Sydnor, mother of Ann Seabrook as aforesaid, died in the winter 1817, at her place in Hanover, & was buried at Dungaroon, same county, [on] the farm of Edward G Sydnor, her son —Blefsed are the righteous for they rest from their labours Edward S Seabrook departed this life at Savannah, in Georgia, of Yellow fever, the Eighteenth day of October, Eighteen hundred & twenty-seven, in his twenty-seventh year

Betsy Seabrook was married to Daniel Trueheart by the Rev John D Blair, at Low Hill, Henrico, the 31st day of August, Eighteen hundred & twenty Their first child was born, in Richmond, the 19th day of August, 1821, and named John Seabrook Their second child, a boy also, was born, at Nosechthos, the 19th July, 1824 & named Gilbert La Fayette—their third child, a daughter, Ann Maria was . . .

Sally Ann was married the 23rd day of November, Eighteen hundred & thirty (1830) to John Mickleberry Sheppard, at the home of her brother-in-law, Daniel Trueheart, (Nosecthos), & departed this life strong in faith, & supported by the hopes & promises of the everlasting Gospel, at the same place on the night of the Twenty-first day of December, Eighteen hundred and thirty-one, aged twenty-three years one Month & twenty-one days Seabrook, the son of the above named John M Sheppard & Sally Ann was born, at Brookfield, the ninth day of September, Eighteen hundred & thirty-one

Camilla T Seabrook was married, in Rockbridge, at her Father's residence, (the old Ship), on the third day of May, Eighteen hundred & thirty-two to Dr Washington Dorsey, of Baltimore, Maryland

Nicholas Brown Seabrook, (Father of Mary Seabrook), eldest born of John & Nancy Seabrook, was married, in Lexington, Virginia to Miss Mary Blair, daughter of the Rev Blair, dec^d, his wife, the sixth day of October, Eighteen & thirty-one

1785, Jan. 8 Will of Nicholas Brown Seabrook, of the City of Richmond, State of Virginia, "in Perfect Health"; proved at Monthly Court, of Henrico County, Sept 7, 1790, mentioned·

Son, John Seabrook, received "my lots of Ground, Known by the Plan of this City, by the Letters AB, with all the Improvements

Son, Nicholas B Seabrook, received "the Corner Lott, by the Market House, with all the Improvements, the Said Lott is Known in the Plan of the City, by the Letter C."

Daughter, Salley Seabrook, received "the Corner Lott of Ground, in Back Street (Known by the Letter 3), and all the Improvements on it"

Daughter, Polley Seabrook, received "the Lott of Ground, in Back Street Known by the letter F & all the Improvements on it"

"a Twenty foot alley be layed off from the back Street down to Pleasant Younghusbands Corner, & from there to Turn to the Market house Common, then one half of the Ground to be allowed from Each lot, & to be kept open forever"

"when my son, John, is of Age, that my Plantation in Hanover County, with all the Stock of Cattle, & Plantation Utensils, be Sold at Public sale, on Such Credit as my Executors Shall judge to the most Advantage, & the amount to be Equally divided among all my Children, as they become of Age, or get married Also when my Son, John, is of Age,   all my Negroes Shall be Equally divided among all my Children, I say Equally in Value"

"Each of my Daughters their Choice in a Feather bed & its Furniture, & the Remaining Part of my Furniture I divide Equally between my Sons, John & Nicholas Brown, my Side Arms, Buckels & Buttons & old Family Cane I leave to my Son, Nicholas Brown"

"If any of my Children die under Age, or without a will, after they become of age, then . . . *there* Fortune Shall be Equally divided among my Surviving Children"

"My Desire is that my Sons be Educated at Williamsburg or Princeton, in the best manner, & be bro^t up to the Study of the Law The Reason that I have Said nothing about my debts is that I Intend to owe a Very few, which I desire may be Paid"

"My Desire is that my Wife, after my Desease, have the whole of my Estate in her Possession, during her Widowhood, & the Profits arising from my Estate to be Used in bringing up my Children & Improving the Childrens' lotts, and any Other Purpose that my Wife, Mary Seabrook, thinks Proper"

Executors "my Wife, Mary Seabrook, with my Son, John Seabrook, Daniel Vandewal and Daniel Lambert

Witnesses: Isaac Younghusband, Pleasant Younghusband and Isaac Younghusband, Junr

The testator signed the will Nich^s Brown Seabrook.

Codicil to above will dated Hanover, October the 29, 1787, mentioned
"to my Son, John Seabrook,   the whole of my Plantation in Hanover County."
"to my Daughter, Polley Seabrook,   that part of my Lott N° E, which follows beginning at the South East corner of Said Lott Joining Market Alley & Running Northwest Parrelel with the Back Street twenty feet, then Southwest Parrelel with Market Alley to the said Alley that leads to the Market House, then South East along that Alley twenty feet to the Corner that Leads to Back Street, Including the Houses that may be built by me (The reason of the above Codesial is owing to the Raise in Value of my Property near the Market House), All the other parts of my will is to remain as wrote at first, except my Executors I Exclude Mefsrs Vandewal & Lambert in this Codecial, & Ordain my Wife, Mary Seabrook & John Seabrook, my sole Executors."

Codicil dated Hanover, November 11th, 1788, mentioned·
"by reason of my late Improvements on my Plantation,   I give   the whole of my Slaves to my Daughters, Sarah & Polley Seabrook, the rest of my will to Continue as above"

Codicil dated Hanover, March 31st, 1789, mentioned:

"By Reason of the Doors & Windows in the N W part of the House Called Mrs Collins', I take from the lott N° E ten feet of Ground, beginning at the N W Corner of Said House, & Running parrelel with the Cross Street to the Extreme part of the Kitchen   I add the above piece of Ground to my Daughter, Polley's lot & Curtail it from my Daughter Sarah's lot N° E "

All three codicils were signed by the testator   Nich^s B Seabrook

Recorded at Richmond, Henrico Co , Va , Vol 2, Wills, pp 162-165

The inventory of his personal estate amounted to £23-4-9, and included Twelve Silver Spoons £10-16-0, One Silver Ladle £1-2-0 = £12-18-0.

1808, Oct 14 Will of Mary Seabrook, of the City of Richmond, proved Dec. 5, 1808, mentioned

"to my Grand Son, Nicholas B Seabrook, one Negro man Named Tom Martin, living with my son, John Seabrook, and also a pair of gold Sleeve-Buttons "

"to my grand Daughter, Maria D Rind, one Negro Woman Named Beck Depriest, and her Son, William, but tis my will that Said Negro woman Beck Depriest be Sold, and the money arising from Said Sale be applied to the purchase of a Negro girl for my grand Daughter, Maria D Rind, and also one Feather bed, Mahogany bed-stead, hair mattrass, one bolster and Two Pillers, Two blankets and Two Counterpins, half a Dozen Silver Table Spoons marked J R , and half a Dozen Tea Spoons marked J R also, and Silver Sugar Tongs unmarked, and also Two Japan'd Teaboards, and one Mahogany Secretary, and my Plain Gold Watch."

'to my grand son, Nicholas B S Rind, one Mahogany Book Case, and one Feather bed, bedstead, hair Mattrass, bolster and Two Pillers, Two blankets, and one New Virginia cloth Counterpin and half a Dozen Silver Table Spoons mark'd H S L , and a gold Repeating Watch, and one old Silver watch also, and one large Family Bible "

'to my grand Daughter, Betsey Seabrook, one Feather bed, bolster and Two Pillers, Two Blankets and a Counterpin "

"to my grand Daughter, Polly Seabrook, one Silver Soup ladle, and half a Dosen Silver Tea Spoons Mark'd N P * S "

"to my grand Son, Edward S Seabrook, one Gold Eagle, and to my Daughter-in-law, Nancy Seabrook, my Silver Snuff-Box "

Executors   "my Son, John Seabrook, and my Nephew, James Seabrook

Witnesses   James Seabrook and Joshua Wise

The testator signed her name to the will

Recorded at Richmond, Henrico Co , Va , Vol 3, Wills, pp 442-443

Issue

55 Mary Seabrook, born, at Portsmouth, Va , Mch. 11, 1764; died aged 17 months
56 John Seabrook, born, at Portsmouth, Va , Feb 17, 1768.
57 Molly Seabrook, born, at Portsmouth, Va , Oct. 22, 1770, died, aged 4 weeks, at Portsmouth
58 Sally Seabrook, born, at Norfolk, Va., Oct 18, 1773
59 Polly Seabrook, born, at Richmond, Va , Feb. 28, 1777.
60 Betsy Seabrook, born, in Hanover County, Va , July 15, 1780, died, Oct. 2, 1783, at Richmond
61 Nicholas B Seabrook, Jr , born, at Dungaroon, Hanover County, Sept 11, 1782; died, Feb 7, 1794, at Richmond   There is, at the corner of St. John's Church, a raised tomb, with brick body and thick dark-stained marble top slab, marked "Nicholas Brown Seabrook, Aged 15 Years, died June 28, 1790." There appears to be some discrepancy in the dates.

17   MARY SEABROOK, daughter of Daniel Seabrook, 4.

Of her I have no exact information, but it is not improbable that she was the Mary Sea-

*A careful reading of this initial makes it conclusive that it *is not* "B," as it might readily be assumed, from their being the property of the wife of Nicholas Brown Seabrook, still it may be an error on the part of the scrivener

brook, who was licensed, May 19, 1767, of Monmouth County, to marry Richard Herbert, and I am impressed with the belief that Obadiah Herbert, who had issue, by his wife, Jane Clark, baptized in the First Reformed Church, Freehold, N J, is, in some way, connected with the above mentioned Mary Seabrook

These children were as follows

Maria Herbert, born July 30, 1793, baptized Sept 22, 1793
John Seabrook Herbert, born Sept 3, baptized Sept 29, 1798
Ruben Brown Herbert, born Oct 8, baptized Oct 18, 1800

"William Clare Seabrook," who appears in Aaron Longstreet's Tax Book, of Middletown, N J, in the year 1794, was, probably, also connected with this line

1786, May 13 Richard Lawrence, Joseph Throckmorton and William Crawford acted as arbitrators in a settlement of the claims of Thomas Seabrook, for himself, and as attorney for his brothers, Nicholas Brown and James Seabrook, and of Thomas McDowell and John Lyell, executors of Andrew McDowell, deceased, who had married one of the daughters of Mary Seabrook, under whose will they all claimed title, and brought an action against John Taylor, Daniel Hendrickson and Eleanor Lyell, executors of Edward Taylor, deceased, and John Stillwell, administrator of Joseph Stillwell, deceased, the said Taylor and said Stillwell being the executors of the will of Mary Seabrook, and dying, without having made a final accounting

As Daniel and Mary Seabrook had but two daughters, Mary and Hannah, if the preceding inference concerning Mary is correct, then of necessity, Hannah was the wife of Andrew McDowell, and mother of Thomas McDowell Original paper in the possession of Dr J E Stillwell.

I have elsewhere among my memoranda, a note that Mary Seabrook, daughter of Daniel Seabrook, died, at an advanced age, unmarried, and that she was simple-minded, from injuries received from falling from a hay-mow, when about ten years of age From all this confusion, I am able to deduce nothing that is accurate

18 JAMES SEABROOK, son of Daniel Seabrook, 4, died about 1815 He was simple-minded, "yet sometimes the smartest of them all"

1787, Jan. 1 A discharge from James Seabrook to his brother, Thomas, for all sums that he may have collected, as attorney for him, in the settlement of his mother, Mary Seabrooks', estate Witnesses Thomas Stout, Thomas Seabrook Jr., and Hannah Seabrook

Thomas Seabrook had, apparently, the care of his younger brother, James Seabrook, during his minority, for I have many papers, mostly releases, for board bills and expenses, from one to the other

42 STEPHEN SEABROOK, son of Thomas Seabrook, 11, was born, probably, between 1759–'64, and died in 1843. He was a private, in the Troop of Light Horse during the Revolutionary War, when a youth, and was bayonetted through the ceiling of his father's house, over the kitchen, where he had withdrawn himself on the approach of the enemy. He was probably his father's eldest son He went to New Albany with his children, but returned to New Jersey He lived near Englishtown He owned the land now known as Lorrillard's Brick Yard, adjacent to Keyport Previously, or later, it belonged to Nathan Brown, who built thereon a brown stone house. Here Stephen Seabrook failed, and his failure broke his health. He was buried in the Tennent Church yard

1778. Stephen Seabrook signed the Monmouth County Articles of Retaliation.

1786, Sept 20 Stephen Seabrook sued James Holmes for a bill of £240, dated Nov. 8, 1785

The Rev A H. Anthony says "It is said a part of the Battle of Monmouth was fought on the Old Seabrook place."

1829, Mch. 9 He wrote to his son, Daniel, a letter in which he stated he was then an old man, upwards of seventy years

He married, first, Nancy Tice, and second, Sally Hankinson, a widow, and a proud old lady. She died, about 1853–1856, aged about ninety-six years She was active, in body and mind, until her death, and was visited by her step-children two years before her death When she married Stephen Seabrook she had been married twice before Her first marriage was to a Mr Hankinson, who was killed at the Battle of Monmouth, and her second was to a husband of the same name It is probable that she had issue by the Hankinson marriages.

Issue by first wife
62 Martha Seabrook; eldest child.
63 Maria Seabrook; second child
64 James Seabrook
65 John Seabrook
66 Daniel Seabrook
67 Anna Seabrook, youngest child

43 THOMAS SEABROOK, son of Thomas Seabrook, 11, was born Nov. 15, 1771, died July 13, 1844; married Ann, daughter of Aaron and Williampe (Hendrickson) Longstreet, Dec 17, 1794 She was born Apr. 8, 1779, and died July 10, 1852

Tombstones in Fairview Cemetery
Thomas Seabrook died, July 14, 1844, aged 72 years, 7 months and 27 days
Anne Seabrook, his wife, died, July 10, 1852, aged 73 years, 3 months and 2 days.

There are pencil sketches of Thomas and Ann Seabrook, also silver spoons, belonging to them, now in the possession of the Rev. Mr. Wilson. At the Bay Shore house there were three guns and a bayonet, three spinning wheels, old china, silver, old chests, two old silver watches, etc., etc.

Issue
68 Aaron Longstreet Seabrook, born Oct 13, 1796, buried May 21, 1800 Tombstone in Fairview Cemetery reads Aaron L Seabrook died, May 19, 1800, aged 4 years, 7 months and 6 days.
69 Mary Seabrook, born Aug 31, 1797, died May 19, 1864. Tombstone in Fairview Cemetery reads Mary Seabrook died, May 19, 1864, aged 67 years, 3 months and 12 days.
70 Aaron Seabrook, born Jan 18, 1802, died Apr. 9, 1872, married Euphemia C., daughter of William and Rebecca (Layton) Wilson. She was born June 7, 1813, living in 1896 He is buried in Fairview Cemetery No issue.
71 Ellen Seabrook, born Oct 3, 1803
72 Lydia H Seabrook, born Oct. 3, 1805 Tombstone in Fairview Cemetery reads Lydia H Seabrook, wife of Rev William V. Wilson, died, Aug 12, 1852, aged 46 years, 10 months and 9 days

SEABROOK OF MONMOUTH COUNTY

73 Thomas Seabrook, born July 26, 1808, died Aug 19, 1818. Tombstone in Fairview Cemetery reads: Thomas Seabrook died, Aug 19, 1818, aged 10 years and 24 days
74 Martha Seabrook, born Feb 17, 1810
75 Henry N Seabrook, born Sept 10, 1813

44 HANNAH SEABROOK, daughter of Thomas Seabrook, 11, was born July 25, 1772, married Dr William Stillwell, Sunday, Oct 20, 1793, (by Rev Benjamin Bennet), who was born Jan. 5-6, 1768, died July 13, 1832 Hannah Seabrook died Apr 18, 1847

Issue

76 Dr. John E Stillwell, of New York City, born 1813.
77 Dr William E. Stillwell, of New York City
78 Julia Stillwell, married Willet Bowne
79 Delia Ann Stillwell, married Enoch Hill

45 MARY [POLLY] SEABROOK, daughter of Thomas Seabrook, 11, died Jan 9, 1795 She married George Crawford, merchant, of Middletown, N J

Issue
80 Kate Crawford, married Edward Burrowes.
Issue
Daughter, married Jacob McLean.
Issue
Catharine McLean; married George Tilton, of Middletown, N J.

46 MARTHA SEABROOK, daughter of Thomas Seabrook, 11, married Tunis Vandevere, of Freehold, N J. He died, aged about eighty years, at Camillas, N. Y He had previously lived at Glen, N Y

Issue
81 Jane Vandevere, married Dr Lee, of Camillas, Onondaga County, who had moved there from Glen, Montgomery County
Issue
William Henry Lee
Seabrook Lee
82 Patty Vandevere, married Shellac Cady, of Camillas
Issue
David Cady, of Chicago, Ill
Miss Cady, married Dr Beach
Miss Cady
83 Arthur Vandevere, married and moved to Cincinnati Had issue
84 John Vandevere, married a daughter of John D Voorhees, of Florida, Montgomery County.
Issue
Tunis Vandevere, of Glen, now living
John Vandevere
William Vandevere, had a son and a daughter.

HISTORICAL MISCELLANY

 Newton Vandevere
 Ruth Vandevere, married Mr Enders
85 Thomas Vandevere, married a Miss Delancy or Delaney
  Issue
  Elizabeth Vandevere; married Mr Liddle She died about 1894 Her son, James S Liddle, was a prominent business man of Lockport, in 1898.
  Martha Vandevere, lived at Lockport, N Y., died, single, in 1892.
  John Vandevere, born in 1821, lived at Lockport, N. Y , living in 1898
  Seabrook Vandevere, oldest child, and single
  Jacob Vandevere, single
  Helen Vandevere, single.

54 JAMES SEABROOK, youngest child of Daniel Seabrook, 12, was born, at Portsmouth, Va , Oct. 24, 1775 He married, Mch 23, 1809, his first cousin, Merriam, daughter of John Lambert and his second wife, Hannah Little, widow of Major Benjamin Dennis, born, in Amwell Township, Hunterdon County, N J , Mch. 18, 1787. James Seabrook died Dec 20, 1852 Merriam, his wife, died July 1, 1868

After the death of his parents, James Seabrook was brought up by his mother's brother in Monmouth County, but returned to Virginia, where, in Richmond, he received his commission, as Lieutenant in the Militia, in 1809 He removed from Richmond, and was living at New Brunswick, N. J , in 1811, at Philadelphia, in 1813, in Amwell Township, in 1815, soon he returned to Philadelphia, where he remained until April, 1823, when he returned to Amwell, where he lived until Apr 1, 1824, when he finally settled at Lambertville, N. J , where he kept an "Apothecary Shop" He was elected an Elder in the Presbyterian Church in 1829.

  Issue
86 John Lambert Seabrook, born, at Richmond, Jan 7, 1810, died, at Philadelphia, Jan. 30, 1821.
87 Nicholas Brown Seabrook, born, at New Brunswick, N. J., Dec. 6, 1811, died, at Philadelphia, Sept. 8, 1813
88 Mary Hannah Seabrook, born, at Amwell, N. J., Dec. 17, 1813.
89 Daniel Seabrook, born Jan. 1, 1816, died July 28, 1816
90 Thomas Seabrook, born, at Philadelphia, June 30, 1817.
91 George Seabrook, born, at Philadelphia, Oct 20, 1819; died, at Philadelphia, Jan 2, 1821

56 JOHN SEABROOK, son of Nicholas B Seabrook, 13, was born, Feb 17, 1768, at Portsmouth, Va. He was educated at Princeton, N J , and married Ann Sydnor, Oct. 18, 1793, who was born Oct 6, 1775.

  Issue
92 Nicholas Brown Seabrook, born, Aug 10, 1799, at Dungaroon, married, Oct 6, 1831, at Lexington, Va
93 Edward Sydnor Seabrook, born, Dec 1, 1800, at Dungaroon, died, Oct 18, 1827, at Savannah
94 Betsy Seabrook, born, Feb. 11, 1802, at Dungaroon, married, Aug 31, 1820, at Low Hill, Henrico County, Va , Daniel Trueheart
  Issue
  John Seabrook Trueheart, born Aug 19, 1821

Gilbert Lafayette Trueheart, born July 19, 1824.
Anna Maria Trueheart

95 John Blair Seabrook, born, Mch 21, 1803, at Dungaroon, died Sept 4, 1804
96 William Seabrook, born, July 28, 1804, at Richmond, died, Aug 12, 1804, at Richmond.
97 Sally Seabrook, born, Aug 1, 1805, at Richmond, died, Oct. 8, 1806, at Oakwell, Hanover County.
98 Polly Seabrook, born, Jan. 29, 1807, at Oakwell
99 Sally Ann Seabrook, born, Nov. 1, 1808, at Oakwell, married, Nov 23, 1830, John Mickleberry Sheppard, of Nosechthos, died, Dec 21, 1831, at Nosechthos.

Issue

Seabrook Sheppard, born, Sept 9, 1831, at Brookfield

100 John Seabrook, born Feb 18, 1810, died November, 1810
101 William Henry Seabrook, born Nov 28, 1811.
102 John Benjamin Thompson Seabrook, born Sept 4, 1813.
103 Camilla Tyrrell Seabrook, born, June 23, 1815, at Richmond Hill, married, May 3, 1832, in Rockbridge, Dr Washington Dorsey, of Baltimore
104 Elizabeth Seabrook, born, at Lambertville, N J, Apr 30, 1824, unmarried and living in 1898
105 William Seabrook, born, at Lambertville, N J, July 29, 1826, died, at Lambertville, Mch. 6, 1830

There are miniatures of James and Meriam (Lambert) Seabrook in the possession of Mrs Ashbel Welch

58 SALLY SEABROOK, daughter of Nicholas B Seabrook, 13, was born, Oct 18, 1773, at Norfolk, Va, died Oct 8, 1803 She married James Rind, Nov 3, 1794, at Dungaroon, Hanover County, Va, who died Aug 4, 1803

Issue

106 Nicholas B Rind, born Mch 13, 1796 Tombstone in St. John's Churchyard reads Nicholas B. S Rind died, Mch. 12, 1845, aged 48 years
107 Maria Duchess Rind, born Jan. 28, 1798.
108 Betsy Rind, born May, 1802; died 1803

59 POLLY SEABROOK, daughter of Nicholas B Seabrook, 13, married, Nov 3, 1794, at Dungaroon, Bartholomew Trueheart She died, at Richmond, May 11, 1796 There is buried at St John's Church "Mary Duchess, consort of Daniel Trueheart, died, 17 August, 1817, in her 20th year"

Mrs Mary Bealle, of 55 McCulloch St, Baltimore, Md., née Mary Trueheart, possesses a Seabrook Family Bible Miss Jessie Gordon, of 3 Grace St, Richmond, Va., also has one.

62 MARTHA SEABROOK, daughter of Stephen Seabrook, 42, was living, in 1877, aged eighty-eight years, hence born in 1789 She married Samuel Mash, of Staten Island, a descendant of an early settler of that name, in Englishtown, N J. They emigrated to New Albany, Ind

MRS MARTHA MARSH

We take the following from the Keyport *Weekly.*—

Died at New Albany, Ind , April, 1878, Martha, widow of Samuel Marsh, and eldest daughter of Stephen Seabrook, aged about ninety-two years

Stephen Seabrook, the father of "Aunt Patty" Marsh, was the eldest son of "Major" Thomas Seabrook, whose name was in the list of Revolutionary soldiers, published the last few weeks in THE MONMOUTH INQUIRER, as Lieut Col Thomas Seabrook Stephen Seabrook assisted at the battle of Monmouth, and dying at Englishtown when more than ninety years of age, was buried in the "Old Tennent" churchyard

Samuel Marsh, accompanied by four of his brothers, and his nephew, Jacob Aumack, moved his family to Cincinnati in 1814, but was induced by his father-in-law, Stephen Seabrook, to go farther down the river—1 e, below the falls of the Ohio, as it would be a better place for his business—that of ship builder New Albany, now a large city—was then a wilderness Daniel Seabrook, who was also of the party, joined Marsh in his business, which they were still engaged in, in 1852 D Seabrook and J Aumack are both still living, aged respectively 88 and 90 years

There are but few, living in this vicinity, who remember Patty *Mash*, as the name was called in the olden time, but there are relatives, nephews and nieces, in Keyport, who will remember her visit here in 1853, at which time she visited her stepmother, Sallie Seabrook, at Englishtown, who was then ninety-four years old

Issue

109 Sarah Ann Marsh, oldest child, born 1806, married Jacob Anthony
110 Alfred Marsh, died leaving issue· George Marsh, etc.
111 Samuel Marsh, married and had a large family
112 Edwin Marsh, married and had a family
113 Augustus Marsh, married and had a family.
114 Harriet Marsh, married, first, Mr Reinhardt or Reinhardt, and twice afterwards.
115 Maria Marsh, married, lives in California.
116 Adelina Marsh, married J K Woodward. She died in August, 1895.

Mrs. Clara Anthony Bley, of 1615 Alleghany Ave, Philadelphia, Pa, wrote, in January, 1894, that she was the youngest daughter of "Sarah Ann Marsh Anthony," who was living "very active and much interested in the life about her. She is the only daughter left of the family and there are yet two sons remaining, Samuel Stephen and Augustus."

In 1890, the Rev. A. H. Anthony, of Winchester, Ky, wrote me concerning his Seabrook ancestry.

63 MARIA SEABROOK, daughter of Stephen Seabrook, 42, married Joseph, son of Nicholas Johnson, of Keyport, N. J *

Issue

117 Stephen Johnson, married Miss Wolfe.
118 William Johnson, married, first, Parmela Walling, second, her sister, Mary Elizabeth Walling. He was deceased in 1877
119 Joseph Johnson, second son, a good man, married Miss Luyster
120 John Johnson
121 James Johnson, unmarried
122 Alfred Johnson; unmarried, in 1877
123 Mary Ann Johnson, married Elijah Walling. He is deceased.

Issue

Fitzroy Walling, married Elizabeth Curtis
Bishop Walling, married a Griffith or Griffin, of Keyport, N J.
Isadore Walling
Theresa Walling
Annie Walling

*Joseph Johnson had two sisters, one, Betsy Johnson, a maiden lady, and a sister who married William Morford, for his second wife, and was the stepmother of the Poet Morford

SEABROOK OF MONMOUTH COUNTY

124 Lucinda Johnson; married Mr Walling, brother of Elijah Walling.
125 Joanna Johnson, living, in 1880, unmarried.
Mrs T. W Seabrook said that the Johnsons had Indian blood in them

64 JAMES SEABROOK, son of Stephen Seabrook, 42, moved to New Albany, in 1814
Issue
126 Daughter   , married Anderson Marsh
127 Leonard Seabrook
128 John Seabrook
[Perhaps the above issue is entirely erroneous]

65 JOHN SEABROOK, son of Stephen Seabrook, 42, married Catharine   . , and lived and died in Keyport, N. J
Issue
129 Stephen Seabrook
130 Ann Seabrook
131 Mary Seabrook
132 Elias Seabrook

66 DANIEL SEABROOK, son of Stephen Seabrook, 42, moved to New Albany, Ind., about 1814, and married twice, both wives being Western women. The family records were lost in the burning of his house, in 1830.
Issue by first wife
133 James Seabrook
134 Alfred Seabrook
135 Ann Maria Seabrook
Issue by second wife
136 John Seabrook
137 Daughter

67 ANNA SEABROOK, daughter of Stephen Seabrook, 42, married, probably in 1820, William Hoff, son of William and Elizabeth (Walling) *Huff* All of their descendants live in Elizabeth, N J , save Daniel S Hoff's widow and children Anna (Seabrook) Hoff probably died about 1855.
Issue
138 Ann Eliza Hoff, born Oct 13, 1821, married Richard Poole Walling
Issue
Mary Ann Walling, married James Van Dike
Issue
Cessie Van Dike
139 Daniel Seabrook Hoff, born Oct 24, 1825. married Mary Ann Collins, of English birth, and died Nov 18, [1877?]
Issue
William Hoff
Ann Hoff
Nellie Hoff

71 ELLEN SEABROOK, daughter of Thomas Seabrook, 43, was born Oct. 3, 1803, died Feb 20, 1877; married William Applegate

72 LYDIA SEABROOK, daughter of Thomas Seabrook, 43, was born Oct 3, 1805, married Rev. William V. Wilson, of Fort Monmouth, N. J., and died, Aug. 13, 1852, aged 46 years, 10 months and 10 days

Issue

140 Mary Anna Wilson, married Capt George Bowne, has issue
141 Mat [Martha?] Wilson, married Capt Benjamin Griggs; no issue

74 MARTHA SEABROOK, daughter of Thomas Seabrook, 43, was born Feb 17, 1810, married Rev William V. Wilson, his second wife, no issue.

75 HENRY SEABROOK, son of Thomas Seabrook, 43, was born Sept 10, 1813, died Mch 30, 1872, married Theresa, daughter of Leonard and Catharine (Aumack) Walling, who was born Aug 8, 1821 Catharine Aumack's mother was a Marsh, a sister to Samuel Marsh, who married Martha Seabrook "My great-grandmother, Gertje Conover, married Jacobus Aumack," said Mrs. T W Seabrook

Issue

142 Annie Seabrook, born Aug 12, 1852, married William Conover.
143 Thomas Leonard Seabrook, born June 16, 1854
144 Henry Seabrook, born Aug 3, 1856, died Oct 12, 1856
145 Elena Seabrook, born Nov 1, 1857, died Mch 15, 1861
146 Harry Seabrook, born Oct 23, 1859, married May Nason
147 Martha Washington Seabrook, born Nov 26, 1863, married John Schenck.

88 MARY HANNAH SEABROOK, daughter of James Seabrook, 54, was born, Dec. 17, 1813, at the home of her grandfather, John Lambert, in Amwell Township, Hunterdon County, N J She married, Oct 25, 1834, Ashbel Welch, a well-known Civil Engineer and railroad man, of New Jersey. He was the son of Ashbel and Margaret (Dorrance) Welch, and was born, Dec 4, 1809, in Nelson, Madison County, N. J, whither his parents had removed from Windham, Conn He resided at Lambertville, N J, where all of his children were born, and where he died Sept 25, 1882. Mary Hannah Welch, his wife, died Apr 1, 1874.

Issue

148 Son, unnamed, born and died Oct 28, 1835
149 Margaret Welch, born Mch 8, 1837, died May 1, 1838.
150 Caroline Corsen Welch, married William Corwin, of Lambertville, N J
151 Mary Merriam Welch, unmarried, living, at Lambertville. N J, in 1898
152 Elizabeth Seabrook Welch, first wife of the Rev. Roswell Randall Hoes, died Apr 7, 1879
153 Margaret Welch, born Sept 21, 1851, died Dec 30, 1853
154 Ashbel Welch, born Feb 5, 1854
155 William Welch, married Marie Lair, who died, Feb. 12, 1897, leaving
Issue
Olivia Welch

SEABROOK OF MONMOUTH COUNTY

90 THOMAS SEABROOK, son of James Seabrook, 54, was born, in Philadelphia, June 30, 1817, married, first, Eveline Barber, adopted daughter of Mrs Tingey, Dec 6, 1842 She died in 1854 He married, second, June 16, 1857, Mrs Sarah (Lambert) Smith, who, in 1898, was still living He died, Feb 24, 1897, in Philadelphia. He was "a civil engineer, prominently identified with the construction and extention of the Penna R R." See Philadelphia Ledger, Feb 27, 1897.

Issue by first wife

156 James Seabrook, died in the Civil War.
157 Ashbel Seabrook, died, in infancy, in 1854
158 *Thomas Seabrook, married, in 1871, Josephine Adams
   Issue
   William Seabrook
   Eveline Tingey Seabrook
   Walter Seabrook
   Thomas Arthur Seabrook
159 Annie Seabrook, unmarried

Issue by second wife

160 Elizabeth Seabrook, married, March, 1885, Henry P Hunter, of Warren, Pa
   Issue
   Marion Hunter, born January, 1886.
   Henry P. Hunter, born January, 1890.
161 Marion Pollard Seabrook, born August, 1865, died Jan 10, 1890

129 STEPHEN SEABROOK, son of John Seabrook, 65, married Mary Walling Mrs T W Seabrook said that he "was intemperate and a fiddler"

Issue

162 Hannah Seabrook } minors in 1877
163 Elias Seabrook

130 ANN SEABROOK, daughter of John Seabrook, 65, married, first, Samuel Walling, second, Josiah Rogers, who is now deceased

Issue

164 Emilius Rogers   }
165 Catharine Rogers } all live in Wisconsin, near Janesville
166 Amelia Rogers   }

131 MARY SEABROOK, daughter of John Seabrook, 65, married Thomas S Clark She was deceased in 1877.

Issue

167 Thomas Clark, he "was intemperate and a fiddler, like his uncle Stephen, and his cousin Steve, but he is not musical," wrote Mrs T W Seabrook

132 ELIAS SEABROOK, son of John Seabrook, 65, married Sarah Walling

---

*Thomas Seabrook is now living at Paterson, N J He has the family records of his father, Thomas Seabrook, and his grandfather, James Seabrook, and can give information relating to his own and his father's family

Issue

168 Elizabeth Seabrook
169 Mary Seabrook, died at the age of fourteen years.
170 Stephen Seabrook, married Harriet Jones.
171 John Seabrook } twins { "steady and industrious"
172 Kate Seabrook } { married [Asbury] Aumack He is deceased

154 ASHBEL WELCH, JR, seventh child and oldest son of Ashbel and MARY HANNAH (SEABROOK) Welch, 88, was born, at Lambertville, N J, Feb 5, 1854, and married, at Lambertville, N J, Jan 1, 1878, Emma D, daughter of John and Eliza Boice (Coriell) Finney, born, May 27, 1855, at Middlebush, Somerset County, N J

In 1898, he was General Manager of the Philadelphia Belt Line R R, and resided at 275 Harvey St, Germantown, Pa

Issue

173 Ashbel Russell Welch, born, at Lambertville, N. J., July 17, 1879.

MISCELLANEOUS NOTES

The following items have been collected from various sources
1569, March 7. "Rob' Seabroke, serv' to Mr Lister," was buried   The Registers of St Thomas, the Apostle, London, from 1558 to 1754

1620. Richard Seabrook issued, in London, a caveat on the eye
Allibone's Dictionary of Authors

1632 [?] Bishop Gibson, in Camden, speaking of the famous church of Gloucester, with its great and stately tower, says Abbot Seabrooke, the designer, dying, left it to the care of Robert Tully, a monk of the place, which is intimated in those verses, written in black letters, under the arch of the *quire*

"Hoc quod digestem specularis, opus que politum,
"Tulli haec ex onere, Seabroke Abbate jubente"

"This fabrick which you see, exact and neat,
"The Abbot charged monk Tully make complete"
New England Genealogical Register, Vol III

1640, July 20   "Isacke Sebrooke, son of Edward Sebrooke," was baptized
1642, Dec 10   "Isaac Seabrooke, son of Edward Sebrooke," was buried
1649, July 18   "Joseph Seabrooke, son of Edward Seabrooke," was buried
1661, Apr 24.   "Sarah Seabrooke, daughter of Edward Seabrooke, Shoemaker," was buried
1663, Nov. 5   "Mr Seabrooke, stranger," buried.
1726, Nov 24. "John Seabrooke, of S' Bartholomeio, the Less, London, Wid', & Mary Drake, of the same place & parish, Sp'," were married
1732, Dec 17. "Edwd Seabrooke, of S' Peter, at S' Albans, Herts, & Ann Langley, of S' Vedast, Foster lane, Lond. Licence," [were married]   The Rejester Booke, of Saynte De'nis, Backchurch parishe, (City of London), Begynnynge in the Yeare of O' Lord God 1538."

1659, January. Will of Joseph Seabrook.

1659, Jan. 15 Will of William Seabrook On record at Somerset House, London, England.

1661, May 16 "Thomas Croxon, of St Nicholas Ackons, & Ann Sebrooke, of Stepney, [were married], by Mr Conyrs" The Parish Registers of St. Mary Aldermary, London, from 1558 to 1754

1728, Sept. 19 "Wm Coombs, of St Giles, Cripplegate, Mid^x, & Mary Seabrook, of St Peters, Cornhill, Lond Licence," [were married] A Register of the Parish of Saint Peters, vpon Cornhill, Beginning at the Raigne of Queen Elizabeth

About 1730, one of this name, an officer in the Royal Navy, died "Gentleman's Magazine."

Peplow and Seabrook, [Milward Seabrook], surgeons, 111 Great Russell St., Bloomsbury, London, W C

Lady Seabrook married a Governor-General, of Dublin.

Sir Charles Seabrook was a Member of Parliament

1879. In the Directory of London, England, of this date, the following references to Seabrooks were found:

    1 John Wm Seabrook, "Panther" P H, [Public House], 15 Turin St, Bethnal Green
    2 Thomas Seabrook, furniture dealer, 98 Back St., Church Lane, E
    3 Wm Seabrook, chandler shop, 1 Graham St, City Road, N.
    4 Reuben Seabrook, bonnet manufacturer, 85 East St, Manchester Sq, W

The first and third of these could not be found The second was visited and proved to be a specimen worthy of Dicken's description The man was unprepossessing, his immediate surroundings still worse, and the section of London that he occupied, notoriously bad However, led astray possibly by a thought that I was seeking heirs to an estate, he became communicative, in a rough way, told me that he hailed from Bairden, County of Essex, about nine miles from Bishop Stortford, and that he occasionally saw passing his door, farmers' wagons with the name, which came by Rumford way. My visit to the last on the list was more pleasing than this Here I met an old gentleman, who was happy to converse concerning those of his name, on the other side of the water He informed me that there had been Seabrooks, in Buckingham, about thirty-five miles from London, but none were there now, that his grandfather was *John Seabrook, of Slapton*, who had a son, Frank, who had among others, my informant, then in his seventieth year He, Reuben Seabrook, was married and his wife was still living Their family consisted of two sons, Frank and William So far as he knew, in his family, at least, Joseph and Robert were not family names, and the peculiar characteristics of all he knew were blue eyes and high foreheads In relating my trip to Dunstable, and its disappointments, it recalled to him that there was a "Seabrook House," surrounded with a moat, and itself old and moss-grown, in shape it was square, built of brick and had a tiled roof It had probably passed from the family of that name to other hands It could be reached by the North Western railway, and lay between Dunstable and London, one having to get out at Cheddington station It was a matter of regret with me that the information came so late as to prevent my visiting the neighborhood, for it seems likely that, from its proximity to Dunstable, that it would furnish a clue to the ancestry of the South Carolina family of Seabrook.

He volunteered, further, that he had the impression that one *Sir Thomas Seabrook*, was living in Bedfordshire; that his own son, "*Mr James F Seabrook*," was "Organizing Master and Inspector, of the Manchester and Salford Church Day School Association," which aimed at the improvement of teachers and the art of teaching. His address was 42 John Dalton St, as appeared on the prospectus of the organization, February, 1880 His father suggested that I should write, as his sons had both become men of means and would, doubtless, take an interest in developing their family history

From another source there was obtained the address of two physicians, viz.:
Thomas Edward Seabrook, M D., 3 Upper Wood St, Brompton, Kent
William Milward Seabrook, M D, Slaidburn, Clitheroe, Yorkshire.

Both were written to The letter, addressed to the former, was returned, marked: "gone away"—left no address"; the other reached its destination, and was politely answered.

Dr William M Seabrook stated "beyond the fact that my father's name was *Thomas Brewster Seabrook*, and that his father was Thomas Seabrook, a clergyman and a schoolmaster, living at Wickhambrook, in Suffolk, twenty-two miles from Cambridge, where he lies buried under the pulpit of the Parish Church, I know nothing. He married, first, ...and had Thomas Brewster Seabrook; second, Miss Cavendish I will forward your letter on to my mother, who lives in London, who will, perhaps, know more about my father's family than I do My father practiced medicine, for thirty-five years, at Brighton, in Sussex." No further information was obtained from this source

The reference to *Dunstable*, in old England, in the will of John Seabrook, of South Carolina, excited hopes that were not realized A visit to this old town, and an interview with its Mayor, the Hon. W. H Derbyshire, who is its historian, as well as several others, resulted in disappointment The name, Seabrook, is nearly unheard of

A hasty search through the priory records, which commence in 1558, was equally unsatisfactory In the Priory Church, which is all that now remains of that once vast and interesting building, are erected tablets to commemorate benefactors. Here, at least, I expected to see the name of John Seabrook enrolled, with others, from the bequest of £100 that he made in his will, to the poor of this parish, A D 1706 Its absence, however, was easily proven and was a source of very great regret, for it seemed that this would, at least, be instrumental in placing the family That it is not there is probably from the fact that it was not entitled to such distinction, from failure on the part of the executors, to carry out the testator's wishes

Among the few tombstones, standing within the enclosure of the Priory yard, is one to "John Puddephatt, who departed this life Sept 23, 1836, aged 57 years," etc

It was copied on account of its resemblance to one of the legatee's names, mentioned in the will of the aforesaid John Seabrook, viz.

"Item I give and bequeathe unto ye Eldest son of Mr Joseph Peddihett, liveing in ye Barbican, near Aldersgate street, London, the sum of fifty pounds sterling money of England," etc.

It is possible that this Dunstable name has gone through a process of reconstruction, and comes out, one hundred and thirty years later, Puddephatt, instead of Peddihett.

One more fact to record, and all the information obtained by the visit is written In conversation with a Dunstable-ite, it was said that, at Luton, not far from this place, was an old church, and in its vicinity might be found possibly Seabrooks, living and dead, but he was not certain

1881. J Seabrook and S. Seabrook played in the cricket match between Ampthill and Wellingboro Grammar Schools, the two Seabrooks being on the latter team.

Bedfordshire Times and Independent, Aug 13, 1881

1888. Sidney Seabrook, a representative of London firms, in New York, and nephew of Mrs Mary Seabrook, of Thames Ditton, Surrey, England, called on me for business orders during this year.

In America, there were, seemingly, several distinct families of this name, one in Connecticut, one in New Jersey, one in Maryland and one in South Carolina.

James Seabrook, mentioned in Mary Matthews' will, New York City, 1687, was not of kin to Thomas Seabrook of Westchester, and the Stuyvesants mentioned therein as her sons were Stephenszens. The situation is a most complicated one and most difficult to unravel, but it all originates from the phonetic spelling of surnames in the transitional Dutch-English Colonial period It is my present belief that Mary Matthews was born Mary Goosen, and that she married, first, Jan Stephenszen. Her children by this marriage are enumerated in her will and are called variously—Peter Stevenson, John, Gosen and Isaac Stuyvesant and Hendrick Jacobs Her daughters are called Christian, wife of Robert Dorkins, Ryntie, wife of Guisbert Guysbertse, and Janitie, wife of Thomas Roberts She likewise mentions her grandchildren Hester Erwin, Marytie Gisbertse, and James Seabrook The will of her second husband, James Matthews, 1685, mentions his wife's children as Isaac and Peter Stevesant and Hendrick Jacobson, all of whom he calls sons-in-law. He likewise mentions the three grandchildren Hester Erwyn, Maria Gerntsen and James Seaborough The will of Henry Jacobs, p 239, Vol I, N Y Hist Soc. Wills, leaves his estate to his wife, and son, Jacob Hendricks, and in the event of their deaths, the same is to be inherited by Johannes Goesens, son of my deceased brother Goesen Stevens, and to James, the son of Clement Seabra, and my sister Judith Stevens Seabra is phonetically Seaborough when tersely pronounced If further evidence were wanting, it would lie in the fact that the Janneckey Stevens, daughter of Mary (Goosen Stephenszen) Matthews, had a license, June 3, 1671, to marry William Erwin, and as Janitie Erwin she had a license to marry, July 16, 1675, Clement Seabra When Clement Seabra, Seaborough or Seabrook died, she married Thomas Roberts for her third husband, and was living at the date of her mother's will, and her two children, Hester Erwin and James Seabrook, half-sister and brother, were under the care of their grandmother, Mary Matthews Janitie, mentioned in the will of Mary Matthews, I take it, is the Dutch name for Judith Stevens, which appears in the will of Henry Jacobs

I have traced the issue of the various Stephenszen children, but I do not conceive that they will be of any further interest here

For verification of these statements, consult the printed New York Wills, N Y Marriage Licenses, and the Dutch Church Record of Marriages and Baptisms, published by the N Y Genealogical Society

1677, Nov 4 Clement Sebrak was on a Coroner's jury New York Wills, Lib B, p 19

1679 Derrick Jansen de Groot or Groodt, sold to Clement Sebrak, a lot of ground, with the mill-house thereon, situated in the city of New York, on the North side of the Sligh Heege, or dirty lane, for 2400 guilders sewant New York Register's Office

1681, Aug. 23. Clement Seabrooke was on a Coroner's jury New York Wills, Lib B., p. 27.

1682. Clement Seabrooke was among the coopers, of New York New York Wills, Lib B, p 19, also New York Documentary History, Vol XIII

"*Stratford*" began to be settled in 1639, under the name of Cupheage, and became a plantation in 1640 The town records commence in 1650 The original territory of Stratford reached back from the sea twelve miles and included the present township of Stratford, Huntington, Monroe, Trumbell and Bridgeport The original proprietors of Stratford, by tradition are reported to have been seventeen. The following large list was taken from the town records, and probably was made before 1650, as William Burritt died that year." Among the names is "*Mr Seabrookes*." "Early Settlers, of Stratford, Conn.," in Historical and Genealogical Register, Vol 27, p 62

"*Seabrook*, Mr was of *Stratford* in 1650 with, (here follows a long list of names) It then continues — These persons with others, were of Stratford in 1651, and previous—unquestionably many others, who were the pioneers of the settlement and had either died or removed—are necessarily omitted by the loss of the first records." Hinman's Catalogue of First Settlers, etc., etc., Hartford, 1846, 1st Edition, p 232

"Robert Seabrook, of Stratford, had several daughters, of whom one married Wm Preston, and one married Thomas Fairchild, and much land he owned there, for, in 1668, are recorded half a dozen persons' shares set off from the grandfather, Robert Seabrook's estate." Savage's New England Genealogical Dictionary, 1862

SEABROOK

OF

SOUTH CAROLINA

ROBERT SEABROOK, an English gentleman, of wealth, position and enterprise, came, with a brother, Benjamin, family tradition puts it, from the County of Kent, England, to Charleston, South Carolina, and settled, in 1682, on the Sea Islands, South of that city. As a matter of fact, I have found no reference to any Benjamin Seabrook, contemporaneous with Robert Seabrook, save Benjamin, the son of Robert Seabrook, who died, in 1716–17, in his nineteenth year, and I am under the impression that, instead of settling on the Sea Islands, Robert Seabrook, and his immediate family, located near what is now known as The Church Flats, St Paul's Parish, on the Stono River, four miles from Rantowles Station, which is fifteen miles from Charleston

Here on the original site of the Parish Church of St. Paul, Robert Seabrook, his wife and son are buried

Here Lyes The Body of Mr Robart Seabrook Dec^d Decr ye 7 1710 in ye 59 year of His age

Here Lyes ye Body of Benjamin Seabrook son of Mr Robart & Sarah Seabrook Dec^d Jan^{ry} ye 17 1716 in ye 19th year if His age

Here Lyes Buried ye Body of Mrs Sarah Seabrook Dec^d June ye 16th 1715 in the 47th year of Her Age

Two other unmarked stones stand in line with the above three

The following stone is still erect

In Memory of Mrs Amerinthia Lowndes wife of Mr Rawlins Lowndes of Charles Town who lies buried here at her own particular desire near her dec^d parents John Thomas and Mary Elliott of this parish She died the 14 of January 1750 aged 21 years

Upon what authority the date, 1682, is given for Robert Seabrook's settlement I do not know, but it may be derived from sources unknown, yet accurate.

The records and Bibles that would have shed light on the history of the family, were destroyed during the Revolution, when they were Tories, and during the Rebellion, when they were Secessionists. The Rev Joseph B Seabrook had progressed so far in his compilation of the history of the family, that he brought with him and showed to Mrs Henry Seabrook, of

Keyport, N. J., when visiting her in 1865, an extensive genealogy of the family, since lost This was during the Civil War.

The oldest records I have found, relating to Robert Seabrook, are in the earliest Book of Wills, at Charleston, S C

"A Warr^t to Mr Robert Seabrook, for one Towne Lott, (by Indenture), dated ye 26th Sept , 1692, vnder hand & Seale of Governo^r Ludwell "

"Received this 15th May, 1697, of Mr Robert Seabrook, for the purchase of two thousand Seauen hundred Acres of Land, in Colleton County, fifty foure pounds for the Right Honorable, the Lords Proprietors
THOMAS CARY, Receiver "

"Received this 16th July, 1697, of Mr Robert Seabrook, for the purchase of One hundred Acres of land, fourty shillings for the Right Honorable, the lords Proprietors
THOMAS CARY, Receiver "

During the invasion of Charleston, by the French and Spanish, in 1706, he, "disregarding the pestilence, yellow fever, marched his men into the town from the islands The French were ingloriously defeated. One ship was taken and between 200 and 300 prisoners, besides many French and Spaniards killed." McCrady's History of South Carolina, 1897, Vol 1, p 398

Capt. Robert Seabrook was an active supporter of the Episcopal Church as were many of his descendants.

In 1704, he was appointed one of the Commissioners to carry out " An Act for the Establishment of Religious Worship in this Province according to the Church of England, and for the Erecting of Churches for the public Worship of God, and also for the Maintenance of Ministers, and the building convenient Houses for them." This act was passed by the South Carolina State Assembly, Nov 4, 1704 Dalcho's History of the Episcopal Church in South Carolina, p 61. Published 1820

In 1706, "Robert Seabrooke, of Colleton County, Esq^e," was appointed sole executor of the will of his son, John Seabrooke

These few records are all that are known. The tombstones show that his wife, Sarah, was seventeen years his junior, and that both died comparatively young The climate and hardships that they were subjected to, shortened the lives of many of the pioneers. Edisto Island, particularly, was destined to curtail the lives of the Seabrooks, for it was malarious, and dysentery frequently prevailed There I noted that the majority of the tombstones recorded interments of people in their prime, many who were still youthful, and only a few of advanced years

Issue

2 Benjamin Seabrook, born 1697; died 1716.
3 John Seabrook
4 Robert Seabrook
5 Joseph Seabrook
6 Ann Seabrook

Other children, alluded to in the will of John Seabrook, 1706, as "my brothers and sisters," to each of whom he willed £20

3 JOHN SEABROOK, son of Robert Seabrook, 1, made his will in 1706, but as no date of probate appears, the time of his death is uncertain He was a large landholder and possessed wealth, but there are few allusions to him

"Received the 15th of may 1697 of Mr John Seabroock, for the purchase of two thousand & Fighty Acres of Land, fourty one pounds twelue shillings, for the right Honorable, ye lords proprietors
THOMAS CARY, receiuer "

1706, Apr. 15. Will of John Seabrooke, of Colleton County, Province of South Carolina, no date of proof mentioned

"unto the poor of the parish of Dunstable, in the County of Bedford, in ye Kingdom of England, the sume of one hundred Pounds, of lawfull money of England, to be paid, by my Executors, to ye Vestry or Church Wardens, or to Such other person or persons for ye time being, as shall have ye Management of the poors Money in Dunstable aforesaid, by them to be paid out in freehold or other Land, for the use of the said poor for ever, & the Annual rents, Yssues & profitts, from thence arising, to be Distributed amongst them, as the persons who may have ye Care & Management thereof may think fitt, but to be applied to no other use or purpose what soever. And . my Execut^s, with all convenient speed, after my Decease, to write to the Church Wardens or overseers of the poor, of the parish aforesaid, or whome it may Perticularly Concern in this behalfe & inform them of this my Legacy & bequest, Desireing their positive Orders how & which way they would have it sent to them in England, but my estate to bear no Risque of ye same to England"

"unto ye Eldest son of Mr Joseph Peddiphett, liveing in ye Barbican, near Aldersgate street, London, the sume of fifty pounds Sterling money of England"

"unto the eldest son of Mr Joseph Fossey, of Hockley, in the Whole, in ye County of Middlesex, ye sume of fifty pounds Sterling money of England, hereby Desireing my Execut^s to make strict and Dilligent Inquiry for ye two last mentioned legacies and to acquaint them of this my will, & and further, to remitt ye s^d several Legacies to them as they & either of them shall Order & Direct, but my Estate to bear no Risque of either of ye said Legacies to England"

' unto my Loveing wife, Ann Seabrooke, the sume of Two hundred pounds Curr^t money of the said province, to be paid by my Execut^{or} hereafter named or by his Execut^{or} or administrator or some of them, immediately after my Decease, in full Considerat^n, Recompence & Satisfaction of her thirds, her dower, which she may have or claim out of any Part of my Estate whatsoever"

"to my Loveing Father, Robt Seabrooke, the sume of Two hundred pounds, Curr^t money, to be paid to him for ye use of my Daughter, Martha, to be paid her at ye age of Sixteen or day of her marriage, which shall first happen, Clear of all Charges for her Education"

"unto my son, James Seabrooke, the full and just sume of five hundred pounds, Curr^t money of ye said Province, to be paid him at the age of Twenty years, Clear of all Charges, for Education . "

"unto ye child my said wife now goes with, ye sume of one hundred pounds, Curr^t money of ye said province, to be paid him or her, at ye age of Fighteen or day of marriage, which shall first happen, Clear of all Charges"

"If it should happen that either of my s^d Children should depart this life before they or any of them have received their Several & Respective Legacies, then and in such Case I appoint ye Legacy or Bequest so by given to ye party so dying to ye Survivour or Survivours of them, that is to say—the Longest Liver to take all"

"I give to amongst my Brothers & Sisters Twenty pounds, Curr^t money of ye said provence, to each of them"

"And this, my last Will May be ye Better & more effectually accomplished and Compelled Legacies & Bequests afores^d paid and Discharged & upon that accout and not otherwise, y^e, the said John Seabrooke, do fully & absolutely Give unto my Loveing father, Robert Seabrooke, of Colleton County aforesaid, Esqr, All and Singular my Lands, Tenements & Hereditaments in the said province, & all & Singular my Negro & Indian Slaves young & Old, Horses, Cattle, Hogs & Stock, what soever or wheresoever, nothing Excepted or Reserved, To have, hold and Enjoy the same and every part thereof, unto ye said Robert Seabrooke, his heirs, for Ever, upon special Trust & Confidence Nevertheless y^t he, the said Robert Seabrooke, his heirs, . or Some of them do well Truly & bona fide pay & Discharge all & every ye Legacies aforesaid herein by me given or intended to be given"

Executor "my said Loveing father sole Executor"

Witnesses. "Martha being first," Evan Mackpherson, Hugh Hest, Benj Lamboll, [his mark], and Henry Wrigington, J

John Seabrook married Ann .

Issue

7 Martha Seabrook, under sixteen years of age in 1706
8 James Seabrook, under twenty years of age in 1706
9 Child, *in utero*, in 1706

4 ROBERT SEABROOK, son of Robert Seabrook, 1, married Mary .... He was, seemingly, the first to settle on the Sea Islands, and owned Wadmalow Island and Seabrook Island. Edisto Island, which lies off the coast, forty miles Southwest of Charleston, and John's Island were, seemingly, later possessions of the Seabrooks On James' Island, and the preceding four islands, Seabrooks may be found in plenty today In 1720, Robert Seabrook died, without issue.

1720, Sept 22 Will of Robert Seabrook, of Colleton County, and Province of South Carolina, "being Sick and weak in body", proved 1720, no other date, mentioned.

Loving wife, Mary, received 14 negro and Indian slaves, named Sampson, Will, Ratt, Little Sambo and July, male negroes, Aphey and her Childe, Jeny, & Lattero, female negroes, Nany, a mulatto girl, Toby, an Indian Boy, & Lucy, an Indian Female, three hundred and seventy-two acres of land, and Plantation, on Wadmelaw, near Edisto Island, lately purchased of his brother-in-Law, Maj Arthur Hall, with his stock of Cattle, horses, mares, sheep & Hogs thereon, & one-half of all his stock of Cattle, Horses, Mares, sheep & hogs "that are on my Island, commonly known by the Name of Seabrook Island" together with all his household goods, furniture, tools, utensils of whatever kind, with all his ready Cash, whether gold, Silver or wrought Plate together with the increase of the above slaves The above was given to his wife by deed dated Aug 8, 1720, which is confirmed by the provisions of the will The widow also had liberty to reside on Seabrook's Island, during her widowhood

To his loving brother, Joseph, all of Seabrook's Island, reserving the above liberty given to his wife, Mary, during her widowhood, and the other one-half of his stock of horses, mares, Cattle, sheep & hogs—on the Island—together with Old Sambo & Peter, negroes, Catherin, Phillis & Florah, Indians, & June, a mulatto Boy, with their future increase The above is given, provided Joseph, his heirs, etc, pay all his debts and funeral charges, "and that he finish, or cause to be finished, for my said loving Wife, Mary Seabrook, in all respects, Workman like the New house now begun on Wadmelaw Island, on the Land and plantation bequeathed to my aforesaid Loveing Wife, Mary Seabrook, and her heirs and assigns forever"

also to my brother, Joseph, my wearing apparel

Sister, Ann Parrott, received two Indian slaves, Jack and Moll

Cousin, Ann Parrott, to receive £50, on the day of her marriage

He gave his mulatto fellow "Sampson," his liberty, immediately after his decease

Executors brother, Joseph Seabrook and the Hon Landgrave Joseph Morton, with instructions to deliver to his Brother-in-law, Willm Parrott, 30 head of year old Cattle, off "my Island," which were bequeathed him by my deceased father, Capt Robert Seabrook

The testator signed his name to the will and sealed with a seal

5 JOSEPH SEABROOK, son of Robert Seabrook, 1, was living in 1720, and was the legatee of his brother, Robert Seabrook He probably is the ancestor of the majority, if not all, of the Seabrooks, living in South Carolina. I have no data concerning him

6 ANN SEABROOK, daughter of Robert Seabrook, 1, married, as per the will of her brother, Robert Seabrook, William Parrott, and had a daughter

Ann Parrott, living in 1720.

JOHN SEABROOK, was the son of .   Seabrook and *Mary*, his wife

1745, Apr 24. John Seabrook, of Colleton County, province of South Carolina, planter, sold to Lieut. John Payne, of his Majesty's Ship, the Rose, now in the port of Charles Town, in the province aforesaid, for 5 shillings, current money of s^d province, "all that Plantation or Tract of Land, containing Three hundred and three Acres, be the same more or less, scituate, lying and being in Colleton County aforesaid, butting & bounding to the westw^d on Lands of Benjamin D'Harriette, to the Eastw^d & Southw^d on Stono River, & to the Northw^d and Northwest on the Lands of the said John Seabrook, together with all & singular the House,

Barns, Stables, orchards, Gardens, Yards, Meadows, Lands, Pastures, Feedings, Commons, Woods, Coppices, Wells, Ways, Waters, Water Courses, Fishings, Fowlings, Huntings, Hawkings, Liberties, Priviledges, Easements, Commodities, Emoluments & Hereditaments."
Lib A A., pp. 526-8, Records in the Secretary of State's Office, Columbia, S C

1746, Mch 17 John Seabrook, of the Province of South Carolina, Planter, sold to George Saxby, of the same place, Gentlemen, for 5 shillings, "All that Plantation on which the said John Seabrook now lives, situate, lying & being on John's Island, and which was devised unto him by the last will and Testament of Colonel Alexander Heat, [Hext?], deceased, Together with all and Singular the Houses," etc   Lib C C, pp 276-7, Records as above.

1746, Mch. 18. John Seabrook, of the Province of South Carolina, Planter, sold to George Saxby, of Charleston, Gentleman, land   Lib C C, pp 277-8, Records as above.

1746, Mch 17 John Seabrook, of John's Island, in Colleton County, South Carolina, Planter, sold to Geo Saxby, Gent, for 10 shillings, three tracts of land, lying contiguous in Colleton County, one tract, containing one hundred acres, purchased of Thomas Elliott, Senr., of said province, planter, deceased, and the tract of seventy-two acres, purchased of Wm Fairchild, of said province, planter, and another tract, containing three hundred and forty acres, which three tracts make a plantation, containing five hundred and twelve acres, also another tract of two hundred acres, lately purchased by the said John Seabrook of Thomas Elliott   Lib C C., pp 279-80, Records as above.

Will of John Seabrook, of Colleton County, Province of South Carolina, Planter, "weak in body, but of sound mind," etc, proved, before the Governor, June 22, 1750, mentioned
Mother, Mary Seabrook, who received £150 current money of South Carolina
To his issue, by his wife Mary, "if any such shall be born of her," the remainder of his estate, real and personal
To each of his executors, £150
Sister, Susannah
Niece, Mary Greene
Sister, Elizabeth, wife of George Saxby
He also mentioned his lands on the North side of Stono River, his lands on John's Island, and some seventy slaves by name
His bequests were large and his wealth great   Wills 1747-1752, pp 295, Records as above

SEABROOK

OF

EDISTO ISLAND

Several lines of the Seabrook family are to be found on Edisto Island, S C, the relationship of which I have not yet determined They descend from John, Gabriel and Benjamin Seabrook They were ardent Episcopalians

1770, Apr 7 The State Assembly passed an act, appointing Commissioners to found a Chapel of Ease,* on Edisto Island, and Joseph and John Seabrook were created two of them.

---
* "Chapels of Ease," according to the original meaning of the term, are not now known in this country In England, there is a distinction between a Chapel of Ease and a Parochial Chapel of Ease Chapels of Ease are founded for the convenience of the people in large Parishes, in Attending Public Worship, where they live at a distance from the Parish Church, to which, however, the Sacraments and Burials are restricted."   Moore, p 267

To aid in the erection of this building, the following amounts were subscribed
John Seabrook $666 , (£150)
Benjamin Seabrook $555 , (£125)
Thomas B Seabrook $444 , (£100)
Joseph B Seabrook $222 , (£50)

Prior to 1774, when the church was built, Edisto was connected with the Parish Church, of St. John's Island.

1804, Feb 20. Benjamin Seabrook was a Delegate, from the Edisto Church, to the 17th Convention of the Episcopal Church, in South Carolina, and to subsequent conventions in 1808, 1809 and 1810, while in 1813, Edisto Church was represented by Thomas B Seabrook

In 1812, the Church had twelve white and three colored communicants, and, 1815, there were twenty white and five colored communicants.

Some of the Edisto Seabrooks were likewise Presbyterians

The following epitaphs are copied from stones, standing in the yard of the Presbyterian Church, on Edisto Island, and I think refer mostly to the descendants of Rich William Seabrook

Mrs Ann Seabrook died, Feb 10, 1809, aged 40   "Erected by her eldest surviving son to the kindest and best of mothers"

Mrs Elizabeth Seabrook died, Feb 1, 1814, aged 20 years   Stone raised to her by her beloved brother

Margaret M Seabrook died, Dec 17, 1837, aged 30 years, 6 months and 3 days   Erected by her husband

Joseph Caldwell Seabrook, son of William B and Elizabeth H Seabrook, died Aug 19, 1836, an infant

Robert Chisholm Seabrook, son of William and Emma E Seabrook, born Aug 31, 1821, died Oct 20, 1852

Emma Elizabeth Seabrook, born May 25, 1831, died Oct 2, 1834

Mrs Emma E Seabrook, born Aug 19 1793, died June 23 1856

There are monuments of public interest, fast going to decay, in the yard of the Presbyterian Church, at Edisto Island, that I copied with a view to their ultimate preservation

Sacred to the Memory of Joseph Russel, William Edings, William Bird, Timothy Hendrick and William Whippy, who, in 1732, gave to this Church certain slaves

Also of

William Cummings, James Clark, Mary Bee and Mary Russel, who, in the year 1740, gave to this Church sundry sums, amounting to near £400, of the Currency of that time.

The preceding inscription appears on a single marble slab, like a tombstone, which is now used as a stepping stone to the side entrance of the church, and is now nearly effaced   It also appears on the following larger monument, as one of the inscriptions with which its four sides are covered

This | Monument | is erected | by the unanimous consent | of the Corporation | of the | Presbyterian Church | of Edisto Island | in testimony | of their gratitude | to the several Benefactors | of their Society | March 1st | 1826

Sacred | To the Memory of | John Bower | who in 1717 endowed this Church | with a Tract of Land containing | three hundred acres | Also of | Mr Wailis | who about the year 1730 | gave to this Church a Tract of | Land   for which in the year 1737 | it received as an equivalent | £2500

Sacred | To the Memory of | Paul Hamilton | who between the years | 1732 & 1755 [or 1735] | gave to this Church certain | Slaves, two Silver Tankards | for the use of the Commission | & £300 10 s

Also of | James Lardant | who gave to this Church | certain Slaves and | £300 | between the years 1732 & 1735

The glory of Edisto Island has departed and the old order of things is now a mere tradition The name of the master is perpetuated by his slaves, for his children have scattered far from the hearth-side, in the struggle for existence   Where once was life and gaiety, there is now oppressive solitude, and I was glad to escape, by Jack Miller's leaky sailboat, rather than wait for the return of the small tug which calls at the island every second day   It was a somewhat hazardous proceeding, for the sail was patched like a quilt and the boat soaked up water like a sponge.   When the vigorous efforts of three negroes and our two selves barely sufficed to keep our feet dry, and we reproached him for it, he simply remarked "that the boat was a little rectified, Boss " At the end of two and one-half hours' sailing, in a stiff breeze, we came to Yonge's Island, where we put up at the house of W C Garraty, who keeps the store, runs the station and owns a fine truck farm Here we were well cared for, modestly charged, and left the next morning for Rantowles, where, at the station, we found the agent gloomily awaiting his chill, and impressed with the belief that he would succumb, like his predecessors, to the malarial scourge which infests the country for miles around

John Seabrook, of Edisto Island, is buried in a small plot, on Edisto Island, which contains half a dozen Seabrook stones and vaults, rapidly going to decay The land, surrounding the graveyard, is owned by a thrifty colored man, Ben Simmons, and his hogs are allowed to roam within the former enclosure It was this Ben Simmons who hired me his forlorn looking carriage, at an exorbitant price, and gave us tasty food out of a varied and scant collection of old and broken china When asked whether any of John Seabrook's descendants still dwelt in this locality, he bumptiously said· "de old folk dey are all gon, but some of the ancestors live hereabout " The epitaphs on these stones are

John Seabrook died, Nov 26, 1783, aged 52 years, [born 1731]
Mrs Sarah Seabrook died, Oct 21, 1798 in her 59th year, [née Lawton?, born 1738].
John Seabrook died, Jan. 10. 1795, in his 29th year, [born 1766]
William Seabrook died, Sept 1, 1836, in his 64th year, [born 1772, flat tombstone, he was known as Rich William Seabrook]
Mrs Mary Ann Seabrook died, July 30 1818, in her 39th year, [born 1779, flat tomb].
William Seabrook Legare died 1850, an infant

1 JOHN SEABROOK and SARAH SEABROOK were the parents of John Seabrook, born in 1766, and of William Seabrook, born in 1772, and Mrs. Mary Ann Seabrook was the wife of William Seabrook, known as "Rich Wilham " This William Seabrook's relatives have intermarried with the Pinckneys, Heywards, Gaillards and others of the best South Carolina blood.

2 "RICH WILLIAM SEABROOK," son of John Seabrook, 1, "was one of the wealthiest and noblest of the name " While he resided on Edisto Island, he owned much land elsewhere, among other pieces, Seabrook Island, now the property of one of his grandsons At one time, he owned over one thousand slaves.

In 1825, he entertained Lafayette, who, while his guest, stood godfather for his daughter, Caroline Lafayette Seabrook, at her baptism. His residence, still standing on Edisto Island, is marked with the letters W S in the house railing, and is distinguished thus from the house of his son, William Seabrook, which was the most pretentious one on the Island in its day It is occupied by his grandson, Marcellus Seabrook, aged about fifty years, a gracious, cultured and refined man, who now supervises the estate for a Charleston lawyer, by the name of Smith.

Rich William Seabrook married, first, Miss Mikell, second, Emma Edings He died in 1836

Issue by first wife
3 William Seabrook
4 E Mikell Seabrook
5 G. Washington Seabrook
6 Sarah Seabrook
7 Mary Seabrook

Issue by second wife
8 Martha Seabrook
9 Caroline Lafayette Seabrook

10 Julia Seabrook
11 Robert Seabrook
12 Chip [Joseph?] Seabrook

3 WILLIAM SEABROOK, son of William Seabrook, 2, inherited his father's wealth. He built, upon Edisto Island, an extremely spacious and elegant house, and sent to England for the landscape gardener, Thompson, who came and laid out his lands, at an expense of $30,000 Thompson made his home here, and, I am told, left his fortune of $100,000, to Charleston, which has perpetuated his memory in calling the auditorium after him.

The fish pond was also a great feature on the old plantation, from which, at command, fish were drawn Now, it is simply indicated by a depression, overgrown with weeds, and the famous gardens are now a mere suggestion The fine house that he built was despoiled of its furnishings, and gutted, even of its mahogany woodwork, during the recent Rebellion, when a sloop sailed directly to its doors and took away everything of value.

William Seabrook, as he appears in a photograph owned by his grandson, Mitchell Seabrook, taken when he was about sixty years of age, was a large, portly man, bald, with a cheery kindly face, finely dressed Photographs of his famous gardens are owned by Mrs. Hopkinson With the War, his fortune was entirely swept away, and his widow spent her declining days in a home for the impoverished ladies of Charleston, founded by the labors of a reverend gentleman, of that city.

Both William Seabrook and his father married sisters, Edings [?], the father having had previous wives His great house is now occupied by his grandson, Mitchell Seabrook, who is aged about thirty-five years, polite, intelligent and refined

Issue

13 William Seabrook, married Miss Whaley
14 Edward Seabrook, married Miss Mitchell

4 E. MICKELL SEABROOK, son of William Seabrook, 2, was an Edisto Island planter of eminence He graduated from Princeton, in 1823.

His tombstone stands, in the Presbyterian Churchyard, on Edisto Island·
Ephraim Mikell Seabrook, born Feb 22, 1797, died Mch. 20, 1846.

5 GEORGE WASHINGTON SEABROOK, son of William Seabrook, 2

Issue

15 William Seabrook

6 SARAH SEABROOK, daughter of William Seabrook, 2, married when a spinster, Colonel Legree. Perhaps the infant, William Seabrook Legare, who died in 1850, and was interred in Rich William Seabrook's plot, was her son

8 MARTHA SEABROOK, daughter of William Seabrook, 2, married Count de Lasteyrie, of Paris, a nephew of Lafayette, and left a daughter and a son, who distinguished himself in the Franco-Prussian War, in 1870

9 CAROLINE LAFAYETTE SEABROOK, daughter of William Seabrook, 2, was godfathered by Lafayette, on his last visit to America, in 1825, while stopping with her father She was then six weeks old She married James, son of Judge Hopkinson, of Philadelphia

Miss Hopkinson, daughter of the Judge, married a Mr. Biddle. At the same time as Caroline L Seabrook's baptism took place, Thomas Wilkes Seabrook engaged himself to his future wife.

James Hopkinson, born May 18, 1810, died Jan 28, 1875.
Caroline Lafayette Seabrook, his wife, born Feb 22, 1825; died Dec 13, 1879
Presbyterian Churchyard, Edisto Island.

10 JULIA SEABROOK, daughter of William Seabrook, 2, married [Bowie?] Legree, a son of Dr Legree, of James' Island.

14 EDWARD SEABROOK, son of William Seabrook, 3, married Miss Mitchell.
Issue
16 Mitchell Seabrook

15. WILLIAM SEABROOK, son of George Washington Seabrook, 5.

WILLIAM SEABROOK

There died in this city yesterday, at the early age of 40, William Seabrook, a gentleman who possessed the high regard and esteem of all who knew him

William Seabrook was the son of George Washington Seabrook, and was reared on Edisto He graduated at the S C College during President Thornwell's administration, taught school at Bluffton and in Charleston, was admitted to the Bar in 1869, and elected corporation counsel last year

Throughout his brief life he was always a useful man, devoting himself to the interests of others to the utter forgetfulness of self, diligent and patient in his pursuits, conscientious in all things, earnest and generous in character, and of so rare a modesty that his few intimates were allowed only an occasional glimpse of his many attainments

He was proficient in classical learning, exact in scholarship and of wide professional knowledge He enjoyed the confidence of his associates at the Bar, and attained the honorable position he lately occupied without seeking it by political arts   [May 13, 1878?]

1 GABRIEL SEABROOK, of Edisto Island, owned large estates, on that Island, between 1792 and 1808

Issue

2 Ephriam Seabrook
3 Henry Seabrook
4 John Seabrook
5 Mary Ann Seabrook } married Henry Seabrook
6 Elizabeth Seabrook

2 EPHRAIM SEABROOK, son of Gabriel Seabrook, 1, married Miss Hanihan; elsewhere he is given a wife, Miss Mikell, and he is then called Ephraim M Seabrook.

Issue

7 John Seabrook
8 Ephraim Seabrook
9 Edward W. Seabrook; married Miss Dawson, of Baltimore, Md
10 Joseph Seabrook, married Phoebe Hamilton, and had two children There was a Joseph W Seabrook, son-in-law to Col Paul Hamilton
11 Henry Seabrook, was engaged to Martha Washington, a lineal descendant of the President's brother. The marriage was never consummated, and neither ever

married Elsewhere I find that Henry Seabrook was a lawyer, of Charleston, S C, and was married, and the father of E H Seabrook

11ª Mary Elizabeth Seabrook, married, first, Paul Hamilton; second, William H Heriot.

11ᵇ Louisa Anastasia Seabrook, unmarried, living, aged about 80 years, in 1908, in Charleston, S C She is the owner of the old homestead on Edisto Island, about twelve miles from the landing

3 HENRY SEABROOK, son of Gabriel Seabrook, 1, [married his cousin, Mary Ann Seabrook?]

Issue

12 Emma Seabrook
13 Elizabeth Seabrook
14 Sarah Ann Seabrook
15 Matilda Seabrook, unmarried
16 Dr Edward Seabrook
17 William Phoenix Seabrook

4 JOHN SEABROOK, son of Gabriel Seabrook, 1, married, first, Miss Murray; second, Martha Meggett.

Issue by first wife

18 Dr Whitemarsh Seabrook
19 Joseph Dill Seabrook
20 James Murray Seabrook
21 Josephine Seabrook; eldest daughter

Issue by second wife

22 Elizabeth Seabrook, married B Scabrook
23 Anna Seabrook
24 Pauline Seabrook
25 Abbie Seabrook, deceased
26 Other children

7 JOHN SEABROOK, son of Ephraim Seabrook, 2, was called "French John," because of his polished manners He married, rather late in life, Miss Turnipseed, daughter of the celebrated Crimean surgeon. He was called Dr John Seabrook, was educated in France, and died, over ninety years of age, at Columbus, S C, but a short time since He left one daughter

8 COL. EPHRAIM SEABROOK, son of Ephraim Seabrook, 2, married, first, Miss Bulow; second, Marian Duboes, third, the widow of Col Bartow.

Issue by second wife

27 Duboes Seabrook I am informed that this gentleman is writing a Seabrook genealogy
28 Julius Seabrook
29 Edgar, or Ernest, Seabrook
30 Marie Seabrook
31 Kate Seabrook [?]

HISTORICAL MISCELLANY

9   EDWARD SEABROOK, son of Ephraim Seabrook, 2, married Miss Dorsey, daughter of Senator Dorsey, of Georgia.

Issue
- 32 Henrietta Hill Scabrook
- 33 Edgar Seabrook
- 34 Marian Seabrook
- 35 Julian Seabrook [?]

1   BENJAMIN SEABROOK, married, first, a daughter of one of the Sea Island families, who was possessed of much wealth, second Miss Baynard

Issue by second wife
- 2 Joseph Seabrook
- 3 Thomas Bannister Seabrook
- 4 Benjamin Seabrook

2   JOSEPH SEABROOK, son of Benjamin Seabrook, 1, was born about 1769, died, in 1815, aged fifty years   He was known as "Sulky Joe," to distinguish him from "Cussing Joe" Seabrook   He married, first, Miss Austin, of England, and had no issue, second, Miss Whaley, third, Martha Beckett

Issue by second wife
- 5 Mary Seabrook, married, first, James Clark, second, Richard Townsend

Issue by third wife
- 6 William Benjamin Seabrook
- 7 Joseph Baynard Seabrook
- 8 James Beckett Seabrook
- 9 Elizabeth Seabrook, married Mr. Hills
- 10 Martha Seabrook, died aged fifteen years
- 11 Francis Seabrook; died aged twelve years.

3   THOMAS BANNISTER SEABROOK, son of Benjamin Seabrook, 1, married Miss Clark

Issue
- 12 Elizabeth Seabrook, married Mr. Miller.
- 13 Caroline Seabrook, married Mr Geddies
- 14 Martha Seabrook, married Mr Faber

4   BENJAMIN SEABROOK, son of Benjamin Seabrook, 1
Issue
- 15 Whitemarsh Seabrook

6   WILLIAM BENJAMIN SEABROOK, son of Joseph Seabrook, 2, married, first, Elizabeth McCloud, second, Elizabeth Royal, who was living in 1881.

Issue by first wife
- 16 William Bannister Seabrook
- 17 Julius Seabrook

Issue by second wife
18 Martha Love Seabrook
19 Cornelia Royal Seabrook
20 Rev Josiah McCloud Seabrook
21 Franklin Pierce Seabrook
22 George Seabrook
23 Jane Seabrook

7 REV. JOSEPH BAYNARD SEABROOK, son of Joseph Seabrook, 2, married, first, Sarah Bailey, second, Lydia Bailey, widow of Mr Whaley; third, Martha Catharine Beckett, living in 1881. He started to make a genealogical investigation of the Seabrook family, and collected a large amount of data, which was destroyed during the late Rebellion. This data he brought with him and showed it to Mrs Henry Seabrook, of Keyport, N. J, when visiting her, about 1860-1865

" Joseph Baynard Seabrook was violently opposed to the late War, and being a man who spoke out boldly and fearlessly his mind on all subjects, did not remain silent here, where he thought so much was at stake He invariably prophesied failure, therefore was looked upon coldly by his more hot-headed relatives and friends But, like a true patriot, went with his state, gave his sons and what of his substance was needed, cast in all, and, like the rest, lost all " Letter of Mrs Joseph B Seabrook, (Mrs Martha C Seabrook), Charleston, S C., June 19, 1878

FROM THE NEW YORK OBSERVER

Rev Dr Seabrook, of Charleston, gave me a very interesting account of his labors among the colored people He is a minister of the Episcopal Church, of one of the old, wealthy families of South Carolina, formerly a slaveholder himself Now he is one of the many whose fortunes were lost in the gulf of war But he continues to preach to the colored people, as he has long done, and he has an attached and faithful people, unable to give him a salary, but he gives them all the energy of his soul and life, to train them for usefulness and glory Of such is the Kingdom of Heaven   *Irenaeus.*

REV JOSEPH B SEABROOK

After a brief illness of ten days, the Rev Jos B Seabrook, for several years past the rector of St Mark's Church and the Superintendent of the city Public Schools, died at his residence, in Spring Street, in this city, yesterday morning Mr Seabrook was born October 10, 1809, on Edisto Island, and was, consequently, at the time of his death, in the 68th year of his age He graduated at Princeton College, studied law under Hugh S Legare, and was admitted to the Bar soon after graduating In consequence of ill health, he abandoned the law, and betook himself to planting and teaching Subsequently he conceived the desire to enter the ministry, and was ordained to the ministry of the Episcopal Church, in 1848 His labors in this field were chiefly among the colored people—a work to which he believed himself called by Divine Providence,—and to which he devoted himself with untiring zeal to the day of his death At his own expense, he erected a church, at Bluffton, in 1840, and another, at St Paul's Parish, in 1859 During his life he accomplished great good as an educator, and, so great was his zeal and enthusiasm on this subject, that he educated a large number of poor boys at his own expense During the War, he was pastor of Grace Church, and the close of the War found him at his post Shortly afterwards, he was called to the rectorship of St Mark's Church, which position he filled up to the time of his death About three years ago, he was chosen Superintendent of the Public Schools of the city, which position he filled with satisfaction to the public In respect to the memory of the deceased, the public schools were closed yesterday, by order of the Board of Commissioners, and will remain closed until after the funeral services, which will take place from St Mark's Church, at 11 o'clock this morning

LATE REV J B SEABROOK —The funeral services of this reverend gentleman, the rector of St Mark's Church, and Superintendent of the public schools of the city, were held yesterday morning, at 11 A M, at St Mark's Church The attendance on the part of the devoted and deeply affected congregation, prominent citizens and clergymen was very large The Rev Messrs Prentiss, Hanckel, Green, Welsh, Steele and Whaley were present in the chancel, and conducted the services, the former clergymen preaching a discourse happily adapted to the occasion The rich floral offerings heaped upon the coffin showed the regard in which the deceased was held by his congregation and friends After the services, the remains were conveyed to Magnolia Cemetery for interment The pall-bearers, six in number, were the vestrymen of the church

HISTORICAL MISCELLANY

Issue by first wife
24 Martha Sarah Seabrook
25 Joseph Baynard Seabrook
26 Caroline Cecile Seabrook
27 Ephraim Baynard Seabrook
28 Theodore Beckett Seabrook
29 Mary Elizabeth Seabrook
30 William Murray Seabrook
31 Pereneau Finley Seabrook
32 Ann Louise Seabrook

Issue by second wife
33 Isabel Seabrook
34 Lydia Seabrook

Issue by third wife
35 Martha Beckett Seabrook, born about 1872

8 JAMES BECKETT SEABROOK, son of Joseph Seabrook, 2, married Elizabeth Clark Bailey, whose sister, Sarah Ann Bailey, married Rev. Joseph B. Seabrook

Issue
36 Elizabeth Moriu Seabrook
37 Kate Ash Seabrook
38 St John Seabrook
39 Matilda Eloise Seabrook
and other children to the total of nine

15 WHITEMARSH SEABROOK, son of Benjamin Seabrook, 4, was a graduate of Princeton College, in 1812, and Governor of South Carolina in 1848-1850 He married Miss Hamilton, daughter of Paul Hamilton, Secretary of the Navy under President Madison.

Issue
40 Archibald Seabrook, married Miss Pinkney, sister of the Rev. Mr. Pinkney, had issue
41 Dr Benjamin Seabrook, married Miss Strobart.
42 Paul Hamilton Seabrook, married Mary Elizabeth Seabrook, daughter of Ephraim Mikell Seabrook
43 Septima Seabrook, living in 1881
44 Julia Seabrook, living in 1881, unmarried

Judge Paul E Seabrook, of Darien, Ga, is a grandson of Governor Seabrook

24 MARTHA SARAH SEABROOK, daughter of Rev. Joseph B Seabrook, 7, was aged forty-two years, in 1881. She supplied me with much information She was then the Vice-principal of a colored school She married William Seabrook, a lawyer, who died Jan 14, 1878. He was a son of G Washington Seabrook and a grandson of "Good William Seabrook."

Issue
45 A daughter

27 EPHRAIM BAYNARD SEABROOK, son of Rev Joseph B Seabrook, 7, was the oldest son. He graduated from Princeton College, in 1861 He died Aug 12, 1877.

"He was a brilliant, unfortunate fellow, broken by ill-health and domestic misfortunes He wrote for the 'Galaxy' for some years and at a very early period of his life His writings were marked by power and a finished elegance, remarkable for so young a man. His genius was very versatile, and, had he lived, would have been a marked man "

42 PAUL HAMILTON SEABROOK, son of Governor Whitemarsh Seabrook, 15, married Mary Elizabeth, daughter of Ephraim Mikell Seabrook

Issue

46 Paul Seabrook, married and had a son
47 Ephraim Mikell Seabrook, (called Ephraim Hamilton Seabrook), my informant, married Miss Booth, of Philadelphia, Pa , and, in 1908, had two adult daughters He was born in Charleston, S. C , resides at Jacksonville, Fla , and is in the transportation business Mr Seabrook has in his possession a ring, finely mounted and engraved, with Seabrook arms, which belonged to his great-grandfather It carries Crest, an arm erect holding a cross crosslett fitcheé in the hand, the Shield a lion rampant carrying a cross crosslet fitcheé

1 JOHN SEABROOK, of Edisto Island, was, probably, a brother of Gabriel Seabrook He married Ann Smiley

Issue

2 Joseph Seabrook
3 Henry Seabrook
4 Smiley Seabrook
5 Robert Seabrook
6 Sarah Seabrook, married, first, Mr. Richardson, second, Mr. Ralston, of Daniel's Island.
7 Elizabeth Seabrook, married, first, Mr Eddings, second Capt L Lightburn, of Bermuda

2 JOSEPH SEABROOK, son of John Seabrook, 1, married Harriet Reynolds

Issue

8 Harriet Seabrook, married, first, John Seabrook; second, Mr Mitchell
9 Sarah Seabrook, married Dr. O O Curtis, of John's Island
10 Nancy Seabrook, married Robert Rivers, of Stono, S C.
11 Elizabeth Seabrook, married Thomas Wilson, of South Carolina.
12 Joseph Henry Seabrook .
13 Robert Seabrook, died unmarried

3 HENRY SEABROOK son of John Seabrook, 1, married, first, Elizabeth Seabrook, his cousin, second, Mary Ann Seabrook, sister of his first wife, a very haughty woman

Issue by first wife

14 Smiley Seabrook, died unmarried
15 Ephraim Seabrook, died unmarried

Issue by second wife
- 16 William Seabrook, unmarried
- 17 Dr Edward Seabrook, unmarried
- 18 Emma Seabrook, married Benjamin Rivers, brother of Robert Rivers mentioned above
- 19 Eliza Seabrook, married Mr. Herriot [?]
- 20 Matilda Seabrook, married Dr Palmer, of South Carolina.
- 21 Sarah Ann Seabrook, unmarried.

4 SMILEY SEABROOK, son of John Seabrook, 1, married Martha Whitaker, of Barnwell District

Issue
- 22 Elizabeth Seabrook, married Henry, a brother of Charles Francis Adams. They live at Columbus, Ohio
- 23 Mary Ann Seabrook, married Mr. Johnson, of Rome, Ga

5 ROBERT SEABROOK, son of John Seabrook, 1.

Issue
- 24 Benjamin Seabrook
- 25 Martha Seabrook; lived in Alabama

12 JOSEPH HENRY SEABROOK, son of Joseph Seabrook, 2, married, first, Miss Hogg, of Beaufort Island, and moved to Quincy, Fla He married, second, the widow of Dr Pue, of Beaufort Island, third a lady from the same place

Issue
26 Sarah Seabrook, married Mr. Coleman, of Beaufort Island.

1 HENRY WHITEMARSH SEABROOK had

Issue
2 Thomas Wilkes Seabrook, "own cousin to Joseph Seabrook."

2 THOMAS WILKES SEABROOK, son of Henry Whitemarsh Seabrook, 1, married Eliza Mary Partridge, of England, whose mother was Miss Lions Thomas Wilkes Seabrook resided at Beaufort, S. C., where he died about 1809. "Mary Elizabeth Partridge" had an uncle, Edward Lecraft, an aide to Benjamin Franklin, when Envoy to France, who was buried at Beaufort, S C His miniature, ornamented by thirteen stars on the reverse side, painted in France, in 1776, and obtained from Honoria Wilkes Seabrook, is now in the possession of Dr John E Stillwell, of New York City

Issue
- 3 Whitemarsh Seabrook, died young
- 4 A daughter
- 5 John Lecraft Seabrook
- 6 Thomas Wilkes Seabrook

5 JOHN LECRAFT SEABROOK, son of Thomas Wilkes Seabrook, 2, died at Grahamville, S C He married, first, Harriet Seabrook, eldest daughter of Joseph Seabrook, of St.

Paul's Parish, near Rantowles' Bridge, S C They had one child, who died young His widow was left a dower, and the balance of his estate, he conveyed to the family of his brother, Thomas Wilkes Seabrook. His widow married Mr Mitchell

6 THOMAS WILKES SEABROOK, son of Thomas Wilkes Seabrook, 2, was born, about 1809, at Beaufort, S C, and died May 1, 1835 He married, in June, 1827, at St Paul's Parish, Martha Mary Seabrook, third daughter of Joseph Seabrook After the decease of her husband, she married J L Rose Both Mr. and Mrs Rose were living in 1882 At the time of their marriage, Thomas Wilkes Seabrook was eighteen years of age and Martha Mary Seabrook was fifteen years of age

Issue
7 Whitemarsh Seabrook
8 Benjamin Alston Seabrook
9 Honoria Wilkes Seabrook

A coat of arms, belonging to the family, is in the garret of Mrs Rose, née Seabrook, also an old family Bible

7 WHITEMARSH SEABROOK, son of Thomas Wilkes Seabrook, 6, was killed in the Confederate service, at the Battle of the Wilderness. He was buried, at Hampton, Va, June, 1864 He married Emily Rivers

Issue
10 Thomas Seabrook, married Miss Craford
11 Olivia Seabrook, married Dr Bailey, of Edisto Island; a cousin

8 BENJAMIN ALSTON SEABROOK, son of Thomas Wilkes Seabrook, 6, died, at Williston, S C., in 1864. He married Miss Derwood

Issue
12 Josephine Seabrook

9 HONORIA WILKES SEABROOK, daughter of Thomas Wilkes Seabrook, 6, was born at St Paul's Parish, and married Mr Fentenheim. She was the eldest of the family and supplied me with much information, while temporarily living in New York City

MISCELLANEOUS NOTES

The South Carolina Seabrooks were, generally, opulent and well educated Among them were lawyers, physicians, clergymen and many college-bred men During the late unfortunate war between the states, many of them died for the cause they served and believed right Of six Seabrooks, all officers, who were in the Virginia campaign, five are lying there today, one a brother of Robert E Seabrook Many were large planters of rice and Sea Island cotton, and became very rich men, but the war sadly wrecked their estates, and now they are working hard for a living   Letter of Robert E. Seabrook

Robert E Seabrook, schoolmaster, residing in Charleston, married, but without issue, has perhaps, given more time to compiling the history of the Seabrook family than any one else When I called upon him, he was absent upon his summer vacation Such data as I present here, no doubt, could be much enriched by his knowledge.

One of the Seabrooks sent his son, Thomas, to Europe for travel and study Upon his return, his father asked him what he liked most while abroad, and he replied, "Paris, father." "I'll buy it for you, my son, I'll buy it for you," was his rejoinder

Polly Seabrook, cousin of Martha, wife of William Seabrook, died aged over one hundred years. She told Mrs Seabrook, who gave the information to me, in 1899, that several brothers, by the name of Seabrook, came, jointly, to America, and settled, one, each, in New York, Virginia and South Carolina. Existing records do not bear out this tradition.

" . . communication is difficult, never as easy as at the North, but singularly difficult now, for the war laid waste and desolated the coast of South Carolina in a fearful manner. The lands have all changed hands and the former masters are dead, their children feebly striving to keep soul and body together Perhaps our sins have found us out God only knows who was most to blame That must be left to wiser heads than ours to decide, but a fearful trouble has fallen on all " Letter of Mrs Joseph B Seabrook, June 19, 1878

In 1782, the estate of Joseph Seabrooke, of South Carolina, was amerced twelve per cent There is reason to believe that, at the outset, he was a Whig

Joseph Seabrooke, Jr , of South Carolina, was in office, under the Crown, after the surrender of Charleston His property was confiscated. Sabine's Royalists in the Revolutionary War.

General Richard Jenkins, who was killed at the Battle of the Wilderness, was the son of a Seabrook mother.

In 1845, Everardus Whalley Seabrook was a graduate of Harvard

SEABROOK

OF

MARYLAND

1 MOSES SEABROOK, born 1743, came, with a brother, to Baltimore, Md , where they separated He died in 1839.

Issue

2 Elijah Seabrook
3 Samuel Seabrook, has a large posterity, among them a son, Moses He lives near Emmetsburg, Md They spell their name *Seabrooks*
4 James Seabrook
5 Moses Seabrook
6 A son, who settled in Ohio

2 ELIJAH SEABROOK, son of Moses Seabrook, 1, moved from Maryland to Pennsylvania.

Issue

7 William Seabrook, married and had two children; one, Alice Seabrook, lived near Emmetsburg, near the Pennsylvania line
8 John Seabrook
9 Nancy Seabrook
10 Jane Seabrook
11 Elizabeth Seabrook; married Mr Zimmerman, of Adams Co , Ill
12 Mary Seabrook, married Mr Andrew.
13 Euphemia Seabrook; married Moses, son of Samuel Seabrook, and live near Gettysburg.
14 Florence Seabrook, married Mr Zimmerman, his second wife

8 JOHN SEABROOK, son of Elijah Seabrook, 2, married, first, Mary Fettrow, second, Kate Deihl. He was living in 1883.

Issue

15 Silas L. Seabrook
16 Clarence Seabrook
17 Carrie Seabrook
18 William Seabrook

15 SILAS L SEABROOK, son of John Seabrook, 8, was born in 1852, married Mary E Hall, and, in 1883, resided at Little Falls, N Y. He is a lawyer, and supplied me with the history of the Maryland Seabrooks.

Issue

19 Harry Seabrook

MISCELLANEOUS NOTES

1759, May 5 John Seabrook and Mary E. Anderson were married.
                          Christ Church Records Philadelphia, Pa , p 227.
1823 Burrowes Seabrook, unlocated
Harrison Seabrook, of 252 South Second St , Philadelphia, Pa

At Colerain, Lancaster County, Pa , is a colony of Seabrooks

On the road between Baltimore and Washington is a station called Seabrook

Frederick County, Md , has a colony of Seabrooks

W. L W Seabrook, Esq , of Anne Arundel County, Md , was nominated, June 26, 1863, for Commissioner of the Land Office, by the Unconditional Union Party

W. L W Seabrook, Esq , of Westminster, Md , made remarks at the 20th Annual Convention, held at Richmond, Va , in 1875

SHEPHERD

OF

MONMOUTH COUNTY

THOMAS SHEPHERD, apparently the first of the name in Monmouth County, married Deborah, daughter of Joseph Grover. He died, May 17, 1751, aged 73 years

1751, May 17. Will of Thomas Shephard, of Middletown, sick, etc., mentioned
Wife, Deborah
Eldest son, Joseph, who received 10 shillings
Two eldest daughters, Sarah Stillwell } each received 10 shillings
Rebeckah Cox
Son, John Shephard, received 10 shillings
Daughter, Deborah Burros, received £50, "with what I have given her already"
Daughter, Hannah Still, received £50, "with what I have given her already"
Daughter, Mary Shephard, received £30, and a negro girl
Executors sons, Thomas and Ebenezer Shephard

The inventory of his personal estate included negroes, an abundance of cattle, and household goods, and amounted to £655-1-4

1759, Dec 19. Will of Deborah Shepherd, widow & Relict of Thomas Shepherd, Late of Middletown, County of Monmouth, "in health", proved Nov 12, 1768, mentioned·
To "Heirs of my Eldeſt Son Joſeph Shepherd Deceased," 10 shillings
Son, Thomas Shepherd, received "all lands and meadows whereof I may die seized of," he paying the legacies
"to Thomas Shepherd son of my son Ebenezer Shepherd Dec'd £200 when he becomes of age"
"to Sarah Shepherd Sister of my s^d Grandson Thomas Shepherd £100 at day of marriage," or at the age of eighteen
If grandson, Thomas Shepherd, does not live to become of age, then the £200, given to Sarah Shepherd, or if Sarah Shepherd should die, then both the £100 and £200 to Grandson, Thomas Shepherd, or if neither live, then their legacies "to my son, Thomas Shepherd," he to pay his five sisters, Sarah Stillwell, Rebeckah Cox, Deborah Burrows, Hannah Stelle and Mary Jonſton, £100, to be equally divided
Personal estate to be equally divided between daughters
Executors "My Son Thomas Shepherd & my friend James Grover, (son of James)"
She signed her name in full
Witnesses Cyrenius Vanmatr, Chrincyonce Van Mater and Joſiah Holmeſ

1768, Nov 12 Thomas Shepherd qualified, at Middletown, as executor

1769, Jan 4. James Grover renounced his executorship. Witness Hugh Patten

SHEPHERD OF MONMOUTH COUNTY

Issue

2 Joseph Shepherd; eldest son.
3 Thomas Shepherd
4 Ebenezer Shepherd, died prior to 1759, as per his mother's will
5 Sarah Shepherd, born May 2, 1708, married Joseph Stillwell, of Nutswamp, Middletown, N J.
6 Rebecca Shepherd, married Mr Cox
7 Deborah Shepherd, married Edward Burrowes.
8 Hannah Shepherd, married Mr Steele   Dr Steele, of Grand or Broome St, New York City, was her descendant.
9 Mary Shepherd, married Mr Johnston.
10 John Shepherd

2   JOSEPH SHEPHERD, son of Thomas Shepherd, 1, married Rebeckah Lippit, May 19, 1733   He died Sept 2, 1753

Joseph Shepherd, in 1715, resided in Nutswamp, about two miles from Leedsville   When her husband died, Rebecca (Lippit) Shepherd moved to the home of her kinspeople in Middletown village, with her small children   Joseph Shepherd possessed the Shepherd trait of tyranny to an extreme degree   Tradition has it that he yoked his negroes to the plough in lieu of cattle

1753, Sept 14   Inventory of the personal estate of Joseph Shepherd, taken this date, by Andrew Winter and Nath' Leonard, amounted to £251-19-8   Among the items were   "½ doz silver spoons & a small tankard £2-5-0"

Issue*

11 Katharine Shepherd, born Aug 11, 1734, married Richard Crawford
12 Deborah Shepherd, born Dec 22, 1735, married John Leonard
13 Sarah Shepherd } a spinster
                  } twins, born Sept 1, 1737
14 Mary Shepherd } married James Winter
15 Hannah Shepherd, born Sept 11, 1739, married Col. John Smock, of Holmdel, for his third wife
16 Thomas Shepherd, born June 22, 1741   He was the founder of Shepherd's Town, W Va   He left with a gun and an axe
17 Capt Moses Shepherd, born Oct 25, 1743   He was the youngest child, and small when his father died

3   THOMAS SHEPHERD, son of Thomas Shepherd, 1, married, Sept 13, 1747, Sarah Dennis, who was born, Apr 18, 1723, about daybreak   She died Mch 14, 1813

Issue†

19 Elisha Shepherd, born July 14, 1750
20 Amelia Shepherd, born Feb 14, 1753, [married William Lippincott]
21 Clemence Shepherd, born Feb 7, 1755; [married Thomas Lloyd]
22 Jacob Shepherd, born Aug 14, 1756.
23 Thomas Shepherd, born Sept 19, 1758
24 Sarah Shepherd, born May 9, 1765

---
*The dates of birth of his issue were copied by Mr George T Beekman, of Middletown, from an old account book of Joseph Shepherd, of his business as miller
†From a Bible owned by Mrs Sarah E Layton, Washington and Borden Streets, Red Bank, N J

4 EBENEZER SHEPHERD, son of Thomas Shepherd, 1.

1759, Nov 14 On the inventory of the personal estate of Ebenezer Shepherd, of Monmouth County, of this date, Cattrina Shepard appeared as administratrix

1759, Nov. 19. Bond for £400, of Catharine Shepherd, widow of Ebenezer Shepherd, of Middletown, and his administratrix, and Thomas Shepherd, yeoman, bondsman Catharine Shepherd made her mark, and Thomas Shepherd signed in full

In 1759, as per the will of his mother he had the following

Issue
25 Thomas Shepherd
26 Sarah Shepherd

5 SARAH SHEPHERD, daughter of Thomas Shepherd, 1, was born May 2, 1709, and married Joseph Stillwell, of Nutswamp, Middletown, N. J , Dec. 28, 1728.

Issue, see Stillwell Family
Thirteen children.

6 REBECCA SHEPHERD, daughter of Thomas Shepherd, 1, married Mr Cox

Issue
A daughter Cox, married Mr. Truex.

Issue
Beck Truex; married Mr. Newel
James Truex, married Miss Ogborne, no issue
John Truex, married Althea Snyder

11 KATHARINE SHEPHERD, daughter of Joseph Shepherd, 2, married Richard Crawford, by license dated Sept 17, 1751. She was born Aug. 11, 1734, and died Jan 13, 1807. He was born Jan 27, 1729, and died Sept. 20, 1798

1794, Oct 1 Will of Richard Crawford, on record at Freehold, N. J , proved Mch. 8, 1806, mentioned.
Wife, Katharine
Sons, Richard Crawford
    George Crawford
Daughters, Catharine Leonard
    Esther Burrowes
    Hannah Crawford

Issue
Richard Crawford
George Crawford
Catharine Crawford, married Mr Leonard
Esther Crawford, married Thomas Burrowes She died, Feb 15, 1836, aged 73 years, 10 months and 26 days He died, Aug 24, 1805, aged 47 years and 24 days
Hannah Crawford

13 SARAH SHEPHERD, daughter of Joseph Shepherd, 2, was born in 1737 She was a twin with Mary Shepherd She was a spinster and known as "Aunt Sally." She died,

Jan. 14, 1835, aged 97 years, 4 months and 3 days, and is buried in the Baptist Churchyard, Middletown, N. J.

She wrote Rev Abel Morgan's epitaph, and broke two cart loads of clam shells in pieces with her hands, which were put beneath and around the first headstone of Rev Abel Morgan, to prevent its sinking It stood in the yard of the defunct Presbyterian Church, in Middletown, but was removed to the Baptist Churchyard, in the same village, where it stands adjacent to the monument recently erected

It was a by-word that Sally Shepherd worshiped God and Abel Morgan

The Rev Mr. Morgan wore enormous big, plug, beaver hats, which were left in the garret of Capt Moses Shepherd, 17, till destroyed by moth and age Capt Moses Shepherd settled his estate Their farms were contiguous, Morgan's house and farm being upon the site of the Col Elias Conover farm, on Middletown Turnpike going to Red Bank

14 MARY SHEPHERD, daughter of Joseph Shepherd, 2, was born Sept 1, 1737 She was a twin with Sarah Shepherd, and married James Winter, who died in the Sugar House, New York, during the Revolutionary War

Issue

Deborah Winter, married Timothy Mount
Andrew Winter, married Rachel Bowne
Sarah Winter
A daughter

16 THOMAS SHEPHERD, son of Joseph Shepherd, 2, was born in 1741 At what time he left Middletown I do not know, but he was of the adventurous type, and left simply with a gun and an axe He founded Shepherd's Town, W Va

MISS ODETTE TYLER MARRIED
THE ACTRESS IS NOW THE WIFE OF MR
REZIN D SHEPHERD, OF SHEPHERDSTOWN, W VA

[By Telegraph to the New York Herald]

Shepherdstown, W Va, April 27, 1897 —Mr Rezin Davis Shepherd and his bride who was Miss Elizabeth Lee Kirkland, daughter of General William W Kirkland, better known by her stage name of Odette Tyler, arrived here this afternoon, and will spend part of their honeymoon at Mr. Shepherd's country home, Wild Goose Farm

Miss Kirkland and Mr Shepherd were married by the Rev Dr Roderick Terry in New York on April 1 The first public announcement of the event was made in the Shepherdstown register last Thursday, Mr Shepherd having communicated the news in a letter to his mother, who resides here

Mr Shepherd was a widower at the time of his marriage His first wife was the well known actress, Marie Prescott, who died in New York city in August, 1893, after little more than a year of married life Mr Shepherd himself was an actor, appearing under the name of McLean, as the leading man in Miss Prescott's company He has not been on the stage since her death

Mr Shepherd comes of an old and distinguished Virginian family, his ancestors being the founders of this town which bears their name He is about thirty-eight years old, and is the eldest son of the late Colonel Henry Shepherd, who was the wealthiest man, probably, in this county From his father he inherited a considerable fortune, including the estate of about four hundred acres of land known as Wild Goose Farm, which is the finest country seat in this section

The Shepherds were very prominent in business circles in New Orleans years ago, and are related to the Brookses, of Boston

Mr and Mrs Shepherd were warmly received here by his mother and brother They will remain at Wild Goose Farm until Thursday evening, when they will go to New York On Saturday they will sail for Europe Mrs Shepherd will fill her contract to play a three weeks' engagement in ' Secret Service" in London

They will then return to the United States, and it is their present intention to settle at Wild Goose Farm, and Mrs Shepherd says she will not go upon the stage again

Mr. and Mrs Shepherd desired that their marriage should be kept secret until they had sailed for Europe, on Saturday, and requested that no announcement should be made until Sunday next

17   CAPT MOSES SHEPHERD, son of Joseph Shepherd, 2, was not quite twenty-one when he married Rebecca, daughter of John and Mercy (Burrows) Stillwell, by license dated Mch 23, 1767, and she was not quite twenty-five   He died Nov 16, 1819, and his wife, Rebecca, died, Nov 2, 1839, aged 98 years, 1 month and 26 days   They are interred in the Stillwell graveyard, on the Joseph Field farm, on the turnpike between Middletown and Red Bank

Capt Moses Shepherd was a Revolutionary officer, and served eight years in the Revolutionary War   Just after the Revolution, he built a house, which is now standing, (1890), next to Elias Conover's farm on the road to Red Bank

Rebecca Stillwell, wife of Capt Moses Shepherd, worshiped her brother, Joseph Stillwell, her father, and the Rev Abel Morgan, "her trinity"   Joseph Stillwell esteemed her judgment, and rode more than once from Trenton, where he was a member of the Legislature, to her home, to obtain her views on matters of public moment

1836, Dec 21   Will of Rebecca Shepherd, "old and feeble," on record at Freehold, N. J, proved Dec 11, 1839, mentioned
Son, Thomas Shepherd
And other children, but not by name

Issue

27   Thomas Shepherd, born Aug 17 or 18, 1780, died, May 24, 1865, in his 85th year
      He was a Judge, Justice, etc
28   Rebecca Shepherd, married Thomas Fields

Issue

Thomas Fields
Joseph Fields   He resided on the old Stillwell farm, near Red Bank, on the Middletown turnpike, and died, Apr. 1, 1897, aged nearly 105 years.
29   Ann Shepherd; married James Lewis.
30   Joseph Shepherd, married Nancy Stillwell
31   Moses Shepherd, married Mary Layton, perhaps a daughter of Isaac Layton
32   Elisha Shepherd, died an infant.
33   Richard Shepherd, died an infant

19   ELISHA SHEPHERD, son of Thomas Shepherd, 3, was born, at Millstone, N J, July 16, 1750, and died, in Ohio, in 1834

He served in the Revolution as Sergeant, fought in the Battle of Monmouth, and was confined, as a prisoner of war, in the Provost's prison   While there he suffered from poor food and cold, and waking one morning, found a dead man on either side of him   He twice escaped from the British soldiers, only to be recaptured, and his descendants still tell of his adventures and hairbreadth escapes

His great-grandson, S M Schanck, Esq, of Hightstown, N J, says that Capt. Elisha Shepherd was taken prisoner, at Colt's Neck, by Capt Tye, and imprisoned in the Hangman's Jail, afterwards the Hall of Records, New York City   In an effort to recapture Elisha Shepherd, the lamented Dr and Col Forman, if I remember rightly, were killed

"Elisha Shepherd was tall and slender, with blue eyes, square forehead, nose inclined to Roman, and a slight catch in his speech when excited   He was a great reader, was kind and affectionate, and very neat"

SHEPHERD OF MONMOUTH COUNTY

He married Alletta, daughter of John and Elizabeth (Conover) Smock, who was born Mch 16, 1753.

Issue

34 Thomas Shepherd, born Oct 12, 1770.
35 John Shepherd, born Mch. 21, 1773
36 Sarah Shepherd, born May 1, 1775
37 Elisha Shepherd, born June 1, 1776
38 Elizabeth Shepherd, born Apr 28, 1778
39 Alletta Shepherd, born Dec. 1, 1779
40 Henry Shepherd, born July 9, 1781
41 Jacob Shepherd, born Apr. 20, 1783.
42 Amelia Shepherd, born Mch 6, 1785, married Thomas Christopher
43 Eleanor Shepherd, born July 20, 1787
44 George Shepherd, born Feb. 20, 1789
45 Clementina Shepherd, born Sept 12, 1791

20 AMELIA SHEPHERD, daughter of Thomas Shepherd, 3, was born Feb 14, 1753, married William Lippincott, by whom she had several sons

Amelia Shepherd also had a son by Shore Stevenson, who was baptized, at Christ Church, Shrewsbury, in 1770, as Benoni—son of my sorrow—Hebrew Under Benoni is written in lead pencil, "now Benjamin of New York " Benoni or Benjamin Stevenson, left off the final syllable "on," of his name, and was the father of John L Stevens, the traveler

21 CLEMENCE SHEPHERD, daughter of Thomas Shepherd, 3, was born Feb 7, 1755, and married Thomas Lloyd.

*Issue**

Thomas Lloyd, born Sept. 11, 1770.
Clementina Lloyd, born Apr. 13, 1775
Clementina Lloyd, born Mch 19, 1777.
John Lloyd, born May 30, 1780.
Sarah Lloyd, born Aug 4, 1782, [single]
Elisha Lloyd, born June 5, 1784.
William Lloyd, born Sept 8, 1786
Charles Lloyd, born Jan 10, 1790
Mary Lloyd, born July 1, 1793, [married Dr Van Meul]
Clemence Lloyd, born Nov 3, 1796
Betsey Lloyd, born June 1, 1798.

27 THOMAS SHEPHERD, ESQ , of Middletown, son of Capt Moses Shepherd, 17, was born Aug. 17 or 18, 1780, died, May 24, 1865, in his 85th year, married, Apr 11, 1802, Helena, daughter of Abraham and Mary (Willett) Stout, who was born Mch 11, 1782 He was the only son of Capt. Moses Shepherd, living, in 1844 He was a Judge, Justice, etc , and Asher Taylor, Esq , said that Thomas Shepherd and his sons "were square men "

Issue

46 Ann Shepherd, born Mch 11, 1803, eldest daughter, died, single, aged 30 years
47 Rebecca Shepherd, born Oct 28, 1804, married Mr Winter

*From a Bible owned by Mrs Sarah E Layton, nee Lloyd, Washington and Borden Streets, Red Bank, N J

48 Joseph Shepherd, born Oct 12, 1806
49 Catharine Shepherd, born Feb. 2, 1809.
50 Lucy Shepherd, born May 6, 1810, married, when well advanced in life, Cornelius Conover No issue.
51 Thomas Shepherd, born Jan 20, 1814.
52 Thomas P Shepherd, born Dec 23, 1816, died, in the South, unmarried, aged 23 years. He was a brilliant man.
53 Helena Shepherd, born June 24, 1819; married Fred H Rickers, of New York
54 Mary Shepherd, born Jan 28, 1822.
55 Mary E. Shepherd, born July 27, 1824, married Silas Shepherd, of New York, who was of no kin. She died, at Middletown, of apoplexy, Friday, Apr. 27, 1894

30 JOSEPH SHEPHERD, son of Capt Moses Shepherd, 17, married Ann (Nancy) Stillwell, daughter of John, son of Thomas, son of Thomas and Alice (Throckmorton) Stillwell They were both wealthy Joseph Shepherd was drowned

Issue

56 William Shepherd, of New York

31 MOSES SHEPHERD, son of Capt Moses Shepherd, 17, married Mary Layton.
1823, Apr 9 Will of Moses Shepherd, of Freehold, N J, proved Apr. 30, 1823, mentioned his children as given below.

Issue

57 Hannah Shepherd, married James Conover.
58 Joseph Shepherd, married Lydia, daughter of Sheriff Craig.
59 Adeline Shepherd, married Stephen Field
60 John Shepherd, married, first, Miss Bedle, second, Lydia Cooper.
61 Thomas Shepherd, married Lucy Field
62 Mary Shepherd, married Mr McChesney.

34 THOMAS SHEPHERD, son of Elisha Shepherd, 19, was born Oct. 12, 1770, and married Nellie Schenck, "one of the chunkies" He removed to Hamilton County, Ohio, and had issue.

35 JOHN SHEPHERD, son of Elisha Shepherd, 19, was born Mch 21, 1773, and married Anne Covenhoven

Issue

63 Barnes Smock Shepherd, baptized May 21, 1793
64 Ida Shepherd; baptized Nov 6, 1798

36 SARAH SHEPHERD, daughter of Elisha Shepherd, 19, was born May 1, 1775, and married Peter Voorhees, son of Koert and Sarah (Voorhees) Schenck
Sarah Shepherd Schenck died about 1807, and was buried near the church, in the yard of the old "Brick Church," Marlboro, N J, and when the church was enlarged, it covered her grave

Issue

Elisha Schenck, married, first, Ida Schenck, second, Catherine Craig
Sarah Schenck, married Hendrick V B Schenck.
Gertrude Schenck, born Jan 31, 1802, married Roger Haddock Whitlock
Henry Schenck, born Jan 24, 1805, married Mary Ann Mount

37 ELISHA SHEPHERD, son of Elisha Shepherd, 19, was born June 1, 1776, and married, Dec 24, 1796, Nelly van Kirk

Issue

65 Elisha Shepherd, baptized Apr 4, 1800
66 Eleanor Shepherd, baptized Sept 25, 1802, "given by her father as her Mother is deceased."

38 ELIZABETH SHEPHERD, daughter of Elisha Shepherd, 19, was born Apr 28, 1778, and married Albert Conover.

Issue

Elinor Conover, married John Lambert
Clementine Conover, married Samuel Gilman
Peter Conover, married Catherine Raymond
Elisha Conover, married Mary D Schenck
Daniel Conover, married Sarah Shepherd
Sarah Conover, single
George Conover, married Agnes Craton

39 ALLETTA SHEPHERD, daughter of Elisha Shepherd, 19, was born Dec 1, 1779, and married David George

Issue

Thomas George
Eliza George
Sarah George
Alletta George, baptized June 1, 1797.
Rachel George, baptized Jan. 4, 1799
Elisha George; baptized Mch. 23, 1801.
Joel George, baptized Apr. 5, 1803.
Peter Schenck George, baptized Apr. 23, 1805.

40 HENRY SHEPHERD, son of Elisha Shepherd, 19, was born July 9, 1781, and married Elizabeth .....

Issue

67 Margaret Shepherd, married Mr. Brokaw.
68 Reune Shepherd
69 Vandervere Shepherd
70 Sarah Shepherd

43 ELEANOR SHEPHERD, daughter of Elisha Shepherd, 19, was born July 20, 1787, and married, first, Francis Gustin, second, Mr Christopher

Issue

Alletta Gustin ⎫
Sarah Ann Gustin ⎬ baptized June 9, 1814, after their father's death.
John Gustin ⎭

48 JOSEPH SHEPHERD, son of Thomas Shepherd, 27, was born Oct. 12, 1806, was a lawyer of Red Bank, N J, and married Elizabeth, daughter of John and Sarah (Hopping) Dorn.

Issue
71 Elmira Shepherd, married James A Greer, of New York City, parents of Mrs. Frank Tilford, of New York City.
72 Mary Elizabeth Shepherd, married Dr Edward Sutton Smith, of New York City.
73 Helen Shepherd, married Grover H Lufborrow, of Middletown, N J, and has two daughters
74 Kate Shepherd, living, single, in 1894
75 Anna Shepherd, married Dr Charles H. White, of Red Bank, N. J

56 WILLIAM SHEPHERD, of New York, son of Joseph Shepherd, 30, married Catharine, daughter of Thomas Conway

Issue
76 Anna Shepherd, married Mr Paulison
77 Matilda Shepherd, married Robert Folds.
78 Charles Shepherd
79 William Henry Shepherd

58 JOSEPH SHEPHERD, son of Moses Shepherd, 31, married Lydia, daughter of Sheriff Craig

Issue
80 Mary Ann Shepherd, married Mr. Patterson.
81 Hannah Shepherd, married Mr. Rogers
82 John Shepherd
83 Charles Shepherd
84 Eveline Shepherd, married Mr Perrine
85 Matilda Shepherd

60 JOHN SHEPHERD, son of Moses Shepherd, 31, married, first, Amy Bedle, second, Lydia Cooper.

Issue by first wife
86 Thomas Edgar Shepherd, born July 16, 1827
87 Louisa Shepherd, born Oct 22, 1825.

Issue by second wife
88 Sarah Ann Shepherd } twins
89 Mary Elizabeth Shepherd, unmarried
90 Emma Shepherd, married Job Compton, his second wife   No issue.
91 Hannah Shepherd, married Job Compton, his third wife   No issue.
92 Rebecca Shepherd
93 William Genry Shepherd; died young.
94 Conover Shepherd; died young.

86 THOMAS EDGAR SHEPHERD, son of John Shepherd, 60, was born July 16, 1827, and married, June 1, 1851, Margaret Pool, daughter of William and Eliza (Pool) Carhart, born

Apr 24, 1831 He was a highly respected citizen, in Matawan, N J , in 1890 They were both living in 1899

Issue

95 Emma Louisa Shepherd, born July 26, 1855, died July 13, 1857
96 Mary Ada Shepherd, born July 21, 1858
97 George B Shepherd, born Mch 3, 1863

87 LOUISA SHEPHERD, daughter of John Shepherd, 60, was born Oct 22, 1825, and married David W. Waters. She was living, in Matawan, N J , in 1899

Issue

Louisa Waters; married Capt Watson H Fisher

88 SARAH ANN SHEPHERD, daughter of John Shepherd, 60, married Joseph Candee, of New York City.

Issue

John Candee
Katherine Candee
Lyman Candee

92 REBECCA SHEPHERD, daughter of John Shepherd, 60, married William Morris

Issue

Burt Morris
Frederick Morris
William Morris

97 GEORGE B SHEPHERD, son of Thomas Edgar Shepherd, 86, was born Mch 3, 1863, and married Sarah Crook

Issue

98 William Shepherd, born Dec 28, 1896

MISCELLANEOUS NOTES

Mrs Mary E. Shepherd, of Middletown, N J , said "The ancestor came from the clothing district of England " That the Shepherds were Irish, i e , those spelling it Shepard, and that one of them, from West Jersey, got the full Shepherd family history some years ago, (1890)

Mrs Shepherd also said that tradition says that John, Thomas and Joseph Shepherd were the first comers to America One settled in New England, one in West Jersey and one in Middletown

"I have found descendants of one of these four brothers David, John, James and Thomas —viz , of Thomas He had a wife, Ann, sons, David and Moses, and daughters, who married Joseph Shepherd and Silas Irland Thomas died in 1739 His descendants are the Shepherds of Penn Yan, and the late Prof Nathan Shepherd, of Saratoga Springs" Letters of Mr E N Shepherd, in 1889, 649 Jersey Ave , Jersey City, N J

Thomas Shepherd had sons
    John
    Joseph
    Thomas
    Ebenezer   See Wyman's Charlestown Estates.

Thomas Shepherd did not go back to Boston "I could never see any connection with the Salem County family." Mr E N Shepherd

While there is some doubt as to the degree, there can hardly arise a doubt as to the fact of kinship between the early Shepherds and Shephards in this country. The great similarity of given names Thomas, Moses, Ebenezer, used alike by them all, would force one to this conclusion, even if other evidence were wanting

For further study of this family see Shourd's History of Fenwick's Colony, and Savage's New England Genealogical Dictionary

John Shepherd, born in Halifax, had a sister, Theresa, wife of a Gov.-General, of Halifax He (i e John Shepherd), married Hannah Neat, of South Carolina. He was confidential dispatch bearer to Washington, while at the headquarters, in Newburgh, N Y He had a son, John, born, in the old house, June 13, 1777 This son became Alderman of 5th Ward, New York City, 1824–25 He married Hannah, daughter of Silas Barber, whose wife was Miss Klein, of Utica, N Y John and Hannah Shepherd had several children, among them Silas, who married Mary E Shepherd, 55, of Middletown These Shepherd families were not related Both John Shepherd and Silas Barber fought at Bunker Hill, and the former also at Lexington.

SPICER

OF

NEW YORK AND NEW JERSEY

THOMAS SPICER, an Englishman, was residing, in Newport, R I , July 16, 1638, where he signed the Civil Compact.   Bartlett's Rhode Island Records, Vol. I, p 70.

In 1642, he was of Portsmouth, R I., where he was chosen to lay out the town and become its Treasurer   Bartlett's Rhode Island Records, Vol I, p 102

It is said that Samuel Spicer was of the party, led by Lady Moody, from New England to New Amsterdam, and who received from the Dutch permission to settle Gravesend, on Long Island   Thompson's History of Long Island

Such is not the case   No Spicer came with Lady Moody   The first of the name was Thomas Spicer, and Samuel Spicer was his son.

Thomas Spicer was one of the thirty-five Associates, who settled on Throg's Neck, with John Throckmorton. When Throckmorton's settlement was destroyed by the Indians, the survivors, among them Thomas Spicer and his family, found their way to the fort and settlement of New Amsterdam   Here they were when Lady Moody and her party arrived from New England   Stuyvesant gave her and her associates a patent, for land on Long Island, Dec 19, 1645, and Feb 20, 1646, a planter's lot, in this new settlement of Gravesend, was assigned to Thomas Spicer.

1643, June 25. Thomas Spicer leased from Arent Van Curler, Secretary of Rensselaerswyck, a bouwery, with a house, barn, tobacco house, etc., with an inventory of what Mr. Van Curler delivered to Mr. Spicer   New York Dutch Manuscripts.

1644, July 8 Court proceedings. Mr Moor vs Mr Spicer
In a case of attachment, on a bark belonging to Peter Lourensen and Mr Throckmorton, Lourensen is condemned to deliver the bark to Spicer agreeably to the power of attorney, on condition that the latter give security for the value of the vessel, in case Mr. Moor hereafter proves that the owner is indebted to him, when the money must be returned

1645, Sept 21 Francis Weeks sued Mr Spicer for the loss of a gun judgment for the defendant.

1645, Oct. 23. Declaration of Adam Mott that he heard William Lachem acknowledge to owe 50 guilders to Tho⁸ Spicer

1646, Dec. 17. Tho⁸ Spicer vs Tho⁸ Sanderson. Plaintiff complains that defendant keeps him out of his land, threatens his life, abuses him as a rogue & *villian* and shot one of his goats. The Court decrees that the first time Tho⁸ Spicer, or any of his neighbors, are insulted, defendant shall be banished from the Plain, the damage complained of to be assessed by the arbitrators.

1646, Dec 17. Thomas Spicer resided on the adjacent plains of Flatlands, where he temporarily moved when the Indian uprising drove him from Gravesend

New York Colonial Records.

1653, Dec 11 Tho⁸ Spicer was a member of a Convention, held at New Amsterdam, to represent the state of the country to the authorities in Holland.

O'Callahan's New Netherlands Register.

1653, Dec 11. Tho⁸ Spicer, as a representative of Gravesend, signed the remonstrance.
Idem.

Monday, 10 March, 1653
Marten Jansen, pltf vs Tho⁸ Spicer, deft
Plft states that deft is trying to eject him from the land he has hired of deft. before the expiration of the time mentioned in the contract, and that the lessor has not fulfilled his condition Wherefore pltf claims to have suffered damages agreeably to his specifications
Referred to Elbert Elbertsen and Peter Clasen, as arbitrators

Marten Jansen, Pltf vs Tho⁸ Spicer's wife, Deft
Pltf states that the deft had slandered him, that he had acted dishonorably in Holland, and was therefore compelled to remove to this country Deft demands the proof of pltf's statement.

1653, March Martin Jansen, from Bruckelen, pltf vs Elbert Elbertsen, Wᵐ. Gerritsen, Jacob Pietersen, Elcke Jansen and Gertie Jacobs, defts
Plft demands evidence of the truth of what defts heard of the slander uttered against him, by Mr Spicer's wife Defts, appearing in court, gave their testimony, yet without deposing anything of moment Martin Jansen requests by petition that since, in the matter between him and Mr Spicer, about the lands, cannot, through Mr Spicer's fault, be settled by arbitration, that their worships would please refer it to two of their board, with costs to be paid by the loser. Petition granted

April, 1653 Respecting the dispute between Martin Jansen and Mr. Tho⁸ Spicer, the arbitrators agree that·
 1 Tho⁸ Spycer consents that Martin Jansen shall have the use of the fields for his horses as he intends to ride to the ferry
 2 Spycer shall deliver a rear and front rail in the waggon
 3 Spycer shall more over deliver one good lock for the door of the dwelling house
 4 and lastly Martin Jansen may build a brew house, and an oven, on the bowery, and remove them at the expiration of the lease, or otherwise they shall remain at the pleasure of Tho⁸ Spicer, provided that said Jansen be paid for them according to appraisal of arbitrators, also Jansen agrees to keep the premises in good repair
Done in Amersfort, on Long Island, April 3, 1653   Signatures

1654, June 2 Judgment on appeal Martin Jansen vs Tho⁸ Spicer, decision of the court, of Midwout, affirmed with costs and 12 guilders fine.

1654, Oct 6 Power of attorney Arent Van Curler to Dirck Van Schelluyne, N. P., to collect rent of a farm from Tho⁸ Spicer.

1654, Oct 15 Complaint Dirck Van Schelluyne, attorney for Arent van Corler, vs Tho⁸ Spicer, for rent of a brewery [bowery?], copy to be served on defendant.

1654, Oct 15 Johannes van Twiller, of Beverwyck, merchant, gives a bond for any judgment that may be obtained by Thos Spicer against Arent van Curler.

1654, Oct. 15. Bond given by Thos Hall for any judgment that may be obtained by Arent van Curler against Thos Spicer

1654, Oct 15. Henry Breeser mortgages his house lot & garden, on Manhattan I^d, as collateral security, to Thos Spicer & John Hall, for a bond signed by them

1654, Oct. 20 Motion To postpone the case of Van Curler vs Spicer, granted.

Burgomasters' Records, City Hall, New York

In 1656, Thos Spicer, with Jacob and Samuel, were Freeholders, at Gravesend

In 1657 and 1658, Thos Spicer was a Magistrate, of Gravesend.

1658, Sept. 30 Will of Thomas Spicer, on record at Gravesend; proved Nov 4, 1658, mentioned:
Wife, Michal
Son, Samuel
Two devisees, undoubtedly his daughters·
Ann, wife of John Lake, who received 60 guilders
Susannah, wife of Henry Brasier, who received 80 guilders.
To the town of Gravesend, he made a bequest for the repairs of the highway
Executors His wife, Machiel, and his son, Samuel.

Mical, the scriptural name with which Thomas Spicer's wife was burdened, has been a source of considerable confusion to genealogists, appearing as it does in many forms of spelling. Bergen, in his work on Kings County, calls her Michael, and makes her, her husband's son

1661, Feb. 17 Proceedings against Mrs Micah Spicer for entertaining George Wilson, a Quaker

1662, Oct. 5. Sentence of banishment against Michal Spicer and Samuel, her son, for harboring Quakers, and distributing seditious and seducing pamphlets, to propagate their heresy.

"Michale Spicer and her son, Samuel, had suffered much for truth, especially Samuel, who had suffered sore imprisonment, even unto death, and much spoiling of their goods, (at Gravesend by the Dutch) " Bishop's "New England Judged," p 423, also quoted by other authors, copying from Bishop, and, perhaps, noticed by Besse, in "Suffering of the Quakers," and Sewall's "History of the Quakers"

1665, Nov. 25 Micah Spicer, for 125 guilders wampum value, sold the property, now known as Bergen's Island, in Flatlands, to Elbert Elbertse Stoothoof. and again, she conveyed her house and lot, in Gravesend, to Carston Johnson

"In 1669, thirty acres of land, on Throckmorton's neck, were granted to Mrs Micah Spicer" Upon the 12 of January, 1686, Spicer's and Brockett's Necks, (commonly called the Grove farm), were confirmed by letters patent, under the great seal of the Province, to Thomas Hunt, etc The Spicers and Brocketts were doubtless some of the associates of John Throckmorton

At a Court of Assizes, held November 15, 1669, Mrs Micah Spicer sued for thirty acres of land, on Throckmorton's Neck Assize Record 225. Bolton's "Westchester," Vol II, p 149

1670. In the Court of the West Riding of Yorkshire, she appeared as pltf , in a suit against Mr Curles for 70 guilders sewant Judgment was given in her favor, when the Court was informed that "Mr Goulding, the vandue master, hath so much in his hands" as would satisfy the debt

1670, June. Memorandum that Mrs Spicer had made good her title to part of Throckmorton's Neck or Spicer's Neck Warrant to lay out for Micah Spicer, thirty acres of land, with meadow in proportion, on Throgmorton's Neck, with assignment of said lands, by Mrs Spicer to Mathias Nicolls, June 19, 1671

1675, June 8 Judgment in the case of Mrs Micall Spicer, widow, against Robert Coe, at the Sessions, at Jamaica, L I ; bill of costs

Issue

2 Samuel Spicer
3 Ann Spicer; married John Lake
4 Susannah Spicer; married first, William Wathems, says Bergen, second, Henry Brasier

2 SAMUEL SPICER, son of Thomas Spicer, 1, was, probably, born, in Rhode Island, about 1640 He was a landholder, in Gravesend, in 1656, which implies he had reached at least the age of sixteen years—for this was the age at which youths were expected to take up arms and which brought with it citizens' rights

His name frequently appears on the records as arbitrator, executor, witness, etc

In 1658, he was an executor of his father's will.

1661, Jan 9. Samuel Spicer was arrested; Jan. 13, indicted; and Jan 20, "Tried and sentenced as a Quaker"; fine £12.

In the Monmouth Patent, in 1664, he is mentioned as a Patentee. He received two allotments of land, in Middletown, in the first division of lands, which occurred in 1667

1670, 29, 4 mo Samuel Spicer was one of the representatives from Gravesend, in settling the boundary of the town, and F De Bruyne's lands.

1673 He was Magistrate, of Gravesend, and held the same position as late as 1684

1680, June 16 Samuel Spicer was sworn as Constable, of Gravesend.

1682, 30, 10 mo Samuel Spicer attended the Friends' Quarterly Meeting, at Flushing

In 1684, Samuel Spicer was a Justice of the Peace, at Gravesend

1684, Nov. 11 A warrant was issued, appointing Samuel Spicer and others, a committee to inspect and audit the accounts of the Sheriffs, of Long Island, since 1674, and also of all fines, rates and public fees, etc , and to make return thereof to his Excellency before the first Monday of November next.

1685, Mch 25, Oct 9, and Oct 20 He was then of Gravesend.

In the spring and fall of 1685, he made three or more considerable sales of his property, in Gravesend, and at the same time purchased from Samuel Cole, a large tract, situated in what is now known as Stockton township, Camden County, N. J This property was described as "lying on the North Side of Cooper's Creek and fronting on the Delaware," and the purchaser thereof was then of Gravesend, L I This last property of Spicers was directly in the line of most travel, to accommodate which, he established a ferry—primitive in the extreme and consisting of one flat bottomed boat—which served, however, for the needs of that day, and was known for years afterwards as Spicer's Ferry

In 1687-8, he was executor to the will of John Tilton.

In 1687, he was appointed one of the Judges of the Courts of Gloucester County, and also to positions of minor importance

"At a Court held at Portland Point, [Middletown, Monmouth County, N. J.], Nov. 2, 1689, William and James Bowne, of the town of Middletown, were appointed to act as Patentees, in the room of John Tilton & Samuel Spicer, of Gravesend, according to an order under both their hands."

Samuel Spicer married Hester or Esther Tilton, daughter of John and Mary Tilton, of Gravesend, at Oyster Bay, 21, 3 mo., 1665. She was born "1647."

Issue

5 Abraham Spicer, born Oct 27, 1666, (27, 8 mo.)* There was an Abraham Spicer who died, at Gravesend, July 26, 1679, (died 26, 5 mo., 1679), "died before his parents."
6 Jacob Spicer, born Mch. 20, 1668, (20, 1 mo.)
7 Mary Spicer, born Oct. 20, 1671, (20, 8 mo.) A Mary Spicer married, in 1706, Joseph Brown. Elsewhere it is said she married Jeremiah Bates.
8 Sarah Spicer, born June 19, 1674, (19, 4 mo.), died 1, 5 mo., *1667* [?]
9 Martha Spicer, born Jan 27, 1676, (27, 11 mo.) Martha Spicer died 29, 2 mo., 1677 Elsewhere Martha Spicer is stated to have married, first, Joseph Brown, second, Thomas Chalkley There were probably two children of this name.
10 Sarah Spicer, born Feb. 16, 1677, (16, 12 mo.), married, in 1695, Daniel Cooper Records of Newtown Meeting
11 Abigail Spicer, born Mch 26, 1683, (26, 1 mo.); married Daniel Stanton
12 Thomas Spicer
13 Samuel Spicer, died unmarried

6 JACOB SPICER, son of Samuel Spicer, 2, was born, at Gravesend, L. I., 1668. He married Sarah ———, who died July 25, 1742

"There is no authentic account at what time he studied law, but it is likely before he left his native state Tradition says he resided a few years near Mullica Hill, Gloucester County, where he owned a large quantity of land A portion of it is now owned by John W Hazleton Jacob Spicer's house stood near the King's Highway, running from Salem to Burlington Spicer in a few years removed to Cape May County and made that county his permanent home He was active in the affairs of West Jersey, and he and Jonathan Leaming wrote a work on the laws of West Jersey It is often referred to by the professional legal men from that time to the present day Jacob Spicer died, near Cold Spring Inlet, Cape May County, 17th 4mo., 1741, aged about 73 years, and was buried in the Presbyterian Graveyard near that place."†
From a newspaper article by Shourd

"In memory of Col Jacob Spicer, who died, April 17, 1741, aged 73 years"
"Death thou hast conquered me
"I by thy darts am slain
"But Christ shall conquer thee
"And I shall rise again"

"Jacob Spicer, Esq, departed this life, Sept. 17th, 1765, in the 49th year of his age."
"If aught that's good or great could save
"Spicer had never seen the grave"

"His wife, who lies by his side, has upon her monument
"Judith Spicer, departed this life, Sept 7th, 1747, in the 33rd year of her age,"
"Virtue and piety give way to death,
"Or else the entombed had ne'er resigned her breath"

"The preceding inscriptions are copied from monuments in an old graveyard, now overgrown with timber, at Cold Spring They commemorate a father and son, who occupied prom-

---

*The Quaker dates are taken from Shourd's Salem County, N J, newspaper articles, while the others were obtained from F G Bergen, Esq ; also from Proceedings N J Historical Society, 2nd Series, Vol 13, p 49, and Friends' Records of New York and Vicinity, published in New York Gen and Biog Record
†This article by Shourd is wrong, he confuses father and son Beesley sets him straight

inent stations in society in their day " From Barber and Howes' Historical Collections of New Jersey, p. 128

Among the constituents who purchased a parsonage for the Cold Spring Presbyterian Church, in 1721, was Col. Jacob Spicer. New York Genealogical Record, April, 1873.

11 ABIGAIL SPICER, daughter of Samuel Spicer, 2, born Mch. 26, 1683; died May, 1714; married, circ. 1707, Daniel, son of Daniel and Elizabeth (Woolley) Stanton, born Apr. 19, 1682, died 1708

Issue

    Daniel Stanton, born 1708, after the death of his father, died June 29, 1770, married, Apr. 5, 1733, Sarah, daughter of John Lloyd.

12 THOMAS SPICER, son of Samuel Spicer, 2, born, according to N J Archives, Vol XX, p. 474, prior to 1686; married Abigail, daughter of Francis and Sarah Davenport. He made his will Jan. 4, 1759, and it was proved Nov. 7, 1759

Issue

14 Samuel Spicer, born Oct. 29, 1720, died 1777, married, first, by license dated Aug. 3, 1743, Abigail Willard, died Apr 24, 1752, second, Sarah Potter, of Shrewsbury.
15 Thomas Spicer, will dated May 4, 1760; proved 1760; married, by license dated Dec. 29, 1740, Rebecca, daughter of Humphrey and Jane Day
16 Jacob Spicer, died Oct. 31, 1779, married Mary Lippincott, no issue.

MISCELLANEOUS NOTES

The best published history of the Spicer family appears in "Sketches of the First Emigrant Settlers, in Newtown Township, old Gloucester County, West New Jersey," by John Clement, of Haddonfield, N J., 1877, pp. 293 to 300.

See also many references in Documentary History of New Jersey.

For many references to the Spicers of Cape May, see "Geological Survey of New Jersey, Cape May County, Trenton, 1857," by Kitchell and Cook, which contains an extensive historical and genealogical article on Cape May County, by Dr Maurice Beesley. See pp 164, 173, 178–9, 180–1, 185, 186, 190, 191, 193, 194, 198, 203 and 205

For Peter Spicer, of New London, in 1666, and family, see Savage; they are, apparently, no kin
"Peter Spicer died, probably, in 1695 He was one of the resident farmers in that part of the township which is now Ledyard. We find him a landholder, in 1666 The inventory of his estate was presented to the Judge of probate, by his wife, in 1695 From her settlement of the estate, it would appear that the children were Edward, Samuel, Peter, William, Joseph, Abigail, Ruth, Hannah and Jane Capt Abel Spicer, of the Revolutionary Army, was of this family " From "History of New London, Conn ," by N. M. Caulkins, p 335

Of Jacob Spicer, who was of Gravesend, in 1656, of Flatlands, in 1684, and again, of Gravesend, in 1691, we have no positive information He is not mentioned in the will of Thomas Spicer, the First, and therefore seems more likely to have been his brother than his son; that he was closely related there can be no doubt

STOUT

of

MONMOUTH COUNTY*

1 RICHARD STOUT, an early settler in this country and the founder of the large family bearing his name, was reputed the son of John Stout, of Nottinghamshire, England Tradition has it that he left England because of friction with his father, who interfered with his love affairs, which drove him to engage on a man-of-war for seven years, at the end of which time he received his discharge at New Amsterdam The tradition may be truthful, but if the printed statement is correct that he was forty years of age when he married Penelope Van Princis, after allowing seven years for ship service and three additional years between his discharge and marriage, he would still have been about thirty years old when this rupture occurred, an age when parental intrusion and discipline in love affairs is hardly likely, but if so, might have been resented in the manner accredited to him The assertion that Richard Stout was of "good family," which implies social caste, and that the cause of the disturbance between father and son was a threatened misalliance also may be true, but we have no proof of the social position of John Stout, and as an argument against it there is the fact that Richard Stout, his son, was not an educated man, when education was common The answer to this is the presumption that Richard Stout was probably a headstrong character, not likely to be coerced into scholarly attainments These statements, and more, are set forth in certain published articles concerning the Stout family, in which Penelope, the wife of Richard, is a conspicuous figure The first of these to appear was the account printed in Samuel Smith's History of New Jersey, published at Burlington, N J., in 1765 A second version appeared in print in Morgan Edwards' Materials Towards A History Of The Baptists in Jersey, published in 1792. These two versions have much in common, but are still so dissimilar that it is evident that their sources of origin were totally different. Edwards projected A History of the American Baptists, in a series of twelve state Baptist church histories The first of these was published in 1770, on Pennsylvania. Then came a long gap, doubtless largely occasioned by the War, and then appeared, in 1792, the volume on New Jersey None followed, as it was a losing venture to the author, though the price was put at one-fourth of one dollar each and the issue limited to five hundred copies. His complaint about neglect was well founded, when the modest

---

*Occasional efforts have been made to compile a genealogy of the Stout family, but in nearly all instances it has been restricted to a single branch The greatness of the undertaking will probably continue to deter all but an enthusiastic genealogist from ever undertaking such a work, which must grow more difficult with time Such incomplete data as I have brought together will, however, be of some assistance if one is ever undertaken I cannot vouch for the accuracy of *all* the names, dates and statements, but believe in the main that they are correct

charge and the labor were considered, but he had entered a field, then as now, unappreciated except by the few historical and genealogical students While his second volume was published in 1792, the preface shows that the work was finished by the writer May 1, 1790, and no doubt its compilation took some years Exactly how long can only be surmised, but as the article on the Stouts, (under the church at Hopewell), was contributed by the Rev Oliver Hart to Mr Edwards, and as his incumbency as pastor of the Hopewell church dates from Dec 16, 1780, it could not have antedated this year 1780, but probably was written between 1785 and 1789

It is from these two sources that later historians, writers and genealogists largely derive their information Benedict, in his History of the Baptists, edition of 1813, (Vol. I, pp. 573-574), draws entirely from Morgan Edwards, as does Barber's Historical Collections of New Jersey, edition of 1868, pp. 259-260 Raum too, in his History of Trenton, N J., 1871, pp 58-59, follows the Edwards text, but misleads in stating that he gives the narrative verbatim. This he does not do, for a superficial comparison shows an embellished text, which, with the erroneous statement that the book was published in 1790, when it was really printed in 1792, leads one to seek another publication when one does not really exist.

The Smith and Edwards publications are reproduced here verbatim, being necessary for a proper appreciation of the dates involved That the tradition concerning Penelope Stout's experience with the Indians is true is, to my mind, as certain as that man now exists. Her hardiness to have outlived, for eighty-four years, her mutilation at the hands of the Indians, her extraordinary longevity reaching one hundred and ten years, and her enormous progeny, would tend to make her a much-talked-of individual, and Smith, who wrote concerning her, less than thirty-three years after her death, must have met many who knew her in life, and Edwards was not far behind him in chronicling the same tale from other sources Then, we have the remarkable verification of her scars by her descendants, as given by Mrs Seabrook Surely there is no room for doubt, and though some seemingly fanciful accretions may have accumulated around the story in time, they are more likely to be facts with misplaced dates, such as the episode of the Indian aiding her escape in the threatened uprising, rather than actual errors.

CASE OF A STRANGER, REMARKABLY SAVED AMONG THE INDIANS

While New York was in possession of the Dutch, about the time of the Indian war in New-England, a Dutch ship coming from Amsterdam, was stranded on Sandy Hook, [2] but the passengers got on shore, among them was a young Dutchman who had been sick most of the voyage, he was taken so bad after landing, that he could not travel; and the other passengers being afraid of the Indians, would not stay till he recovered, but made what haste they could to New Amsterdam, his wife however would not leave him, the rest promised to send as soon as they arrived They had not been long gone, before a company of Indians coming down to the water side, discovered them on the beach, and hastening to the spot, soon killed the man, and cut and mangled the woman in such a manner that they left her for dead She had strength enough to crawl up to some old logs not far distant, and getting into a hollow one, lived mostly in it for several days, subsisting in part by the excrescences that grew from it, the Indians had left some fire on the shore, which she kept together for warmth having remained in this manner for some time, an old Indian and a young one coming down to the beach found her, they were soon in high words, which she afterwards understood was a dispute, the former being for keeping her alive, the other for dispatching After they had debated the point a while, the first hastily took her up, and tossing her upon his shoulder, carried her to a place near where Middletown now stands, where he dressed her wounds and soon cured her After some time the Dutch in New-Amsterdam hearing of a white woman among the Indians, concluded who it must be and some of them came to her relief, the old man her preserver, gave her the choice either to go or stay, she chose the first. A while after marrying to one Stout, they lived together at Middletown among other Dutch inhabitants, the old Indian who saved her life, used frequently to visit her, at one of his visits she observed him to be more pensive than common, and sitting down he gave three heavy sighs, after the last she thought herself at liberty to ask him what was the matter? He told her he had

STOUT OF MONMOUTH COUNTY

something to tell her in friendship, tho' at the risk of his own life, which was, that the Indians were that night to kill all the whites, and advised her to go off for New-Amsterdam, she asked him how she could get off? he told her he had provided a canoe at a place which he named. Being gone from her, she sent for her husband out of the field, and discovered the matter to him, who not believing it, she told him the old man *never deceived her*, and that she with her children would go, accordingly going to the place appointed, they found the canoe and paddled off When they were gone, the husband began to consider the thing, and sending for five or six of his neighbours, they set upon their guard About midnight they heard the dismal war-hoop, presently came up a company of Indians, they first expostulated, and then told them, if they persisted in their bloody design, they would sell their lives very dear Their arguments prevailed, the Indians desisted, and entered into a league of peace, which was kept without violation From this woman, thus remarkably saved, with her scars visible, through a long life, is descended a numerous posterity of the name of Stout, now inhabiting New-Jersey At that time there were supposed to be about fifty families of white people, and five hundred Indians inhabiting those parts

z Other accounts say in Delaware, nigh Christeen, but this is most likely to be true.

History of New Jersey, Samuel Smith, Burlington, 1765, pp 65 et al

The family of the Stouts are so remarkable for their number, origin and character in both church and state that I cannot forbear bestowing a post-script upon them, and no place can be so proper as that of *Hopewell*, where the bulk of the family resides We have already seen that Jonathan Stout and family were the seed of Hopewell church, and the beginning of *Hopewell* settlement, and that of the 15 which constituted the church, nine were Stouts. the church was constituted at the house of a Stout, and the meetings were held chiefly at the dwellings of the Stouts for 41 years, viz from the beginning of the settlement to the building of the meeting-house, before described Mr Hart is of the opinion "That from first to last, half the members have been and are of that name, for, in looking over the church book, (saith he), I find that near two hundred of the name have been added, besides about as many more of the blood of the Stouts, who had lost the name by marriages the present two deacons and four elders, are Stouts the late Zebulon and David Stout were two of its main pillars the last lived to see his offspring multiplied into a hundred and 17 souls " The origin of this Baptist family is no less remarkable, for they all sprang from one woman, and she as good as dead her history is in the mouths of her posterity, and is told as follows "She was born at Amsterdam, about the year 1602 her father's name was Vanprincis she and her first husband, (whose name is not known), sailed for New-York, (then New Amsterdam), about the year 1620 the vessel was stranded at Sandy Hook. the crew got ashore, and marched towards said New York but Penelope's (for that was her name) husband being hurt in the wreck, could not march with them, therefore, he and the wife tarried in the woods they had not been long in the place before the Indians killed them both, (as they tho't), and stripped them to the skin however, Penelope came to, tho' her skull was fractured, and her left shoulder so hacked that she could never use that arm like the other she was also cut across the abdomen so that her bowels appeared, these she kept in with her hand she continued in this situation for seven days taking shelter in a hollow tree, and eating the excres-cence of it the seventh day she saw a deer passing by with arrows sticking in it, and soon after two Indians appeared, whom she was glad to see, in hope they would put her out of her misery, accordingly, one made towards her to knock her on the head, but the other (who was an elderly man) prevented him, and throwing his match-coat about her, carried her to his wigwam, and cured her of her wounds and bruises, after that he took her to New York, and made a present of her to her countrymen, viz an Indian present, expecting ten times the value in return It was in New York that one Richard Stout married her he was a native of Old England, and of a good family she was now in her 22d year, and he in his 40th she bore him seven sons and three daughters, viz Jonathan, (founder of Hopewell), John, Richard, James, Peter, David, Benjamin, Mary, Sarah, and Alice the daughters married into the families of the Bounds, Pikes, Throgmortons and Skeltons, and so lost the name of Stout the sons married into the families of Bullen, Crawford, Ashton, Truax, these had many children, but I could not come at the names of the families into which the other brothers married The mother lived to the age of 110, and saw her offspring multiplied into 502 in about 88 years " Morgan Edwards' Materials Towards A History Of The Baptists in Jersey.

We may pass Bergen, (Early Settlers of King's County, pp 286-287), who quotes Raum and cavils at the accuracy of the tradition, and Franklin Ellis, (History of Monmouth County, N. J, pp 66-68), who follows Smith and Edwards, and, while properly taking exception to palpable errors in dates, is in error himself when he criticises the Indian attitude, which, at times, was intensely hostile With Salter and Stockton following Smith and Edwards, we may now close the list These printed histories are reinforced by manuscript histories and oral traditions Of these, a manuscript history of the Stouts was made, in 1823, by Nathan Stout. It was from a copy of this work, made by Mr. Joseph D. Hoff, of Middletown, N. J., in 1885, that I made a copy in 1892, which so far as the genealogy goes, is incorporated, as far as possible, in corrected shape, in the following contributions to the Stout family history. The narrative concerning Penelope Stout, which was the introduction to this manuscript family history, is produced in its original language further on, and is practically the same as those that have appeared in print

Of the oral traditions, those derived from the late Mrs Henry Seabrook, of Keyport, née Therese Walling, are, doubtless, the most accurate, original and entertaining. Mrs. Seabrook was an intellectually gifted woman, steeped in local genealogical lore, derived from her great ancestors. Upon their laps she sat when young, or with the assembled elders at the nearby hearthside, to be entertained by their constant repetitions of tales of exposure, hardship, love and war The old are garrulous, live in the past, delight in the young, and with contracted lives and thought they become the local historians of the past to young but willing ears, upon whose excited imagination the stories remain indelibly impressed Thus it was that Mrs Seabrook passed onward the tales of her childhood. Perhaps the most important of these was the following:

"My grandmother, Helena Huff, told me how her grandfather, John Stout, had felt the wounds of Penelope Stout, and that he blushed like a school boy She wished the knowledge of the Indian assault transmitted to her posterity and it has been done, for *there are but two hands between Penelope and me* "

"Richard Stout having passed seven years on a man of war schooner, which he had entered when he forsook his father's house, after the failure of his first love speculation, married Penelope Van Prince After a time the little Dutch woman prevailed in inducing her husband to consent to come to the future site of Middletown to settle They were accompanied by four families, tradition states, by the name of Bowne, Lawrence, Grover and Whitlock about the year 1648 The Stouts were in Middletown and Pleasant Valley, the Bownes from Chigarora Creek west and north, owning what is now Union, East and West Keyport, Brown's Point, Cliffwood, etc The Lawrence family settled at Colt's Neck, and extended north probably to Holmdel, but generally going further south, where they swarmed The Whitlocks settled at the Bay Shore near the site of the present Port Monmouth, and later between Middletown and Holmdel "

"There was the best of understanding between Penelope Stout and her Indian 'father' as she called him, although all was not rose color between the settlers and Indians A great-great-grand-daughter of hers used to relate to us grandchildren of her own, the following incident Once the Indian father refused to eat with the family which he was always in the habit of doing when coming to see them, and Mrs Stout followed him when he left the house and learned from him that his people had made arrangements to surprise and murder all the whites on the following night She lost no time in gathering the white people together, and they made their way to the Bay Shore, and entering their canoes, lay all night in them off shore, it being too dark to go to any place across the water The next day peace was made with them Later in their history, the whites of Middletown and vicinity were several weeks in a Block house which stood on the ground now occupied by the Baptist Church of that village In the Block house or fort, were born twin great grand-daughters of Penelope, one of whom was immediately named Hope Still, after a treaty of peace with the besiegers, the other was called Deliverance, the first name is still in the family, the last, we think was not repeated, owing perhaps to her dying unmarried, as our ancestors were sure to name the first children for their parents There has never failed a Richard among the Hartshornes, a Richard and John among the Stouts—a Thomas, Joe or John among Wallings,—a Hendrick in the Hendrickson and Longstreet families—or a Wilhemus in Covenhoven "

Mrs T W. Seabrook

"Richard Stout, the first of the name in America, was born in Nottinghamshire, England, and his father's name was John The said Richard when quite a young man paid his addresses to a young woman that his father thought was below his rank, upon which account some unpleasant conversation happened between the father and son, upon account of which the said Richard left his father's house and in a few days engaged on board a ship of war, where he served about seven years, at which time he got his discharge at New Amsterdam, now called New York About the same time a ship from Amsterdam in Holland, on her way to the said New Amsterdam was drove on the shore that is now called Middletown in Monmouth County in the state of New Jersey, which ship was loaded with passengers who, with much difficulty got on shore But the Indians not long after fell upon them and butchered and killed the whole crew as they thought, but soon after the Indians were gone a certain Penelope Van Prince, whose husband the Indians had killed, she found herself possessed with strength enough to creep in a hollow tree, where she remained some days with a number of severe wounds in her head and back   An Indian happening to come that way whose dog barking at the tree occasioned him to examine the inside of the tree, where he found the said Penelope in this forlorn and distressing condition which moved his compassion   He took her out of the tree and carried her to his residence, where he treated her kindly and healed her wounds, and in a short time conveyed her in his canoe to New Amsterdam where he sold her to the Dutch who then owned that city   The man and the woman from whom the whole race of Stouts have descended are now in the city of New Amsterdam where they became acquainted with each other and were married and notwithstanding it may be thought by some they conducted [themselves] with more fortitude than prudence, they immediately crossed the bay and settled in the aforesaid Middletown where Penelope had lost her first husband by the Indians and had been so severely wounded herself   There was at this time but six white families in the settlement, including their own which was in the year 1648   Here they continued until they became rich in property and rich in children "—From the manuscript written, in 1825, by Capt Nathan Stout, and corrected by Joseph D Hoff, of Middletown, N J , in August, 1885   This manuscript contained many errors.*

Setting aside, temporarily, his traditional history, we now come to Richard Stout's known history   This starts about 1643, when, in June of that year, Lady Deborah Moody, accompanied by her son, Sir Henry Moody, and a number of English families of good condition, arrived at the fort, at New Amsterdam, fresh from religious persecutions in New England, to seek and found an asylum under the Dutch   They were hospitably received and permitted to select such lands as they wished   At the date of their arrival, Richard Stout was probably among the English settlers, who, prior to that time, had located among the Dutch upon Manhattan Island, attracted thither from the religious intolerance of New England, or for purposes of trade, or in the spirit of adventure   These English speaking bodies soon joined to found the new settlement of Gravesend, upon Long Island, whither they probably at once commenced to remove   By 1645, with some intervening vicissitudes, they were well organized and the Director-General, Kieft, issued them a patent dated Dec 19th, of that year   Among the thirty-nine patentees enumerated was Richard Stout

An entry in the Town Book of the new settlement throws some light upon the life and times of Richard Stout   Unfortunately it is incomplete

May 7, 1647. "Richard Stoute being sworn deposeth yt in the   his being a soldiere at the ffort with Penneare and other his fellow soldieres," etc

Twice, in 1643, the English were employed as soldiers by the Dutch   The unparalleled stupidity and barbarity of the Dutch Director-General, Kieft, and certain of his followers, jeopardized the very existence of the Dutch settlements, by embroiling them with the Indians

About the first of *February, 1643*, the warlike Mohawks descended upon the tribes inhabiting the shores of the lower Hudson, to enforce the tribute of dried clams and wampum which had been withheld at the instigation of some of the Long Island Indians   Fleeing like sheep before wolves, consumed with cold, hunger and fright, some four or five hundred fugitives sought the protection of the whites upon Manhattan Island, where, under the walls of the fort, these pitiable objects were fed and sheltered by the hospitable settlers for a fortnight

Recovering confidence, they broke up into two parties, one of which ventured across the river to Pavonia, on the way to their friends, the Hackensacks, while the other removed to the vicinity of Corlear's Hook, where a number of Rockaway Indians had lately set up their wigwams

At this juncture, the Director, when heated with wine, yielded to the appeals of his Secretary to revenge a murder committed, some time previously, at Hackensack, and the failure of

---

*The original is now owned by Mr J Hervey Stout, of Stoutsburg, whose father had it printed in a small edition, by the Hopewell Herald, to save it from destruction   Copies of the book are now scarce

the Westchester Indians to surrender the murderer of one of the settlers, Claes Schmidt, likewise an affair many months old Volunteers and soldiers thereupon were led to the two Indian encampments, where, under cover of darkness, they fell upon the trusting savages and foully murdered eighty in one place and forty in the other, sparing neither infants, women nor the decrepid Never was there fouler butchery When they realized that it was not the Indians of Fort Orange, but the Dutch who had attacked them at Pavonia and Corlear's Hook, they joined the Long Island tribes, who had recently been plundered of their corn by Dutch farmers, made bold by recent events, and who had killed two of the savages while defending their property These two factions now made an alliance with the River Indians, and eleven tribes, numbering two thousand warriors, burning to avenge the massacre of their people, rose in open war and every white man upon whom they could lay hands was killed They laid waste the whole country from the Raritan River to the banks of the Connecticut The fort became the sole refuge of the panic stricken inhabitants, who, huddled together, bewailed their utter ruin through the folly and criminality of Kieft, and they now threatened to abandon the colony in a body In this emergency, the Director-General saw no resource to prevent a depopulation of New Amsterdam, but to take all the settlers into the service of the Company, for two months, until peace could be reestablished, "as he had not sufficient soldiers for public defense "
Life and Times of Nicholas Stillwell, p 86

This uprising was of short duration, for the savages, who had glutted their revenge, felt the need of planting their maize, and made overtures of peace, which were eagerly accepted by Kieft, and a treaty was concluded, first, with the Long Island Indians, on Mch 25, 1643, and with the River Indians on Apr 22, 1643

The second uprising, in 1643, occurred some months later, and again was the result of Kieft's maladministration Notwithstanding the fearful experience he had just passed through, his cupidity and dishonesty were such that he embezzled the gifts that were to ratify the late treaty with the River Indians, which occasioned such dissatisfaction and discontent that the outraged Indians seized several boats laden with peltries in retaliation and as an offset. In doing this, ten white men were killed Then followed war in its most terrible shape The settlements of Anne Hutchinson, John Throckmorton and the Rev Francis Doughty were all destroyed, some of their settlers killed or taken into captivity, while the balance, amounting to over an hundred families, quickly made their way to the Fort at New Amsterdam Lady Moody's settlement, at Gravesend, alone was able to withstand their assault Here, the townsmen, many of whom had served during the two months in the Indian outbreak in the Spring, under Lieut Nicholas Stillwell, Ensign George Baxter and Sergeant James Hubbard, well organized into a trained band, gave them so brisk and severe a reception that they were soon in full retreat So great was the need of protection at the Fort that Kieft again found it necessary to take "into the public service all the able bodied English inhabitants of the neighboring villages, the Commonalty of New Amsterdam having agreed to provide for one-third of their pay, and a company of fifty was immediately enrolled from their number, armed and drilled."

About March, 1644, the Indians were vanquished, and on Apr 6, and Apr. 16, 1644, Sachems from various tribes concluded a new peace at Fort Amsterdam. It was in one of these two enlistments that Richard Stout served with Robert Pennoyer and other fellow soldiers, and I am inclined to think it was in the first one.

At that time, Lady Moody and her party had not arrived and he was naturally free, but during the second enlistment, Gravesend having been settled and he, doubtless, one of its inhabitants, it was naturally incumbent upon him to remain with its defensive company.

The supposition that Richard Stout was employed at the Fort in the Spring uprising of 1643, rather than in the Fall and Winter of 1643 and 1644, and that he left New Amsterdam, with Lady Moody, in the Summer of 1643, to found Gravesend, is confirmed by the following record from the Calendar of New York Historical Manuscripts, which establishes a date for his residence at Gravesend

"Octoberr 13th, 1643, Richard Aestin, Ambrose Love [?] and Richard Stout made declaration that the crew of the Seven Stars and of the privateer landed at the farm of Anthony Jansen, of Salee, in the Bay, and took off 200 pumpkins, and would have carried away a lot of hogs from Coney Island had they not learned that they belonged to Lady Moody "

Thus far we have ascertained that Richard Stout was a resident of New Amsterdam in the Spring of 1643, when he was employed by Governor Kieft as a soldier in the February uprising of that year; that he accompanied Lady Moody, with other settlers, to found Gravesend, between her arrival in June, and October of this same year

How much earlier than February, 1643, Richard Stout may have been in New Amsterdam, it is idle to speculate upon

In the first allotments of house lots and farms in Gravesend, Feb. 20, 1646, he received Plantation lot No 16, upon which he evidently grew tobacco, for Oct 26, 1649, John Thomas bought, for two hundred and ten guilders, Richard Stout's crop of tobacco

Gravesend Town Records

In 1657, of his twenty acre farm he had seventeen acres under cultivation.

1661, Apr 5 He bought an adjoining farm of Edward Griffin

1663, Oct 8 Richard Stout was plaintiff in a slander suit in Gravesend, and won his case

Even with his double farm of forty acres, Richard Stout realized its insufficiency to maintain and settle a rapidly growing family, so that he, with other neighbors, similarly situated, turned to the adjacent and easily reached country, whose wooded hills could be seen towards the South, which was the spot where his wife had had her bitter experience among the Indians, and of whose attractions she had doubtless spoken, prompting him to scout its woods in search of game, and finally in search of land for a new home for himself and family That this settlement occurred before 1664, I doubt, though the Stout manuscript, and Mrs. Seabrook, probably from the same source, say explicitly, that it was in the year 1648, and that Stout was associated with five additional settlers, among whom Mrs Seabrook named Bowne, Lawrence, Grover and Whitlock To this earlier settlement, Edwards makes no allusion, nor can it be said that Smith does, but to the contrary, he fixes the date of Stout's settlement practically about the time of 1665, or a little later, for he mentions the event, as does Edwards, of an uprising when Penelope's oldtime Indian friend saved her by a timely warning, which Smith says occurred, when there "were supposed to be about fifty families of white people, and five hundred Indians inhabiting these parts." Surely this must relate to a later date than 1648, for so many white families could only have been assembled in this district after the Monmouth Patent had been issued by Governor Nicolls, further, a study of the movements of the Stouts, Bownes, Lawrences, Grovers and Whitlocks does not encourage the belief that they were permanently settled on the Monmouth Tract much before 1665 At times members of these families may have been temporarily camped out in this district for hunting or prospecting, and it may have been on one of these occasions that Penelope Stout received the warning from her Indian friend of the threatened uprising, and the need of her immediate removal, and, indeed, this event, given by Smith, Edwards and the Stout manuscript, could only have occurred during such a temporary occupation, for, in 1665, or later, Penelope's Indian saviour would have been more than twenty-two years older than he was in 1643, the date of Penelope's supposed arrival, when he was already an old man. Add these years to this old man's age and he would have been pretty patriarchal Again, Smith's account says Penelope took her children with her, which would probably refer to a late, rather than to an early event, as in 1665, her family was largely grown, yet some were young, being born after 1654

Another statement in Smith's account contradicts the idea of a 1648 settlement, for he states that, "A while after marrying to one Stout, they lived together at Middletown among other Dutch inhabitants " As a matter of fact, the accredited associates of Stout, in his 1648 settlement, were English from Gravesend, and there is no knowledge of any Dutch in this locality till long after the Monmouth Patent was granted

When the conclusion was reached that it was vital to abandon the crowded settlement of Gravesend, a number of the settlers from that village, and a few from adjacent towns, to the number of twenty, sailed in a sloop, in the early part of December, 1663, up the Raritan River, and began negotiations with the Sachems for the purchase of lands These proceedings were interrupted by a company of Dutchmen, who, cruising about in one of the company's sloops, heard of the presence of the English, and suspecting their purpose, notified the Sachems, of the Raritans and the Navesinks not to bargain with them, whereupon the English went to the shores at the mouth of the Navesink, where, again, for a second time, a sharp passage at words occurred between them The Dutch, for some time, had realized the desire of the English to throw over their allegiance, and were alert to impress them with the need of fealty, so that no progress was apparently made by the English settlers in their negotiations for lands, at this time. It was, probably, however, in anticipation of the expected overthrow of the Dutch, that this expedition was undertaken, and the consummation of this event, in the year following, 1664, with the proclamation of Governor Stuyvesant's successor, Richard Nicolls, of certain concessions, promptly brought about organized effort to locate in the territory which they had so recently prospected. Among those who moved to avail themselves of this golden opportunity, was Richard Stout, who, with others, patentees and associates, bought the Sachems' rights to the land embraced in the future Monmouth Patent, Apr 8, 1665, which was confirmed to twelve of them, of whom he was one

When ready to remove to this new tract, Richard Stout disposed of his Gravesend property to Mr. Thomas Delaval, a prosperous merchant of New York, who seems to have meditated making his residence at Gravesend, and perhaps actually did so, as he is named as a Patentee in at least one of the patents of the town

After the death of Thomas Delaval, this property became vested in his son, John Delaval, whose widow, Hannah, sold it to John Lake, and thence on it became part of the Lake estate

The date of Richard Stout's arrival, and permanent settlement on the Monmouth Tract, was 1664, as established by his claims for lands under the Grants and Concessions These set forth the rights of the settlers

GRANTS AND CONCESSIONS.

Before January, 1665, i e, between 1664 and 1665, To every freeman (he or she) and for his able bodied man servants, if equipped, going from the port with the Governor, properly equipped, each 150 acres; and for weaker servants or slaves, exceeding fourteen years, each 75 acres, and the Christian servant, at the expiration of his service, 75 acres

To any master or mistress going before January, 1665, 120 acres, and to every able bodied servant taken with them, 120 acres, and for weaker servants, i e over fourteen years, each 60 acres, and to Christian servants, upon the expiration of their time, each 60 acres

Between January, 1665, and January, 1666, To every free man or woman, 90 acres, and for every able bodied servant, 90 acres, and 45 acres for the weaker servants, and 45 acres to every Christian servant, upon the expiration of his time

From January, 1666, to January, 1667, To every free man or woman, 60 acres, and to able bodied servants, 60 acres, to weaker servants, 30 acres, and to Christian servants, upon the expiration of their time, 30 acres.
Leaming and Spicer

1675. Here begins the Rights of Lands due, according to Concessions
Richard Stout brings for his rights, for the year 1665, for his wife, two sons, John and Richard, 120 acres each, total 480 acres

Items for his sons and daughters yt are come voyge [of age?] since the year 1667, namely, James, Peter, Mary, Alice and Sarah, each 60 acres, total 300 acres
John Stout, of Middletown, for himself and wife, , 240 acres
Richard Stout, Jr , of Shrewsbury, for himself and wife, 120 acres
James Stout for his owne right 60 acres
Peter Stout for his owne right 60 acres
Sarah Stout for her owne right 60 acres
James Bowne, in right of his wife, Mary Stout, 240 acres
John Throckmorton, in right of his wife, Alice Stout, 240 acres.

Lib 3, East Jersey Deeds, A side, p 1

As already stated a careful study of Richard Stout's claim proves that he and his wife, with their two sons, John and Richard, came to the new country in 1664, while the remainder of their children probably dwelt in Gravesend till about 1667, when they too came to the Monmouth Tract to join their parents in their newly made home This is a reasonable deduction, as some roof had to be erected to receive this large family, whose presence, in the absence of such an one, would be a hindrance rather than a help to their parents, especially as some of the children were still young It is easy to conceive that the Gravesend house was presided over by one of the daughters and one of the sons, aided by frequent visits from the parents, till their removal took place in 1667

Richard Stout's application for land was recorded in 1675, in which he lays claim, in right of himself, wife and children for 780 acres, i. e., 120 acres, each, for himself, wife, son John and son Richard, who were master, mistress and able-bodied servants, [not necessarily twenty-one years of age however], settling on the land *before* January, 1665, and 60 acres, each, for his children, James, Peter, Mary, Alice and Sarah, who *voyged* thither, about 1667, and who were classified as free men and women, arriving between January, 1666 and 1667 If they had settled on the Monmouth Tract with their father, prior to 1665, they too would have received this same amount of land, 60 acres, each, as weaker servants being over fourteen years of age, but the record expressly states *from 1667*, and the matter of their birth is not involved if the word *voyge* is read as *travel*, rather than *age*, as has been done heretofore The younger, known but unmentioned, children were evidently under the age of fourteen in 1675, as they had not reached the period of being classified as "weaker servants," which had they been, would have entitled their father, Richard Stout, to additional lands at thirty acres per head, and for proof of which he put in no claim.

The influx of settlers was rapid and large, for in the astonishingly short time of about five years, from 1664 to July, 1669, further settlement was restricted especially of transients, "considering the towne to be now wholly compleated beeing full acording to their number."

Upon the settlement of the Monmouth Tract, the settlers grouped themselves in three bodies, one settling at Portland Point, now the Navesink Highlands, one at Shrewsbury, on Narumsunk Neck, and one at Middletown, on Newasink Neck, so named because of lying between the first two settlements Before and after town organization was complete the Patentees met, with Deputies elected from their associates, in an *Assembly*, at various times in these towns, and made laws for the government of the towns, by the erection of a Constable's Court, the distribution of town lands, the election of officers, laying out of roads, etc , and in this Assembly Richard Stout frequently sat, as one of the Patentees, during 1669, 1670 and 1671

Shortly after this, the local Assembly was abolished and the direction of the town's affairs were left largely to themselves, while matters of large import were directed by General Assemblies and the Proprietary Governor which had been the order of things for some years

The settlers, as we have seen, had assigned to them, by the village commonalty, under the direction of the Local Assembly, town lots and farms adjacent to the village, and it was only after some years, when the whole tract became better peopled, that they applied for and received large grants from the Proprietors, in conformity with their rights under the Grants and Concessions

At the first division of the town lots, Dec 30, 1667, Richard Stout drew lot No. 6, which would correspond closely to the present site of Squire Henry Taylor's house, on the South side of the Middletown highway, and beyond him, at the Eastern end of the town, probably on the North side, his son, John Stout, drew lot No. 19. The next day, Dec. 31, 1667, he was chosen, with James Ashton, to assist James Grover in laying out, in lots, the Poplar and the Mountainy fields, No 12 falling to him, and No. 5 falling to his son, John Stout.

1668, Jan 4 He recorded his cattle-mark, which passed, Aug. 25, 1710, to his son, Benjamin Stout, and, in 1721, to John Burrows, as Benjamin Stout and his family had moved away.

Richard Stout enjoyed the confidence and respect of his fellow townsmen and was frequently elected to fill responsible positions in the conduct of the town's public business. He was one of the six who were to give answer to the Governor's men in the town's behalf, in their resistance to Proprietary aggression; he was commonly Overseer, and thus a member of the Constables Court

In 1669, "the equality of the division of the meadows is putt to the Judgement of Richard Stoutte" and two others.

In 1678, he was chosen one of the Overseers of the Highways, and this is seemingly his last public office, for age had overtaken him, and his children had come to the fore, especially his son, John Stout

Richard Stout received various grants of lands from the Proprietors, upon which he was compelled to pay taxes These Middletown lands are variously alluded to in warrants, surveys and tax lists, and while, perhaps, they are in some instances here duplicated, were apparently as follows

1675, Nov 2 Richard Stout had seven hundred and eighty acres, at Middletown.

1676, Feb 24 Richard Stout had four hundred acres, he having purchased the same from ye Indians in the Lord Proprietor's name

1676, May 31 Richard Stout had five hundred acres, and meadow, as being one of the first purchasers

1676, June 23 Richard Stout had four hundred and sixty acres
1676, June 28 Richard Stout had four hundred and sixty acres
1676, June 30 Richard Stout had one hundred and eighty-four acres, in Middletown, which he sold later to William Leeds, Sr , of Burlington
1677, May 7 Richard Stout had two hundred and eighty-five acres
1686, July 20 Richard Stout had four hundred and sixty acres.

1686, Oct 15. Quit Rents of Middletown
Richard Stout 460 acres at 19 s 2 d pr. An   9 11 8
Cr. By Pardons order payd to   1·15·0
By 20 bushells of wheat at 4 s pr bushel   .   4:00:0

By 26 bushells of Indian Corn at 2 s   2:12 08 } 9·11·8
By abatement the man is very old   1·04:00 /

In the Quit Rent Roll, for the year 1686, he received an abatement of his tax, as "the man is very old." This brings us to a discussion of the probable year of Richard Stout's birth and death. The Rev Mr. Hart, of Hopewell, drawing his information from the descendants of Jonathan Stout, and supplying it to Morgan Edwards, gave a series of dates which are wrong upon their face and extremely confusing He stated that Penelope, the wife of Richard Stout, was born in 1602, and sailed for New York about 1620, and was wrecked That she met and married, in New York, Richard Stout, when she was in her twenty-second year, and he in his fortieth, and that she lived to the age of one hundred and ten years, and saw her offspring multiplied into five hundred and two in about eighty-eight years Allowing one year for her widowhood, Penelope Stout would have married Richard Stout, according to these dates, in 1621, in her twenty-second year, which would make her born about 1600, and he, at this date, in his fortieth year, would have been born about 1582, she, living to one hundred and ten years of age, would have died about 1710

If Penelope Stout was born in 1602, she was sixty-three years old when the settlement of Middletown occurred, and as only two of her children, John and Richard, had arrived at age, and were presumbly about twenty and eighteen years, respectively, she must have been aged forty-three years when she bore her first child, and as we know that she had ten children that grew to adult life, and perhaps others who died young, it would have prolonged her child-bearing period till she was near, if not over, the age of sixty, when, as a matter of fact, it should have encompassed thirty years, between the ages of sixteen years and forty-six years, or thereabouts Evidently there is a mistake in Mr. Hart's dates, and I think it lies in the fact that he erroneously gave the date of birth, 1602, to Penelope Stout instead of to Richard Stout, her husband If we accept this as likely, and fit her marriage to the date of 1644, which we have proved was the probable date of her arrival, then we can intelligently apply the other figures, given by Mr. Hart, and the results would be

Richard Stout was born 1602; married 1644, died 1705.

Penelope Stout was born 1622-23, married 1644, died 1732-3

The correctness of the dates assigned Richard Stout is sustained by the fact that he was *very old in 1686*, and that he became *inactive*, in town affairs, *about 1670*

We have little knowledge of him in his later days

1679-80, Feb 26 Richard and Penelope Stout sold to Thomas Snowsell, Sr , sixteen acres of land, with dwelling house, barn and orchard, and nine acres of upland, in the Poplar Field, and other small parcels, for £66-5-3 This land later passed to John Crafford and then to Peter Tilton.

In 1690, he conveyed to his son, Peter Stout, land on Hop River, and six and two-thirds acres of meadow, at Conesconck, joining David Stout.

In 1690, he conveyed to his son, James Stout, land on Hop River, on whose boundaries was Jonathan Stout, and another piece of land, at Conescunk, adjoining David Stout.

1703, June 9th Will of Richard Stout, of Middletowne, County of Monmouth, proved, by attestation of Richard Hartshorne, one of the witnesses, and also to the signatures of witnesses, John Weekham, [Meekham?], and Peter Vandevandetere, before Edward, Vifcount Cornbury, Governor, Perth Amboy, ye 23th, 8[ber], 1705, mentioned

"unto my loving wife deuring her naturall life All my orchard and that part or rome of the houfe fhee now lives in with the cellar and all the land I now Improue   unto my loving wife all my horfe kind excepting one mare and coult my Sonn Beniamin is to haue for wintering my cattell laft yeare"

"to my Sonns, John, Richard, James, Johnathan, Dauid, Beniamin, one fhilling each of them"

"to my Daughters, Mary, Alce and Sarah, each of them, one fhilling"

"to my daughter in law, Marey Stoute, and to her fonn, John, one fhilling each of them"

"unto my kinswoman, Mary Stoute, the daughter formerly of peter ftouts, one Cow to be paid within fix days After my wifes death"

Residue "of personall eftate   unto my loving wife, and   I mak my fonn John and my fonn Johnathan my Exseceters to fee this my will performed."

Witnesses Richard Hartshorne, John Weekham [Meekham?]* and Peter Vandevandeter
He signed with his mark.
1705, 8ber, 23th Oath of executors, John and Jonathan Stout, before Edward, Viſcount Cornbury, Perth Amboy

Richard Stout, as has been deduced, probably married in 1643 or 1644, and had by his wife, Penelope, issue, most, if not all of whom, were born in Gravesend, Long Island. If no account is taken of any deceased children, or the exact order of succession, the dates of birth of the known children would be about as follows

Issue

2 John Stout, born about 1644-5.
3 Richard Stout, born about 1646.
4 Mary Stout, born about 1648
5 James Stout, born about 1650.
6 Alice Stout, born about 1652.
7 Peter Stout, born about 1654, died between 1702 and 1703
8 Sarah Stout, born about 1656
9 Jonathan Stout, born about 16—, 1646, says James Hervey Stout.
10 Benjamin Stout, born about 1669?
11 David Stout, born about 1667 or 1669

That these children are given with some semblance of proper succession is likely, as their arrangement here conforms to their order in the Grants and Concessions, as well as in Richard Stout's will

LINE OF JOHN STOUT

2 JOHN STOUT, son of Richard Stout, 1, was born, by deduction, at Gravesend, Long Island, about 1644-45 He was married, at Middletown, N J, by John Bowne, Justice of the Peace, Jan 12, 1671-72, to Elizabeth   . ., whose surname is omitted in the record.

He was probably the first born, and his birth can be fixed by the deduced date of marriage of his parents, by the fact he is first enumerated in his father's claim for lands under the Grants and Concessions, and that he was an able-bodied man, though not necessarily of age, at the date of the settlement of Middletown in 1664-65.

In the first division of lands, in Middletown, Dec 30, 1667, he drew lot No 19, on the main street, and the following day, in the distribution of the outlying Poplar and Mountainy fields, he drew lot No 5 He erected a house upon his town-lot, stocked his farm with cattle, some of which were allowed to herd, in common with others, and to designate which, he recorded his cattle-mark Sept 4, 1672

John Stout remained at Middletown, and died some time prior to 1740, as at this date, his cattle-mark was assumed by his grandson, John Stout, the newly-elected Town Clerk; and, July 23, 1742, Richard Stout, son and heir-at-law to John Stout, late of Middletown, is alluded to in a deed, with Zephaniah White, as a witness   Freehold Deeds, Lib H , p 317

If it were he who died prior to 1740, he must have attained a very advanced age and sustained the family's reputation for longevity

John Stout acquired a considerable estate

---

*In the will the name "John Weekham" appears like "*John nauhan,*" [Vaughn] In the proof of the will it is spelled "Weekham," or "Meekham"

LINE OF JOHN STOUT

From the Proprietors, as alluded to in Warrants, Surveys and tax bills, he received

1675, Nov. 2, one hundred and twenty acres, at Middletown
1676, Oct 6, two hundred and forty acres.
1678, Feb 7, two hundred and nine acres
1678, Feb 10, two hundred and nine acres, in and about Middletown
1687, Mch 25, two hundred and nine acres
1696 John Stout, of Middletown, yeoman, and Elizabeth, his wife, sold land at Crosswicks
1697, July 17 He bought lands of James Grover

Some of these may be duplicates, appearing, as is common, in various quit-rent taxes. No doubt he acquired other lands as well, by succession and purchase

1697, July 17 James Grover, carpenter, conveyed to John Stout, yeoman, property. James Bollen was a witness and made his acknowledgment to this deed in 1710

1705, Oct 5 John Stout, of Middletown, yeoman, for reasonable causes and considerations, conveyed to Benjamin Stout, of Middletown, yeoman, land on Hop River, bounded by land formerly David Stout's, and land formerly Peter Stout's, as also land at Conesconk, belonging "to my late father, Richard Stout"

1710, Apr. 6 John Stout, of Middletown, for £15, conveyed to Richard Hartshorne, six acres of meadow, on Haitshorne's Neck, known as Conneskunk, which was granted to the said John Stout by Richard Hartshorne, May 6, 1705

Thomas and Jane Higham the said Jane being the widow of Richard Sadler, of Middletown, who gave her, by his will, a proprietary right, conveyed the same, for £40, to John Stout, of Middletown

Of his estate, he gave as follows

1703, Apr. 30 John Stout, of Middletown, for £20, sold to his son, Richard Stout, two hundred acres, lying, in Middletown, adjacent to William Layton's line

1704, May. John Stout conveyed land, lying at Shoal Harbor, to his son, Richard Stout, cordwinder, alias shoemaker

1704, Jan. 30 John Stout, of Middletown, sold lands, for £6, to Jonathan Stout, patented July 16, 1700

1704 John Stout, of Middletown, sold land, at Hop River, for £6

Trenton, N J, Conveyances

John Stout became a man of prominence in the Middletown settlement.

In 1675, he, with James Bowne, his brother-in-law, was chosen a Magistrate of a Monthly Court of Small Cases

1679–80, Feb 20 He was chosen, with the same individual, a Deputy, to represent Middletown, in the Local Assembly

1681, July 4 John Stout was appointed ensign in the military company of Middletown, of which John Bowne was Captain and James Grover was Lieutenant

1684–5 He was appointed Constable for Middletown

Of his wife, little is known

In 1712, there was an Elizabeth Stout, of Middletown, a member of the Baptist Church, which may be she, or this may apply to Elizabeth, the wife of James Stout· Before the erection of their church, in 1712, "they met at first in a private house belonging to Mr John Stout."

Issue

3 Richard Stout
4 John Stout
5 Hope Still Stout ⎱ born in Middletown Block House, as given by Mrs Seabrook
6 Faith Stout ⎰
  Probably others

3 RICHARD STOUT, son of John Stout, 2, was called his son and heir, in a conveyance dated 1742

1742, July 23 Richard Stout, of Middletown, son and heir to John Stout, late of Middletown, yeoman, for £28, conveyed to Timothy Waeir, of Shrewsbury, yeoman, thirty acres, at Barnegat, in Shrewsbury, granted to the deceased John Stout by patent from the Proprietors. Richard Stout signed his name.

Richard Stout was, by trade, a cordwainer or shoemaker, in 1704, when he received, from his father, land at Shoal Harbor

He resided in Middletown, on his estate, of two hundred acres, bought from his father Apr 30, 1703

In 1695, he recorded his cattle-mark, and, in 1712, he recorded his brandmark

1714, Apr. 10. Capt Richard Stout, of Middletown, gent, for 10 shillings, sold a four acre right to Hugh Hartshorne

1714, Aug 21 Richard Stout, of Middletown, planter, for £20, sold to Garvine Drummond, of Shrewsbury, a right to three hundred acres He signed the deed Richard Stout

1714, Aug 26 Richard Stout acknowledged the above deed and was styled Capt Richard Stout

1717, 17th of 11th mo Richard and Mary Stout signed the marriage certificate of John Woolley and Patience Lippit, at the house of Sarah Lippit, Middletown

1724, May 26 Richard Stout, Esq, of Middletown, for £20, sold land to John Woolley, Jr

1724 Richard Stout was a Justice, in Middletown

1729, Dec. 19 Richard Stout conveyed to son, John, land adjoining widow Lippet and George Taylor

Richard Stout was, probably, among the first born children, as he had a daughter, Esther Stout, born prior to her brother, John Stout, who was born in 1701, say in 1699, and who married Benjamin Woolley about 1716, which necessitates their father, Richard Stout, being born not later than 1678, and perhaps earlier.

Richard Stout was probably married twice, and unless another husband can be found for Esther, daughter of Peter and Rebecca (Brazier) Tilton, born Aug. 5, 1678, I judge her to have been the first wife of Richard Stout, and his second wife was Mary Tilton, born Feb 2, 1681, his first wife's sister

At what time his first wife died I do not know, but Mary was his wife in 1704, when they both signed the marriage certificate of Walter Harbert and Sarah Tilton, her cousin, at the house of Rebecca Tilton, the 2 of 4 mo, of that year John Stout, his son, was born in 1701, and Jonathan Stout, his son, in 1704. The latter was therefore the son of Mary, but Esther Stout, his daughter, was born prior to John, for she was married to Benjamin Woolley, about 1716, according to dates of birth of their children

1749, Dec. 28 Richard Stout made his will, which was proved Jan 17, 1749, in which he recites that he was of Middletown, Esquire, and mentioned:

Son, John Stout, to whom he gave land, bought of Thomas Cox, and along the line of Sarah Lippit, William Bowne's line, and thence to the highway by the graves, etc

Son, Jonathan Stout

Negroes, Harriet and Bess to be freed and to have the use of one-half of my father's field, other negroes were also provided for

Daughters, Mary, Catharine, Rebecca, and three daughters of my deceased daughter, Esther Woolley

He appointed his two sons executors, and signed his name to the will.

Issue

7 Esther Stout, born about 1699
8 John Stout, born 1701.

9 Jonathan Stout, born 1704
10 Mary Stout, married James Grover
11 Catharine Stout, married, by license dated Nov 2, 1730, John Stout, son of Joseph, eldest son of Jonathan, son of Richard Stout, 1.
12 Rebecca Stout, married George Taylor.
13 Daughter Stout, (perhaps), said to have married Samuel Tilton, but very doubtful

4 JOHN STOUT, JR , son of John Stout, 2, recorded his cattle-mark, in Middletown, Oct 31, 1698, which passed, May 12, 1753, to Richard, his son, whence it passed to George Taylor, Jr , in 1761, and then, in 1809, to John Stout, carpenter, son of the last-named Richard Stout, and then, in 1844, to Richard W Stout, son of John Stout, carpenter

Issue
14 Richard Stout

7 ESTHER STOUT, daughter of Richard Stout, Esq., 4, was born about 1699, and died prior to Dec 28, 1749 She married, about 1716, Benjamin Woolley, born 12mo , 25, 1692-3, son of John and Mercy (Potter) Woolley.

Esther Stout was Benjamin Woolley's second wife, the name of his first wife being unknown to me Upon the death of his wife, Esther Stout, Benjamin Woolley married, third, 7mo , 19, 1744, Catharine (West) Cook, widow of Edward P Cook, and upon her demise, he married, fourth, May 31, 1758, Phebe Cooper, widow For their issue see Woolley Family in Historical Miscellany.

8 JOHN STOUT, son of Richard Stout, Esq , 3, was "born Dec 4, [?], and is now, Jan 8, 1782, aged 80 years " He died, Aug. [16 probably], 1783, aged 81 years, 7 months and 8 days, as per Bible record, and Aug. 16, 1782, aged 81 years and 7 months, as per his tombstone in the Old Presbyterian Churchyard, at Middletown He married Margaret, daughter of Thomas Taylor, who died June 5, 1793, (Baptist Church Record), leaving a will dated Apr 25, 1793

In 1740, he was Town Clerk of Middletown

1740, Apr. 16 He recorded his cattle-mark, at Middletown, which was the same as that of his grandfather, John, the son of Richard and Penelope.

1749/50, Feb 10 John Stout, son of Richard, 3, deceased, gave to be recorded for his son, Richard, the earmark that George Taylor said, Jan 17, 1770, "formerly belonged to Captain Richard Stout "

1776, Apr 25 John Stout made his will, in which he mentioned his wife, Margaret, and sons, William and Thomas, while that of his wife, Margaret Stout, was written Apr 25, 1793

Issue
15 John Stout, Jr , born, Sept 12, 1732, about 9 o'clock in the morning, died, Mch 9, 1758, aged 25 years, 5 months and 16 days His cattle-mark was recorded Aug 1, 1755, and was formerly Sarah Lippit's, and passed to his brother, Thomas Stout, Oct 21, 1761 He probably married Mary   , as per his mother's will, and had a daughter, Mary Stout
16 Helena Stout, born, Dec 2, 1734, between 12 and 1 o'clock, married, by license dated May 2, 1758, John, son of William Hoff She was a legatee in the will of Zephaniah White in 1758
"But two hands between Penelope and me", "My grandmother, Helena Huff, told how her grandfather, John Stout, felt the wounds of the old lady and that he blushed like a schoolboy "   Mrs T W Seabook

Issue

Leonard Hoff; killed, at Middletown Point, May 23, 1779, aged 19, in Revolutionary War
John Hoff
William Hoff
Thomas Hoff
Christian Hoff
Margaret Hoff
Elizabeth Hoff
Helena Hoff

17 Lydia Stout, born, Apr 4, 1737, about 12 or near 1 o'clock.
18 Richard Stout, born, Oct 10, 1738, about 10 at night, died, June 1, 1759, aged twenty years, seven months, twenty-one days.
19 Thomas Stout, born Apr 13, 1741, died May 13, 1806
20 Sarah Stout, born Feb 14, 1743-4, married, by license dated May 15, 1766, John Pierson.
21 Joseph Lippit Stout, born Nov 24, 1746, married Jane   . , was a Tory and removed from Middletown His daughter, Peggy, born 1787, died Aug 27, 1787, is buried, with her grandfather, John Stout, in the Presbyterian Churchyard, Middletown, N J He also had an adult son, in 1797, William Stout, as per his mother's will, and a daughter, Peggy Stout, born May 22, 1787, died Aug. 27, 1787.
22 Mary Stout, born June 16, 1749 [?].
23 Catharine Stout, born Mch 9, 1752, married George Yard, when thirty years of age. She was living, aged eighty years, in 1831.
24 William Stout } born Oct 26, 1755
25 Anne Stout   } She married, by license dated Mch. 26, 1778, William West. Apr. 10, 1799, Cateline Yard and Anne West conveyed to Thomas West, their brother, their Proprietary rights in land left by will of Margaret Stout, widow, dated Apr 25, 1793, to Joseph Stout Signed by William West and Cataline Yard.
26 Hester Stout, solely upon the authority of the late Asher Taylor, Esq., who married William Taylor, but it is likely an error Was it boatman Joe?

9 DR JONATHAN STOUT, son of Richard Stout, Esq , 3, was born Mch 26, 1702, died, Apr 27, 1773, aged 71, 1, 1, buried in the Old Presbyterian Churchyard, Middletown, N J , married Leah, daughter of Amos and Hannah (Mills) White, prior to 12mo , 27, 1728-9, since Amos White, in his will of that date, calls him son-in-law. Leah White, his wife, was born in 1704, and was living at the date of his will, 1773. Both Jonathan Stout and his wife, Leah, were baptized, at Shrewsbury, N. J., in 1759 She must have been the mother of all of his children

1729, Aug. 6 He recorded his cattle-mark, which passed to his son, Peter, in 1775, thence to Peter's brother, Abraham, in 1789, and then, in 1834, to Esther and Mary, daughters of Abraham Stout, and finally, in 1854, to William Carhart

1773, Oct 13 Jonathan Stout made his will, which was proved Apr 1, 1775, which seems from the inscription on his tombstone, to be an erroneous date, and in which he mentioned:
Wife, Leah
Son, Richard, land adjacent Edward Burrowes and Andrew Layton
Second son, Jonathan, land adjacent Edward Taylor and widow Mary Stout

LINE OF JOHN STOUT

Third son, Peter
Fourth son, Jehu
Fifth son, Abram.
Daughter, Esther Stout
Daughter, Rebecca.
Grandchildren, Leah Benjamin and Stout Benjamin, not 21 years
Four daughters, Leah, Esther, Rachel and Rebecca
Executors. sons, Peter and Abram
He was a man of considerable wealth, and made liberal provision for all of his family

His children were also legatees in the will of their uncle, Zephaniah White, who died in 1758.*

Issue

27 Richard Stout, born 1728, died 1807, was a legatee in the will of his uncle, Zephaniah White, in 1758.
28 Jonathan Stout, living, as Jonathan Stout, Jr, in 1758, and a legatee in the will of his uncle, Zephaniah White
29 Jehu Stout, not mentioned, in 1758, in the will of Zephaniah White
30 Peter Stout, born 1734; died 1828, not mentioned in the will of Zephaniah White, in 1758.
31 Abram Stout, born 1750; died 1830, not mentioned in the will of Zephaniah White, in 1758.
32 Hannah Stout, born 1732; died 1757
33 Esther Stout, mentioned in the will of her uncle, Zephaniah White, in 1758
34 Mary Stout, mentioned in the will of her uncle, Zephaniah White, in 1758
35 Rebecca Stout, married, by license dated Oct 5, 1763, Alexander Grant
36 Leah Stout, mentioned in the will of her uncle, Zephaniah White, in 1758, married, by license dated Oct 12, 1761, Samuel Taylor
37 Rachel Stout, born 1746, married James Patterson, born 1733

Issue

Jehu Patterson, born 1765, married at the age of twenty.
Rebecca Patterson, married Mr Crawford
Leah Patterson; married Robert Patterson, her first cousin
James Patterson, married Mary Conover.

14   RICHARD STOUT, son of John Stout, Jr., 4.

1753, May 12   He had recorded, at Middletown, the earmark which had been his father's, and which, passing to George Taylor, Jr, in 1761, was resumed, in 1809, by his son, John Stout, "carpenter"

Issue

38 John Stout; "carpenter."

15   JOHN STOUT, JR., son of John Stout, 8.

There seems to have been some connection between the Stouts and the Lippits, which gave rise to the taking of Sarah Lippit's cattle-mark, Aug 1, 1755, by John Stout, Jr., (15), and the

---

*Amos White married Hannah Mills   In his will, of 1728, he appoints his son-in-law, Jonathan Stout, an executor   Amos White had children Zephaniah White, who died in 1758, Amos White, Andrew White, Avis White, who married John Fisher, Hannah White, who married William Layton, and Leah White, who married Jonathan Stout   Zephaniah White, who died in 1758, alludes to his nephews and nieces, as cousins, the oldtime phraseology for that kindred   They were Leah Stout, deceased cousin Hannah Stout, Richard Stout, Jonathan Stout, Jr, Mary Stout, Hester Stout, the other children of Jonathan Stout, for some reason, were omitted

naming of his brother, Joseph Lippit Stout, (21), who was born Nov 24, 1746 See also under No. 8

He probably died prior to Oct. 21, 1761, as his cattle-mark was then taken up by his brother, Thomas Stout, 19

19 THOMAS STOUT, son of John Stout, 8, was born Apr 13, 1741, and died May 13, 1806, and was buried in the Wall and Stout plot, in Middletown He married Catharine Cooper 1761, Oct 21. He took up the cattle-mark of his brother, John Stout

1805, Apr 19 Thomas Stout made his will, which was proved May 26, 1806.

Issue

39 John Stout, born Sept 28, 1772
40 Richard Stout, born Sept. 20, 1781.
41 Thomas T. Stout, born 1785, died, Apr. 21, 1871, single
42 Deborah Stout, born 1770; died Mch 22, 1803, married James Reynolds.

Issue

George Reynolds, born 1803, died 1869.

43 Hope Stout, born Feb 5, 1776, died June 1, 1825, married James Reynolds, his second wife

Issue

Catharine Reynolds, born June 4, 1805, died Sept 19, 1822
Hope Reynolds

44 Margaret Stout, born Oct 17, 1778, died Aug 10, 1841, married John Carroll.

Issue

Deborah Carroll, born June 10, 1803, died July 22, 1888, married Leonard Walling

45 Helena Stout, married George Dorset.

Issue

James Dorset
Joseph Dorset
Eliza Dorset
Catharine Dorset
Sarah Ann Dorset

27 RICHARD STOUT, son of Jonathan Stout, 9, was born in 1728, died Mch 6, 1807, and married, by license dated Nov 20, 1751, Anna Tenbrook*, born in 1735 Nov 17, 1806, Nancy, wife of Richard Stout, died (Baptist Church Record, Middletown, N J) Her tombstone reads that she died, Dec 18, 1806, aged seventy-one years.

1791, May 23 Richard Stout made his will, which was proved Mch. 27, 1807, in which he mentioned.

Father, Jonathan Stout, deceased.
Wife, Ann
Son, Wessels Tenbrooke Stout
Son, Richard Stout
Son, Jonathan Stout
Daughter, Elizabeth
Daughter, Rhoda Burdon
He owned property at Shoal Harbor and Frosts

---

*In the will of Dirck DeWitt, of Kingston, Ulster Co , N Y , recorded in New York City, Anna Tenbrook is mentioned as, "my grand daughter Ann, wife of Richard Stout," to whom he gives £10, further the testator gives to my three grandchildren, children of Wessell Jacobson TenBroeck, by my daughter Neeltie, viz Jacob, Dirck and Elizabeth, £200, and calls his daughter, Neeltie, the wife of Samuel Stout, and gives her £10, by which it would appear that Neeltie DeWitt married, first, a TenBroeck, and second, a Stout, and that her daughter, Anna, likewise married a Stout. Dirck De Witt was rich and left a good-sized family

LINE OF JOHN STOUT

Issue

46 Wessel Tenbrooke Stout
47 Richard Stout
48 Jonathan Stout
49 Elizabeth Stout
50 Rhoda Stout, married Mr. Burdon

30 PETER STOUT, son of Jonathan Stout, 9, was born in 1744, died in 1828, and married, by license dated Nov 16, 1767, Charity Williams

1775, Aug 20 He recorded his father's cattle-mark, and, in 1789, transferred it to his brother, Abram Stout.

Peter Stout was a Royalist, as appears in the Report of the Bureau of Archives, of Ontario, Part 1, p 119

Claim of Peter Stout of Middletown, N J, stated he had a brother, Abraham Stout Peter received 200 acres under the will of his father, dated October, 1773, and the property was confiscated and sold, and one, Burrows, bought it

He doubtless returned to Middletown from New Brunswick, (Canada), as appears by his will.

1827, Oct 22 Peter Stout made his will, which was proved July 12, 1828, and mentioned his children, and his nephew, Abram Stout, Jr

Issue

51 Peter Stout
52 Jonathan Stout
53 John Stout
54 Leah Stout*, wife of Mr Martin in 1827
55 Charity Stout, married, Sept 1, 1799, Asher Vaughan, and was living in 1827.

31 ABRAM STOUT, son of Jonathan Stout, 9, was born in 1750, died in 1830, and married Mary Willet, born in 1762; died in 1844.

1789, May 28 He recorded his cattle-mark

1828, Mch. 18. Abram Stout made his will, which was proved Sept 27, 1830, and mentioned his wife, Mary, and children by name

Issue

56 Abram Stout, born 1804, died 1832.
57 Helena Stout, married, Apr. 11, 1802, Thomas Shepherd, Esq, and was living in 1828.
58 Thomas Stout
59 Charles Stout
60 Catharine Stout ⎫ recorded cattle-mark, in 1834, which, in 1854, passed to William
61 Esther Stout   ⎭ Carhart.
62 Mary Stout
63 Other children

32 HANNAH STOUT, daughter of Jonathan Stout, 9, was born Dec. 15, 1732, died Sept 18, 1757; buried in the Presbyterian Churchyard, Middletown, N J, and had a romantic history She was engaged to Lawrence Smyth, who had gone to England to settle his father's

---

*Lieba [Leah] Stout married, Dec 13, 1795, David Moorehouse

estate When returning, his ship was wrecked, and none, save himself and the Captain, were saved Hastening home, he found his fiancée, Hannah Stout, had been dead two weeks.

33 ESTHER STOUT, daughter of Jonathan Stout, 9, married, first, Mr Frost, and second, Mr. Hedden

There was a James Frost, Esq., born Jan. 1, 1769, died Mch 23, 1821, with wife, Lydia, daughter of Benjamin and Lydia (Crawford-Compton) Morris, who died, Nov 23, 1863, aged ninety years, nine months and twenty-eight days, who had three children, Rachel, Eliza Ann, and Caroline This James Frost, Esq., may have been a son of Esther by her first husband.

By Mr Hedden, she probably had Jonathan Hedden, born Jan 31, 1780, died Apr. 15, 1882, who married Mary . . . . ., born Aug 5, 1791, and died Apr 28, 1847 They had a daughter, Esther Hedden, who died, Nov 23, 1843, aged 21 years and 6 months, and a daughter, Caroline Hedden, born Sept 11, 1829, died Nov. 29, 1841

34 MARY STOUT, daughter of Jonathan Stout, 9, was married, by license dated Mch. 6, 1764, to Herrick Benjamin, of Morris County, New Jersey, and was dead at the time her father's will was made, which refers to her children, Leah Benjamin and Stout Benjamin She was a legatee in the will of her uncle, Zephaniah White, in 1758.

Issue
Leah Benjamin
Stout Benjamin

38 JOHN STOUT, son of Richard Stout, 14, was born July 2, 1766, died May 28, 1844; married Esther . . . . ., born June 26, 1770; died Aug 26, 1837

1809, Mch 4 He, as the son of Richard Stout, recorded the earmark that had been his father's, in 1753, and his grandfather, John's, 4, in 1698. He was a carpenter

Issue
64 Leah Stout, born 1797, died May 12, 1829
65 Richard W Stout, married Mary, daughter of Jehu and Hannah (Gordon) Patterson, born Apr 28, 1804; died Sept. 21, 1837

Issue
Jacob Tenbrook Stout, born Nov 23, 1832; died Jan 5, 1835
66 Sarah Stout, born Jan 24, 1804, died Sept 29, 1847, married John Patterson.

Issue
John Jacob Timbrook Patterson, born June 28, 1835; died Apr. 29, 1852.
67 James F Stout, born 1808, died July 23, 1851.
68 Jacob Tenbrook Stout, born 1812; died June 2, 1830.

39 JOHN STOUT, son of Thomas Stout, 19, was born Sept 28, 1772, and died 1838 He married, Feb 8, 1798, Martha, daughter of Thomas and Amy Bedel, who was born Mch. 25, 1780

1801, May 13 He recorded his cattle-mark, derived from his grandfather, John Stout

1837, Dec 19. John Stout made his will, which was proved Dec 19, 1838, in which he mentioned that he was of Middletown

LINE OF JOHN STOUT

Issue

69 Joseph Stout, born Nov 22, 1798, deceased, prior to 1837, leaving

Issue

John Stout
William Stout
James Stout

70 Douglass C Stout, born May 25, 1800; married, Dec. 11, 1822, Rachel McLean, and died May 22, 1834.
71 John Stout, born Oct. 2, 1801, in 1837, he had a daughter, Desire Stout
72 Richard B Stout, born Jan. 16, 1803
73 Catharine Stout, born Aug 26, 1804; in 1837, she was Catharine Stricker.
74 Elijah Stout, born Feb 23, 1806
75 Thomas Stout, born Dec. 17, 1807, probably married Amelia . . . .

Issue

Elizabeth Stout, who died, Apr 2, 1838, aged 4 years, 7 months and 11 days
76 Joel Stout, born May 18, 1809
77 Sarah Ann Stout, born Jan. 17, 1812, in 1837, she was Sarah Ann Sprowl
78 Jarret S Stout, born, Oct 9, 1813, on the old Stout Farm, at Centreville, near Keyport, died Feb. 20, 1906. He married, in 1831, Sarah Jane Dickerson, who died in 1894. He was the oldest resident of Keyport at the time of his death, and was the last of a family of fourteen children At the time of his death he left

Issue

Daughter . , married Francis Van Gieson.
William H Stout, of Forrest Hill.

79 Elizabeth Stout, born Oct. 6, 1815, in 1837, she was Elizabeth Walling
80 Lucy Stout, born Mch 1, 1819, in 1837, she was unmarried.
81 Maria Stout, born Sept 6, 1820, unmarried in 1837.
82 William Stout, born Feb. 27, 1823.

40 RICHARD STOUT, "at the Sawmill," son of Thomas Stout, 19, was born Sept 20, 1781, died Oct. 31, 1828, married, Apr 21, 1812, Sarah, daughter of Thomas Bedel, born 1793, died Mch. 23, 1849.

1824, Nov 13 He recorded his cattle-mark, formerly that of his father

Issue

83 William Stout, born Apr 16, 1813, died, Jan. 9, 1815, aged 1 year, 9 months and 23 days
84 Peter Stout, married Lucy Stout
85 Tenbrook Stout, born April 30, 1822, died, June 12, 1838, aged 16 years, 1 month and 12 days
86 Thomas Stout
87 Edward Stout, born Apr 2, 1824, died, July 29, 1844, aged 20 years, 3 months and 27 days
88 Ann Stout

46 COLONEL WESSEL TENBROOKE STOUT, son of Richard Stout, 27, born Nov 2, 1752, died Nov 11, 1818, buried in the Presbyterian Churchyard, at Allentown, N. J. He

was an officer, of reputation, in the Revolution, and probably made a Montgomery or Wikoff alliance

    Issue
- 88ª Elzabeth Stout; died Mch 4, 1850, buried at Allentown
- 88ᵇ Richard Montgomery Stout, born Nov 12, 1789, died Jan 19, 1857, buried at Allentown, N. J , married Mary . , and had

      Issue
    Caroline Holmes Stout, died, May 14, 1840, in her 17th year
    Peter Wikoff Stout, died Apr 9, 1860
    Wessel T Stout, M. D., died Feb 26, 1862
    Mary Stout, died Feb 10, 1883

47 RICHARD STOUT, son of Richard Stout, 27, married . .

    Issue
- 89 Richard Tenbrook Stout, born Jan 18, 1821, died May 19, 1853; married Elizabeth Bek

48 JONATHAN R STOUT,* son of Richard Stout, 27, born Mch 5, 1758, died, Sept 25, 1834, aged 76 years, 6 months and 20 days; married Hannah . . . . . ,* born Dec. 30, 1764; died Sept. 10, 1853
 1834, Sept 20 He made his will, which was proved Oct. 24, 1834, and in which he mentioned.
Wife, Hannah
Son, James D Stout
Daughter, Elizabeth D Stout
Son, Richard Stout
Daughter, Susan M Stout
Daughter, Nancy Forman
Daughter, Rachel Borden
Daughter, Lucy Giberson
Daughter, Eleanor Perrine
Grand-daughter, Mary Borden
Brother, John Stout.

    Issue
- 90 James D. Stout,* born Oct 5, 1786, died Sept 30, 1857
- 91 Elizabeth D. Stout,* born Sept 28, 1788, died Apr 3,1863
- 92 Richard T Stout,* born Nov 8, 1796; died Feb 11, 1868.
- 93 Susan M. Stout
- 94 Nancy Stout, married Mr. Forman
- 95 Rachel Stout, married Mr. Borden.
- 96 Lucy Stout,* born Apr 7, 1794, died Apr. 17, 1869; married Gilbert Giberson, Jr ,* born Sept 20, 1792, died Feb 2, 1832
- 97 Eleanor Stout, married Mr Perrine.
- 97ª Maria Stout,* born Mch. 20, 1804; died Sept 5, 1814.

51 PETER STOUT, son of Peter Stout, 30, was born 1767, died May 25, 1835, married Catharine . , born Jan 6, 1777; died May 20, 1847 Buried in the Baptist Churchyard, Middletown, N J
 His will was proved June 3, 1835.

---
*Buried at Allentown, N J , in the Presbyterian Churchyard

84 PETER STOUT, son of Richard Stout, 40, married Lucy Stout
    Issue
    98 Crawford Stout, born 1849; died May 5, 1850
    99 William Edward Stout, born 1847, died June 30, 1848
    100 Sarah Stout, died, Aug 16, 1845, aged 8 months and 21 days

89 RICHARD TENBROOK STOUT, son of Richard Stout, 47, born, at Tom's River, Jan 18, 1821, died May 19, 1853, married Elizabeth Bek
    Issue
    101 Wesley B. Stout, married June 6, 1888, Mary E. Lord
        Issue
        Richard Weslord Stout
    102 Joseph C W Stout
    103 Richard T Stout

LINE OF RICHARD STOUT

3 RICHARD STOUT, son of Richard Stout, 1, was born, by deduction, at Gravesend, Long Island, about 1646, or a little later. He doubtless accompanied his father in the migration to Middletown, in 1665, for his father bases an application for lands on this fact, yet, in December, 1667, upon the first division of lands, in Middletown, he, personally, was ignored, which was probably from the fact that he was still a youth and living at home with his parents

Richard Stout, 3, had two wives, an early one by the name of Frances, and a later one by the name of Mary I cannot say, with certainty, what their surnames were, but one was, I think, a Seymour and the mother of Frances was Frances   who married, for her first husband, a man with name yet unknown   As the wife of this unknown man, she had this daughter, Frances [Stout], and as the widow of this unknown man, she became the second wife of Robert West, whose first wife, Elizabeth, joined him [Robert West] in a deed, Oct 18, 1663, in Rhode Island. Upon Robert West's death, she, Frances, married, third, Edmond Lafetra*, and was probably his sole wife This Frances had issue by all three of her husbands, by the first, a daughter, called Frances   , who became the wife of Richard Stout, certainly prior to

---

*The will of Edmund Lafetra has been variously interpreted The following, I believe, is its correct explanation, viz Robert West, Sr , of Rhode Island, and afterwards of Shrewsbury, married twice, first, Elizabeth   , by whom he had
    Issue
    Robert West, Jr , who took the Oath of Allegiance with his father, in 1667-8
    Joseph West, married, May 12, 1692, Mary Webley
    Elizabeth West, erroneously assumed by many to have been a daughter of Edmund Lafetra, and the wife of John West
    Ann West, who married Henry Chamberlain
    Mary West, who married Nathaniel Cammock
Robert West married, second, Frances   , a widow, whose maiden and widowed names are alike unknown, she was the mother by her first husband (unknown) of a daughter Frances, who became the wife of Richard, the son of Richard and Penelope Stout, and is referred to in the will of Edmund Lafetra, as Frances Stoutt   And by this marriage to Frances   , Robert West had
    Issue
    John West, an only child, so far as we know, by this marriage
Afterwards this same Frances, upon the death of her husband, Robert West, took for her third husband, Edmund Lafetra, by whom she had
    Issue
    Edmund Lafetra
    Sarah Lafetra
Under the generous roof of the kind-hearted Quaker, Edmund Lafetra, were reared these four separate sets of children, and in his will the noble man called each one of them "son" or "daughter" or "child "

1679-80, and probably prior to 1676, which, if we do not allow, would necessitate Richard Stout having an earlier wife with name unknown, which I hardly think is likely.

In a letter, in my possession, written by William Leeds, about 1736, to   . Cox, concerning a title to land in dispute between them, he says

"Richd. Stout married a girl in Shrewsbury and settled there and his father lived in Middletown and passing and repassing from one to the other he took a liking to some land at Swiming River   The Gen'l Surveyor then being a measuring land thereabouts to the people Stout got him to measure him a piece the 1 June 1676, in order to settle it, but Stout's wife would not go so far unless he would get a neighbor to go with her "   He then asked Thomas Wright, of Shrewsbury, with his wife, to settle on the tract he had just obtained and he would sell him part.

"In the Fall the patent was sent to Stout from Elizabethtown   Then they went to Leonard to read it to them for neither of them could read," etc , etc

That Richard Stout secured this land is certain, as "Richard Stout, Jr , was on the boundary of Grover's Inheritance, in 1676," which lay on Swimming River, and he also made good his offer to Wright, in a deed dated June 22, 1676, which he signed alone, not being joined by his wife. New Jersey Archives, Vol XXI, p. 232

Wright repudiated the deed when he ascertained that he had to pay quit-rent on the lands, and the claims of his supposed descendants, the Walls and the Coxes, rested upon the question of his rights, in their contention with William Leeds

At all events, whether Wright settled on the land as his neighbor, or not, Stout, himself, did, and took with him to this home, in 1676, a wife. She was probably Frances, as Feb 7, 1679-80, Richard Stout, Jr , and wife, Frances, jointly signed a conveyance to William Leeds, of Shrewsbury.

Richard Stout acquired considerable land in Monmouth County   Among the Warrants, Surveys and Conveyances, from the Proprietors, appear

1675 to 1686, he paid quit-rents on one hundred and twenty acres of land

1675, Nov 2 He had one hundred and twenty acres at Shrewsbury

1676, June 23. He had one hundred and eighty-four acres granted to him

1676, June 28. He had one hundred and eighty-four acres granted to him, later conveyed to William Leeds

In 1676, Richard Stout, Jr., was still of Middletown, when he divided with Thomas Wright land surveyed about the first of June, 1676

1686 He paid quit-rent on Middletown lands

1687, June 20. He had one hundred and twenty acres granted him, adjacent to Richard Stout, the elder.

1689, June 24 Samuel Leonard, of Colt's Neck, bought lands from the Indian Sachems, of Manasquan, lying at Manasquan, beginning at Squancum, for various goods, rum, etc., which he assigned to Richard Stout, Jr , Dec 19, 1689

Richard Stout, 3, and his descendants, settled at Shrewsbury, and bought lands at Long Branch, Deal, Manasquan and Barnegat, all places to the South along the shore.

He had little opportunity to acquire education, and there was little need for it, so, that like many others among the early settlers, he made his mark, as did his wife, Mary

On the other hand, John Stout, 2, the brother of Richard Stout, 3, resided at Middletown, where he and his descendants owned land and bought to the Northward, towards the Bay Shore   John Stout's son, Richard Stout, also married a wife, Mary, and was contemporary with

Richard Stout, 3, and Mary, his wife, but they may easily be separated, for Richard Stout, 3, with wife, Mary, were identified with Shrewsbury and made their marks to documents, while Richard Stout, son of John Stout, 2, with wife, Mary, were identified with Middletown, and both signed their names to documents

The following items shed light upon Richard Stout's later years and upon his children

1687, Dec. 3. Richard Stout, Jr, received land from Samuel Leonard, which he conveyed, 1, 10, 1691, (calling himself planter, of Manasquan, at which time he signed by his mark), to Ananias Gifford This transfer may have been the result of a suit brought by Richard Stout, Jr., of Middletown, Nov 21, 1687, against Samuel Leonard, of Colt's Neck

1704 Richard Stout and Mary Stout witnesses to a marriage.

1705, Dec. 20. Richard Stout, Sr., of Shrewsbury, yeoman, and Robert Stout, own son of the said Richard Stout, also of Shrewsbury, singleman, conveyed, for £30, to Joseph Hulett, singleman, of Shrewsbury, fifty-five acres of land, in Shrewsbury, which Richard Stout, Sr, purchased from Hananiah Gifford, Mch. 10, 1691, and conveyed to his son, Robert Stout, Apr 7, 1703 Richard Stout and Robert Stout both signed the deed by their marks.

1709, Sept 26 Richard Stout, Sr., yeoman, of Shrewsbury, and Mary, his wife, conveyed to Ebenezer Cook, yeoman, of Shrewsbury, for £175, land, at Long Branch, and six acres of meadow, at Portapeck, being in all two hundred and thirty-five acres, reserving a piece of ground three rods square, where the said Richard Stout's former wife lies buried, which land was conveyed to Richard Stout, Sr, by Ananias Gifford Mch 4, 1691 Signed by Richard Stout and Mary Stout by their marks Recorded 1736

1709, Nov 11 Richard Stout, Sr, yeoman, of Shrewsbury, conveyed to his loving son, Joseph Stout, of Shrewsbury, carpenter, for the love and fatherly care "I have for his Advantage & Preferment in this World," land and meadow, lying at Manasquan River, being one-half of the tract of land conveyed to Richard Stout by Ebenezer Cook, Sept 26, 1709, bounded by David Stout's line, etc. Signed by Richard Stout and Mary Stout by their marks Witnesses John Gifford, Joseph Gifford and Samuel Dennis, Jr Recorded 1734

1713, Apr 28 Richard Stout, yeoman, of Shrewsbury, and Mary, his wife, exchanged with William Jefferys, yeoman, of Shrewsbury, his land, known as Deal, containing one hundred and twenty acres, bounded by lands of Francis Jeffery, Whale Pond Brook, Thomas Potter's land, etc, excepting a burying place "where Benjamin Rogers, deceased, lyes buried," which land was conveyed to Richard Stout by Benjamin Rogers May 1, 1712, for land belonging to William Jeffery, which he had derived from Francis Jeffery Feb 21, 1712 Signed by Richard Stout by his mark Witnesses Jonathan Allen, Joseph Wardell, Jacob Dennis, Thomas Bently Recorded 1731-2

1714, June 19 Richard Stout, of Shrewsbury, yeoman, and Mary, his wife, for £300, sold to William Jeffery, yeoman, of Shrewsbury, property at Deal, which was conveyed to said Stout, Apr 28, 1713, by the said Jeffery William Jeffery was the son of Francis Jeffery, of Shrewsbury, who also had another son by name, Francis Jeffery Richard Stout signed by his mark Mary, his wife, did not sign Registered 1731-2

1717, May 8 Richard Stout, yeoman, of Shrewsbury, conveyed to Gabriel Stelle, and Elizabeth, his wife, land, at Deal, which said Stout had from Jeffries, in 1713, for land, on the South side of Manasquan River, which had been deeded to Stelle, in 1717

Back of Lib H, p 29, Freehold, N J, Records

Issue

4 Richard Stout; married Eve   , prior to 1718, and probably was he who was called "Squan Dick"

5 Robert Stout, single, in 1705, when he received lands from his father, bought land in 1709
6 Joseph Stout, received land, from his father, in 1709
7 David Stout, died, intestate and unmarried, prior to 1718
8 Seymour Stout
9 Penelope Stout (supposed)
10 Lucy Stout
11 John Stout (supposed)
12 Rebecca Stout (supposed)

Of these sons, one married and had a daughter, Frances Stout, who married, 11 mo , 6, 1734, Wilbur Lippincott, son of William [son of Remembrance] and Hannah (Wilbur) Lippincott, born 1 mo , 18, 1710; died 10 mo , 1775 and had

Issue

Margaret Lippincott, born 10 mo., 17, 1735
Ann Lippincott, born 8 mo., 7, 1737, married Mr. Ford
Jediah Lippincott, born 4 mo , 9, 1740, married   and had

Issue

Hannah Lippincott, married, by license dated Nov. 20, 1782, Abraham Vanderveer
James Lippincott

(?) Patience Lippincott, married Mr Middleton
Richard Lippincott, born Jan 2, 1745, died May 14, 1826; married, first, 9 mo., 5, 1769, Mary Scull; second, Mch 4, 1770, Esther, daughter of Jeremiah and Esther (Tilton) Borden (This was the Captain Richard Lippincott engaged in the Huddy affair He settled in Canada, and from his daughter, Esther Borden Lippincott, who married George Taylor Dennison, is descended a Dennison who had the old Family Bible)

There was, *presumably*, another Frances Stout, who was perhaps a daughter of one of Richard and Frances Stout's sons, and hence their grand-daughter. This assumption, for such it is, rests upon the fact that there was a *Frances*   , who became the wife of Job Throckmorton, of Shrewsbury, which given name, Frances, was apparently confined to the Stouts of Shrewsbury This Job Throckmorton was the son of Job and Sarah (Leonard) Throckmorton, and also was a resident of Shrewsbury Job Throckmorton and Sarah Leonard were married in 1685, and Job, their son, was born, by deduction, about 1690-95, and married, by deduction, Frances   . , about 1712 If this reasoning be correct, Frances would have been born too late to have been the daughter of Richard and Frances Stout, of Shrewsbury, but would have been the issue of one of their children

4 RICHARD STOUT, son of Richard Stout, 3, resided at Barnegat, N. J. He married Eve

1718, Oct 11 Richard Stout, (in the body of the deed he is called Richard Stout, Jr), yeoman, of Shrewsbury, and Eve, his wife, as heir to his loving brother, David Stout, late of Shrewsbury, who died intestate, conveyed eighty acres of land, on Shark River, bounded by John West, and ten acres of meadow, on the beach at Barnegate, bounded by Ananias Gifford's land, Stephen West, etc , to William Woolley, son of William Woolley, of Shrewsbury, yeoman, for the sum of £20, and the land bought by William Woolley, May 24, 1718, from William

LINE OF RICHARD STOUT

Brinley Richard Stout made his mark to the deed. Witnesses: Arch: Innes, Sam: Dennis, William Havens and Jacob Dennis. Recorded 1728 Book H , p. 49, Freehold, N J , Records.

1724, May 26 Richard Stout sold land to John Woolley, Jr.

That this individual, Richard Stout, Jr., was the son of Richard Stout, 3, and of the third generation is clear when it is recalled that the first Richard Stout died in 1705, and that the second Richard Stout's brother, David, was living, and moved to Amwell in 1725 He could not have been a son of Jonathan Stout, for Jonathan, in his will of 1722, speaks of his son, David, as yet alive, so that, by exclusion, he must have been a son of Richard, John, James or Peter Stout, of the second generation, and though I have no knowledge that James Stout had no son, David, or that Peter Stout, of the second generation, who died during his father's lifetime, and who left a wife, Mary, had other than a daughter, Mary, and a son, John, though reputed to have had a large family, still I am inclined to assign the Richard Stout, under discussion, to Richard Stout, of the second generation, and consider him the individual called "Squan Dick."

Squan Dick Stout settled at Squan and is reputed to have raised a large family, who dwelt at Barnegat and along the shore, where still their descendants may be found

Issue

13 Benjamin Stout; reputed son.

5 ROBERT STOUT, son of Richard Stout, 3.

1715, Oct. 10. Robert Stout, of Shrewsbury, yeoman, for £5, sold to Thomas Chambers, of Shrewsbury, yeoman, land on the South side of Shark River, which the said Robert Stout received by deed from Nicholas Wainwright July 20, 1709 Robert Stout signed by his mark Witnesses Samuel Dennis, William Exeen, Samuel Dennis, Jr Acknowledged by Robert Stout in 1720.

1734, Sept 5 Robert Stout, of Shrewsbury, yeoman, conveyed to Peter Le Conte, of Freehold, physician and chirurgeon, for £30–10–0, one hundred acres of land and meadow, which said Stout received from George Lafetra by deed dated June 28, 1732, the land being situated in Shrewsbury, at Barnigat Robert Stout signed by his mark Witnesses Samuel Dennis, Anthony Pintard and Obadiah Williams Acknowledged by *Robt Stout, 1784.*

1779, Feb 17 There was a Robert Stout whose property was confiscated because of his Toryism, and advertised for sale at this date His neighbors were those who were settled around Shrewsbury, and to the South thereof, which makes it probable that he was a descendant of Richard Stout, 3, and was likely the above mentioned Robert Stout, 5, or a son of his

6 JOSEPH STOUT, son of Richard Stout, 3, received from his father, in 1709, a deed of land at Manasquan River, in which he is mentioned as "carpenter, of Shrewsbury "

1728/9, Jan 22 Will of Joseph Stout, "of Shrewsberry," proved, by Adam Woolley and William Kneeburn, Mch 22, 1729 In it he mentioned·
Hannah, his beloved wife
"Cousen Jonathan Jacock, the son of Thomas Jacocks "
And made Jonathan and his father the executors.
His servant girl, Mary Burk, to be set free at his death
Witnesses Adam Woolley, William Kneeburn, Samuel Leonard

7 DAVID STOUT, son of Richard Stout, 3, bought lands from William West and Margaret, his wife, Sept 2, 1712, when he is alluded to as *singleman* and yeoman In 1718, he was dead, and his brother, Richard, was his heir-at-law.

8 SEYMOUR STOUT, son of Richard Stout, 3

1739, Aug 8 Seymour Stout, of Shrewsbury, singleman, sold to Henry Herbert, yeoman, the one-half part, or Easterly moiety of the same tract which was "conveyed to me by my loving father, Richard Stout, deceased, July 10, 1717" Signed his name "Seimour Stout"

Back of Book H , p. 30, Freehold, N J , Records

1747, Mch. 25 The above deed was acknowledged by Isaac Herbert, one of the witnesses.

It is my belief Seymour Stout married and had a family, though as against this, he was single, in 1739, twenty-two years after his father had established him in life with real estate It is likely that the group of children named in the following will belongs to him; if not, they belong to one of his brothers Certainly they are descendants of Richard Stout, 3.

Will of Abraham Stout, of New York, cordwainer, mentioned wife, Sarah, to whom he gave two houses in Water St , and all his household goods, and created her executrix, brothers, David and Seymour Stout, and sisters, Rebecca, Elizabeth and Mary Stout, an equal share in two houses adjacent to the above, and £20 more to his sister, Rebecca Written Sept 29, 1780, proved Oct 2, 1780

1779, Aug 10 Seymour Stout was a witness, in New York, to the will of John Bogart.

9 PENELOPE STOUT, supposed daughter of Richard Stout, 3.

On the authority of O B. Leonard, Esq , a daughter of this name was given to John, the son of Richard Stout, 1, but as this Penelope Stout was reputed to be of Shrewsbury, it is more than likely she was the daughter of Richard Stout, son of Richard Stout, 1, as he, and not his brother, John Stout, was the ancestor of those bearing the name Stout in Shrewsbury and further Southward

In 1731, Henry Jacobs Falkinburg, the first child born in Little Egg Harbor, N J., and the son of a father of the same name, married Penelope Stout, reputed of Shrewsbury, N. J.

Issue
John Falkinburg
David Falkinburg
Jacob Falkinburg
Henry Falkinburg; non compos
Hannah Falkinburg
Mary Falkinburg

10 LUCY STOUT, daughter of Richard Stout, 3, became the wife of Elisha Lawrence, who was born in 1666, and died in 1724. She was reputed to have been born in Shrewsbury, N. J.

1754, Aug 6 Elisha Stout, Jr., of Manasquan, bought land of William Burnet, of Amboy. It seems nearly certain, because of his location, that Elisha Stout, Jr , was a descendant of Richard Stout, 3, and, because of his name, Elisha, strongly corroborative of Lucy Stout, wife of *Elisha* Lawrence, being of Shrewsbury origin

11 JOHN STOUT, a supposed son of Richard Stout, 3

It has been customary to assign a John Stout, who was a sea-faring man, and called "Sailor John" to John Stout, 2. This "Sailor John" Stout married and had a large family, among whom was a daughter, Penelope Stout If the tradition concerning the existence of such a man be true, then the locality, the occupation and the fact that John, son of John Stout, 2, was of Middletown, and is accounted for, contradicts the assertion that John Stout, 11, was a son of John Stout, 2, and makes him of necessity a son of Richard Stout, 3.

LINE OF RICHARD STOUT

Issue
14 Penelope Stout

12 REBECCA STOUT, supposed daughter of Richard Stout, 3.

John Cramer, of Little Egg Harbor, N J, married, first, in 1721, Mary Andrews, who shortly died, and, in 1726, he and Rebecca Stout laid their intention of marriage before the Little Egg Harbor Monthly Meeting. She is not styled as "of Shrewsbury," though Mrs Blackman, in her account of the Cramer and Falkinburg families, says that she, and her sister, Penelope Stout, who married Henry *Jacobs* Falkinburg, in 1731, at Little Egg Harbor, came from Shrewsbury The descendants of these two Stouts were compiled by William Francis Creeger, of Philadelphia, in 1882, who then conjectured they were the descendants of David Stout. See History of Little Egg Harbor in Proceedings of the Surveyors Association of West Jersey and the Ancestry of the Children of James William White, M D

John Cramer and Rebecca Stout had

Issue
John Cramer
Semon Cramer [i. e. Semor Cramer.]*
Rachel Cramer
Elizabeth Cramer
Rebecca Cramer
Hannah Cramer

13 BENJAMIN STOUT, a son of Richard Stout, 4, on the authority of the Rev Mr. Schenck, married Mary Johnson

In a small cemetery, on the main road, Bayville, Ocean Co., N. J., are a number of modern stones erected to members of the Lewis, Long, Potter, Tilton, and other families. The earliest among them commemorate

Benjamin Stout died, Nov 5, 1821, aged 76 years, 4 months and 9 days
Mary Stout, wife of do., died, Mch 12, 1824, in her 78th year.

Issue
15 Capt. Benjamin Stout

14 PENELOPE STOUT, daughter of John Stout, 11, married John Sutphin, who removed later to Amwell, near Neshanic

In the Freehold, N J, Dutch Church, John Sutphen, Jr., and his wife, Pieternella Stout, had Jan Sutphen baptized Oct 25, 1741, which suggests that Penelope and Pieternella may have been the same individual.

Issue
Derick Sutphin
John Sutphin
Stout Sutphin
Sarah Sutphin

---
*Though the name Semon, printed in Mrs Leah Blackman's History of Little Egg Harbor Township, runs through several generations of the Cranmer family, I think it started originally with the spelling *Semor*, which if so, proves the kinship of Penelope and Rebecca Stout, of Shrewsbury, to Seymour Stout, of the same place, and it is worthy of mention as corroborative of this supposition, that Mrs Blackman, on page 295, of her work, mentions, in distinguishing the titles of several of the John Cranmers, that some of them were known as "John's John and *Semor's* John, Long John and Short John, Poplar Neck John and Beach John, Over-the-Plains John and Patty's John, Captain John and Bank John, Neddy's John and Bass River John"

15 CAPT BENJAMIN STOUT, son of Benjamin Stout, 13, married Sarah Breese He came from Squan, and bought the noted Thomas Potter farm, at Goodluck, where he died, Feb 13, 1850, aged 69 years, 7 [4] months and 5 days His wife died, Apr. 23, 1866, aged 82 years, 4 months and 20 days.
Capt Benjamin Stout was not in the War of 1812, but he had a substitute in Thomas Chadwick, the first husband of Amelia Bodine and brother of the wife of Esquire Daniel Stout.

Issue

16   Joseph Stout
17   Benjamin B. Stout, of Goodluck, 1878, wrote to Edwin Salter concerning his family
18   Daniel Stout
19   James Stout
20   John Stout
20ª Jane Stout, married Garret Stout. She was born Mch. 12, 1812, and died Nov. 16, 1895
20ᵇ Eliza Stout, died, Oct. 22, 1856, aged 37, 2, 0; married Forman Stout, who died, Aug, 18, 1852, aged 28, 4, 6 He was the son of Garret Stout, Sr , and his wife Elizabeth.
20ᶜ Sarah Stout
20ᵈ Rebecca Stout; married Francis Letts. She was born May 27, 1807, and died, Apr 26, 1828, aged 20 years and 11 months.

16   JOSEPH STOUT, son of Benjamin Stout, 15, born Oct. 3, 1803, died July, 3, 1863, or 1883; married Amelia, daughter of James and Sarah Falkinburg, died, Aug 22, 1870, aged 69 years, 8 months and 7 days

Issue

Charles Stout; living at Glenoka, Ocean Co , 1912; married Sylvia Grant.
Benjamin F Stout, born 1837, died, June 17, 1863, aged 26 years, 5 months and 8 days.

PROBABLE DESCENDENTS OF RICHARD STOUT, 3.

1   JAMES STOUT, son of   Stout, made his will Jan 31, 1760, which was proved Mch. 28, 1760, and in which he mentioned that he was of Shrewsbury, N. J , and named the following individuals.
Son, John Stout, executor
Daughter, Mary Potter, 10 shillings
Daughter, Penelope (Stout), 10 shillings
Grandson, John Stout
Grandson, Daniel Stout
Grandson, James Wells
Witnesses. John Potter, Jeams Wells, his mark, and Jacob Baker
The testator made his mark to the will His inventory amounted to £100-15-9

Issue

2   Mary Stout, married Mr Potter
3   Penelope Stout

LINE OF MARY STOUT (BOWNE)

    4 John Stout
    5 Daughter Stout, married Mr Wells, probably James Wells, and had
        Issue
        James Wells

4 JOHN STOUT, son of James Stout, 1, born about 1735, resided at Shrewsbury, N J. He married, by license dated Nov 28, 1752–3, Ruth Ellison He was called Capt. John Stout in the Revolutionary War. He died, in 1791, at Dover, N. J., intestate, and his wife administered on his estate

In 1795, Ruth Stout, widow of John Stout, with Amos Pharo, executors of the estate of James Stout, executed a deed to Daniel Stout, for land, in Dover, the plantation formerly belonging to John Stout, deceased.

    Issue
    6 John Stout
    7 Daniel Stout

7 DANIEL STOUT, son of John Stout, 4, was born Nov. 14, 1758, and died Sept. 3 [2], 1843. He married, Dec 25, 1792, Ann, daughter of Capt. Thomas and Elizabeth (Woolley) Chadwick, of the Revolution, born Dec 9, 1772, and died Oct 29, 1858. He resided at Goodluck, N J, he also lived for a while at Dover, N J He was a Revolutionary soldier and a Justice of the Peace. The square brackets enclose different dates, obtained from the Pension Office, otherwise the Bible and Pension Office dates are alike

Daniel Stout had a brother, John, killed in the Revolution, wrote Judge D I C. Rogers to Edwin Salter in 1877 Daniel Stout's farm was on the south side of Stout's Creek, Forked River, and ran to the Bay.

    Issue
    8 John Stout, born Oct 5, 1793, died Apr 2 [5], 1795.
    9 Elizabeth Stout, born Nov. 6, 1794, died, Jan 16, 1883, unmarried
   10 Hannah Stout, born Nov 16, 1796, married, Feb 28, 1818, William Rogers
   11 Rachel Stout, born Nov. 11, 1798; married John Williams
   12 Caroline Stout, born Nov. 16, 1800, died November, 1853; married, May 15, 1818, John, or Joseph, Henderson
   13 Catharine Stout, born Nov 8, 1802, married William Holmes
   14 Anna Stout, born Feb 25, 1805, died 1880, married, Feb 14, 1824, Joseph Holmes.
   15 Alice C. [Chadwick] Stout, born May 16, 1807; died, Apr 19, 1868, aged 61, 11, 3, married, Nov. 12, 1856, Randolph Dye
   16 Margaret Stout, born Nov. 29, 1809, married John Applegate
   17 Sarah [Cravel] Stout, born Sept. 11, 1812, died 1894, married David I C. Rogers

LINE OF MARY STOUT (BOWNE)

4 MARY STOUT, daughter of Richard Stout, 1, was born, I deduce, about 1648, and was married, at Gravesend, Long Island, according to various readings of the records of that town, either Nov 26, 1665, Dec 26, 1665, or Dec. 26, 1668, to James, the son of William Bowne

James Bowne moved from Gravesend and was among the first settlers of Middletown. He died prior to 1697, for in that year his son, James Bowne, took up lands in right of his deceased father. (See Bowne Family)

1675, Nov. 2. As a settler on the Monmouth Tract, prior to 1667, Mary Stout was alloted sixty acres in Middletown.

"James Bowne in right of his wife, Mary Stout, two hundred and forty acres."

Lib. 3, East Jersey Deeds, A side, page 1.

Issue
James Bowne
Samuel Bowne
William Bowne
John Bowne
Probably others.

LINE OF JAMES STOUT

5 JAMES STOUT, son of Richard Stout, 1, was born, by deduction, at Gravesend, Long Island, about 1650.

1675, Nov 2 As a settler on the Monmouth Patent, about 1667, he received sixty acres of land in Middletown

1685, Feb 16 He recorded his cattle-mark, at Middletown, but no further reference is found concerning it.

In 1686, he paid quit-rent on one hundred and forty-two and one-half acres of land, at Middletown.

1690, June 29 Richard Stout, of Middletown, gave land to his son, James Stout, of the same place, that was situated at Romanis or Hope River, and he also gave him five acres of meadow at Conescunk, described as "adjoining Dan. Stout" This is undoubtedly an error, and should have read David, in lieu of Dan, for I have no knowledge of the existence of any such an individual as Daniel Stout at this early date And an analysis of the lands, deeded by Richard Stout, Sr , to his sons of this date, sustains the conclusion This error is to be found on page 288, of Volume xxi, of the New Jersey Archives

1705, Mch. 18 James Stout bought land of George Willocks

1706, Apr. 6 James and Elizabeth Stout were of Middletown, and, Aug 11, 1707, of Freehold Both James and Elizabeth Stout made their marks

1711, May 8. James and Elizabeth Stout, of Freehold, sold land

1714, Jan 29 James Stout, of Freehold, yeoman, and Elizabeth, his wife, for £250, conveyed to Thomas Williams, of Freehold, yeoman, land, in Freehold, "where James Stout now lives," bounded by David Clayton, Jno Warford, etc , reserving one-half of an acre of land where John Clayton and his wife are buried, which land the said James Stout bought from George Willocks, Mch 18, 1705. James Stout and his wife, Elizabeth, both signed by their marks

1714, Jan. 29. James Stout, of Freehold, yeoman, and Elizabeth, his wife, for £40, sold to John Warford, yeoman, of Freehold, land in said town James and Elizabeth Stout both signed by their marks

He married Elizabeth . . . , who may have been the Elizabeth Stout, of Freehold, who was a member of the Baptist Church, at Middletown, in 1712.

There was another Elizabeth Stout, *of Middletown*, also a church member, at this date. ese two individuals were the wives of James and John Stout.

LINE OF JAMES STOUT

Issue

6 Benjamin Stout
7 James Stout
8 Joseph Stout
9 Penelope Stout, married William Jewell, and had Sarah Jewell, who married William Parke.
10 Mercy Stout, married Mr Warner, and had a large family
11 Ann Stout, married Cornelius Johnson, had a large family, and lived to a great age She outlived, by many years, all the other grand-children of Richard and Penelope Stout.
12 Elizabeth Stout; married Mr Warford

1705 The Grand Jury, of Monmouth Co., N. J, present Elizabeth, daughter of James Stout, of Middletown, for a bastard child by James Hid, late of Middletown. She was fined £5 and costs, or to be whipped ten lashes on her bare back The fine was paid by her father, James Stout

6 BENJAMIN STOUT, son of James Stout, 5, married Ruth Bogart. I doubt if Benjamin Stout was the son of James Stout, 5, though he is so reputed, but believe a generation has been dropped and that he was his grandson The dates of marriage of his following children I think prove the error

Issue

13 Sarah Stout, married John Taylor.

Issue

Peter Taylor

14 Joseph Stout, married, by license dated Dec 11, 1765, Theodosia, daughter of Gabriel Hoff.

Issue

John Stout
Mary Stout

15 Benjamin Stout; married Elizabeth, daughter of William Anderson, [marriage license dated Dec 11, 1765], and had many children
16 Elizabeth Stout; married John, son of Francis Quick Had seven children
17 Sarah Stout, married, by license dated Oct 11, 1762, Zebulon Stout, son of Zebulon, 3, Jonathan, 2, Richard, 1, no issue
18 Mary Stout; married Mr. Hunt
19 Rachel Stout, married Stephen Howell.
20 Ruth Stout, married ———
21 Ann Stout, married Abram Stout, by whom she had a daughter, Sarah Stout.

7 JAMES STOUT, reputed son of James Stout, 5, married Joanna Johnson.

Issue

22 Sarah Stout; married Samuel Furman, and had Sarah and James Furman.
23 Elizabeth Stout, married Abram Prall, and had William, Elizabeth and Hannah Prall.
24 Jemima Stout; married Thomas Hankison, and had children
25 Joanna Stout, married Rulif Sutphin, and had Col Abram, James, and three daughters

26 Thomas Stout, married twice, many children
27 Cornelius Stout, married Miss Longstreet
28 James Stout, married, by license dated Apr 25, 1775, Louisa Hart [Lois Weart?], by whom he had a daughter, and a son, Thomas, who married Elizabeth Burroughs.

8 JOSEPH STOUT, son of James Stout, 5, moved to Philadelphia; followed the sea, married, and had many children, among them

Issue

30 Joseph Stout, a sea captain, in 1779.

LINE OF ALICE STOUT (THROCKMORTON)

6 ALICE STOUT, daughter of Richard Stout, 1, was born, by deduction, at Gravesend, Long Island, about 1652. She was married, Dec. 12, 1670, to John, son of John Throckmorton, at Middletown, N J, second, to Robert Skelton, by license dated Oct. 30, 1691, and third, to Mr Jones

John Throckmorton died in the summer of 1690
1692 Robert Skelton was on the Petit Jury, for Monmouth County
Alice Stout was living with her husband, Robert Skelton, in Monmouth County, April, 1696-7
1704, Apr 13 Letters of Administration were granted to Alice Jones, mother of Joseph Throckmorton, lately deceased, intestate.
1704, May 15 Robert Skelton's Inventory was filed, he left an estate of large size. It was sworn to by Alice Jones, his relict and administratrix   New York Wills.

Issue by first husband, John Throckmorton:

7 Joseph Throckmorton, died unmarried.
8 Rebecca Throckmorton, married John Stillwell, Esq, of Staten Island.
9 Alice Throckmorton, married Thomas Stillwell
10 Patience Throckmorton, married, first, Hugh Coward, by license dated July 6, 1703; second, Mr. Lake.
11 Sarah Throckmorton; married Moses Lippit in 1697
12 Deliverance Throckmorton; died single

Issue by second husband, Robert Skelton

13 Susanna Skelton; married Barnes Johnson
14 Alice Skelton [?]

8 REBECCA THROCKMORTON, daughter of John Throckmorton and ALICE STOUT, 6, married John Stillwell, Esq, of Staten Island

Issue

15 Richard Stillwell
16 John Stillwell
17 Joseph Stillwell
18 Thomas Stillwell

19 Daniel Stillwell
20 Rebecca Stillwell
21 Mary Stillwell
22 Alice Stillwell

9 ALICE THROCKMORTON, daughter of John Throckmorton and ALICE STOUT, 6, married Thomas Stillwell, of Middletown, N. J.

Issue

23 Thomas Stillwell
24 John Stillwell, born 1709.

11 SARAH THROCKMORTON, daughter of John Throckmorton and ALICE STOUT, 6, married, in 1697, Moses Lippit.

Issue

25 Sarah Lippit, born 1705
26 John Lippit
27 Patience Lippit
28 Alice Lippit
29 Ann Lippit

13 SUSANNA SKELTON, daughter of Robert Skelton and ALICE STOUT, 6, married Barnes Johnson

Susanna Skelton was spoken of as the sister of the half blood of Joseph Throckmorton, her brother. She was living, and the wife of Barnes Johnson, of Monmouth County, in 1726, and, in 1750, was deceased, leaving a son and heir, Skelton Johnson

Issue

30 Skelton Johnson

14 ALICE SKELTON, daughter of Robert Skelton and ALICE STOUT, 6.

Whether such a daughter existed or not is problematical

Patience Lippit, a grand-daughter of Alice Stout Throckmorton-Skelton, married, at Shrewsbury, 11 mo., 17, 1717, John Woolley Her marriage certificate was signed by an Alice Skelton, at which time her grandmother was known to have been the wife of Mr Jones, so that the grandmother either erroneously signed her name *Skelton*, instead of Jones, or she had a daughter, Alice Skelton.

LINE OF PETER STOUT

7 PETER STOUT, son of Richard Stout, 1, was born, by deduction, at Gravesend, Long Island, about 1654, and died, at Middletown, N J, between 1702 and 1703, for, May 23, 1702, he recorded his cattle-mark which he "had held many years," and, June 9, 1703, in his father's will, he is mentioned as deceased

1675, Nov. 2. He was granted sixty acres of land, at Middletown, in right of his being a settler on the Monmouth Tract, in 1667.

1690, June 29. He received land by deed from his father, Richard Stout

HISTORICAL MISCELLANY

Peter Stout resided in Middletown, and is reputed to have been very rich, possessed of an excellent disposition, and much respected. He married Miss Bullen, perhaps Mary, if it is she who is spoken of in the will of Richard Stout, 1, as the wife of his son, Peter Stout, in 1703. He is reputed to have had a large family who settled in Monmouth County, along the seashore.

Issue

8 Mary Stout } as per will of Richard Stout, 1
9 John Stout }

9 JOHN STOUT, son of Peter Stout, 7.

1716, Oct. 9 John Stout, of Middletown, yeoman, son and heir of Peter Stout, of Middletown, deceased, for £500, sold land to Obadiah Holmes, of Middletown, yeoman, on Hop River, and meadow, at Conescunk, which land was conveyed to Peter Stout by his father, Richard Stout, June 29, 1690. The deed was signed by John Stout and Sarah Stout. Witnesses: Rebekeh Tilton, William Lawrence, Jr, Mercy Lawrence [daughter of Richard Hartshorne, born 1693] and Rachel Clark.

In 1716, Benjamin Stout, 10, an uncle of the aforesaid John Stout, had recently removed from Middletown to Delaware, where a number of families from East Jersey had settled on George's Creek, and it is supposed that they were drawn hither partly by the proximity of the Welsh Tract Baptist Church. Among these were three of the name of Stout.

John Stout, "of the township of Freehold, County of Monmouth, and Province of East Jersey," who bought land there on the north side of Dragon Swamp, May 8, 1708, Samuel Stout, with wife, Margaret, who bought land on George's Creek, in 1720; and "Elizabeth Stoute," who signed the marriage certificate of William Farson and Rachel Vail, in 1719.

The John Stout, whose name appears in Delaware, I believe corresponds to John Stout, 9, son of Peter Stout, 7, though he may be descended from some other one of the older sons of Richard and Penelope Stout. He signed the Confession of Faith of the Welsh Tract Baptist Church, in 1719, and disappears from the records in 1726.

LINE OF SARAH STOUT (PIKE)

8 SARAH STOUT, daughter of Richard Stout, 1, was born, by deduction, at Gravesend, Long Island, about 1656. She married, at Middletown, N. J., Feb 2, 1675, John Pike, of Woodbridge, N. J., son of John Pike, of the same place. He was born in 1639, and died, Aug 13, 1714, aged 75 years.

The Pikes were eminent in Woodbridge, N. J. Dally, in his history of that town, says of John Pike, the husband of Sarah Stout:

"The astute Judge John Pike, who having attained the age of seventy-five years, died in August, 1714, whether buried near his father, the distinguished Capt John Pike, we do not know, as no stone marks the tomb of the elder Pike Here, however, is Zebulon's grave and that of the third John"

Issue

9 John Pike, born Apr 9, 1677, died May 14, 1677
10 Sarah Pike, born Jan 15, 1679, died Dec 17, 1681
11 Joseph Pike, born Oct 18, 1680; died Dec 28, 1680
12 John Pike, born Dec 5, 1681
13 Joseph Pike, born Oct 24, 1683.
14 Sarah Pike, "ye 2nd," born Oct. 17, 1686.
15 Mary Pike, born Nov 9, 1687

16 Hannah Pike, born Dec 18, 1689
17 Zebulon Pike, born Aug 17, 1693, died Feb 6, 1763; buried, at Woodbridge, N J, in Presbyterian Cemetery

In 1680, John Pike, the First, had a daughter, Ruth, the wife of Abraham Tappin.
Historical Society Records, Newark, N J

John Pike, Jr, formerly of Newberry, in Essex County, New England, now of Woodbridge, N. J., planter, gave Letter of Attorney to his father, Capt. John Pike, to sell his lands in said place. No date

The Children of John and Sarah (Stout) Pike married and left a numerous progeny.

Joseph Pike, perhaps No 11, the son of John and Sarah (Stout) Pike, married, Dec 27, 1716, Elizabeth Frazee, at Woodbridge, N. J.

Issue
John Pike, born Jan 4, 1718.
Timothy Pike, born Apr. 3, 1720
Sarah Pike, born July 29, 1722.
Elizabeth Pike, born Apr. 23, 1725

FROM THE INSCRIPTION BOOK, HISTORICAL SOCIETY RECORDS, NEWARK, N. J:
Jane Pike died, May 15, 1761, aged 39, 0, 0.
James Pike died, Feb 18, 1759, aged 32, 11, 0.
Joseph Pike died Feb 16, 1730, aged 36, 0, 0
John Pike died, Feb 1, 1761, aged 43, 0, 0
Nathaniel Pike died, Sept. 22, 1766, aged 42, 0, 0.

All are buried at Woodbridge, N. J.

LINE OF JONATHAN STOUT

9 JONATHAN STOUT, son of Richard Stout, 1, was one of the younger children He married, Aug 27, 1685, Anna, daughter of James Bollen, Secretary of the Province, who died, at Woodbridge, N J, in 1682 James Bollen's daughter, Anna, and son, James, in May, 1683, selected Samuel Moore and Nathaniel Fitzrandolph as guardians

1685, Feb. 16 He recorded his cattle-mark, of which no later transfer is recorded
1686 He paid quit-rent on one hundred and forty-two and one-half acres, at Middletown, N J.
1698–9 He was Overseer of the Poor of Middletown, N. J.
1703, Jan. 26 John Chapman, yeoman, of Chesterfield, in Burlington County, N. J, sold to Jonathan Stout, yeoman, of Middletown, three hundred acres of land, lying above the Falls of the Delaware, for £65
1704, Jan 1 Jonathan Stout and Anna, his wife, of Middletown, sold to James Hubbard, of the same place, two hundred and fifty acres of land, in Middletown, and Meadow at Conasconck, for £328

The preceding sales and the following purchase were, apparently, made with the intention of moving to the Hopewell district, where, with two other families, he was about to found a settlement in the wilderness

1705, July 20 William Crouch, of London, and William Bills [Biles], of Bucks County, sold to Johathan Stout, of Burlington County, one sixteenth of one one-hundredth part of the Province of West Jersey.

1714, Mch 12. He and his wife, Anna, acknowledged a deed.

Jonathan Stout and his family were a devout set of people The first Baptist Church in Columbia village, Township of Hopewell, was organized, Apr 23, 1715, with Mr Stout and his family representing eight or nine of the fifteen constituent members. The church was constituted at his house, the meetings were chiefly held at the dwelling of the Stouts, from the foundation of the settlement till the erection of a meeting house, a period of forty-one years, and it was estimated that the total membership of the church, from first to last, contained, up to 1790, nearly two hundred of the Stout name, besides as many more of the blood of the Stouts, who had lost their name by intermarriage with others.

In 1790, two deacons and four elders of the church were Stouts, and the late Zebulon and David Stout had been main pillars of the church The last lived to see his descendants number one hundred and seventeen souls

In the early career of the Hopewell Church Edwards says that Joseph, Sarah, Benjamin, Hannah, David and Zebulon Stout were reputed to have gone to Pennsylvania for baptism, while the other children of Benjamin Stout, viz , Samuel, Jonathan and Ann Stout were baptized in Hopewell, although the church books do not give the names.

1722, Nov 24. Jonathan Stout made his will, which was proved Mch. 25, 1723, and mentioned.

Son, Joseph
Daughters, Sarah, Hannah, and
Sons, Benjamin, Zebulon, Jonathan and David, to each of whom he gave one shilling.
Son, Samuel, received a negro girl
Daughter, Ann, received a negro girl
Executor Andrew Smith
The inventory of his estate amounted to £362-2-10¾

Some of the descendants of Jonathan Stout are reputed to have moved to Kentucky, and the South, about the time of the Revolutionary War.

Issue

10 Joseph Stout, born, Oct. 25, 1686, in Middletown.
11 Sarah Stout, born, Sept 10, 1689, in Middletown.
12 Benjamin Stout, born, Dec. 14, 1691, in Middletown
13 Hannah Stout, born, Mch 29, 1694, in Middletown.
14 David Stout, born, in 1706, as per Asher Taylor, Esq.*
15 Zebulon Stout, born, in 1699, as per Nathan Stout
16 Samuel Stout, born, in 1709, as per Asher Taylor, Esq
17 Jonathan Stout, born, 1701, as per Nathan Stout, pamphlet written in 1823.
18 Ann Stout, born, in 1704, married Nehemiah Bonham, and had a daughter Anne, who married Benjamin Reeder Her mother was nigh on to sixty years old at her birth

10 COL. JOSEPH STOUT, son of Jonathan Stout, 9, was born Oct 25, 1686, and died Oct 22, 1766 He married Ruth, daughter of Dr Henry Greenland. She was a constituent member of the Hopewell Church, in 1715, with her husband and his family

---

*Asher Taylor, Esq , the early Middletown genealogist, and Nathan Stout, give the date of Benjamin Stout's birth as 1696, which is wrong, unless the Benjamin Stout, who was born in 1691, died, and a second son was so called Asher Taylor also gives to Sarah Stout, 11, a husband, Andrew Smith

LINE OF JONATHAN STOUT

1722 Joseph Stout was on the Hopewell Tax Roll, and had twenty-eight cattle, eighteen sheep, two hundred and thirty acres of land, and was married.

In 1731, Joseph Stout was one of many defendants to popular land ejectment suits.

1749, Aug 29 Jos Stout, Esq, of Hopewell, N J, gave a deed to John Stout, his son. Witnesses were David and Jonathan Stout.

In 1753, Col Joseph Stout was assessed in Hopewell

Issue

19 John Stout
20 Joseph Stout
21 Col Jonathan Stout
22 James Stout
23 Mary Stout; married Harmon Rosenkranz She had issue. Alexander, Joseph, John, Catharine, Mary and Rachel
24 Ann Stout; married Mr Worth, and had children.
25 Ruth Stout; married Mr Leonard, and had children.
26 Rachel Stout, married Mr Stockton, and had issue. Joseph and Richard Stockton. Upon the death of Mr. Stockton, Rachel Stout married Mr Reddal, by whom she had a daughter, Ann

11 SARAH STOUT, daughter of Jonathan Stout, 9, was born Sept. 10, 1689, married Andrew Smith

Issue

Ann Smith; married Thomas Hirst, or John Titus
Jonathan Smith; married Miss Hixon.
Andrew Smith, married Miss Mershon
George Smith, married, and had a family.
Charles Smith, married ———
Timothy Smith, married Miss Lott

12 BENJAMIN STOUT, son of Jonathan Stout, 9, was born Dec 14, 1691, married Hannah Bonham.

There was a Benjamin Stout, Sr., on the Assessment Roll, of Hopewell, in 1753, and a Benjamin Stout, Jr., who may have been his son

Issue

28 Jonathan Stout, married Miss Jewell, lived one hundred years, and had a large family
29 Hezekiah Stout, married, first, Widow Smith, second, Widow Sorter, lived to nearly one hundred years No issue
30 Benjamin Stout; married, first, Rebecca Dulhangel, second, Sept 17, 1772, by license, *Marthew* Schihok [Skyhawk] He had large families by both wives
31 Nathaniel Stout; married Charity Furman; had a daughter, Rhoda Stout, who married, first, Zephaniah Stout, second, Burges Allison, and had issue by both husbands
33 Ezekiel Stout, married Miss Drake; had many children
34 Hosea Stout, married in Virginia, had many children
35 Mary Stout; married William Heabron, had issue
36 Hannah Stout; married David Ollivant
37 Sarah Stout, married Andrew Bray.

13 HANNAH STOUT, daughter of Jonathan Stout, 9, was born Mch. 29, 1694; married Jediah Higgins

Issue

Mary Higgins, married her mother's first cousin, Benjamin, son of David Stout, son of Richard Stout, the First
Joseph Higgins
Jonathan Higgins
Joshua Higgins
James Higgins
Rachel Higgins

14 DAVID STOUT, son of Jonathan Stout, 9, was born in 1706, and married Elizabeth Garrison. Of him Nathan Stout wrote, in 1823. "He was reputed an honest man and a Christian, which I believe to be the two highest traits of which human nature is susceptible."

In 1722, David Stout was assessed on the Hopewell Tax List, for ten cattle, one sheep, two hundred and fifty acres of land, and was married.

There was a David Stout, Sr., on the Assessment Roll, of Hopewell, in 1753, and another David Stout, who may have been his son

Issue

38 Jonathan Stout
39 Andrew Stout
40 James Stout
41 David Stout, married Charity Burrows and had Mary Stout, who married Jared Saxton, and Elizabeth Stout, who married Nathaniel Burrows
42 Elizabeth Stout, married Freegift Stout, her second cousin.
43 Ann Stout, married Timothy Merrill, or Merrit.
44 Mary Stout, married John, son of Lewis Chamberlain.
45 Sarah Stout, married Moses Randolph
46 Hannah Stout, married James Wyckoff, by license dated Apr 2, 1765, and had a son, Peter Wyckoff, who had a daughter, Mary, who married John I. Updike, of Hopewell, son of Jesse, grandson of Laurence.

15 ZEBULON STOUT, son of Jonathan Stout, 9, was born in 1699, and married Charity, daughter of Thomas Burrows, of Hopewell, N. J

There was a Zebulon Stout on the Assessment Roll, of Hopewell, in 1753.

Issue

47 John Stout
48 Zebulon Stout
49 Ann Stout; married, by license dated July 23, 1744, Ichabod Leigh
50 Hannah Stout, married John Bunson [Brinson?]
51 Mary Stout; married, by license dated Mch. 14, 1770, Francis Carbine.
52 Rachel Stout, married, by license dated Dec 22, 1747, Stephen Barton [Bartow?]
53 Charity Stout; married Nathaniel Stout, son of David and Ann (Merrill) Stout
54 Sarah Stout, married, first, Abraham Skillman; second, by license dated June 4, 1764, Nathaniel Stout

LINE OF JONATHAN STOUT

16 SAMUEL STOUT, son of Jonathan Stout, 9, was born in 1709, and married, first, in 1729, Catharine Simpson, widow of his cousin, James, son of David Stout, second, Widow Limbrook, perhaps Tenbrook.

There was a Samuel Stout, Esq, on the Assessment Roll, of Hopewell, for 1753.

Issue by first wife

55 Samuel Stout, born February, 1732

Issue by second wife

56 Jonathan Stout, married, by license dated Apr 1, 1775, Sarah Phillips; raised a large family of children.
57 Andrew Stout, died single

17 JONATHAN STOUT, son of Jonathan Stout, 9, married Mary Lee.

In 1731, Jonathan Stout of Hopewell, was one of many defendants to popular land ejectment suits

Issue

58 Zebulon Stout; single.
59 Samuel Stout, married, and had many children.
60 Jonathan Stout; married Miss Swym, had several children
61 David Stout, married Sarah Park; had several children, moved West
62 Ann Stout; married Andrew Stout, son of David and Elizabeth (Garrison) Stout.
63 Sarah Stout, married, first, Moses Morgan, second, by license dated June 22, 1777, Andrew Stout, her cousin, son of David and Elizabeth (Garrison) Stout.

19 JOHN STOUT, son of Joseph Stout, 10, was born in 1706; died July 27, 1761, married, by license dated Nov. 2, 1730, Catharine Stout, daughter of Richard and Mary (Tilton) Stout, son of John and Elizabeth Stout, son of Richard and Penelope Stout

Issue

64 Richard Stout; married Penelope Park
65 Jehu Stout
66 Daniel Stout; married Charity Brinson
67 Mary Stout, born 1727, died Apr 23, 1773, married, by license dated Jan 27, 1749, Samuel Holmes, born Oct. 4, 1726, died Nov 29, 1769
68 Ruth Stout, married John Sutton, a Baptist minister in Virginia The Rev John Sutton was born, at Basking Ridge, N. J., Feb. 12, 1733, and probably descended from William Sutton, of Eastham, Mass, which, however, is not assured He married Ruth Stout, second daughter of John and Catharine Stout, between 1780 and 1785, whose home was at Hopewell, N J Their descendant, D R Browning, Esq, of Lewisburg, Logan Co, Ky, wrote me in 1897, on the subject of his family.
69 Rebecca Stout, married Henry Sorter
70 Rachel Stout; married Nehemiah Stout, son of David and Ann (Merrill), son of David and Rebecca (Ashton), son of Richard and Penelope Stout

20 JOSEPH STOUT, son of Joseph Stout, 10, married Rebecca Grover, probably a granddaughter of Safety Grover

There was a Joseph Stout on the Assessment Roll, of Hopewell, for 1753.
1785, Nov 14 Richard Stout and Joseph Stout, both of Burlington Co, sold land, bought by them, to Daniel Ellis

Issue

71 Grover Stout, married, by license dated Mch. 16, 1775, Frances Mitchel.
72 Safety Stout, single.
73 Esther Stout; married Peter Sorter.
74 Joseph Stout, married a daughter of George Garrison or Garretson, and had many children

21 COL. JONATHAN STOUT, son of Joseph Stout, 10, married Elizabeth, daughter of Wilson Hunt

Issue

75 Joseph Stout
76 Wilson Stout
77 Daniel Stout
78 Ruth Stout

22 JAMES STOUT, son of Joseph Stout, 10, married, in Maryland, a lady with an honorary social title.

Issue

79 St Leger Cod Stout. Feb 1, 1755 St Leger Cod Stout, of Amwell, yeoman, signed a receipt for £50, paid by his grandfather, Col. Joseph Stout, the executor of "my father's estate." Signed Sint Leger Cod Stout.

38 JONATHAN STOUT, son of David Stout, 14, married Rachel Burrows.

Issue

80 David Stout; married, first, Amy, daughter of Nehemiah Stout, son of David and Ann (Merrill) Stout, son of David and Rebecca (Ashton) Stout, son of Richard and Penelope Stout; second, Rachel, daughter of Nehemiah Stout.
    Issue by second wife
    Jonathan Stout
    Nathan Stout
81 Moses Stout
82 Job Stout; married a daughter of Abner Howell, of Ohio, and had several children.

39 ANDREW STOUT, son of David Stout, 14, married Anna, and Sarah, widow of Moses Morgan, and both daughters of Jonathan Stout

If Anna and Sarah *were* daughters of Jonathan Stout, as here stated, then Sarah must have been the widow of Moses Morgan But the question arises, was it this Andrew Stout who married her, or was it Andrew Stout (5), Samuel (4), Samuel (3), Jonathan (2), Richard (1). Note that in each instance these records say Sarah "Stout," while the license reads Sarah "Morgan."

Issue by first wife
83 Andrew Stout, married Miss Golden, moved West; had issue.
84 Mary Stout; married Mr. Leigh

LINE OF JONATHAN STOUT

85 Anna Stout; married, by license dated Dec. 30, 1778, Johnson Titus.
86 Sarah Stout, married John Bryant, and had children.

Issue by second wife

87 David Stout
88 Jonathan Stout
89 Ruth Stout, married Amos Hart

40 JAMES STOUT, son of David Stout, 14, married Catharine Stout

Issue

90 Jesse Stout
91 Amos Stout; married Catharine, daughter of Wm. Drake; of the New York Lakes, had many children
92 Charles Stout, married Arlissa, daughter of Jared Saxton, had many children.
93 Rachel Stout; married, by license dated Mch. 17, 1780, John Manners, had issue.
94 Elizabeth Stout, married, first, David Stout, 52, son of Benjamin, 16, son of David, 11, son of Richard, second, John Hoagland; no issue.*
95 Catharine Stout, married James Bryant, of the New York Lakes
96 Ann Stout; married Philip Lewis [Servis?]

47 JOHN STOUT, son of Zebulon Stout, 15, married Mabel Saxton.

Issue

97 Zephaniah Stout; married Rhoda Stout. She married, second, Burges Allison.

Issue

Ebenezer Stout; a lawyer.
98 Amos Stout; married Miss Morgan, of the New York Lakes.
99 Elizabeth Stout, married, by license dated May 2, 1770, Nathaniel Hart
100 Mabel Stout married James Campbell
101 Keziah Stout; married Lewis Gordon
102 Rachel Stout, married Jonathan Stout, son of Samuel, son of Samuel, son of Jonathan, son of Richard
103 Charity Stout; married John Park.

48 ZEBULON STOUT, son of Zebulon Stout, 15, married, by license dated Oct 11, 1762, Sarah Stout, daughter of Benjamin Stout and Ruth Bogert, who was the son of James, son of Richard, 1. He married, second, Widow Sutphin, née Demott.

Issue by second marriage

104 Zebulon Stout

55 SAMUEL STOUT, ESQ., son of Samuel Stout, 16, was born February, 1732, died Sept. 24, 1803. He married Anne, daughter of John Van Dyke, who was born in 1732, and died Sept. 12, 1810. Both buried in Hopewell Churchyard.

Samuel Stout was a Justice of the Peace and a Member of the New Jersey Legislature

---

*There is a marriage license, dated Jan 7, 1774 of an Elizabeth Stout with a Joseph Stout, which may be confused with this Elizabeth Stout, 94

HISTORICAL MISCELLANY

Issue

105 Abraham Stout, married, by license dated May 10, 1777, Jean Pettit, and had many children He served throughout the Revolutionary War, as an officer, with distinction
106 Samuel S Stout, born in 1756
107 John Stout
108 Jonathan Stout; married Rachel Stout, daughter of John, son of Zebulon, son of Jonathan, son of Richard, 1. They had several children.
109 Col Ira Stout; died, Aug. 11, 1851, aged 81 years; married Sarah Burroughs; died, Sept 14, 1825, in her 55th year; Hopewell Churchyard
110 Andrew Stout, married Sarah Stout
111 Jacob Stout, married Ann Burtis.
112 Catharine Stout; married Peter Smith, a Baptist clergyman.
113 Ann Stout; married Benjamin Stout.
114 Sarah Stout; married John Wycoff.

64 RICHARD STOUT, son of John Stout, 19, married Penelope Park.

Issue

115 Jehu Stout; married Miss Runyon, and moved west.
116 Elhanan Stout, married, Dec 7, 1798, Mary Hurley.
117 Richard Stout; married Miss Pinkerton

Issue
Penelope Stout
Job Stout
Abraham Stout

118 Nathan Stout; no issue.
119 Rachel Stout; married Isaac Whitenack.
120 Penelope Stout, married Frederick Van Liew, New York Lakes.
121 Sarah Stout, married John Van Liew, of Long Island.
122 John Stout
123 William Stout

65 JEHU STOUT, son of John Stout, 19, was a physician; moved to Carolina, and died without issue. He was educated, as per Morgan Edwards, at the school of the Rev. Isaac Eaton, at Hopewell, between 1756 and 1767 He was deceased in 1790.

66 DANIEL (OR DAVID) STOUT, son of John Stout, 19, married, first, Charity Brinson, second, Miss Heron

Issue by first wife
124 Jonathan Stout
125 David Stout; married Miss Ott.

Issue
Zebulon Stout
Henry Stout

126 Elijah Stout; married Miss Van Zandt.

LINE OF JONATHAN STOUT

Issue
Lucretia Stout
Mary Stout
127 Catharine Stout; single

Issue by second wife
128 Charity Stout; married Jonathan Walters.

87 DAVID STOUT, son of Andrew Stout, 39, married Margaret Weart. He was a Judge in Hunterdon County, New Jersey David Stout, Esq , died, Sept 19, 1849, aged 71, 3, 19; Margaretta, his wife, died, July 23, 1854, in 73rd year; buried in Hopewell Baptist Churchyard.

Issue
129 Henrietta Stout; married Abraham Skillman.
130 Charles Stout
131 Mary Stout
132 Susan Stout; married Caleb Baker.
133 Monroe Stout; married Jane Van Dyke.
134 Jacob W. Stout
134ª Gilbert Stout [?], married Adelaide Van Dyke, and had issue.

88 JONATHAN STOUT, son of Andrew Stout, 39, married Miss Buckalew, moved North. He was a Colonel of Militia.

Issue
135 Andrew Stout
136 Furman Stout; married, and had issue.
137 Abraham Stout
138 Charlotte Stout
139 Mary Stout
140 Margaret Stout
141 Sarah Stout

90 JESSE STOUT, son of James Stout, 40, married Abigail, daughter of Felix Lott.

Issue
142 Spencer Stout
143 Jonathan Stout
144 Peter L Stout
145 Charles G. Stout
146 Abraham L. Stout
147 Susan Stout; married John Weart, Jr.
148 Charity Stout; married Michael Blue.
149 Naomi Stout; married Amos Gibbins.
150 Betsey Stout; married Daniel Luther.
151 Theodosia Stout, married Joseph Hart
152 Kitty Stout; married Jacob Weart
153 Abigail Stout; married Zephaniah Stout, son of William and Ann (Sexton) Stout; no issue.

106 SAMUEL S STOUT, son of Samuel Stout, 55, was born in 1756, and died Apr. 22, 1795 He married, as Samuel Stout, minor, by license dated Apr. 24, 1779, Helenah Cruser, born June 1, 1759; died Jan 30, 1821 Both buried in Hopewell Churchyard

Issue

154 Abraham Cruser Stout, born May 26, 1780

107 JOHN STOUT, son of Samuel Stout, 55, married Rachel, daughter of Harmon and Mary (Stout) Rosenkrans

Issue

155 Washington Stout, married Hannah Stout
156 Montgomery Stout; married Miss Wyckoff.
157 Samuel Stout; married Mary Labaw *
158 Hezekiah Stout; single.
159 Mary Stout; married Philip Lewis
160 Catharine Stout, married William Little

108 JONATHAN STOUT, son of Samuel Stout, 55, married Rachel Stout, daughter of John and Mabel (Saxton), son of Zebulon and Charity (Burrowes), son of Jonathan, 9, son of Richard Stout. They had several children

May not this be the Jonathan R Stout whose will may be found on record at Freehold, dated Sept. 20, 1834; proved Oct, 24, 1834? In it he calls himself of Upper Freehold, and mentioned·

Wife, Hannah
Brother, John Stout
Son, James D. Stout
Daughter, Elizabeth D. Stout
Son, Richard Stout
Daughter, Susan M Stout
Daughter, Nancy Forman
Daughter, Rachel Borden
Daughter, Lucy Giberson
Daughter, Eleanor Perrine

Issue

161 James D. Stout
162 Elizabeth D. Stout
163 Richard Stout
164 Susan M. Stout
165 Nancy Stout, married, Mch 31, 1802, Michael Forman
166 Rachel Stout, married Mr Borden, and had

Issue

Mary Borden

167 Lucy Stout, married, Dec 18, 1816, Gilbert Giberson
168 Eleanor Stout, married Mr Perrine.

115 JEHU STOUT, son of Richard Stout, 64, married Miss Runyon. She is supposed to be Naomi, daughter of Reuben and Maria (Gordon) Runyon, and, as in the Pound and Kerster

---

*In Hopewell Baptist Church Yard are two stones which may represent this Samuel and Mary Stout Samuel I Stout died, June 30, 1852, in 60th year, and Mary, his wife, died, March 24, 1859, in 72nd year

LINE OF JONATHAN STOUT

Genealogy, a Reuben C. Stout, and a Sarah Naomi Stout are mentioned, it is thought that the descendants of Jehu Stout may be found in the State of Indiana

116 ELHANAN STOUT, son of Richard Stout, 64, married, Dec. 7, 1798, Mary, daughter of Dennis Hurley

Issue

169 John P. Stout, died single
170 Elhanan H Stout, married Mary Lippincott.
171 Lydia Stout, married Thomas King
172 Mary Ann Stout, married, first, Benjamin Harris, second, Robert I. Finley
173 Samuel Corlies Stout
174 William L Stout, died May 6, 1892, married Hannah Youmans.

117 RICHARD STOUT, son of Richard Stout, 64, married Miss Pinkerton.

Issue

175 Penelope Stout
176 John Stout
177 Abram Stout

122 JOHN STOUT, son of Richard Stout, 64, was a Judge in Somerset County, New Jersey

Issue

178 William Stout; married Anna Sexton, descendant of Richard Stout's third son, and had

Issue

Richard Stout, married Abigail, daughter of George H. Stout

Issue

John W Stout, married Sarah M Tuttle and Virginia G Martin
William Stout; died single.
George H. Stout; married Nettie Frost, no issue
Richard Stout, married Mary Dodd.
Anna A. Stout, single.
Emily Stout, married Sumner A Kingman
Maria Louise Stout; single.

Zephaniah Stout
Abraham Stout
Runkle Stout

179 Richard Stout
180 Rachel Stout; married Albert Sutphen.
181 Penelope Stout, married John, son of David Manners

123 WILLIAM STOUT, son of Richard Stout, 64, married Rachel Carr or Carle

Issue

182 John M Stout
183 Chalion Stout, married Sarah, daughter of Joshua Stout
184 Daniel Stout; married Miss Fisher

185 Nathan Stout, unmarried
186 Thomas Stout, unmarried.
187 Catharine Stout, married Zeb. S. Randolph.
188 Ruth Stout, married Isaac Brown, and moved West.
189 Penelope Stout, unmarried.
190 Rebecca Stout, unmarried.

124 JONATHAN STOUT, son of Daniel (or David) Stout, 66, married Miss Howell; moved West

Issue

191 Benjamin Stout
192 Daniel Stout
193 Charity Stout
194 Mary Stout
195 Catharine Stout

130 CHARLES W. STOUT, son of David Stout, 87, married Sarah Merrill.

Issue

196 D. Webster Stout; married Hannah Waters.

Issue

Charles W. Stout
Harry H. Stout
Sarah M. Stout
197 Furman Stout
198 David Stout; married Miss Hoagland
199 Charles Stout, married Miss Holcombe.
200 Mary Ann Stout, married Abraham Manners.
201 Carrie Stout; married Mr. Holcombe.
202 Addria Stout; married Israel Hunt.

142 SPENCER STOUT, son of Jesse Stout, 90, married Mary Weart.

Issue

203 John Stout
204 Jacob Stout
205 Lafayette Stout
206 Weart Stout
207 Mary Stout
208 Cherry Ann Stout

143 JONATHAN STOUT, son of Jesse Stout, 90, married Jane Blue.

Issue

209 Spencer Stout
210 Amy Stout
211 Abby Stout
212 Jane Stout

LINE OF JONATHAN STOUT

144 PETER L STOUT, son of Jesse Stout, 90, married Watty Luther.
   Issue
   213 Hart Stout
   214 Algernon W Stout
   215 Norton Stout
   216 Luther C. Stout
   217 Horace R. Stout
   218 Sarah Stout
   219 Electra Stout
   220 Cornelia Stout
   221 Adele Stout

145 CHARLES C. STOUT, son of Jesse Stout, 90, married Ure Hart.
   Issue
   222 Amos Stout; married Caroline Benedict, second, Isabel Jolly.
       Issue by first wife
       Marion Stout
           Issue by second wife
       Charles W. Stout
       Mary E. Stout
       Myrta B. Stout
   223 Gorden Stout; married Calista Knowlton.
           Issue
       Etherald E. Stout
       Addison A Stout
   224 James M. Stout; married Helen Corbin.
           Issue
       Addie I. Stout
       Libbie R. Stout
   225 Andrew Stout; single
   226 George W. Stout, served in the Union Army, and died from exposure and wounds.
   227 John P Stout; married Alice Main
           Issue
       Lena W. Stout
   228 Ambrose N. Stout, married Susan Winslow, no issue.
   229 Katurah R Stout; married Chauncey Sterns.
   230 Abby J Stout; single
   231 Mary A Stout, married Oliver Cooley.

146 ABRAHAM L STOUT, son of Jesse Stout, 90, married Sarah Crittenden
   Issue
   232 Norman Stout
   233 Jesse Stout
   234 Jared Stout
   235 Albert Stout
   236 Hannah Stout
   237 Clarissa Stout

HISTORICAL MISCELLANY

154 ABRAM CRUSER STOUT, son of Samuel S Stout, 106, was born May 26, 1780, died Aug. 23, 1849; married, Sept 24, 1801, Anna, daughter of Rudolph Hagaman and Catharine Holmes, born Apr 17, 1783; died Sept 26, 1854 Abram C. Stout was a Member of the New Jersey Legislature.

Issue

238 Helen Stout; married Dr James H. Baldwin.
239 Samuel Holmes Stout, born Feb. 20 1809.

170 ELHANAN H STOUT, son of Elhanan Stout, 116, married Mary Lippincott. His grandson is now living in Red Bank, N. J.

Issue

240 Capt. Samuel L. Stout; married Jane Edgar; lost at sea, leaving Mary and Samuel Stout
241 John H Stout, single.
242 Melvina Stout, married Lybran Sill.
243 Johanna Stout, married John S. Ripley.
244 Abby Stout; married William P. Romaine.
245 Mary E. Stout, died single.

173 SAMUEL CORLIES STOUT, son of Elhanan Stout, 116, was born in 1811, and died Nov. 11, 1892 He married Mary Packer, who died aged eighty years. She was the widow of Charles Packer, and daughter of Garret and Rebecca (Lippincott) White

Issue

246 Winchester White Stout, born Jan 22, 1841, married, Sept. 12, 1866, Georgianna Hitchcock, born Oct. 6, 1838. Of Red Bank, N J, in 1908.
247 Charles Packer Stout; married Abigail Wardell
248 Richard Stout; married Susan Shultz, no issue.
249 Rebecca Stout, married James B. Sherman.

Issue
Mary Arline Sherman
Stout Sherman
Georgeanna Sherman

250 Margaret Ashby Stout; single, of Hamilton, N. J, she has the old Bible

174 WILLIAM L STOUT, son of Elhanan Stout, 116, married Hannah Youmans. He died May 6, 1892.

Issue

251 William H Stout; single.
252 Mary J Stout, married, first, Wesley M. Rogers, second, Frederick Lane.
253 Sarah E Stout; single
254 Penelope Stout; single
255 Anna Stout, married George T. Morris
256 Henrietta Stout, married Oscar S Hurley.
257 Lydia Stout, married Alexander Van Note.
258 Caroline Stout; single.

LINE OF BENJAMIN STOUT

182   JEHU OR JOHN M STOUT, son of William Stout, 123, married Miss Conover
> *Issue*
> 259 James Nelson Stout, died single
> 260 Stryker Stout, married Miss Bergen, has issue.
> 261 Jane Stout
> 262 Ira Stout, married, and left issue

Another memorandum says   Jehu (Jno in another account), son of William Stout, 123, married Miss Conover, and had Nelson Stout and three daughters

183   CHALION STOUT, son of William Stout, 123, married Sarah Stout
> *Issue*
> 263 William Stout, moved to California; married Miss Davenport
> 264 Catharine Stout; married Richard Servis
> 265 Rhoda Stout, married Jef. Shepherd
> 266 Abby Stout; married Richard Hankins.
> 267 Lucy Stout; married Theodore Duryee
> 268 Randolph Stout; married Miss Manning.
> 269 Ann Augusta Stout; single.
> 270 Jacob W Stout, married Miss Bulmer, of California, had issue

239   SAMUEL HOLMES STOUT, son of Abram Cruser Stout, 154, born Feb. 20, 1809, died Dec. 31, 1886, married, Feb. 14, 1883, Deborah Van Kirk Drake, born Oct 29, 1806, died Dec. 26, 1852.
> *Issue*
> 271 Helen Baldwin Stout, married David L. Blackwell.
> 272 Sarah Drake Stout
> 273 Anna Hagaman Stout, married Nelson D. Blackwell
> 274 James Hervey Stout, single, of Stoutsburg, N J.
> 275 Mary Titus Stout, married Edward Updike

LINE OF BENJAMIN STOUT

10   BENJAMIN STOUT, son of Richard Stout, 1, born about 1669
1690   Richard Stout, Sr., conveyed to his son, Benjamin Stout, land at Hopp River.
1699, Nov 11   To Benjamin Stout for boarding Denis Garetson, one year, £2 19 2
Middletown Town Records

1705, Oct. 5 Benjamin Stout, yeoman, of Middletown, bought land from John Stout, of Middletown, lying on Hop river.

ANN by the grace of God of grate Brittan France and Ireland and defender of the faith &c
  To our high sheriff of our county of Monmouth greeting   wee command you that you give warning forthwith to the freeholders of your balywick having severally one hundred acres of freehold in his own right or that if worth fifty pounds Starling money in Money goods and chattels that they assemble at such convenient time and place as you shall think meet to elect and choose by plurality of voices one able sufficient man having one thousand acres of land of an estate of freehold in his own especial right or if worth five hundred pounds starling in money goods or chattels to be a representative of our said county in the room of Gershom Mott so that he be and appear at Burlington the twenty eighth day of this January to assist our governor and comander in cheif of our said province of new Jersey in a general Assembly of our said province and that you

return then and there the name of the representative so chosen as aforesaid under your hand and seal and the hands and seals of five at least of the princable freeholders of the said county by   between you and them to be maid for that purpose, and none of you are not to fale at your peroll witness our trusty and well-beloved Robert Hunter Esqr our Captin ginerall and comander in cheif of our province of New Jersey at Burlington this nineteenth day of January in the ninth year of our Reigane
January 27th day 1710-11

JR. BAff
BENJA STOUT Sheriff

Cherry Hall Papers

1710, Aug 25. Benjamin Stout recorded the cattle-mark that formerly belonged to his father, Richard Stout, 1.

1715. He was a resident of Delaware.

1721, May. The above cattle-mark was assumed by John Burrows, Benjamin Stout and his family, having moved away

Dr Thomas Hale Streets, of the U S Navy, [133 East Mount Airy Ave., Mount Airy, Philadelphia], who has given some time to the study of this line of the Stouts, says Benjamin Stout migrated to Delaware and became the ancestor of the Stouts of that State. He also asserts that he is unable to find any documentary evidence to show that, as has been claimed, Benjamin Stout ever lived in Maryland The statement to this effect may have arisen from the fact, ("a falsity has usually a nucleus of reality"), that he owned land on the Maryland road, (it is so called in deeds), running from Appoquinimink Creek, (Delaware), to Bohemia (Maryland). He is described in deeds as of George's Creek, in the vicinity of the Dragon Swamp. He afterward moved further down the County to Appoquinimink Creek

In 1721, while he was of George's Creek, he gave lands to his sons, Charles and Benjamin, Jr., calling the former "his son and heir."

In 1727, he conveyed land on George's Creek that he had purchased, in 1715, the earliest date when his name appears in the Delaware records, though the deed for this land is not found, perhaps because some of the old books of New Castle County were lost during the Revolutionary War

It is known that Benjamin Stout had a wife Agnes, whose name appears among the members of the Baptist Church, Middletown, N. J., in 1712. She was living, Feb 16, 1734, when, as Agnes Stout, widow of Benjamin Stout, late of Appoquinimink Hundred, Delaware, she petitioned the Orphan's Court for authority to sell his dwelling plantation, and was joined in the petition by her son Jacob Whether Benjamin Stout had any earlier wife than Agnes I do not know, nor do I know her surname, but inasmuch as Morgan Edwards, in his Contributions to a History of the Baptists, states that an intermarriage occurred between one of the sons of Richard and Penelope Stout with a Truax, and, as members of the Truax family, migrated about the same time as Benjamin Stout, and settled, as his neighbors, in Delaware, it raises the presumption that Agnes, the wife of Benjamin Stout, might have been a Truax by birth

Benjamin Stout made his will Apr 25, 1734, which was proved June 10, 1734, wherein he stated that he was in a "low condition," and bequeathed all his property to his son Jacob, his wife, unnamed, to be subsisted out of the estate

Issue

11 Charles Stout
12 Benjamin Stout, Jr., married Elizabeth Lewis.
13 Jacob Stout

11 CHARLES STOUT, son of Benjamin Stout, 10, was mentioned, in 1721, in a deed of gift from his father, Benjamin Stout, wherein he was called "son and heir" of his father.

12 BENJAMIN STOUT, JR, son of Benjamin Stout, 10, in association with his brother Charles, received land in a deed of gift from his father, in 1721 He married, in 1714/15, Elizabeth, daughter of John and Sarah (Price) Lewis, born 10 mo., 25, 1696, (Haverford Meeting), and she was made administratrix on his estate Mch 16, 1740, by letters issued in Kent County, Delaware.

Issue

14 Peter Stout
15 Emmanuel Stout, of New Castle Co, Delaware, died 1781, married, first, Lurana Owen, second, Mary Griffin, widow of Mr. Leech and Mr. Jones

Issue

Jacob Stout
Sarah Stout
Martha Stout; married John Cowgill.
Rebecca Stout
Peter Stout
Ann Stout, died aged 104 years, married William Denny.
Lydia Stout, married Robert Regester.

13 JACOB STOUT, son of Benjamin Stout, 10, was living at the time of his father's death, in 1734, on Blackbird Creek, in Appoquinimink Hundred.

LINE OF DAVID STOUT

11 DAVID STOUT, son of Richard Stout, 1, was born, it is said, about 1669, which seems to me a little late, and I prefer the date of 1667

In 1690, his father, Richard Stout, Sr, conveyed land to him at Hopp River.

1701, April 3. David Stout, with consent of his wife, Rebecca, sold land in Monmouth County

1706, August 19. David Stout, yeoman, of Freehold, sold lands, with the consent of his wife, Rebecca.

1712 David and Rebecca Stout were members of the Middletown Baptist Church

1714, Apr. 20. David Stout, of Freehold, yeoman, and Rebecca, his wife, in land transaction.

"He moved, about 1725, to Amwell, N J, bought lands there and died there very old, buried on his farm The old David Stout house, at Amwell, is still standing" Where he is interred, still remains a Stout burying-ground.

David Stout married Rebecca Ashton, in 1688, said Asher Taylor, Esq

His residence, in Middletown, was said to have been on land, part of which was, in 1823, in the possession of Denise Hendrickson, which was near the property of Obadiah Holmes, the husband of his wife's sister, Alice Ashton He remained in Middletown until two of his elder children, James and Rebecca, had married, upon whom he bestowed one hundred acres in Upper Freehold.

Issue

12 James Stout, of Upper Freehold, born, by deduction, about 1694.
13 Freegift Stout, born 1693.
14 David Stout, born 1695.
15 Joseph Stout, born 1698

16 Benjamin Stout
17 Rebecca Stout, born 1691, married John Manners, of Upper Freehold.
18 Deliverance Stout; married Francis Labaw, and had children.
19 Sarah Stout, "single, handsome and sensible."

12 JAMES STOUT, son of David Stout, 11, married, in 1712, Catharine Simpson * Between 1715–20, he moved to Amwell, where he bought seven hundred acres and built a house. He died aged thirty-six years, and as his will was proved in 1731, it would appear that he was born about 1694 His widow married his cousin, Samuel, youngest son of Jonathan Stout.

1727, Apr. 21 James Stout made his will, proved Apr. 26, 1731, in which he stated that he was of Amwell, and mentioned:
Wife, Catharine, pregnant.
Son, John
Six sons
Uncle, James Aston, as executor, and if he cannot serve, then his cousin, Joseph Stout, of Hopewell
He signed with his mark   J S

The inventory of James Stout, yeoman, of Hunterdon County, dated July 29, 1731, amounted to £46:6:3

Issue
20 John Stout
21 James Stout, born 1715.
22 Joseph Stout, born 1717.
23 David Stout, born 1719.
24 Jonathan Stout, born 1723.
25 Jacob Stout, born 1721
26 Rebecca Stout, born 1725; married Nathan Drake; had a son, James Drake.

13 FREEGIFT STOUT, son of David Stout, 11, was born in 1693; married Mary Higgins. He lived at Clover Hill, Hunterdon County, New Jersey.

Issue
27 Jediah Stout, married, by license dated Jan. 13, 1744–5, Philina Chamberlain, who was the daughter of John Chamberlain, by his wife, Rebecca, daughter of Lewis Morris, of Passage Point. They lived near the seashore 1755, Oct 24 Jediah Stout, yeoman, of Winson [?], sold land to Matthias Mount.
28 Freegift Stout; married Elizabeth, daughter of David Stout, son of Jonathan, son of Richard; had many children
29 James Stout, married, first, a daughter of Jacob Mattison, second, Rachel, daughter of . . Higgins, had a son, Samuel Stout, by his first wife.
30 Joshua Stout, married Miss Hames 1781. Joshua Stout, yeoman, of Amwell, made a deed. He had a family
31 Obadiah Stout, married Mary McBride, had a large family
32 Isaac Stout, born about 1740, married, by license dated Sept 30, 1765, Mary Quinby.
33 Sarah Stout; married Ephraim Oliphant; had children

---
*In Hopewell Baptist Churchyard lies a "Catharine Stout, died, Dec 8, 1749, in 58th year", hence born 1692 If the dates assigned to James Stout, 12, are correct, he married at an uncommonly early age.

LINE OF DAVID STOUT

34 Mary Stout, married Richard Chamberlain, probably brother to Philina, above.
35 Rebecca Stout, married Edward Taylor; had children
36 Rachel Stout, married Richard Rounswell, had Freegift and Isaac

14 DAVID STOUT, son of David Stout, 11, settled at Amwell He married Ann, daughter of William Merrill.

Issue

37 Nehemiah Stout
38 Nathaniel Stout
39 Rebecca Stout; married Isaac Eaton, pastor, for twenty-six years, of the Hopewell Baptist Church, who died, July 4, 1772, in the 47th year of his age Stone in Hopewell Baptist Churchyard, New Jersey They had issue

15 JOSEPH STOUT, son of David Stout, 11, was born in 1698, and married, first, Mary Ashland, second, Martha Reeder, of New Brunswick, N J*

Issue by first wife

40 Mary Stout

Issue by second wife

41 Job Stout; married, and had a family
42 Jacob Stout
43 Noah Stout; married Miss Thacher
44 Martha Stout; married Mr Bennet
45 Abner Stout; married Miss Stout
46 Reeder Stout
47 Joseph Stout; married Miss Titus.
48 Benjamin Stout

16 BENJAMIN STOUT, son of David Stout, 11 His tombstone, in Hopewell Churchyard, reads: died, May 23, 1789, in his 82nd year Adjacent to it is that of Mary Stout, who died, Aug. 5, 17 , in her 72nd year He settled at Amwell, N. J, and married, when about seventeen years of age, first, Widow Ketchum, second, Mary, daughter of Jediah Higgins. He had no issue by his first wife, but she had children older than he

---

*The following item, taken from the Newark Evening News for Nov 19, 1910, evidently related to the descendents of Joseph Stout, 15

No 3274—BRYANT—LANNING—STOUT—Extract from the will of Benjamin Bryant, dated 1803, on file in State House, Trenton, No 3050, Hunterdon, which gives his wife as Elizabeth , sons Daniel, John and William, and daughter Elizabeth, the wife of Joab Stout, Ann, the wife of Edward Lanning, and Margaret, the wife of Abner Stout

Was this Benjamin Bryant the son of Cornelius Bryant, of Westfield? Was Elizabeth , Elizabeth Tucker or Trotter, of Elizabeth? Whom did the sons marry? Who were the parents of Joab Stout? Please give, if possible, particulars, dates, etc , and references

Also wanted the parentage of Martha Reeder, second wife of Joseph Stout, grandfather of above mentioned Abner Stout

Benjamin Bryant died about 1820 Elizabeth and Ann, and their husbands, are mentioned in Ege's "Pioneers of Old Hopewell " A Benjamin Bryant is mentioned as the son of Cornelius Bryant by Mrs Baetjie in the Bryant-Carteret Book
C.

Issue

49 Elihu Stout*, [died young?]. There is a field stone in the Baptist Churchyard, Hopewell, N. J., roughly inscribed Elihu Stout died Oct. 3, 1762.
50 Jediah Stout, married, by license dated Mch 21, 1781, Mary Stout, and had a family.
51 Benjamin Stout, married Rachel Stout, sister to Mary, wife of Jediah Stout. After her death he married, second, Ann, daughter of Samuel Stout, and, third, Mary, daughter of Oliver Hart.

Issue

Rachel Stout
Ann Stout
Mary Stout

52 David Stout; married Elizabeth, daughter of James and Catharine Stout, 40, line of Jonathan Stout.
53 Hannah Stout, died young. There is a field stone, bearing this name, adjacent to Elihu Stout in Hopewell Churchyard
54 Sarah Stout; married Elijah, son of James Stout.
55 Rachel Stout; married Paul Hill; had children.
56 Mary Stout, married Garrison Prall, and moved to Kentucky. According to the Nathan Stout manuscript Elihu, Hannah and Sarah, children of Benjamin Stout, all died under twelve years of age.

17 REBECCA STOUT, daughter of David Stout. 11, born 1691; married John Manners, of Upper Freehold, N J, born in Yorkshire, England, and had

Issue

John Manners
Rebecca Manners
Elizabeth Manners
Lydia Manners, married James Stout, who called himself "Turler."

Issue

Isaac Stout
Jesse Stout
Antony Stout
Elizabeth Stout
Rebecca Stout
Ann Stout
Rachel Stout

20 JOHN STOUT, son of James Stout, 12, married Rachel, daughter of William Merrill, in 1734

Issue

57 Abraham Stout
58 Amos Stout, born in 1741; died, single, 1762.

---

*There was an Elihu Stout, of whom the following was written
Elihu Stout was induced by Gen William Henry Harrison, afterwards President, to settle at Vincennes, Ind He founded the "Western Sun," a newspaper, July 4, 1804, the pioneer newspaper within the territory now embraced by the State of Indiana He continued its publication under difficulties, until November, 1845, for many years after its first publication, transporting his materials on pack horse from Lexington, Ky He died, at Vincennes, in April, 1860, and was laid to rest in the public cemetery, "leaving behind no evidence of any necessity for taking an inventory of his estate."   Saltar

LINE OF DAVID STOUT

  59 Aaron Stout, died aged two years
  60 William Stout, died aged six years
  61 Nathan Stout
  62 Moses Stout
  63 Levi Stout, died, single, aged twenty-one years
  64 Catharine Stout; married James Stout.
  65 Ann Stout, married, as his second wife, John Manners, who was a son of John Manners and his wife, Rebecca Stout, had issue
  66 Rachel Stout; married Isaac Prall, had issue

21 JAMES STOUT, son of James Stout, 12, was born in 1715, and married Jemima Reeder.

Issue

  67 Abel Stout, married Williampe Wyckoff, and had many children
  68 Caleb Stout; married Elizabeth, daughter of Francis Labaw, and had many children.
  69 James Stout; married first, (Pennie?), daughter of James Osborne, and had many children, second, Esther, daughter of Jediah Higgins, by whom he had two children.
  70 Amy Stout, married Abraham Clayton
  71 Mary Stout; married David Labaw, had issue.
  72 Elinor Stout, married Elijah Larrison

22 JOSEPH STOUT, son of James Stout, 12, married Mary Hixson.

Issue

  73 Elijah Stout; married Martha, daughter of James Matthews, moved to Virginia, and had many children.
  74 Benijah Stout, married Elizabeth Hyde, moved to Ohio, and had many children
  75 Timothy Stout, married, first, Sarah Shrieve, second, Sarah J Reed, and had many children They lived in Shimokin
  76 Elisha Stout, single
  77 Catharine Stout; married Obadiah, son of Thomas Hunt
  78 Elizabeth Stout, married John Whitehead, large family.
  79 Rebecca Stout; married Abraham Hoagland; had family
  80 Mary Stout, married Benjamin Grey, and moved to Virginia, large family.
  81 Rachel Stout, married Clear Oxly, and moved to Virginia, had family.

23 DAVID STOUT, son of James Stout, 12, was born in 1719 He married his first cousin, Mary, daughter of Joseph Stout, second, Sarah, daughter of Joseph Higgins

Issue by first wife

  82 George Stout; died single.
  83 Mary Stout, married Phineas Riggs, had family.

Issue by second wife

  84 James Stout; died single
  85 Joseph Stout, married, and had one child
  86 John Stout, married a daughter of Freegift Stout, and had one child, who married Benjamin Merrill.

    87 Jacob Stout
    88 David Stout; married Sarah Acker, and had two children.
    89 Amos Stout, died aged three years
    90 Joshua Stout
    91 Sarah Stout, married, by license dated Apr. 19, 1779, Abraham Runkle; had family.

  24 JONATHAN STOUT, son of James Stout, 12, was born 1723, and married Elizabeth Hixson.
          Issue
    92 Benjamin Stout, married Miss Hutchinson, daughter of John
    93 Jonathan Stout
    94 Reuben Stout
    95 Aaron Stout
    96 Enoch Stout
    97 Rachel Stout, married Peter Van Dyke, had family.
    98 Mary Stout, married Garret Van Dyke, had one child
    99 Rebecca Stout, born 1753, died, Jan. 29, 1788, in 36th year, (Hopewell Baptist Churchyard), married Ralph Drake, had family
    100 Ann Stout, married Ephraim Hart; had family.
    101 Catharine Stout, died single.

  25 JACOB STOUT, son of James Stout, 12, married Grace, daughter of Dr. Rodger Park. He died Sept. 20, 1785.
          Issue
    102 Samuel Stout
    103 Aaron Stout
    104 William Stout, married, by license dated Dec. 27, 1780, Elizabeth Hutchinson, and had two children.*
    105 John Stout; died, 1816, in his 57th year; married, by license dated Dec. 7, 1782, Keziah Brush, who died, in 1822, in her 78th year. They had one child.
    106 Elizabeth Stout, married John Vankirk; had family.
    107 Ann Stout, born Sept. 14, 1754, died Sept 9, 1831; married Benjamin, son of Joseph Stout, son of David, son of Richard, the First, which would make him, her father's first cousin He, Benjamin Stout, was born Feb 12, 1750, and died 1824
    108 Sarah Stout; married, by license dated June 20, 1779, Azariah Higgins; had family.
    109 Catharine Stout, married Enoch Drake, had family

  32 ISAAC STOUT, son of Freegift Stout, 13, was born about 1740, and died, in 1823, at Clover Hill, Hunterdon County, New Jersey. He married, by license dated Sept. 30, 1765, Mary, daughter of Isaiah Quinby.
          Issue: all born at Clover Hill, Hunterdon County, New Jersey.
    110 Isaiah Stout
    111 Josiah Stout, married a daughter of Isaac Prall

---
*William Stout died, Aug 31, 1833, aged 51, 11, 12   Hannah H Stout died, June 8, 1849, aged 42, 10, 18
Hopewell Baptist Burying-ground

LINE OF DAVID STOUT

112 Aaron Stout. He was the youngest child, and born in 1780 He married a daughter of Nathaniel Nixson.
113 Rachel Stout, died single
114 Sarah Stout } married Elisha Sharp.
115 Mary Stout

37 NEHEMIAH STOUT, son of David Stout, 14, married Rachel, daughter of John and Catharine Stout, in the line of Jonathan Stout, son of Richard Stout, 1.

Issue

116 Wilkes Stout
117 Anne Stout; married Andrew Anderson
118 Rebecca Stout, married Lloyd Holmes.
119 Amy Stout, married David Stout.
120 Rachel Stout, married David Stout.

38 NATHANIEL STOUT, son of David Stout, 14, married Charity and Sarah Stout, daughters of Zebulon and Charity (Burrows) Stout

Issue

121 Lavinia Stout
122 Elijah Stout
123 Charity Stout; married, by license dated Oct. 22, 1780, Henry Solter. And others.

42 JACOB STOUT, son of Joseph Stout, 15, married Miss Huff, of Kingwood, N. J.

Issue

124 Mary Stout, married Mr Boon
125 Jacob Stout, married Catharine Eick
126 David Stout, married Letitia Roberts He was a Baptist minister.
127 Martha Stout, married Daniel Tucker

46 REEDER STOUT, son of Joseph Stout, 15, died, aged eighty years, at Kingwood, N J He married Hannah Kinney, who died aged eighty-three years

Issue

128 Joseph Stout; married Neeley Hoagland They resided at Cincinnati, O
129 Mary Stout, born 1773, died 1834, married George Opdyke, Mayor of New York.
130 John Stout, died, single, in 1832.
131 Elizabeth Stout; died, single, in 1867.
132 Ann Stout, married Cyrus Slack
133 Abner Stout, died in 1828 He married Parmela Hoagland.
134 Hester Stout, married Peter Stout, grandson of Reeder's brother, Jacob

48 BENJAMIN STOUT, son of Joseph Stout, 15, born Feb 12, 1750, died 1824; married Ann Stout, daughter of Jacob, son of James, son of David, son of Richard Stout, the First. She was born Sept. 14, 1754, and died Sept 9, 1831 They resided at Amwell, N. J.

Issue

135 Abner Stout, born Feb. 12, 1774
136 Aaron Stout, born Dec 5, 1771; married a Bryant

137 Grace Stout, married Peter Hortman.
138 John R. Stout, born Jan. 11, 1780, probably died young
139 Amos Stout, born Sept. 23, 1783, probably died young.

52 DAVID STOUT, son of Benjamin Stout, 16, married Elizabeth Stout, daughter of James and Catharine Stout, 40, of the line of Jonathan Stout. He left no issue

David Stout, Esq, Deacon of 1st Baptist Church, at Hopewell, died, Sept 30, 1806, in his 38th year
Elizabeth Hoagland, formerly widow of David Stout, died, July 23, 1844, in her 77th year From tombstones in Baptist Churchyard, Hopewell, N J

57 ABRAHAM STOUT, son of John Stout, 20, was born in 1735, and died in 1776. He married, first, Elizabeth, daughter of Thomas Houghton, second, by license dated Jan. 19, 1774, Alice Houghton, third, by license dated Oct. 26, 1775, Ann, daughter of Benjamin Stout. Elizabeth and Alice Houghton were daughters of Thomas Houghton It has also been stated that his first wife was Elizabeth Herbert, whom he married by license dated Sept. 27, 1755.

Issue by first wife
140 Solomon Stout
141 Joab Stout
142 Eli Stout
143 Mary Stout
144 Rachel Stout

Issue by second wife
145 John Stout

Issue by third wife
146 One daughter.

61 NATHAN STOUT, son of John Stout, 20, was born in 1748. He was the author of the Stout manuscript family history finished, in 1823, in his seventy-fifth year, which was first printed in Philadelphia, then in Hopewell, and lastly in Illinois Such notes as I have used from his history of the family were obtained from a copy of his original manuscript, as I have elsewhere stated, and not from any of the printed editions. I have been told that quite a number of errors have been discovered in his work, valuable as it is, which would not be unlikely, as it was not started until he was seventy-three years of age. He married, by license dated Oct 24, 1767, Esther, daughter of Jonathan Ketchum.

Issue
147 John Stout; died aged about forty; married, first, Hannnah, daughter of John Price, second, Ann, daughter of Daniel Holmes, a Scotch Baptist minister, and had ten children.
148 Levi Stout
149 Zephaniah Stout
150 William Stout
151 Robert Stout
152 Mary Stout, married Philip Housel, had issue
153 Sarah Stout, died aged six years.
154 Rachel Stout; died, single, Sept 17, 1833, in her 56th year.
155 Catharine Stout, married William, son of William Golden, and left issue.
156 Rhoda Stout, married Reuben, son of John and Deliverance (Labaw) Golden.

LINE OF DAVID STOUT

62 MOSES STOUT, son of John Stout, 20, married Abigail, daughter of John Hart, by license dated Mch 17, 1773.

Issue

157 John Stout, died aged two years.
158 Asher Stout, married Miss Egbert, daughter of Paul Egbert
159 Edward Stout
160 Simson Stout
161 Scudder Stout; went to sea
162 Parmelia Stout, died aged sixteen years.
163 Rachel Stout, married Abraham, son of Jacob Quick; large family
164 Theodosia Stout, married John Schenck, large family.
165 Deborah Stout, married John, son of Edward Hart; went to Virginia; large family
166 Sarah Stout, married Sidney, son of Isaac Prall, had children.

87 JACOB STOUT, son of David Stout, 23, married Abigail, daughter of Thomas and Abigail Hance

Issue

167 George H. Stout
168 John W Stout
169 Jacob Stout, married and moved to Ohio, had children.
170 Thomas Stout, living, in 1798; married Eliza Ashmead; no issue
171 Margaret Stout; married James Priestly.

90 JOSHUA STOUT, son of David Stout, 23, married Catharine, daughter of Philip Servis.

Issue

172 Philip Stout
173 David Stout
174 John Stout
175 Thomas Stout
176 Amos Stout
177 Joshua Stout
178 Sarah Stout
179 Mary Stout
180 Parmelia Stout

102 SAMUEL STOUT, son of Jacob Stout, 25, married Hannah Drake.

Issue

181 Nathan Stout
182 John Stout
183 Elizabeth Stout
184 Sarah Stout

103 AARON STOUT, son of Jacob Stout, 25, married Mary Drake.

Issue

185 Andrew Stout
186 Daniel Stout

HISTORICAL MISCELLANY

110   ISAIAH STOUT, son of Isaac Stout, 32, married a daughter of Henry Kennedy. He died in prime of life

Issue
187 Isaac Stout
188 Henry Stout
189 Joseph Stout; he was the only child living in 1879
190 Isaiah Stout

111   JOSIAH STOUT, son of Isaac Stout, 32. He was a prominent business man in New Brunswick, N J

Issue
191 Josiah Stout
192 Steward Stout
193 Mary Stout; eldest daughter, married Samuel Metler. She was dead in 1890
194 Daughter

112   AARON STOUT, son of Isaac Stout, 32, married, and his issue were all born in New Jersey, except the two youngest children.

Issue
195 Tacy Stout
196 Nathaniel Stout
197 Moses Stout
198 Ebenezer Stout
199 Isaac Stout
200 Theodore Stout   I received a letter, 1890, containing information on this branch of the family, from his daughter, Mary A Stout, of 504 North Street, Bloomington, Ill.
201 Mary Stout
202 Rachel Stout

135   ABNER STOUT, son of Benjamin Stout, 48, born Feb 12, 1774, died 1847, married, first, Margaret Bryant, second, Rachel Coles, daughter of James Hill, born 1790, died 1865

Abner Stout raised a large family. His sixteenth and youngest child, Rachel Ellen Stout, was born when he was fifty-seven years old His oldest child was born in 1801, and died six years prior to this sixteenth child's birth, leaving an only child, who was five and a half years her aunt's senior

148   LEVI STOUT, son of Nathan Stout, 61, married Mary, daughter of Col David Bishop. She was born Mch 16, 1788, died Apr 18, 1869, and is buried in the Baptist Churchyard, Middletown, N J

Issue, among several
203   Rev David B. Stout
203ª Mary Stout, married John A. Prall
203ᵇ Esther Stout, married Mr Blodget
203ᶜ Sarah Stout; married Augustus W. Barber

LINE OF DAVID STOUT

149 ZEPHANIAH STOUT, son of Nathan Stout, 61, married Eleanor, daughter of Henry Lane. He died when his son was two years old, and his widow married his brother, William Stout.

Issue

204 John L Stout

150 WILLIAM STOUT, son of Nathan Stout, 61, married Eleanor Lane Stout, the widow of his brother, Zephaniah

Issue

205 Nathan Stout, married Mary A Fisher
206 Henry L Stout, moved to Dubuque, Iowa, married Eveline Dening
207 Catharine L Stout, married James S. Fisher.
208 Mary Ann Stout; married William H. Smock.
209 Caroline Stout, married Garret G Brokaw
210 Zephaniah Stout, married Cornelia Smock; moved to Independence, Iowa.

Issue
Ella J. Stout
Ida Stout

211 Maria L Stout, single
212 Ellen Stout; married O H. Hazzard, a Presbyterian minister.

151 ROBERT STOUT, son of Nathan Stout, 61, married, first, Mary, daughter of Arthur Prall; second, Elizabeth Duffries.

Issue

213 Sarah Stout, married Abraham Lawshe; moved to Pennsylvania
214 Mary Stout
215 Ann Stout, single
216 William Stout; single.

159 EDWARD STOUT, son of Moses Stout, 62, married Catharine Brees

Issue

217 Parmela Stout; married Dr. Harris
218 Sarah Stout, married John Wyckoff
219 Susan Stout, married Garret Servis
220 Clementina Stout, married John Wortman
221 Elizabeth Stout, married Asher Kinney.
222 John Stout
223 Scudder Stout, born Oct. 18, 1814, died Aug. 27, 1844; married Rebecca Bowne, born Aug. 24, 1818, died July 3, 1891
224 Moses S. Stout, married Sarah A. Fine.
225 Henry Stout; married Hannah Emmons
226 William O. Stout; married Jerusha Brewer.

Issue
Charles Stout
Caroline Stout
Alice Stout
Bertha S. Stout

160 SIMSON STOUT, son of Moses Stout, 62, married Abigail Bryant.
> *Issue*
> 227 Eliza A. Stout; married George Van Dyke.
> 228 Maria Stout
> 229 Sarah Stout; married John West.
> 229ª Zephaniah S. Stout; married, first, Mary A Benward, second, her sister, Rebecca.
>> *Issue*
>> Simpson Stout
>> James Stout
>> Ellen Stout
>> Jenny Stout
>> All of Ohio.

167 GEORGE H. STOUT, son of Jacob Stout, 87, married Phebe Randolph.
> *Issue*
> 230 Lewis Stout; married Jane Woodruff
>> *Issue*
>> George Stout
>> Randolph Stout
>> Elizabeth Stout
>> Phebe Stout
>> Lucetta Stout
> 231 John W. Stout, married Elenor Baudoine; moved to Newark, and had several children
> 232 Augustus T. Stout He was Mayor of New Brunswick, N. J., and married Jane Dunham.
> 233 Abigail H Stout, married Richard, son of William and Ann (Sexton) Stout.
> 234 Anna Stout
> 235 Maria Stout

168 JOHN STOUT, son of Jacob stout, 87, married Eliza Woodruff.
> *Issue*
> 236 Jacob Stout; single.
> 237 Thomas H Stout, married Sarah Coffin
> 238 Gideon Lee Stout; married Rebecca Conger; had three children.
> 239 Amelia Stout; married John McIntosh, a Major General in the U. S. Army.
> 240 Margaret Stout; married John S. Seabury.
> 241 Augusta Stout, married Samuel Appleton, an Episcopal clergyman
> 242 Abbie Stout, married, Feb 1, 18—, Martin A Howell, Jr., son of Martin A. and Mary Jane (White) Howell. She died Apr 12, 1890

188 HENRY STOUT, son of Isaiah Stout, 110, married   .
> *Issue*
> 243 A daughter; married and living in Newark, N. J.

LINE OF DAVID STOUT

189 JOSEPH STOUT, son of Isaiah Stout, 110, was living, aged about eighty years, in 1879. He had then, living in Newark, one son.

Issue

244 George Stout

203 DAVID B STOUT, son of Levi Stout, 148, was born Jan 12, 1810, died May 17, 1875 He was a Baptist minister at Middletown, N. J He married, first, Susan Brown, second, Jane Merrill, born Dec. 22, 1806, died Sept 3, 1877.

Issue by first wife

245 Elizabeth Stout; married Mr. Hoagland.

Issue by second wife

246 Levi Stout, born June 8, 1833, died Dec 30, 1872, married Sarah Ann ...., born Mch. 13, 1826, died Dec. 9, 1864
247 William B Stout, born Aug 2, 1847; died Sept 4, 1877.

204 JOHN L. STOUT, son of Zephaniah Stout, 149, married, first, Margaret Williams, second, Margaret Titus He settled in Virginia.

Issue by first wife

248 Ellen C. Stout, married George M. Fry.
249 Maria L Stout, married Joshua Fry
250 Charles W. Stout, married Ann M. Kindwell
251 Sydnah Stout, married Mary C. Wicklow
252 Israel Stout; married, in New Jersey, Keziah Geddes
253 Caroline Stout, died young
254 Zephaniah Stout
255 Henry C. Stout; married Anna C Bates

Issue by second wife

256 Mary C. Stout; married Charles W Umbaugh
257 Sarah A. Stout
258 Robert W. Stout
259 Nathan Stout
260 Amanda E Stout

205 NATHAN STOUT, son of William Stout, 150, married Mary A Fisher.

Issue

261 William F. Stout, of Independence, Iowa, married Martha A Harriman. He died in his 35th year.
262 Henry H. Stout; was killed, in the Union Army, during the Rebellion
263 Simson S. Stout
263ª Lucretia F. Stout, died single
263ᵇ Mary Y Stout; married Augustus Young.

206 HENRY L STOUT, son of William Stout, 150, married Eveline Dening, of Syracuse, N. Y. He moved to Dubuque, Iowa.

Issue
264 James H. Stout; married Kitty J Morrell
265 Jenny E. Stout; married A. W. Dougherty.
266 Frank Stout; married [Miss Faney?]

MISCELLANEOUS ITEMS

The following items may refer to the descendants of James Stout, son of Richard Stout, 1.
In 1752, Richard Stout, of New Brittan, Bucks Co , Penn , made his will, in which he mentioned:

Daughter, Elizabeth Stout
Daughter Sarah Stout, wife of John Lambet, to her "a gownd which was her mothers," and to her husband, John Lambet, £400
Son, Joseph Stout

1778, Feb 21 Jonathan Stout took the Oath of Allegiance, before Joshua Anderson, in Bucks Co , Penn
1778, June 8 Jacob and Daniel Stout took the Oath of Allegiance, before Joshua Anderson, in Bucks Co , Penn
1783, Oct 14 James Stout took the Oath of Allegiance, before Joshua Anderson, in Bucks Co , Penn

Mary Stout, widow, died Oct 21, 1806. Baptist Church Records, Middletown, N J.
1801, May 15 Mary Stout, *widdow*, of Middletown, N. J., made her will, which was proved Nov. 10, 1806, and mentioned children:
Mary Stout
Lydia Stout, wife of William Morford, whose eldest son is John Morford   [Lydia Stout was born in 1768. See Ellis' History of Monmouth County for their children.]

1 . . . . . STOUT married . . . . .
   Issue
   2 Elijah Stout
   3 Joseph Henry Stout, who died in 1834. He married Rebecca . . . , and had issue.
   4 James Stout
   5 John W. Stout

5 JOHN W. STOUT, son of Joseph Henry Stout, 3, born 1824 or 1826, died 1903. He married, first, Apr 19, 1846, Emeline Hurley, born 1827, died Feb. 19, 1898, second, August, 1898, Ada L. Thomson.

   Issue
   6 Joseph Stout; married . . . . .
      Issue
      Estella Stout
      A son
      Another daughter

STOUT MISCELLANEOUS ITEMS

    7 Henry Stout
    8 Elijah Stout, of Red Bank, N. J.
    9 Ella Stout, born 1863; married William A. Bicknell
  10 John W Stout, born 1855; died Sept. 16, 1906; married ..

Issue

Rennie Hendrickson Stout, married a daughter of Sidney B Conover

1 .... STOUT married and had

Issue

2 Stephen Stout
3 John Stout
4 Sarah Stout

2 STEPHEN STOUT, son of .... Stout, 1

1816, Mch 2 Stephen Stout, of Freehold, N. J., made his will, which was proved Mch 13, 1816, and in which he mentioned:

Brother, John Stout
Sister, Sarah, wife of Thomas Parker, Sr
"my nephew or sister's son, Sylvenis T Bills"

4 SARAH STOUT, daughter of . Stout, 1, married, first, Mr Bills, second, Thomas Parker, Sr.

Issue by first husband

Sylvanus T. Bills

1787, October Term Monmouth County Orphans' Court Sarah Parker, mother of Sylvanus Bills, (aged 11 years), petitioned, and Thomas Parker was appointed his guardian

Issue by second husband, (if he had no other wife)

Charles Parker, born 1787, an eminent man, married Sarah Coward, and was the father of Gov. Joel Parker, born 1816 See Ellis' History of Monmouth County.
Joseph Parker
Anthony Parker, married Phebe, daughter of David Stout

Issue

Thomas Parker
David Stout Parker, born 1808.
Abigail Parker; married David Salter
John Parker
Joseph Parker

1821, Oct. 11. Benjamin Stout, of Dover, in Monmouth County, N J, made his will, which was proved Nov. 16, 1821, and in which he mentioned·

Wife, Mary.
Son, Benjamin
Daughters, Mary Havens, Lydia Akins, Elizabeth Britton, Deborah Lewis, Ann Britton, Hannah Brown and Actsah Stout

1 ABRAHAM STOUT married, and had
> *Issue*
> 2 Abraham Stout; married Elizabeth Hires
> > *Issue*
> > 3 Garret Stout, Sr , born 1802; died, May 15, 1888, aged 86 years, kept a hotel at Cedar Creek, N. J   He married, first, Elizabeth Jeffrey, died, May 7, 1848, aged 50, 2, 7, second, Ann Jane Stout, born 1812, died 1895
> > > *Issue* by first wife
> > > Forman Stout, born 1824, died 1852; married Eliza, daughter of Benjamin and Sarah Stout.
> > > Abraham Stout
> > > Garret Stout

"The original Stouts were largely a red-haired race, not an offensive red, but one with a touch of gold "

"Penelope Stout was buried on the farm of Mr Kelly, who purchased the same from Mr. Carman, which lies between Holmdel and Annie Ogborn's Corner "

Perhaps this can be reconciled with the following

"Penelope Stout's grave can be seen from the windows of the house of Charles Conover (Big Charley)   This farm is, or was, until recently, known as the Obadiah Stillwell farm and formed part of the homestead of Richard Stout, the first."

At one time I was inclined to think that Penelope Stout was buried in the Lippit Burying-ground, but later evidence convinces me that this was an error

"The maiden name, perhaps married name, of Penelope Van Princis was Kent or Lent," as Mrs Seabrook recalls it

"Penelope was a Dutch woman, and her name I always supposed was Van Prince, either by birth or marriage, but I think my grandmother called her by another name which I do not remember. My grandmother never told me whom she married, merely gave the story of the wreck and her subsequent history "   Mrs T W Seabrook, Nov. 4, 1881

Hope Still and Deliverance were twins and grandchildren of Penelope Stout, who were born, during an Indian excitement, in the block house which was situated on the site of the of the present Episcopal Church, in Middletown, N J

Mrs Seabrook states that her grandmother, Helena Huff, said that Penelope Stout was bandaged with withes (the inside bark of a tree) and sewed with gut, and that the Indian who preserved her life, when he saw her lying, walked backwards and threw his blanket over her as a sign that he protected her   This occurred at Long Branch

On one occasion, when there was a threatened Indian uprising, he called upon her, at Middletown, and refused to eat supper that night as was his custom. They took the hint from this suggestion, and lay off in the bay, in a boat, until the excitement abated.

1687, Aug 12 Henry Stout is named as a legatee in the will of Gawen Lawrie, late Governor of East Jersey.   New Jersey Archives, Volume XXI, page 101

1738, Jan 14 Hannah Stout, of Shrewsbury, N J., died.   Episcopal Church Record

STOUT MISCELLANEOUS ITEMS

The following four items are from the Shrewsbury, N J , Town Poor Book
1743 Hannah Stout one of the Town Poor, 1744-5, 1746
1772. Robert Stout on the Tax List.
1774. Benjamin Stout on the Tax List.
1762. John Stout mentioned as an Overseer.

1777, Apr 10. Mercy Stout, of Hunterdon County, late Mercy Vaughan, (with others), executrix of late William Vaughn, of Upper Freehold, conveyed land to William Mount

1793, Apr. 1 David Stout and wife, Hannah, of Middletown, sold to Job Layton, for £6-13-0, one-third of a four acre lot of meadow, at Shoal Harbor, late property of Timothy Mount, deceased, and which descended to said Hannah Stout and her two sisters, Jemimah and Elizabeth, all daughters of said Timothy.

1813, Aug. 13. Acknowledged by Hannah, relict of said David Stout
1794, Jan 3. John Eldrith sold one-third of the preceding land to Job Layton.

From Tom's River, Ocean Co., Marriage Records
1852, Feb. 17. Garret Stout and Mary G. Irons
1852, July 14. James Stout and Ann Grant
1854, Dec 28. James P. Dye and Mary E. Stout
1858, Nov 30 John Stout and Louvinna Taylor.

From Freehold, N J , Marriage Records
1795, Dec. 13. Lieha Stout and David Moorehouse
1796, Jan. 31. Ruth Stout and Garret Covenhoven.
1797, Mch 2 Nancy Stout and Jeremiah Anderson.
1798, Feb. 8. John Stout and Martha Bealei, [Bedel?]
1799, Oct. 27. Jonathan Stout and Hester Morris.
1800, Oct. 26. John Stout and Rebecca Hambleton.
1802, Mch 27. Joseph Stout, of Howell, and Jane Brinley, widow, of Shrewsbury.
1802, Nov. 28. Anne Stout, of Dover, and Richard Britton, Jr., of Howell.
1803, June 26. Hannah Stout and Charles Fisher, at Howell.
1803, Oct. 26. Elizabeth Stout and Jesse Chamberling.
1804, Aug. 15. Elcey Stout and Peter Clayton
1804, Sept. 19. Rachel Stout and Francis Wheeler, both of Howell.
1805, Dec. 25. Jonathan Stout and Elizabeth Jeffree
1806, Mch. 2. Sarah Stout and William Aumack; both of Howell.
1806, Nov. 16. Lucy Stout, of Middletown, and Oliver Hix, of New York
1807, Nov. 20 Anne Stout and Henry Herbert.
1808, Jan. 9. Jacob Stout and Catharine Schenck
1809, Jan. 12. Betsy Stout and John Clayton
1809, Aug 6. Richard Stout and Elizabeth Airs
1811, Feb. 27. Richard Stout and Ann Allen; both of Howell.
1813, Dec 16 Thomas Stout and Maria Leffertson
1815, Mch. 5. Charles Stout and Phebe Compton, both of Middletown.
1815, June 1 Robert Stout and Jane Newman, both of Howell
1816, Feb. 4. Anna Stout and Edward Wilbur.
1817, Feb 17 Rebecca Stout, at house of Benjamin Stout, and Francis Leets
1818, Feb 28 Hannah Stout, at house of Daniel Stout, Esq , and William Rogers.

1818, Nov 5 Joseph Stout and Williampe Dorset, both of Howell, at house of James Dorset.
1818, Nov. 11. William Stout and Margaret Pearce; both of Howell.
1819, Feb. 18 Jacob Stout and Getty Truax, both of Howell.
1819, Apr. 22 John Stout and Delilah Allen, both of Howell.
1819, Oct. 15. Abraham Stout and Catharine Bennet; both of Dover.
1820, Apr 9 Betsy Stout and Thomas Beard
1820, Apr 16 Rachel Stout and John Williams, both of Dover, at Goodluck.
1822, May 9 Joseph Stout and Rebecca Wilson.
1822, Nov. 17. David Stout and Isabel Curtis, both of Howell.
1822, Dec. 11. Douglas Stout and Rachel McLean.
1823, Feb. 22 Garret Stout and Eliza Jeffrey.
1823, June 26 Hannah Stout and Charles Fisher, at Howell.
1823, Aug. 10 Lydia Stout, of Burlington Co., and Wesley Southard, of Stafford, at Manahawkin. Elsewhere date is Feb. 9, 1826
1823, Dec 21. Richard Stout and Hannah Stricklands
1824, Feb 14 Ann Stout and Joseph Holmes, both of Howell, at Goodluck
1824, June 26 Mary Stout and John Jones, both of Dover.
1826, Feb 9. James Stout and Harriet Snedecker
1827, Jan. 27 Rebecca Stout and James Pearce, at the house of William Stout.
1827, Feb 20 Catharine Stout and Daniel Stryker, both of Middletown.
1827, May 24 Orphau Stout and William Van Note.
1828, Jan. —. Elizabeth Stout and Jacob Conover, both of Middletown.
1828, Feb 27. Joseph Stout and Amelia Falkinburg, both of Dover, at John Tilton's, in Dover.
1829, Jan 23 Elizabeth Stout and Elijah Vanderhoof, both of Howell.
1852, July 6 Jonathan Stout and Elizabeth Morris
[1873?] Jan 1 James W. Stout and Adelaide Morris

From New Brunswick, N. J., Marriage Records.

1795, Nov. 25 Amos Stout and Margaret Morgan.
1796, Aug. 31. Luce Stout and Timothy Core.
1799, Sept 1 Charity Stout and Asher Vaughan
1800, Nov. 5. David Stout and . . . . Breese.
1802, Mch. 31. Michael Forman and Ann Stout, at Hightstown.
1802 [1809?] Sept 2 Randolph Stout and Margaret Perkins.
1802, Nov. 10 Elizabeth Stout and William Hutchinson, of Hightstown.
1803, Oct. 8. Charlotte S Stout and Ezekial Dodge
1809, Feb. 16 Eunice Stout and Robert Ayers
1811, Jan. 12. Charles Stout and Sarah Gulick.
1816, Dec 18. Lucy Stout and Gilbert Giberson

New Brunswick, N. J , Deeds.

1785, Nov 14. Richard Stout, [his mark], and Joseph Stout, of Burlington County, give deed
1794, June 4. John Stout and Mabel, his wife, of South Amboy, give deed.
1800 Daniel Stout and Ann, his wife, of East Windsor, are mentioned.

STOUT MISCELLANEOUS ITEMS

1802. Samuel Stout, Sr , of Windsor, N J , made his will, which was proved in 1811, and which directed that he be buried by the side of his wife, Eunice, in the burying-ground where his wife and children are buried, and mentioned

Second wife, Mary
Six children, male and female
Daughter, Mary, deceased, wife of Jacob Post, left a child   Executor· Friend, Joseph Stout, of Penn's Neck

1733, Feb. 22. Herman Stout, of Perth Amboy, sail-maker, appoint "my wife Mary Stout my attorney."

1755, Oct 24. Jediah Stout, of Windsor, yeoman, to Matthias Mount, of same, yeoman
Trenton Records.

1731. Joseph Stout, of Hopewell, was with many others, a defendant to popular land ejectment suits.

1722   Joseph Stout, married, had 28 cattle, 18 sheep, 230 acres
David Stout, married, had 10 cattle, 1 sheep, 250 acres   Hopewell Tax Roll.

1753. Benjamin, Sr., Benjamin, Jr , David, David, Sr , Joseph, Col Joseph, Jacob, Samuel, Esq , and Zebulon Stout were on the Hopewell Tax Roll

David Stout, born Jan 28, 1734, died Feb 8, 1826; married, by license dated Nov 28, 1760, Catherine, daughter of John Barclay. He resided, during the latter part of his life, at *Cranberry*, Middlesex County, N. J

Issue, baptized at Christ Church, Shrewsbury, N. J
Ann Stout; baptized Nov 1, 1761
Elizabeth Stout, baptized May 1, 1763
John Barclay Stout; baptized Dec 9 1764

Abel Stout, Sr , born, in New Jersey, in 1734, died Aug 24, 1797; married Elizabeth . . ., who died, at White Oak Springs, Va., Feb 28, 1842   Abel Stout is the great-grandfather of S H. Stout, Division Freight Agent of the Louisville and Nashville R. R Co

April, 1908, Mr S H. Stout writes   "I have succeeded in tracing the line back to John Stout, Nottinghamshire, England, through James and Catharine (Simpson) Stout " See 67, 12 and 11

1739, Nov. 9 Samuel Stout was the administrator of Jas [Ashton?] The inventory amounted to £51-6-3

1758, Jan "fourteenth " Administrator's Bond, signed by Samuel Tilton, [sig], administrator and principal creditor of *John Stout*, [probable descendant of John Stout, 2, of Richard Stout, 1, of Middletown], late of Middletown, Boatman, and William Compton, [sig Will Comton?], both of Middletown, yeomen. Witness   Tho® Bartow   On the back of the bond appears the affirmation of Samuel Tilton, "being one of the People called Quakers," to administer

1758, Jan 17. Inventory of John Stout, appraised by Samuel Carman, Cornelius Compton, Samuel Legg and Samuel Tilton, amounted to about [£13-4-6?]

1766. William Compton, in his will of this date, mentioned his son-in-law, Jacob Stout

1766, Oct 23 Rachel Stout married Wm Clawson   North and Southampton Church Records, in Gage Library, New Brunswick, N. J

1803, Sept 8. Benjamin Stout, reputed son of Abner Stout, was married, in New Jersey, to Ruth Prall

1774, Jan 7 Joseph Stout was licensed to marry Elizabeth Stout. They may be No 52, of the line of David Stout, and No 94, of the line of Jonathan Stout, in which case the David Stout should read· Joseph Stout had a license to marry, Jan 7, 1774, Elizabeth Stout, but it is all supposition

John Stout moved from Squancum to Herbertville. By his wife, Psyche, (so pronounced), he had
Issue
David Stout, an only son who went West

Lydia Stout; married, first, Osborn Garretson, and second, Hugh Burdge, by whom she had Billy Burdge, who married Jane Havens In 1910, Billy Burdge was living, aged about 80 years, at Herbertville, N. J

1813, Oct. 9. Garret S. Stout born .. ; died Feb. 20, 1906; married, 1831, Sarah Jane Dickerson, who died 1894 They had a daughter, Mrs Francis Van Gieson, and a son W^m H Stout, of Forrest Hills.

1860, May 1. Richard Stout died, aged 82 years, 5 months and 11 days

1831, May 18. Mrs Alice Stout died, aged 52 years and 9 days. Old Cemetery, Tom's River

UNPLACED NEW YORK STOUTS

1698–9. Abraham Walker, of Jamaica, appointed John Stout, of Port Royal, Gent , his attorney, to sue and recover debts due him by Wm Huddlestone, Gent , of New York.

1699 Administration on estate of John Stout, late of Jamaica, who died on a voyage to New York, on board the sloop Content, granted to Thos Wenham, of New York, his trustee. See interesting letter among New York Wills.

1700, June 19 Petition of Amareus, widow of John Stout, late of the Island of Jamaica, praying that the lands, on Staten Island, purchased by her husband, Andrew Norwood, to whom the same were patented, be surveyed.

1714 Amerantie Stout, formerly widow of John Stout, of the Island of Jamaica, and afterward widow of Benjamin Beagrave, died intestate and letters of administration were granted to her eldest son, John Stout. In 1717–18, Amantie, daughter of John Stout, was a legatee, for £10, in the will of Peter Christianse, a New York boatman.

1721, May 16 Harman Stout, of New York, sail-maker and mariner, apprenticed John Cooper, son of John Cooper, mariner, deceased, Sept. 15, 1743

1728 Harman Stout was witness to a New York will.

1751 John McEvers, in his will, alludes to land purchased from Mary, wife and attorney of Herman Stout, amounting to 607 acres, situated in Middlesex Co., N. J., near Millstone River.

In 1757, there was in Monmouth County, N. J., a Harman Stout, with wife Mary, daughter of David and Catharine Lyell, who were the parents of one son and two daughters.

1814, Feb 18 James H Stout, Frankfort St., died, aged 22 years, and is buried in Trinity Churchyard

1816, Jan. 14 Sarah Stout died, in Grand St., New York City, aged 1 year amd 6 months, and is buried in Trinity Churchyard

1816, May 19 Jacob Stout was married to Miss Mary Mount, by the Rev Dr Spring, of New York

Samuel Livingston Breese, son of Arthur Breese, Rear Admiral of U S. Navy, married first, Frances S Stout, second, Emma Lovett He died Dec 17, 1870

UNATTACHED LINES

A branch of the Stout Family settled in New York City. Without any strong reason therefor, I believe they are descendants of John Stout, son of Richard and Penelope Stout The following data concerns them

1 JOHN STOUT, ship-captain, married, June 24, 1714, Abigail, daughter of Benjamin Bill She was baptized Nov 13, 1695, and was nineteen years of age at the time of her marriage In 1718, Abigail Stout was a witness to a New York will.

Issue

2 Anna Maria Stout; baptized Mch. 4, 1715
3 Benjamin Stout, baptized June 2, 1717.
4 John Stout; baptized Feb 10, 1720

3 BENJAMIN STOUT, son of John Stout, 1, was baptized June 2, 1717; married, May 6, 1738, ffamitie de Froseest [Phoebe De Fosest?].

1805, Sept 28 Died, at Brooklyn, Mrs. Phoebe Stout, in the 94th year of her age [Widow of Benjamin Stout, 3?]

1783, Nov 10 Benjamin Stout made his will which was proved May 7, 1788

The following items may refer to Benjamin Stout, 3, or to Benjamin Stout, 5
1751 Benjamin Stout was a witness to a will   New York Wills

1768, Jan 21. Benjamin Stout, James Waterman, and sixteen others, petitioned for a tract of eighteen thousand acres of land, on the West side of the Connecticut River

1770, 1771, 1773 Benjamin Stout was appointed executor in New York Wills.

1770, July 9 Benjamin Stout and associates petitioned for a grant of thirty thousand acres of land, about eighteen miles to the West of the Connecticut River, and South of Kent, and that the same be erected into a township by the name of Virgin Hall

1770, July 27. Return of Survey of Benjamin Stout and his associates, of a tract of twenty-six thousand five hundred acres of land, on the West side of the Connecticut River, in the County of Cumberland, adjoining the township of Kent, (Andover, Windham County Vt), with a map of the same (Virgin Hall)

1776, July 23. Gov Henry Moore granted to John Stout, Benjamin Stout, and twenty-three others, for 2s. 6d , quit-rent per hundred acres, a tract of land, on the West side of the Connecticut River, in the County of Cumberland, erected into a township by the name of Hertford.

Issue

5 Benjamin Stout, born 1745
6 John B. Stout, married, Jan. 23, 1772, Effee Van Varck [Effie Varick]
7 Jacob Stout, married, first, Elizabeth Carpender, second Frances Carpender
8 Abigail Stout, married, first, by license dated June 19, 1758, John Agnew, second, Apr. 12, 1762, Caleb Hyatt, his second wife.

9 Sarah Stout married, first, James Taggart; second, John Carpender
10 Eleanah [Helen] Stout, married, September, 1766, William Grigg, no issue

4 JOHN STOUT, son of John Stout, 1, and Abigail Bill, was baptized Feb 10, 1720, and married Ann Dodameed, who was baptized, in the First Presbyterian Church, of New York City, Aug. 24, 1766. He was a sea captain and commanded the British privateer "Harlequin," of 16 guns, in the Revolutionary War

The following items may refer to John Stout, 4:
1745, and again in 1758, John Stout was a witness to wills in New York City.
1773, Mch 1. John Stout, shipmaster, a member of the Marine Society
1775. John Stout was of the township of Durham, N. Y
1776, March John Stout was 1st Lieutenant of the 22nd Regiment, New York City Militia In 1776, he was also a fireman of the city.

Issue

11 John Stout, born Nov 1, 1765, baptized, Aug. 7, 1766, in the First Presbyterian Church, New York City.

5 BENJAMIN STOUT, JR, eldest son of Benjamin Stout, 3, was born in 1745, and married, Aug 24, 1766, Jemima Brevoort*, of New York He died, June 12, 1799, aged 54 years, and Jemima, his wife, died, Feb 18, 1812, aged 65 years Sarah, their daughter, died, Apr. 21, 1808, aged 37 years, and Charlotte Rainteaux, their grandchild, died, May 15, 1808, aged 2 years On a single slab in Trinity Churchyard, New York City

Allusion to his death in local papers gave his death as at Greenwich, but late of Maiden Lane In this last-named locality he appears to have kept a boarding-house in his latter days. His wife died, of apoplexy, at 160 Greenwich St, New York City.

1760, Jan 14 Benjamin Stout, late of this County [New York], innholder, was administrator on the estate of the widow, Catharine Hubbell.

1766, August There was a Benjamin Stout who was an innkeeper, and kept a tavern on the Bloomingdale Road, near the six mile stone It was a favorite resort of those who were inclined to be loyal to the King.

The following squib is from the New York Journal, of June 8, 1791:

"We hear from the six mile stone, north river, that on Saturday last, a select company of the Loyal Subjects of George the Third, merchants, &c, from this city, had a high glee kick up at Stouts, in celebration of their master's birth-day Protected by the laws, favored by the domestic patronage—, and enjoying every other blessing of a free and plentiful country—with mock effrontery—they geer its simple manners—and in its teeth, they chant their "Rule Britannia"'
LO' these are they who lur'd by follies—
Left all, and follow'd great Cornwallis"'

1776 There was a Benjamin Stout, a dealer in wines, groceries, dye woods, etc., doing business in Queen, now Pearl St, near Peck Slip, who was a signer to the address of the Loyalists to Lord Howe his son, Benjamin Stout, Jr, and John B Stout, Richard Stout and Robert Stout were also signers

Benjamin Stout's house was searched by authority of the resolve of Congress of Mch 10, 1776, he being well known as a person disaffected Two pistols, of the value of £1-16-0, were found

*Elias Brevoort, in his will dated 1774, proved 1777, left to his daughter, Jacamyntie, wife of Benjamin Stout, Jr, his dwelling house and other real estate in New York, and appointed his son-in-law, Benjamin Stout, Jr, one of his executors

STOUT UNATTACHED LINES

1776, June 15 He is also included in the list of suspected persons, furnished to the committee to detect conspiracies, of this date

1780, Feb 2 Benjamin Stout was 1st Lieutenant in Company 1, New York City Volunteers, and promoted to a Captaincy vice Bayard, Mch 23, of the same year

1782 Benjamin Stout was appointed administrator. New York Wills

1783 Benjamin Stout, Jr, was executor on the estate of Edward Smith, tinman

1785, Mch 22. Benjamin Stout, Jr, merchant, and Jacomentye, his wife, sold land, in Smith's Fly, to John Lovell, butcher.

1800, Dec 16. Jemima Stout, widow of Benjamin Stout, late of New York, gentleman, deceased, and Jacob Stout, of Phillisburg [?], Westchester County, Gent, are mentioned, probably in a conveyance

1810, Aug. 11. Jemima Stout, widow, gave to her daughter, Eliza, wife of Amos Butler, a negro girl The indenture was witnessed by Abigail Mervin and Wm. G. Stout

Issue

12 Lunah Stout, married John William Delaney [or Delancey], a merchant of New York She died while on a voyage from St Croix, in February, 1799.
13 Sarah Stout, born 1771, died, Apr. 21, 1808, and buried from 31 Courtlandt St, New York City
14 Benjamin Stout
15 Phoebe Stout, married Anthony Rainetaux, a merchant of New York
16 Abigail Stout, married Francis Menier
17 Samuel Stout
18 Elizabeth Stout, married, July 31, 1804, Amos Butler, who, with John Crookes, was the proprietor of the Mercantile Advertiser.
19 Charlotte Stout
20 William Stout

6 JOHN BENJAMIN STOUT, son of Benjamin Stout, 3, followed the business of a baker, in New York City, to which he was admitted freeman in 1773 He married, Jan 23, 1772, Effee, daughter of Andrew Varick, a hatter

1830, June 2 Mrs Effee Stout died, in her 79th year, at 79 or 99 Ludlow St Her husband must have died in 1791 or 1792 She worked as a seamstress or tailoress

Issue

21 Phebe Stout, died unmarried Her will was proved Sept 4, 1855
22 Andrew V. Stout, married, first, Jane. . ; second, Almira H . . . . .

Issue

Abigail Stout, died aged 4 years, and lies buried in Trinity Churchyard, New York City
23 James D Stout; married, first, Jane Disney She died, Dec. 25, 1815, aged 34 years, and lies buried in Trinity Churchyard, New York City. He married, second, Susan Smith

Issue

Edwin Stout, died, Oct 9, 1814, aged 10 months
James Disney Stout, died, Aug 24, 1816, aged 9 months.
24 Helen Stout, married Mr Sickels
25 Effee Stout, married Mr. Hyatt.

HISTORICAL MISCELLANY

Issue

Nancy Hyatt
Phebe Caroline Hyatt
Mary Jane Hyatt; married Isaac Hatch [?]

7 JACOB STOUT, son of Benjamin Stout, 3, married, first, Elizabeth Carpender, second, his sister-in-law, Frances Carpender

Jacob Stout, during the War of the Revolution, commanded the following privateers, belonging to New York

"Lively" of 14 guns. "Britannia" of 20 guns. "Delight" of 8 guns. "Triumph" of 16 guns

1798, July 31 A Jacob Stout mentioned his residence, at Philipsburg, on a farm, in the town of Yonkers, in the Daily Advertiser of this date

Issue by first wife

26 John Stout
27 Jacob Stout, married Susan, daughter of Arthur Breese. After his death, she married Rev Dr Pierre Alexis Proal, Rector of Trinity Church. She died about 1863
28 Catharine Stout, born 1782, married, Oct. 6, 1808, Asher Marx. She died July 2, 1811.

Issue by second wife, [half-sister of Elizabeth.]

29 Sarah Ann Stout, born 1804; died, Apr. 13, 1808, aged 4 years and 2 months, and lies buried in Trinity Churchyard
30 Matthew White Stout
31 Aquilla G Stout, married his cousin Ann, daughter of William W Morris. His will was proved June 27, 1857.

Issue

Sarah Morris Stout
Francis A Stout, a merchant, in 1826, at 14 Broad St. He resided, with his mother, at 100 Chambers St.
32 William C Stout, married Miss Henry He was living in 1857
33 Charles Rainteaux Stout
34 Frances Stout, married Michael Hogan, son of William Hogan, who married Miss Clendening, and probably had a daughter, Frances Hogan
35 Lenox Stout
36 Arthur Breese Stout, living in 1857.

23 JAMES D STOUT, son of John Benjamin Stout, 6

1868, Feb 3 The will of James D. Stout, Gent., which was proved July 16, 1868, and recorded in New York, sets forth the following relationships

Issue

37 John B. Stout
38 George Stout
39 James V. Stout In his will of July, 1859, which was proved May 4, 1860, he stated that he was of New York City, and mentioned his brother, John B Stout, and the grave of his brother, George, in Greenwood. His estate was left to Mary Otten

STOUT UNATTACHED LINES

37 JOHN B STOUT, son of James D. Stout, 23, resided in Franklin County, Kentucky
   Issue
   40 Anna M Stout, married Charles S Todd, of New Albany, Ind , and had two children
   41 Addie M. Stout, married George O. Hart, of Paducah, Kentucky, and had two children

"The Stout family, descended from the two old ship captains, Jacob and John, were numerous, but at this day the race is nearly extinct

Captain Jacob Stout [died 1821] had several children In 1795, he lived at Amboy, where he had the yellow fever He was so near death that his family felt justified in ordering his coffin

Jacob, Jr., was a son of his first wife, so was John

Catharine, his daughter, married Asher Marx, Oct 8, 1808 [She died 1811] They were married by Rev Doctor Beach. Mr Marx was a very eminent merchant for years, under the firm of Marx & Linsley, at No 74 Queens street, where he kept for over twenty years, or until he died, in his house, No 673 Broadway, in 1824 He married a second time, I think, a Miss Carroll She lived many years after his death, and left several children"

"The second wife of Capt Jacob Stout was a Miss [Frances] Carpender [half-sister of his first wife] Before he married her—or in 1796, when he quit sea life—he went up to Westchester, and bought a place at Yonkers It was the old Stone Mills He afterwards sold it to Joseph Howland, the father of G G Howland Old Captain Stout was, as I have said, an Englishman by birth He sailed, first, from London in one of the East India Company's ships, the 'Sampson,' from Ostend to Calcutta He was taken a prisoner in the French war He had charge, at the time, of a letter of marque He was a prisoner on board the flag-ship of the Count de Grasse, when Admiral Rodney took the French fleet

His second wife was a daughter of William Carpender, a shipmaster The latter married a daughter of William Grant, the first person who ever imported potatoes from abroad He used always to be found at King's Coffee House

Capt Jacob had by his second wife, Miss Carpender, the following children Matthew White Stout, [born 1796], named after old Henry White, a great merchant as early as 1769, before the war and afterwards His daughters, the Miss Whites, I have already written about The next son was Aquilla Giles Stout, [born 1799] He was named after Col Aquilla Giles, who was a very celebrated man in his day, lived for many years at 54 Broadway, and had a country seat in the upper part of Greenwich village Another son was William Carpender [Stout], [born 1801], named after his mother's father, Capt William Carpender, who married Miss Grant

Capt Jacob Stout's fourth child was Sarah Ann, [born 1804, died 1808] She died young The fifth was Charles Raintaux Stout, [born 1802] He was named after an old merchant Anthony [Raintaux]

Frances Hogan, [born 1806], was the sixth child She married Captain Breeze of the navy

The seventh child was named Lenox Stout, [born 1809], after old Robert Lenox, who was an intimate friend of old Robert

The eighth child was Arthur Breeze Stout, [born 1814, died, unmarried, 1898, in San Francisco]

All of these children are deceased, except William Carpender Stout, [died 1870], and A Breeze Stout [All dead, in 1832, except William, Rainteaux and others]

Old Capt Jacob Stout, after he sold his mills at Yonkers, purchased a place at Belleville, where he put up a flouring mill He ground for the city and for the country He had two mills He bought of Doctor Ogilvey, the Episcopal minister He lived out there in the summer, and resided in the city in the winter He died about 1823

Jacob, the eldest son of old Capt Jacob, married [Susan], a daughter of Arthur Breeze, of Utica They had two children—a son [Edward] and a daughter [Sarah Lansing Stout] The son entered the navy He married a daughter of Commodore Aulick He was a lieutenant, and lost in [on] the Levant He left a widow and two children They are in France [His issue were deceased in 1905]

Aquilla G Stout, left a son Francis A , who is still alive Also a daughter, Sarah Morris Stout She married a Monsieur De Veatt Gringues, [Baron de Vaugrigneuse], of the French Legation [He died during the siege of Paris, she died Apr 22, 1904]

Consul Ridgway, of Santa Cruz, married the widow of old Captain Jacob Stout [first]

Captain W C Stout married Miss Henry, daughter of old Captain Henry, one of the oldest captains out of this port forty years ago Old Captain Henry married Miss Harved She was a daughter of Jonathan Harved They lived in Pearl street Mr Harved was one hundred years old when he died, and his wife ninety-three They lived together sixty years He died in Charles street

Captain Henry had three daughters He always said that they never should marry sailors Yet all did One married Captain Stout, another married Com Montgomery, U S N, now in command at Boston, another married Dr Hosea Edwards, of Bridgeport, a Surgeon in the Navy Old Captain Henry was in the Liverpool trade

Captain Stout I have given a full history of in another chapter He has a place at Huntington, Long Island, where he spends his summers, and in the winter he stops at the New York Hotel He has no children [He died in 1870, and his wife, Delia, died in 1877]

Nearly all of the Stout family descended from old Captain Jacob are dead There were descendants from Captain John, but I believe they are dead too That family lived in Courtlandt street One son was Ben Stout. He was lost in the West Indies His body was buried in Trinity Churchyard

Amos Butler, who was one of the owners of the *Daily Mercantile Advertiser* thirty years ago, married one of the Miss Stouts I believe his descendants are living in the city "

The Old Merchants of New York City—Walter Barrett, Edition 1885, Vol III, pp 87, 92, 93, 94 and 95, also Vol IV *

Franklin Ellis, in his History of Monmouth County, New Jersey, (Philadelphia 1885), pp 66, 67 & 68, writing of Richard Stout and his wife, Penelope, quotes Smith's allusions to them in full, introducing his account as follows·

"* * * * * the following account is found in a 'History of New Jersey,' published in 1765 "

Having finished Smith's account, he gives a portion of the Stout history as it appears in Benedict's History of the Baptists, and a little erroneously, and forthwith proceeds to comment upon it in the following language:

"There is, beyond doubt, a good deal of romance and inaccuracy in both these accounts, though in their main features they are probably correct The statement that they lived 'among other Dutch' at Middletown is clearly incorrect, as there were no Dutch among the early settlers there The story of the intended Indian massacre, too, is undoubtedly the product of a fertile imagination, as it is well known that the Indians of this region were always friendly to the English settlers, and never gave them any trouble except an occasional drunken brawl, which the white men punished by placing the noble red man in the stocks or pillory, just as they did the same class of white offenders,—a fact which in itself shews that they had no fear of any Indian massacre. As to Benedict's statement, if it is true that she was born in 1602, and was married to Richard Stout when she was twenty-two, the time of their marriage must have been the year 1624, at which time he was forty years of age They went to Middletown, with the first settlers, in 1664, at which time, (if this statement is correct), her age was sixty-two, and his eighty years At that time, and for several succeeding years, Richard Stout was a prominent man in the public affairs of the Navesink settlements, which would hardly have been the case at such an age, and in 1669, when, (according to the above supposition), he was eighty-five years old, Richard Stout, Jonathan Holmes, Edward Smith and James Bowne were chosen 'overseers' of Middletown, and Stout made his X mark to the 'Ingadgement' in lieu of signature,—which last mentioned fact makes it improbable that he was, as stated, an Englishman 'of good family,' according to the usual English understanding of that term Richard Stout was, however, one of the most respectable and respected men in his day in the Monmouth settlements "

"STOUT or STOUCE, RICHARD, one of the first settlers of G^d in 1643, and allotted plantation-lot No 18 in 1646, as per town rec, d about 1688 He also bought Apl 5, 1661, plantation-lot No 26 of Edward Griffen With a number of his neighbors he left G^d and settled at Middletown, Monmouth Co, N J, of which place he was one of the patentees or original purchasers of the Indians, as per p 73 of Vol 1, of Raum's N J There is a story, founded on tradition, on p 76, etc, of said Vol, of the shipwreck of a Dutch ship on Sandy Hook, of the crew and passengers leaving a sick young Dutchman and his wife there while they went for relief, of the Indians tomahawking the man, mangling the wife and leaving her for dead, of her recovering

---
*The interpolations were made by me from data supplied by Charles L Craig, Esq, 22 William St, New York City

and crawling into a hollow log and subsisting for several days on berries, and then being discovered and taken prisoner and her life preserved by an old Indian, ransomed by the Dutch of N Y, where she married *Richard Stout*, being at the time in her 22d year and he in his 40th They settled at Middletown, where the old Indian often visited her, and on one occasion, by informing her of a plot to massacre the whites, put them on their guard and saved the settlement from destruction This woman, whose maiden name was *Penelope Van Prince*, lived to the age of 110 years, her posterity numbering 502 at the time of her death The compiler gives this tradition as he finds it, having little faith therein Issue (per Rev G C Schenck) —John, Richard, Jonathan, Peter, James, Benjamin, David, Deliverance, Sarah, and Penelope, whose descendants are numerous in N J Made his mark to documents "

From Early Settlers of Kings Co —Bergen—pp 286, 287, Ed 1881

"In a small pamphlet published in 1790, a very interesting account is given of this family "

"Mrs Stout was born in Amsterdam, about the year 1602 Her father's name was Vanprinces She and her first husband (whose name is not known) sailed for New York (then New Amsterdam) about the year 1620 The vessel was stranded at Sandy Hook The crew got ashore, and went toward New York, but the husband of Penelope being hurt in the wreck, could not travel with them, and they both tarried in the woods

They had not been long left before the Indians came upon them and killed them as they thought, and stripped them of their garments However, Penelope revived, although her skull was fractured and her left shoulder so injured that she was never able to use it like the other, besides she was so cut across the body that her bowels protruded, and she was obliged to keep her hand upon the wound

In this situation she continued for seven days, taking shelter in a hollow tree, living on what she could pick off from the tree On the seventh day she saw a deer pass with arrows sticking in it, and soon after appeared two Indians whom she was glad to see, hoping that they would put her out of her misery Accordingly, one made towards her, to knock her in the head, but the other (who was an elderly man), prevented him, and throwing his watchcoat about her, took her to his wigwam and cured her of her wounds Afterwards he took her to New York and presented her to her countrymen, expecting a present in return, no doubt It was in New York that Richard Stout married her, in her twenty-second year He was from England, of a good family, and in his fortieth year They had several children, and Mrs Stout lived to the age of one hundred and ten years, and saw her offspring multiplied to five hundred and two in about eighty-eight years "

*From Raum's History of the City of Trenton, N J Trenton, N J, 1871, pp 58 and 59

NEW YORK CITY DIRECTORIES

1786 Benj Stout, merchant, 6 Golden Hill.
1789 John Stout, Baker, Cryers Wharf (Crugers Wharf? which?).
1789 Harman Stout, 2 Thomas St.
1790 John Stout, Baker, 2 Rutgers St
1791 John Stout, grocer and baker, Cor. Church and Warren Sts
1792 Benj. Stout, Boarding House, Cor Great Dock and Broad Sts
1792 Widow Stout, 22 Little Dock St
1793 Benj Stout, Boarding House, 19 Maiden Lane
1793 Mrs Stout, 62 Maiden Lane
1794 Wid. Effey Stout, 27 Fair
1794 B Stout, boarding house, 55 Maiden Lane
1796 Andrew Stout, baker, 36 Gold St
1796 Benj Stout, baker, 36 Gold St
1796 John Stout, *stevadore*, 89 Catharine
1797 Wid Stout, seamstress, 59 Ann St
1797 Benj Stout, 55 Maiden Lane
1798 Benj Stout, 55 Maiden Lane.

*"I give," Raum writes, "the narrative *verbatim*, as published in 1790 "

1798 Wid Stout, seamstress, 49 Partition St.
1798 Andrew Stout, baker, 62 Partition St
1799 John Stout, Tailor, 47 Chatam St.
1799 Wid Stout, seamstress, 85 Warren St.
1800 Mrs Stout, 5 Golden Hill, 1801 also.
1800 Wid. Stout, 4 Courtlandt St.
1801 Andrew Stout, baker, 4 Lombard St
1802 Andrew Stout, copper plate printer, 4 Lombard St
1802 Jacob Stout, 60 Greenwich St
1802 Mrs Stout, 24 Courtlandt.
1803 Charlotte Stout, mantua-maker, 117 William St
1803 Wid Euphemia Stout, 63 Ann St
1803 Jacob Stout, Jr , merchant, 16 Front St
1804 James D Stout, engraver, 51 Ann St.
1804 Wid. Effee Stout, 51 Ann St
1804 Wid Euphemia Stout, 51 Ann St.
1809 Andrew V Stout, cartman, rear 8 Pump.
1810–12 Andrew V. Stout, Baker, rear 8 Pump
1812 Jacob Stout . .
1813 James D Stout, engraver & seal cutter, 23 Courtlandt St
1814 Wid Effee Stout, 4 Orchard St
1814 M. Hogan, 52 Greenwich St
1817 Stout & Cowgill, curriers, 15 Jacob St.
1818 John Stout, currier, 13 Jacob St
1819 John W Stout, ... 13 Jacob St
1819 Jacob Stout, Jr , merchant, 11 Chatam, Stout & Platt, merchants, 11 Chatam St
1821 Effee Stout, 39 Frankfort St.
1823 Andrew V. Stout, baker, Eldridge cor Delancy Sts , in 1824, at 6 Pump St.
1823 Wid Effee Stout, tailoress, 39 Frankfort St
1826 Aquila G Stout, merchant, 14 Broad St
1826 Frances, wid of Jacob Stout, 86 Chambers
1827 Aquila G Stout, h 86 Chambers
1827 Effee, wid of John B , 15 Frankfort St
1829 And V. Stout, baker, 290 Walker St.
1829 Aquila G Stout, 281 Pearl, h 100 Chambers.
1829 Frances Stout, wid of Jacob, 100 Chambers
1832 Effee Hyatt, wid of Jacob, 35 Allen St.
1832 Caleb Hyatt, carpenter, 35 Allen St
1833 Andrew V. Stout, baker, 290 Walker.
1834 Andrew V Stout, teacher, 290 Walker St.
1836 Andrew V Stout, teacher, 36 Ridge

ADDENDA AND ERRATA
VOL. III

p 71 *Philip Bowne, 90*, married, first, by license dated Mch 11, 1765, Mary Taylor She died soon thereafter He married, second, in 1768, Thomasin Pancoast. He married, third, by license dated Jan 10, 1778, Sarah Wilson Issue by second wife Thomas Bowne, who married Susan Beck and died without issue, and James Bowne, who married Priscilla Boulton and died without issue Issue by third wife· Philip Bowne, who married Phebe Poinsett and had ten children, viz   Samuel, Mary, Sarah, Elizabeth, William, Philip, James, Nathan C , Phebe and Margaret

p 132 *Mary* Brown, 31, is the name given this woman in the will of Abiah Edwards, page 148, Vol XXIII, New Jersey Archives, but under the Edwards Family, p 230, of Vol III, of my Historical and Genealogical Miscellany, I call her *Naomi*

p 132 *Preserve Brown*, 10, died, 4, 26, 1744, aged 65   Quaker Burying Ground, Bordentown, N J.

p 200 *Thomas Curtis, 2*, had, in addition to the seven children assigned to him, a daughter, Anne, and a son, Jonathan   Jane, the widow of Thomas Curtis, had a fourth husband by the name of Thomas Cross, for William Pancoast testified, in 1699, "that before Jane Pancoast was married to Thomas Cross he was present when there were 5 cows that belonged to Anne and Abigail Curtis" The will of Thomas Cross, of Burlington Co , 1698, mentioned his daughter-in-law, Abigail, and his sons-in-law, Jonathan and Thomas Curtis, and the children of William Atkinson.

p. 201. John Day, a Quaker and administrator of *Peter Harvey*, accounted Aug 5, 1707 He charged himself with the total of the estate £148, 16, 01, and credited himself with many disbursements, among them coffins for Peter Harvey and his wife and a coffin for their child To Will Atkinson he paid for nursing the youngest child one month; to keeping a girl of 2 years for six months, for keeping Hannah Harvey 1 year and 18 weeks, to Dr Peachley £10 13.6 Mention is made of Elizabeth, daughter of Peter Harvey, and nursing Hannah Harvey when she had the small-pox

p 201. Elizabeth Curtis bound herself out to *Elias Farr* Study his will printed in Vol XXIII, New Jersey Archives, p. 159

VOL. IV

p 5   24   William Morford, *baptised May 27, 1764*
      25   Lydia Morford, *baptised Nov 15, 1761.*
      17. Thomas Morford had *marriage license* with Esther Holmes *April 3, 1768*

p 10 49   Under issue read. George Taylor *Morford* and Essie Taylor *Morford*

p. 87. Under 32. *Jacob Mott, 32,* should read Married *probably* Kesia, daughter of Nathaniel Seaman, born 1699, *by his wife* Sarah Powell Jacob Mott, 32, *did certainly* marry Abigail Jackson

p 110ª 27th line, should read Deborah *Sands*

p 123 26. Abiel Cook, son of Ellis and Martha, had Abiel who died 1740 This last Abiel had Ellis Cook and Abiel Cook, and this last Abiel (the third) was the father of Frances Cook who married Samuel Mount.

p. 151. 22nd line should read of Life worthy *of* Imitation

p 153 The will of John Ogborne, 1, as quoted in the New Jersey Archives, (volume of wills), gives him also a *granddaughter "An,"* daughter to his deceased son John, which is concurred in by the Rev Elias Boudinot Stockton Also *eliminate* in this will *the name Hocton*.

p. 154 John Ogborne, 2, married, about 1697, *Ann Kendall,* born about 1677 and died, July 25, 1745, aged 68 years. Following the death of John Ogborne, and about 1715, Ann Kendall married, second, John, son of Richard and Abigail Stockton, born, in Flushing, about 1674, and died, in Springfield township, Burlington Co, Mch 29, 1747 Ann Kendall, the wife of John Ogborne, 2, and John Stockton, was the daughter of Thomas Kendall, bricklayer, of Burlington Co, who married, first, Dec. 25, 1685, Mary, daughter of Anthony and Susanna Elton by whom he had Mary Kendall, who married Samuel Cole and the above mentioned Ann Upon the death of his wife Mary Elton, Thomas Kendall married, second, 6, 1mo, 1690, Ann Jennings, possibly widow of Peter Jennings, of Burlington Co, who had recently died Thomas Kendall died 1709, leaving a will. Ann Kendall probably had no issue by her husband John Stockton His will, dated Aug 31, 1745, proved Apr 4, 1747, gave his daughters-in-law, (i e, stepdaughters), Sarah Woolston and Anna Lippincott each £2, and to the three children of his other stepdaughter, Hannah Butterworth, viz David, Joseph and Benjamin, Jr., £4, when 21. He further mentioned his sons, Daniel and David, whom he appointed executors, and his daughters Rebecca Lippincott, Rachel Briggs and Mary Wetherell The son, David Stockton, died, Nov 14, 1763, aged 55 o 26, hence born 1708 and a son of John Stockton by his wife Mary Leeds (Baptist Meeting Yard, Pemberton, Burlington Co, N J).

p 154 John Ogborne, 2, *resided at Springfield Township,* Burlington Co, N J In addition to Sarah and Anna he had likewise a daughter Ann. The following deed is substantiative of her existence Jonathan Wright, of Burlington City, conveys to John Mathis Apr 23, 1741 In the deed it is set forth that "Whereas *John Ogbourne,* late of said County deceased was lawfully seized in four hundred acres of land lying at a place called little Egg harbour and County aforesaid and the said John Ogbourne being seized as aforesaid died and the same descended *to his three daughters Sarah, Ann* and *Anna* as coheirs of him the said John Ogbourn and the said three daughters were married to the following persons vizt Sarah was married to Michael Woolston, Ann was married to Benjamin Butterworth and Anna was married to Job Lippincott and whereas the said Michael Woolston and Sarah his wife, Benjamin Butterworth and Ann his wife and Job Lippincott and Anna his wife by their Indenture of Bargain and Sale under their hands and seals, dated 25th day of Sept 1731, for the consideration therein mentioned did Grant Bargain and sell the aforesaid four hundred acres of land unto George Douglas of Chesterfield and county aforesaid," etc, etc (Book G. of Deeds, p 358, Trenton.)

It is thus absolutely established that John Ogborne, 2, had two daughters of like name, Ann and Anna, which in turn raises the query whether he may not have had two wives, giving him an Ann by one wife and an Anna by the other wife Or is it that she may have been originally called Hannah and time and usage changed it to Anna In the Mott family this extraordinary duplication of names likewise occurs for Adam Mott, the first, alludes in his will to my oldest son Adam and my youngest son Adam, who were his children by different wives

p 154 *Sarah Ogborne*, 5, daughter of John Ogborne, 2, was born about 1699, died, Dec 24, 1771, aged 72 years; buried in St Andrew's Yard, Mount Holly; married, first, about 1720, Jacob Carman, of Springfield township, Burlington Co, who died intestate prior to Dec. 14, 1724, when his estate was inventoried at about £90 Administration granted, Jan 29, 1725, to his widow, had an only son John Carman, who was sole executor of the will of his mother Sarah Woolston, dated Oct 8, 1771, proved Jan 6, 1772, and was mentioned in the will of his stepfather Michael Woolston John Carman married Ann, daughter of Daniel and Hannah (Fisher) Stockton. Sarah Ogborne married, second, about 1725, Michael, son of John and Lettice (Newbold) Woolston, who was born about 1698, and who died, in Northampton township, Burlington Co, Feb 27, 1753, aged 55. In his will, Feb. 23, 1751, proved Mch 5, 1753, he named his children, relatives, wife Sarah and stepson John Carman Her will, (Sarah Woolston), Oct 8, 1771, proved Jan 6, 1772, named her two daughters Lettice Hinchman [wife of Isaac Hinchman] and Ann Briggs, her granddaughters Sarah Briggs, Sarah Hinchman and Sarah King, and her great-granddaughter Susanna King The inventory of her estate amounted to £285,10,5 In addition to the children above mentioned the grave stones in St Andrew's Yard, Mount Holly, tell of several more, who were apparently carried away in the winter and spring of 1753, by some epidemic Job Woolston died, Jan. 27, 1753, aged 23 years, Joseph Woolston died, May 21, 1753, aged about 18 years, Joshua Woolston died, May 28, 1753, aged about 27 years, Barzillai Woolston died, Aug 25, 1753, aged about 20 years. Also stones to her son-in-law Levi Briggs, who died, Oct 31, 1766, aged 26 8 0, [born Jan 20, 1739-40], and to her granddaughter Sarah, only daughter of Levi and Ann (Woolston) Briggs, who died, July 9, 1777, aged 17, 4, 27.

p 154 William Ogborne, 3, must have had a *son William*, if the New Jersey Archives, (Vol 23, p. 344), correctly state that Mary Ogborne had guardianship given to her brother William Ogborne Dec 18, 1721 That such a son existed is not impossible, as John Ogborne, 1, in his will makes no allusion to any grandson John, son of his son William Ogborne, though we know that such a son existed, so there is no greater call for John Ogborne, 1, declaring the existence of this supposed grandson William Ogborne, of the third generation But it is passing strange that William Ogborne, 3, the father, should he have had a son William, should not have made provision for him in his will, 1708-9, when the said child was less than ten years of age, especially when he provided for his other minor son John If error be eliminated, it creates the supposition that William Ogborne, 3, had a wife prior to Mary Cole, whom he married in 1698.

p 154 Elizabeth Ogborne, 7, married John, son of Joseph and *Thomasin (Scattergood)* Pancoast, *Oct 20, 1724.*

p 155 Mary Ogborne, 8, married, Joseph, son of William and *Hannah (Scattergood)* Pancoast.

p 155 Hannah Ogborne, 9, died January 1736-7, married, in 1722, Jonathan, son of Aaron and Elizabeth (Shaw) Sleeper. Hannah Sleeper was a cousin of Gov Belcher, of New York. Jonathan Sleeper came from New Hampshire and became an early settler in Mount Holly, Northampton township, Burlington Co, N J "In company with eight others he built the first saw mill and grist mill and built and lived in the house since known as Lion's house." Administration upon his estate was granted to his wife, May 10, 1736. His wife, Hannah, died shortly after, for January, 1736-7, her will was proved, and Thomas Shinn was appointed administrator in her place upon the estate of her late husband, Jonathan Sleeper, and also guardian of their son John Sleeper

Jonathan and Hannah (Ogborne) Sleeper had issue· John, Leah, Mary and a posthumous son Jonathan Sleeper Of these children *Mary Sleeper* died, unmarried, leaving a will, Oct. 13, 1752, of Burlington Co , N J , in which she devised her estate to her brothers, Jonathan and John Sleeper, and to her sister since Leah Atkinson Concerning *the son John Sleeper*, it is known that he was born 10 mo , 14, 1731, and from the same source, (Burlington Monthly Meeting), that he was living at Bridgetown, Northampton township, Burlington Co , carpenter, when he married, 9 mo , 26, 1754, at Chester Meeting House, Hannah, daughter of Nehemiah and Ann Haines, of Chester township, in said county They had seven sons and five daughters, whose births are recorded in the Friends' Records He removed, in 1768 or 1770, to Otsego Co , N. Y., with several of his children Concerning *Leah Sleeper*, the daughter of Jonathan and Hannah (Ogborne) Sleeper, it is known that she married, first, A M. Atkinson, by whom she had one son, and that upon the death of her husband, Mr. Atkinson, she married, second, Samuel Atkinson, of Mount Holly, by whom she had two boys and three girls Of *Jonathan Sleeper*, the son of Jonathan and Hannah (Ogborne) Sleeper, it is known that he married Sybilla, daughter of Joseph Lippincott, of near Mount Holly, by whom he had four sons and three daughters. For further information concerning the Sleeper family, see Hoyt's First Families of Salisbury and Amesbury, Mass., History of Hampton, N. H., Manuscript "History of our family by Benjamin Sleeper, only son of John and Mary Sleeper, as given by my father and others," which, in 1898, was in the possession of his granddaughter Anna M Sleeper, in Lamberton, Burlington Co , N J

p 155 *Anna Ogborne*, 6, daughter of John Ogborne, 2, *married Job, son of Samuel and Ann (Hulitt) Lippincott* In her marriage license she is called Anna. Job Lippincott was of Springfield, in his will, written 1759, which mentioned his son Job, and his daughters Ann, wife of Revel Elton, and Sarah Lippincott. Likewise his brother Samuel Lippincott. His daughter later married her first cousin, Joseph, son of Benjamin and Hannah (Ogborne) Butterworth "3 mo 7, 1763, Joseph Butterworth made acknowledgement for marriage out to his first *cousin*." (Friends' Meeting Records of Burlington and Mount Holly, contained in one volume in Penn Hist Soc)

Further light upon Anna Lippincott's descendants may be found in Mount Holly Transfers, Book C , p 386, which contains an indenture, 11 May, 1793, which recites. that Anna Lippincott became "seized of a certain messuage, tenement and lot of land with the appurtenances situate in the town of Mount Holly" through purchase from Hugh Hollinshead, Jr , and Mary his wife, who took title from Samuel Stockton, who took title from William Stockton, his brother, who became seized of it through his sister Sarah, who died under lawful age, who received the same from her grandfather Benjamin Brain, who bought the same from Josiah White, who bought from Samuel Gaskill, who bought from his father Edward Gaskill, who with Josiah Southwick purchased the same from Samuel Jennings That the said Anna Lippincott, by her will, devised the use of the same for life to her daughter Sarah, wife of Joseph Butterworth, with remainder to Mary, wife of John Black, surveyor, of Mansfield, Elizabeth, Anna and Patience Lippincott, of Springfield, daughters of her son Job Lippincott, dec^d, to Anna, wife of John Mullen, carpenter, of Northampton, Mary, wife of Josiah Dungan, of Philadelphia, Sarah, Lettice and Elizabeth Butterworth, of Mt Holly, daughters of Joseph and Sarah Butterworth; to Anna, wife of William Rogers, Jr , and daughter of Revell Elton, dec^d This lot of land was conveyed by the executors of Anna Lippincott, joined by the above interested parties to John Butterworth, farmer, of Northampton, and John Ross, Practitioner in Physic and surveyor.

Ann Ogborne, was a daughter of John Ogborne, 2, as established by the preceding evidence While in the will of her stepfather, John Stockton, she is called Hannah, in her grandfather's will she is called An, and in her marriage license to Benjamin Butterworth, Sept 11, 1729 Ann, and in the deed of 1741, Ann, so that we can safely eliminate Hannah and call her *Ann* She became the *first wife of Benjamin Butterworth*, 1729, who, following her decease, married, second, Nov. 18, 1735, Ann McCarty, probably daughter of Dennis McCarty, who died, intestate, in Burlington Co, 1736 Benjamin Butterworth was a weaver by trade and farmer as well He was living as late as Aug. 12, 1742, upon what was apparently the property of Jonathan Wright, whose executors at this date advertised the sale of the same in the Penn Gazette It comprised 250 acres of land lying within three miles of the City of Burlington, with a good log house, a small barn, an orchard, etc It is from Ann Ogborne and Benjamin Butterworth that practically all of the name now living in Burlington Co are descended They had issue (1) David, who probably died young, (2) Joseph, and (3) Benjamin. Of these children (2) Joseph was a tanner by trade and in the latter part of his life a brewer in Mount Holly He married twice, first, about 1759, his first cousin Sarah, daughter of Job and Anna (Ogborne) Lippincott by whom he had all his issue, second, Elizabeth, daughter of Francis and Zilpha Venicomb, and widow of Isaac Lippincott They, Joseph Butterworth and his wife Anna Ogborne, had issue (a) John Butterworth, born about 1760, died, Jan 23, 1839, married, first, Rachel, daughter of Joseph and Charity Eayre, second, June 26, 1796, Rachel Corlies, widow of Caleb Ridgway, she being born Oct 31, 1770, and died Mch 24, 1847; (b) Joseph Butterworth, Jr, married Sarah, daughter of Thomas and Miranna (Ridgway) Moore, (c) Ann Butterworth married John Mullin, (d) Mary Butterworth, born Nov 14, 1770, died June 22, 1818, married, first, about 1793, Josiah Dungan,* born Mch 20, 1771, died Aug 20, 1811; second, about 1814, Major John Curtis, of Mansfield, Burlington Co, (e) Samuel Butterworth died 1812, married Anna, daughter of Joseph and Mary (Coates) Ridgway, born Dec. 24, 1775; (f) Sarah Butterworth, (g) Lettice Butterworth, (h) Elizabeth Butterworth married Francis Prickett.

Benjamin Butterworth, (3), son of Benjamin Butterworth and Ann Ogborne, married, by license, July 26, 1757, Sarah Likens I have no further information concerning him All three of Ann Ogborne Butterworth's children, David, Joseph and Benjamin, were mentioned in the will of their step-grandfather, John Stockton

p 156 3 *Mary Ogborne*, married, *9 mo.*, 1707, John Engle, *who died 1722*, then married, *5 mo*, 1727, Jonas Cattell, then married, *8, 9 mo*, 1732, Thomas French *Robert Engle*, her son, married, *5, 17, 1728*, Rachel Vinicomb, Jane Engle married, *8 mo*, 1729, John Turner.

p 157. John Engle *married, Nov 1, 1737*, Hannah Middleton, Mary Engle, born 8, 14, 1716, died 12, 1, 1787, *married, 4 mo, 1736, Nathaniel Lippincott*, Hannah Engle married, *11 mo, 1739, Isaac* Lippincott.

Sarah Ogborne, 4, (wife of Edmond Kinsey) *died, 6 mo, 25* ——, *aged 97 years Edmond Kinsey died 12, 21, 1759*. Concerning their issue Samuel Kinsey, born 10, 20, 1710, married, 7 mo, 1733, Elizabeth Crew, David Kinsey, born 9, 3, 1712, married, 11, 30, 1734, Tamer Fell, Mary Kinsey, born 2, 20, 1715, married, 12 mo, 1735, Joseph Fell, Jr, Elizabeth Kinsey,

---

* Josiah Dungan was born, in Oxford Township, Philadelphia Co, Pa, Mch 20, 1771, died Aug 20, 1811 He was the son of Capt Benjamin Dungan (Revolutionary War) by his wife, Esther Cottman born in Somerset Co, Maryland, who, dying when her son Josiah was still young, her husband, Capt Benjamin Dungan, married again in 1779 Capt Benjamin Dungan was a deacon of the Pennypack Baptist Meeting, in Lower Dublin Township Philadelphia Co, for thirty-four years, and was a descendant in the fourth generation of the Rev Thomas Dungan, who came from Rhode Island, in 1683, and settled at Cold Spring, Bucks Co, Pa, where he established the first Baptist church in Pennsylvania Josiah Dungan, by his wife, Mary Butterworth, had seven children, four of whom married

born 4, 23, 1717, married 10, 1, 1742, Thomas Smith, John Kinsey, born 2, 5, 1719, Joseph Kinsey, born 6, 21, 1722, died 1764, married, 3, 17, 1749, Hannah Yates; Sarah Kinsey, born 11, 13, 1724, married, 2, 17, 1746, Timothy Smith, Jr., Benjamin Kinsey, born 10, 22, 1727, died 1789, married, 3, 23, 1749, Susannah Brown, Jonathan Kinsey, born 3, 12, 1731, married, 1751, Jemima Heston.

Concerning the children of *Joseph Hampton and Mary Canby* Sarah Hampton, born, 9, 30, 1723, married, 9, 19, 1744, Isaac Wilson, John Hampton, born, 1, 12, 1724-5, died 9, 10, 1775, Benjamin Hampton, born 7, 15, 1728, married, 9, 28, 1750, Ann Wildman, Jane Hampton, born 1, 26, 1731, died 1, 31, 1809, Joseph Hampton, born 1, 29, 1735-6, David Hampton, born 8, 22, 1737, died, 1, 3, 1757, Mary Hampton, born 2, 12, 1739, died 11, 13, 1804, married James Stokes.

Jane Curtis married, third, 4 mo., 12, 1706, Nathaniel Fitz-Randolph.

p 158   *John Sharp died Oct. 23, 1726*

p. 168.   Joel E Ogborn   Mrs J E Ogborn, of New Sharon, Iowa, in 1900, wrote that an obituary of Edwin Ogborn, her husband's brother, appeared in an old newspaper and stated that he was born at Egg Harbor, N J, and that he was seven years old when his father went West.

Students of the Ogborne family are Howard Deacon, Esq., of Philadelphia, Pa., Mr. H. Clifford Campion, Jr, of Media, Delaware Co, Pa., and the Rev E Boudinot Stockton, of 161 South Arlington Ave, East Orange, N J

p. 171.   Erase *Issue by second wife*   So far as I know all Thomas Potter's children were by his first wife

Mercy Potter, 3, died prior to Aug. 12, 1730, when John Woolley, her husband, married Rachel Clark

p 175.   *William Bickley*   Add the following notes to those that appear on pages 170 and 175   Despite the statements of a writer of relatively recent date* which besmirch the character of William Bickley, there remains convincing evidence that he was an upright Quaker much esteemed by his neighbors and fellow merchants of New York   He was frequently a witness to wills, an executor, an administrator, and a scholarly man with some legal attainments, for he declared to the Court that it was he who drew, in 1690, the will of Col Lewis Morris *Charles Lambert*, a New York shop keeper, or merchant, died on the Barquentine, St Mary, on a journey from Jamaica to New York and made a nuncupative will, Nov 8, 1691, which gave part of his estate to his mother and sister residing in the City of Exeter, and the remainder to his loving uncle William Bickley, in consideration of many kindnesses, excepting his trunk of books, which he willed to Lewis Morris   His will was then proved and letters of administration were issued, June 7, 1691 [1692], to William Bickley   Herein may lie some evidence of the English origin of Bickley   Between Bickley and Col Lewis Morris there existed a strong bond of attachment.   The latter in his will, Feb. 7, 1690, gave him a negro, half his interest in the ship *Friends Adventure*, and made him one of his executors   He was apparently Morris' neighbor in Westchester, yet he at some time probably resided in New York City   He made his will, 3, 5 mo., 1707   An abstract of it is given on page 175 of this volume from which was omitted the following items   should his grandson William Cook fail to serve out his indented time he only receives 2 pieces of 8, to his daughters-in-law one *Arabian* piece of gold of 12 shillings value to Thomas Ives and his wife Susannah £5 to purchase a small piece of plate in consideration of their kindness to me and mine, to Dr John Redman, Hugh Cowperthwaite

* Historical and Genealogical Miscellany, Vol IV, p 18

and Samuel Bowne, of Flushing, each £10, and to George Curtis, John Lippincott, Sr , and William Worth, of Shrewsbury, N. J , each £5 Appoints his son Abraham his executor   He had a wife Susannah, living in 1698, but who predeceased him

The allusion to William Bickley's daughters-in-law [step-daughters?] justly raises the presumption that he may have had a second wife, a widow with daughters, but she must have predeceased him for he makes no provision for any wife   His own children Sarah, Elizabeth and Abraham married and had issue, in all a goodly number, and to these he willed each 12 shillings   *Sarah, his daughter,* married, first, *Mr Lawrence,* second, *Thomas Potter* (see Potter Family) and, third, *Henry Graves*   Mr Lawrence I have not been able to identify   Thomas Potter was about 65 years old when he married, in 1695, Sarah Bickley Lawrence, and it is noteworthy that their marriage certificate had none of his children among the witnesses   Her kindred on the other hand were present.   Potter's previous wife, Ann, did not die till 1694, which is good reason to believe that she was the mother of all of his issue   If this is correct deduction her four children were most likely Lawrences, perhaps Graves   They were hardly likely to have been Thomas Potter's children for he would have been between 66 and 72 years of age at the time of their birth and they would have been minors at the date of his death, in 1702, and no provision was made for any minor child in his will

Sarah Bickley outlived her third husband, for Aug 23, 1720, for £50, Sarah Graves, of Shrewsbury, widow of Henry Graves, sold land on Rumson Neck to Timothy Halstead, late of Orange Co , N Y , that had been conveyed to her by her father, William Bickley, dec^d, by deed Mch 10, 1704. By her own deed of Dec. 19, 1709, as Sarah, widow of Thomas Potter, she conveyed to Thomas White, single man, land at Rumson "where she now lives" likewise derived from her father, probably part of a joint tract

Concerning William Bickley's *daughter, Elizabeth,* not much is known, but she was married to Thomas, of Thomas Cook, prior to 29, 1 mo , 1695, when they, Thomas and Elizabeth Cook, were present as witnesses at the marriage of her sister Sarah Bickley Lawrence to Thomas Potter. Thomas Cook died leaving a will dated 1698 and proved 1699, wherein he mentioned his eldest son William Cook, his son Thomas Cook and his daughter Elizabeth Cook, a minor, and his wife Elizabeth, whom he made executrix   She apparently married after his decease Nicholas Brown, for her father, in his will, 1707, calls her Elizabeth Brown, and gives 12 shillings to his son-in-law Nicholas Brown and £20 conditionally to his grandson William Cook   She was ignored in the will of her brother Abraham Bickley, 1725, but her three children, William and Thomas Cook and Elizabeth, their sister, and Matthew Birchfield, (probably her husband), whom he calls kinsman, received legacies, hence she was probably dead.

The difficulty which now presents itself is to determine which Nicholas Brown married Elizabeth Bickley. It would appear that he was Nicholas, son of Abraham, son of Nicholas Brown, who died 1723-4, leaving a will wherein he named his wife Elizabeth, but unfortunately she is known to have been Elizabeth, daughter of Abiah Edwards, which is confirmed by the fact that the rare name of Abiah occurs among the children of Preserve Brown and that there is a Neomy Brown, of Burlington Co , who had a license to marry James Killgore, Dec 14, 1730, and this name, Naomi, is likewise an Edwards family name   In possible explanation of this situation it may be possible that Nicholas Brown had two wives by the name of Elizabeth, one Elizabeth Edwards and the other Elizabeth Bickley Cook

Concerning *Abraham, the son of William Bickley,* some information may be extracted from his will, written Oct 13, 1725, proved Mch 28, 1726   In his father's will, 1707, he is alluded to as of Philadelphia, but in his own will he calls himself, merchant, of Burlington, and alludes to his "present wife Dorothy," and the following children   William, Elizabeth, Polgreen, Samuel, Hannah, Susannah, Abraham, Mary, his sister, Sarah Graves, and her four children, kinsman, William Cook, his brother, Thomas Cook, and sister, Elizabeth, and Mathew Birchfield (who was probably Elizabeth's husband); his brother-in-law, William Hudson. Who the last wife, Dorothy, was I do not know, but his first wife was *Elizabeth, daughter of Thomas Gardner*, and brother to John and Thomas Gardner, to whom he was married, prior to 1696, for in that year and again in 1698, William Bickley and Susannahh, is wife, joined by Abraham Bickley and Elizabeth, his wife, made conveyances. (N J Archives, Vol. XXI, pp 294, 537.)

The record of the births of some of Abraham and Elizabeth Bickley's children is to be found in the Philadelphia Quarterly Meeting Records, and no doubt the record of the others is spread upon the books of the Friends in other localities This record gives likewise the date of death of his wife Elizabeth Gardner, 3 mo, 15, 1714, apparently six days after the birth of her son Benjamin with which event it was doubtless associated. Susanna, born 3, 11, 1702, buried, 7, 16, 1702. Samuel, born 4, 2, 1703, (an executor in his father's will and who advertised for claims against his father's estate May 5, 1726); Hannah, born, 9, 9, 1704, Susanna, born 1, 19, 1705-6, (married, 5, 25, 1728, Hodge, son of Henry Knight, Arch St Meeting, Phila); Abraham, born 2, 24, 1707, Mary, born 1, 21, 1708-9, died 4, 8, 1708, Mary, born 8, 5, 1710; Isaac, born 6, 6, 1712; Benjamin, born 3, 9, 1714 Ye mother died ye 15th.

p 211 *Mary Saltar, 4, married Thomas Leaming*
Sarah Saltar, 5, married Isaiah and not Thomas Leaming, so Mrs Scollay wrote, but gave no authority for either this or the preceding statement.

p 212. Thomas Britton, born 1739, married, first, Sarah, daughter of Thomas Harvey, born 1745, second, prior to 1798, Sarah, widow of Thomas Saltar, uncle to Thomas Briton (Orphan's Court Record Book 17, pp. 427-430 From Mrs Scollay)

p 247 The fifth line from the top should read.—*This issue was*, and *not* These children were as follows·

p 251. *Nos. 104 and 105 are children of James Seabrook, 54* Likewise the reference which follows them belongs to No. 54

p 252 *Mary Seabrook*, 63, not Maria, married Joseph Johnson *Jan. 4, 1822*

p. 253. *John Seabrook*, 65, married Catharine *Hoffmire Sept 15, 1810*
Anna Seabrook, 67, married William Hoff *Nov. 15, 1821*.

p 254 *Lydia Seabrook*, 72, married Rev. William V. Wilson, of *Port* Monmouth, N. J , *Sept 16, 1841*
Martha Seabrook, 74, married Rev William V Wilson *Jan 2, 1854*

p. 254 4th line, 7th word should read *Port* Monmouth

p. 255 *Stephen Seabrook*, 129, married Mary Walling *Aug 9, 1854*
Ann Seabrook, 130, married Samuel Walling *Dec 1, 1833*.
Mary Seabrook, 131, married Thomas S Clark *Nov 29, 1835*
Elias Seabrook, 132, married Sarah Walling *June 25, 1842*

p 259 13th line, 5th word from end of line should read Robert *Darkins*.

p 293 Sarah, wife of Jacob Spicer, 6, died, July 25, 1742, *aged 65*. (From the oldest monument in Cold Spring Cemetery.)
Col Jacob Spicer died, Apr 17, 1741, aged 73, 2, 27 He removed from Long Island to Cape May in 1691, member of Legislature 1709-1723, Surrogate 1723-1741, for many years a Justice.

Jacob Spicer, *Esq*, left a will, Oct. 9, 1765, which disposed of a large estate and mentioned therein his children and a *wife Deborah* Judith *Spicer*, who lies next to him and died, Sept 7,

ADDENDA AND ERRATA 383

1747, in her 33rd year, was *a daughter of Humphrey Hughes,* while *Deborah,* his wife, who outlived him, and whom he married, in 1751, was a *Hand* and the *widow of Christopher Leaming*

The tombstones of Col Jacob Spicer and his son Jacob Spicer, Esq, and his wife Judith stood in the grove North of Vincent Miller's house at Cape May.

Jacob Spicer, Esq, was as eminent as his father. With Aaron Leaming he revised the State Laws, which became known as *Leaming and Spicer's Collection.* He was member of the Legislature from 1744 to 1765 In 1756, he purchased for himself from Dr Johnson, agent, the interest of the West Jersey Society, in Cape May, known as the *Vacant Right,* for the small sum of £300, for which he was severely attacked and criticised He was a very successful, industrious, energetic business man carrying on large enterprises He had *issue:* (a) Sarah Spicer, who married Christopher Leaming and had eight children, (b) Sylvia Spicer, married, first, Rev Samuel Jones, second, Rev Mr Harris; (c) Judith Spicer married Elijah, son of Elijah Hughes, 2nd.,* (d) Jacob Spicer, 3rd, became a prominent merchant in Philadelphia, but failed He died, Dec. 5, 1806, and left, it is said, no male issue "I am told that a person named Walter Spicer was a highly educated man, married Rachel Goff, of West Creek, and was a successful school teacher in Cape May Co, that they had no children and that he was the last male of the name of Spicer They lived at Tuckahoe, N J, where they died and were buried at West Creek, Cape May Co." (Communication from the Rev Daniel L Hughes, Cape May City, N. J, August, 1896, to Dr John E Stillwell)

Walter Spicer departed this life, Dec. 12, 1874, aged 87, 10, 0. Rachel Spicer departed this life, Aug 13, 1876, aged 79, 11, 17.

p 322 Seymour Stout, 8 There was a George Seemur witness, Apr 10, 1731, to the will of William Layton, of Freehold, N J.

p 328. Alice Stout, 6 Letters of administration upon the estate of Robert Skelton, of New York, lately deceased, were granted to his widow *Alice Jones* Apr 13, 1704

May 12, 1704 An inventory of the estate of Robert Skelton, late of New York, was taken by Jeremiah Tothill and William Anderson Value not given

Robert Skelton was a witness to the will of Peter Jacob Marius, merchant, of New York City, July 7, 1701, also to will of Allard Anthony, of the same place, Dec 12, 1685, and an appraiser on the inventory of the goods of Nathaniel Thompson Borrow, of New York City, Sept. 1, 1688

p 329. Skelton Johnson, 30 The fourth volume of Burke's or Stith's History of Virginia was edited by one, Skelton Johnson

p 345 6th line from bottom of page, should read —"or that if worth "

---

* Elijah Hughes, 3rd, was Clerk of Cape May Co, 1762-1768, Surrogate, 1768-1787, Member State Legislative Council, 1781-1782, and again 1785-1786 They had issue (a) Spicer Hughes, of Cold Spring, unmarried, (b) Nancy Hughes (c) Sarah Hughes, who married Mr Mulford no issue Nancy Hughes (b) married John Bennett and had George, who married Prescilla Eldridge, John, unmarried and Elijah Hughes Bennett, who married Mary Hand and had John Spicer Bennett

INDEX*

A

ABBOTT, Lucy, w, 190
   Samuel, md, 190
ABEL, Eleanor Hines, granddau, 98, res, 98, her Bible, 98
ABERDEEN, William, Earl of, fa, 43
ACKER, Sarah, md, 352, mo, 352*
ADAMS, Charles Francis, bro, 274
   Elizabeth Seabrook, w, 274, res, 274
   Hannah, dau, 159, leg, 159
   Henry, md, 274, bro, 274, res, 274
   John, res, 20, detr, 20, leg, 20
   Josephine, md 255, mo, 255**
AFFERE (see ALFERE, ALFREE), Thomas, bondsm, 173
AGNEW, Abigail Stout, w, 367
   John md 367, m l, 367
AKINS, Lydia, dau, 361, leg, 361
ALBANY, State Library, manuscripts, 85
ALDRIX, Ephraim, mark, 221, wit, 221
   Peter, deft, 22
ALEXANDER, Capt, husb, 98, of Navy, 98
   Mr, md, 235
   Elinor, wid, 98, md, 98
   James (Jas), endorsed by, 187, surxey genl, 78, 224, sig, 224, as Hon, Esq, ment, 44, res, 44
   Mary, w, 235
ALFERF (see AFFERE, ALFREE), Thomas, bondsm, 173
ALFREE (see AFFERE ALFERE), Mr land of, 173, mast, 173
   Thomas bondsm 173
ALLOWAYES CREEK, alias Monmouth River, 18
ALLEN (ALLIN ALLYN,† ALYN,†† see ALLEN), Ann, md, 363, res, 363
   Charles G, s 4
   Charlotte, md, 141, b, 141, d, 141, age, 141
   David bill pd 230, proxy, 230
   Deborah, w, 51, mo, 51, grandmo, 51**

ALLEN, Continued
   Delilah, md, 364, res, 364
   Elisha wit, 170
   Elizabeth, md, 59, 92, b, 59, d, 59, 92, mo, 59, 92**, 93**, dau, 92*, leg, 92, exrx, 92
   Enos, bro, 135, s, 135 grands, 135
   Ethan, bro, 127
   Hannah, md, 127, sis, 127, d, 127, age, 127, mo, 127, bur, 127
   Henry, his wid, 92, fa, 92, grandfa, 92**, 93**
   James P md, 4, fa, 4*
   Jedediah, just, 26, seizure of, 26, prison, 26
   John, prchs, 84†
   John, Jr, husb, 81††
   Jonathan wit, 319
   Lewis, md, 137
   Lydia Mount, w 137
   Margaret, md, 135, sis, 135, dau, 135, b, 135, d, 135, granddau, 135, age, 135
   Martha, w, 81, leg, 81††
   Mary, w, 4, 135, mo, 4*, 92*, 135*, wid, 92, will, 92, res, 92, grandmo, 92**, 93**
   Nathan md, 183, res, 183
   Capt Robert, s, 4
   Sarah, w, 183
   Theodosia, w, 119, mo, 119, md, 142, b, 142, d, 142, age, 142
   Thomas, fa 135*, husb, 135
   Rebecca md, 142
ALLENTOWN, bur, 316*, Mount of, 143, Presbyterian Cemetery, bur, 144**, do, Churchyard, bur, 137*, 315, 316, Yellow Meeting House, bur, 137
ALLEN (see ALLEN), Miss, dau, 204, md 204
   Laurent, md, 204, fa, 204
   Lavinia Louise, w 204, mo, 204
ALLISON, Burges, md, 333, 337, fa, 333
   Rhoda Stout, w, 333, 337, mo, 333

ALMY, Audrey, w, 35, mo, 35, res, 35, grandmo, 35**
   Cathrine w, 23, mo, 23, grandmo, 23**
   Christopher, res, 38, his land, 38
   Elizabeth, dau, 35, mo, 35**, md, 35*
   William, fa, 35, husb, 35, grandfa, 35**, res, 35
ALSOP, Richard, md, 92
   Sarah w, 92
AMBOY (see PERTH AMBOY), Sec of, letter to, 125, sloop cleared for, 88
AMELIA SPRINGS, Battle of, 109
AMERSFORT, ment, 290
ANDERSON (ANDERION), Mr re candidacy, 103, md, 129
   Andrew, md, 353
   Anne Stout (Nancy Stout†), w, 353, 363†
   Elizabeth, md, 327, dau, 327, m l, 327, mo, 327**
   Jane, w, 137, admrx, 137*
   Jeremiah, md, 363
   John, wit, 116, judge, 116, as Esq, ackn before, 185
   Joshua, oath before, 360**
   Lewis, md, 137, his est, 137
   Mary E, md, 277
   Sarah Mount, w, 129
   William, fa, 327, grandfa, 327**, took invt, 383
ANDREW Mr, md, 277
   Mary Seabrook, w, 277
ANDREWS, Elizabeth (Betsy†), sis, 168†, md, 168†, dau, 168†
   Esther, md, 168*, dau, 168, b, 168, mo, 168**, grandmo, 168**, sis, 168, d, 168
   Isaac, fa, 168*, husb, 168*, grandfa 168**
   Mary, md, 323, d, 323
   Rebecca, w, 168*, mo, 168*, grandmo 168**

One * denotes more than one reference on a page
Two ** denote more than two references on a page
One or two †† denote varied spellings of Christian and surnames
Names of Cities Counties, Countries, States, etc, have been purposely omitted

ANDROSS, Gov, pat from, 18
  Gov C appnt admrs, 24
ANNIE OGBORN S CORNERS (AN-
  NIE OGBORN S CORNER),
  ment 153, 362
ANSLEY, Elizabeth, res, 49, m 1, 49
  Mary, m 1, 47, res, 47, mo, 47, 48**
ANTHONY, Allard will, 383, res, 383
  Rev A H, author, 248, res, 252, re
    ancestry, 252
  Alice, md, 62
  Jacob, md, 252
  Sarah Ann, w 252
  Sarah Ann Marsh, mo, 252, living,
    252, dau, 252
ANTILL (ANTIL), Anne Morris, w, 33,
  35, mo, 35, godmo, 43
  Edward, md, 33, 35, res, 33, b, 35,
    d, 35, fa, 35
  Sarah, dau, 35, b, 35, 44, md, 35,
    44, mo, 44, 45*
ANTONIDES, Sarah, w, 60*, mo, 60**,
  grandmo, 60*
APPLEGATE, ment, 164
  Mr, md, 144
  Mrs, decd, 102, dau, 102, mo, 102*
  Ann (Nancy†), md, 145†, b, 145†,
    d 145†, granddau, 162, leg, 162
  Caroline, md, 148, b, 148, mo,
    148*, 149**, wid, 148, d, 148
  Ebenezer, bndry, 45
  Elizabeth Ogborne, w, 164, mo, 164**
  Ellen Seabrook, w, 254
  Hannah, dau, 144, leg, 144
  Hannah Mount, w, 144
  John, md 325
  Margaret Stout, w, 325
  Richard, s, 164, md, 164
  Mrs Richard, w, 164
  William (Wm), admr, 160**, relative,
    160, sig, as bondsm, 160*, res,
    160, yeom, 160, md, 164, 254, fa,
    164**
APPLETON, Augusta Stout, w, 358
  Samuel, md, 358, clergyman, 358
APPOQUINIMINK CREEK, ment,
  346**
APPOQUINIMINK HUNDRED, ment,
  346 347
AQUACKENON, ment, 189
ARMSTRONG. Margaret, md, 203, mo,
  203**
ARNOLD, General, re capture, 132
  Isaac N, res, 185, author, 185
  James, m 1, 84, 110°, res, 84, 110°
ASHFIELD, negroes, ment, 44
  Ann Morris, mo, 38 45, cousin, 38
  Catharine, dau, 38, md, 38
  Elizabeth, dau, 38, md, 38, w, 38,
    mo, 38**
  Euphemia, dau, 38, leg, 38*, age,
    38, sis, 38, md, 38
  Helene, dau, 38, w, 38
  Helene Morris, dau, 45
  Isabella, dau, 38, b, 38, m 1, 38,
    res, 38
  Isabella Morris, w, 34, 38, b, 38,
    mo, 38**, grandmo, 38**, d, 38
  Lewis Morris, s, 38, b, 38, fa, 38, 45,
    cousin, 38, md, 38, d, 38, will, 38,
    fa, 38**
  Mary, dau, 38*, b, 38, d, 38, do,
    s p, 38, sis, 38, leg, 38*, md,
    38, age, 38, frees negro, 44, res,
    44

ASHFIELD, Continued
  Patience, dau, 38, granddau, 38
  Pearce, s, 38, grands, 38
  Redford, s, 38, leg, 38, bro, 38**,
    res, 38, d, s p, 38, test, 38*
  Richard, md, 34, 38, s, 38, grands,
    38, b, 38, d, 38, res, 38, mer, 38,
    sell, 38, fa, 38**, grandfa, 38**
  Sarah Morris, w, 36, 38
  Vincent Pearse (Vincent P †), md,
    36, 38†, m 1, 36, 38†, s, 38†, cou-
    sin, 38†
ASHLAND, Mary, md, 349, mo, 349
ASHMEAD, Eliza, md, 355, s p, 355
ASHTON (see ASTON), family, md,
  297
  Alice, w, 90, 347, mo, 90, grandmo,
    90**, sis, 347
  Catharine, w, 3
  Catharine Morford, w, 3
  James (Jas), res, 196, trust, 196,
    survey, 304, est admn, 365, as
    Esq, prchs, 183, res, 183
  John, md, 3
  Joseph, wit, 159
  Rebecca, w, 335, 336, mo, 335, 336,
    347**, 348**, md, 347, sis, 347,
    grandmo, 348
ASSEMBLY, re business of, 303, dis-
  putes, 77, Colonial, memb of, 84,
  do, ment, 76, Provincial, memb
  of, 88
ASTON(AESTIN†,see ASHTON),ment,
  176
  James, exr, 348, uncle, 348
  Richard, declr, 301†
ATKINSON, Mr, husb, 378, fa, 378,
  d, 378
  A M, md, 378, husb, 378, fa, 378,
    d, 378
  Elizabeth, w, 156
  Leah, w, 378*, wid, 378, mo, 378**,
    md, 378, sis, 378, leg, 378
  Samuel, md, 378, res, 378, fa, 378**
  William (Will†), md, 156, res, 156,
    yeom, 156, bondsm, 156, nurse,
    375†, his chldn, heirs, 375
AUCHMUTY, Parson, rector, 43
AULICK, Commodore, fa, 371, grandfa,
  371*
  Miss, dau, 371, md, 371, mo, 371*,
    res, 371
AUMACK, Asbury, md, 256, decd, 256
  Catharine, w, 254, mo, 254, grand-
    mo, 254**, dau, 254
  Catharine Seabrook (Kate Sea-
    brook†), w, 256†
  Gertje, w, 254
  J, living, 252, age, 252
  Jacob (Jacobus†), neph, 252, re-
    mov, 252, md, 254†
  John, md, 69
  Mary Morris, w, 69*
  Sarah Stout, w, 363, res, 363
  William, md, 363, res, 363
AUSTIN,Miss,md, 270, res, 270, s p, 270
  Patience m 1, 110°, res, 110°
AYRES (AIRS†, AYERS††), Abigail,
  md, 216††, mo, 216††
  Elizabeth, md, 214, 216, 363†, d,
    216, age, 216, mo, 216 [?]
  Ellen Morris, w, 58
  Lunice Stout, w, 364††
  Joseph C, md, 58, b, 58, d, 58
  Robert, md, 364††

B

BAEL, Miss, md, 119
BAERUM (see BOERUM)
BAETJIE, Mrs, author, 349
BAILEY, Dr, md, 275, res, 275, cousin,
  275
  Elias, md, 147, fa, 147
  Elizabeth Clark, md, 272, mo, 272;
    sis, 272
  Lydia, md, 271, wid, 271, mo, 272*
  Mary, w, 147, mo, 147
  Olivia Seabrook, w, 275, cousin, 275
  Sarah, md, 271, mo, 272**
  Sarah Ann, md, 272, mo, 272, sis,
    272
  William, s, 147, b, 147
BAKER, Tract, ment, 180
  Mr, md, 52
  Caleb, md, 339
  Jacob, wit, 324
  Sarah Morris, w, 52*
  Susan Stout, w, 339
BALDWIN, Geneal, ment, 176
  Agnes, dau, 176, bp, 176
  Alice, w, 176, leg, 176, mo, 176**,
    grandmo, 176**, testa, 176
  Anna, w, 128
  Helen Stout, w, 344
  Henry, will, 176, husb, 176, fa.,
    176**, grandfa, 176
  Israel, md, 128
  Dr James H, md, 344
  Lydia, w, 128
  Mary, dau, 176*, md, 176, leg, 176,
    mo, 176*
  Richard, exr, 176, will, 176, bro,
    176, uncle, 176**
  Thomas, md, 128
BALLANTRAIL, a property, 198
BALLY, Nicholas, wit, 221
BANKS, Eliza, md, 64, mo, 64*
BAPTISMS, Dutch Church, 73, Mott,
  88, 97, 110**, 110°**, 110°, New
  Amsterdam, 72*, St George's
  Church, 110**, 110°**, 110°
BAPTIST (BAPTISTS), Hist of, ment,
  212, 295, 296, "Society of People
  called," deed to, 196, Church,
  First, dea, 107, do, rec, ment,
  309
BARBADOES, Parish of St Michael's,
  b, 25*
BARBER (BARBIER†), Augustus W.,
  md, 356
  Claude, convey, 71†
  Cornelia, md, 143
  Elizabeth Morford, w, 12
  Eveline, md, 255, dau, 255, d, 255,
    mo, 255**, grandmo, 255**
  Hannah, md, 288, dau, 288, mo, 288
  Henry, md, 12
  Joseph, res, 12, md, 12
  Rachel Morford, w, 12
  Sarah Stout, w, 356
  Silas, sol, 288, fa, 288, md, 288;
    grandfa, 288
  Mrs Silas, w, 288, mo, 288
BARCLAY (BARKLEY†), Catherine,
  md, 365, dau, 365, mo, 365**
  Hannah Mount, dau, 126†, w, 126†,
    127, leg, 126†
  James, husb, 126†, md, 127
  John, fa, 365, grandfa, 365**
  Lydia, w, 142, mo, 142

INDEX 387

BARKER, Joshua, prchs , 166
BARNARD, John, bro , 222*, res , 222, emig , 222, age, 222, husb , 222, freeman, 222, remov , 222*, uncle, 222*, testa , 222, d , 222, s p , 222, kinsman, 222
 Mary, sis , 222**, w , 222*, md , 222, mo , 222, age, 222, emig 222, s p , 222, wid , 222, d , 222, testa , 222
BARNEGAT (BARNIGAT), ment , 44, 78, 308, 318, 320, 321*
BARNEGAT (BARNEGATE, BARNIGAT) BEACH, ment , 23, 320
BARNES, Susannah, m l , 110*
BARNIT, Mr , md , 130
 Mary Mount (Polly Mount), w , 130†
BARTHOLOMEW, Ann, w , 212, mo , 212 grandmo , 213**
BARTON, Rachel Stout, w , 334
 Stephen, md 334, m l , 334
BARTOW, Col , his wid , 269
 Mrs , wid , 269, md , 269
 Rachel Stout, w , 334
 Stephen, md , 334, m l , 334
 Thomas (Tho*), wit , 365
BASS RIVER, John of, ment , 323
BASSE (BAif), Governor, demand re writ, 27, sits, 27
 Jeremiah (Jr), letter of, 26, sig , 26, 346, replaced as gov , 27, as Gov , 26, re factional disputes, 26, 27
BATES, Mr , md , 115
 Anna C , md , 359
 Jeremiah, md , 293
 Mary Spicer, w , 293
 Rebecca Mount, w , 115, d , 115
BATTLE HILL, called Madison, 201
BATTLES, Amelia Springs, 109, Baton Rouge, 108, Brandywine, 98, Chancellorsville, 109, Germantown, 98, City of Mexico, 109, of Monmouth, ment , 52, 98, 147, 248*, 252, 282, of Monterey, 53, of Pittsburgh Landing, 206, of Quebec, 98, Second Bull Run, 109, Springfield, 98, Trenton, 98, Valley Forge, 98, of Vera Cruz. 109, of the Wilderness, ment , 275. 276
BATTY (see BEATTY), Abigail, dau , 93, md , 93
 David, fa , 93, res 93
BAUDINE (see BODINE)
BAY, BAYS, Chingaroras, 78, Massachusetts, 226, The, 113, 301, Wallabout, 12
BAY SHORE, house, old relics at, 248, alias Port Monmouth, 223
BAYARD, Captain, in his place, 369
 Balthazar, comm , 17*, guard , 17
 N , Secry , 17, sig , 17
BAYLIS, Abigail, w , 128, b , 128, d , 128, age, 128, wid , 128, bur , 128, will, 128, mo , 128**
 Ellen, md , 113
 John, fa , 120, 131, husb , 120, res , 131, grandfa , 131**
 Mary, md , 120, 131, dau , 120, 131, b , 120, mo , 131**
 Susannah, w , 120, mo , 120
BAYNARD, Miss, md , 270, mo., 270**
BAYVILLE, Cemetery, ment , 323
BAXTER, Ensign George, sol , 300

BEACH, Dr , md , 249, as Rev , officiating clergy man, 371
 Mrs , w , 240
BEACON LIGHTS, re firing of, 187
BEAGRAVE, Amerantie (Amaritie), w , 366, wid , 366, d intest , 366, mo , 366, leg , 366, dau , 366
 Benjamin, his wid , 366
BEALEI, Martha, md , 363
BEALLE, Mrs Mary, res , 251, has Bible, 251
BEARD, Elizabeth Stout (Betsy Stout†), w , 364†
 Thomas, md , 364
BEATTY (see BATTY), James, md , 130
 Rhoda Mount, w , 130
BEAVERS, fine of eight, 21
BECK (see BEK), Susan, md , 375
BECKETT, Martha, md , 270, mo , 270**
 Martha Catharine, md , 271, living, 271, mo , 272
BEDIENT (BEADIENT†, BEDENTE††), Francis, fa , 222, kinsman, 222, exr 222
 John, step s , 222, leg, 222
 Mary, w , 222**, md , 222, mo , 222**, admrx , 222, res , 222, oath, 222
 Mordicay, step-s , 222, leg , 222
 Morgan, prchs , 220, 221†, sell , 220, right to enter property, 221, singleman, 221†, res , 221*†, 222**, convey , 221, 222, mark, 221, bill of sale, 221†, s 222**, b , 222, neph , 222, leg , 222, fa , 222**, husb , 222, bro , 222, deft , 222, d , 222
 Morgan, Sr , husb , 222*
 Thomas (Thoms†), s , 222**, b , 222, neph , 222, leg , 222**, res , 222**, release, 222*, seal, 222, step-s , 222, sig , 222††, yeom , 222, bro , 222, pltf , 222, heir, 222, intest , 222, husb , 222, d , 222
BEDLE (BEADLE, BEDEL, BEDELL), Governor, ment , 109, sis of his mo , 161, as Ex Governor, ment , 153, res , 153
 Miss, md , 284
 Amy, md , 286, mo , 286*. 314, w , 314, grandmo , 315**, g grandmo , 315**
 Catharina, w , 61, mo , 61, grandmo , 61
 David, res , 110*, will, 110*, fa , 110*
 Hannah, w , 164
 James, md , 132, b , 132, d , 132
 Margaret Mount, w , 132
 Martha, md , 314, 363, dau , 314, b , 314, mo , 315**, grandmo , 315**
 Sarah, md , 315, dau , 315, b , 315, d , 315, mo , 315**
 Sylvanus C , md , 164
 Thomas, fa , 314, 315, husb , 314, grandfa , 315**, g grandfa , 315**
BEDSON, Mary, res , 152, sis , 152*, leg , 152*, wid , 152
BEE, Mary, tombs , 265, donor, 265
BEEKMAN, Mr George T, author , 279, res , 279
 Maria, dau , 43, md , 43, mo , 43, grandmo , 43**
 William, fa , 43, grandfa , 43
BEERE, Jonathan, prchs , 22, res , 22, gent , 22
BEESLEY, Dr Maurice, author, 294

BEK (see BECK), Elizabeth, md , 316, 317, mo , 317**, grandmo , 317
BELCHER, Gov , cousin, 377, res , 377
BELL, Mr , md , 165
 George W , Esq , has port , 165, res . 165
 Lauretta, w , 165
 Mary Catharine, w , 204, mo , 204, grandmo , 204**, decd , 204
 Rosa, md , 204, mo , 204**
 Thomas, appr , 168, convey , 172, trust , 172, md , 204, fa , 204, grandfa , 204**
BEMBRIDGE, Mary, w , 193, née Clark, 193
BENEDICT, Caroline, md , 343, mo , 343
BENJAMIN, Herrick, md , 314, m l , 314, res , 314, d , 314, fa , 314*
 Leah, granddau , 314, dau , 314*
 Mary Stout, w , 314, living, 314, dau , 314, mo , 314*, leg , 314, niece, 314
 Stout, grands , 314, s , 314*
BENNET (BENNETT), Mr , md , 349
 Ann (Nancy†), w , 383†, mo , 383**†, grandmo , 383†
 Benjamin wit , 239, as Rev , re md , 249
 Catharine (Catherine), md , 57, 364, mo , 57**, 58*, res , 364
 Charles, md , 66
 Deborah, md , 54, 57, mo , 57**
 Elijah Hughes, w , 383, md , 383, fa , 383
 George, s , 383, md , 383
 Hannah, md , 65, 66, mo , 66**, 67**, grandmo , 66**
 John, s , 383, unmd , 383, md , 383, fa , 383**, grandfa , 383
 John Spicer, s , 383, grands , 383
 Lydia Morris, w , 66
 Martha Stout, w , 349
 Mary, w , 61, 383, mo , 61, 383
 Prescilla, w , 383
BENT, Mr , md , 165, fa , 165, disappeared 165
 Rachel Ogborne, w , 165, mo , 165, d , 165, age, 165, port , 165
BENTHALL (BENTHALS†), Walter, land pat to, 115, land ment , 186†, bndry, 186†
BENTHAM, JOSEPH, cred , 85, admn granted to, 85
BENTLY, Thomas, wit , 319
BENWARD, Mary A , md , 358, mo , 358**, sis , 358
 Rebecca, md , 358, sis , 358, mo , [?], 358**
BERGEN, County of, re riots, etc , 29
 Miss, md , 315, mo , 345
 Elias, md 119
 Hannah Mount. w , 143
 Mary, md , 119
 Peter C , admr , 139, md , 143, b , 143, d , 143
 Phebe w , 119
 T G , author , 74, 292, as Esq , do , 293
BERGEN'S ISLAND, ment , 291
BERRY, Capt , bro , 196
 Miss, sis , 196
 Mr , guard , 16
 Elizabeth St Clair, md , 56, 59, mo , 59**
 Capt John, admr , 25

INDEX

BETHANY, in Middletown, ment, 147, 148**, 149
BETTS, Mary, w, 56, mo, 56
BEVERWYCK, ment, 201
BICKFORD, Dorothy, md, 215, b, 215, d 215
  Elizabeth, md 215, mo, 215**, g grandmo, 215
BICKLEY (see WHARTON), English family, 380, est., ment, 202, Quakers, 380, 382, ref, 382
  Abraham (Abram†), wit, 170†, prchs, 170, res, 170*, 175, 381*, convey 170, 382, s, 175, 381**, 382, leg, 175 381, bro, 175, 381**, exr, 381, grands, 381, will, 381**, 382, mer, 381, husb, 381, 382**, md, 381, 382, fa, 381**, 382**, uncle, 381**, b, 382, est, 382, bro law, 382
  Abraham W, s, 202, md, 202
  Agnes, w, 202
  Benjamin, s, 382*, b, 382*
  Dorothy, w, 381, 382, mo, 381**
  Elizabeth, dau, 381**, granddau, 381, md, 381**, mo, 381**, 382**, leg, 381, wit, 381, sis, 381*, w, 382*, convey, 382, d, 382*
  Hannah, w, 202, dau, 381, 382, granddau, 381, b, 382
  Howell, s, 202, md, 202
  Isaac, s, 382, b, 382
  Laura, w, 202
  Lloyd, change of name, 202, s, 202, md, 202, fa, 202**
  Lloyd W, s, 202, md, 202
  Margaret A, w, 202, mo, 202**
  Mary, dau, 381, 382*, granddau, 381, b, 382*, d, 382
  Miriam, w, 202
  Polgreen, dau, 381, granddau, 381
  Robert, s, 202, md, 202
  Samuel, s, 381, 382**, grands, 381, b, 382, exr, 382, advertised, 382
  Sarah md, 170*, 381**, mo, 171**, 381, dau, 381**, recd land, 381, leg, 381, w, 381
  Susannah (Susanna), wit, 170, convey, 170, 382, dau, 381, 382*, granddau, 381, w, 381 382, living, 381, decd, 381, b, 382*, md, 382, bur, 382
  William (Wm), res, 18, 170, 171, 175*, 380, recd land, 18, leg, 19, 20, 380, declr, 20, wit, 20, 380, friend, 20, exr, 20, 380*, mer, 170, 380, prchs, 170, shopkeeper, 170, 175, convey, 170, 381, 382, decd, 171, 381, testa, 175, 381, mast, 175, will, 175, 380, 381*, fa, 171, 175**, 381**, grandfa, 175**, 380, 381**, fa-law, 175*, 380, 381*, Quaker, 175, 380, cor, 380, ref, 380, admr, 380*, character, 380, uncle, 380, drew will, 380, orig, 380, friendship, 380, neighbor, 380, s, 381, grands, 381, husb 381*, 382, gave land, 381, step-fa, 381
BICKNELL, Ella Stout, w, 361
  William A, md 361
BIDDLE, in Rev War, 236*
  Captain, prison, 236, autobiog, 236, re luggage, 236
  Mr, md, 268
  Mrs, w, 268

BIDDLE Continued
  Charles, friend, 213, exr, 213, Vice-Pres, 236, auto biog, 236
BIG BLUE RIVER, ment, 197
BILES (see BILL, BILLS), Anne, md, 99, mo, 99**
  Sarah Mott, w, 89
  William, md, 89, m l, 89, res, 332, convey, 332
BILL (see BILES, BILLS), Abigail, dau, 367, md, 367, bp, 367, age, 367, wit, 367, mo, 367**, 368, w, 368, grandmo, 368
  Benjamin, fa, 367, grandfa, 367**
BILLS (see BILES, BILL), Mr, md, 361, fa, 361
  Lydia, md, 145, mo, 145, 173, w, 173
  Sarah Stout, w, 361, mo, 361
  Sylvanus, s, 361, age, 361, re guard, 361
  Sylvanus T (Sylvenus T), s, 361, neph, 361, leg, 361
  William, res, 332, convey, 332
BINES, Mary Elizabeth, md, 63
BINGLA, Mary, md, 175
BIRCHFIELD, Elizabeth, w, 381, 382
  Matthew (Mathew), husb, 381, 382, leg, 381, kinsman, 381, ment, 381
BIRD, William, tombs, 265, donor, 265
BIRDSALL, Benjamin, md, 88, 110ᵇ
  Miriam Mott, w, 88, 110ᵇ
BISHOP, Capt, husb, 163, res, 163
  Col David, fa, 356, grandfa, 356**
  Mrs Eliza, dau, 163, wid, 163
  Mary, md, 356, dau, 356, b, 356, d, 356, bur, 356, mo, 356**
BLACK, John, husb, 378, survey, 378, res, 378
  Mary, leg, 378, w, 378
BLACK HORSE, property, ment, 195, Staten Island, ment, 195
BLACK POINT, ment, 187
BLACKBIRD CREEK, ment, 347
BLACKMAN, Mrs, author, 323, author, 323
  Mrs Leah, author, 323
BLACKWELL, Anna Hagaman, w, 345
  David L, md, 345
  Helen Baldwin, 345
  Jacob, bro law, 110ᵃ, exr, 110ᵃ
  Nelson D, md, 345
BLAIR, Rev, decd, 245, fa, 245
  Rev John D, bp by, 244*, md by, 244
  Miss Mary, md, 245, dau, 245
BLAKLLY, Charles, md, 12
  Lucy Morford, w 12
BLLA, Mrs Clara Anthony, res, 252, letter of, 252, dau, 252
BLOCK HOUSE, Middletown, b, 307, a fort, Middletown, 298
BLOCK ISLAND, Livermore's hist of, ref, 110
BLODGLT, Mr, md, 356
  Esther Stout, w, 356
BLOOMINGDALL ROAD, tavern, 368
BLOWERS, Joseph, convey, 153
BLUE, Charity Stout, w, 339
  Jane, md, 342, mo, 342**
  Michael, md, 339
BLUE ANCHOR, "At the sign of the," ment, 190

BODINE (BAUDINE†), Amelia, w, 324
  Elenor, md, 358†, remov, 358†, mo, 358*†
  Margaret J, md, 206, res, 206, b, 206, mo, 206
BOEL (BOLF), Thomas, bndry, 180, line, bndry, 180**
BOERUM (BAERUM†, BOORUM††), Catharine, wid, 87†, md, 87†, 110ᵃ††
BOGART (BOGLRT), Ruth, md, 327, mo, 327**, 337, grandmo, 327**, 337, w, 337
  John, will, 322
BOGGS, Elizabeth, dau, 44
  James, s law, 44, md, 44, fa, 44**, as M D, md, 44
  Mary Morris, w, 44, mo, 44**
BOKENHAMIS, manor called, 176
BOLINGBROKE, Lord, ment, 240
BOLLEN (see BULLEN), Anna, dau, 331*, md, 331, re guard, 331
  James, wit, 307, ackn, 307, s, 331, re guard, 331, secry, 331, fa, 331*, d, 331
BOLTON (see BOULTON), Eleanor, md, 217, mo, 217*
BONHAM, Anne, dau, 332, md, 332
  Ann Stout, w, 332, mo, 332, age, 332
  Hannah, md, 333, mo, 333**, grandmo, 333**
  Mary, md, 121, d, s p, 121
  Nehemiah, md, 332, fa, 332
BOONE (BOON†), Mr, md, 353†
  Ann, md, 191, cousin, 191, grandmo, 191
  Benjamin, fa, 187, husb, 187
  Daniel, cousin, 187, 191, pioneer, 191
  Dinah, md, 187, cousin, 187, dau, 187, b, 187, descendant, 187
  Mary Stout, w, 353†
  Susannah, w, 187, mo, 187
BOOTH Miss, md, 273, res, 273, mo, 273*
BORDEN, relations, 111
  Miss, w, 111, dau, 111
  Mr, md, 58, 316, 340, fa, 340
  Mrs, ment, 91
  Abigail, w, 111
  Amey, dau, 90, md, 90**, mo, 90**
  Benjamin, prchs, 111, recd pat, 111, husb, 111
  Charles Dennis, md, 58, s, 58, b, 58, d, 58
  Esther, dau, 320, md, 320, mo, 320, w, 320, grandmo, 320
  Francis, wit, 35, fa, 58, husb, 58
  Jane, w, 47, mo, 47, grandmo, 47**
  Jeremiah, fa, 320, husb, 320, grandfa, 320
  John, s, 111, emig, 111
  Margaret, w, 50, mo, 58
  Margaret Emma, w, 67
  Mary, granddau, 316, leg, 316, dau, 340
  Mary Ann, w, 58
  Matthew, will, 111, res, 111, fa, 111*
  Rachel, dau, 58, 316, 340, leg, 58, 316, 340
  Rachel Morris, w, 58
  Rachel Stout, w, 316 340, mo, 340
  Richard, md, 67, emig, 111, s, 111, wit, 183, bndry, 183

INDEX 389

BORDEN, *Continued*
 Safety, fa , 90, res , 90, grandfa , 90**, convey , 185
BORDENTOWN, Quaker Burying Ground ment . 375
BORRADAILL, John, prchs , 157, res , 157
BORROW, Nathaniel Thompson, in v t , 383, res , 383
BOSTON, Newspapers, re shipwreck, 234, jail, keeper of, 178
BOSTWICK, Mr , md , 105
 Ann, letter of, 103, detr , 103
 Ann Mott, w , 105
 John, ment , 102
BOUND (see BOWNE)
BOULTON (see BOLTON), Priscilla, md , 375
BOWER, John, tombs , 265, donor, 265
BOWERS, John Calvin, md , 205
 Lemuel, pltf 89
 Sarah Elizabeth, w , 205
BOWKER, Anne Mount, w , 127
 Levi, m l , 127
BOWLES, Ann Salter, w , 215
 Samuel, md , 215
BOWMAN, Isabella, md , 112
BOWNE (BOUND†), Bible, ment , 121, family, emig , 298, do , geneal of, 72, do , md , 297†, do , ment , 326, do , ref , 72, do , set , 298, 301*, in Militia, 307* Papers, ref , 76
 Capt , expelled, 181
 Miss, dau , 72, 76, md , 72, 110, mo , 72, 76, w , 76
 Andrew, sig , 28, just , 77, md , 223, as Capt , as proxy, 27
 Anne, dau , 181, re trust, 181, leg , 182
 Ann Seabrook, w , 223
 Catharine, w , 88, mo , 88, grandmo , 88, 89**
 Easter (see Hester); md , 4, m l , 4, res , 4, mo , 4**
 Elizabeth, w , 194, dau , 375
 Frances, w , 181, re trust, 181, leg , 182
 Capt George, md , 254, s p , 254
 Hester (see Easter), md , 4
 Hester Morford, w , 12†
 Jacob I , res , 110, author , 110
 James (Geamest), md , 12†, 134, 325, 375, re trust, 182, debt discharged, 182, res , 292, pat , 292, husb , 303, 326, land grant, 303, bro law 307, magist , 307, s , 325, 326*, 375*, re lands, 326, fa , 326**, remov , 326, set , 326, d , 326, do , s p , 375, o\sr , 372
 John, res , 20*, 181, leg , 20, 182, friend, 20, exr , 20, bro , 76, 181*, decd , 76, uncle, 76, 181**, 183*, 185, bndry , 113, s , 181, 182 326, re trust, 181, deed, do , 181, husb , 181, mer , 181, 224, gave bond, 181, will, 181, 183*, 185, convey , 223, his est , 224, cred , 224, just , 306, as Captain, re pat rights, 181, fa , 181*, grandfa , 181**, 182**, in Militia, 307
 Julia, w , 249
 Lydia, granddau , 121, statement, 121, dau , 181, re trust, 181, w , 181, mo , 181*, grandmo , 181**, 182**, leg , 182

BOWNE, *Continued*
 Lydia Mount, w , 134, d , 134
 Margaret, dau , 375
 Mary, dau , 375, w , 375, d , 375
 Mary Anna, w , 254, s p , 254
 Mary Stout, w , 303, 325, 326, land grant, 303, line of, 325, 326, mo , 326**, re land 326
 Nathan C , s , 375
 Obadiah, wit , 181, fa , 181**, 182, admr , 185, pltf , 185
 Phebe, dau , 375, w , 375, mo , 375**
 Philip, cor , 375, m l , 375*, s , 375*, md , 375**, fa , 375**
 Priscilla, w , 375, d , s p , 375
 Rachel, md , 281
 Rebecca, md , 357, b , 357, d , 357
 Robert, md , 194
 Samuel, friend 175, leg , 175, 381, res , 175 381, s , 326, 375
 Sarah (Sally†), her Bible, 121†, res , 121†, md , 181, dau , 181, 375, b , 181, living, 181, sis , 181, mo , 181**, 182**, 375*, w , 375
 Susan, w , 375, d , s p , 375
 Thomas, s , 375, md , 375, d , s p , 375
 Thomasin, w , 375
 William, fa , 72, 76, 325, res , 72, 292, grandfa , 72, 76, 326**, pat , 292, bndry , 308, s , 326, 375
 Willet, md , 249
BOYD, Kate A , md , 129, mo , 129
 Julius md , 129
BRADFIELD, Annie Mount, w , 129
BRADFORD, William (Will†), clk , 77*†, printer, 86, cred , 86, admr , 86
BRAIN, Benjamin, prchs , 378, grandfa , 378, testa , 378
BRANNON James, md , 164
 Rhoda, w , 164
BRANSON, Maria, md , 133, dau , 133, b , 133, d , 133
 Capt Ware, fa , 133
BRASIER (BRAZIER†, see BREESER), Henry, husb , 291, md , 292
 Rebecca, w , 308†, mo , 308*†, grandmo , 308*†, 309**†
 Susannah, dau , 291, w , 291, leg , 291
 Susannah Spicer, w , 292
BRAY, Andrew, md , 333
 Amelia, granddau , 162, leg , 162
 Ann, md , 149, 165, b 149, d , 149, mo , 149**, dau , 165*, sis , 165**
 Ann Seabrook, w , 223
 Catharine, granddau , 162, leg , 162
 Catharine Winter, dau , 165, d , 165, age, 165
 David, s , 165
 Elizabeth, w , 165, d , 165, age, 165
 James, s law, 162, exr , 162, md , 165, d , 165, age, 165, poisoned, 165, fa , 165**
 John, wit , 159, as Rev , md , 223
 Louette, granddau , 162, leg , 162
 Mary, granddau , 162, leg , 162, dau , 105
 Mary Ogborne (Polly Ogborne), w , 164, wid , 164, mo , 165**
 Rachel, dau , 165
 Rachel Ogborne, w , 165, wid , 165, mo , 165**
 Samuel, md , 164, fa , 165**, s , 165
 Samuel Ogborne s , 165*, d , 165*, age, 165*, md 165
 Sarah Stout, w , 333

BRAZIER (see BRASIER)
BREARLEY, in Militia, 90
 David, Esq , Col , 90
BREESE (BRES, BREEZE†), Captain, md , 371†, of navy, 371†
 Miss, md , 364
 Arthur, fa , 367, 370, 371, Rear Admiral, 367, res , 371†, grandfa , 371*†
 Catharine, md , 357, mo , 357**, grandmo , 357**
 Emma, w , 367
 Frances Hogan, w , 371†
 Frances S , w , 367
 Samuel, sell , 122, res , 122*, gent , 122
 Samuel Livingston, s , 367, md , 367*, d , 367
 Sarah, md , 324, d , 324, age, 324, mo , 324**
 Susan, md , 370*, 371†, dau , 370, 371†, wid , 370, d , 370, mo , 371*†
BREESER (see BRASIER), Henry, mort , 291, house, 291
BRENTHALL'S BROOK, bndry , 114
BREVOORT, Elias, will , 368, fa , 368, house, 368, fa law, 368, grandfa , 369**
 Jacamyntie (Jacomentye), dau , 368, w , 368, leg . 368
 Jemima md , 368, res , 368, d , 368*, age, 368, mo , 368, 369**, grandmo , 368, tombs , 368
 Mary, dau , 204
 Rosa, w , 204, mo , 204**
 Samuel, md , 204, res , 204, fa , 204**
BREWER, Bible rec , 51*
 Aaron Robbins, s , 51, res , 51, b , 51, d , 51, md , 51
 Adam, house of, 46, res , 46, fa 46, 51, will, 50, res , 50, s , 51, b , 51, d , 51, husb , 51, grandfa , 51**
 Anne, md , 58, b , 58, d , 58, mo , 58**
 Deborah, dau , 51, b , 51, d , 51, md , 51, w , 51, 58, mo , 51, 58, grandmo , 51**
 Elazarus (Elazerus), admr , 41, res , 41, 51, exr , 50, md , 51, m l , 51, cordwainder, 51, s , 51, b , 51, d , 51, age, 51, fa , 51**, husb , 51, tombs , 51
 Elizabeth, res , 46, dau , 46, 51, md , 46, 51, mo , 46**, 47**, b , 51
 Elizabeth Cooper, w , 51
 Elizabeth Morris, w , 69
 Frances, mo , 51**, w , 51**
 Frances Morris, b , 51, d , 51
 George, s , 51, b 51, d , 51, md , 51*
 Jerusha, md , 357, mo 357**
 John s , 51*, b , 51*, d , 51, md , 51
 Joseph md , 69
 Lydia Hulet, w , 51
 Mary, dau , 51, 58, d , 51, 58, md , 51, 58, res , 58, mo , 58**
 Rebecca Schenck, w , 51
BRIDGES, John, will, 85, chief-just , 85
BRIGGS, gravestones, 377
 Ann dau , 377, w , 377, mo , 377
 Levi, ta , 377, husb , 377, s law, 377, d , 377, age, 377, b , 377, tombs , 377
 Rachel, dau , 376, leg , 376
 Sarah, dau , 377, granddau , 377*, d , 377, age, 377, tombs , 377
BRINDLEY, Euphame, m l , 50, res , 5

INDEX

BRINKERHOFF, George D , md , 38,
  res , 38
  Euphemia Ashfield, w , 38
BRINLEY, Elizabeth, md , 121, m 1,
  121, dau , 121, mo , 121**, w , 121,
  grandmo , 121**
  Jane, wid , 363, res , 363, md , 363
  John, re quit-claim, 121
  William, fa law, 121, res , 121, esq ,
  121, prchs , 121, fa , 121. husb,
  121, grandfa , 121**, convey , 320-
  321
BRINSON, Charity, md , 335, 338, mo ,
  338*, 339, grandmo , 338*, 339*
  Hannah Stout, w , 334
  John, md , 334
BRITANNIA, Privateer, ment , 370
BRITISH ARMY, ment , 98, Morris in, 43
BRITISH NAVY, ment , 98
BRITTON (BRITAIN†, BRITON,
  BRITTAIN††), Miss, md , 117,
  mo , 117
  Ann, w 117, sis , 117, aunt, 117,
  dau , 361, leg , 361
  Ann Mount, w , 118†, 137, d , 137,
  bur , 137
  Anne Stout, w , 363, res , 363
  Benjamin, s , 213, decd , 213
  Catharine, w , 212
  Mrs Charles P , author , 136, res , 136
  Flenor, w , 212, mo , 213**
  Elizabeth dau , 361, leg , 361
  Hannah sis , 210*, mo , 210*, decd ,
  210*
  Hannah Saltar, w , 212**, res , 212,
  ch memb , 212**, do , transferred,
  212, dau , 212, mo , 212**
  John, neph , 210*, 212*, leg , 210,
  212, 213, do , revoked, 210, 212, s ,
  210, 212**, 213, b , 212*, remov ,
  212, living, 212, md , 212, fa
  213**, exr , 213, prchs , 213**,
  res , 213**, will, 213, sig , 213,
  mer , 213, pet , 213
  John, Senior, mer , 213, res , 213,
  fa law, 213, will, 213, res , 213,
  fa , 213**, aged, 213
  Joseph, wit , 113, 116††, 118, s law,
  113, husb , 117, 118, uncle, 117,
  md , 118†
  Lyonell, prchs . 156, res , 156
  Margaret Mount, w , 137, d , 137,
  bur 137
  Mary, dau 213, decd , 213
  Nathaniel, md , 137, b . 137, d , 137,
  bur 137, will, 189††, res , 189††
  Nicholas, md , 137, h , 137
  Rachel, w , 161††, mo , 161††, grand-
  mo , 161**††, 162**††
  Richard (Rich^d), md , 212, husb ,
  212**, res , 212, fa , 212**, bndry ,
  213, convey , 235††
  Richard, Jr. md , 363, res , 363
  Saltar s , 213, leg , 213
  Samuel, est admn , 96, decd , 96,
  res , 96
  Sarah, dau , 212, md , 212, w , 382
  Thomas, neph , 210**, 212, 382, s ,
  210, 212*, leg , 210**, 212, do , re-
  voked 210, bro 210*, exr , 210,
  212, md , 211††, 212*, 382*, b , 212,
  382, res , 212, pet , 212, cor , 382
  Mrs Thomas, w , 211††
  Rebecca, dau . 212, md , 212
  William, s. 213, exr , 213, leg , 213

BROCK, Burbridge, husb , 175, sworn,
  175, mark, 175
  Mary, mo , 175*, dau , 175, w , 175,
  sworn, 175
  William Potter, grands , 175, leg , 175
BROCKETS associates, 291
BROCKETT'S NECK, alias Grove farm,
  291
BROKAW, Mr , md , 57, 285
  Caroline Stout, w , 357
  Charlotte Ann, w , 57
  Garret G , md , 357
  Margaret Shepherd, w , 285
BROMBICH, Anna, md , 234
BRONCK'S, land, alias Haerlem, 18,
  plantation, 17, 22
BROOKE, Lord, ment , 243
  D J B , md , 202, res , 202
  Maria, w , 202
BROOKFIELD, ment , 245, 251
BROOKLYN (see BRUCKELEN)
BROOKS, in U S Army, 52, of Boston,
  281
  Captain, md , 52
  Frances Morris, w , 52
BROOKS (see CREEKS, RIVERS,
  RUNS), Brenthall's, 114, Bug,
  156, Cranberry (Cranbury†), 113,
  116, 186†, Gravell (Gravill†), 185†,
  Hop, 180, Jumping, 45, Main,
  Freehold 180, Mill. 113, Pine,
  185, Rocky, 114, 115, Whale Pond,
  319
BROWER, Cornelius, fa , 65, husb , 65
  Deborah Morris, w , 65
  Elias, md , 69, res , 69
  Elizabeth, w , 69
  Elizabeth More, w , 69, res , 69
  Elizabeth Morris, w , 69, res , 69
  Gilbert, md , 65, s , 65
  Jane, mo , 65, w , 65
  John, md , 57
  Margaret Morris, w , 57
BROWN (BROWNE), bog, ment , 238,
  Quakers, 375
  Abiah, re name, 381
  Abraham, fa , 171, 381, grandfa ,
  172, 173**, s , 381
  Elizabeth, dau , 175, 381, leg , 175,
  381, w , 381**, mo , 381
  Frederick, grands , 117, leg , 117
  Hannah, dau , 361, leg , 361
  Isaac, md , 342, remov , 342
  Jane, w , 210, leg , 210
  John, recpt for coffin, 112, sig , 112,
  md , 119, husb , 210, joiner, 210
  Joseph (Joseph), md , 293*
  Margaret, w , 119
  Martha, md , 157, mo , 157**
  Martha Spicer, w , 293
  Mary, wid , 171, 172*, md , 171, 172,
  225*, dau , 172**, 225, 226*, 227,
  mo , 172*, 226, 232**, leg , 172**,
  226, 375, w , 172*, 225, 226*, 232,
  re convey , 172, re md , 172, con-
  vey , 172, 226, sis , 172*, re trust,
  172*, sig , 172, b , 225, 226, re
  land, 227, grandmo , 232**, cor , 375
  Mary Spicer, w , 293
  Naomi (Neomyt), cor , 375, leg , 375,
  res , 381†, m 1 , 381†, re name, 381
  Nathan, land owner, 247, house, 247
  Nicholas (Nich , Nicolas), took invt ,
  23, wit , 24, mark, 24, his wid ,
  171, 172*, his goods, 172, res , 172,

BROWN, Continued
  226*, convey , 172, d , 172, 381,
  husb , 172, 225, 226, 381**, testa ,
  172, 227, will, 172*, 381, leg , 175,
  381, s law, 175, 381, fa , 225, 226*,
  227, 232, 381, md , 225, 381*,
  decd , 226, pat , 226, prchs , 226,
  227*, propn 227, grandfa , 232**,
  381, re land, 232, his atty , 247,
  bro , 247, s , 381
  Preserve, cor , 375, d , 375, age, 375,
  bur , 375, Quaker, 375, fa , 381**
  Ruth Stout, w , 342, remov , 342
  Sarah, md , 171, dau , 171, b , 171,
  d , 171, mo , 172, 173**
  Susannah (Susan†), md , 359†, 380,
  mo , 359†
  William, fa , 11, grandfa , 11**
  Zilpha Maria, md , 11, dau , 11, b.,
  11, d , 11, mo , 11**
BROWN'S POINT, ment , 298
BROWNING, D R , Esq , res., 335, de-
  scendant, 335, letter of, 335
BRUCKELEN, ment , 290
BRUSH, Keziah, m 1 , 110°, md , 352;
  m 1 , 352, d , 352, age, 352, mo ,
  352
BRYANT-Carteret Book, ment , 349,
  -Lanning-Stout, item, 349, ref , 349
  Miss, md , 353
  Abigail, md , 358, mo , 358**, grand-
  mo . 358**
  Ann, dau , 349, md , 349, ment , 349
  Benjamin, will, 349, husb , 349, fa ,
  349**, s , 349*, d , 349, ment , 349
  Catharine Stout, w , 337
  Cornelius, fa , 349*, res , 349
  Daniel, s , 349
  Elizabeth, dau , 349, md , 349, ment ,
  349, w , 349*, mo , 349*
  James, md , 337, res , 337
  John, md , 337, fa , 337*, s , 349
  Margaret, dau , 349, md , 349, 356,
  mo , 356*
  Sarah Stout, w , 337, mo , 337*
  William, s , 349
BUCK, Aaron, detr , 100
BUCKALEW (BUCKELEW), Miss,
  md , 339, remov , 339, mo , 339**,
  grandmo , 339
  Col I S , s , 208, res , 208*, letter of,
  208, author , 208
  James, md , 208, fa , 208*
  John M , md , 139
  Lydia Mount, w , 139
  Margaret Chambers, w , 208, mo ,
  208*
BUCKINGHAM (BUCKINGAM†),
  County, ment , 72†, Seabrooks in,
  257
BUDD, Mr , just , 88
  Deborah, md , 125, dau , 125, b ,
  125, d , 125
  George, s law, 213, exr , 213
  Hannah, w , 125, mo , 125
  Irene, md , 62
  Samuel, fa , 125, husb , 125
  Susan, dau , 213, leg , 213
BUGBROOK, ment , 156
BULL RUN, Battle of, second, 109
BULLEN (see BOLLEN), family, md ,
  297
  Miss, md , 330, mo , 330*
  Mary, md , 330, leg , 330, w , 330,
  mo . 330*

BULMER, Miss, md , 345, res , 345, mo , 345
BULOW, Miss, md , 269
BUMBO SPRING, ment , 77
BUNSON, Hannah Stout, w , 334
   John, md , 334
BURDGE (BURGE†), David, fa , 131, husb , 131, grandfa , 131**, 132**
   Elizabeth, w , 131, mo , 131, grandmo , 131**, 132**
   Elizabeth Layton, w , 131
   Hannah, dau , 2, md , 2, mo , 2*, 3*, bp 2
   Hugh, md , 366, fa , 366
   Isaac, s , 131, md , 131, b , 131, d , 131
   Jane, w , 366
   Jonathan, fa , 2, grandfa , 2*, 3*, md , 41, m l , 41, res , 41
   Joseph, s law, 40, exr , 40, res , 40, 41, md , 41, wit , 46
   Lydia Stout, w , 366, mo , 366
   Mary, dau , 40, leg , 40
   Mary Morris, w , 41
   Phebe, md , 148†, b , 148†, d , 148†, mo , 148**†
   Richard (Rich⁴), bill pd , 230
   Rebecca, dau , 40, leg , 40
   Sarah Morris, w , 41
   William (Billy†), s , 366†, md , 366†, living, 366†, res , 366†, age, 366†
BURDON, Mr , md , 313
   Rhoda, dau , 312, leg , 312
   Rhoda Stout, w , 312, 313
BURGES, Deborah, md , 56
BURGOINE, his Army ment , 101
BURGOMASTERS' REC , New York, ment , 291
BURK, Emma L , md , 166, 167, dau , 166, 167, mo , 167**
   Col James, husb , 166, 167**, fa , 166, 167, grandfa , 167**
   Mary, servt , 321
   Sarah, w , 166, 167, mo , 166, 167, grandmo , 167**
BURLEIGH Benjamin, testa , 86, will, 86, husb , 86, res , 86, bro law, 86
   Hannah, exrx , 86, w , 86
BURLING, Edward, Jr , s , 75, exr , 75
   Edward, Sr , fa , 75, exr , 75
   Jane md , 75, res , 75
BURLINGTON First Div of lands, 153, Friends' Rec , 378, High St , ment , 153**, 154, 156*, hist of 132, Market House, ment , 153, Monthly Meeting, ret , 378, Quaker Rec , 155*, 156, 167, St Mary's Church, Rec , 12, 189, do , churchyard, bur , 154*, 155**, 190, City, highway, ment , 155, Co , Court, 107, do , jail, poison ,191, do , Mott of, 84, do , murder by "Old Si," 161, Path meat , 290
BURNETT (BURNET),Governor,ment , 30, his successor, 30
   Mr , clk , 233
   Robert, land ment , 186, bndry , 186
   William, convey , 322, res , 322, as Esq , Gov, 167
BURNHAM, Mary E , md , 149, b , 149
BURRITT, William, d , 260
BURROWES (BURROS†, BURROUGHS††, BURROWS), Miss, dau , 249, md , 249, mo , 249
   Mr , prchs , 313

BURROWES, Continued
   Catharine (Kate†), w , 249†, mo , 249†, grandmo , 249†
   Charity, md , 334*, mo , 334**, 340, 353*, dau , 334, w , 340, 353*, grandmo , 340, 353**, g grandmo , 340**
   Deborah, dau , 278†, leg , 278*†, sis , 278
   Deborah Shepherd, w , 279
   Eden, prchs , 112, 113, husb, 113, s , 113, emig, 113, fa , 113
   Edward, fa , 113, 249, res , 113, md , 249, 270, grandfa , 249, bndry , 310
   Elizabeth, md , 328††
   Elizabeth Stout, w , 334
   Esther, dau , 280, leg , 280, w , 280, b , 280, d , 280, age, 280
   John, cattle-mark, 304, 346
   Jonathan P , md , 131††
   Margaret Mount, w , 131††
   Mercy, w , 163, 282, mo , 163, 282, grandmo , 163**, 282**
   Nathaniel, md , 334
   Rachel, w , 113 md , 336, mo , 336**, grandmo , 336*
   Rebecca, dau 113
   Sarah, md , 338††, d , 338††, age, 338††, bur, 338††
   Thomas, md , 280, d , 280, age, 280, fa , 334, res , 334, grand'a , 334**
BURIIS (BURTES†), Ann, md , 338
   Susannah, w , 120, mo , 120
   Jane, md , 110⁶
   Margaret, m l , 110⁶
BURYING-GROUNDS (see CEMETERIES, CHURCHYARDS, YARDS), Baptist, Freehold, 13, do , Hopewell, bur , 352, Clayton, 326, Disboro, 75, Lippit, 362, Morford, 1, Mott, 75, 75, 86, 99, Quaker, bur , 99, 375, Richbell, 73. 75, Rogers, 319, St Paul, Parish Church, 260, Spicer, 383, Stout, 319, 347*, 362*, bur , 365, Topanemus, 4, Wall, Middletown, bur , 161, Willson's, 210, Woburn, 178
BUSH, Jame, md , 60
   Sarah wid , 197, md , 197, b , 197
BUTCHER, Ann, b , 156, dau , 156
   Hester, w , 156, mo , 156
   Thomas, fa , 156, husb , 156
BUTLER (see ULRICH), Amos, md , 369, 372, propri , 369, 372, husb , 369, descendants, 372
   Mrs Amos, w , 372
   Eliza Stout, w , 369, recd negro, 369, dau , 369
   Elizabeth Stout, w , 369
   Susannah, md 209
BUTTERNUTS, valley of the, 52
BUTTERWORTH, Quakers, 378
   Ann (Anna†), w , 376, 379**†, convey , 376, dau , 379, md , 379, mo , 379**†, decd , 379
   Benjamin, m l , 167, 379*, md , 376, 379*, husb , 376, 378, 379*, convey , 376, fa , 378, 379**, s , 379**, step-s , 379, leg , 379, weaver, 379, farmer, 379, res , 379
   Benjamin, Jr , s , 376, leg , 376
   David, s , 376, 379*, leg , 376, 379, d , 379, step grands , 379
   Elizabeth, dau , 378, 379, leg 378, sis ,378*, res , 378, md , 379, w , 379

BUTTERWORTH, Continued
   Hannah, step-dau , 376, dau law, 376, mo , 376**, 378, w , 378
   John, s , 379, b , 379, d , 379, md , 379*, prchs , 379, farmer, 379, res , 379
   Joseph s , 376, 378, 379*, leg , 376, 379, md , 378*, 379*, cousin, 378*, 379, husb , 378*, 379 fa , 378**, 379**, ackn , 378, Quaker, 378,* stepgrands , 379, farmer, 379, brewer, 379
   Joseph, Jr , s , 379, md , 379
   Lettice, leg , 378, sis , 378*, dau , 378, 379, res , 378
   Mary, dau , 379, b , 379, d , 379, md , 379*, w , 379, mo , 379**
   Rachel, w , 379*
   Samuel, s , 379, d , 379, md , 379
   Sarah, dau , 378*, 379, leg , 378*, w , 378**, 379**, mo , 378**, 379**, sis , 378*, res , 378

C

CADY, Miss, dau , 249*, md , 249
   David, s , 249, res , 249
   Martha (Patty†), w , 249†, mo , 249**†
   Shellac, md , 249, res , 249, fa , 249**
CAMMOCK, Mary, w , 317
   Nathaniel, md , 317
CAMPBELL, James, md , 337
   John, Esq , judge, 183
   Mabel Stout, w , 337
   Robert (Rob⁴), jr , declr , 90, 91, sig , 91
CAMPION, Mr H Clifford, Jr , res , 380, author , 380
CANADA, expedition agnst , 77
CANBY, Mary, md , 157, mo , 157**, 380**, w , 380
CANDEE, Katherine, dau , 287
   John, s , 287
   Joseph, md , 287, fa , 287**, res , 267
   Lyman, s , 287
   Sarah Ann, w , 287, mo , 287**
CANNON (CONON†), Jemima Mott (Jemine Mott), dau , 87†, w , 87†, 110⁶, leg , 87
   John, husb , 87†, m l , 110⁶, md , 110⁶
CAPE MAY, Spicers of, 294
CARBINE, Francis, md , 334, m l , 334
   Mary Stout, w , 334
CARHART, Eliza, w 286, mo , 286, grandmo , 287**
   Margaret Pool, md , 286, dau , 286, b , 286, living, 287, mo , 287*
   William, fa , 286, husb , 286, grandfa , 287**, cattle-mark, 310, 313
CARLE, Rachel, md , 341, mo , 341**, 342**
   Uriah, judgmt agnst 90, re dispute, 90
CARLISLE, Catherine, md , 138, mo , 138**
CARMAN (CARMEN), family ment ,84
   Mr , convey , 362, farm, 362
   Ann, w , 377
   Daniel, husb , 86*
   Deborah, md , 99, m l , 99, d , 99, mo , 99*
   Jacob, md , 377, res , 377, fa , 377, d intest , 377, est invt , 377

CARMAN, Continued
    John bill pd 230, s 377*, exr, 377,
        step-s, 377*, leg, 377, rid, 377
    Joseph, dep 84, md 110ᵇ
    Martha Mott, dau, 86, w 86*, leg,
        86
    Ruth Mott, w, 110ᵇ
    Samuel appr, 365
    Sarah w, 377, wid, 377, admrx,
        377, mo, 377
CARPENDER (see CARPENTER),
    Miss, mo, 371**, w, 371
    Elizabeth, md, 367, 370, half-sis,
        370, mo, 370*
    Frances, md 367, 370, half-sis, 370,
        sis law, 370 mo, 370**, grandmo,
        370**, as Miss, w, 371 half-sis,
        371
    John md, 368
    Sarah Stout, w, 368
    William, fa, 371, shipmaster, 371,
        md 371, his dau, 371, as Capt,
        named for, 371, fa, 371, md, 371
CARPENTER (see CARPENDER),
    Ann w 92, mo, 92
    Rebecca Mott, w, 110ᵇ
    Samuel, md, 110ᵇ
    Sarah, md, 43, as Miss, md, 52,
        mo, 52**, 53**
CARPENTER'S GUILD, London, leg,
    152*, poor of, do, 152
CARR (KARR†), Andrew, md, 70†
    Ann Morris (Nancy Morris†), w,
        70*†
    Rachel, md, 341, mo, 341**, 342**
    Robert, address by, 73, commr, 73,
        expedition, 73
CARROLL (CARYL†), Miss, md, 371,
    living 371, mo, 371*
    Deborah, dau, 312, b, 312, d, 312,
        md, 312
    John md, 312, fa, 312
    Margaret Stout, w, 312, mo, 312
    Mariana Mott, w, 83†
    Mary Ann (Mary Anne), dau, 83**,
        w, 83 leg, 83, mo 83
    Patrick md, 83†, husb, 83†
CARTER, Isaac, md, 66
    Lawrence, oath 222
    Sarah Ann, w, 66
CARTERET-Bryant Book, ment, 349
    Philip, grants land, 25
CARY, Martha Jefferson, md, 53, cou-
    sin, 53, res, 53, d, 53, mo, 53**
    Thomas, recpt, 261**, sig, 261**
CASH (see COOK), Major James, md,
    129
    Margaret w, 129
CASTLE HILL ment, 220
CATHARINE, a sloop cleared, 88
CATSKILL (see KATSKILL)
CATTELL, Jonas, md, 156, 379
    Mary w 379, md, 379
    Mary Ogborne, w, 156
CAULKINS, N M, author, 294
CEDAR, ship, ment, 178
CEDAR CREEK ment, 362
CEMETERIES (see BURYING-
    GROUNDS, CHURCHYARDS,
    YARDS), Allentown Presbyterian,
    144**, Atlantic View, Manasquan,
    141, Bayville, 323, Cold Spring,
    382, Fairview 8, house near, 120,
    tombs, 238, 248**, 249, do, Mid-
    dletown, 121, 131, do, bur, 131,

CEMETERIES, Continued
    Greenwood, Trenton, 137, King's
    Chapel-yard, bur, 178, Magnolia,
    271, Maplewood, Freehold, 139,
    Old, Tom's River, bur, 366, Pres-
    byterian, Woodbridge, bur, 331,
    Seabrook, 238, Topanemus, bur,
    119*
CENSUS, of Hempstead, 72 74, 75, So
    83, 219, Mott in, 91, of Westches-
    ter, Mott in, 75
CHADWICK, in Rev War, 325, in War
    1812, 324
    Amelia w, 324
    Ann, md, 325, dau, 325, b, 325, d
        325, mo, 325**
    Elizabeth, w, 325, mo, 325, grand-
        mo, 325**
    Margaret, md, 65, b, 65, d, 65, mo,
        65**, grandmo, 65
    Mary, w, 8, mo, 8, b, 8, grandmo,
        8*
    Thomas, substitute, 324, husb, 324,
        bro, 324, as Capt, husb, 325, fa,
        325, grandfa, 325**, sol, 325
CHALKLEY, Martha Spicer, w, 293
    Thomas, md, 293
CHAMBERLAIN (CHAMBERLAYNL,
    CHAMBERLIN†, CHAMBER-
    LING††), Ann, w, 42†, 317, mo,
    42†, grandmo, 42**†
    Elizabeth Stout, w, 363††
    Enoch, md, 123, d, 123, age, 123,
        wit 139
    Ezekiel, s, 138, d, 138, age, 138,
        bur, 138
    Hannah, dau, 135, sis, 135*, md,
        135, 139, b, 135, 139, d, 135, 139,
        dau, 139
    Harriet, dau, 138, md, 138, mo, 139
    Henry, s, 42, b, 42, md, 42, 317,
        fa, 42*, remov, 42, husb, 42,
        grandfa, 42**
    Jane Mount w, 135, 139
    Jesse, md, 363††
    John, md, 35, 42†, 135, 138, 139, 334,
        est admn, 41, his wid, 41, res,
        41, 128, s, 42*†, 135, 139, 334, re-
        mov, 42, bur, 42†, 138†, admn,
        42†, fa, 42**†, 135**, 138*, 139**,
        348, bondsm, 42, s law, 123, exr,
        123, prchs, 128, bro, 135*, husb,
        135, 348, b, 138, d, 138, age, 138,
        grandfa, 139, as Esq, letter to, 30
    Joseph, s, 42, remov, 42
    Lewis, s, 42, md, 42, 123, remov,
        42, d, 123, age, 123, fa, 334
    Lucretia Wolsey, w, 42
    Mary, dau, 123, leg, 123, md, 136,
        b, 136, d, 136, age, 136
    Mary Mount, w, 123, d, 123, age,
        123
    Mary Stout, w, 334, 340
    Philena (Philina), dau, 42*, 348, m 1,
        42, 348, md, 348, res, 348,
        grandmo, 348, sis, 349
    Rachel, dau, 123, leg, 123
    Rachel Mount, w, 123, d, 123, age,
        123
    Rebecca (Rebecka), wid, 41, admrx,
        41, res, 41, dau, 123, 135, 139,
        leg, 123, md, 134, 139, sis, 135*,
        w, 348, mo, 348
    Rebecca Morris, w, 35, 42†, admrx,
        42, mo, 42**

CHAMBERLAIN, Continued
    Rebecca Mount, w, 135, 138, mo,
        135**, 138*, 139**, d, 138, age,
        138, grandmo, 139
    Richard, s, 42, remov, 42, md, 340;
        bro, 349
CHAMBERS, Alexander, md, 99
    Ann, wit, 23, w, 23, md, 120, m 1,
        120
    Elizabeth, md, 142, mo, 142**
    Hannah, dau, 226, b, 226
    John, fa, 171, 225, husb, 171, 225,
        m 1, 175, grandfa, 225, yeom,
        226, res, 226, prchs, 226, g grand-
        fa, 232**
    Margaret Mott, w, 99
    Mary, md, 171, 172, 225, wid, 171,
        dau, 171, w, 171, 225*, mo, 171,
        172*, 225**, intended w, 172, re
        trust, 172, release, 172, sis, 172,
        grandmo, 225, 232**, b, 226, g-
        grandmo, 232**
    Richard (Richᵈ), md, 23, wit, 170,
        bro, 172*, trust, 172, releases,
        lands, 172, exr, 172, as Esq, bro,
        172, trust, 172, sig, 172
    Thomas (Thoˢ), fa, 226, prchs, 321,
        res, 321, yeom, 321
CHAMPLICE, Rebekah, md, 173
CHANCELLOR, Mary, servt, 210, leg,
    210
CHANCELLORSVILLE, Battle of, 109
CHANDLER Elizabeth, m 1, 68
    Lauretta, md, 149
    Lydia, w, 47, 51, mo, 47, 51
    Mary Morris, w, 47
CHANNELHOUSE (CHANEL-
    HOUSE), Adam, fa, 170, decd,
    170
    Mary, res, 170, convey, 170, 171,
        dau, 170
CHAPELS OF EASE, ment, 264, 265
CHAPMAN, Isaac, md, 99
    John, yeom, 331, res, 331, convey,
    331
    Mary Mott, w, 99
CHARLESTON (CHARLSTON), inva-
    sion of 261, Wills, ment, 261
CHARLTON, Richard (Rich), wit,
    221
CHARLOTTE PRECINCT, ment, 87
CHASEY, Bible rec, 50
    Mr, md, 50
    Audery, w, 120
    Elizabeth, w, 121
    John, fa, 41, md, 120, 121, wit,
        235, mark, 235
    Margaret, dau 41
    Rebecca, mo, 50, ment, 50*
    Rebecca Cox, w, 50
CHEPSTOW CASTLE, ment, 21
CHERRY HALL, ment, 78, Papers,
    ment, 79*, 80, 90, 91*, 100**, 162*,
    163, 192, 346, do, rei, 77**, 78,
    101*, 102**, 103**, 104**
CHESHIRE, Joel, exr, 48
CHESTER, Meeting House, md, 378,
    township, ment, 378
CHESTERFIELD, Monthly Meeting,
    ment, 116, 132, do, md, 155*
CHIGARORA (CHINGARORAS)
    CREEK, ment, 298
CHINGARORAS BAY, ment, 78
CHRIST CHURCH (see SHREWS-
    BURY)

CHRISTEEN (CHRITEEN), ment, 297
CHRISTIANSE, Peter, will, 366, res, 366, boatman, 366
CHRISTOPHER, Mr, md, 285
   Amelia Shepherd, b, 283, w, 283
   Eleanor Shepherd, w, 285
   Thomas, md, 283
CHURCH, CHURCHES, contributions to, 107, educational purposes 95, land donated, at Manasquan, 146, leg of slaves 265*, recd half tine, 21, re service, pageanty, 30, Arch St Meeting, 382, Baptist, erection of 307, established, 379, do, hist, 295, do, Meeting Yard, 376, do, memb of, 112, 307, do, site 298, do, rec, 309, do, Hightstown, ment, 134, do, rec, 146, do Hopewell, dea of, 354, do, pastor of, 349, do, Middletown, memb of, 112, 212, 226, 233, 326, 346, 317, do, ment, 46, 182, 188, 224, do, rec, 41, 312, 360, do, rec book, 212, do, trust of, 162, do, Montgomery County, ment, 212, do, Pennypack ment, 379, rec, 212, do, Upper Freehold, ment, 46, do, Welsh Tract, 330*, First Baptist, dea, 107, do, Columbia village, 332, do, Philadelphia, bp regist, 213, do, md book, 212, do, md rec, 212, do, rec, 212, do, regist of memb, 212, Brick, Marlboro, bur, 284, Burlington Monthly Meeting, 378, Chester Meeting House, 378, Chesterfield Monthly Meeting, 132, Christ, md at, 183, do, rec, 45, do, Philadelphia, md, 183, 209, 212, 213 do, rec, 277, do, Shrewsbury, bp, 2, 3, 4, 23, 24, 39, 44**, 45, 46, 69, 122**, 133, 283, 365, do, bur and d, 24, do, md, 24, do, rec, 54, do, regist, rec, 4, Dunstable, poor leg, 262, do, Priory, rec, 258, tablets, 258, Dutch, bp, 73, 74, 81, do rec, 54, 72, 110, 258, do, Freehold, bp, 323, do, New York City, 118, Edisto, ment, 265**, of England, leg, 96, Episcopal, ment, 261*, 265, 271*, do, hist of, 261, do, Middletown, ment, 302, Shrewsbury, rec, 362, Friends' Meeting, ment, 107, do, leg, 15, do, rec, 378, of Gloucester, ment, 256, Grace, pastor of 271, at Hopewell, ment, 296*, 297, 332*, do, bp, 332, Luton, ment, 258, North, bp, 214, do, rec, 365, Parish, Jamaica, ment, 76, do, re dissenters, 31, re ejectment suits, 31, Pennypack Baptist, ment, 379*, Philadelphia Quarterly Meeting, rec, 382, Presbyterian, elder of, 250, do, leg, 96, do, monument to donors, 265, do, rec, 106, 110, 110*, 110b, do, Cold Spring, ment, 293, do, Cranbury, elder of, 126, do, Indianapolis, ment, 129, do, Middletown, ment, 281, do, New York, rec, 122, do, Shark River, ment, 232, do, First Presbyterian, Cranbury (Cranberry), ment, 117, 128, do, elder of, 127,

CHURCH, CHURCHES, *Continued*
do, New York, bp 368*, Quaker Meeting House, ment, 81, Reformed, ref, 12, do Freehold, 12, do, First Reformed, bp, 247**, Ryement, 75, St Andrew (St Andrew's), ment, 177, do, Parish, 177, do, Yard, 377, St Buttolph, Parish, 178, St Ethelred, ment, 177, St George's (St George), ment, 76, 83, 87*, 88, 110**, 110**, 110b**, do, bp 97, 110°, md, 86, 97, 98, 110°, do, Parish, ment, 96, 177, St John's, bur, 251, St Mark's, ment, 271**, rector of, 271, St Mary (St Mary's), recment, 12, Parish of Vestrym, 95, do, Burlington, rec, 189, Southampton, rec, 365, Tennent, bp, 117**, 118, 126**, 130*, Old Tennent, ment, 127, hist of, 126, bp, 126, Tottengen ment, 176, Trinity, Rector of, 43, 195, 370, do New York, Vestrym of, 32, Westbury Monthly Meeting, 96, Yellow Meeting House, ment, 13, memb of 173, do, Allentown, ment, 137
CHURCH FLATS, The, ment, 260
CHURCH HILL bp 244
CHURCHILL, Mary, dau, 152, leg, 152
   Ogborne, grands, 152**, leg, 152**
   Richard, grands, 152, leg, 152
   Sarah, granddau, 152*, leg, 152*
CHURCHYARDS (see BURYING GROUNDS, CEMETERIES, YARDS), Baptist, Hightstown, ment, 133, 140, do bur 166, Baptist, Holmdel, ment, 164, do, bur, 339, 354, do, tombs, 350, Baptist, Middletown, bur, 281*, 316, 356, Christ, bur, 199*, do, Shrewsbury, bur, 198*, Crosswicks Methodist, ment, 155, Edisto Island, Presbyterian, ment, 265, 267, 268, Episcopal, Shrewsbury, bur 198*, Hopewell, bur, 337, 338, 340 do tombs, 349, 350, do, Baptist, bur, 340, 348, 349, 352, Presbyterian, Allentown, ment, 137*, do, bur, 315, 316, do, Edisto Island, ment, 267, do, bur, 268* do, Manasquan, ment, 7, do, Middletown, bur, 310, 313, do, Old, tombs 309, 310, Priory, Dunstable tombs, 258, Ryerson, bur, 195, St John's, tombs, 251, St Mary's, Burlington bur, 154*, 155**, 190, Tenrent, ment, 4, do, bur, 119, 247, do, Old, bur, 252, Trinity, bur, 366*, 370, 372, do, rector of, 43, do, New York, bur, 360*, tombs 368
CINCINNATI, Society of, ment, 109
CITY ISLAND, alias Mineford, ment, 219
CIVIL WAR, Henry in, 202, Longstreet in, 235, Mott in 107, 109, Salter in, 205, 206, Seabrook in, 275
CLARK (CLARKE), Miss, w, 193, dau, 193, md, 270, mo, 270**
   Mr, fa, 193, husb, 193
   Mrs, w, 193, mo, 193
   Abigail (Abby†), md, 200†, dau, 200†, d, 200†, age, 200†, mo, 200*†
   Hon Abraham, signer of Declaration

CLARK, *Continued*
of Independence, 200†, fa, 200†, grandfa, 200*†
   Alexander, will, 117, 232, res, 117, 232, yeom, 232, husb, 232, fa, 232**
   Benjamin, s, 232, leg, 232
   Elizabeth (Elisabeth), dau, 94, 232, leg, 94, 232
   Elizabeth Mount, w, 145
   George, md, 145
   Mr Henry, oath before, 222
   James, tombs, 265, donor, 265, ind, 270
   Jane, w, 247, mo, 247**
   John, test, 220†, res, 220†, age, 220†, sojourner, 220†, s, 232, leg, 232
   Joseph (Jo†), wit, 221†
   Mary, dau, 232, leg, 232, w, 382
   Mary Applegate, w, 148
   Mary Seabrook, w, 255, 270, decd, 255, mo, 255
   Peter, appr, 68
   Rachel, wit, 330, md, 380
   Richard, s, 232, leg, 232
   Robert B, md, 148
   Sarah, w, 232, mo 232**, exrx, 232, sis, 232, leg, 232
   Thomas, s, 255
   Thomas S, md, 255, 382, fa, 255
   William, prchs, 38, s, 232, leg, 232
CLASEN, Peter, arb, 290
CLAWSON, Rachel Stout, w, 365
   William (W^m), md, 365
CLAY, Helene Ashfield, w, 38
   Helene Morris, w, 45
   Richard, husb, 38, md, 45
CLAYTON, burying-ground, ment, 326
   Abraham, md, 351
   Alice, mo, 76, w, 76
   Amy Stout, w, 351
   Catherine D, md, 141, b, 141
   David, bndry, 326
   Licey Stout, w, 363
   Elizabeth Stout (Betsy Stout†), w, 363†
   Hannah, md, 140
   Harriet (Hetty†), md, 136†, dau, 136†, remov, 136†
   John, fa, 76, 136, husb, 76, 326, md, 139, 363, bur, 326, w bur, 326
   Martha, ment, 78*
   Peter, md, 363
   Phebe Mount, w, 139
   Sarah, dau, 76, m 1 76, md, 76, 77
CLEMENT, John, author, 294, res, 294
CLENDENING, Miss, md, 370
CLERGY (see MINISTERS), attack of, 30
CLINE (CLYNE, KLEIN†, KLINE††), Miss, md, 288, mo, 288†, res, 288†
   Mr, md, 199, res, 199, fa, 199**
   Charles, neph, 198, leg, 198
   Ephraim, md, 99, 102, fa, 99**
   Frances (Fanny†), dau, 199, res, 199, niece, 199
   Frances S, niece, 198*, 199††, leg, 198*, 199††
   Jesse L, neph, 198, leg, 198
   Joseph, s, 199
   Julius, md, 229†
   Mary Tom, w, 129†
   Rachel, w, 99, 102, mo, 99**

INDEX

CLINE, *Continued*
  Rachel Saltar, w, 199, mo, 199**
  Rebecca, dau, 199, md, 199, remov, 199
  Richard S, neph, 198, leg, 198
CLINTON in Militia, 44
  Governor, his Co, 44
CLOVER HILL, ment, 318, 352*
CLOWS (CLOWES), Catharine, md, 110b
CLUNG, John, his place, 243
COATTS, Mary, w, 379, mo, 379
CODWISE, Edward Bertie (Edward B), s 204 207, b, 207, md, 207, fa, 207*, as Mr, res, 207, author, 207
  Elisha R, md, 204, fa, 240*
  Emma, w, 207, mo, 207*
  Harrietta Frances, dau, 207, b, 207
  Harrietta Matilda, w, 204, mo, 204*, 207, grandmo, 207*
  Henry Rogers, s, 207, b, 207
  Louisa Saltar, dau, 204, b, 204
COE, Robert, judgm agnst, 292, deft, 292
COFFEE HOUSES, ment, 101
COFFIN, Charles Carleton, author, 186
  Sarah, md, 358
COGWELL, Harriet, md, 106, dau, 106, mo, 106
  Dr James, fa, 106, grandfa, 106; res, 106
COIL, James, md, 69, res, 69
  Rachel Morris, w, 69*
COLD SPRING, Cemetery, monument, 382, Graveyard, bur, 293, Presbyterian Church, re parsonage, 293
COLD SPRING INLET, ment, 293, Graveyard near, bur, 293
COLE Elizabeth, md, 69
  Mary md, 154*, 377, m 1, 154, mo, 154, 155**, w, 376, 377
  Samuel, convey, 292, md, 376, husb, 376
COLE'S CREEK, ment, 116
COLEMAN, Miss, has letters, 193
  Mr, md, 274, res, 274
  Mrs, mo, 203, author, 203
  Annie F, w, 203, mo, 203**
  Annie Saltar (Annie S †), dau, 203, as Miss dau, 203†, author, 203†
  Caleb, md, 108
  James Pearson (J P, J Pearson), s, 203, as Dr, md, 203, res, 203, 207, fa 203**, 207, grandfa, 207
  Dame Joyce, w, 152*, leg, 152, exrx, 152
  Phebe Rose Mott, w, 108
  Sarah Pearson (Sallie Pearson), dau, 203, as Miss, md, 207, dau, 207, mo 207
  Sarah Seabrook, w, 274
  Walter s law, 152*, leg, 152, draper, 152, res, 152, adjust, 152, husb, 152*, exr 152
COLES, Anne (Nancy†), md, 88†, 97, b, 97, d, 97, mo, 97**, grandmo, 97**
  Gloriana res 97, md, 97, mo, 97
  Ruth Mott w, 88
  Stephen md, 88
COLGATE Romulus R, md, 204
  Susan, w, 204
COLLINS Mrs house, 246
  Mary Ann, md, 253, b, 253, mo, 253**

COLTON, family, hist of, ment, 218
COLT'S NECK, ment, 1, 282, 298, 318, 319
COLUMBIA, S C, rec, 264**
COLUMBIA, College of Medicine, 106*, village, First Baptist Church, organized, 332
COLVE, Anthony (A), issues pass, 16*, sig, 16*, as Gov Genl, letter to, 17*
COMBS (COOMBS†), Mr, md, 234
  Amy, md, 143, mo, 143**
  Ann, md, 119*, mo, 119**
  Elizabeth, md, 142
  Huldah, w, 234
  Joseph, fa, 119
  Phebe, md, 119*, b, 119*, d, 119*, age, 119, mo, 119**, 134, grandmo, 119**, w, 134
  Rebecca, md, 142
  Rebecca Mount, w, 142
  Thomas, md, 142
  William (W^m), md, 257†, m 1, 257†, res, 257†
COMMISSIONS (COMMISSIONERS, see under LOAN)
COMPTON (COMTON†), Cornelius, m 1, 62, md, 62, d, 62, appr, 365
  Cornelius, Jr, md, 118, m 1, 118, d, 118, will, 118
  Emma Shepherd, w, 286, s p, 286
  Hannah Mount, w, 118, md, 118
  Hannah Shepherd, w, 286, s p, 286
  Job, md, 286*, s p, 286*
  Judah, wit, 232†
  Lydia, w, 62, 314, wid, 62, mo, 314, grandmo, 314**
  Mary, md, 70
  Phebe, md, 363, res, 363
  William (Will†), sig, 365†, bondsm, 365†, res, 365†, yeom, 365†, will, 365, fa law, 365
COMPTON'S CREEK, bndry, 224
COMSTOCK, Julia A, md, 64, b, 64, d, 64, mo 64**
CONASCUNK (CONASCONCK, CONLSCONCK, CONESCONK, CONESCUNK, CONNESKUNK), bndry, 78
CONCKLIN, Catharine Elizabeth, w, 149, d, 149
  William, md, 149
CONEY ISLAND, hogs on, 301
CONGER, John S, wit, 239
  Rebecca, md, 358, mo, 358**
CONNECTICUT RIVER, ment, 367**, Indian war re, 300
CONNELLY, Col John, res, 241, md, 241, as "Uncle Connelly," re his w's d, 241, fa, 241, md, 241, s, 241
CONNER (see CONYRS), Commodore David md, 99, d, 99, fa, 99
  P S P, s, 99, res, 99, grands, 99
  Susan, w, 99, mo, 99
CONNESKUNK NECK, alias Hartshorne's Neck, 307
CONOVER (see COVLNHOVEN), Miss, md, 345*, mo, 345**, grandmo, 345*
  Mr, md, 128, fa, 128
  Agnes, w, 285
  Albert, md, 285, fa, 285**
  Anna, dau, 128, mo, 128
  Ann Mount, w, 128, mo, 128, d, 128

CONOVER, *Continued*
  Anne Seabrook, w, 254, b, 254
  Catharine, w, 285
  Catharine Morris, w, 41, age, 41
  Charles (Big Charley), house, 362
  Clementine, dau, 285, md, 285
  Cornelius, md, 284, s p, 284
  Daniel, s, 285, md, 285
  Eleanor (Elinor, Nellie†), md, 119†, 285, dau, 285
  Elias, his farm, 282, as Col, his farm, 281
  Elisha, s, 285, md, 285
  Elizabeth, w, 283, mo, 283, grandmo, 283**
  Elizabeth Mount (Betsy Mount†), w, 121†
  Elizabeth Shepherd, w, 285, mo, 285**
  Elizabeth Stout, w, 364, res, 364
  George, s, 285, md, 285
  Gertrude (Gertjet), g grandmo, 254†, md, 254†
  Hannah Shepherd, w, 284
  Jacob, md, 364, res, 364
  James, md, 284
  John, md, 41, s, 128, grands, 128, s, 128, leg, 128
  Lucy Shepherd, b, 284, w, 284
  Maria, mo, 9, w, 9, grandmo, 9*, 10*
  Mary, w, 119, md, 311
  Mary D, w, 285
  Matthias, md, 121
  Peter, md, 119, 285, s, 285
  Rennie Hendrickson, w, 361
  Sarah, dau, 285
  Sarah Ann (Sarah A †), md, 6†, 9, dau, 9, mo, 9*, 10**, obit, 10, age, 10
  Sarah Shepherd, w, 285
  Sidney B, md, 361
  Tylee, fa, 9, husb, 9, grandfa, 9*, 10*
  William, md, 254
CONREY, John, m 1, 69
CONTENT, sloop, ment, 366
CONWAY, Catharine, md, 286, dau, 286, mo, 286**
  Thomas, fa, 286, grandfa, 286**
CONYRS (see CONNER), Mr, md by, 257
COOK (COOKE, see CASH), Abiel, fa, 123*, 376**, grandfa, 123, 124**, 376, cor, 376, s, 376**, d, 376, as the third, fa, 376
  Amor (Amos?), s, 51, md, 51, b, 51, d, 51, fa, 58, 60, husb, 58, 60
  Caroline, md, 8, dau, 8, b, 8*, mo, 8*, d, 8
  Catharine, wid, 309, md, 309, d, 309
  David, md, 60, s, 60
  Deborah, w, 58, mo, 58
  Deborah Brewer, w, 51
  Ebenezer, prchs, 319, yeom, 319, res, 319, convey, 319
  Edward Patterson (Edward P †), exr, 46, 47, res, 47, wit, 17, fa, 47, 51, husb, 47, 51, his wid, 309†
  Elias (see Ellis), appli of, 89
  Elizabeth, wit, 170, dau, 381**, leg, 381**, sis, 381**, w, 381**, exrx, 381, md, 381, wit, 381, mo, 381**, d, 381

INDEX 395

COOK, Continued
Elizabeth Bickley w , 381
Ellis (see Elias), appli of, 89, fa , 376, s , 376, husb , 376, grandfa , 376
Frances, w , 59, 134, mo , 59, 123, 124**, 134, m 1 , 115, b , 115, 123, d , 115, 123, bur , 115, md , 123, sis , 123, dau , 123, 376
Hannah, md , 120, wit , 120, grandmo , 120**
Major James, md , 129
John, md , 58, 69, s , 58, b , 58, d , 58, res , 60
Joseph, bndry , 232
Louise Catherine, w , 60
Lydia, w , 47, 51 , mo , 47, 51
Margaret, w , 48, 129, mo , 48, md , 134
Martha, mo , 376, w , 376, grandmo , 376
Mary, md , 205, res , 205, mo , 205
Mary Ann, w , 60, mo , 60
Mary Chadwick, w , 8, mo , 8, grandmo , 8*
Mary Morris (Molly Morris), w , 47, 58, as Mrs , 69*†, res , 69†
Nathaniel, fa , 48, husb , 48, bro , 123, s 123
Parthenia, dau , 12, leg , 12
Penelope, age, 220, test , 220
Peter md , 47, s , 47
Rev'd Mr Samuel, ment , 37
Sarah, leg , 48, dau , 48, granddau , 48
Thomas (Tho°), wit , 170, s , 381**, leg , 381*, bro , 381**, md , 381, fa , 381**, wit , 381, husb , 381, d , 381*, will, 381
William, fa , 8, husb , 8, grandfa , 8*, grands , 175, 380, 381, leg , 175, 380, 381**, app , 175, 380, s , 381*, bro , 381**, kinsman, 381
COOLEY, Mary A , w , 343
Oliver, md , 343
COOPER, farm of, ment , 1, graveyard on farm, 1
Mrs , letter by, 104*, res , 104
Abigail, md , 133, bp , 133, mo , 133*
Benjamin, md , 132
Catharine, md , 312, mo , 312**, grandmo 312**
Daniel, md , 293
Elizabeth, md , 51, dau , 51
Euphame, w , 164
Euphame Layton, w , 132
Ezekiel m l , 110°
Isaac md , 52, res , 52, bro , 52
J Fenimore, author, 52, bro , 52
Jacob, bro , 168, res , 168
John app , 366, s , 366, fa , 366, mariner, 366, decd , 366
Jonathan, md , 69, res , 69
Joseph, md , 132 164*, res , 164, husb , 164
Lydia, md , 284, 286, mo , 286**
Margaret, w , 51, mo , 51
Martha, w , 164
Mary, md , 54, mo , 54*
Mary Morris, w , 52
Phebe, wid , 309, md , 309
Philip, bondsm , 3, res , 3, fa , 51, husb , 51
Rebecca 5 , w , 132
Sarah Morris, w , 69*, res , 69

COOPER, Continued
Sarah Spicer, w , 293
Simon, convey , 34, chirurgeon, 38, sell , 38
Thomas (Tho°), res , 180*, mer , 180, issued power atty , 180*
COOPER'S, BRIDGE, ment , 1
COOPER'S CREEK, ment , 292
CORBETT, Mary, sis , 37, will, 37, aunt, 37
CORBIN, Helen, md , 343, mo , 343*
CORE, Luce Stout, w , 364
Timotny, md , 364
CORIELL, Eliza Boice, w , 256, mo , 256, grandmo , 256
CORLEAR'S HOOK, ment , 299, Indians attacked at, 300
CORLIES (CURLES†, CURLEIS††, CURLICE†††, CURLIS††††, see CURTIS) Mr , deft , 291†
David, fa , 57
Elizabeth, w , 121, mo , 121, grandmo , 121**
Elizabeth Mount, w , 132, tombs , 132, d 132, age, 132
George, age, 171††, res , 171††, test , 171††, friend, 175††††, leg , 175††††, took int t , 171††
Gertrude Ann, w , 57
Hannah Hartshorne, w , 194, d , 194
Jacob, fa , 56, husb , 56, md , 194
John, buy , 39†††
Joseph, md , 57, s , 57
Lucy G , w , 61, mo 61
Rachel, w , 56, mo , 56, md , 379, wid , 379, b , 379, d , 379
Richard md , 132, b 132, d , 132
Sarah White, md , 56, dau , 56, b , 56, d , 56
CORNBURY, Lord, his Council, 28, letter of, 28, offended, 28, commanded 28, opinion of, 28, ment , 33, suspended by, 33, apology to, 33, as Gov, 181*
Edward, Viscount, ackn before, 305, 306
CORNELL (CORNEL), family, geneal of, 110
Ann, w , 76, leg , 76, dau , 76
Ann Mott, w , 76
Rev John, author, 110
Miriam Mott (Meriam Mott), w , 76, 110°, res , 76
Rebecca, wit , 74
Richard, md , 76, husb , 76, as Mr , ovsr , 222
Samuel, md , 76, husb , 76*, 105, bro , 87, exr , 87, decd , 105
Sarah, w , 105, wid , 105
Thomas C (T C †), author, 93†, 94†, author, 110, as Mr , author, 93†
Tennis (Tunnis†), his acct , 100†
William, Jr , md , 110°
CORNWALLIS (CORN WALLIS†), ment , 368, capture of, 242†
CORNWELL, John magist , 72
CORSEN (CORSON), Christian, will, 234, fa law, 234
Daniel, husb , 234, b , 234, d , 234
John, pet , 189, re admn est , 189
Mary, w , 234, exrx , 234, dau law, 234
CORWIN, Caroline Corsen, w , 254
William, md , 254, res , 254

COSBY, Gov , arrival, 30, letter of, 30*, 31, revolt agnst , 30, re remov , 31
COTTERLLL (COTTRELL), Ann, w , 119
Samuel (Sam†), re seeds, 103†
William, md , 119
COTTMAN, Esther, w , 379, mo , 379, b 379, d , 379
COUNCIL OF SAFETY, ment , 90, order of, 191
COUNTY, COUNTIES, (see County names and under families), Monmouth, rec , 77
COURT, Orphans', rec , 382
COVENHOVEN (see CONOVER), Mr , md , 120
Anna (Anne), md , 233, 284, remov , 233, mo 284*
Eleanor (Nelly†), md , 69†
Elizabeth, guard , 132, sis , 132
Garret, md , 363
Jacob, s , 238, guard , 238, fa , 238, decd , 238, res , 238
Mary, w , 120
Matthias W , prchs , 162
Nelly (see Eleanor)
Peter, bndry , 213
Ruth Stout, w , 363
William (Wilhemus†), ment , 298†
COW NECK (COWNECK), ment , 74, 80**, 81, 82**, 87, 92*, 93*, 94, 105, Survey of Highways, 83
COWARD, Deliverance, md , 234, mo , 234, grandmo , 234
Hugh, md , 328, m 1 , 328
John, s , 189, quit-claim, 189, heir, 189
Patience, w , 328
Sarah, md , 361, mo , 361
COWGILL, - & Stout, curriers, 374, res , 374
John, md , 347
Martha Stout, w , 347
COWPERTHWAITE, Ann dau , 175, w , 175, mo , 175*, leg , 175
Hugh, friend, 175, leg , 175, 380
John, husb , 175, fa , 175*
COX (COXE), claims of, 318, family, letter re, 114
Dr , remov , 179
Miss, md , 280, mo , 280**
Mr , md , 134, 279, 280, remov , 134, fa , 280, grandfa , 280**, letter to, 316
Aaron, s , 210, 212, leg , 210
Anne, dau , 210, 212, leg , 210
Anne Mount, w , 131
Benjamin, uncle, 114, letter to, 114
Daniel (Dan), memb council, 28, address, 28
Elijah, s , 210, 212, leg , 210
Elisha, s , 210, 212, leg , 210
Elizabeth dau , 210, 212, leg , 210
Eseck, s , 125, md , 125, b , 125, d , 125
Frederick, md , 131, res , 131
James, appr , 112, took invt , 112, bro , 115, div est , 115, bndry, 189, md , 189, res , 189, d , 189, fa , 212, grandfa , 212**
John, s , 115, 212, leg , 115, 210, res , 115, 210, 212, will, 115, bro , 115, 210, fa , 115**, 210**, 212**, husb , 115, grandfa , 175**, step-s , 209, leg , 210, step-bro , 210, 212
John, Jr (John, minor), m l , 09

INDEX

COX *Continued*
Joseph farmer 114, res, 114**, 125, md, 114**, grandfa, 114, b, 114, d, 114*, age, 114, s, 115, leg, 115, fa, 125, husb, 125, will, 125
Margaret Mount, w, 134, remov, 134
Mary, md 43, 52, 119, mo, 52**, 115, 110**, 125 w, 115, 110, 125, grandmo, 115**, dau, 210, 212, leg, 210, m l, 211, step-sis, 211, re b, 211
Mary Mount, w, 114**, b, 114, dau, 114, grandmo, 114*, res, 114, d, 114
Paul, s, 210, 212, leg, 210
Rachel, md, 115, dau, 115, 210, 212, mo, 115**, w, 125, leg 210
Rebecca (Rebeckah), m l, 50*, md, 50, 135, ment, 50*, dau, 135, 210, 212, 278, mo 135** 136**, w, 189, living, 189, leg, 210, 278*, sis 278
Rebecca Shepherd w, 279, 280, mo, 280, grandmo, 280**
Samuel s 115, leg 115
Samuel J, nepb, 114, letter of, 114, 122, res, 122
Sarah w, 135, mo, 135, grandmo, 135**, 136**
Susanna, dau 210, 212, leg 210
Thomas, bndry, 113*, fa 135, husb, 135, grandfa, 135**, 136**, wit, 185, convey, 308
COX S CORNERS ment, 187
COXHAKKI, Co, Militia at, 178
CRAIG, Sheriff, fa, 284, 286, grandfa, 286**
Catherine, md, 284
Charles L Esq, author, 372, res, 372
Lydia md 284 286, dau, 284, 286, mo, 286**
CRAMER (see CRANMER), family, account of, 323, Quakers, 323
Elizabeth, dau 323
Hannah dau 323
John, s, 323, fa, 323**, res, 323, md, 323, banns, 323
Mary, w, 323, d, 323
Phebe, m l, 84 110°
Rachel, dau, 323
Rebecca, dau, 323
Rebecca Stout, banns, 323, mo, 323**, res, 323, descendants, 323
Semon (Semort) s, 323†
CRANBURY (CRANBERRY†), bp, 128*, 142**, 143*, 144, bur, 126, 128, congregation, 142, rec, 128, tombs, 128, in city of Perth Amboy ment 113 116, Presbyterian Church, elder of, 126, First Presbyterian Church, do, 117, 127, 128†, do, Yard, bur, 117, do, graves in 129
CRANBURY (CRANBERRY†) BROOK ment, 186, bndry, 113†, 116†
CRANE, Sarah (Sally), her Bible, 121, res 121
CRANMER (see CRAMER), family, ment, 323
John, nicknames, 323**
CRATON (see CREIGHTON)
CRAWFORD (CRAFFORD†, CRAFORD†), family, md, 297
Miss md 275†
Mr, md, 311

CRAWFORD, *Continued*
Annie Morris, w, 41, age 41
Catharine (Catherine, Kate†), w, 130, mo, 130, 249†, dau, 238, 249†, 280, granddau, 238, leg, 238, md, 249†, 280, grandmo, 249†
Catharine Shepherd (Katharine Shepherd), w, 279, 280, b, 280, d, 280, mo, 280**, leg, 280
Esther, dau, 280, md, 280, d, 280, age, 280
George, md, 249, mer, 249, res, 249, fa, 249, grandfa, 249, g grandfa, 249, s, 280*, leg, 280
Hannah dau, 7, 130, 280*, mo, 7, md 130, leg, 280
James S, Esq, res, 190, orig paper, 190, decd, 190
Job, md, 41
John, re land, 305††
Lydia, md, 62*, m l, 62*, mo, 63**, 314, w, 314, grandmo, 314**
Margaret, b, 182
Mary Seabrook (Polly Seabrook), w, 249, mo, 249, grandmo, 249, g grandmo, 249
Rebecca, w, 311
Richard (Rich⁴), fa, 7, 130, 280**, grandfa, 7, will, 7, 280, husb, 130, appr, 160, his corner, 162, bond pd, 229, 231*, md 279, 280, s, 280*, m l 280, b, 280, d, 280, res, 280, leg, 280
William, friend, md, 249, exr, 40, 49, renounces as do, 49, res, 40, 49, appr, 160, wit, 240, arb, 247
Mrs William, ill, 102
CRAWFORD'S CORNER, ment, 162
CREAM RIDGE, Yellow Meeting House, graveyard, 183
CREEGER, William Francis, compiler, 323, res, 323
CREEKS, (see BROOKS, RIVERS, RUNS), frozen over, 102, Allawayes, 18, Appoquinimink, 346**, Blackbird, 347, Cedar, 362, Chingarora (Chingaroras), 298, Cole's, 116*, Compton's, 224, Cooper's, 292, Doctor's, 49, 183, 209, 213, Dover, 84, George's, 330*, 346**, John Reves', 224, Lupakitunk, 77, Maple, 156, Millstone, 134, Reve's (see John Reve's), Smith's 240**, Stout's, 325, West, 383*
CREIGHTON (CRATON†), Agnes, md, 285†
CREW, Elizabeth md 379
CRITTENDON, Sarah, md, 343, mo, 343**
CROMWELL, Oliver, The Protector, 14
CRONLY, Eliza Loskiel Bernardo, w, 201, s p, 201
John, md, 201, s p, 201
CROOK, Sarah, md, 287, mo, 287
CROOKES John, propr, 369
CROSS, Jane, w, 375
Thomas, md, 375, husb, 375, will, 375, res, 375, step-fa, 375**, testa, 375
CROSSWICKS (CROSWICKSUM†), "Indian Wright at", 23†, Indian prchs, 23, Methodist Churchyard, bur, 155

CROUCH, William, res, 332, convey, 332
CROXON, Thomas, res, 257, md, 257, m l, 257
CRUSER, Helenah, md, 340, m l, 340, mo, 340, b, 340, d, 340, bur, 340
CUBBERLY, David, md, 127
Elizabeth (Betsey†), md, 204†, mo, 205**†
Elizabeth Mount, w, 127
CUMMINGS (CUMINS†, CUMMINS††), Elizabeth, m l, 125*††, re do, 125†, md, 125, d, 125, mo, 125
William tombs, 265, donor, 265
CUNLIFF, Mr John, re smallpox, 243
CUNNINGHAM, Catherine (Katharine†), md, 174, m 1, 174, mo, 174**, w, 174†, leg, 174†
CUPHEAGE, alias Stratford, 259
CURTIS (see CORLIES), in Militia, 379
Abigail, dau law, 375, owner, 375, dau, 375
Ann (Anne), md, 141*, dau, 141, 375*, b, 141, d, 141, wid, 141, owner, 375
Asher, fa, 141, husb, 141
Charlotte, md, 141, b, 141, d, 141, age, 141
David, fa, 48*, husb, 48*
Elizabeth, md, 48, 156, 252, b, 48, dau, 48, cor, 375, app, 375
George, friend, 175*, leg, 175, 381
Isabel, md, 364, res, 364
Jane, dau, 156, w, 156**, b, 156, mo, 156, 157*, 375*, md, 157*, 375, 380, grandmo, 157**, wid, 375, cor, 380
Jean, wid, 156, md, 156**, mo, 156*, 157**, grandmo, 156*, 157**
Major John, md, 379, res, 379
Jonathan, s law, 375*, s, 375
Lydia, w, 48, mo, 48
Lydia White, w, 48, mo, 48
Mary, w, 379
Dr O O, md, 273, res, 273
Sarah, w, 141, mo, 141
Sarah Seabrook, w, 273
Thomas, fa, 156, 375**, husb, 156, cor, 375, s law, 375, his wid, 375
CUSHMAN, Maria Jane, w, 215
Hon Samuel, md, 215
CUSTIS-MOORE, Caroline, w, 66, mo, 66 grandmo, 66**
CUTHBERT, Thomas, prchs, 192
CYRUS, Lida, m l, 110°

D

DALY, Mr, md, 164, res, 164
Mrs, w, 164
DALZELL, in Militia, 42, in Rev War, 42, Regiment, ment, 42
DANGLER Hannah Maria, w, 67
Samuel C, md, 67
DANIEL'S ISLAND, ment, 273
DANSER, George, wit, 235
DARBY, Hannah Mott, w, 110
John md, 110
DARKINS (DORKINS†), Christian, w, 259†, dau, 259†
Robert, husb, 259, cor, 382
DAVENPORT, Miss, md, 345
Abigail, md, 294, dau, 294, mo, 294**

DAVENPORT, Continued
    Francis, fa , 294, husb , 294, grandfa , 294**
    Sarah w , 294, mo . 294, grandmo , 294**
DAVID, Nicholas, convey , 170
DAVIDSON Mr , md , 242
    John, md , 110b, res , 110b
    Rebecca, w   242
    Rebecca Mott, w , 110b, res , 110b
DAVIS, Mr , md , 54, 57
    Dr Charles, res , 203, extr , 203
    Elizabeth w 131 mo , 131, grandmo , 131**, 132**
    Henry, md , 119
    John, md , 120, remov , 120
    Lydia Morris, w , 54
    Mary E , md , 143
    Mary Elizabeth, w , 57
    Phebe, w , 119
    Rebecca, w , 120, remov , 120
DAVISON, Lydia md , 119
    Lydia A , md , 66
DAWS, Mary, md , 54, mo , 54**, 55*, m l , 68
DAWSON Miss, md , 268, res , 268
DAY Quakers, 375
    Humphrey fa , 294, husb , 294
    Jane, w , 294, mo , 294
    John, cor 375, admr , 375, his acct , 375, Quaker, 375
    Mary, md , 88
    Rebecca, md , 294, m l , 294, dau , 294
DAYTON Charlotte, md , 200, dau , 200, b , 200, d , 200, mo , 200**
    Jonathan, fa , 200, grandfa , 200**
DEACON, Howard Esq , author , 380, res , 380, as Mr author , 183, 211, res 183
DEAL (DEALL), Elizabeth, md , 98, 107, b , 107, d , 107, mo . 107*
DEAN Sarah md 139
DE BONREPOS, Martha, will, 189, res , 180
DEBOW (DEBOGH, DE BOGH), Catharine, dau 46*, leg, 46
    Frances dau , 117†, leg 117†
    Frederick. testa 117, land for sale, 117, res , 117**†, his extr , 117†, will, 117†, husb , 117†, fa , 117*†, grandfa , 117†
    Hannah w , 117*†, leg , 117, mo , 117**, dau , 117, grandmo , 117, extr , 117†
    Lawrence, s , 117†, exr , 117†
    Van Hook, s , 117†, leg , 117†
    Sarah dau , 117†, leg , 117†
    Solomon s 117, leg 117
DE BRUYNE, F , re land bndry , 292
DE FOREST (DE FROSEEST†), Phoebe (flamitiet), md , 367, mo , 367**, 368*
DE GRASSE, Count, his flagship, 371
DE GRAY, Theodosia, w , 122, mo , 122
DE GROOT (DE GROOT, see GROODT), Derrick Jansen sell , 259
    Julia A , md , 60, d , 60
    Richard (see Dernick)
D'HARRIETTE Benjamin, bndry , 263
DEHART (DE HART), Commander, shipwreck, 234
    Capt James, shipwrecked, 234, drowned, 234

DIEHL Kate, md , 277, mo , 277
DELANCY (DELANCEY, see DELANEY), Miss, md , 250, mo , 250**, grandmo , 250
    Mr James, judge, 30
    John William, md , 369, mer , 369, res , 369
    Lunah Stout, w , 369, d , 369
DELANEY (see DELANCY), Miss, md , 250, mo , 250**, grandmo , 250
    John William, md , 369, mer , 369, res , 369
    Lunah Stout, w , 369, d , 369
DE LASTEYRIE, Count, md , 267, res , 267, neph , 267, fa , 267*, his s in war, 267
DELATOSH, Henry, fa , 130, grandfa , 130
    Sophia, md , 130, dau , 130, mo 130
DELWAL (DELAVALL), Mr , guard , 16
    Hannah, s , 302, wid , 302, convey , 302
    John, s , 302, heir, 302, husb , 302
    Thomas (Tho*), as Capt , admr , 24, as Mr , prchs , 302, mer , 302, res , 302, pat , 302, d , 302, fa , 302
DELAWARE, Falls of, ment , 80, 331
DELAWARE RIVER, ment , 18, 25, 202, bndry , 187
DELGADO, Caroline Salter, w , 217
    Marcelo M md , 217
DELIGHT, Privateer, ment , 370
DEMOTT, Miss, md 337, mo , 337
DENING, Eveline, md 357, 359, res , 359, remov , 359, mo , 360**
DENNIS (DENNES†), Anthony, wit , 37, cedar swamp, 238*†
    Major Benjamin, md , 241, res , 241, his wid , 250
    Catherine, md , 136
    Cornelia, wit , 239
    Hannah, w , 241, wid , 241, 250, md 241, 250
    Jacob wit , 319, 321
    Joseph, cooper, 113, prchs 113, wit , 182
    Samuel (Sam †), king's atty , 26, secry , 26, clk 26, shrf 26, prison , 26, just , 171, wit , 321**†
    Samuel, Jr , wit , 319, 321
    Sarah, md , 279, b , 279, d , 279, mo , 279*†
DENNISON Esther Borden L , w , 320, re Bible, 320
    George Taylor, md , 320, fa , 320, re Bible, 320
DENNY, Ann Stout, w , 347, d , 347, age, 347
    Captain Richard, rescue by , 244
    William md , 347
DENTON David, agrmt , , 1
    Deborah, md , 110b
DENYSE Helena, md 235
DERBYSHIRE, Hon W H , Mayor, 258, hist 258
DERWOOD, Miss, md , 275, mo , 275
DE VAUGRIGNEUSE (DE VEATT GRINGUES), Baron, 371, d , 371, Monsieur, md , 371
    Sarah Morris, w , 371, d , 371
DE WITTS, Eleanor, dau , 213, md , 213, leg , 213
    William, md , 213
DE WETT (see DE WITT), Morgan, prchs , 179

DEWITT (see DEWETT), Neeltie, dau , 312, md , 312*, mo , 312
    Richard (Dirckt), will, 312†, res , 312†, grandfa , 312**†, fa , 312†, rich, 312†
DEY (DYE†), Alice Chadwick, w , 325†
    Daniel, md , 134
    Elizabeth, md 139
    Elmer L , s , 166
    Enoch, md , 166, fa , 166**
    James, md , 119
    James P md , 363†
    Lydia, md , 133, b , 133, d , 133, bur 133*, w , 133, 139, 143, mo , 134**, 139, 143, grandmo , 139** 143**
    Margaret, w , 182, b , 182, d , 182, res , 182
    Margaret Mount, w , 119
    Mary E , dau , 166, w , 363†
    Phebe Mount w , 134
    Randolph md , 325†
    Rebecca Ogborne, w , 166, mo , 166**
    Viola md , 166
    William, prchs , 186*†, res , 186†, yeom , 186†
    William, Sr , md , 182, res , 182*, b , 182, d , 182
DIARY, Mott, ment , 88, 91, extract, 78
DICKERSON (DICKESON†), John, husb , 175†, leg , 175†
    Sarah Jane, md , 315, 366, d , 315, 366, mo , 294, mo , 369**
    Susanna, dau , 175†, w , 175†, leg , 175†
DIRTY LANE, alias Sligh Heege, 259
DISBOW, burying-ground, 75
    Benjamin, s , 75, bro , 75**, re bur plot, 75, res , 75
    Henry (Henery), s , 75, bro , 75**, re bur plot, 75, res , 75
    John s 75, bro 75**, re bur plot, 75, res , 75
    Margaret, mo , 75**, re bur plot, 75, res 75
DISBROW, Miss, dau , 127, sis , 127
    Ann md 110, res , 110
    Joseph, bro , 127, fa , 127, guard , 127, admr , 127
DISNEY, Jane, md , 369 d , 369, age, 369, bur 369, mo , 369*
DOBBS, Aaron, fa , 121, grandfa , 122**
    Adam fa , 121, grandfa , 122**
    Ann, md , 122, d , 122, age, 122, cousin, 123
    Margaret md , 121, dau , 121, mo , 122**
DOCKWRA (DOCWRA), heirs of, convey , 115*
    William (Wm), heirs of, convey , 114, res 180, issued power atty , 180*, re comm issued 180
DOCTORS, Bailey 275, James H Baldwin 344, Beach, 249, Maurice Beesley, 294, James Boggs, 44, James Cogwell, 100, J P Cokman, 203, Simon Cooper, 38, Cox, 179, O O Curtis, 273, Charles Davis, 203, Washington Dorsey, 245, 251, Enoch Edwards, 193, Hosea Edwards 377, Ennis, 33, Forman, 282, Aaron Forman, 235, Henry Greenland, 332, Harris, 357, Th (Th*) Henderson, 100*, Jaquish,

DOCTORS, Continued
240. Johnson 383, Laird, 7, Robert Laird, 7, William Lawrence, 98, Peter Le Conte. 79 So, 321, Lee, 240 Legree 268, John Morford, 7, Richard Lewis Morris, 53, Henry Mott, 106*, Valentine Mott, 106*, Timothy Murphy, 147, Nelson, 201, Palmer, 274, Rodger Park 352 Ebnck Parmly, 36, Peachley, 375, Mr Peplow, 257, William Perrine, 129, William Williamson Perrine, 129, Pitney, 102, Pue, 274, John Redman, 380, John Rodman, 175, John Ross 379, Frederick Henry Beesley Saltar, 203, George H Colton Salter, 217, Jos Ely Salter, 207, Thomas Barton Saltar, 203, Nathaniel Scudder, 4*, Benjamin Seabrook, 272, Edward Seabrook, 269, 274, John Seabrook, 269, Milward Seabrook, 257, Thomas Edward Seabrook, 258, Whitemarsh Seabrook, 269, William M Seabrook, 258, William Milward Seabrook, 258*, Slack, 143, Edward Sutton Smith, 286, Samuel Staats, 36, Steele, 279, H H Stevens, 53, Stillwell, 153*, 241, John E (J E) Stillwell, 220, 243*, 247, 249, 274, 383, Richd Stillwell, 231, William Stillwell, 163, 243, 249, William E Stillwell, 249, Jehu Stout, 338, Jonathan Stout, 310, Wessel T Stout, 316, Thomas Hale Streets, 346, Studdiford, 243, Stephen (Stephan, Steven) Talman, 121, 229, 231*, 237, Turnipseed, 269, Van Meul, 283, James Wasse, 22, Charles H White, 286, James William White, 323, Daniel Morris Woolley, 60
DOCTOR'S CREEK, ment, 49, 209, bndry, 183, 213
DODAMEED, Ann, md , 368, bp , 368, mo , 368
DODD, Mary, md , 341
DODDS, Fanny, md , 129, mo , 129
DODGE Charlotte S , w , 364
 Deborah, md , 105
 Ezekial, md , 364
 Phebe, w , 82
 Tristam, md , 82, his exr , 92
DONGAN (see DUNGAN), Gov , his Council, 18
DORKINS (see DARKINS)
DORLAN (DORLENSEt), Elias, uncle, 87, exr, 87
DORN, Elizabeth, md , 286, dau , 286, mo , 286**, grandmo , 286*
 John, fa , 286, husb , 286, grandfa 286**
 Sarah, w , 286, mo , 286, grandmo, 286*
DORRANCE, Margaret, w , 254, mo , 254, grandmo, 254**, remov , 254
DORSET (DORSETT, DORRETT, DORITT, DOSETT), ment , 164
 Miss, has orig papers, 161, res , 161, sis , 161, has silver, etc , 161, 162
 Ann, granddau , 162, leg , 162, dau , 165
 Catharine, dau , 312
 Eliza, dau , 312

DORSET, Continued
 Elizabeth (elifabetht), dau , 162, her guard , 162, re education, 162†
 George, md , 312, fa , 312**
 Hannah, dau , 165
 Helena Stout, w , 312, mo , 312**
 James, s , 312, house, 364
 John, ment , 78†, wit , 78, bondsm , 162, exr , 162
 Joseph, bndry , 78, wit , 78, s law, 162, exr , 162, md , 165, res , 165, fa , 165**, s , 165, 312, arb , 226
 Mary, dau , 162, re guard , 162, re education, 162
 Rachel, leg , 162, w , 162, wid , 162, mo , 162*
 Samuel, decd , 162*, fa , 162*, will, 162, husb, 162, his est , 162
 Sarah Ann, dau , 312
 Sarah Ogborne (Sally Ogbornet), w , 165†, mo , 165**†
 Williampe, md , 364, res , 364
DORSEY, Miss, md , 270, dau , 270, mo , 270**
 Senator, fa , 270, res , 270, grandfa , 270**
 Camilla Tyrrell (Camilla T †), w , 245†, 251, dau , 245†
 Dr Washington, md , 251, res , 251
 Dr William, md , 245, res , 245
DOTY (see DOUGHTY), William, m 1, 110^b
DOUGHERTY, A W , md , 360
DOUGHTY (see DOTY), Deborah, md , 105, leg , 105, mo , 105**, exrx , 105
 Rev Francis, settlement attacked, 300
DOUGLASS (DOUGLAS), geneal , 190
 Charles, s , 190, res , 190
 Earle, md , 204, res , 204
 Mrs Earle, w , 204
 George, res , 376 prchs, 376
 John, bro , 190, 210**, leg , 190, 210, cousin, 190, 210
 John Saltar, s , 190, admr , 190
 Lydia, dau , 190, cousin, 190, 210, leg , 190, 210, sis , 190, 210**
 Lydia Saltar, w , 190, mo , 190**
 Richard, s , 190, cousin, 190, 210, bro , 190, 210**, leg , 190, 210, md , 190, res , 190*, d , 190*, fa , 190**, admn of est , 190
 Sarah, dau , 190, res , 190, cousin, 190, 210, leg , 190, 210, sis , 190, 210**
 Thomas bondsm , 190
DOVER CREEK, ment , 84
DOVER HUNDRED, ment , 30, 84
DOVER RIVER, ment , 84
DOWNS, Helena, md , 138, b , 138, d , 138, age, 138, mo , 138**, bur , 138
DOXLE, Margaret Mott, w , 110^b
 Samuel, md , 110^b
DRAGON SWAMP, ment , 330, 346
DRAKE, Miss, md , 333, mo , 333**
 Benjamin (Benjamen), md , 225, 232, bond, 229, bill pd due w , 229, husb , 231*, 233, fa , 233, grandfa , 233
 Catharine, md , 337, dau , 337, mo , 337**
 Catharine Stout, w , 352, mo , 352*
 Deborah Van Kirk, md , 345, b , 345, d , 345, mo , 345**

DRAKE, Continued
 Enoch, md , 352, fa , 352*
 Hannah, mo , 233*, 355**, d , 233*, g grandmo , 233, b , 233, dau 233, w , 233, grandmo , 233, md , 355
 Hannah Seabrook, w , 225, 231*, 232, bond pd , 231*
 James, s , 348
 Mary, res , 256, md , 256, 355, spinster, 256, mo , 355*
 Nathan, md, 348, fa , 348
 Ralph, md , 352, fa , 352*
 Rebecca Stout, w , 348, 352, mo , 348, 352*, b , 352, d , 352, age, 352, bur , 352
 William (Wm), fa , 337, res , 337, grandfa , 337**
DREXEL, Elizabeth (Bessiet), dau , 202†
 Catharine, dau , 202
 Joseph W , res , 202, banker, 202, md , 202, fa , 202**
 Josephine, dau , 202
 Lucy, dau , 202, w , 202, mo , 202**
DRUMMOND, Gawin (Garvinet), convey , 227, prchs , 232, 308†, grandfa , 232, grands , 232, bro law, 232, demand, 232, res , 308†
 Rebecca Morford, w , 7, b , 7, d , 7
 Robert, md , 7, b , 7, d , 7
DU BOIS (DUBOES†, DU BOIS), Abraham, fa , 120
 Ann Mount, w , 120
 Jane, w , 120
 Lewis, res , 17, his atty , 17*, pltf , 17, re negroes, 17
 Marian, md , 269†, mo , 269**†
 Nicholas, md , 120*, b , 120, d , 120, bur , 120
DUFFRIES, Elizabeth, md , 357
DUKE OF YORK, his commrs , 73
DULHANGEL, Rebecca, md , 337, mo , 333**
DUNBAR, Joseph, md , 110^b, res , 110^b, Phebe Mott, w , 110^b
DUNCAN, Ann, md , 129
DUNGAN (see DONGAN), of Maryland, 379, of Pennsylvania, 379, of Rhode Island, 379, in Rev War, 379
 Capt Benjamin, sol , 379 fa , 379, husb , 379*, b , 379, md , 379, dea , 379, ancestors, 379
 Esther, w , 379*, mo , 379*
 Josiah, husb , 378, 379, res , 378, b , 379*, d , 379*, s , 379*, fa , 379**, md , 379, footnote, 379
 Mary, w , 378, 379*, leg , 378, md , 379, mo , 379**
 Rev Thomas, his descendants, 379, emig , 379, set , 379
DUNHAM, Content, md , 54, mo , 54*, 243
 Jane, md , 358
DUNMORE, John, Earl of, his fleet, 242, 243
DUNSTABLE, Church of, poor, leg , 262, Parish Poor of leg , 262, Priory Church, rec , 258, tablets, 258, Priory Churchyard, tombs , 258
DURFEE, Patience, w , 186, mo , 186, grandmo , 186
DURRANT, Abigail, md , 178
DURYEA (DURYEE†), Aaron, s , 110^b; b , 110^b*, grands , 110^b, md , 110^b, fa , 110^b*, res , 110^b

INDEX 399

DURYEA, Continued
Abraham, s, 110ᵇ, b, 110ᵇ, grands, 110ᵇ
Lucy Stout, w, 345†
Mary Mott, dau, 110ᵇ, w, 110ᵇ, mo, 110ᵇ*, res, 110ᵇ
Theodore, md, 345†
DUTCH, accession of, 16, age to take up arms, 292, attack Indians, 300, capture by, 15, re term of contempt, 29, demands of, 16, re disputes, 222, 223, employ sol, 299 explore for set, 302, farmers plundered, 300, Gov, agrmt signed, 71, re change of do, 24, invaders, 21, maladministration, 300 manuscripts, ment, 289, overthrow of, 73, ransom set, 299, riots, disputes, etc, 29, set, ment, 289, ship, wrecked, 296, 297, 372, term of contempt, 29, subjugate Province, 21, on Manhattan Island, 299, at Middletown, 302, 372, re Monmouth Pat, 223, 302, at New Amsterdam, 299, in New York, 296*, of do, ransomed by, 373, Church, bp, 73, 74, 81, do, rec, 72, 110, 259
DUTCH NECK, ment, 119
DUTCHESS, Mary, md, 242, 243, b, 242, 243, remov, 243, mo, 243, 246**
DYE (see DEY)
DYMOCK, Clara Gertrude Mott, w, 98, mo, 98
William, md, 98, res, 98, fa, 98

E

EAGLES (EGLE†), Alexander (Alexʳ), exrs of 89, do, plif, 89
William H, Esq, hist, 185†
EARLE, Elizabeth Morris, w, 58
Lawrence, md, 58
EAST JERSEY, Deeds, 302, 303, 326, Proprietors, under, 70
EAST NECK, ment, 73*, 74
EATON, Isaac, minister, 349, md, 349, res, 349, d, 349, age, 349, tombs, 349, fa, 349, as Rev, his school, 338, res, 338
Rebecca Stout, w, 349, mo, 349
EATONTOWN (EDENTOWN†), ment, 65, 230*†
EAYRE, Charity, w, 379, mo, 379
Joseph, fa, 379, husb, 379
Rachel, md, 379, dau, 379
EDDINGS (EDINGS), Miss, sis, 267, md, 267
Mr, md, 273
Elizabeth Seabrook, w, 273
Emma, md, 266, mo, 265*, 267**
William, tombs, 265, donor, 265
EDDY, Hannah, w, 195
Thomas, md, 195
EDGAR, Jane, md, 344, mo, 344*
EDGERTON, Sarah, md, 108, Quaker, 108, remov, 108, mo, 108**
EDINBURGH (EDINBURG), alias Scots Chester Burg, 104
EDISTO ISLAND, bur plot, 266, ment, 266**, Church, ment, 265*, Presbyterian Church, monument to donors, 265, do, Churchyard, ment, 267, do, bur, 268*, do,

EDISTO ISLAND, Continued
tombs, 265*, homestead 269, Seabrook, of, 264-276, ment, 273
EDMONDS, Nicholas, s, 173, app, 173
Robert, bastardy, 173, fa, 173, consent, 173
EDWARDS, family, ment, 375, do, name, 381
Mr, author, 112, 332, author, 301*
Abiah, wit, 23, will, 375, testa, 375, fa, 381
Abigail (Abe†), m 1, 175†
Alexander, fa, 136, husb, 136, grandfa, 137**
Ann, w, 136, mo, 136, grandmo, 137**
Catharine w, 23
Elizabeth, dau, 381, w, 381
Enoch, physician, 193, husb, 193
Frances, w, 193, leg, 193, dau, 193
Dr Hosea, md, 372, res, 372
Mrs Hosea, w, 372
James, md, 69
Margaret, md, 136, dau, 136, b, 136, d, 136, res, 136*, mo, 137**
Mary, md, 122, 133, dau, 122, b, 122, d, 122, mo, 133
Morgan, author, 212, 295, 296, 304, 346, author, 338
Philip, md, 23
Richard fa, 122, husb, 122
Mˢ Sarah Morris, w, 69*
Theodosia, w, 122, mo, 122
EGBERT, Miss, md, 355, dau, 355
Paul, fa, 355
EICK, Catharine, md, 353
ELBERTSEN, Elbert, arb, 290, deft, 290
ELDERT, Lucas m 1, 110
Martha Mott, w, 110
ELDRED, Lucas, md, 110
Martha Mott, w, 110
ELDRETH (ELDRITH†), Mr, md, 118, fa, 118
Elizabeth Mount, w, 118, mo, 118
John, s, 118†, convey, 118†, 363
ELDRIDGE, house, ment, 4
Prescilla md 383
ELIZABETHTOWN (ELISABETH TOWN†, ELIZABETHTOWNE), re disputes, etc, 29†
ELLIOTT (ELLIOT, see THOMAS), Ann, md, 43, 51, 130, 144, res, 43, 51, mo, 51, 145**, b, 130, 144, d, 130, 144
Anna S, md, 12, b, 12, mo, 13
Elizabeth, md, 145
Mary, w, 260, md, 260, res, 260
Thomas, Senʳ convey, 264*, res, 264, planter, 264, decd, 264
ELLIS, Miss, md, 196, mo, 196**
Daniel, prchs, 238
Franklin, author, 297
ELLISON, Elizabeth, md, 42, 97, dau, 42, m 1, 42, s p, 97
Thomas, fa, 42
Ruth, md, 325, m 1, 325, mo, 325*
ELLITHORPE, Elizabeth Morris, w, 60
O S, md, 60
ELMER, Elizabeth, w, 65, mo, 65, grandmo, 65
ELSINBURGH (ELSSENBURGH), ment, 67, 68

ELTON, Ann (Anna†), dau, 378†, w, 378, leg, 378
Anthony, fa, 376, husb, 376, grandfa, 376*
Mary, dau, 376, md, 376, mo, 376*, d, 376
Revel (Revell), husb, 378, fa, 378, decd, 378
Susanna, w, 376, mo, 376, grandmo, 376*
ELY, Mr, md, 140
Achsah Mount, w, 135
Ann Mount (Nancy Mount†), w, 134†
Catharine Ann, md, 207, dau, 207, mo, 207
Elizabeth, dau, 123, leg, 123
Elizabeth Mount, w, 123, 139*, mo, 139**, leg, 139
Ezekiel, s, 139, age, 139, leg, 139
George, md, 123, 135, 139, remov, 135, s, 139, leg, 139, res, 139, will, 139, fa, 139**
James, s, 139, age, 139 leg, 139
John, s, 139, leg, 139
John J, md, 135, b, 135, d, 135
John L, husb, 140, fa, 140
John R, md, 167
Joseph J (Jos J) fa, 207, grandfa, 207
Martha Rebecca, dau, 140, d, 140, age, 140
Mary C, w, 135, remov, 135
Parmelia (Permelia†), w, 140†, d, 140†, tombs, 140†, age, 140†, mo 140†
Parmelia A, w, 140
Rachel Ogborne, w, 167, living, 167, res, 167, correspondent, 167, dau, 167, her Bible, 167
Rebecca, md, 119, w, 119, mo, 119*
Richard, s, 139, age, 139, leg, 139
Samuel, prchs, 122, res, 122, md, 134, buy, 134
Saxton, s, 139, age, 139, leg, 139
Thomas (Tomas†), admr, 139†
William, s, 139, age, 139, leg, 139
EMERSON, Ann, w, 73, mo, 73*
Govey, prchs, 95, 107
John, md, 73, res, 73, fa, 73*
EMERY, Mary Salter, w, 215, d, 215, age, 215, grandmo, 215
Titus Salter, grauds 215, res, 215
William, md, 215, res, 215, grandfa, 215
EMLEN, Deborah, dau, 99, d, 99, unmd, 99
Elizabeth, dau, 99, md, 99, mo, 99, grandmo, 99
Samuel, md, 99, fa, 99**, grandfa, 99
Sarah Mott, w, 99, mo, 99*, grandmo, 99
EMLEY (EMBLY†, see IMLAY), Mr, md, 125, fa, 125*
Ann, md, 235, dau, 235, g grandmo, 235
Ann L, md, 143†, d, 143†, age, 143†
Ann Mount (Nancy Mount†), w, 137†
Elizabeth, w, 125, d, 125, mo, 125*
John, admr, 140 friend, 184, exr, 184, fa, 235, husb, 235
Joseph, s, 125, md, 137
Sarah, w, 235, mo, 235

INDEX

EMMONS, David, md, 69, res, 69
  Francis Asbury, md, 58
  Hannah, md, 357
  Lydia Ann, w, 58, d, 58
  Minnie, md, 66, mo, 66**
  Parmelia (Permeliaf), md, 143†, mo, 143**†, grandmo, 143†
  Rosannah Morris, w, 69†, res, 69
ENDERS, Mr, md, 250
  Ruth, w, 250
ENGLE, Hannah, granddau, 157, md, 157, 379, dau, 157, w, 379
  Jane, dau, 156, 379, md, 156, granddau, 159, leg, 159, mo, 379
  John, md, 156, 370*, fa, 156*, 157**, 379*, grands, 157, s, 157, d, 379
  Mary, granddau, 157, md, 157, 379* dau, 157 b, 379 d, 379, w, 379, mo, 379**, wid, 379
  Mary Ogborne, w, 156, mo, 156*, 157**
  Rachel, w, 379
  Robert, s, 156, 379, md, 379
ENGLISH, re change gov, 24, employed as sol, 299, explore for set, 302, inhabitants as sol, 300, set, New Amsterdam, 299, set, re agrmt, 71, Pat, ment, 73
ENNIS, Dr, re apology, 33
ERRICKSON (ERICKSON), Alice, w, 55, wid, 55
  Francis, b, 55, d, 55
  Susan, md, 161
ERWIN (ERWYN†), Janitie, m 1, 259, wid, 259
  Hester, dau, 259, half-sis, 259, granddau, 259**†
  William, m 1, 259
ESSEX, County of, jail, 29, do, escape of criminals, 29, re riots, etc, 29
ESTH Matilda Morris, w, 70*, res, 70
  Samuel, md, 70, res, 70
ESTILL, John comm, 116, res, 116
  William (Wm) bndry, 185*
EVANS Enoch comm, 107
EVERINGHAM, William, pltf, 182
EVISHAM, Meeting, 156
EWEN (IWAN†), Juhus, m 1, 110*†
  Mary md 216, b 216, d 216, res, 216, mo, 216, 217**
EXCFEN, Elizabeth, b, 226
  John, b, 226
  Mary, w, 172, convey, 172, mo, 172, b, 226
  William, husb, 172*, convey, 172, b, 226, wit, 321

F

FABER Mr md, 270
  Martha Seabrook, w, 270
FAIRCHILD, Mrs, w, 260
  Thomas, md, 260
  William (Wm), convey, 264, planter, 264 res 264
FAIRVIEW CEMETERY, house near, 120 tombs 238, 248**, 249, Midletown, ment, 121, do, bur, 131
FALKENBURG family, acct of, 323
  Amelia, md, 324, 364, dau, 324, d, 324, age, 324, mo, 324*, res, 364
  David, s, 322
  Hannah, dau, 322
  Henry, s, 322
  Henry Jacobs, b, 322, s, 322, fa,

FALKENBURG, Continued
322**, md, 322, 323, grandfa 322**
  Jacob, s, 322
  James, husb, 324, fa, 324, grandfa, 324*
  John, s, 322
  Mary, dau, 322
  Penelope Stout, w, 322, 323, mo, 322**, res, 322 323, descendants, 323
  Sarah, w, 324, mo, 324 grandmo, 324*
FALLS, of Delaware, ment, 331, Monthly Meeting, Minutes of, 158**
FALLS RIVER, ment, 18
FANEY, Miss, md, 360
FARMINGDALE, called Squankum, ment, 41
FARR Elias, mast, 375, will, 375
  Thomas, friend, 124, exr, 124*, res 124, convey, as exr, 124
FARSON, William, md cert, 330
FEEKS, Charles Coles, md, 97, fa, 97
  Mary Ann Mott, w, 97, mo, 97
FELL, Mr, md, 157
  Elizabeth, wit, 159
  Joseph, exr, 159
  Joseph, Jr, md, 379
  Mary, w, 157, 379
  Tamer, md, 379
FENILNHLIM, Mr, md, 275
  Honoria Wilkes, w, 275, author, 275, res, 275
FENTON, Eleazor, prchs, 153
  Eliza Ogborn, w, 168
  Elizabeth Ogborn, w, 168
  Samuel, md, 168
FENWICK, Colony, ment, 22
  John, testa, 18, exrs of, 18
FERRIS, Grace, w, 81, mo, 81, res, 81, grandmo, 81**, 82**, g grandmo, 81**, 82**
  Hannah, dau, 81 md, 81, d, 81, leg, 81, mo, 81**, 82**, grandmo, 81**, 82**, will, 81
  John, fa, 81*, res, 81*, husb, 81, grandfa, 81**, 82**, g grandfa, 81**, 82**, will, 81
FETTROW, Mary, md, 277, mo, 277
FIELD (FIELDS†), Adeline Shepherd, w, 284
  E, md, 195
  Isaac md, 133
  Joseph, farm of, 4, do, graveyard on, 282, s, 282, res, 282, d, 282, age, 282
  Lucy, md, 284
  Martha Woodward w, 133
  Rebecca Shepherd, w, 282†, mo, 282*†
  Rebecca Woodward, w, 132
  Stephen, md, 284
  Thomas, md, 132, 282†, res, 132, s, 282†, fa, 282*†
FINE, Sarah A, md, 357
FINLLY, Mary Ann, w, 341
  Robert I, md, 341
FINNEGAN Mary, md, 60
FINNLY, Eliza Boice, w, 256, mo, 256, grandmo, 256
  Emma D, dau, 256, md, 256, b, 256, mo, 256
  John, fa, 256, husb, 256, grandfa, 256

FISCAL, The, pltf, 21, re fine, 21
FISH, Mrs w, 52*, social note, 52*
  Hamilton, fa, 52, md, 52*, Sec of State, 52
  Mrs Hamilton, w, 52
FISHER, Miss, md, 341
  Avis, w, 311
  Catharine L, w, 357
  Charles, md, 363, 364
  Hannah, w, 377, mo, 377
  Hannah Stout, w, 363, 364
  James S, md, 357
  John, md, 311
  Louisa, w, 287
  Mary A, md, 357, 359, mo, 359**
  Capt Watson H, md, 287
FITCH, Catharine Murphy, w, 148, wid, 148, md, 148
  Francis B, md, 148, d, 148
FITZ-RANDOLPH (FITZ-RANDOLPH, FITZRANDLE†, FITZ RANDOLPH, FITZRANDOLPH, FITZ-RANDOLPH, FITZ RANDOLPH),
  Anna, w, 234
  Benjamin, s, 157, 158**, 159†, 234, b, 157, leg, 158**, 159†, re maintenance, 158, md, 234
  Daniel, s, 234, md, 234
  Deliverance, w, 234, mo, 234, grandmo, 234
  Edward, wit, 158
  Elizabeth, dau, 235
  Grace, wit, 158
  Hannah, dau, 234, md, 234, mo, 234, 235, w, 234
  Huldah, dau, 234, md, 234
  Isaac, grands, 158**, leg, 158**, s, 234, md, 234*, b, 234, fa, 234**, 235, grandfa, 234, g grandfa, 234, 235
  James, md, 225, s, 234, md, 234, fa, 234, grandfa, 234
  Jane (Jean†), w, 156†, 157, 158*, 380, mo, 157*†, 159**, wid, 157†, 158†, leg, 158, exrv, 158*†, req cert remov, 158, re do, 158, mo-law, 158*, cert remov, 158, md, 158†, declr of, 158†
  Joseph (Jofeph), s, 158, re mone s, 158
  Margaret, w, 234
  Nathaniel, md, 156, 157, 158, 380, res, 156, 158*, d, 156, fa, 157*, 158**, mark, 158, will, 158, planter, 158, grandfa, 158, fa law, 158, husb, 158*, est admn, 158, guard, 331
  Rebecca, dau, 234
  Rebecca Seabrook, w, 225, 234, mo, 234**, d, 234, grandmo, 234, g-grandmo, 234, 235*
  Rhoda, dau, 234, md, 234
  Ruth, dau, 234, md, 234
  Samuel (famuell), s, 158*, re moneys, 158, ovsr, 158
  Stephen, s, 234
FLAG, Mr, letter by, 101
FLAT-ROCK-BATTERY, ment, 44
FLEESON, Rebecca, sis, 210**, leg, 210**, mo, 210*, w, 212
  Thomas, md, 212
FLEMING, Anna Morris, w, 68
  Caroline, md, 67
  Stephen, md, 68
FLITCROFT, Annie, md, 60

INDEX 401

FLOWERS, Ann, md , 86
FLUSHING (fFLUSHING, see MID-WOUT), Friends' Quarterly Meeting, 292
FOLDS, Matilda Shepherd, w , 286
  Robert, md , 286
FOLWELL, Mary, dau , 91 , to be md , 91
  William, fa , 91
FORBES, Catharine, md , 212
FORD (FORDE), Mr , md , 320
  Ann, w , 320
  Clarissa Murphy, w , 149
  George H , md , 149
  Jacob, Esq , exr , 89, pltf , 89
  Mary, md , 145, res , 145
  Sarah, dau , 213†, leg , 213†
FORKED RIVER, ment , 196, 201, 202, 205*, 206, 325
FORMAN (FORMAN, FURMAN†), Loyalists, 236†, in Rev War , 236†
  Captain, res , 236*†, friend, 236†, fa , 236†, relative, 236†, sol , 236†, re capture, 236†, re pension, 236†
  Col , killed, 282
  Dr , killed, 282
  Mr , convey , 227, md , 316
  Aaron, s , 235, leg , 235, as Dr , s , 235, set , 235, md , 235, g grandfa , 235
  Andrew, fa , 135, grandfa , 135*
  Ann (Nancy†), w , 235, g grandmo , 235, dau , 316†, 340†, leg , 316†, 340†
  Ann Stout (Nancy Stout†), w , 316*†, 340†, 364
  Charity, md , 333†, mo , 333†
  General E , ment , 236†, relative, 236†
  Eleanor, dau , 136, unmd , 136
  Elizabeth, w , 115, 173, mo , 115**, 123, will 115*, grandmo , 123**, dau , 136, 235*, md , 136, test , 182, wit , 232, leg , 235
  Elizabeth Seabrook, w , 225, 235*, mo , 235**, md , 235, leg , 235, exrx , 235, qual as do , 235
  Ezekiel, (Lzekial), bur , 49, md , 115, 225, 235, 236*†, b , 115, 235, d , 115, 235, fa , 123, 235**, 236†, husb , 123, 235, grandfa , 123**, s , 235*, will, 235, res , 235, 236†, bro , 235, bro law, 235, prchs , 235, friend, 236†, mer , 236†, intemperate, 236†, sol , 236†, re capture, 236†, re pension, 236†
  Mrs Lzakiel, w , 236†
  Hannah, dau , 235*, leg , 235
  Helena, w , 235
  James, s , 327†
  Jane, w , 235, mo , 235*, grandmo , 235
  John (Jon†), qual as exr , 5, exr , 5*†, prchs , 227, res , 227, blacksmith, 227
  Jonathan (Jon†), bro , 235†, exr , 235†, qual as do , 235†
  Margaret ment 103
  Mary (Mollet, Millet†), w , 13, 135, md , 123, 136†, 144††, 235, dau , 123, 135, 136†, 144††, 235**, b , 123, d , 123, will, 123, mo , 123**, 135*, 136*†, 144**††, leg , 235
  Michael, s , 136*, res , 136, grands 136, md , 340, 364
  Peter, s , 136, md , 136, fa , 136

FORMAN, Continued
  Rebecca, dau , 136**, leg , 136, sell , 136, res , 136, w , 144, mo , 144, grandmo , 144**
  Rebecca Mount, w , 136, 144, mo , 136**, 144**, dau , 136, grandmo , 136*, will, 136, d , 136
  Samuel (Sam¹), s , 235**, leg , 235*, res , 235, md , 235, 327, fa , 327*
  Samuel P , md , 136, fa , 136**, 144, grandfa , 136*, 144**, husb , 144
  Sarah, dau , 327†
  Sarah Stout, w , 327†, mo , 327*†
  Susan Mount, w , 140
  Thomas, md , 140, 235, s , 235*, leg , 235, cousin, 235, remov , 235, fa , 235*, grandfa , 235, g grandfa , 236
  Thomas Seabrook, s , 235, b , 235, d , 235
FORSYTH, Annie, md , 60
FORT, FORTS (fFORT), Block House, Middletown, 208, 307 , at Manhattan Island, 299, at New Amsterdam, 289, 299*, 300**, George, ment , 104, James, in New Yorke, Office of Rec , 221 do , New Yorke, Rec , 220 Ontario, ment , 178, Orange, Indians of, 300, Moultrie, ment , 52, Stanwix, ment , 101**, William Henry (Willem Hendrick), ment , 16**, 17**, 21, 72, William and Mary, ment , 215
FORTUNE, schooner, int in willed, 95
FOSSET, Mr , New Store, ment , 243
FOSSEY, Mr Joseph, fa , 262, res , 262
FOSTER (fFOSTER), Abigail, dau , 87, leg , 87
  Josiah, convey 197
  Mary E , md , 64*, b , 64, mo , 64**, 65*
  Miles leg , 20, friend, 20, res , 20, exr , 20
FOWLER, Thomas, deft , 233, res , 233, Marriner, 233, warrant for, 233
FOX George, entertained, 15
FRANCE war with, ment , 105
FRANCIS ship, ment , 222
  Ann Morris, w , 69*
  John, md , 69
FRANKFORT, bur , 120
FRANKLIN, Benjamin, his aide, 274, envoy, 274
  Sarah, md , 106, res 106, mo , 106**
FRAZEE, Elizabeth, md , 331, res , 331, mo , 331**
FRAZIER, Sarah mo , 201, b , 201, md , 201, mo , 201**
FREEHOLD (fFRLEHOLD, see LOWER FREEHOLD, UPPER FREEHOLD, WEST FREEHOLD), Baptist Burying-ground, ment , 13, Dutch Church, bp , 323, Reformed Church, ment , 12, First Reformed Church, bp , 247**, Court Rec , ment , 41*, 62, 76, 113 173*, 180 182, 183, 184, 187, 188*, Deeds, ment , 1, 115*, 135, 182, 306, Loan Comm , at, 209, main brook, 186, Maplewood Cemetery, ment , 139, md rec , 69 70, 363, 364, Morris, md . 69, 70, mort ment , 49, Rec , ment , 134, 159, 182, 185, 223, 319 321, 322, do Common Pleas, 182, wills at, 123,

FREEHOLD, Continued
  do , ment , 161, 192, 239, 340
FREEMAN, Bible rec , 51*
  Anne, dau , 51, b , 51
  Asahel (Asahal, see Essec), md , 51, m 1 , 51, 69, fa , 51**
  Essec (see Asahel), s , 51, b , 51, md , 51, m 1 , 51, fa , 51**
  Hannah, md , 127, b , 127, d , 127, mo , 128**, 134, w , 134
  James, s , 51, b , 51
  Lydia (Ledia), dau , 51, b , 51
  Mary Morris w , 51, mo , 51**
  Mercy (Marsscy†), dau , 51†, b , 51†
  Morris, s , 51, b , 51
  Richard, s , 51, b , 51
FRENCH (fFRENCH), in Rev War, 110ᵇ
  Capt , his Co , 110ᵇ
  Anna J , w , 10
  Anna J Morford, b , 10, w , 10
  Francis (ffrancis), mark, 221, wit , 221
  John, prchs , 2, res , 2
  Mary, w , 379
  Mary Ogborne, w , 156
  Thomas, md , 156, 379
  Walter md , 10
FRESH KILL, ment , 84
FRIENDS (see QUAKERS, also under names of places), Meetings, leg , 15, do , Rec , ment , 378, do , New York, leg , 20, do , Westbury, do , 107, minister, 93, 108, Mott, 86, 92, 93, do, preacher, 98, do , of N Y and N J , 108, Phila , Arch St Meeting, 382, Rec , Plainfield 157*, Quarterly Meeting, Flushing, 292, Rec books, ment , 382, Rec , ref , 378, do , New York, 105, 293*, do , Westbury, 92, 93**, Soc of Rec , 85, 110, Service, ment , 168, Shrewsbury, leg , 19, Women's Monthly Meeting, Philadelphia, leg , 104, Willis, ment , 93
FRIENDS' ADVENTURE, ship, 20, 380
FROST (FROSTS†), family, hist of, ment , 218, land at, 312†
  Mr , md , fa , [?] 314
  Abigail, md , 217, mo , 217
  Adelaide Morford, w , 8
  Benjamin, md , 8*
  Caroline, dau , 314
  Dorothy Salter, w , 215, d , 215
  Eliza Ann, dau , 314
  Elizabeth Morford b , 8, w , 8
  Esther Stout, w , 314, mo , [?] 314
  James, md , 63, b , 63, d , 63, friend, 239, exr , 239, as Esq² , exr , 239, b 314, d , 314, husb , 314, fa , 314**, s , 314
  James H , md , 8, res , 8
  Jane, md , 215, b , 215, d , 215, mo , 215**
  John, md , 215
  Lydia Morris, w , 63
  Nettie, md , 341, s p , 341
  Rachel, dau , 314
  Sarah, md , 216, mo , 216
  Sarah Morford, w , 8
FRY Elizabeth Morris, b , 42, w , 42
  Ellen C , w , 359
  George M , md , 359
  John, md , 42, res , 42
  Joshua, md , 359
  Maria L , w , 359

INDEX

FRY, *Continued*
    Mary, w , 93**, mo , 93**, grandmo , 93**
FRYLEY, William, res , 156, carpenter, 156, convey , 156
FURMAN (see FORMAN)

G

GAA Mr , md , 116
    Rebecca Mount, w , 116
GAGE, Library, New Brunswick, ment , 363
GAILLARDS, of South Carolina, ment , 266
GALLOWAY, sold lands, 84
    Elizabeth, w , 84, convey, 84, res , 84
    Peter, convey , 84, husb , 84, res , 84
GARDNER Elizabeth, dau , 382, sis , 382*, md , 382, w , 382, d , 382, mo , 382**
    Hannah, md , 69
    John, bro , 382
    Thomas, fa 382**, bro ,382, s , 382
GARRAT'S HILL, ment , 164
GARRATY, W C house, 266, store, 266, farm, 266
GARRETSON (GARETSON, GARRETSONS†, GERRITSEN††, see GARRISON), Miss, md , 336, mo , 336**
    Denis, town poor, 345
    George, fa , 336
    John, prchs , 189†, res , 189†
    Lydia Stout, w , 366
    Maria, granddau , 259††
    Osborn, md , 366
    William (W m), deft , 290†
GARRISON (GARRISONS†, see GARRETSON), Miss, md , 336, mo , 336**
    Abigail, dau , 147, b , 147
    Abraham, md , 147, d , 147, fa , 147**, his wid , 147, husb , 147, grandfa , 147**, 148*
    Catharine, dau , 147, b , 147
    Elizabeth, dau , 147, b , 147, md , 334, mo , 334**, 335*, grandmo , 334**, w , 335*
    George, fa , 336
    Hartshorne, s , 147, b , 147
    John, s , 147, b , 147
    Mary, md , 147, dau , 147*, b , 147*, d 147*, age, 147*, mo , 147**, 148*, grandmo , 147**, 148**, w , 147*, wid , 147
    Matthew (Matt, Matts), his Neck, 219*†
GASKILL, Edward, fa , 378, prchs , 378
    Samuel, sell , 378, prchs , 378, s , 378
GASTON, Jane, md , 137*, b , 137, d , 137, mo ,137**, w , 137, grandmo , 137**
    John, fa , 137, husb , 137, grandfa , 137**
    Margaret, md , 137, b , 137, d , 137
GAUNT (see GRANT), Johanna, wit , 23
GEDDIS (GIDDIS†), Mr , md , 270†
    Caroline Seabrook, w , 270†
    Keziah, md , 359, res , 359
GEDNEY (GIDNEY†), Ann, granddau , 73*, leg , 73
    Phebe, md 110*†
GEORGE, Alletta, dau , 285, bp , 285
    Alletta Shepherd, w , 285, mo , 285**

GEORGE, *Continued*
    David, md , 285, fa , 285**
    Elisha, s , 285, bp , 285
    Eliza, dau , 285
    Joel, s , 285, bp , 285
    Peter Schenck, s , 285, bp , 285
    Rachel, dau , 285, bp , 285
    Sarah, dau , 285
    Thomas, s , 285
GEORGE'S CREEK, ment . 330*, 346**
GIBBINS, Amos, md , 339
    Naomi Stout, w , 339
    Richard, bndry , 113
GIBBS, Mr , re mutiny, 15, guard , 16
    Thomas (Tho⁸), as Mr , admr , 25
GIBERSON, Gilbert, md , 340, 364
    Gilbert, Jr , md , 316, b , 316, d , 316, bur , 316
    Lucy, dau , 316, 340, leg , 316, 340
    Lucy Stout, w , 316*, 340, 364, d , 316, bur , 316
    Mary, dau , 46*, leg , 46
GIBSON, Bishop, author , 256
    Robert, his est , 72, res , 72, cred , 72, mvt , 72
GIFFORD, Ananias, prchs , 319, convey , 319, bndry , 320
    Elizabeth, md , 59, dau , 59
    Hananiah, convey , 319
    John, wit , 319
    John B , fa , 59
    Joseph, wit , 319
GILDERSLEEVE, Richard, his exrs , 86
GILES, Col Aquilla, named for, 371, res , 371
GILL, Hannah, w , 125, mo , 125
GILLAM, Margaret, w , 169, mo , 169, grandmo , 169**
    Mary Ann, md , 169, b , 169, dau , 169, mo , 169**
    Rev Rany, husb , 169, fa , 169, grandfa , 169**
GILMAN, Clementine, w , 285
    Samuel, md , 285
GILMORE, Ellen, md , 202, mo , 203*
GITHENS, Caroline Morford, w , 6, mo , 6**
    John, md , 6, b , 6, d , 6, fa , 6**
    Joseph, s , 6, bp , 6
    Mary W, dau , 6, b , 6, d , 6
    Sarah, dau , 6, bp , 6
GLENN, Tho⁸ Allen, author , 212
GLOUCESTER, Church of, ment , 256
GODDARD, Benah, res , 226, agrmt , 226
GODLEY, Anne, md , 99, mo , 99
GOIT, Rachel, md , 383, res , 383, s p , 383, d , 383, bur , 383
GOLDEN, Miss, md , 336, remov , 336, mo , 336
    Anne, dau , 67, md , 67
    Ann Morris, w , 65, 67, mo , 67**
    Caroline Fleming, w , 67
    Catharine, dau , 67, b , 67, d , 67
    Catharine Stout, w , 354, mo , 354*
    Charles, s , 67, d , 67, md , 67
    Cyrenius, md , 65, 67, fa , 67**
    Deborah, dau , 67, md , 67
    Deliverance, w , 354, mo , 354
    George, s , 67, b , 67, d , 67
    John, fa , 354, husb , 354
    Joseph, s , 67, b , 67, d , 67, appr , 160*, convey , 163
    Reuben, md , 354, s , 354
    Rhoda Stout, w , 354

GOLDEN, *Continued*
    Sarah, dau , 67
    William, s , 67, 354, md , 67, 354; fa , 354**, grandfa , 354**
GOLDSMITH, Amelia, md , 121
GOMEZ, Mr , pltf , 184
GOODLUCK, ment , 324*, 325, 364*
GOODMAN, Charles, comm issued to, 180, res , 180, depy secry , 180
GOOSEN (GOESENS†, see STEPHENSZEN), Johannes, s , 259†, leg , 259†
    Mary, b , 259, md , 259, mo , 259**, grandmo , 259**
GORDON, Miss, granddau , 193, age, 193, living, 193
    Alexander, fa , 193, res , 193
    Mrs Alexander, w , 193, mo , 193
    Lady Catherine, md , 43, m 1 , 43, dau , 43, wid , 43, d , 43
    Cathrene Morford, w , 4, mo , 4*, grandmo , 4*
    Charles, Esq , md , 4, fa , 4*, grandfa , 4*
    Cosmo George, Duke of, 43, his wid , 43, b , 43, d , 43
    Dolly (see Mary), md , 194*, w , 194, s p , 194
    Dorothy, dau , 193*, w , 193*, leg , 193, md , 194
    Elizabeth, dau , 193**, w , 193, 194, leg , 193, md , 193, granddau , 193, mo , 193**, letters of, 194
    Epenetus, dau , 208, md , 208, mo , 208**
    Frances, dau , 193, w , 193, leg , 193
    George, s , 203, leg , 193
    Hannah, dau , 4, md , 4, w , 314, mo , 314, grandmo , 314
    Jane, md , 145
    Janet, w , 193, 208, mo , 193, 208, grandmo , 193**, 208**, dau , 193
    Miss Jessie, res , 251, has Bible, 251
    Keziah Stout, w , 337
    Lewis, md , 337
    Maria w , 340, mo , 340
    Mary (see Dolly), dau , 4, 193, md , 4, mo , 4*, w , 193, leg , 193
    Patience, w , 124, admrx , 124, mo , 124**
    Patience Mount, w , 124, mo , 124**
    Rebecca, dau , 193*, leg , 193*, w , 193
    Robert, m 1 , 124, est admn , 124, husb , 124, decd , 124, fa , 124**
    Thomas, King's atty , 26, surro , 158, s , 193**, leg , 193, husb , 193*, 208, mcr , 193, res , 193*, fa , 193**, 208, grandfa , 193**, 208**, gent , 193, decd , 193, will, 193*, descendants, 193, parents, 193
GOULDING, Mr , vandue mast , 291
GOUVENEUR, Nicholas, fa , 43, grandfa , 43, god-fa , 43
    Sarah, niece, 36, md , 36, b , 36, d , 36, mo , 36**, 38 , w , 38
GOVERNOR, GOVERNORS, ment , 15, 292, 302, 345, insulted, 27, letter to, 84, do , re, 85, men, answer to, 304, of New York, 33, order of, 17, re position for Lieut , Militia, 96; Proprietary, ment , 303, and Council, ment , 26*, 27, 28, 36*, do., opinion of, 27, order of, 27, sits, 27; -General, ment , 16, 21, 257, Andross, 18*, E Andross, 24, Basse,

INDEX 403

GOVERNOR, Continued
26, 27**, Jeremiah (Jr) Basse, 26, 27, 346, Bedle, 109, 153, 161, Belcher, 377, Burnett, 30*, William Burnet, Esq, 167, Clinton, 44, Gen Anthony Colve, 16, 17*, Lord Cornbury, 181,* do, as Edward, Vifcount, 305, 306, Cosby, 30**, 31*, Dongan, 18, Hamilton, 26**, 27*, 28*, as Col, 28*, Andrew Hamilton, 76, Hardy, 187, Hunter, 29, 30*, Robert Hunter, 30, do, as Esq', 346, Ingoldsby, 72, do, as Lieut Gov, 28,* Kieft, 301, Gawen Lawrie, 18, 362, Leisler, 72, Wm Livingston, 238, Lovelace, 28, Ludlow, 109, Ludwell, 261, Montgomerie, 30**, 36, Henry Moore, 367, Morris, 26, Lewis Morris, 22, 23, 25, 26, 28, 31, 33, 34, 36*, 37*, 187, Robert Hunter Morris, 36, 37, 44*, 45, as Lieut Gov, 44, James Atwell Mount, 129, Nicolls, 301, Richard Nicolls, 302, Ogden, 195, Parker, 109, Joel Parker, 361, Thomas Rudyard, 18, Seabrook, 272, Whitemarsh Seabrook, 272, Stuyvesant, 289 302

GRAHAM, Arabella Morris, w, 33
Isabella, md, 33, 37, m 1, 33, b, 33, d, 33, mo, 33**, 34**, sis, 37, will, 38, grandmo, 38**
James, md, 33, d, 33, fa, 33, atty-genl, 33, grandfa, 33**, 34**

GRANDIN, Daniel, res, 49, sell, 49, bndry, 209

GRANT (see GAUNT), General, ment, 52
Miss, md, 371
Alexander, md, 311, m 1, 311
Ann (Annie†), b, 7†, d, 7†, w, 7†, md, 363
Catharine, md, 149, b, 149, d, 149
Hester Ann, w, 7, called "Annie," 7
Hester Ann Morford, b, 7, d, 7, w, 7
Johanna, wit, 23
Mary, md, 207, s p, 207
Rebecca Stout, w, 311
Sylvia, md, 324
William, his dau, 371, fa, 371, ment, 371
William H, md, 7, b, 7, d, 7

GRANTS AND CONCESSIONS, qual, 302, 303

GRAVELL (GRAVILL) BROOK, ment, 185*

GRAVES Henry, md, 170, 381, d, 170, husb, 381, d, 381
Sarah, w, 170, 381*, mo, 381**, sis, 381, res, 381, wid, 381, convey, 381

GRAVESEND (Gᵈ), first allotments, 301, bndry, 292, English set, 302, founded, 301, Freeholders of, 291, pat issued, 299, rec, 325, first set, 372, set of, 299, re do, 289*, 302, slander suit, 301, Town Book, entry, 299, town of, leg, 291, do, Rec ment, 301

GRAVEYARDS (see BURYING-GROUNDS, CHURCHYARDS, YARDS), on Cooper farm, 1, Edisto Island, 266, Cold Spring, bur, 293, Cold Spring Inlet, Presbyterian, 293, on Joseph Field farm,

GRAVEYARDS, Continued
282, Robbins' farm, 187, Stillwell, 282, Stout, 308, do, bur, 312, Wall, bur, 312, Yellow Meeting House, 183

GRAYSON, Paralee, md, 129, mo, 129**

GREAT NECK, alias Madnam's Neck, ment, 81

GREAT SWAMP, bndry, 156

GREEN (GREENE), Mr, md, 55, as Rev, ment, 271
Mrs, w, 55
Caroline Estelle, w, 66
Elizabeth, w, 159, leg, 159
Elizabeth Morris, w, 69
James Monroe, md, 66, res, 66
John, md, 69
Mary niece, 264, leg, 264

GREENLAND, ment, 215
Dr Henry, fa, 332, grandfa, 333**, g grandfa, 333**
Ruth, md, 332, dau, 332, ch memb, 332, mo, 333**, grandmo, 333**

GREENWICH, village, ment, 371

GREENWOOD, Adeline, dau, 149, b, 149
Amelia, md, 148, 149, res, 148, b, 148, 149, dau, 149
Benjamin, s, 149, b, 149
Eliza Booth, dau, 149, b, 149
Henry, s, 149, b, 149
Joseph B, s, 149, b, 149
Mary Hannah, dau, 149, b, 149
Mary Murphy, w, 149, mo, 149**
Richard, md, 149, b, 149, d, 149, fa, 149**
Richard B, s, 149, b, 149
Sophia, dau, 149, b, 149
William Murphy, s, 149, b, 149

GREER, Elmira Shepherd, w, 286, mo, 286*
James A, md, 286, res, 286, fa, 286*

GREGORY, Hortense, md, 8

GREY, Benjamin, md, 351, remov, 351, fa, 351*
Mary Stout, w, 351, mo, 351**, remov, 351

GRIFFIN (see GRIFFITH), Miss, md, 252, res, 252
Edward, convey, 301, 372
Mary, md, 347, wid, 347, mo, 347**

GRIFFITH (see GRIFFIN), Miss, md, 252, res, 252

GRIGG (GRIGGS†), Capt Benjamin, md, 254†, s p, 254†
Eleanah (Helen) Stout, w, 368, s p, 368
Helen (see Eleanah)
Martha (Matt), w, 254†, s p, 254†
William, md, 368, s p, 368

GROODT (see DE GROOT), Derrick Jansen, sell, 259

GROVE FARM, alias Brockett's Neck, 291

GROVER, family, emig, 298, line, bndry, 213, re hist, 111, in Militia, 307, set, 301*
Mr, re mines, 18
Abigail, sis, 111, w, 111
Deborah, md, 278, w, 278, grandmo, 278**, leg, 278, mo, 278**, 279**, will, 278, sig, 278
Elizabeth, w, 136, 160, mo, 136, 160, grandmo, 161**, dau, 224, sis, 224, b, 224

GROVER, Continued
Hannah, dau, 161, 224*, 225, 227, mo, 161, 224*, 225**, w, 224, md, 224, b, 224, sis, 224, d, 224, grandmo, 225**, leg, 225, 227
James, bndry, 39, 45, exr, 49, 118*, 278, renounces as do, 49, 278, friend 49, 228, res, 49, prchs, 116*, 224, yeom, 116, sig, 118, fa, 161, 278, grandfa, 161, test, 182, re propn, 224, re land, 224, bro, 224*, uncle, 226, convey, 226, 307*, s, 278, survey, 304, carpenter, 307, Lieut, in Militia, 307, md, 309
James, Jr (James, Juncr, James, Jun'), appr, 227, 229, sig, 229
Joseph, fa, 224**, 225, 227, 278, re daus leg, 224, husb, 224, grandfa, 225**, 278**, 279**, testa, 225, 227
Mary Stout, w, 309
Rebecca, md, 335, granddau, 335, mo, 336**, grandmo, 336**
Safety (Safty, Safty), took invt, 112, pays money, 112, bndry, 113, 125, his land, 116, decd, 116, grandfa, 335, g grandfa, 336**

GROVER'S INHERITANCE, bndry, 318

GUILFORD, Library, ment, 152

GULICK, Catharine (Kathanne†), w, 159†, convey, 159†
Hendrick, husb, 159, convey, 159
Sarah, md, 364

GUSTIN, Alletta, dau, 285, bp, 285
Eleanor Shepherd, w, 285, mo, 285**
Francis, md, 285, fa, 285**, d, 285
John, s, 285, bp, 285
Sarah Ann, dau, 285, bp, 285

GUYSBERTSE (GISBERTSE†), Guisbert, husb, 259
Marytie, granddau, 259†
Ryntie, w, 259, dau, 259

H

HACKENSACK, Indians, visited, 299, murder by do, 299, revenged, 299

HADDONFIELD, Monthly Meeting, Rec, 158

HADLEY, Rec, ment, 222

HAGAMAN, Anna, md, 344, dau, 344, b, 344, d, 344, mo, 344*
Catharine, w, 344, mo, 344, grandmo, 344*
Rudolph, fa, 344, husb, 344, grandfa, 344*

HAINES, Quakers, 378*
Ann, w, 378, mo, 378, Quaker, 378, res, 378, grandmo 378**
Hannah, md, 378, dau, 378, mo, 378**
Nehemiah, Quaker, 378, fa, 378, husb 378, res, 378, grandfa, 378**

HALL, Mr, md, 214
Miss, md, 108
Maj Arthur, bro law, 263, prchs, 263
John, mo, 57, bondsm, 291
Lydia Morris, w, 57
Margery, dau, 214, leg, 214
Margery Salter, w, 214
Mary L, md, 277, res, 277, mo, 277

INDEX

HALL, *Continued*
Thomas (Tho⁸), wit , 73, gives bond, 291
HALL OF RECORDS, re Hangman's Jail, 282
HALLET, John, res , 110ᵃ, will , 110ᵃ, husb , 110ᵃ, fa , 110ᵃ**, bro , 110ᵃ, bro law, 110ᵃ
Sarah, w , 110ᵃ, mo , 110ᵃ**
HALLOWOOD, Deborah Mott, w , 110ᵃ
Thomas, md , 110ᵃ
HALSTEAD (HOLSTED†), Jacob, exr , 94
Rebecca ment , 78†
Timothy, prchs , 381, res , 381
HAMES, Miss md , 348, mo , 348
HAMILTON (HAMBLETON†), a place, ment , 344, in U S Navy, 272
Col illegal power, 26 , as Gov , 27, 28**
Gov , his Council, 26 , 27*, 28*, seizure of, 26 , prison , 26, ment , 27*, 28, grants land, 28, Scotch Gov , 28*
Miss, md , 272, dau , 272, mo , 272**
Gov Andrew, comm from, 76
John, pres , 187, decd , 187
Mary Elizabeth, w , 269
Paul, tombs , 265, donor, 265, md , 269, fa , 272, Secry ,272, grandfa , 272**, as Col , fa law, 268
Phoebe, md , 268, mo , 268*
Rebecca, ment , 363†
Robert, succeeded as clk and rec , 22
HAMILTON SQUARE, (Nottingham), ment , 142
HAMPTON (HAMTON†), a place, ment , 378
Mr , md , 57
Andrew res , 27, *cryed* out, 27, s , 157, leg , 157
Ann, w , 380
Benjamin, s , 157, 380, grands , 157, b , 380, md , 380
David s. 157*, 380, leg , 157, grands 157, b , 380, d , 380
Elizabeth, dau , 157, leg , 157
Gertrude Ann, w , 57
Jane (see Janet and Jean), dau , 157, 380, granddau 157, unmd , 157, w , 157**, mo , 157**, leg , 157, sold house, 157, grandmo, 157**, exrx , 157, md , 158, res , 158, b , 380, d , 380
Janet (see Jane and Jean), w , 157, mo , 157
Jean (see Jane and Janet), w , 156, wid 156, mo , 157, grandmo , 157**
John, md , 156, 157**, res , 156, d , 156, 157, 380, fa , 157**, grandfa , 157**, s , 157*, 380, leg , 157, grands , 157, will, 157, husb , 157, res 157†, sold house, 157, b , 380
Jonathan, s , 157, leg , 157
Joseph (Jo†), s , 157**, 159*, 380, d , 157, md 157, fa , 157**, 159, 380**, leg , 157, 158, 159*†, grands , 157 , s law, 158†, b , 380, husb , 380
Lydia, dau , 157, leg , 157
Martha, w , 157, mo , 157**
Mary, dau , 157, 380, granddau , 157, md , 157, 380, w , 157, 380, mo , 157**, 380**, b , 380, d , 380
Noah, s., 157, leg , 157

HAMPTON, *Continued*
Sarah, dau , 157, 380, md , 157, 380, granddau , 157, b , 380
HANCE, Abigail, md , 355, dau , 355, mo , 355**, w , 355, grandmo , 355**
Caroline, w , 10, mo , 10
Elizabeth A , w , 10
Elizabeth A Morford, b , 10, w , 10
John, appr 3 , friend, 20, res , 20, exr , 20, just , 170, md by, 170
Joseph E , md , 10, s , 10, b , 10
Mrs Joseph E , dau , 10, res , 10
Joseph L fa , 10 husb , 10
Thomas, fa , 355, husb , 355, grandfa , 355**
Rev William White, late, 146, friend, 146, geneal , 146
HANCKEL, Rev Mr , ment , 271
HAND, Deborah, md , 383
Mary, md , 383, mo , 383
HANGMAN'S JAIL, New York, 282
HANIHAN, Miss, md , 268, mo , 268**, 269*
HANKINS, Mr , sell , 117, husb , 117
Mrs , sell , 117, w , 117
Abby Stout, w , 345
Richard, md , 345
HANKINSON (HANKISON†), md ment , 248, in Rev War, 12, 248
Mr , md , 248*, killed, 248, fa , 248
Eleanor, dau , 132, md , 132, d , 132, mo , 132
Jemima Stout w , 327†, mo , 327*†
Capt Kenneth, his co , 12*
Robert, mort , 209†
Sarah (Sally†), wid , 248†, d , 248†, age, 248†, step-mo , 248†, md , 248*†, mo , 248†
Thomas, fa , 132, 327*†, grandfa , 132, md , 327†
HANKS, Ann (Nancy†), dau , 197†, md , 197*†, cousin, 197†, d , 197†, mo , 197*†, w , 197†
Joseph, md , 197, fa , 197
HANNAWAY, Samuel, md , 141, b , 141, d , 141
Susannah Mount, d , 141, w , 141
HANOVER (HANNOVER†), Township, ment , 38, 99†
HARDBARGAIN HOUSE, Richmond, 244
HARDY, Gov , comm by, 187
HARE, Mr , md , 61
Elizabeth Morris, w , 61
HARIMAN, Martha A , md , 359
HARLEM (HAERLEM†), alias Bronck's land, 18†
HARLEM RIVER, ment , 15, 21
HARLEQUIN, Privateer, ment , 368
HARRINGTON, Annie E , md , 10, 11, dau , 10, 11, mo , 12**
John, fa , 10, 11, husb , 10, 11, grandfa , 12**
Lucy, w , 10, 11, mo , 10, 11, grandmo , 12**
HARRIS, Dr , md , 357
Mr , md , 165, as Rev , md , 383
Benjamin, md , 341
Edward Doubleday, author, 110, res , 110
Hannah Mount, w , 140
Harriet Ogborne, w , 163, mo , 163
John, md , 140, 163, fa , 163
Lauretta, w , 165

HARRIS, *Continued*
Lydia w , 60, mo , 60, grandmo , 60**
Mary Ann, w , 341
Parmela Stout, w , 357
Sylvia, w , 383
HARRIS and McCRAY, school of, 243
HARRISON, Georgianna, md , 218, mo , 218
Gen William Henry, Pres , 350, ment , 350
HART, Mr , opinion of, 297, error, 305*, as Rev , author , 304
Abigail, md , 328, m l , 355, dau , 355, mo , 355**, grandmo , 355**
Addie M , w , 371, mo , 371*
Amos, md , 337
Ann Stout, w , 352, mo , 352*
Deborah Stout, w , 355, mo , 355**
Ebenezer, md , 130
Edward, fa , 355, grandfa , 355**
Elizabeth Stout, w , 337
Ephraim, md , 352, fa , 352*
George O , res , 371, md , 371, fa , 371*
John, md , 355, s , 355, remov , 355, fa , 355**, grandfa , 355**, g grandfa , 355**
Joseph, md , 339
Louisa, md , 328, m l , 328, mo , 328*
Lydia, sis , 68, leg , 68
Margaret White, w , 130
Mary, md , 350, dau , 350
Nathaniel, md , 337, m l , 337
Oliver, fa , 350, as Rev , author, 296, 297, pastor, 296
Ruth Stout, w , 337
Theodosia Stout, w , 339
Ure, md , 343, mo , 343**, grandmo , 343**
HARTSHORNE (HARSHORN†, HARTSHORN), Mr , re candidacy, 103†
Abigail, w 195
Ann Mount, w , 127
Catharine, w , 88, mo , 88, grandmo , 88, 89**
E , w , 195*
Elizabeth, dau , 194*, md , 194*
Elizabeth Saltar, w , 194, mo , 194**
Esek, md , 194, fa , 194**
Ezekiel, s , 194, md , 194
Hannah, dau , 194, 195, md , 194*, 195, d , 194, w , 194, 195
Hugh, recpt , 79, prchs , 308
Jane, w , 194
John, md , 194, 195*, s , 195, fa , 195**, prchs , 197
Lawrence, s , 195, md , 195*
Lucy Saltar, w , 194, mo , 195*
Margaret, dau , 88, 182, md , 88, granddau , 88, mo , 88, 89**, 130, w , 130, grandmo , 130**, re trust, 182, leg , 182
Mary, md , 147*, b , 147, d , 147, age, 147, mo , 147**, w , 147, grandmo , 147**, 148*
Rachel, md , 192, 197, w , 197, mo , 197, grandmo , 197*, 198*, wid , 197, g grandmo , 197
Richard (Rich), friend, 20, res , 20, 180, exr , 20, sig , 28, 112, of Council, 28, recpt , 112, convey , 113, bndry , 113, atty , 180, bondsm , 181, trust , 181; re do ,

INDEX   405

HARTSHORNE, Continued
    182, s , 182, 194, dwelling, 182,
      leg , 182, md , 194, ment , 298,
      attest , 305, wit , 305, 306, prchs ,
      307, grant by, 307, fa , 330, b ,
      330
    Richard Saltar, s , 194, md , 194
    Robert, md , 194, fa , 194**
    Samuel Wright, m l , 127
    Sarah (Sally†), dau , 194†, md , 194†
    Sarah Saltar, w , 194, mo , 194**
    Susan, w , 194*
    William, wit , 39, husb , 88, fa , 88,
      182**, grandfa , 88, 89**, s , 182,
      194*, re trust, 182, leg , 182, md ,
      194*
HARTSHORNE'S NECK, alias Conne-
    skunk, 307
HARVARD COLLEGE, ment , 276
HARVLD, Miss, md , 372, dau , 372,
    res , 372
    Mrs , w , 372, res , 372, d , 372,
      mo , 372
    Jonathan, ia , 372, age , 372, res ,
      372, d , 372, his w d , 372
HARVEY (HARVIE†), Elizabeth, ment ,
    375, dau , 375
    Hannah, her keep, 375, nursing of,
      375
    Peter, bro law, 156, trust , 156, asst ,
      156, husb , 375, fa , 375*, coffin
      for, 375, do , for w , 375, admr of,
      375
    Sarah, wit , 156†, b , 382, md , 382,
      dau , 382
    Thomas, fa , 382
HARWOOD, John, res , 156, yeom , 156,
    convey , 156, prchs, 156
HATCH, Isaac, md , 370
    Mary Jane, w , 370
HATFIELD, Caroline Knott, w , 149
    Catharine (Katie†), md , 60†
    Frank, md , 149
HATHAWAY, Abel, admr , 89, deft , 89
    Jonathan, his admr , 89
HAVENS, Jane, md , 366
    Mary, dau , 361, leg , 361
    William, wit , 321
HAVERFORD, Meeting, ment , 347
HAWKINS, Julia, md , 145, w 145, mo ,
    145**
HAY, George, md , 58
    Harriet Morris, w , 58
    Mary, md , 117, m l , 126, spinster,
      126, res , 126, mo , 126*, exrx , 126
HAYDEN, Henrietta, md , 124
HAZELTON, John W , his land, 293
HAZZARD Ellen Stout, w , 357
    O H , md , 357, minister, 357
HEABRON, Mary Stout, w , 333, mo ,
    333
    William, md , 333, fa , 333
HEADDY (see HEDDEN), Patience,
    md , 196, res , 196, mo , 196**
HEAT, Colonel Alexander, will, 264,
    testa , 264, decd , 264
HEATHCOTE, Col Caleb, prchs , 73,
    exr , 73
HEDDEN (HEADON†, see HEADDY),
    Mr , md , 314, fa , 314, grandfa ,
      314*
    Caroline, dau , 314, b , 314, d , 314
    Esther, dau , 314, d , 314, age, 314
    Esther Stout, w , 314, mo , 314,
      grandmo , 314*

HEDDEN, Continued
    Jonathan, s , 314, b , 314, d , 314,
      md , 314, fa , 314*
    Marcus, bndry , 121†
    Mary md , 314, w , 314, b , 314, d ,
      314, mo , 314*
    Patience, md , 196, res , 196, mo ,
      196**
HEISLEY, Judge Wilbur Arthur, md ,
    66
    Myrtilla De Graw, w , 66
HELLINGS, Rebecca, dau , 213, leg ,
    213
HEMONES, Hulden, m l , 39
HEMPSTEAD (HAMSTED†, see SOUTH
    HEMPSTEAD), Cen of, 72, 74,
      75, 76*, 80, 82, 83, 91, 219, Harbor,
      ment , 82, 83, 88, 97, town of,
      ment , 87, do , Rec , 110, 219
HENDERSON (HENDERSON), Rev
    Mr , re Helebore, 30
    Caroline Stout, w , 325
    Jacob, missionary, 30, res , 30, letter
      of, 30
    John, admr , 68, cred , 68, md ,
      325
    Joseph, md , 325
    Michael, appr , 5
    Thomas (Th, Th°), cred , 100, recpt ,
      100, sig , 100
    Timothy, tombs , 265, donor, 265
HENDRICKS, Jacob, s , 259, leg 259
HENDRICKSON, remov of tombs , 238,
    Seabrook controversy, 238
    Catharina, w , 61, mo , 61, grandmo ,
      61
    Charles I , Esq , res , 238, decd , 238
    Cornelius, bndry , 213
    Daniel, fa , 136, husb , 136, bndry,
      213, deft , 247, exr , 247, as Capt ,
      fa , 61, husb , 61, grandfa , 61
    Denise, land, 347
    Elizabeth, mark, 103, gives power
      atty , 103, res , 103, w , 136**,
      mo , 136*, grandmo , 136*
    Elizabeth Mount, w , 136, mo , 136*
    Forman, s , 136, md 136
    Gilbert, fa , 136, husb , 136, grand-
      fa , 136*, admr , 136
    Hannah Morris, w , 70
    Hendrick, ment , 298
    Jacob, md , 136*, m l , 136, s , 136*,
      b , 136, d , 136*, fa , 136*
    Mrs James C , w , 11
    James C , md , 11
    James G , md , 70
    John Lawrence, md , 136
    Lydia M , w , 9
    Margaret, md , 134
    Mary (Marcy†), md , 58, 61†, dau
      61†, mo 61†
    Oke, convey , 213
    Rachel, convey , 213
    Samuel T , md , 9
    Sarah, w , 136
    Theodosia, md , 136, dau , 136, b ,
      136
    William, convey , 213
    Williampe, w , 248, mo , 248, grand-
      mo , 248**, 249**
HENRY, Capt , fa , 372**, sea captain,
    372, md , 372, res , 372
    Miss, md , 370, 372**, dau , 372**
    Mrs , w , 202, 372, d , 202, mo , 372**
    Fanny, w , 202, d , 202

HENRY, Continued
    Guy V , md , 202, Brig Genl , 202,
      nickname, 202, d , 202
HERBERT (HARBERT†, HAR-
    BURT††), Mrs , dau , 242, nurse,
      242
    Amey, md , 90**, m l , 90, d , 90,
      dau , 90, mo , 90**
    Anne Stout, w , 363
    Daniel, fa , 8, husb , 8, 90, grandfa ,
      9**, md , 90, s , 119*, leg , 119
    Elizabeth, md , 354, m l , 354
    Francis, took invt , 112††
    Henry (Hen†), wit , 174†, prchs ,
      322, yeom , 322, md , 363
    Isaac, md , 69, res , 69, ackn , 322,
      wit 322
    James, fa , 63, 119**, grandfa , 63**,
      md , 114, m l , 115, yeom , 118,
      res , 118, 119*, s , 119*, leg , 119,
      husb , 119*, will, 119*, testa , 119,
      bro , 119
    Jane, w , 247, mo , 247**
    John Seabrook, s , 247, b , 247, bp ,
      247
    Margaret, mo , 8, w , 8, grandmo ,
      9**
    Margaret Mount, w , 114, 118, 119,
      res , 118, spinster, 118, dau , 118,
      mo , 119**, leg , 119, md , 119
    Maria, dau , 247, b , 247, bp , 247
    Obadiah, fa , 247**, husb , 247
    Patience, md , 63, d , 63, mo , 63**
    Richard, s , 119*, leg , 119*, bro ,
      119, m l , 247
    Ruben Brown, s , 247, b , 247, bp , 247
    Sarah, w , 308
    Sarah Morris, w , 69, res , 69
    Susan, md , 8, dau , 8, b , 9, d , 9,
      mo , 9**
    Thomas, propri deed, ment , 1
    Walter, md cert , 308†
HERRING, Jon, wit , 174
HERRIOT (HERIOT), Mr , md , 274
    Eliza Seabrook , w , 274
    Mary Elizabeth, w , 269
    William H , md , 269
HERRON (HERON†), Miss, md , 338†,
    mo 339†
    Elizabeth (Betsey†). md , 241†, dau ,
      241†, step-mo , 241†
HESSIANS, in Rev War, 237
HEST, Hugh, wit , 262
HESTON, Jemima, md , 380
HEWLETT (HULET, HULETT, HU-
    LIT, HULITT), Ann, md , 154;
      res , 154, w , 378, mo , 378, grand-
      mo , 378**
    Catharine, w , 65, mo , 65
    Constant md , 51, b , 51, d , 51,
      age, 51
    Daniel, fa , 65, husb , 65, md , 110*
    Elizabeth, md , 110*
    Jane (Jennet), md , 72†, res , 72†,
      mo , 72**†, 73, w , 73
    Johnnah, m l , 48, res , 48
    Joseph, prchs , 319, singleman, 319,
      res , 319
    Lydia, md , 51
    Mary Ann, w , 65
    Mary Mott, w , 110*
    Michael, md , 65, s , 65
    William, exr , 49, bro law, 49
HEXT, Colonel Alexander, will, 264,
    testa , 264, decd , 264

INDEX

HEYWARDS, of South Carolina, ment., 266
HICKS (see HIX), Abigail, w, 90, mo, 90, grandmo, 90**
  Benjamin, will, 76, res, 76, 86, his exrs 86, m 1, 110°
  John, m 1, 110°
  Thomas, magist, 72
HID (see HYDE)
HIGBIE (HIGBEE), Mifs, ment, 102
  Henry, m 1, 110°
HIGGINS, Mifs, md, 119
  Mr, fa, 348
  Azariah, md, 352, m 1, 352, fa, 352*
  Esther, md, 351, dau, 351, mo, 351*
  Hannah Stout, w, 334, mo, 334**, cousin, 334
  James, s, 334
  Jediah, md, 334, fa, 334**, 349, 351, grandfa, 350**, 351*, g-grandfa, 350**
  Jonathan, s, 334
  Joseph, s, 334, fa, 351, grandfa, 351**, 352**, g grandfa, 351*, 352**
  Joshua, s, 334
  Mary, dau, 334, 349, md, 334, 348, 349, mo, 348**, 349**, 350**, grandmo, 348**, 349**, 350**, d, 349, age 349, tombs, 349
  Rachel, dau, 334, 348, md, 348, Richard, wit, 174
  Sarah, md 351, dau, 351, mo, 351**, 352, grandmo, 351*, 352**
  Sarah Stout, w, 352, mo, 352*
HIGHAM, Jane, w, 307, convey, 307
  Thomas convey, 307, husb, 307
HIGHLANDS, aliases, 4
HIGHTSTOWN, bur, 115, 127, 134**, 135, 138**, 139**, Baptist Church, trust of, 134, do, Rec, 146, do, Churchyard, bur, 133, 166, do, tombs, 140, yard, bur, 138*
HILDRETH Margaret, md, 45
HILL (see HILLS), family, res, 237, re silver, 237
  Catharine w, 131, mo, 131, grandmo 131**
  Cornelia, md, 131, b, 131, d, 131, mo, 131**, grandmo, 131
  Delia Ann, w, 249
  Enoch, md, 249
  James, fa, 356, grandfa, 356*
  John, wit, 159, made invt, 159
  Paul, md, 350, fa, 350*
  Rachel Coles, md, 356, dau, 356, b, 356, d, 356, mo, 356*, grandmo, 356
  Rachel Stout, w, 350, mo, 350*
  Robert, fa, 131, husb, 131, grandfa 131**
  Samuel S, md, 107
  Sarah Mott, w, 107
HILLMAN, Elizabeth, md, 125
HILLS (see HILL), Mr, md, 270
  Elizabeth Seabrook, w, 270
HINCHMAN, Isaac, husb, 377
  Lettice, dau, 377, w, 377
  Sarah, granddau, 377
HINMAN, Andrew, deft, 225
HIRES (HIREf), Llinot Mott, w, 107
  Elizabeth, md, 362, mo, 362, grandmo, 362**
  John vandue Master, 229†, 231†, bill pd, 229†, 231†

HIRES, Continued
  Rev W D, md, 107
HIRST, Ann, w, 333
  Thomas, md, 333
HITCHCOCK, Georgianna, md, 344, b, 344, res, 344
HIX (see HICKS), Lucy Stout, w, 363, res, 363
  Oliver, md, 363, res, 363
HIXSON (HIXON), Mifs, md, 333
  Elizabeth, md, 352, mo, 352**, grandmo, 352**
  Mary, md, 351, mo, 351**, grandmo, 351**
HOAGLAND, Mifs, md, 342
  Mr, md, 359
  Abraham, md, 351, fa, 351**
  Cornelia (see Neeley)
  Elizabeth, wid, 354, d, 354, age, 354, tombs, 354
  Elizabeth Stout, w, 337, 359, s p, 337
  John, md, 337, s p, 337
  Neeley, md, 353, res, 353
  Parmela, md, 354
  Rebecca Stout, w, 351, mo, 351**
HOBART, Bishop, re his family, 193
  Mifs, w, 193, mo, 193, of Bishop's family, 193
HOBBS (HUBSf, HUBBSf†), Elizabeth, w, 72, mo, 80†ized, release, 80††
  Robert, md, 72†
HOBBY, Maria Mott, w, 106, leg, 106
  S M md, 106
  Sette M, husb, 106
HOCTON (see STOCKTON), name cor, 376
  Anna, w, 153, dau law, 153, leg, 153
  John, husb, 153, md, 154
HODSON, William (Wm), cert, 125, sig, 125
HOES, Elizabeth Seabrook, w, 254, d, 254
  Rev Roswell Randall, md, 254
HOFF (HUFF†), in Rev War, 310
  Mifs, md, 353†, res, 353†, mo, 353**†
  Ann (Annat), dau, 253, w, 382†
  Ann Eliza, dau, 253, b, 253, md, 253, mo, 253, grandmo, 253
  Anna Seabrook, w, 253, descendants, 253, d, 253, mo, 253*, grandmo, 253**, g grandmo, 253
  Christian, s, 310
  Daniel S, his wid, 253, fa, 253*
  Daniel Seabrook, s, 253, b, 253, md, 253, d, 253, fa, 253**
  Eleanor (Nellief), dau, 253†
  Elizabeth, mo, 253†, w, 253†, grandmo, 253**†, g grandmo, 253**†, dau, 310
  Gabriel, fa, 327, grandfa, 327*
  Helena, grandmo, 298†, 309†, 362*†, anecdote, 298†, 309†, granddau, 298†, 309†, dau, 310, statement, 362†
  Helena Stout, w, 309, leg, 309, mo, 310**
  John, s, 309, 310, md, 309, m 1, 309, fa, 310**
  Joseph D, corrects manuscript, 299, res, 299, as Mr, res, 298, author, 298
  Leonard, s, 310, killed, 310, sol, 310, age, 310

HOFF, Continued
  Margaret, dau, 310
  Mary Ann, w, 253, mo, 253**
  Theodosia, md, 327, m 1, 327, dau., 327, mo, 327**
  Thomas, s, 310
  William, md, 253, 382, s, 253*, 310, fa, 253*†, 309, grandfa, 253**†, 310**, g grandfa, 253**†, descendants, 253, husb, 253†
HOFFMIRE, Catharine, md, 382
  Lydia (Lidyt), m 1, 50†
HOG NECK, ment, 39
HOGAN, Frances, dau, 370, granddau, 370
  Frances Stout, w, 370, mo, 370
  M, res, 374
  Michael, md, 370, s, 370, fa, 370
  William, fa, 370, grandfa, 370
  Mrs William, w, 370
HOGARTH, Margaret, md, 64, b, 64
HOGG, Mifs, md, 274, res, 274, mo, 274
HOLBROOK, Mrs Levi, res, 182, author, 182, descent, 182
HOLCOMBE, Mifs, md, 342
  Mr, md, 342
  Carrie Stout, w, 342
HOLEMAN, Joseph, prchs, 115
HOLLINSHEAD, Hugh, Jr, prchs, 378, sell, 378, husb, 378
  Mary, prchs, 378, sell, 378, w, 378
HOLMDEL, bur, 161, 164*, homestead near, 153, Baptist Churchyard, bur, 164
HOLMES (HOLMEf), Bible, 191, 192, family, ment, 91, in Rev War, 101
  Mr, ment, 102
  Mifs, md, 129
  Alice, w, 90, 347, mo, 90, 150**, grandmo, 90**, md, 149, 165, b, 149, d, 149, dau, 165
  Ann, md, 354, dau, 354, mo, 354**
  Ann Eliza, md, 59, 67, b, 59, d, 59, mo, 59**, 67
  Ann Stout (Anna Stoutf), w, 325†, 364, res, 364
  Asher (Afher), s, 99, ment, 100, cousin, 103, 104, admr, 103, pd acct as do, 103, letter to, 104, as Col, letter to, 101, res, 101, as Mr, cousin, 103, letter to, 104, res, 104, 191, 192, his Bible, 191, 192
  Catharine, w, 344, mo, 344, grandmo, 344*
  Catharine Stout, w, 325
  Daniel, fa, 354, minister, 354, grandfa, 354**
  Esther, dau, 5, md, 5, age, 5, d, 5, mo, 5*, 6**, m 1, 375
  Huldah, dau, 161, md, 161, mo, 161
  Huldah Mott, b, 91, d, 91, mo, 91**, w, 91*
  James, admr pd acct, 103, res, 103, his est, 103, deed, 103, deft, 238, 248
  James M, s, 99
  John W, res, 104
  Jonathan, s, 161, fa, 161, grandfa, 161**, ovsr, 372
  Jonathan, Jr (Jonatn, Mnr†), appr, 79†
  Joseph (Jofeph), his admr, 90, do, dispute, 90, decd, 90, md, 99, 325, 364, m 1, 99, fa, 99**, res, 364

HOLMES, *Continued*
  Josiah (Josiah), fa , 5, grandfa , 5*, 6**, wit , 278
  Lloyd, md , 353
  Lydia, dau , 165, md , 165, w , 181, mo , 181*, grandmo , 181**, 182**
  Mary, dau , 90, md , 90, d , 90, mo , 90**
  Mary Ogborne (Polly Ogborne), w , 164, wid , 164, bur , 164, mo , 165*
  Mary Stout, w , 335, d , 335
  Obadiah (Obediah), writ agnst , 27, shrf , 27, husb , 90, 347, fa , 90, 161**, grandfa . 90**, 161, md, 161, m l , 161, s , 161*, grandfs , 161, d , 161, prchs , 330, res , 330, yeom , 330, land 347, as Rev fa , 161, res , 161, grandfa , 161
  Obadiah, Jr (Obediah, Junr), appr , 79
  Rebecca Stout, w , 353
  Rhoda, dau , 161, md , 161, remov , 161
  Robert, bndry , 78
  Samuel, Acct Book. 41, md , 91*, 335, b , 91, 335, d , 91, 335, fa , 91**, 191, 192, wit , 99, husb , 192, grandfa , 192, m l 335
  Sarah (Sally†), md , 191†, dau , 191†, b , 191†, d , 191†, mo , 192†, as Miss, ment , 91†
  Sarah Mott, w , 99, mo , 99*
  Sarah Ogborne, w , 161, mo , 161**, grandmo , 161, d , 161
  Stout, md , 164, b , 164, d , 164, age, 164, bur , 164, fa , 165*
  William, md , 325
HOOTON, John, m l , 110ᵉ
HOOPER (see HOOPS), James, shrf , 233
  Nicholas, sell , 134
  Phebe, md , 142
  Robert Lettis, convey , 116, sell , 126
HOOPS (see HOOPER), James, shrf , 233
HOP BROOK, branch of bndry , 180
HOP (HOPE†, HOPP††), RIVER, ment , 19, 23, 305*, 307*, 330, 345*††, 347††, alias Romanis, 326††
HOPEWELL (see OLD HOPEWELL), Assess Roll, ment , 333, 334*, 335, 336, Baptist Burying-ground, bur , 352, do , Church, dea of, 354, do , pastor of, 349, do , Churchyard, bur , 339, 340, 348, 349, 352, 354, do , tombs , 350, Church at, ment , 296*, 297, 332, do , bp , 332, do , re memb , 332, Churchyard, bur , 337, 338, 340, do , tombs , 349, 350, founder of, 297, Herald, ment , 299, a ketch named, ment , 73*, set , ment , 297, Tax List, ment , 334, do , Roll, ment , 333, 365*, Township of, ment , 332
HOPKINS, Hannah, md , 195
HOPKINSON, Judge, fa , 267, 268, res , 267
  Miss, dau , 268, md , 268
  Mrs , owns photos , 267
  Caroline Lafayette, w , 267, 268, b , 268, d , 268, bur , 268
  James, s , 267, md , 267, b , 268, d 268, bur , 268, husb , 268
HOPLER, Conrad, deft , 178, res , 178
HOPPING, Sarah, w , 286, mo , 286, grandmo , 286**

HORNE, Edward, md , 42, res , 42
  Henrietta Morris, b , 42, w , 42
HORTMAN, Grace Stout, w , 354
  Peter, md , 354
HORTON, in Militia, 73
  Lieut John, exr , 73
HOUGHTON, Alice, md , 354, m l , 354, dau , 354, mo , 354
  Elizabeth, md , 354, dau , 354*, mo , 354**
  Thomas, fa , 354*, grandfa , 354**
HOUSEL, Mary Stout, w , 354, mo , 354*
  Philip, md 354, fa , 354*
HOWARD, Deborah, sis , 194, her chn leg , 194
  Harriet Salter, w , 217
  J Freeman, md , 217
  John, fa , 194, leg , 194
HOWE Lord, address to, 368
  Sir William, order of, 44
HOWELL (HOWEL), Miss, md , 336, 342, dau , 336, mo , 336*, 342**, remov , 342
  Abbie Stout, w , 358, d , 358
  Abner, fa , 336, grandfa , 336*
  Arthur md , 90
  Benjamin, pltf , 89
  George, md , 136, res , 136
  Hannah Mount, w , 136, res , 136
  Margaret, md , 200, dau , 200, mo , 200**
  Margaret A , md , 202, dau , 202, mo , 202**
  Martin A , husb , 358, fa , 358
  Martin A , Jr , md , 358, s , 358
  Mary Jane, w , 358, mo , 358
  Mary Mott, w , 90
  Rachel Stout, w , 327
  Samuel, fa , 202, res , 202, grandfa , 202**, as Esq, fa , 200, grandfa , 200**
  Stephen, md , 327
HOWLAND, C G , s , 371
  Joseph, prchs , 371, fa , 371
HUBBARD, James, prchs , 331, res , 331, as Sergeant, sol , 300
HUBBELL, Catharine, wid 368, est admo , 368
HUDDLESTONE, William (Wm), gent , 365, res , 366, detr , 366
HUDDY, affair, ment , 320
  Capt , murder of, 237
  William, bro law, 382
HUDSON RIVER, Indians of, 299, lower, Indians of, attacked, 299
HUFF (see HOFF)
HUGHES, Mr , ment , 101
  Ann (Nancy†), dau , 383*†, md , 383†, mo , 383**†, grandmo , 383†
  Rev Daniel L, author, 383, res , 383
  Elijah, md , 383, s 383, as 2ⁿᵈ, fa , 383, as 3ʳᵈ, fa , 383**, footnote, 383, clk , 383, surro , 383, memb Legislative council, 383
  Humphrey, fa , 383
  James Cristy, md , 64
  John, md , 137
  Judith, dau , 383, w , 383, mo , 383**
  Mary Mount, w , 137, bur , 137
  Sarah, dau , 383, md , 383, s p , 383
  Sarah Tilton, w , 64
  Spicer, s , 383, unmd , 383, res , 383
  Rev Thomas, bp by, 244
HULETT (see HEWLETT)

HULICK, Abigail B , md , 144, d , 144, age, 144, bur , 144
  Abigail Mount, dau , 144, b , 144
  Anna Mount, w , 128, 144, mo , 144**
  Catherine Amanda, dau , 144, b , 144
  Daniel Mount, s , 144, b , 144
  Hamilton, s 144, b , 144
  Humphrey Mount, s , 144, b 144
  John, md , 128, 144, fa , 144**
  Mary Ann, dau , 144, b , 144
HULL, Mr , md , 61
  Elizabeth Morris, w , 61
  John, bndry , 121
  Jonathan Dayton, cousin, 203, res , 203, exr , 203
HULSE (HULIT†, HULTS††), Benjamin, husb , 86*
  Richard, wit , 5*††, mark, 5†
  Sarah Mott, dau , 86, w , 86*, leg , 86
HUMPHREYS (HUMPHARY†, HUMPHRIES), Elizabeth, md , 58, 61, mo , 58, 61**, 62**
  Thomas, agent, 114, atty , 114
  Walter, prchs , 153†, res , 153†, carpenter, 153†
HUNLOKE, Joshua, wit , 84
HUNT, Mr , md , 327
  Addria Stout, w , 342
  Catharine Stout, w , 351
  Elizabeth, md , 336 dau , 336, mo , 336**
  Isabella Ashfield, w [?], 38
  Israel, md , 342
  Leonard, convey , 18
  Obadiah, md , 351, s , 351
  Mary Stout, w , 327
  Samuel, m l , 38, res , 38
  Thomas, aged, 20, ment , 20, pat, 291, fa , 351
  Wilson (Willson), prchs , 135, bond, 229, fa , 336, grandfa , 336**
HUNTER, Gov , letter of, 29, ment , 30, appnt by, 30, attacked, 30*
  Elizabeth, dau , 83**, w , 83, leg , 83*, mo , 83, her heir, 83
  Elizabeth Mott, w , 83
  Elizabeth Seabrook, w , 255, mo , 255*
  Henry P , s , 255, b , 255, md , 255, res , 255, fa , 255*
  Marion, s , 255, b , 255
  Robert, Esqʳ, Captⁿ ginerall, etc , 346, as Gov , letter of, 30
HUNTERDON CO , Mott of, 88, recruiting, 98
HURLEY, Mr , md , 58
  Dennis, fa , 341, grandfa , 341**
  Emeline, md , 360, b , 360, d , 360, mo , 360, 361**, grandmo , 360**, 361
  Henrietta Stout, w , 344
  Mary, md , 338, 341, dau , 341, mo , 341**
  Mary Morris (Polly Morris), w , 58
  Oscar S , md , 344
HUTCHESON (see HUTCHINSON)
HUTCHINSON (HUTCHESON†), Miss, md , 143, 205, 352, twin sis , 143, b , 143, d , 143, age, 143, dau , 205, 352
  Anne, her set attacked, 300
  Elizabeth, md , 352, m l , 352, mo , 352*
  Elizabeth Stout, w , 364

408 INDEX

HUTCHINSON, *Continued*
  George, convey, 154, res, 154, town lot, 156†
  John, fa, 352
  Mary B, md, 143, b, 143, d, 143, twin sis, 143
  Robert, bro, 205, preacher, 205
  Sylvester, fa, 205, res, 205, bro, 205, preacher, 205
  William, md, 364, res, 364
HUTCHINSON S MILLS, ment, 127
HYATT, Mr, md, 369, fa, 370**
  Abigail Stout, w, 367
  Ann (Nancy†), dau, 370†
  Caleb, md, 367, husb, 367, carpenter, 374, res, 374
  Effee, wid, 374, res, 374
  Effee Stout, w, 369, mo, 370**
  Mary Jane, md, 370, dau, 370
  Phebe Caroline, dau, 370
HYDE (HID†), Mr, md, 59
  Caroline Morris, w, 59
  Elizabeth, md, 351, remov, 351, mo, 351**
  James, bastardy, 327†, res, 327†

I

IMLAY (see **EMLEY**), Ann, leg, 48, sis, 48, dau, 48, granddau, 48
  Euphemia, w, 213, convey, 213, res, 213
  John, indenture, 213, bndry, 213
  Leah, leg, 48, sis, 48, dau, 48, granddau, 48
  Meribah, w, 48, mo, 48*
  Peter, convey, 213, yeom, 213, husb, 213, res, 213
  Peter, Jr, convey, 213, husb, 213
  Robert (Rob†), bndry, 187, 213, decd, 213
  Samuel, fa, 48*, husb, 48
IMLAY'S MILLS, ment, 189
IMLAYSTOWN (IMLAYTOWN), ment, 114, 187, mills at, 180
INDIANS (INDYANS†), aids escape, 296, 297, re alarm, 220†, assault, 298, attack, 297, 298, do, set, 298, 299, attacked, 300, blood, Johnsons, 253, re condition, 197, comm re lands, 197, Deed, ment, 73, destroy set, 289, escapes from, 202, kill set, 296, 297, killed by, 197, excitement, ment, 362, experience with, 301, of Fort Orange, 300, Hackensack, 299, of Long Island, 299, 300, of lower Hudson, attacked, 299, Mohawks, 299, in New York, killed by, 123, 124*, River, 300*, Rockaway, 299, Seminole, War, 98, Westchester, 300, lands, re prchs of, 18, 226, do, from, 111, 170 304, line of Pocahontas, 43, make peace, 297, massacre, 269, 372, 373, murders by, 299, 300, mutilated by, 296, 297, number in war, 301*, *Wright*, ment, 23, do, at Croswicksum, 23, Sachems, peace treaty, 300, do, sell land, 302, do, of Manasquan, convey, 318, do, of Navesinks, 302, do, of Raritans, 302, do, of Raritan River, 302, saved by, 296, 297, saved friend, 301, saves life, 362, 373, saved set, 299, seize

INDIANS, *Continued*
  boats, 300, sell lands, 23, 73, 372, re selling liquor to, 74, sell prison, 299, *Servant*, 259, 291, slaves, 262, 263*, Catherin, 263, Florah, 263, Jack, 263, June, 263, Lucy, 263, Moll, 263, named Peter, servt, 173, re killing pigs, 173, indict, 173, Phillis, 263, Toby, 263, treaties, 187, tribute of dried clams, 299, do, of wampum, 299, uprising, 290, 299, 300*, 301*, 362, wampum, ment, 291, war (see also Seminole), ment, 296, King Philip's, do, 178
INGOLDSBY, Gov, ment, 72
  Lieut -Gov, suspends memb, 28
  Richard, Lieut Gov, address, 28
INGRAHAM, Anna Murphy, w, 148, mo, 148*
  George, md, 148*, res, 148, b, 148, d, 148*, fa, 148*
  Lauretta Michell, w, 148
  Mary Michell, w, 148
  Rebecca, dau, 148, b, 148, md, 148
  Samuel, md, 148
  Timothy Murphy, s, 148, b, 148, d 148
INIANS, Mr John, pltf, 222
INNES, Alexander, convey, 172, trust, 172, clk, 172
  Archibald (Arch), wit, 321
IRLAND, Silas, md, 287
IRONS, Garret, prchs, 198
  Mary G, md, 363
  Thomas, prchs, 106, res, 106
ISLANDS, Antigua, 35, 42*, Barbadoes, 14, 15, 16, 17, 18*, 22, 24, 25 38, 72, Beaufort, 274**, Bergen's, 291, Block, 110, Cape Devards, 233, Carrihees, 17, City, 219*, Coney, 301, Daniel s, 273, Demarara, 38, Edisto, 261, 263*, 265, 266**, 267**, 268**, 269, 271, 273, 275, do, Presbyterian Churchyard, 265*, Hispaniola (Haiti), 14, Jamaica, 42*, 366**, 380, James's, 263, 268, Java, 53, John's, 263, 264**, 273, Long, 20, 38, 71*, 72, 73*, 75, 76, 82, 83*, 85, 87*, 92*, 95, 98, 101, 103, 106*, 107, 110, 110°, 111, 145, 219**, 222, 234*, 289, 290, 292, 299*, 300, 306*, 317, 325, 326, 328, 329, 330, 338, 382, Madeira, 44, Manhattan, 291, 299*, Minnieford (Mineford†), 219*†, New Providence, 126, Rhode, 35, 38, 71, 92, 98, 110**, 111, 148, 161, 170, 177, 186, 216, 234, 289, 292, 317*, 379, St Christopher, 73, St Croix, 369, Santa Cruz, 371, St John's 265, St Lucia, 15, Salter's, 213, 214 Sea, 260*, 263, 275, do, families, 270, Seabrook, 263**, 266, Sedge, 78, of Shoals, 213, Silvester's, 17, Spanish West Indies, 14, Staten, Block House, 195, do, Coll of, 195, re British, 195, do, first Court, 195, Wadmalow, 263, West Indies, 73, Yonge's, 266
IVES, Susannah (Susanah) w, 175, 380, leg, 175, 380, friend, 175
  Thomas, friend, 175, husb, 175, 380, leg, 175, 380

J

JACKSON, Abigail, b, 87, d, 87, md, 87*, 376, sis, 88*, leg, 88*, mo, 88**
  Ann, md, 47
  Benjamin (Ben†), ment, 241†
  Elizabeth, sis, 198, md, 198, mo, 198**
  Hugh, husb, 47, s, 48, md, 48, 173, 174, bro law, 173, 174, prchs, 173, 174
  Keziah Mott, w, 81
  Marcy (see Mary), dau, 172, 173, leg, 172, 173, md, 173
  Marcy Potter, w, 173, living, 173
  Mary (see Marcy), mo, 48
  Rebecca, w, 47, leg, 47, md, 69
  Rebecca Morris, b, 48, d, 48, w, 48
  Richard, md, 81, est admn, 81, res, 81
  Samuel, fa, 94, decd, 94
  Thomas, bro, 88, res, 88, bro law, 88, s, 94, friend, 94, exr, 94
JACOBS, Gertrude (Gertief), deft, 290†
  Henry (Hendrick†), s, 259†, will, 259*, husb, 259, fa, 259, bro, 259**
JACOBSON, Hendrick, step-s, 259
JACOCK (JACOCKS†), Jonathan, *cousen*, 321, s, 321*, leg, 321, exr, 321
  Thomas, fa, 321*†, exr, 321†
JAMAICA, re remov of minister, 30, Parish, re dissenters, 31, re ejectment suits, 31, do, Church, md, 76, Rec, ment, 74, 83, 219, Sessions, 202
JAME'S ISLAND, ment, 263, 268
JAMES RIVER, falls of, 243
JANSEN, Anthony, farm of, 301, robbed, 301
  Eicke, deft, 290
  Martin (Marten), pltf, 290**, res, 290, pet, 290, dispute set, 290*
JAQUINS, Lorenzo, md, 205, shrf, 205, res, 205, s p, 205
  Mary Salter, w, 205, s p, 205
JAQUISH, Dr, bndry, 240
  Richard (Rich⁴), his land, 240
JAUNCEY, James, pltf, 89
JEFFREY (JEFFRY, JEFFERYS, JEFFREE, JEFFRY), Eliza, md, 364
  Elizabeth, md, 362, 363, d, 362, age, 362, mo, 362**
  France, prchs, 170, res, 170, 319, fa, 319*, s, 319, convey, 319, bndry, 319
  William, s, 319, re land, 319, prchs, 319, yeom, 319*, res, 319*, exch land, 319*, convey, 319
JENKINS, Genl Richard, killed, 176, s, 276
JENNETT, Miss, dau, 241
  Nathan, md, 241, d, 24, widr, 241, fa, 241
JENNINGS, Mr, ment, 28
  Ann, md, 376, wid, 376
  Peter, res, 376, his wid, 376, d, 376
  Samuel (Sam), ment, 28, peace disturber, 29, sell, 378, as Mr, factional disputes, 29

INDEX 409

JEREMIAH STILLWELL'S CORNER, bndry, 213
JEROE, Anthony, convey, 71
JEROME, Catharine (Kathariner), md, 109†, dau, 109†
Fay Purdy, mo, 109
JERSEY, sloop, wrecked, 234
JEWELL (JEWEL), Miss, md, 333, age, 333, mo, 333**
Elisha, md, 142, res, 142
Mary Mount, w, 142
Penelope Stout, w, 327, mo, 327
Richard, prchs, 180
Sarah, dau, 327, md, 327
William, md, 327, fa, 327
JIMMERSON, Mr, md, 190
Elizabeth, w, 190
JOB Mr, md, 123, remov, 123
Mrs, w, 123, remov, 123
Ann, wid, 133, md, 133, mo [?], 134**, w, 134
Mary Mount, w, 134, d, 134, bur, 134
Peter, his wid, 133, fa, 134, husb, 134
Redford, md, 134, s, 134, d, 134, age, 134, bur, 134
Richard, prchs, 142*
Samuel, wit, 78
JOHANNA, a ship, wrecked, 234
JOHN REVES' CREEK, bndry, 224
JOHNES, Hannah, md, 143, mo, 143**; grandmo, 143
JOHN'S ISLAND, ment, 263, 264**, 273
JOHNSON, Indian blood, 253
Dr, agent, 383
Miss, sis, 252, md, 252, step-mo, 252
Mr, md, 4, 274, res, 274
Mrs, w, 4
Albert, res, 84, will, 84, fa, 84*, testa, 84
Alfred, s, 252, unmd, 252
Ann Stout, w, 327, mo, 327**, age, 327, granddau, 327
Barnes, husb, 189, 329, res, 189, 329, md, 328, 329, fa, 329*
Carston, prchs, 291
Catharine, md, 130, dau, 130, mo, 130, b, 130, d, 130
Cornelius, fa, 130, 327**, grandfa, 130, md, 327, age, 327
Daniel, his wid, 197
Effy, wid, 143, md, 143
Elizabeth (Betsy†), dau, 190, md, 190, sis, 252*†, spinster, 252†
Euphemia Mount, w, 134, d, 134
Isaac, will, 87, 88, res, 87, bro, 88*
James, md, 189, fa, 190*, s, 252, unmd, 252
James M, his wid, 143
James Montgomery, md, 134
Jeronimus, his admr, 87, res, 87
Joanna, dau, 8, 253, md, 8, 327, b, 8, d, 8, mo, 8*, 327**, 328**, living, 253, unmd, 253
John, md, 69, s, 252
Joseph, s, 252*, md, 252*, 382, bro, 252*, fa, 252**, 253*, grandfa, 252**
Mrs Joseph, w, 252
Lucinda, dau, 253, md, 253
Lucy Saltar, w, 189, mo, 190*
Maria, cor, 382

JOHNSON, Continued
Maria Seabrook, w, 252, mo, 252**, 253*, grandmo, 252**
Mary, w, 8, 382, mo, 8, 323, grandmo, 8*, dau, 190, md, 190, 323
Mary Ann, dau, 252, md, 252, mo, 252**, w, 274
Mary Elizabeth, w, 252
Mary Seabrook, cor, 382, md, 382
Nicholas, fa, 8, 252, husb, 8, grandfa, 8*, 252**, 253*, res, 252
Parmela, w, 252
Sarah, wid, 197, md, 197
Skelton, wit, 227, 231, 232, s, 329*, heir, 329, cor, 383, author, 383
Stephen, s, 252, md, 252
Mrs Stephen, w, 252
Susannah (Susanna), w, 189, 328, prchs, 189, res, 189
Susanna Skelton, w, 329*, mo, 329*, decd, 329
Valeriah Morris, w, 69
William, acct of, 100, s, 252, md, 252*, decd, 252
JOHNSTON (JONITON†), Mr, md, 279
Andrew, ackn before, 186
Deborah Morris, w, 70, res, 70
Elinor, md, 98, wid, 98, mo, 98*, grandmo, 98, bur, 99
Ezekiel, md, 70, res, 70
James, mast, 112
Mary, sis, 278†, leg, 278†
Mary Shepherd, w, 279
JOLLY, Isabel, md, 343, mo, 343**
JONES, Mr, md, 169, 328, husb, 329, his wid, 347
Abigail, md, 106, dau, 106
Alice, mo, 328, admrx, 328*, 383, relict, 328, sworn, 328, w, 329, re sig, 329, grandmo, 329 wid, 383
Alice Stout, w, 328
Emma Ogborn, w, 169
Harriet, md, 256
John, md, 364, res, 364
Mary, md, 145, md, 347
Mary Stout, w, 364, res, 364
Richard, mer, 20, res, 20*, leg, 20, friend, 20, extr, 20
Rev Samuel, md, 383
Sylvia, w, 383
Walter, fa, 106
JOY, James, bill pd, 230, 231, gravedigger 230
JUMPING BROOK, bndry, 45
JUMPING RIVER, ment, 39

K

KAKIAT, alias New Hempstead, ment, 83, 95
KARR (see CARR)
KATSKILL, Co Militia at, 178
KEAN, Peter, md, 52
Sarah Morris, w, 52
KEARNY (KEARNEY), land, bndry, 77, 78, line, ment, 77
Michael (Mich), md, 34, b, 34, d, 34, pltf, 62
Ravaud, pltf, 178
Sarah Morris, w, 34, d, 34
Thomas (Tho*), pltf, 62, bndry, 78, 88
KEELER, Mary E, md, 217, mo, 217**
KEENER, Sophie, md, 129, d, 129, mo, 129**

KELLY, Mr, farm, 362, prchs, 362
Mary, w, 98, mo, 98
KELSEY, James, inform, 238*
KEMBLE, Charlotte Morris, w, 53
Richard, md, 53
KEMISH, Sir Nicholas, King's genl, 21
KENDALL, Ann, pet, 154, dau, 376*, md, 376*, b, 376, d, 376, age, 376, w, 376*, s p, 376
Mary, dau, 376, md, 376, w, 376, mo, 376*
Thomas, bricklayer, 153, 376, convey, 153**, res, 153**, fa, 376**, md, 376*, testa, 376, d, 376, will, 376
KENNEDY, Miss, md, 356, dau, 356, mo, 356**
Henry, fa 356, grandfa, 356**
KENT, Co, Mott of, 84, 95, 96, 106, 107
Penelope, md name, 362
KERR, Samuel, md, 69
Sarah Morris, w, 69
KERSTER, geneal ment, 340, 341
KESHOW, Margaret, md, 110ᵇ, res, 110ᵇ
KETCHUM, Widow, md, 349, mo, 349*
Esther, md, 354, m l, 354, dau, 354, mo, 354**, grandmo, 354**
Hannah, dau, 166
Joanna Ogborne, w, 166, mo, 166
Jonathan, fa, 354, grandfa, 354**, g grandfa, 354**
Joseph, md, 166, fa, 166
KETTLE, Jonas, s law, 159, leg, 159
Mary, dau, 159**, leg, 159*, mo, 159**
KEYNELL, Sir Christopher, fa, 42, test, 42, grandfa, 42**
Elizabeth, md, 42, dau, 42, heiress, 42, mo, 42**, d, 42
KIEFT, Director-General, barbarity of, 299, dishonesty, 300, issues pat, 299, his secry, 299, revenges murders, 299, 300, treachery, 300, treaty, 300
Governor, ment, 301
KILDARE, plantation called, 133*
KILLEND, Thomas, est admn, 75, res, 75
KILLGORE, James, m l, 381
KINDWELL, Ann M, md, 359
KING, Joseph, prchs, 133, res, 133
Lydia Stout, w, 341
Sarah, md, 206, mo, 206, granddau, 377
Susanna, g granddau, 377
Thomas, md, 341
KING PHILIP'S WAR, Salters in, 178
KINGMAN, Emily Stout, w, 341
Sumner A, md, 341
KING'S, Chapel-yard, bur, 178, Coffee House, ment, 371, Highway, 293
KINGSBURY, farm called, 33
KINNAN, Thomas, wit, 232
KINNEY, Asher, md, 357
Elizabeth Morris, w, 357
Hannah, md, 353, d, 353, age, 353, mo, 353**
KINSEY (KINEY), Benjamin, s, 157, 380, grands, 157, b, 380, d, 380, md, 380
David, s, 157, 379, grands, 157, b, 379, md, 379

KINSEY, *Continued*
 Edmond, md, 157, fa, 157**, 379**, 380**, s law, 158*, 159*, req cert remov, 158, re do 158, husb, 158*, 379, leg, 139**, exr, 159, d, 379
 Elizabeth, dau, 157, 379, granddau, 157, md, 157, 380, leg, 159, w, 379, b, 380
 Grace, wit, 158
 Hannah, w, 380
 Jemima, w, 380
 John, s, 157, 380, grands, 157, friend, 158, ovsr, 158, wit, 158**, b, 380
 Jonathan, s, 157, 380, grands, 157, b, 380, md, 380
 Joseph, s, 157, 380, grands, 157, b, 380, d, 380, md, 380
 Mary, dau, 157, 379, md, 157, 379, granddau, 157, leg, 159, b, 379
 Samuel, s, 157, 379, grands, 157, b., 379, md, 379
 Sarah, w, 157, 379, mo, 157**, 159**, 379**, 380**, dau, 157, 159**, 380, granddau, 157, md, 157, 380, leg, 159*, b, 380
 Susannah, w, 380
 Tamer, w, 379
KIRBY, Ann (Nancy†), md, 135†, b, 135†, d, 135†
 Mary, md, 70
KIRK, Hannah Mount, w, 143, mo, 143
 Jesse A, md, 143, res, 143, fa, 143
 Mount Emmons, s, 143, grands, 143
KIRKLAND, Miss Elizabeth Lee, dau, 281, actress, 281, honey moon, 281, md, 281
 Genl William W, fa, 281
KISNER, Isabella S, md, 149, b, 149
KISSAM, Ann Mott, w, 81
 Daniel, grands., 81, leg, 81, md, 81
 Elizabeth, md 110*
KITCHEN, Mary, m l, 110*, res, 110*
KLAWBERG, Fred, md, 61
 Julia Morris, w, 61
KLINE (see CLINE)
KLOTTS, Charlotte A, w, 7
 Charlotte A Morford, w, 7, b, 7, d, 7
 George, md, 7
KNAPP, Mr, md, 10
 Essie Taylor w, 10
KNEEBURN, William, wit, 321, pr will, 321
KNIGHT, Harriet B Morford, w, 11
 Henry, fa, 382
 Hodge, md, 382, s, 382
 Susanna, w, 382
KNOTT, Ann, md, 129
 Catharine, m l, 190
 Catharine Potter, w, 173
 David, admr, 3*, qual as do, 3, res, 3, 232, exr, 232, release, 232, inform, 232, bndry, 232, re land, 232, atty, 232, claim, 232, brolaw, 232
 Knott, Peter, md, 173, b, 173, d, 173, bndry, 232, prchs, 240, res, 240
 Rebecca (Rebekah), m l, 50
KNIGHT, Mr, md, 11
 Harriet B, w, 11
 Peter friend, 210, exr, 210
KNOWLTON, Calista, md, 343, mo, 343*

L

LABAW, David, md, 351, fa, 351
 Deliverance, w, 354, mo, 354
 Deliverance Stout, w, 348, mo, 348
 Elizabeth, md, 351, dau, 351, mo, 351**
 Francis, md, 348, fa, 348, 351, grandfa, 351**
 Mary, md, 340, d, 340, age, 340
 Mary Stout, w, 351, mo, 351
LACHEM, William, ackn, 289, detr, 289
LAFAYETTE, Genl, guest, 266, god-fa, 266, 267, uncle, 267, his visit, 267
LAFETRA, Quakers, 317
 Edmund (Edmond†), md, 317†, fa, 317**†, error, 317, s, 317, husb, 317, Quaker, 317, will, 317**
 Frances, w, 317*, mo, 317**
 George, convey, 321
 Sarah, dau, 317
LAING, John, wit, 158, friend, 158, ovsr, 158
 William, wit, 158
LAIR, Marie, w, 254, d, 254, mo, 254
LAIRD, Dr, d, 7
 Dr Robert, md, 7, d, 7
 Eliza Osborn, w, 7, d, 7, age, 7
LAKE, est ment, 302
 Mr, md, 328
 Ann, dau, 291, w, 291, leg, 291
 Ann Spicer, w, 292
 John, husb, 291, md, 292, prchs, 302
 Patience, mo, 189, decd, 189, w, 328
LAMAR, Justice, decd, 235, fa, 235
 Miss, dau, 235, md, 235
LAMB, Caroline M, md, 63, b, 63, d, 63, mo, 63**, grandmo, 63*
LAMBERT (LAMBET†), Mr, excluded exr, 245
 Charles, bro, 380, s, 380, shopkeeper, 380, ment, 380, d, 380, will, 380, his books, 380
 Daniel, exr, 245
 Elinor, w, 285
 Hannah, w, 241, 250, mo, 241, 250, grandmo, 250**
 John, fa law, 240, farm, 240*, md, 241, 285, fa, 241, 250, husb, 250, 360*†, grandfa, 250**, 254, res, 254, home, 254, leg, 360†
 Merriam (Meriam†), dau, 241, 250, md, 241, 250, cousin, 241, 250, sis, 241, b, 250, d, 250, mo, 250**, miniature, 251†
 Mrs Sarah, md, 255, living, 255, mo, 255*, grandmo, 255*
 Sarah Stout, w, 360, dau, 360, leg, 360
LAMBERTON, Port of, Coll of, 109
LAMBERTVILLE, bur, 131*, Presbyterian Church, elder of, 250
LAMBOLL, Benjamin (Benj), wit, 262, mark, 262
LAMLRY (see LANFRY), Susannah, md, 69
LAMOIN, Cynthia Mount, w, 133
 John, md, 133
LANE (LAIN†), Catharine, md, 69
 Cornelious, mast, 173†
 Eleanor, md, 357**, dau, 357, wid, 357*, mo, 357†
 Frederick, md, 344

LANE, *Continued*
 Henry, fa, 357, grandfa, 357
 Mary J, w, 344
LANFRY (see LAMERY), Susannah, md, 69
LANGDON, in Rev War, 216
 Col John, his Co, Light Horse, 216
LANGFORD, Isabella, w, 112
 John, md, 112
LANGLEY, Ann, md, 256, res, 256
LANNING-Bryant-Stout, item, 349, ref, 349
 Ann, w, 349*, ment, 349
 Edward, husb, 349*, ment, 349
LARDANT, James, tombs, 265, donor, 265
LARDNER, Alexander, s, 199
 Edward, s, 199
 Elizabeth, dau, 199
 Henry, s, 199
 James Lawrence, s, 199
 John, s, 199, md, 199, d, 199, res, 199, fa, 199**
 Lawrence Saltar, s, 199
 Lynford, grands, 193, exr, 193, s, 199
 Margaret Saltar, w, 199, d, 199, res, 199, mo, 199**
 Penn, s, 199
 Richard, s, 199
LARRISON, David, md, 130
 Elijah, md, 351
 Elinor Stout, w, 351
 Fanny Mount, 130
LA RUE, Mary, w, 137, mo, 137
LASSCELLSES (LASCASSES, LASSCASSES, LAfSCELLSES), in Militia, 37, 44, Reg officer in, 37, do, ment, 44
LATOURETTE, Amy, md, 201, d, s p, 201
 Mary, md, 201, mo, 201**
 Paul, Sr, res, 205*, prchs, 205
LAVALL, Captain, house, 17, re secreted goods, 17
LAWRENCE (LAURENCE, LAWRANCE), Cherry Hall Papers, 77, disputes, 77, family, emig, 298, do, set, 298, set, 301*
 Mr, ment, 77, 381, his wid, 170, md, 381
 Catharine Morris, w, 43
 Deborah, md, 98, dau, 98, mo, 98**
 Ed, took invt, 112
 Elisha, gent, 183, prchs, 183, res, 183, 189, 196, fa, 184, 188, exr, 184, 235, bro, 184, husb, 188, 322*, grandfa, 188**, convey, 189, trust, 196, friend, 235, renounces exr, 235, b, 322, d, 322, as Col, s, 38, md, 38, res, 38, as Mr, his reasons, 77
 Elizabeth, md, 184, dau, 184, d, 184
 Hannah, dau, 188, b, 188, md, 188, mo 188**, 225**, w 224, grandmo, 225**
 John, guard, 17*, resgn as do, 17, fa, 38, res, 38, 194, exr, 184, bro, 184, bndry, 189, admr, 194
 Jordan, md, 88; res, 88
 Lucy, w, 188, mo, 188, grandmo, 188**
 Lucy Stout, w, 322*, res, 322, orig, 322
 Martha Morris, author, 70

INDEX

LAWRENCE, Continued
Mary Ashfield, w , 38, d , s p , 38
Mary Morris, w , 36, 43, d , 43
Mercy, wit , 330, dau , 330
Richard, arb , 247
Robert, wit , 184, bndry , 189
Ruth Mott, w 88
Sarah, md , 170*, 194, res , 170, wid 170, w , 235, 381, mo , 235, 381**
Sarah Bickley, sis , 381, md , 381*, do , cert , 381, relatives, 381
Thomas, res , 37, 43, leg , 37, md , 43*, cousin, 43
Thomas, Jr , md , 36, res , 36
William (W^m), wit , 181, oath, 181, dwelling,182, as Capt , ovsr 222, as Dr , fa , 98, grandfa , 98**
William , Jr (William, Junr, Willm, Junr), wit , 113, 159, 232, 330, div est , 115, survey, 224, res , 232, exr , 232, as Mr , survey , 77
William, Sr , bondsm , 181, trust , 181
LAWRENCE LANE, ment , 152
LAWRENSON, Johannes, convey , 80, res , 80
LAWRIE (LAURIE† see LOWRIE), Benjamin, wit 113†
Gawen, testa , 362, will, 362, Gov , 362, as Gov , ment , 18
W , wit , 113†
LAWSHE, Abraham, md , 357, remov , 357
Sarah Stout, w , 357
LAWSON, Mr , md , 57
Lydia Jane, w , 57
LAYTON, land, bndry , 113, hne, do , 113
Mr , md , 57
Mrs , w , 57
Andrew, bndry , 310
Anthony, prchs , 163
Elizabeth, dau , 131, b , 131, d , 131, md , 131, w , 132
Euphame, dau , 132, d , 132, wid , 132, w , 164
Hannah, w , 311
Isaac, fa , 282
Job, prchs , 118, md , 121, 131, will, 131, fa , 131**, 132**, s , 132*, prchs , 363*
John, b , 132, d , 132, md , 132
Mary, md , 282, 284, dau , 282, mo , 284**
Obadiah, m l , 39
Rebecca, md , 39, 131, m l , 45, 68, dau , 131, b , 131, d , 131*, epi , 131, bur, 131, w , 248, mo , 248
Rebecca Mount (Becky Mount†) w , 121†, 131, mo , 131**, 132**
Sarah (Sally†), dau , 132†, b , 132†, d , 132†, md , 132†
Mrs Sarah E , her Bible, 279, 283, res , 279, 283
Thomas, bndry , 121
William, bndry , 113, 307, md , 311, will, 383, res , 383
LEACH (LEECH†), Mr , md , 214, his wid , 347†
Charity, dau , 214, leg , 214
Chanty Salter, w , 214
Mary, wid , 347†
LEADBETTER, Letitia, m 1 , 110*
LEAMING (LEMING†, see LIMING), -& Spicer's Collection, ment , 383
Mr , md , 211, fa , 211**

LEAMING, Continued
Aaron, revised laws , 383
Christopher, md , 383, fa , 383**, his wid , 383
Deborah, wid , 383, md , 383
Ephraim, s , 210, 211, neph , 210, leg , 210
Hannah, wit , 37†, dau , 210, 211, niece, 210, leg , 210
Isaiah, s , 210, 211, neph , 210, leg , 210, res , 210, 211, md , 382
John, s , 210*, 211*, neph , 210**, 211, leg , 210**, 211, res , 210, 211
Jonathan, author, 293
Lucy, dau , 210, 211, niece, 210, leg , 210
Mary, sis , 210* 211, leg , 210*, mo , 210**, 211, res , 210, w , 382
Mary Saltar, w , 211, mo , 211**, living, 211
Menbah, m 1 , 68†, dau , 210, 211, leg , 210, niece, 210
Ossa, dau or s , 210, 211, niece or neph , 210, leg , 210
Rebecca, dau , 210, 211, niece, 210, leg , 210
Sarah dau , 210, 211, niece, 210, leg , 210*, sis , 210, mo , 210**, 383**, w , 382, 383
Sarah Saltar, w , 211, sis , 211, res , 211, mo , 211**
Thomas, wit , 37†, s , 210, 211, neph , 210, leg , 210*, bro law, 210, md , 211, 382, res , 211, fa , 211**, cor , 382
LE COUNTE (LE COMT†, LE CONTE, see M^{c}COMT), Miss, ment , 103
Mr James, re saltpetre, 101†
Margaret, her exr , 84
P , recpt , 80
Peter, bill, 79, prchs , 321, res , 321, physician, 321, surgeon, 321
LECRAFT, Edward, uncle, 274, aide, 274, bur , 274, miniature, 274
LEE (see LEIGH), in Rev War, 52
Dr , md , 249, res , 249, remov , 249, fa , 249*
General Charles, his staff, 52
Hannah, md , 234, mo , 235
Jane, w , 249, mo , 249*
Joseph, wit , 222
Mary, md , 335, mo , 335**, grand-mo , 335*
Seabrook, s , 249
William Henry, s , 249
LEEDS, Daniel, just , 154, md by, 154, house, 154, res , 154, 156, gent , 156, bondsm , 156
Mary, w , 376, mo , 376
William, contention of, 318, prchs , 318*, res , 318, letter of, 318
William, Sr , prchs , 304, res , 304
LEETS (see LETTS), Francis, md , 363
Rebecca Stout, w , 363
LEFFERTS, Maria, md , 58, 61, b , 58, 61 d , 58, 61, mo , 61**
LEFFERTSON, Maria, md , 363
LEGARE (see LEGREE), Hugh S , lawyer, 271
William Seabrook, tombs , 266, d , 266, 267, s , 267, bur , 267
LEGG, Samuel, appr , 355
LEGREE (see LEGARE), Colonel, md , 267, fa , 267

LEGREE, Continued
Dr , res , 268, fa , 268
Bowie, md , 268, s , 268
Julia Seabrook w , 268
Sarah Seabrook, w , 267, mo , 267
LEIGH (see LEE), Mr , md , 336
Ann Stout, w , 334
Ichabod, md , 334, m 1 , 334
Mary Stout, w , 336
LEISLER, Gov , ment , 72
LENOX, Robert, named for, 371
LENT, Penelope, md name, 362
LEONARD, in militia, 101
Captn, recd goods, 101, of reg , 101
Mr , md , 53, 280, 333, ment , 318, fa , 333*
Ann, dau , 35, leg , 35
Catharine, dau , 280, leg , 280, w , 280
Christopher, s , 35, leg , 35
Deborah Shepherd, w , 279
Elizabeth, dau , 12, leg , 12, w , 35, wid , 35, mo , 35**, exrx , 35
Henry, bro , 12, will, 12, husb, 12, fa , 12**, bro law, 12, cousin, 35, power to sell, 35, s , 35, leg , 35
John, s , 35, leg , 35, step-fa , 38, prchs , 38, md , 279, as Esq , md , 35, d , 35, will, 35, fa , 35**, step-fa , 35, 38, res , 38, prchs , 38, buy , 39
Lydia, w , 12*, leg , 12, mo , 12**
Margaret, dau , 12, leg , 12
Mary, dau , 12, leg , 12, age, 12, md , 97, d , 97, mo , 97**
Nathaniel (Nathl), took invt , 279
O B , Esq, author , 322
Parthenia, dau , 12, leg , 12
Ruth Stout, w , 333, mo , 333*
Samuel, s 12, 35, exr , 12*, bro , 12, convey , 18, 319, just , 26, seizure of 26, prison , 26, leg , 35, bndry , 50, wit , 40, 321, res , 318, 319, prchs , 318, deft , 319
Sarah, dau , 12, 35, leg , 12, 35, w , 320, mo 320*, md , 320
Sarah Morris, w , 53
Susannah, w , 1, exrx , 1, mo , 1**, dau , 12, leg , 12
Thomas (Tho), appr , 5, s , 12, exr , 12
LE ROY, Edward, md , 53
Louisa Morris, w , 53
LETTS (see LEETS), Francis, md , 324
Rebecca Stout, w , 324, b , 324, d , 324, age, 324
LEVERICH, Hannah Mott, w , 110^b, d , 110^b, mo , 110^b
James md , 110^b, d , 110^b, husb, 110^b, fa , 110^b
LEVERIDGE, Hannah, md , 236
Margaret, dau , 236, w , 236
Mary, w , 236
Temperance, dau , 236, w , 236
William (Wm), s , 236, husb, 236, tutor , 236, 236*, decd , 236, feltmaker, 236, fa , 236**
LEWIS (LEWES†), tombs , 323
Ann, w , 65, mo , 65, grandmo , 65**
Ann Shepherd, w , 282
Ann Stout, w , 337
Benjamin, md , 141
Deborah, dau , 361, leg , 361

LEWIS, Continued
  Elizabeth, md , 346, 347, dau , 347,
    b , 347, admr , 347, mo , 347*,
    grandmo , 347**
  Elizabeth Mount, w , 141
  Elizabeth Morris, w , 69 res , 69
  Hannah, dau , 87†, leg , 87†
  Jael, w , 68
  James, md , 282
  John md , 68, fa , 347, husb , 347,
    grandfa , 347*, g grandfa , 347**
  Mary Stout, w , 340
  Philip, md , 337, 340
  Robert md , 69, res , 69
  Sarah, w , 347, mo , 347, grandmo ,
    347*, g grandmo , 347**
LIDDLE, Mr , md , 250, fa , 250
  Elizabeth, w , 250, mo , 250
  James S , 250, res , 250
LIGHTBURN, Elizabeth Seabrook, w ,
    273
  Capt L , md , 273, res , 273
LIKENS, Sarah, md , 379
LILLIES (see LILLY)
LIMBROOK , Widow, md , 335, mo ,
    335**, grandmo , 335**
LIMING (see LEAMING), Ephraim, s ,
    210, neph , 210, leg , 210
  Hannah, dau , 210, niece, 210, leg ,
    210
  John, s , 210*, neph , 210*, leg , 210*,
    res , 210, m l , 211
  Lucy, dau , 210, niece, 210, leg , 210
  Mary, sis , 210, leg , 210, mo , 210**
  Ossa, dau or s , 210, niece or neph ,
    210, leg , 210
  Thomas, s , 210, neph , 210, leg , 210
LINCOLN (LINCON), family, ment ,
    187, geneal ,185*, of Penn , 185,191
  Mr , grands , 191, re author , 191
  Abraham, bro , 184, emig , 184, 185,
    197, res ,184, 197, d , 184, 187,
    191, s ,185**, 186, 187, 191*, 197*,
    b , 185*, 187, 191, 197, will, 185,
    fa , 185**, 191*, 197**, set , 185,
    blacksmith, 185, convey , 185,
    prchs , 185, md , 185, 191, 197,
    life of, 185, 186, ancestry, 185, leg ,
    186, remov , 191, Pres, 191, 197,
    grandfa , 191, 197, taxed, 191
    memb assemb , 191, age, 197, his
    w b , 197
  Ann (Nancy†) dau , 185, 186**, 197†,
    leg , 185, md 186, mo , 186, 197†,
    sis , 186, w , 191, 197†, grandmo ,
    191, b , 197†, d , 197†
  Daniel, s , 184
  David J , res , 186, decd , 186, author ,
    186
  Deborah (Deborah), dau , 187†,
    tombs , 187†, d , 187†, age, 187†
  Hannah, dau , 185, 186*, leg , 185,
    w , 185, d , 185, md , 186
  Mrs Hannah Loomis, md , 59, res ,
    59
  Hannah Saltar, w , 184, 185*, 186**,
    191*, d , 185, niece, 185, mo ,
    186**, 191*, grandmo , 186, 191**,
    emig , 191
  Isaac, s , 185, 191, leg , 185, res ,
    191
  Jacob, s , 185, 191, leg , 185
  John, s , 185, 186**, 191**, leg ,
    185, 186**, res , 186, weaver, 186,
    heir, 186, convey , 186*, b , 186,

LINCOLN, Continued
  ackn , 186, bro , 186**, descent,
    186, emig , 191, taxed, 191,
    remov , 191, fa , 191**, 197,
    ancestor, 191, grandfa , 191, 197**,
    g grandfa , 197
  Josiah, s , 197, living, 197, d , 197,
    res , 197
  Martha, w , 184, mo , 184**, 185**,
    dau , 185, grandmo , 185*
  Mary, dau , 184, 185, 186, 197, leg ,
    185*, w , 185, 186** 197, md ,
    186**, living, 186, wid , 186, mo ,
    187*, 197**, g grandmo , 197
  Mordecai, s , 184**, 185**, 186, 187,
    197*, md , 184, 185**, b , 184,
    185**, 187, 197, fa , 184, 185**,
    186**, 187**, 191**, 197*, res , 184,
    185, blacksmith, 184, bro , 184,
    emig , 184, 185, 191, d , 184, 197,
    prchs , 185, leg , 185, 186, deft ,
    185, pltf , 185, husb , 185, 186**,
    191*, will, 185, 186, testa, 186,
    decd , 186, his wid , 186, grandfa ,
    191**, remov , 197, killed, 197,
    age, 197
  Rebecca, dau , 185†, leg , 185
  Samuel, s , 184, emig , 184, res , 184,
    md , 184, fa , 184**, 185**, grandfa , 185*, descendants, 185
  Sarah, dau , 184*, 185*, 187, leg ,
    185†, w , 197
  Thomas, s , 184*, 185, 186, 187, 191,
    197*, leg , 185, 186, fa , 191, 197,
    grandfa , 191, md , 197**, cousin,
    197, d , 197, res , 197
LINDSLEY (LINDELEY†, LINSLLY††), -& Marx, firm, 371††
  Chrity (Charety†), md , 88**†
LINING, John, deft , 185
LIONS (LION'S†), House, ment , 378†
  Miss, mo , 274, grandmo , 274**
LIPPINCOTT (LIPINCOTT), Quakers,
    378
  Mr , md , 157*
  Abigail (Abigall), recpt , 112, sig ,
    112
  Amelia Shepherd, w , 279, 283, mo ,
    283**
  Ann (Anna†, Anne), w , 56, 155*,
    376*†, 378*†, 379†, mo , 56, 155,
    378**†, 379†, grandmo , 56**,
    378**†, 379†, d , 155, bur , 155,
    dau , 320, 378*†, b , 320, md , 320,
    convey , 376†, dau law, 376†, stepdau , 376†, leg , 376†, 378*†, sis ,
    378*†, res , 378†, will, 378†, testa ,
    378†, prchs , 378†, descendants,
    378†, exrs convey , 379†
  Deborah Morris, w , 69
  Elizabeth, leg , 378, dau , 378, sis ,
    378*, res ,378, wid ,379, md , 379
  Esther, w , 320, mo , 320
  Esther Borden, dau , 320, md , 320,
    descent, 320
  Frances Stout, w , 320, mo , 320**,
    grandmo , 320*
  Hannah, consent, 120, mo , 120, 320,
    mo law, 120, will, 120, grandmo ,
    120**, 320**, w , 157, 320, 379,
    dau , 320, md , 320, g grandmo ,
    320**
  Isaac, md , 379, his wid , 379
  Jacob, md , 69
  James, s , 320

LIPPINCOTT, Continued
  Jediah, s , 320, b , 320, md , 320, fa ,
    320*
  Mrs Jediah, w , 320, mo , 320*
  Job (Jobe), m l , 155, 378, fa , 155,
    378**, 379, d , 155, age, 155, bur ,
    155, s , 378**, bro , 378, res , 378*,
    leg , 378, decd , 378, will, 378, md ,
    378, husb , 379, grandfa , 379**
  John, bill pd , 229, 231, md , 376;
    husb , 376*, convey , 376
  John, Jr (Jno , Jr), exr , 172
  John, Sr , friend, 175, leg , 175, 381
  John W , md , 70
  Joseph, s , 155, d , 155, age, 155, bur ,
    155, fa , 378, res , 378, grandfa ,
    378**
  Margaret, dau , 320, b , 320
  Mary, w , 157, 320, 379, md , 294,
    341, 344, s p , 294, mo , 344**,
    grandmo , 344*
  Nathaniel, md , 379
  Patience, dau , 320, 378, md , 320,
    leg , 378, sis , 378*, res , 378
  Rebecca, w , 344, mo , 344, grandmo , 344**, g grandmo , 344**,
    dau , 376, leg , 376
  Remembrance, fa , 320, grandfa ,
    320**, g grandfa , 320**
  Remembrance, Jr , m l , 50
  Restore, res , 170, convey , 170
  Richard, s , 320, b , 320, d , 320, md ,
    320*, set , 320, fa , 320*, as Captain, re Huddy affair, 320, set ,
    320, fa , 320
  Samuel, yeom , 51 surety, 51; md ,
    154, res , 154, exr , 154, bro , 378,
    leg , 378, fa , 378, husb , 378,
    grandfa , 378**
  Sarah, dau , 378*, 379, leg , 378, md ,
    378, 379, cousin, 378, mo , 379**
  Sarah Morris, w , 70, res , 70
  Susannah, md , 69
  Sybilla, md , 378, dau , 378, mo ,
    378**
  Thomas, md , 120, will, 120
  Wilbur, md , 320, s , 320, grands ,
    320, b , 320, d , 320, fa , 320**,
    grandfa , 320*
  William, wit , 35, will, 50, res , 50,
    appr , 68, md , 279, 283, fa , 283**,
    320, s , 320, husb , 320, grandfa ,
    320**, g grandfa , 320*
LIPPIT (LIPPET), burying-ground,
    ment , 362, re connection, 311
  Widow, bndry , 308
  Alice, dau , 329
  Ann, dau , 329
  John, s , 329
  Moses, md , 328, 329, fa , 329**
  Patience, md cert , 308, dau , 329,
    granddau , 329*, md , 329, md
    cert , 329, mo [?], 329
  Rebecca (Rebeckah), md , 279, mo,,
    279**, remov , 279, kin-folk, 279
  Sarah, bndry , 308, house, 308, res ,
    308, cattle-mark, 309, 311, w , 328,
    dau , 329, b , 329
  Sarah Throckmorton, w , 329, mo ,
    329**
LISK, Alice Saltar, w , 196
  James, md , 196, res , 196*, m. l ,
    196, bondsm , 196, sig , 196
  John, bondsm , 196, res , 196
LISTER, Mr , mast , 256

LITTEL (see LITTLE)
LITTLE (LITTEL†), Absalom, detr., 94, res., 94
  Ann, sis 241, md, 241
  Caroline Morford, w, 6, b, 6, d, 6, mo. 6**, md, 6
  Catharine Stout, w, 340
  Charles W, md, 6, b, 6, d, 6, fa 6
  Lurania S, dau, 6, b, 6
  Hannah, sis, 241, md, 241, as "Aunt Hanah," ment, 241
  Isabel (Isabella†), dau, 226†, b, 226†, bond pd, 231
  John (Jno), exr, 174†, res, 174†, fa, 240*, d, 240, grandfa, 240*, 242**, husb, 240
  Mary (see Mercy), w, 226, 240, 242, mo, 226, 240**, 242**, m l 240, dau, 240* b, 240, d, 240*, remov 240, md, 241, grandmo, 242**
  Mercy (see Mary), mo, 240 w, 240, grandmo, 242**
  Theophilus, bro, 241, res, 241, se, 241, as "Uncle Thops," ment, 241, re his *famely*, 241 fa, 241, as Major, uncle, 240, guard, 240
  Thomas (Tho⁹), fa, 226, husb, 226
  Tobias, s, 241
  William, md, 340
LITTLE CREEK HUNDRED, alias York, 96
LITTLE CREEK NECK ment 107
LITTLE EGG HARBOR (LITTLE EGG HARBOUR), hist of, 323*, Monthly Meeting, 323
LIQUOR, re Indians, 74, re at funerals, 75*
LIVELY, Privateer, ment, 370
LIVINGSTON, William (Wᵐ), Gov, appnt, 238
LLOYD, Mr, md, 54
  Charles, s, 283, b, 283
  Clemence, dau, 283, b, 283
  Clemence Shepherd w, 279, 283, mo, 283**
  Clementina, dau, 283*, b, 283*
  Elisha, md, 70, res, 70, s, 283, b, 283
  Elizabeth (Betsey†), dau, 283†, b, 283†
  James, fa, 13
  John, fa 294, s, 283, b, 283
  Mary, dau, 283 b, 283, md, 283
  Mary Morris (Polly Morris†), w, 54†, 70*, res, 70
  Melinda, leg, 13, dau, 13
  Richard bndry, 213
  Sarah dau, 283, 294, b, 283, md, 294
  Sarah F, has Bible, 283
  Thomas md 279, 283, s, 283, b, 283, fa, 283**
  William s, 283, b, 283
LLOYD S NECK, ment, 73
LOAN COMMISSIONS, re mort, 39*, 41 45, Freehold, ment 209
LOAN COMMISSIONERS ment, 187*, 188 at Freehold, 209, re mort, 39
LOAN OFFICE, Comm of, 187*, do, sell land, 188, mort in, 235
LOCKE, in Rev War 215
  Capt Francis, his Co, 215
LONG, tombs, 323
  Jacob, exr, 46

LONG, *Continued*
  Capt Robert, god-fa, 37
LONG ISLAND, habitation, 73, hist of, ment, 289, Indians instigators, 290, do, plunder farmers, 300, treaty, 300, ref, 92, 110, Rocks, ship wrecked, 103
LONG ISLAND SOUND re shipwreck, 234*
LONG MEADOW RUN, bndry, 185*
LONG NECK (LONGE NECK), ment, 227
LONGSTREET (LONGSTREET), in Civil War 235, family, ment, 235, silver, 161, 248,
  Judge, decd, 235, g grands, 235, grandfa, 235
  Miss, md, 161, 328
  Mr. re candidacy. 103
  A B, s, 234, as Hon, author, 235, g grands, 235
  Aaron, exr, 239, his Tax Book, 247, fa, 248, husb, 248, grandfa, 248**, 249**
  Abigail, w, 234, mo 234, grandmo, 234
  Alice, dau, 167, leg, 167
  Ann (Anne) md, 248, dau, 248, b, 248, d, 248*, tombs, 248, age, 248, sketch, 248 her silver, 248, mo, 248**, 249**
  Christopher (see Stoffel)
  Hannah w, 234, mo, 234
  Henry (Hendrick†), ment, 298†
  Henry H, res, 161, has silver, 161
  Gen'l James, descent, 235, g grands, 235
  John, ment 103
  Mary (see Mercy), mo 240, w, 240, grandmo, 242**
  Mary Morris, w, 54
  Mercy (see Mary), mo, 240, w, 240, grandmo, 242**
  Samuel, exr, 168
  Stoffel (Christopher), md, 54, fa, 234, husb, 234, grandfa, 234
  William, s 234, md, 234, fa, 234
  Wilhampe w 248, mo, 248, grandmo, 248**, 249**
LOOMIS, Mrs Hannah, md 59, res, 59
LORD, Mary E, md, 317, mo, 317
LORDS OF TRADE, ment 28* 29 30
LORRILLARD'S, Brick Yard, ment, 247
LOTT, Miss, md 333
  Abigail, md, 339 dau, 339, mo, 339**
  Felix fa, 339, grandfa, 339**
  Gershom grands, 94, s, 94, leg, 94
  Mary (Molly†), dau, 94†, leg, 94†, w, 94†, mo, 94†
  Peter, fa 94, husb, 94
LOURENSEN Peter, bark attached 289
LOVE, Ambrose, decir, 301
LOVELACE Governor, address to, 28
  Lord. proposed by, 28*, letter of, 28
LOVELL, John, prchs, 369, butcher, 369
LOVETT, Emma md 367
LOW HILL ment, 244, 250
LOWNDES, Mrs Amerinthia, w, 260, tombs, 260, d, 260, dau, 2 o
  Mr Rawlins, res, 260, husb, 260
LOWRIE (see LAWRIE), James, s, 190, d, 190
  Lucy, dau 190, md, 190
  Sarah Saltar, w, 190, mo, 190**

LOWRIE, *Continued*
  Thomas, md, 190, fa, 190**
  William, s, 190, d, 190
LOYAL LEGION, ment, 109
LOYALISTS List of, in Lenox Library, 140, Captain Furman, 236, Motts, 110ᵇ, Mounts, 140, 141, Stouts, 368 369
LUDLOW, Gov, ment, 109
  Henry, fa, 43, mer, 43, grandfa, 43**, Chief-Just, 43
  Sarah, md, 43, dau, 43, b, 43, d, 43, mo, 43**
LUDWELL, Governor, seal of, 261
LUFBORROW, Elizabeth, md, 67
  Grover H, md, 286, res, 286, fa, 286*
  Helen Shepherd, w 286, mo 286*
LUPAKITUNK CREEK, ment, 77
LUTHER, Daniel, md, 339
  Elizabeth Stout (Betsey Stout†), w, 339†
  Watty md, 343, mo, 343**
LUYCK, Egidius, reed goods, 17
LUYSTER, Miss md, 252
  Cordelia Morris, w, 67
  George C, md, 67
LYELL, Catharine, w, 366, mo, 366, grandmo, 356**
  David, fa, 366, husb, 366, grandfa, 366**
  Eleanor, deft, 247, exrx, 247
  Eleanor Taylor w, 160
  Fenwick (Fenw'k), md, 160, atty, 233
  John, exr, 247
  Mary, dau 366, w, 366, mo, 366**
LYLLY (LILLIES†), David (Davied), oath, 20, wit, 20*†
LYRE, Manuel, Esq, tenant, 210

M

McBRIDE, Mary, md, 348, mo, 348**
McCARTY, Ann, md 379, mo, 379
  Dennis, fa, 379, d, 379, intest, 379
McCAUSLAND, Hannah White Morford, b, 7, d, 7, w, 7
  James rid, 7, b, 7, d, 7
McCHESNEY, Mr, md, 284
  Mary Shepherd, w 284
McCLAIN (see McLEAN), Mr, md, 57
  Deborah Patterson, w, 57
  Sidney, md, 164
  Mrs Sidney, w, 164
McCLOUD, Elizabeth, md, 270, mo, 270*
McCOMB, in U S Army, 108
  General, fa, 108
  Miss, dau, 108 md, 108
  Bridgett Mott, w 110*, mo, 110*
  Eleazer, s, 110*, bp 110*
  James fa, 110*, husb 110*
McCOMB (see LLCOUNIL), Mr James, re saltpetre 101
McCRAY AND HARRIS, school of 243
McDONALD, Clarissa md 207, mo, 207**
McDOUGALL, Mr, md, 129 res, 129
  Pauline Bertha, w, 129
McDOWELL (MACK DOWALL†) of Shrewsbury, ment, 236
  Andrew md, 236, 247, husb, 236†, 247, fa, 247, decd, 247, his exrs, 247

INDEX

McDOWELL, Continued
　Alexander, Mariner, 236†, res , 236†
　Eleanor, md , 225, 236, b , 225, 236;
　　res , 236
　Hannah Seabrook, w , 247, mo , 247
　Margaret, w , 236†
　Thomas, s , 247, exr , 247
McEVERS, Mr , atty , 233
　John will, 366, prchs , 366
McILVAINE, Ernest W , s , 166, md ,
　166, fa , 166
　Lydia M , w , 166, mo , 166
McINTOSH, in U S Army, 358
　Amelia Stout, w , 358
　John, md 358, Major-Genl , 358
McKINSTRY, in U. S Navy, 108
　Capt , md , 108
　Mary, w , 108
McLEAN (see McCLAIN, SHEPHERD),
　Judge, md , 109
　Catharine, dau , 249 md , 249
　Jacob, md , 249, fa , 249
　Mrs Jacob, w , 249, mo , 249
　Marie Mott, w , 109
　Rachel, md , 315, 364, d , 315
　Rezin D , actor, 281, family, 281, s ,
　　281
McMENOMY, Eliza Loskiel Bernardo,
　dau , 201, md , 201, decd , 201,
　s p , 201
　Eliza Saltar, w , 195, 200, 204*, mo ,
　　195, 200, 201*, leg , 195, 204*,
　　grandmo , 204*, g grandmo , 204**
　Lavinia Louise, dau 201, 204, md ,
　　204, mo , 204
　Mary Catharine, dau , 200, 204,
　　md , 204, decd , 204, mo , 204,
　　grandmo , 204**
　Robert, opinion agnst , 195, md ,
　　195, 200, clk , 200, auctioneer,
　　200, fa , 195, 200, 201*, 204*,
　　husb , 204*, grandfa , 204*, g
　　grandfa , 204**
McMICHAEL, John, md , 129
　Rebecca, w , 129
McMURTRIE, Ann, w , 193, dau , 193,
　leg , 193
　Rebecca, w , 193, leg , 193
　William, husb , 193, mer , 193
MACKPHERSON, Evan, wit , 262
McROBERTS, Mr , md , 129
　Mary Frances, w , 129
MACE, Mr , md , 214
　Mary, dau , 214, leg , 214
　Mary Sater, w , 214
MACHAPONIX (MATCHEPONIX†),
　ment , 130†
MACHAPONIX RIVER, ment , 185,
　bndry , 185
MADDEN (MADDON), Mr , md , 130
　Hannah Mount, w , 130
　Mary, w , 63, 64, mo , 63, 64, grand-
　　mo , 64**
MADDOCK (see MATTOCKS), William
　(Wm), wit , 235
MADISON, called Battle Hill, 201
　President, ment 272
MADNAM'S (MADNAN'S) NECK,
　ment , 80, 81, 84, alias Great Neck,
　ment , 81
MAGEE (MAGHEE, MEGHEE), Amey,
　w , 90, mo , 90**
　Anne Golden, w , 67
　Catharine, dau , 90, b , 90
　Henry, md , 67

MAGEE, Continued
　James, s , 90, b , 90
　Safety, s , 90, 91*, b , 90, re md , 91,
　　letter of, 91**, sig , 91*, bro , 91*
　William (Billy†), s , 90, b , 90, md,
　　90, fa , 90**, bro , 91†, d , 91†,
　　bur , 91†
MAGNOLIA CEMETERY, bur , 271
MAIN, Alice, md,, 343, mo , 343
MALCOLM, Edwin, s , 207
　Frederick, s , 207
　Capt George, prchs , 195, md , 206,
　　res , 206, fa , 207**
　Horatio, s , 207
　Ida, dau , 207
　Leslie, s , 207
　Matilda, dau , 207
　Rachel Salter, w , 206, md , 206, d.,
　　206, mo , 207**
　Washington Irving, s , 207, decd ,
　　207
MANAHAWKIN, ment , 364
MANASQUAN, Atlantic View Cemetery,
　bur , 141, Indian Sachems of, con-
　vey , 118, land donated for ch ,
　146, Presbyterian Churchyard,
　ment , 7
MANASQUAN BEACH, ment , 33
MANASQUAN RIVER, ment , 319*,
　321, branches of, 226
MANHATTAN ISLAND, Dutch on,
　299, protection of fort, 299
MANLOVE, in Rev War, 107
　Capt , his battalion, 107
　George, md , 96, res , 96
　Matthew (Mathew), md , 96, admn
　　granted, 96
　Sarah, admn granted, 96, sis , 107,
　　leg , 107, mo , 107*
　Sarah Mott, w , 96
MANNERS, Abraham, md , 342
　Ann Stout, w , 351, mo , 351
　David, fa , 341
　Elizabeth, dau , 350
　John, md , 337, 341, 348, 350, 351,
　　m l , 337, fa , 337, 350**, 351*,
　　s , 341, 350, 351, res , 348, 350, b ,
　　350, grandfa , 350**, 351 husb ,
　　351
　Lydia, dau , 350, md , 350, mo , 350**
　Mary Ann, w , 350
　Penelope Stout, w , 341
　Rebecca, dau , 350
　Rachel Stout, w , 337, 348, 350, 351,
　　mo , 337, 350**, 351, grandmo ,
　　350**, 351
MANNING-and Bray, Hist , ment , 152,
　do , of Surrey, 152
　Miss, md , 345
　Amos R , Esq , Supreme Court, 153,
　　res , 153
MANUSCRIPTS, Colonial, Calendar of,
　85
MAPLE, Ladies, ment , 104
MAPLE CREEK, bndry , 156
MAPPA (see MAPPIE, MAPPS), Mr ,
　md , 197
　Mrs , w , 197
　Elizabeth, leg , 198
　Jane, dau , 198, leg , 198
　John, fa , 198
　Sarah, mo , 198
MAPPIE (see MAPPA, MAPPS), Mr ,
　md , 197
　Mrs , w , 197

MAPPS (see MAPPA, MAPPIE), Mr ,
　md , 197
　Mrs , w , 197
　Elizabeth, leg , 199
　John, leg , 199
MARCH (see MARSH), Elizabeth, md ,
　215, res , 215, b , 215, d , 215, mo ,
　215
MARIUS, Peter Jacob, will, 383, mer ,
　383, res , 383
MARKET ALLEY, Richmond, 245*
MARKET HOUSE, Richmond, 245**,
　do , Common, 245
MARLBORO, Brick Church, bur , 284
MAMARONECK (MARMARONECK,
　MARONECK†, MOMORON-
　ACK, MOMORONECK), Rec ,
　Town of, 110
MARQUETTE, Bishop of, ment , 108
MARRIAGES, Mott, 110°, Licenses,
　Mott, 110°**, New Jersey, 110,
　110°, New York, 110, 110°**, 110b,
　110°, Rec , Freehold, 363, 364,
　do , New Brunswick, 364, do ,
　Tom's River, 363
MARSH (MASH†, see MARCH), old
　spelling, 252
　Miss, mo , 254, sis, 254
　Adelina, dau , 252, md , 252, d , 252
　Alfred, s , 252, d , 252, fa , 252
　Anderson, md , 253
　Mrs Anderson, w , 253
　Augustus, s , 252*, md , 252, fa.,
　　252**
　Edwin, s , 252, md , 252, fa , 252**
　George, s , 252
　Harriet, dau , 252, md , 252**
　Maria, dau , 252, md , 252, res , 252
　Martha (Patty†), aunt, 252†, dau ,
　　252†, relatives of, 252†, step-dau ,
　　252†, as Mrs , obit , 251, 252, d ,
　　251*, wid , 251, age, 251, 252†
　Martha Seabrook, w , 251, 254, age,
　　251, b , 251, emig , 251
　Samuel, md , 251†, 252, 254, res ,
　　251†, descendant, 251†, emig , 251†,
　　his wid , 251, s , 252, fa , 252**,
　　bro , 252**, 254, remov , 252;
　　uncle, 252, s law, 252, shipbuilder,
　　252, grandfa , 252**
　Samuel Stephen, s , 252
　Sarah Ann, dau , 252, b , 252, md ,
　　252
MARSHALL, Ann, w , 136, mo , 136,
　grandmo , 137**
MARTIN, Mr , husb , 313
　John (Jno), wit , 152
　Leah Stout, w , 313
　Rhoda, md , 163, 166, b , 166, d ,
　　166, age, 166, bur , 166, mo , 166**
　Virginia G , md , 341
MARX-& Linsley, firm, 371
　Asher, md , 370, 371*, res , 371,
　　partner, 371, mer , 371, fa , 371*
　Catharine Stout, w , 370, 371, b ,
　　370, d , 370, 371
MARYLAND ROAD, ment , 346
MASKER, Emeline, md , 11, dau , 11,
　mo , 11**
　Hannah, mo , 11, w , 11, res , 11,
　　grandmo , 11**
　Jacob H , fa , 11, husb , 11, res , 11,
　　grandfa , 11**
MASON, Elizabeth, md , 60
MASON'S HALL, Richmond, bp , 244

INDEX 415

MASSACHUSETTS, State of, difficulties of, 109
MASSACHUSETTS BAY, ment., 226, Colony, ment., 177
MASTERS, Miss, md., 42
  Dorothy, md., 42, d., s p., 42
MATHIS (see MATTHEWS), John. prchs., 376
MATINECOCK (MATTINICOT†), ment., 20 73, 110
MATOROPAN BRIDGE, ment., 156
MATTACOPENY, ment., 153
MATTGAIRISON'S (MATTSGAIRISONS) NECK, ment., 219*
MATTHEWS (see MATHIS), James, will, 259, husb., 259, step-fa., 259*, fa., 351, grandfa., 351**
  Lydia md., 55, 69
  Martha, md., 351, mo., 351**, remov., 351
  Mary, mo., 259**, will, 259**, w., 259, grandmo., 259**, guard., 259
  Mary Brewer, w., 51
  William, md., 51
MATTISON, Miss, md., 348, mo., 348
  Jacob, fa., 348, grandfa., 348
MATTOCKS (see MADDOCK), Jerusha Mott, w., 97
  Richard, md., 97
MAVERICKE, Samuel, address by, 73, commr., 73, expeditions, 73
MAXSON (MAXIN†), Mr., md., 131, 164, fa., 131, 164, grandfa., 164
  Anne, dau., 164†, md., 164†, mo., 164†, grandmo., 164†
  Hannah Ogborne, w., 164†, mo., 164**†, grandmo., 164*†, md., 164†
  Margaret Amelia, w., 131, mo., 131
  Timothy, s., 131, res., 131
  Timothy M., his Bible, 120, res., 120
MAXWELL, in Rev War, 98, Brigade, ment., 98
MAYER, Emeline Laura Mott, w., 98, mo., 98
  Frederick, md., 98, fa., 98
MAYES, Edward, Esq., lawyer, 235, res., 235, md., 235, author, 235
MEDICAL, bill, 100, Columbia College, 106*, prescriptions, 79, treatment, 102; 103
MEEKER, Mrs., md., 119
MEEKHAM, John, wit., 305 306, sig., 305
MEGGETT, Martha, md., 269, mo., 269**
MEIRS, Appollo, buy., 136
MENIER, Abigail Stout, w., 369
  Francis, md., 369
MERMAID, Majesty's ship, ment., 44
MERRILL (MERRELL†, see MORRELL), Ann, w., 334, 335, 336, mo., 334, 335, 336, 349**, md., 349, dau., 349, grandmo., 349
  Ann Stout, w., 334
  Benjamin, md., 351
  Jane, md., 359, b., 359, d., 359, mo., 359*
  Rachel, md., 350, dau., 350, mo., 350*, 351**, grandmo., 351*
  Richard, bond, 195**†, ycom., 195†, res., 195†
  Sarah, md., 342, mo., 342**, grandmo., 342**
  Timothy, md., 334
  William, fa., 349, 350, grandfa., 349**, 350*, 351**, g grandfa., 319, 351*

MERRIT, Ann Stout, w., 334
  Timothy, md., 334
MERRY, Mr Deputy, res., 152, educated, 152, testa., 152
MERSEREAU, Elizabeth, md., 132
  John, bondsm., 195
  Peter, md., 132
  Sarah Layton (Sally Layton†), w., 132
MERSHON, Miss, md., 333
MERVIN, Abigail, wit., 369
MESPATH KILL, ment., 71
METHODISTS, of New Jersey, preachers of, 205
METLER, Mary Stout, w., 356, d., 356
  Samuel, md., 356
MEXICO City of, Battle of, 109
MEXICAN WAR, ment., 108, Mott in, 109, Morris in, 53
MICHEAU, John, friend, 85, exr., 85
MIDDLE NECK, ment., 72
MIDDLESEX, Deeds, ment., 143, Rec., ment., 138, County of, attack on jail, 29, do., Clayton's Hist of, 129, do., Court Rec., 225
MIDDLETON, Mr., md., 320
  Hannah md., 379
  Hester, mo., 56, w., 56
  Patience, w., 320
MIDDLETOWN (MIDDLETON†), Assess List, 160, Baptist Church, erection of, 362, do., ment., 46, do., memb. of, 112, 182, 188, 212, 224, 226, 233, 307, 326, 346, 347, do., Rec., 41, 312, 360, Rec. Book, 212, do., site, 298, do., trust of, 162, do., Churchyard, bur., 281*, 316, 356, Block House, a fort, 298, do., b., 307, do., site, 362, bridge between Red Bank, 1, Court at, 25, 112, do., Sessions, 26, do., Book, 224, re desecration of Sabbath, 34, first div of, 292, Episcopal Church, ment., 362, Fairview Cemetery ment., 131, do., bur., 121 re fighting, drinking and immorality, 32, highway, ment., 304, homestead near, 111, Local Assemb., 307, Militia, 307, minister at, 359, Monthly Court, 307, Patentees, controversy, 181, Poor of ment., 331 Presbyterian Church, defunct, 281, do., Churchyard, bur., 310, 313, do., Old, do., tombs, 309, Quit Rents, 304, road, ment., 1, set., 305, shore, shipwreck 298, Stout, plot, 312, Tax Book, ment., 247, Town Rec., ment., 345, Township, ment., 67, 112, Wall Burying-ground, bur., 161, do., plot, 312, village, ment., 237, 238
MIDDLETOWN POINT, ment., 91, 105, 136, 310
MIDWOUT (see FLUSHING), Court at, 290
MIKELL, Miss, md., 266, 268, mo., 266**, 268**, 269*
MILITIA (see REGIMENTS), age to take up arms, 292, Baxter in, 300, Brearley in, 90, Company of foot, 74, Clinton in, 44, Curtis in, 379, Dazell's Regiment, 42 Troop Light Dragoons, 12; 163, in Dutch employ, 299, English employed by

MILITIA, Continued
  Dutch, 299, English in, 300, Capt Kenneth Hankinson's Reg., 12*, Horton in, 73, Hubbard in, 300, Lascellses Reg., 37, 44; Capt Francis Locke's Co., 215, Middletown, 307, Monmouth, 90, Morris in, 24*, 25, 34, 37, 42, 43 67, Col Lewis Morris, (England), 14, Mott in, 73*, 75**, 84, 85, 86*, 90**, 96, Mount in, 113, 117, 133, movements of, 101, New Jersey Battalion, 44, Capt Jos Parson's Co., 216, Penneare in, 299, Pennoyer in, 300, Pothook, 178, Read in, 237, Richmond Co., 96, Salter in, 180, Seabrook in, 236, 237, 252, Seaman in, 75, Lieut Barnes Smock, his Troop, 163, Stillwell in, 300, Stout in, 299, 300, 301, 307, 339, 368, 369, Underhill in, 71, Waddle in, 237, Capt John Walton's Dragoons, 12, Westchester Co., 43
MILL BROOK, ment., 113
MILL RUN, bndry., 113
MILLARD, Hannah, w., 186
  Joseph, md., 186, bro law., 186, living, 186
MILLER, Mr., md., 11, 270
  David, fa., 202
  Elizabeth Seabrook, w., 270
  Gilbert, md., 56
  Gordon, md., 145, d., 145
  Hannah, md., 202, dau., 202
  John (Jack†), his boat, 265†, negro, 265†
  Julia Adelaide, w., 11
  Julia Adelaide Morford, b., 11, w., 11
  Martha Mount, w., 145
  Rachel, md., 145
  Sarah, md., 105, mo., 105**
  Vincent house, 383, res., 383
MILLS, Elizabeth Salter, w., 214
  Hannah, w., 310, mo., 310, grandmo., 310*, 311**, g grandmo., 311**, md., 311
  John, pltf., 182
  Richard, md., 214
MILLSTONE CREEK, ment., 134
MILLSTONE RIVER, ment., 114, 366
MINISTERS (MISSIONARY†, see CLERGY), Friends of, Presbyterion, land for use of, 181, Quaker, 82, do., preacher, 98, Bishop of London, 32, Bishop of Marquette, 108, Rector of Bramerton, 177, Rev A H Anthony, 248, 252, Samuel Appleton, 358, Parson Auchmuty, 43, Rev Doctor Beach, 371, Rev Benjamin Bennet, 249, Rev Mr Blair, 245, Rev John D Blair, 244**, Rev John Bray, 223, Rev'd Mr Samuel Cook, 37, Rev John Cornell, 110, Rev Francis Doughty, 300, Rev Thomas Dungan, 379, Rev Isaac Eaton, 338, 340, Mr Edwards, 301, 332, Morgan Edwards, 21, 295, 296, 297, 304, 338, 346, George Fox, 15, Rev Tho' Foxcraft, 178, Bishop Gibson, 256, Rev Rany Gillam, 169, Rev Mr Green, 271, Rev William White Hance, 146, Rev Mr Hanckel, 271, Rev Mr Harris, 383, Mr Hart, 305, as Rev,

INDEX

MINISTERS, *Continued*
304, Rev Oliver Hart, 206, 297, O H Hazzard, 357. Rev Mr Henderson, 30, Jacob Henderson, 30†, Rev W D Hires 107, Bishop Hobart 193, Rev Roswell Randall Hoes, 244, Daniel Holmes, 354, Rev Obadiah Holmes, 161, Rev Daniel L Hughes, 383, Rev, Thomas Hughes, 244, Robert Hutchinson, 205, Sylvester Hutchinson, 205, Rev Samuel Jones, 383, Benjamin Moore, 195, Rev Abel Morgan, 281**, 282, Jacob L Mott (Quaker), 98, Phebe Mott, (Quaker), 82, Richard Mott, (Quaker), 108† Rev Harry N Mount, 129, Rev W N Ogborn, 169, Rev Willard N Ogborne, 166, Doctor Ogilvey, 371, Parson Oren, 37, Rev Humphrey M Perrine, 129, Rev Mr Pinkney, 272 Rev Alfred Povah, 151, Rev Mr Poyer, 30, Rev Mr Prentiss, 271, Rev Dr Pierre Alexis Proal, 370, Mr Reading, md by, 96, Rev Jacob Reckhow, 69, Rev John H Rice, 244, Rev Charles C Salter, 177, Rev David B Salter, 201, 204 205*, 207**, Rev Samuel Salter, 177, William Salter, 201, as Rev, 177, 216, 218, Rev Mr Schenck, 323, Rev. G C Schenck, 373, Rev Thomas Schrieve, 38, Abbot Seabrooke, 256, Rev Joseph B Seabrook, 260, 272*, 273, Rev Joseph Baynard Seabrook, 271**, Rev Josiah McCloud Seabrook, 271, Thomas Seabrook, 258, Peter Smith, 338, Rev Garner Snyder, 149, Rev Dr Spring, 367, Rev Mr Steele, 271, Rev E Boudinot Stockton, 380, Rev Elias Boudinot Stockton 376, David Stout, 353, David B Stout, 356, 359, Rev George Strebeck, 98, Rev John Sutton, 335, Rev Dr Roderick Terry, 281, Robert Tully, 256, Rev Mr Welsh 271, Rev Mr Whaley, 271, Bishop Williams, 108, Bishop Gershom Mott Williams 108, John Willis, (Quaker), 93, Phebe Willits, (Quaker), 82, Rev Mr Wilson, 248, George Wilson, 291, Rev William V Wilson, 248, 254*, 382*

MINNEFORD (MINEFORD†), ISLAND ment 219, alias City, 219†

MINTON, Archibald, md, 61, d, 61
Cornelia Morris, w, 61
Emily Morris, w, 61
James, md, 61, b, 61, d, 61
Philip tenant 221*

MINUTE MEN, Capt Jos Parson's Co, 216

MINVIELLE (MINVIELL, MINVILLI), Gabriel, appr, 17, compt, 17, res 17, atty, 17*, answer, 17, pltf, 74

MISSIONARY (see MINISTERS)

MITCHELL (MICHELL†, MITCHEL), Miss, md, 267, 268, mo, 268
Mr md, 273, 275
Mrs w, 275
Anna Murphy, w, 148†, mo, 148*†

MITCHELL, *Continued*
Catharine Murphy, 148
Frances, md, 336, m 1, 336
Harriet Seabrook, w, 273
Joseph, md, 148†, fa, 148*†
Lauretta, dau, 148†, b, 148†, md, 148†
Mary, dau, 148†, b, 148, md, 148†
Winfield S md., 148

MODIFORD, Thomas, agrmt, 72, mer, 72, res, 72

MOHAWK (MOHOCK, MOHOCKS) RIVER, ment, 37, 101

MOHAWKS, warlike descent 299

MOLLENNEX, Thomas (Tho), wit, 221

MOMPESSON, Mr, chief-just, 30, d, 30
Roger, memb council, 28, address, 28

MONELL, Elizabeth, md, 50

MONMOUTH, Battle of, ment, 52, 98, 147, 248*, 252, 282, Co , Council of Safety, 90, re expulsion of representative, 77, do, election of, 77, re forfeited est, 237, Genl Assemb, 237, hist of, ref, 110, m 1, 68, 69, Medical Soc, ment, 7*, Morris md, 69, 70, naming of, 18, Rec, ment, 77, Reg of Foot, 90, re riots, disputes, etc, 29, Troop of Dragoons, 163, Troop of Light Horse, 247, Court, ment, 90, do, House, ment, 117, Militia, ment, 90, Pat, ment, 222, 223, 292, 302, 326, do, issued, 301, do, re prospecting, 222, do, prchs of, 302, ref, 70, set, ment, 372, Tract, ment, 34, 303**, 326, 329, do , prchs of, 111, do , set of, 111, 301, 302

MONMOUTH RIVER, alias Allawayes Creek, 18, ranges of, 178

MONTEREY, Battle of, 53

MONTGOMERY (MONTGOMFRIE), Com , U S N, md, 372
Governor, ment, 30, 36, reduces salary, 30, d, 30
Miss, md, 316, mo, 316*, grandmo, 316**
Mrs, w, 372
Gertrude (Gertruydt††), md, 42, 50†, b, 50, mo, 50**

MONTGOMERY COUNTY, Baptist Church, ment, 212

MOODY (MUDIE†), Lady, arrival, 289, 300, emig , 300, her hogs, 301, her party, 289, recd pat, 289, her set, 300, 301
David, fa, 193†, 208†, grandfa, 193†, 208†, g grandfa, 193†, 208**†
Lady Deborah, mo, 299, arrival, 299, persecuted, 299, set, 299
Janet, dau, 193†, 208†, md, 193, mo, 193†, 208†, grandmo, 193**†, 208**†, w, 208†
Sir Henry, s, 299, arrival, 299, persecuted, 299, set, 299

MOORE (MOOR†, MORL††, see MORRIS), Mr, pltf, 289†
Rev Benjamin, trust, 195, friend, 195, minister, 195
Britton, md, 134, remov, 134
Eliza, md, 64††, mo, 64**††
Elizabeth, md, 69††, res, 69††
Gov Henry, land grant, 367

MOORE, *Continued*
Matthew (Matt), age, 27, test on oath, 27
Miranna, w, 379, mo, 379
Rebecca Mount, w, 134, remov, 134
Samuel, guard, 331
Sarah, md, 379, dau, 379
Thomas, fa, 370, husb, 379

MOORE-CUSTIS, Caroline, w, 66, mo, 66, grandmo, 66**

MOOREHOUSE, David, md, 313, 363
Leah Stout (Lieha Stout†), w, 313†, 363†

MORFORD (MAURFOOT, MORFOOT, MORFORT, MORPHET), burying-ground, ment, 1, miscellaneous notes, 12–13, Oath of Alleg, 12, in Rev War, 12, of Monmouth County, 1–13, bp, 2, 3**, 4, 7, 11, bur, 13, hist, 1, invt, 3, 4, 5, md, 12, negroes, 3**, on Patriotic Comtee, 5, ref, 1, 3, 9, 10**, 11, 12**, 13**, res, 9, in Rev. War, 12, silver, 3, 5*, spelling, 13, tombs, 1, tradition, 12, will, 1, 2*, 3, 5*, 6, 7, 12, 13, of Freehold, 13; of Lynchburg, Va , 12, of Middletown, 12, of Pa , Oath of Alleg, 12, of Princeton, 12, of Va , 12
Miss, res, 12*, author, 12*, dau, 12
Poet, step-s, 252
Essie Taylor, cor, 375
Garrett (see Jarrat), appr, 118, d, 118
George Taylor, cor, 375
Jarrat (Jarratt, see Garrett), surety, 42, admr, 130
John, md, 41, s, 41, 360, prchs, 115, bndry, 115
Joseph (Joseph), house of, 90
Lydia, cor, 375, bp, 375
Lydia Stout, w, 360, mo, 360, b, 360
Margaret, dau, 40, leg, 40
Margaret Morris, w, 41
Mary, w, 41, mo, 41
Sarah, md, 133, dau, 133, b, 133, d, 133, mo, 133*†
Thomas, fa, 41, 133, husb, 41, appr, 68, bndry, 113, 122, friend, 124, exr, 124*, res, 124, 133, convey as exr, 124, grandfa, 133**, test, 133*, his land, 133, will, 133, prchs, 133, cor 375, m 1, 375
William, md, 252, husb, 360, fa, 360, cor, 375, bp, 375
Mrs William, w, 252, step-mo, 252

MORGAN, Miss, md, 337
Rev Mr, his hats, 281, his house, 281
Abel, ment, 281, as Rev, epi, 281, re tombs, 281, do , remov, 281, ment, 282
Margaret, md, 364
Moses, md, 335, his wid, 336*
Sarah, m 1, 336, wid, 336, md, 336
Sarah Stout, w, 335, 336, wid, 336, md, 336, mo, 337**

MORRELL (see MERRILL), Kitty J, md, 360
Richard, bond, 360

MORRIS (see MOORE), Bible rec, 43, 50*, 51, British line, 43, land grants, 52, manor house, 52, m 1, 68, 69, 70, md rec, 69, 70, ment,

INDEX 417

MORRIS, Continued
110°, Memorial Chapel, 52, miniatures, 52, miscellaneous notes, 62–68, Papers, ref , 70, ref , 70, in Reg , 44, relics, 52, in Rev War, 35, 37, 43**, 52, 65, 67, in U S Army, 53*, in War of 1812, 63, of Monmouth County, 14–70, acct book, 68, anecdote, 36*, 37**, do , re gaming, 34, bp , 44, 49, 69, Bible, 37, 43, 50**, do , rec , 50, 51, in British Army, 43, crest, 21*, re factional disputes, 25–32, est confiscated, 15, farm, graveyard on, 54, Friends, 19, re funereal details, 32, 33 homestead, hist of, 14, 36, 46, in t , 20, 40, 47, 48, manor house, 18, 24, 33, 34, md , 69, 70, md rec , Freehold, 69, 70, m l , 68, 69, in Mexican War, 53, military appointment, 24, do , honors, 25, in Militia, 24*, 25, 34, 37, 42, mines, 18, negroes, 15*, 17, 18**, 19**, 20**, 22**, 34**, 44, 47, papers destroyed, 18, Quakers, 15, 30*, 32, 48, 67, in open rebellion, 29, ref , 14, 15**, 16**, 17**, 18**, 20**, 21**, 22 25**, 26**, 27, 36, 37*, 38, 41**, 44**, 49, 50*, 53**, 54, 62, 70, re religion, 32, re removing remains, 37, res , 15*, 16, 17, 18, 19, 20*, 22, 24, 26, 29, 33, 36, 37, 45, in Rev War, 21, 42, 43 44** 52, 65, Royalists, 44*, silver, 18*, 19*, 20*, 22**, troop of horse, 14, re vaults, 37, War 1812, 63, will, 19, 20, 35, 37, 40, 45, 46, 47*, 48*, 49*, 68, of England, 25, of N J , Quakers, 67, of N Y , 15–32 43, of Wales, 14*, do , est confiscated, 14, do , raised troop of horse, 14, of Westchester Co , 14, Judge, resgn , 187
Mr , md , 186
Adelaide, md , 364
Ann, md , 370, cousin, 370, dau , 370, mo , 370*
Anna Stout, w , 344
Benjamin, fa , 314, husb , 314, grandfa , 314**
Burt, s , 287
Elizabeth, w , 202, mo , 202*, d , 202, md , 364
Frederick, s , 287
George T , md , 344
Hester, md , 363
Joseph (Jos), prison , 12, res , 12
Lewis, res , 348, fa , 348, grandfa , 348, leg , 380, as Col , friendship, 380, ship-owner, 380, neighbor, 380, will, 380*, his negroes, 380
Lydia, w , 314*, dau , 314, d , 314, age, 314, mo , 314**, grandmo , 314**
Margaret, md , 3, dau , 3
Maria, dau , 202, md , 202
Mary, w , 186, bill pd , 230, 231
Mary B , md , 108
Rebecca, dau , 348, mo , 348, w , 348
Rebecca Shepherd, w , 287, mo , 287**
Richard, fa , 3**
Robert, his Claim, ref , 70
Robert Hunter, Esq*, Chief-just , 233
Thomas, md , 202, fa , 202*, res , 202
Wharton, s , 202

MORRIS, Continued
William, s , 287, md , 287, fa , 287**
William W , md , 370, grandfa , 370*
MORRIS COUNTY, Courts of, 89, Court Rec , 178
MORRIS RIVER, called Quahocking, 22
MORRISANIA, Manor of, 24, 33
MORRISSON (see MOURISON)
MORTON, Hon Landgrave Joseph, exr , 263
Margaret, w , 65, mo , 65, grandmo , 65*, 66
MOSES, Mrs John, g granddau , 235, res , 235
MOTT (MAET, MOOT, MOOTE, MOT), Ancestry, ment , 93, bp , 110**, 110ᵃ**, 110ᶜ, in Civil War, 107, 109, Diary, 88, descendants, 110ᵇ, English family, 71, exch of prison , 101, family, hist of, 109, do , manuscript hist of, 110; do , re names, 377, geneal of, 110**, Iron Works, ment , 107, md , 110**, 110ᵃ**, 110ᵇ**, 110°, m l , 84, Quakers, 191, in Rev War, ref , 110, 110ᵇ, spool cotton, manufacture of 108, Street, re naming, 98 of New York and New Jersey, 71–110*, re accts , 100, bp , 72*, 73, 74, 87, 88, 97, Bible, 83, 88, do , rec , 80, 98, bur , 78, do , plot, 73*, 75, burying-ground, 86, 99, in Cen , 72, 74, 75*, 76*, 80, 82, 83, 91, Cherry Hall Papers, 77**, diary, 78, 91, disputes, 77, est , 95, family affairs, 100, 101, 103, Friends 86, 92 93, 98, 108, homestead, 71, 73, 78, 80, 81, 82, 83, 86*, 87, 92, 93, 94, 96**, 99, 105, in Indian War, 98, invt , 78, 79, 84, 88, 90, letters, 100, 101, 102, 103, 104, Loyalists, 110ᵇ, md 87, m l , 110ᵃ**, in Mexican War, 109, in militia, 73*, 74, 75**, 84, 85, 86*, 90**, 96, 101, miscellaneous notes, 110-110ᵇ, negroes, 78*, 80*, 81*, 82, 83**, 90, 96, pat , 78, pewter, 71, 79, 81, plate, 106, Quakers. 81, 82, 96, 99, in Rebellion, 109, ref , 71, 74**, 75**, 77**, 78, 79, 80, 82, 85, 86, 92**, 93, 94, 97, 102*, 103**, 104**, 105, 109, 110**, 110ᵇ, in Rev War, 98*, 99, 103, 104, 105, res , 74, 75*, servt , 80, silver, 90, 93, 94, slaves, 80, 87, survey, 77, will, 71*, 75*, 76, 78, 80*, 81*, 82*, 83**, 84, 85, 86, 87**, 88*, 91, 92**, 94**, 95**, 96, 107, 110ᵇ, Whigs, 98, 88*, of Baltimore, 94*, of Boston, 71, invt , 84, of Burlington, m 1 , 84*, of Burlington Co , ment , 84**, will, 84, of Cape May, 84, of Delaware, ment , 84, 95, 96**, 106 107, in Rev War, 107, of Dutchess Co , ment ,81, 87, 110ᵇ, of Hunterdon Co ment , 88*, 98, 99, of Iowa, Bible, 88, ment , 80, 88*, of Kent Co , ment , 84, 95**, 96**, 106, 107, of Long Island, ment , 71, of Manhattan, ment , 71, of Monmouth Co , ment , 88, 89, 99, name extinct, 80, of New Amsterdam, ment , 71, of Ohio, ment , 108*, Quakers, 108, of Onondaga Co , 110ᵇ, of Orange Co ,

MOTT, Continued
ment , 94† 95, lands, 94, of Penn , ment , 84, of Queens Co , ment , 80, 87, 106, 110ᵇ, of Rhode Island, ment , 71, ref , 110**, of Richmond Co , ment , 96*, of Staten Island, ment , 80, 84, will, 84, of South Carolina, ment , 88*, of Ulster Co , ment , 110ᵇ, of Westchester Co , in Cen , 75
Abigail, w , 376
Adam declr , 289, s , 377*, leg , 377*, as the first, will, 377, fa , 377*, husb , 377*
Catharine, error, 190
Catharine A (Kate A †), author, 109, 110*
Cornelius, deft , 219
Gershom (Garcham, Garsham, Garshom, Gershum, Girshom), representative 345
Huldah, w , 188, 191, Quaker, 191, md , 192, d , 192, mo , 192**
Jacob, cor , 376, md , 376*
James, bondsm , 162**, 163, exr , 162**, 163, uncle, 198, letter to, 198, wit , 227, 231, 232, as Mr , letter to, 192
Kesia, w , 376
MOULTON, John, md , 214
Mehitable Salter, w , 214
MOUNT, Bible, ment , 116, 120. 121, 135*, do , rec , 112, 115, family, ment , 225, do , English, ment , 111, killed by Indians, 123, 124, Loyalists, 140, 141, in Militia, 133, ref , 146, relations, 111, in Rev War. 113, 117*, 127*, 128, 130, 132, 142, do , property confiscated, 125, Unconnected, 145, 146, of Monmouth County, 111–146, anecdote, 145, 146, Bible rec , 112, 116, killed by Indians, 123, Loyalists, 140, in Militia, 113, 117, in Navy, 137, Quakers, 116, ref , 112, 115, 126, 128, 129, 132, 142, 146, in Rev War, 125, 127*, 132, 145, of Allentown, 143, of Long Island, 111, of Salem, Mass , 111
Deborah, w , 281
Edward, grands , 5, s , 5, 8, leg , 5, bro , 5
Elizabeth, dau , 363, sis , 363**, leg , 363
Elizabeth Seabrook, w , 225, 235, d , 225
Frances, w , 376
George, grands , 5, s , 5, 8, leg , 5, bro , 5
Hannah, granddau , 5, leg , 5, 363, sis , 5, 363**, dau , 5, 8, 363
Hiram, prchs , 166
Horatio, grands , 5, s , 5, 8, leg , 5, bro , 5
Mr J R , author , 129
Jemimah, dau , 363, sis , 363**, leg , 363
Joseph fa , 5**, 8**, husb , 5, 8*, md , 8
Miss Mary, md , 367
Mary Ann, md , 284
Matthias (Mathias), cred , 40, prchs , 348, 305, res , 365, ycom , 365
Paul W , Esq* , author , 129
Rebecca, granddau , 5, leg , 5, sis , 5, dau , 5, 8, md , 183

418   INDEX

MOUNT, Continued
  Richard, md, 225, 235, b, 235, d, 235
  Samuel, md, 376
  Sarah, dau, 5, 8, w 5*, 8, leg, 5,
    mo, 5**, 8**
  Sarah Mortord, w 8, mo, 8**
  Timothy, md, 281, fa, 363**, testa,
    363, deed, 363, his land, 363
  William, prchs, 363
MOUNT HOLLY, Friends' Rec, ment,
  378 rec, 121, 142, will rec, 140,
  St Andrew's Yard, bur, 377, do,
  tombs, 377, transfers, 378
MOUNT MISERY, shipwreck, 234
MOUNTEN HILL ment, 238
MOUNT'S CORNER, West Freehold,
  hotel at, 145
MOURISON, Isaac, appli of, 89
MUIJTIENS, Elsje, wit, 73
MULATTOES (see INDIAN SLAVES,
  SLAVES)
MULFORD, Mr, md, 383, s p, 383
  Sarah, w, 383, s p, 383
MULLICA HILL ment, 293
MULLIN (MULLEN), Ann (Anna†),
  w, 378†, 379, leg, 378†
  John, husb, 378, 379, carpenter, 378,
    res, 378, md, 379
MURPHY, orig, 147, in Rev War, 147,
  of Monmouth co, 147-150
  Judge, md, 165, res, 165
  Mr, md, 165
  Alice, w, 165
  Amelia, w, 165
  Ann, granddau, 162, leg, 162, w,
    165
  Henry C, md, 149
MURRAY, Miss md, 269, mo, 269**
MUSKETS COVE, landing, ment, 238
MUSTER ROLL, ment, 113, 117, Capt
  Francis Locke's Co, 215
MYERS, Barbara, md, 141, b, 141, d,
  141

                N

NARROWS, ship wrecked near, 103
NARUMSUNK (NORRAMSONT,
  NORRANSONT, see RUMSON),
  alias Passage Point, 34, 38
NARUMSUNK NECK, ment, 303
NASON, May, md, 254
NAVESINK (NAVESINKS, NEVER-
  SAND, NEWASINK), alias High-
  lands 4, or Witch Hollow, ment,
  4, first prchs of, 15, 16, 34
NAVESINK HIGHLANDS, re beacon
  lights, 187, Sachems of, notified,
  302, set, 372
NAVESINK (NEWASINK†) NECK,
  ment, 303†
NAVESINK (NAVRSAND†) RIVER,
  ment, 1, 114*†, 187, mouth of, 302
NAVY, Mount in, 137
NAYSMITH (see NESSMITH)
NEAL, Elizabeth, md, 166, res, 166,
  mo, 166**, grandmo, 166**
NEAT, Hannah, md, 288, res, 288
NEGROES (see SERVANTS, SLAVES),
  corrected, 15, dispute re, 17, murder by, 34, trial of, 34, preached to,
  271, stealing, 15, suit re, 22, theft
  of, 34, Abba, 20, Abraham, 3,
  Alphey, 263, Beck Depriest, 246,
  Bess (beas) 3, 22, 19*, 308, Betty,

NEGROES, Continued
  90, 244, Buckey, 20, Cate, 78,
  Docia, 244, Esther (Easter†) 244†,
  do, and child, 90, Esabel, 238,
  Francke, 18, Hannah, 3, Harriet,
  308, Isaac, 90, Jack, 19, 78, Jennie
  (Jeny), 78, 263, July, 263, Lattero,
  263, Maria, 19, Tom Martin, 246,
  Mott's, 90, Nany, 263, Nell, 20,
  Oliver, 90, Peter, 90, 263, Philis,
  90, Ratt, 263, Sambo (Little), 263,
  Sambo (Old), 263, Sampson, 263*,
  Samuel, 90, Tom, 210, Toney, 20,
  William (Will), 263, 246, Yaff,
  19*, Yeabba, 20
NELSON, ment, 254
  Dr, md, 201, res, 201
  Mrs, w, 201
NESBIT (NESBITS, NISBETT, NIS-
  BIT), memb of Scotch commun-
  ity, 117
  Miss, md, 117
  Dorothy, wit, 117, 232, mark, 117,
    232
NESHANIC, ment, 323
NESSMITH (NAYSMITH), Thomas,
  leg, 158
NEW AMSTERDAM (NEW AMTER-
  DAM), bp, 72*, Church, Dutch,
  ment, 74, do bp, 73, do, Rec,
  72, 110, city of, 299, Convention
  at, 290, Dutch Church, 72, 73, 74,
  110, Dutch in, 296, do, ransom
  set, 299, do, treat kindly, 299,
  fort, ment, 289, do, arrival at,
  299, do, refuge, 300**, uprising,
  301
NEWARK, Court of Sessions, Rec, 29,
  Hist Soc, Inscription Book, d,
  331, do, Rec, 331
NEW BRUNSWICK, Deeds, ment, 364,
  365, md rec, 364, rec, 116, 225,
  365, ship belonging to, wrecked,
  234, Wills, 117, 140
NEW CASTI F (NEWCASTLE), pet for
  bridge, 216
  Duke of, letter to, 30, 31
NEW ENGLAND, Indian War in, 296,
  religious intolerance, 299
NEW HEMPSTEAD, alias Kakiat,
  ment, 83, 95
NEW JERSEY (see JERSEY), Archives,
  ment, 294, 326, 375, ref, 375, 376,
  377, 382, Assemb affected, 28,
  do, re factional disputes, 32, do,
  re sale of land, 154, Battalion, 44,
  re boundary line, 36, re consolida-
  tion, 28, Deeds, 110, Eastern Div
  of, ment, 76, do, sale, 226, factional fights, 76, Genl Assemb,
  345, list of, 295, 297, m 1, 110,
  110^s, Methodists of, 205, National
  Guard, 109, Provincial Courts of,
  ref, 70, State Prison, ment, 109,
  Wills, 110
NEWKIRK, Ellen, md, 70
NEWMAN (NEWMON), Jane, md,
  363, res, 363
  Jedidah md, 70
NEW NETHERLANDS, expedition
  agnst, 73, Gov Genl of, 17**,
  hist of, ref, 71
NEW STORE, Mr Iosset's, ment, 243
NEW YORK, Assemb, re expulsion, 30,
  do, re factional disputes, 32, re

NEW YORK, Continued
  bndry line, 36, Burgomasters'
  rec, 291, Colonial manuscripts, 16,
  17**, do, rec, ment, 290, re con-
  solidation, 28, Deeds, ment, 110,
  Documentary hist, 219, Dutch in
  possession, 296, do, Church rec,
  54, do, manuscripts, 289, Friends'
  Meeting, leg, 20, do, rec, 105,
  293, Geneal and Biog Rec, 53,
  Gov of, 33, Hall of Rec, 282,
  Hangman's Jail, 282, hist manuscripts, 301, do, Soc, wills, 259,
  Indians, killed by, 123, 124*,
  Lakes, ment, 337**, 338, m l,
  110, 110a**, 110b, 110s, 259;
  Mayor's Court, 22, Presbyterian
  Church, Rec, 122, do, First,
  bp, 368*, Privateers of, 370,
  Prov of, captured, 15, do, Chief-
  Just, 85, do, re Dutch subjuga-
  tion, 21, Stouts, unplaced, 366-
  367, Sugar House Prison, 281,
  Trinity Church, Vestrym of, 32,
  do, Churchyard, bur, 369*, do,
  tombs, 368, University of, ment,
  7, Wills, ment, 20, 75, 110, 175,
  203, 221, 259**, 328, 367, 369, in-
  teresting letter, 366, ref, 86
NEW YORK CITY, Directories, Stouts
  in, 373-374, Dutch Church, ment,
  118
NEWBERRY (see NEWBRAY), ment,
  331
NEWBOLD, Lettice, w, 377, mo, 377;
  grandmo, 377
NEWBRAY (see NEWBERRY), Wil-
  liam, wit, 174, mark, 174
NEWELL (NEWALL, NEWEL), Mr,
  md, 62, 280
  Emma Jane, w, 62
  Ezuba, md, 134†
  Rebecca (Beck†), w 280†
NEWS RIVER, ment, 240, 241
NEWTON, Alice, w, 73, wit, 73
  Capt Bryan, husb, 73
NEWTOWN, Meeting Rec, ment, 293
NICOLLS (NICHOLS†, NICOLL††),
  Governor, issues pat, 301
  Mr, guard, 16††, ment, 25††
  Matthias (Mathias), letter of, 15††,
    ment, 15††, sig, 15††, Secry, 221,
    prchs, 292, as Mr, Mayor, 24††,
    res, 24††, admr, 24††
  Richard, Gov, proclamation, 302
  Silleck, md, 141†
  William, prchs, 74††
NINE PARTNERS, ment, 87
NIPPER, Alexander (Elexander†),
  bndry, 180*, land ment, 180†
NIVERSON, Jacob, md, 163, fa, 163*
  Sarah Ogborne, w, 163, mo, 163*
NIXSON, Mr, md, 353, dau, 353
  Nathaniel, fa, 353
NOKES, John, sheep at, 158
NORRIS, Euphemia Morris, w, 33
  Sir John, fa, 33
  Capt Matthew, s, 33, md, 33
  Sarah, w, 131, mo, 131
NORTH CHURCH, bp, 214, Rec,
  ment, 365
NORTH NECK, ment, 219*
NORTH RIVER, ment, 201, 368
NORTHAMPTON, Monthly Meeting,
  Rec, 156

NORTON, Richard, exr , 138
NORWOOD, Amareus, wid , 366, w , 366, pet , 366
    Andrew husb 366, prchs , 366
NOSECHTHOS (NOSECTHOS†), ment , 244*†, 251*
NOTTINGHAM, (Hamilton Squan.), ment , 142, 155, 187, 188, 191, 192, 103
NUIJTING, Brian, wit , 74
NUTSWAMP, ment , 39**, 41, 45, 62, 163, 164, 279*, 280

O

OATH OF ALLEGIANCE, ment , 21, 31†, Morford, 12, Stout, 360**
ODIORNE, Elizabeth, md , 214, b , 214, d , 214, mo , 214**
ODIORNE'S POINT, ment , 177, 213, 214
OGBORNE (OGBORN, OGBOURN†, OGBOURNE†, OGBURN, see OGDEN, OSBORN), Bible, ment , 150, 160, do , family, 167, cpi 151, family, ref , 380, do , English. 151, 152, 167, homestead, 153, miscellaneous notes, 155, 167†, 169†, a place, 169†, Quakers, 153, 158, 168, 169, ref , 151, in Rev War, 163, silver, 161, similar names, 167, tombs , 151, wills, 152, 160, of England, ment , 151, 152, 169, silver, 152, of Iowa, 380, in the South, 169, in Wales, 169, hist of, 169, Quakers, 169, of Monmouth County, 151-169, Bible, 159, 167, port , 165, Quakers, 152, 155, 156, 157, 158, 167, 168, 169, ref , 152, 153, 154, 155, 156, 157, 158, 162, 163, in Rev War, 163, silver, 159, 161*, 168, various spellings, 167
  Miss, md , 280, s p , 280
  Ann (An, Anna†, Annie††, see Hannah), her Corner, 362††, dau , 376**†, 377*†, 379, granddau , 376, 379, ment , 376 md , 376**†, 378†, w , 376*, 379**†, wid , 376, co heir, 376*†, re name, 377, 379, cor , 378†, m l , 378†, 379, mo 378**†, 379**†, leg as Hannah, 379, grand-mo , 379**, in deed, 379
  Edwin, obit , 380, bro , 380, b , 380, age, 380, s , 380
  Elizabeth, cor , 377, md , 377, dau , 377, re name, 377, 379, d , 377, md , 377, w , 378**, mo , 378**, step-dau , 379
  Hannah (see Ann), cor , 377, dau , 377, re name, 377, 379, d , 377, md , 377, w , 378**, mo , 378**, step-dau , 379
  Mrs J E , res , 380, letter, 380, w , 380
  Joel F , cor , 380, bro , 380
  John, cor , 376, md , 376, d , 376, husb , 376**, 377, fa , 376**, 377**, 378, 379, s , 376, 377, decd , 376*†, res , 376**†, d , 376**, his heirs, 376†, owner, 376†, will, 376, 377, grandfa , 376, 377**, 378**, leg , 377, age, 377, grands , 377
  Mary, cor , 377, 379, md , 377, 379**, guard , 377, sis , 377, w , 377, mo , 379*
  Samuel (Sam¹¹), appr , 227, 229, bondsm , 227, bill pd , 229, 231, sig , 229
  Sarah, dau , 376*, 377, md , 376,

OGBORNE, Continued
377*, co-heir, 376, cor , 377, 379, b , 377, d 377, 379, mo , 377, 379**, 380**, age, 377, 379, bur , 377, w , 379
  William, cor , 377, fa , 377**, s , 377**, will, 377, leg , 377, husb , 377, md , 377, his guard , 377, bro , 377, grands , 377, age, 377
OGBORNE'S CORNERS, ment , 162, 165, Annie, ment , 153, corruption of name, 153
OGDEN (see OGBORNE, OSBORN), Governor, his place sold, 195
  David, friend, 37, exr , 37
  David, Jr , deft , 178
  Euphemia Morris, w , 36
  Hannah Mott, w , 110, mo , 110
  Joseph, md , 190
  Mary, dau , 110, b , 110, bp , 110, w , 190
  Mary Saltar, w , 190
  Moses, md , 190
  Nathaniel, md , 110, fa , 110
  Colonel Samuel, md , 36
OGDEN'S CORNERS, corruption of name, 153
OGILVEY, Doctor, convey , 371, minister, 371
OHIO RIVER, falls of, 252
OKESON (O KESON, OKESON), Elizabeth, her mark, 83, convey , 83, w , 83
  John, sig , 83, husb , 83, res , 83, convey , 83, oath, 181, wit , 181
OLD FORGE POND, hndry , 213
OLD HOPEWELL, Pioneers of, 349
OLD SHIP, res , 245
"OLD SI," hanged for murder, 161
OLD TOWN, ment , 189
OLDEN, Mary, md , 121, d , s p , 121
OLIFFT, Marie Mott, w , 109
  William M , md , 109, Park commr , 109, res , 109
OLIPHANT (OLLIVANT†), David, md , 333†
  Ephraim, md , 348, fa , 348*
  Hannah Stout, w , 333†
  Sarah Stout, w , 348, mo , 348**
ONDERDONK, Harriet Mott, w , 106
  William H , md , 106
ONEANICKSON, ment , 153
ONEIDA LAKE, ment , 197
O'NEIL, Mary, m 1 , 177
OPDYKE, George, md , 353, Mayor, 353, res , 353
  Mary Stout, w , 353, b , 353, d , 353
ORANGE, Brigantine, re voyage, 233, Brigg, do , 233
OREN, Parson, christened by, 37
OSBORN (ORSBORNE†, OSBORNE, OSBURN††, see OGBORNE), similar names, 167
  Capt , house, 220
  Col Abraham fa , 7
  Ann, invt , 168, res , 168
  Caleb Jewell, fa , 59, husb , 59
  Eliza, md , 7, dau , 7
  Hester Ann, md , 59, dau , 59, d , 59
  James, fa , 351, grandfa , 351**
  Mary, md , 7, 10, b , 7, 10, d , 7, 10, mo , 11**
  Pennie, md , 351, dau , 351, mo , 351**
  Roger, took invt , 84†

OSBORN, Continued
  Samuel, appr , 167††, res , 167, will, 167, fa , 167
  Sarah, w , 141, mo , 141
  Susan, w , 59, mo , 59
  William, est of, 167††, res , 167††, invt , 167††, decd , 167††
OTT, Miss, md , 338, mo , 338*
OTTEN, Mary, leg , 370
OVDENAARDE, Hendrik, pltf , 89
OVENS, Eliza, w , 7, 10, mo , 7, 10, grandmo , 10**
  George, fa , 7, 10, husb , 7, 10, grandfa , 10**
  Mary Ruth, md , 7, 10, dau , 7, 10, b , 7, 10, d , 7, 10, mo , 10**
OWEN, Lurana, md , 347
  Sarah Wills, md , 168, 169, mo , 169**
OXLY, Clear, md , 351, remov , 351, fa , 351
  Rachel Stout, w , 351, remov , 351, mo , 351
OYSTER BAY (OYSTERBAY) neighbors' dispute, 73

P

PACKER (see PARKER), Charles, his wid , 344
  Mary, md , 344, d , 344, age, 344, wid , 344, mo , 344**, grandmo , 344**
PAGE, Anthony, sold land, 170, prch , 170
  Mary Ann, w , 60, mo , 60
PALMER (PARMER†), family, release, 72
  Dr , md , 274, res , 274
  Mr , md , 127*†
  Mrs , w , 127*†
  Matilda Seabrook, w , 274
  Samuel (Sam¹), leg , 20
  Sarah, md , 64, mo , 64**
  William, clk , 75
PANCOAST, Elizabeth, w , 377
  Elizabeth Ogborne, w , 154
  Hannah, w , 377, mo , 377
  Jane, md , 375
  John, md , 154, 377, s , 155, 377
  Joseph, fa , 154, 377, md , 155, 377, s , 155, 377, husb , 377
  Mary, w , 377
  Mary Ogborne, w , 155
  Thomasin, md , 375, w , 377, mo , 377
  William fa , 155, 377, res , 155, husb , 377, test , 375
PAQUANACK, Township, ment , 89
PARCIPANY, ment , 38
PARDON (see PURDAND), Mr , order pd , 304
PARENT, Amy Mott, w , 110
  John, md , 110, res , 110
PARIS, Ferdinand John, suggestion of, 187
PARK (PARKE), Charity Stout, w , 337
  Grace, md , 352, dau , 352, mo , 352**, grandmo , 352**
  John, md , 337
  Penelope, md , 335, 338, mo , 338**, grandmo , 338**
  Dr Rodger, fa , 352, grandfa , 352**, g grandfa , 352**
  Sarah, w , 377, md , 335, mo , 335**, remov , 335
  William, md , 327

420   INDEX

PARKER, ref , 361
  Gov , ment , 109
  Abigail, md , 205, 361, cousin, 205,
    mo , 205**, d , 205, dau , 361
  Ann, md , 168, dau , 168, mo , 168**
  Anthony, s , 361, md , 361, fa , 361**
  Benjamin, md , 168
  Charles, s , 361; b , 361, md , 361,
    fa., 361
  David Stout, w , 361, b , 361; as
    Capt , md , 205, res , 205, fa , 205
  Emeline Salter, w , 205, mo , 205, d ,
    205
  George, wit , 183
  Jacob Corlies, md , 6, b , 7, d , 7
  Jane Dodge, w , 10
  Jane Dodge Morford, w , 10, b , 10,
    d , 10
  Gov Joel, s 361, b , 361, as Hon ,
    res , 205, cousin, 205
  John, mast , 62, res , 62, s , 361
  Joseph, fa , 168, grandfa , 168**, s ,
    361*
  Julia Ann Morford, w , 6
  Margaret, w , 58, mo , 58
  Mary, w , 183, convey , 183, mark,
    183
  Phebe Ogborn, w , 168
  Phebe Stout, w , 361, mo , 361**
  Robert White, md , 10, b , 10
  Sarah, w , 361, mo , 361*, pet , 361
  Sarah Elizabeth, dau , 205, md , 205
  Sarah S , md , 138, b , 138; d , 138
  Sarah Stout, sis , 361, w , 361*, leg ,
    361, mo , 361**, grandmo , 361**
  Thomas, convey , 183*, husb , 183,
    mark, 183, s , 361, guard , 361
  Thomas, Sr , convey , 183, res , 183,
    mer , 183, husb , 361, md , 361,
    fa , 361**, grandfa , 361**
  William, Jr , exr , 46
PARMLY, Dr Ehnck, res , 36
PARROTT, Ann, s , 263, living, 263,
    sis , 263, leg , 263*, cousin, 263
  Ann Seabrook, w , 263, mo , 263; sis ,
    263
  William (Willm), md , 263, fa , 263,
    bro law, 263, re cattle, leg , 263
PARSELL (see PEARSALL), Nathaniel,
    leg in trust, 96
PARSONS (PARSON†), in Rev War,
    216†
  Mrs , convey ,73, mo ,73*, grandmo ,
    73
  Ann, mo , 72, 74, w , 72, grandmo ,
    72**, 75*, dau , 73, will, 74
  Joseph (Jos), as Capt , his Co , Min-
    ute Men 216†
  Margery, mo , 73*, advanced goods,
    73, recd land, 73, bur , 73
  Mary Morford, w , 6, d , 6, age, 6
  Walter C , md , 6, d , 6
PARTRIDGE, Eliza Mary, md , 274,
    res , 274, mo , 274**
  Mary Elizabeth, niece, 274
PASSAGE POINT, alias Norransont, 34,
    called Norramsont, ment , 38
PATENTEES, re factional disputes, 32,
    one of, 170
PATRIOTIC COMMITTEE, Shrews-
    bury, ment., 5
PATTEN (PATTAN†), Mr , md , 126,
    remov , 126
  Hugh, wit , 278
  Martha Mount, w , 126, remov , 126

PATTEN, Continued
  William, mort , 45†
PATTERSON (PATTERION), in Rev
    War, 98
  Capt , his Co , 98
  Miss, md , 10, 164
  Mr , md , 164, 286, fa , 164**
  Catharine (Katy†), dau , 164†
  Charlotte Smith Mott, w , 98, mo , 98
  Elizabeth, w , 39, 45, consent, 39,
    mo , 45
  Hannah, w , 4, 314, mo , 314, grand-
    mo , 314
  Hester, md , 39, 65, spinster, 45,
    m l, 45, res , 45, dau , 45, mo ,
    45**, 65
  James, s , 311, md , 311*, b , 311
    fa , 311**
  Jehu, bndry , 121, s , 311, b , 311,
    md , 311, age, 311, fa , 314, husb ,
    314, grandfa , 314, as Judge, fa , 4
  Capt John W , md , 98, fa , 98
  Joanna (Johannah†), md , 39, m l ,
    39, 69†
  John, md , 314, fa , 314, as Esq , exr ,
    239
  John Jacob Timbrook, s , 314, b.,
    314, d , 314
  Joseph (Joseph), bondsm , 39, friend,
    174, exr , 174, renounces as do , 174
  Leah, dau , 311, md , 311, cousin,
    311, w , 311
  Lydia, md , 54, dau , 54, d , 54, age,
    54, mo , 54**
  Mary, w , 128, mo , 128, 314, md ,
    314, dau , 314, b , 314, d , 314
  Mary Ann, w , 128
  Rachel Stout, w , 311, mo , 311**
  Rebecca, dau , 164, 311, md , 311
  Robert, husb , 39, 45, consent, 39,
    fa , 45, 54, grandfa , 54**, md ,
    311, cousin, 311
  Sarah, md , 69, w , 164, mo , 164**
  Sarah Stout, w , 314, mo , 314
  Stillwell, s , 164
PAUL, Mr , business of, 102
PAULISON, Mr , md , 286
  Anna Shepherd, w , 286
PAULUS HOOK, ment , 205
PAVONIA, Indians attacked at, 300
PAYNE, Lieut John, prchs , 263, of
    ship Rose, 263
PLACHLEY, Dr , bill pd , 375
PEAIRS (PEARS†, see PEARCE), Jona-
    than, wit , 162
  Rachel, wit , 162, 163†
PEAK, Mr , md , 58
  Martha, dau , 58, leg , 58
  Martha Morris, w , 58
PEARCE (PEARSE, PIERCE†, see
    PEAIRS), Amos, fa , 60†
  Benjamin Davenport, fa , 66, husb ,
    66, grandfa , 66**
  Caroline, w , 66, mo , 66, grandmo ,
    66**
  Elizabeth Louise, b , 66, d , 66, md ,
    66, dau , 66, mo , 66**, grandmo ,
    66**
  James, md , 364
  Jane, md , 60†, dau , 60†, b , 60†
  John, convey , 223
  Margaret, md , 364, res , 364
  Mary Morris, w , 33†, bur , 33†,
    s p , 33†
  Rebecca Stout, w , 364

PEARCE, Continued
  Samuel, will, 93, his exr , 93
  Capt Vincent, md , 33†, d , s p , 33†
PEARCEFIELD, est of, 21
PEARSALL (see PARSELL), Deborah,
    md , 95, mo , 95**
  Nathaniel, friend, 82, exr , 82, res , 82
  Sarah, dau , 92, md , 92, b , 92, d ,
    92, w , 92, leg , 92, mo , 92*,
    grandmo , 92
  Thomas, husb , 92, fa , 92, res , 92,
    105, grandfa , 92, 105, fa law, 92,
    exr , 92, will, 105
PECK, Aaron, md , 149
  Catharine Elizabeth, w , 149, wid ,
    149
PECKHAM, Ella V , md , 13, res , 13
PEDDIPHETT (PEDDIHETT†, PUD-
    DEPHATT††), John, tombs ,
    258††, d , 258††, age, 258††
  Mr Joseph, fa , 262, res , 262, his
    s leg , 258†
PELHAM NECK, ment , 219
PELL, Hannah, granddau , 81, 82, leg ,
    81, dau , 81, 82
  Hannah Mott, b , 82, dau , 82, md ,
    82, mo , 82**
  John, sworn before, 220*, sig , 220*
  Martha, granddau , 81, 82, leg , 81,
    dau , 81, 82
  Philip, s law , 81, leg , 81*, grands ,
    81, 82, s , 81, 82, leg , 82, res , 82,
    d , 82, bro law, 82, fa , 82**
PEMBERTON, Baptist Meeting Yard,
    376
PENN, Admiral, ment , 14
  William, friend, 19, leg , 19
PENNEARE (see PENNOYER), Mr ,
    sol , 299
PENNOYER (see PENNEARE), Rob-
    ert, sol , 300
PENN'S NECK, ment , 142, 365
PENNYPACK, Baptist Church, Rec ,
    212, Baptist Meeting, dea of, 379
PENTAR (see PINTARD), Sarah, sis ,
    140
PEPLOW, Mr , surgeon, 257
PEPPERELL, family, hist of, ment , 218
PERCIVAL, Mr , md , 67
  Mrs , w , 67
PERKINS, Margaret, md , 364
PERRINE (PARINE†, PERINE), Bible,
    ment , 128, in Rev War , 128
  Mr , md , 6, 286, 316, 340, fa , 6
  Ann (Anna†), m l , 117†, dau , 128†,
    d , 128†, md , 128†, w , 129*
  Ann Mount, w , 128, bp , 128, b ,
    128, tombs , 128, mo , 128*, 129*
  Catharine Mount, w , 137
  Daniel, s , 129, b , 129, md , 129
  David, friend, 13†, leg , 13†
  Eleanor, dau , 316, 340, leg , 316, 340
  Eleanor Stout, w , 316*, 340
  Elizabeth (Betsey†), w , 129†
  Eveline Shepherd, w , 286
  Fanny, w , 129, mo , 129
  Hannah, dau , 5, 129, mo , 5, 6, leg ,
    5, w , 6, b , 129
  Hannah Morford, w , 6, mo , 6
  Hannah Mount, w , 128, bp , 128,
    b , 128, tombs , 128, mo , 128*,
    129**
  Howland, his Bible, 128
  Rev Humphrey M , s , 129, b , 129,
    professor, 129, md , 129, fa , 129

INDEX

PERRINE, Continued
 John, s, 129, b, 129, md, 129, fa, 137, husb, 137
 Lydia, dau, 128, d, 128, md, 128
 Lydia Mount, w, 127
 Margaret, dau, 129, b, 129, md, 129
 Mary, w, 137; mo, 137
 Matthias, s, 129, b, 129, md, 129
 Peter, md, 129, 137, s, 129, 137, b, 129, 137, d, 137
 Rebecca, md, 119*, 129, 135, 163, mo, 119**, dau, 129, b, 129, res, 163, mo, 163**, grandmo, 163**
 Sarah, w, 129, mo, 129*
 Thomas Morford, s, 5, 6, grands, 5, leg, 5
 William, signed bond, 4, res, 4, 128, md, 5, 128, will, 128, sol, 128, b, 128, d, 128, fa, 128*, 129**, as Dr, s, 129
 William J, md, 127, b, 127, d, 127
 Dr William Williamson, s, 129, b, 129, md, 129, fa, 129*, remov, 129
PERRIT, Jane, m 1, 110°
PERTH AMBOY, Citty of, ment, 233*, Court at, 18, Court of Common Right, 27, Court trials, 34, Cranbury (Cranberry), m city of, 113, 116, Deeds, 172, Gen Assemb, 27, re Morris fight, 27, Rec, 78, 227, 236, re ship sailing, 234
PETTINGER, Hester, md, 140, b, 140, mo, 140*, 141**, grandmo, 141
PETTIT, Jane (Jean†), md, 110°, 338†, m 1, 338†, mo, 338**†
PEW, James, appr, 227, 229, bondsm, 227, mark, 229, bill pd, 229, 230, 231
PHARO, Amos, exr, 325
PHILADELPHIA, First Baptist Church, Bp Regist, 213, do, md Book, 212, do, md Rec, 212, do, Rec, 212, do, Regist of Memb, 212, Christ Church, md, 209, 212, 213, do, Rec, 277, Deeds, 192, 193, 209, Quarterly Meeting, Rec, 302, Rec, ment, 190, Wills, ment, 193, 211, Women's Monthly Meeting, Friends, leg, 194
PHILBROOK, Frances, md, 218, mo, 218
PHILIPSBURG, ment, 370
PHILLIPS (PHILIPS, PHILIPSE†, PHILLIPSE††), Mr, md, 169, res, 169
 Catharine Morris, w, 70
 Elizabeth Ogborn, w, 169, res, 169
 Eve, dau, 72†
 Frederick, Ia, 72†, as M', Judge, 30
 Sarah, md, 335, mo, 335**
 Thomas, w, 70
PHILLIPSE MANOR (MANNOR), ment, 242††, 243
PHILLISBURG, ment, 369
PHYSICK, Elizabeth, w, 99, mo, 99, grandmo, 99
 Philip Syng, md, 99, fa, 99, grandfa, 99
 Susan, dau, 99, md, 99, mo, 99
PIERCE (see PEARCE)
PIERSON, John, md, 310, m 1, 310
 Sarah Stout, w, 310
PIETERSEN, Jacob, deft, 290

PIKE, d and bur, 331, family, md, 297, ref, 330, 331, of Woodbridge, ment, 330
 Elizabeth, dau, 331, b, 331, w, 331, mo, 331**
 Emma L, md, 9, 11, mo, 11**
 Hannah, dau, 331, b, 331
 James, d, 331, age, 331, bur, 331
 Jane, d, 331, age, 331, bur, 331
 John, s, 330**, 331, b, 330**, 331, d, 330*, 331, md, 330, res, 330*, fa, 330**, 331**, age, 330, 331, husb, 330, 331, bur, 331, as Capt, fa, 330, re tombs, 330, recd power atty, 331, as Judge, age, 330, d, 330, bur, 330, s, 330, as the First, fa, 331, as third, grave, 330
 John, Jr, res, 331*, planter, 331, re power atty, 331, s, 331
 Joseph, s, 330*, 331, b, 330*, d, 330, 331, md, 331, fa, 331**, age, 331, bur, 331
 Mary, dau, 330
 Nathaniel, d, 331, age, 331, bur, 331
 Ruth, dau, 331
 Sarah, dau, 330*, 331, b, 330*, 331, d, 330
 Sarah Stout, w, 330, 331, mo, 330**, 331**, line of, 330, 331
 Timothy, s, 331 b, 331
 Zebulon, grave, 330, s, 331, b, 331, d, 331, bur, 331
PILES GROVE, ment, 46, 55
PINE BROOK, bndry, 185
PINHORNE, William, memb Council, 28, address, 28
PINKERTON, Miss, md, 338, 341, mo, 341**
PINKNEY (PINCKNEY), of South Carolina, ment, 266
 Miss, md, 272, mo, 272, sis, 272
 Rev Mr, bro, 272
PINTARD (PINTAR†, see PENTAR), exrs, pltf, 62
 Mr, md, 126†
 Anthony, wit, 321
 Sarah Mount, w, 126
PISCATAQUA, ment, 35, 116
PITCH, tar, etc, making of, 33
PITNEY Doctor, ment, 102
PITTSBURGH LANDING, battle of, 206
PLAINFIELD, Friends' Rec, 157
PLATT, Elizabeth Mott, w, 110*
 Philip, md, 110*
 Philip Smith, m 1, 110*
PLEASANT VALLEY, ment, 298
PLEASANT YOUNG HUSBAND'S CORNER, ment, 245
PLUMSTEAD (PLUMSTED), Caleb, issued power atty, 180, convey, 180
POCAHONTAS, descendants of, 43
POINSETT, Joseph, md, 140
 Phebe, md, 375, mo, 375**
 Sarah Mount, w, 140
POLE (see POOL), Miss, md, 24, res, 24, mo, 25
POTHEMUS, Elizabeth, w, 136, mo, 136, grandmo, 136*
POMPTON, ment, 201
PONTERRY, ment, 14
POOL (see POLE), Eliza, w, 286, mo, 286, grandmo, 287**
POOLE'S BRIDGE, ment, 210

POPHAM, in Rev War, 43*
 Mary Morris, w, 43
 Major William, md, 43, res, 43
POPLAR FIELD (POPLAR FIELDS†), ment, 113, 304, 305, 306†
POPLAR NECK, John of, ment, 323
PORT MONMOUTH, alias Bay Shore, 223, cor, 382*
PORT ROYAL (PORT ROYALL), ment, 178, 366
PORTAPECK (POTAPECK†, POTOPECK††), ment, 170†, 319
POTOPECK NECK, ment, 121††
PORTER, Alice Mount, w, 116
 John, md, 116, m 1, 116
 Mary, md, 39, spinster, 39, m 1, 39, mo, 40**
 Mary Salter, w, 217
 Richard G, md, 217
PORTLAND POINT, Court at, 292, Genl Assemb at, 111
POST, Jacob, husb, 365, fa, 365
 Mary Stout, w, 365, dau, 365, decd, 365, mo, 365
POTHOOK, Co Militia at, 178
POTTER family, ment, 381, Quakers, 174, miscellaneous notes, 175, tombs, 323, of Monmouth County, 170-175, Quakers, 171*, ref, 171, 172, 173, 175, silver, 172, of Rhode Island, 170, 175, of Woodbridge, 175
 Mr, md, 324
 Ann, w, 381, d, 381, mo, 381**
 Catherine, mo, 56, w, 56, grandmo, 56, 57**
 John, wit, 324
 Mary, dau, 324, leg, 324
 Mary Stout, w, 324
 Mercy, w, 309, mo, 309, cor, 380, d, 380
 Sarah, md, 294, res, 294, 381, w, 381*, wid, 381, convey, 381
 Thomas, bndry, 319, farm ment, 324, cor, 380, fa, 380, 381**, his w, 380, md, 381**, age, 381*, husb, 381, md cert, 381, d, 381, will, 381, his wid, 381
POTTS, Elizabeth, md, 119, w, 119, mo, 119*
 Joseph, m 1, 110°, res, 110°
 Rebecca Mount, w, 124, mo, 124**
 Thomas, ment, 78
 William, his house, 91, md, 124, fa, 124**
POUND, geneal, ment, 340, 341
POVAH, Rev Alfred, author, 151
POWELL, Abigail, w, 82, mo, 82, res, 82, grandmo, 82**
 Ruth, dau, 110, leg, 110
 Ruth Mott, leg, 110
 Sarah, wit, 35, md, 87, w, 376, mo, 376
 Thomas, fa, 110, res, 110
POYER, Rev Mr, installed, 30
PRALL (PROAL†), Miss, md, 352, dau, 352
 Abram, md, 327, fa, 327**
 Arthur, fa, 357, grandfa, 357**
 Elizabeth, md, 327
 Elizabeth Stout, w, 327, mo, 327**
 Garrison, md, 350, remov, 350
 Hannah, dau, 327
 Isaac, md, 351, fa, 351, 352, 355; grandfa, 355*

INDEX

PRALL, *Continued*
  John A, md, 356
  Mary, md, 357, dau, 357, mo, 357**
  Mary Stout, w, 350, 356, remov, 350
  Rev Dr Pierre Alexis, Rector, 370†, md, 370†
  Rachel Stout, w, 351, mo, 351
  Ruth, md, 366
  Sarah Stout, w, 355, mo, 355*
  Sidney, md, 355, s, 355, fa, 355*
  Susan, w, 370†, d, 370†
  William, s, 327
PRATT, Jacob, md, 110ᵃ, res, 110ᵃ, m l, 110ᵃ
  Mary Mott, w, 110ᵃ, res, 110ᵃ
PREMIUM POINT, ment, 105
PRENTISS, Mr, md, 52, as Rev, ment, 271
  Catharine Morris, w, 52
PRESBYTERIANS, leg for educational purposes, 96, Church Rec, 106, 110, 110ᵃ, 110ᵇ
PRESCOTT Mane, w, 281, actress, 281; d, 281
PRESTON, Mrs, w, 260
  William (Wᵐ), md, 260
PRICE, Capt, letter by, 100*
  Mr, md, 198
  Cornelia, md, 66
  Hannah, md, 354, dau, 354
  Huldah, niece, 198*, 199, dau, 198, 199, leg, 198*, 199
  Huldah Saltar, w, 198
  John, fa, 354
  Patience, md, 122, m l, 122, bp, 122, mo, 122**
  Sarah, w, 347, mo, 347; grandmo, 347*, g grandmo, 347**
  William, wit, 3*
PRICKETT, Elizabeth, w, 379
  Francis, md, 379
PRIESTLY, James, md, 355
  Margaret Stout, w, 355
PRINCE, in USA, 204
  Annie Coolidge, dau, 204
  Gertrude, dau, 204
  Louise Gordon, dau, 204
  Maria Louisa, w, 204, mo, 204**, d, 204
  Susan Lyman, dau, 204, md, 204
  Col William E, md, 204, fa, 204**
PRINCETON (PRINCE TOWN†), ment, 101*†, 131, 148, 245, 250, College, ment, 153, 267, 271, 272, 273, do, professor of, 129
PRINGLE, Miss, md, 52, mo, 52*
PRIVATEERS (see SHIPS), ment, 178, 301, of New York, 370, theft by crew of, 301, Britannia, 370, Delight, 370, General Sullivan, 216, Lively, 370, Triumph, 370
PROAL (see PRALL)
PROPRIETARY, Aggression, 304
PROPRIETORS, re disputes, 32, 181, Last Jersey under, ref, 70, grants and concessions, 304, grants, 307, 308, land grants, 304, i e Proprietary Party, 181**, re quit-rents, 181, rights, etc, 28, warrants, surveys, etc, 318
PROVOST'S PRISON, ment, 282
PUBLIC HOUSE, appli for, 89**
PUDDEPHATT (see PEDDIPHETT)
PUDNEY, Mary, cousin, 81, wid, 81, leg, 81

PUE, Dr, his wid, 274; res 274
  Mrs, wid, 274; md, 274
PURDANE (see PARDON)
  Will, recpt for digging grave, 112, sig, 112
PURDY, Fay, mo, 109
  Katharine Jerome, dau, 109, md, 109
  William, his mill dam, bndry, 183, convey, 183
PURE, Simon, mess, 103
PYLE, Emeline Morford, w, 7
  Samuel L, md, 7

Q

QUAKERS (see FRIENDS), Burlington, Rec, 155*, 156*, 167*, do, Regist, Monthly Meeting, 156, Buryingground, bur, 99, 375, Chesterfield Monthly Meeting, 116, 132*, do, Rec, 155**, dates of b, 293, Evesham Meeting, 156**, Falls Monthly Meeting, ment, 158**, George Fox, preacher, 15, Haddonfield Meeting, ment, 158, do, Rec, 158, harboring of, 291, Haverford Meeting, ment, 347, leg, to Friends' Meetings, 15, letter re, 30, Meeting House built, 81, minister, 82, Mott, 96, 99, 108, 191, do, of Great Neck, 81, Newtown Meeting Rec, 293, Northampton Monthly Meeting, ment, 156, do, Rec, 156, Ogborns, 168, 169, of Ratcliffe Meeting, leg, 152, Rec, ment, 171, 312, do, Shrewsbury, 171**, 175, ref to, 291, Robins' Meeting, 48, Salter, 191, Seaman, 85, sentenced, 292, Shrewsbury Meeting, ment, 158, do, House, 154, do, Rec, 158, strife re, 32, Westbury Monthly Meeting, 96, Willis, 93, Woodbridge Meeting, ment, 158**
QUARY, Robert, memb council, 28, address, 28, as Col, letter of, 28
QUEENS COUNTY, Court of Sessions, 72, Mott of, 80, 106, Rec, 219
QUEBEC, battle of, 98
QUIAHOCKING RIVER, alias Morris, 22
QUICK, Abraham, md, 355, s, 355, fa, 355**
  Elizabeth Stout, w, 327, mo, 327**
  Francis, fa, 327, grandfa, 327**
  Jacob, fa, 355, grandfa, 355**
  John, md, 327, s, 327, fa, 327**
  Rachel Stout, w, 355, mo, 355**
QUICKSALL, John, Jr, will, 155, res, 155
QUINBY, Isaiah, fa, 352, grandfa, 352*, 353**
  Mary, md, 348, 352, m l, 348, 352, dau, 352, mo, 352*, 353**

R

RAHWAY (RAWAY†), NECK, ment, 158†
RAINBURGH, Rebecca, dau, 136, mo, 136
RAINTEAUX (RAINETAUX, RAINTAUX), Anthony, md, 369, mer, 369, 371, res, 369, named for, 371

RAINTEAUX, *Continued*
  Charlotte, granddau, 368, d, 368, age, 368, tombs, 368
  Phoebe Stout, w, 369
RALSTON, Mr, md, 273, res, 273
  Sarah Seabrook, w, 273
RANDALL, Mr, md, 214
  Mrs, w, 214
  John, grands, 214, leg, 214
  Thomas (Thᵒ), letter of, 192, sig, 192
RANDOLPH, Ann Cary, dau, 43, d, 43, mo, 43, 44
  Catharine Stout, w, 342
  Eliza, md, 70
  Moses, md, 334
  Phebe, md, 358, mo, 358**, grandmo, 358**
  Sarah Stout, w, 334
  Thomas Mann, fa, 43, res, 43, grandfa, 43, 44
  Zebulon S (Zeb S), md, 342
RANTOWLES, ment, 266, Bridge, ment, 275, Station, ment, 260
RARITAN (RARITANS†), Sachems of, notified, 302
RARITAN RIVER, ment, 300, 302
RASCARRICK (see RESCARRICK)
RAY (REAY†, see RHEA), Catharine (Katharine†), m l, 175†
  Janet, dau, 157, leg, 157, mo, 157**
  John, pltf, 89
  Robert, exr, 157
  Sybil (Sybyl), w, 92, 110ᵃ, mo., 92, 110ᵃ, grandmo, 92** 110ᵃ
RAYMOND, Catherine, md, 285
RAYNOR (REYNER†), James, md., 110ᵃ†, m l, 110ᵃ
  John, md, 110ᵇ
  Rebecca Mott, w, 110ᵇ
  Sarah Mott, w, 110ᵃ*†
READ (READE, REED†, REID††), in Militia, 237, in Rev War, 237
  Col, his Battalion, 237
  Mr, md, 144†, fa, 144†
  Andrew, fa, 126†, grandfa, 126†
  Charles, convey, 153, res, 153
  Eliza, md, 70†
  Elizabeth, md, 126†, dau, 126†, mo, 126**†
  Ellen, dau, 143†, 144†, granddau, 143†, leg, 143†
  James, bondsm, 196†, res, 196†
  John, survey genl, 77††, convey, 172††, trust, 172††, oaths before, 181††, wit, 232†, as Esq, convey, 185††
  Lydia Ann, dau, 143†, leg, 143†, mo, 143†, 144†, w, 144†
  Sarah J, md, 351†, mo, 351**†, res, 351†
  William F, Esq, res, 185†, author, 185†
READING, Mr, minister, 96, md by, 96
  Richard (Richᵈ), prison, 101, exch. of, 101, his sons prison, 101
REAPE, Sarah, bndry, 113
REBELLION (see REGIMENTS, REVOLUTIONARY WAR), ment, 29, of Colonies, re disorders, 29, Morris in, 21, Mott in, 109, Stout in, 359
RECKHOW, Isabel Morris, w, 69
  Rev, Jacob, md, 69
RECORDS, Bible, Mott, 80, 98, 107, Dutch Church, ment, 72, 110,

RECORDS, Continued
Freehold Court, 76, do, md, 363, 364, Friends', ment, 93**, 378, do, New York, 105, do, Westbury, 92, Geneal and Biog, ref, 70, 74, 75, 82, 85, 86, 97, 110**, Hempstead, ment, 110, Jamaica, ment, 74, 83, Mamaroneck, ment, 110, md, Freehold, 363, 364, do, New Brunswick, 364, do, Tom's River, 363, Monmouth County, 77, New Brunswick, md, 364, Orphans' Court, 382, Perth Amboy, ment, 78, Presbyterian Church, ment, 110, 110b, 110b, do, ref, 106, Quaker, 382, St George's Church, 110**, 110***, 110b**, Soc of Friends, ment, 85, 110, Southampton, 73, Tom's River, md, 363, Westbury, 93**, Westchester ment, 110, do, Town, 75, White Plains, ment, 110

RED BANK, bridge at, 1

REDDAL, Mr, md, 333, fa, 333
  Ann, dau, 333
  Rachel Stout, w, 333, mo, 333

REDFORD, Elizabeth, md, 38, dau, 38, mo, 38**
  John, fa, 38, grandfa, 38**

REDMAN, Mr, husb, 72, fa, 72, d, 72, grandfa, 72**
  Ann, mo, 72, 73**, 74, wid, 72, 73, md, 72, 73, grandmo, 72**, 75*, dau, 73*, will, 74
  Elizabeth, md, 72**, 73, dau, 72, 73, mo, 72**, 83, living, 72, w 72, 83, wid, 72, testa, 83
  Dr John, leg, 380
  Mary, dau, 73*, 74**, md, 73, 74, w, 73, recd land, 73, 74, m 1, 74, d 74, mo, 75*

REEDER, Anne, w, 332
  Benjamin, md, 332
  Jemima, md, 351, mo, 351**, grandmo, 351**
  Martha, md, 349, res, 349, mo, 349**, grandmo, 349*, re parentage, 349, w, 349

REGESTER, Lydia Stout, w, 347
  Robert, md, 347

REGIMENTS (see MILITIA, REBELLION REVOLUTIONARY WAR), ment, 104, 109, 110b, 3rd Artillery 108, 47th British Line, 44, Delaware battalion, 107, of Foot, Mon Co 90, Lafscellses, 44, Captn Leonard's, 101, marching of, 101, Maxwell's Brigade, 98, Morris in, 44, Mott in, 101, New Jersey Battalion, 44, Capt Patterson's Co, 98

REINHARDT (see REMHARDT), Mr, md, 252
  Mrs, w, 252

REMHARDT (REINHARDT), Mr, md, 252
  Mrs, w, 252

RENSELAER, Mr, brought ejectment suit, 31, pltf, 31

RENSSELAERSWYCK ment, 289

RESCARRICK (RASCARRICK†), George, wit, 116†

REVELL, Thomas, controversy, 73

REVES, John, his creek, bndry, 224

REVOLUTIONARY WAR (REVOLUTION†, see REBELLION, REGIMENTS), Biddle in, 236*, books lost during, 346, Burgoine in, 101, Chadwick in 325, commencement of, 243†, Dalzell in, 42, demnified for loss, 52†, Dungan in, Edward, 12*, 248, Hessians in, 237, Hoff in, 310, Holmes in, 101, Langdon in, 216, Locke in, 215*, Lee in, 52, Manlove in, 107, Maxwell in, 98, Morford in, 12** do, Oath of Alleg, 12, Patriotic Comtee, 5, Morris in 21, 35, 37, 42, 43**, 44**, 52*, 65*, 67, Mott in, 98*, 99, 103, 104, 105, 107, 110, 110b, Mount in, 113, 117*, 127**, 128, 130, 132*, 142†, 145, Murphy in 147, Oath of Alleg, Morford, 12, Ogborne in, 163*, opening of, 98, Parsons in, 216, Patterson in, 98, Patriotic Comtee, Morford on, 5, Perrine in 128* Popham in 43*, property confiscated, 125†, Read in, 237, Rhea in, 102, salt petre kittles, 101, Salter in, 177, 178*, 180, 191, 195*, 215*, 216*, Seabrook in, 236, 237, 247* 252 260, 276, Schuyler in, 104 Shepherd in, 282**, Smith in, 105, Smock in, 163 Spicer in, 294, Stout in, 316, 325*, 338, 368, 370, Gen Sullivan in, 98, Waddle in 237, Wallen in, 101, Walton in, 12*, Gen Washington in, 98, Winter in, 281

REYNOLDS, Ann, m 1, 126, d, 126, mo, 126*
  Catharine, dau, 312, b, 312 d 312
  Deborah Stout, w, 312, d, 312, mo, 312
  George, s, 312, b, 312, d, 312
  Harriet, md, 273, mo, 273**
  Hope, dau, 312
  Hope Stout, w, 312, mo, 312*, d, 312
  James, md, 312*, fa, 312**

RHEA (see RAY), in Rev War, 102
  Col ment, 102, husb, 102
  Mrs, w, 102, ill, 102

RHEESE (RHESE), Rachel, w, 188, md, 193, d, 193, mo, 193

RHINELANDER, Mr, employ, 121, res 121

RHODE ISLAND, Expedition to, 216, Motts, 110**, Rec, ment, 289**, ref, 92, 110, re shipwreck, 234

RICE, James, wit, 118
  John H, bp by, 244
  Margaretta, md 62, mo, 62**
  Margaretta V, md, 61

RICEVILLE, alias Highlands, 4

RICHARDSON, Mr, md, 273
  Richard, gives power atty, 18, res, 18
  Sarah Seabrook, w, 273
  William (Wm), leg, 19, res, 20, exr, 20, friend, 20

RICHBELL, lands 72, burying-ground, 73, 75, will, 73, 75
  Mr, warrant for horse, 73, addressed, 73
  Mrs, w, 73**, recd land, 73, dau, 73, testa, 73, mo, 73, convey, 73*, heir, 73

RICHBELL, Continued
  Ann, w, 72, 73**, dau, 73*, recd land, 73, trust deed, 73, mo, 73*, 74*, grandmo, 73*, 75*, 80, wid, 73 bur, 73*, will, 73, 74, 75, res, 73, 80, gentlewoman 73, 80, testa 73, mo law, 73, gave land, 74, her exr, 80
  Edward, s, 72, heir, 72*, res, 72*, grands, 72, release, 72*, g neph, 72, as Esq, s, 72, neph, 72, res, 72, fa, 72
  John husb, 72, 73**, mort, 72, res, 72**, 73**, ref, 72, detr, 72, agrmt, 72, bro, 72, uncle, 72, g uncle, 72*, testa, 72, const, 73, his arrival, 73, deeded land, 73, address to, 73, mer, 73*, trust deed, 73, s p, 73, controversy, 73*, prchs 73**, pat, 73*, wit, 73, d, 73, bur, 73, as Mr, bur, 75, husb, 75, s law, 75
  Robert, bro, 72, res, 72, heir-at-law, 72, fa, 72, grandfa, 72

RICHMOND, Hardbargain House, 244, Market Alley, 245*, Market House 245**, do, Common, 245, Mason's Hall, bp, 244, Pleasant Young Husband's Corner, 245
  Lydia, md, 58, mo, 58

RICHMOND COUNTY, Militia, ment', 84, 96, Mott of, 84

RICHMOND HILL, ment, 244, 251

RICKERS, Fred H, md, 284, res, 284
  Helena Shepherd b, 284, w, 284

RIDGWAY, Consul, res, 371, md, 371
  Anna, md, 379, dau, 379, b, 379
  Caleb, his wid, 379
  Frances, w, 371
  Joseph fa 379, husb, 379
  Mary, mo, 379, w, 379
  Miranna, w, 379, mo, 379
  Rachel, wid, 379
  Richard res, 153, 156, convey, 153, prchs, 156

RIGGS, Elizabeth (Betsey†), md, 129†
  Mary Stout, w, 351, mo, 351
  Phineas, md, 351, fa, 351

RIKER Hannah, md, 98, dau 98, b, 98, res, 98
  Mary, w, 98, mo, 98
  Peter, fa, 98, husb, 98, res, 98

RILEY, Catharine Murphy, w, 148, wid, 148, md, 148
  Horatio C, md, 148, d, 148

RIND, Elizabeth (Betsey†), dau, 243†, 251†, b, 243†, 251†, d, 243†, 251†
  James, md, 243†, 251, atty, 243, fa, 243**, 251**, house, 213, husb, 243, remov, 243, d, 243, 251, bur, 243, as Mr, his s 241
  Maria Dutchess (Maria D†), dau, 243 251, b, 243, 251, granddau, 246*†, leg, 246*†
  Nicholas B (N B †), s, 243†, 251, b, 243†, 251, tombs, 251, d, 251, age, 251
  Nicholas B S (N B S †, see Nicholas B), cousin, 244†, re strength, 244†, grands, 246, leg, 246
  Sarah Seabrook (Sally Seabrook) sis, 243, md, 243, w, 243*, 251, mo, 243**, 251**, remov, 243, d, 243 251, bur, 243, b, 251

RIPARIAN COMMISSION, ment, 10

424   INDEX

RIPLEY, Mr , md , 55
  Elizabeth Morris, w , 55
  Johanna Stout, w , 344
  John S , md , 344
RIPSEY, Elizabeth, sis , 58, leg , 58
RIVER INDIANS, alliance of, 300, badly treated, 300, treaty, 300
RIVERS, Ann Seabrook (Nancy Seabrook), w , 273†
  Benjamin, md , 274, bro , 274
  Emma Seabrook, w , 274
  Emily , md , 275, mo , 275*
  Robert, md , 273, res , 273, ment., 274, bro , 274
RIVERS (SEE BROOKS, CREEKS, RUNS), Bass, 323, Big Blue, 197, Connecticut, 300, 367**, Delaware, 18, 25, 187, 292, Dover, 84, Falls, 18, Forked 196, 201, 202, 205*, 206, 325, Harlem, 15, 21, Hop (Hopp), 18, 23, 305*, 307*, 330, 345*, 347, Hope, 326, Hudson, 299, James, falls of, 243, Jumping, 39, Machaponix, 185*, Manasquan, 226, 319*, 321, Millstone, 114, 366, Mohawk (Mohockt, Mohockst), 37†, 101†, Monmouth, alias Allawayes Creek, 18*, 178, Morris, 22, Navesink, 1, 187, 302, Neversand, 114*, News, 240, 241, North, 201, 368, Ohio, falls of, 252, Quahocking, 22, Rantan, 300, 302, Romanis, 326, Shark, 23, 226, 232, 320, 321, Shrewsbury, 33, 121*, 140, do , North, 10, do , Ice Yacht Club, 10, South, 119, Stone, 260, 263, 264, Swimming (Swiming), 18, 19, 23, 26, 318*, Tom's, 103, 167, 198, 317, 363 366, do , Bridge, 44, Vatauga, 191, White, 73
ROBBINS (ROBINS†), Friends' Meeting, leg , 48†, farm, graveyard, 187
  Mr , husb , 211†, res , 211†
  Ann (Nancy†), dau , 48†, leg , 48*†, w , 48*†, granddau , 48†
  Ann Morris, w , 48
  Esek, md , 234†
  Ezekiel (Ezekial), md , 48, husb, 48*†, s , 210, 211, neph , 210, leg , 210
  Isaiah, s , 211
  Jacob, s , 210, 211, neph , 210, leg , 210
  John, s , 48, 210, 211, leg , 48, 210, neph , 210
  Jonathan (Jonothont), wit , 183†, ackn sig , 183†
  Joseph, s , 48, leg , 48, exr , 48†, husb , 210, fa , 210**, 211**, brolaw, 210, md , 211
  Leah, will, 48, res , 48, mo , 48**, grandmo , 48**
  Martha, w , 155†, mo , 155†
  Mary, md , 48†, m 1 , 48†, leg , 210†, dau , 211
  Meribah, sis , 210**, 211, res , 210*, 211, w , 210, 211, leg , 210*, 211, mo , 210**
  Meribah Saltar, w , 211, mo , 211**, living, 211
  Moses, bndry , 189†, md , 234†
  Priscilla, dau , 210, 211, niece, 210, md , 210, 211, leg , 210
  Rebecca, dau , 210, 211, niece, 210, leg , 210*†, res , 210

ROBBINS, Continued
  Rhoda, w , 234†
  Ruth, w , 234†
  Samuel, s , 210, 211, neph , 210, leg , 210
  Sarah, dau , 210, 211, niece, 210, md , 210, 211, leg , 210
  Susannah, dau , 210, 211, niece, 210, md , 210, 211, leg , 210
  Thomas, s , 210, 211, neph , 210, leg , 210
  Zebulon, s , 48, leg , 48
ROBERTS, Mrs , md , 53, mo , 53**
  Janitie, w , 259*, dau , 259
  Letitia, md , 353
  Mary Eliza, md , 129, d , 129, mo , 129**
  Susannah (Susanah), wit , 20*, mark, 20, oath, 20
  Thomas, md , 259, husb , 259
ROBINSON, Catharine M Mott, w , 97
  James (Jaˢ), wit , 5*, appr , 68
  John, sold mill, 82
  Rachel, née Hartshorne, 192, md , 192, 197, s p , 192, w , 197, mo , 197, wid , 197, grandmo , 197*, 198*, g grandmo , 197
  Sarah, leg , 37, md , 197, dau , 197, mo , 197*, 198*, grandmo , 197
  Thomas, fa , 197, husb , 197*, grandfa , 197*, 198*, d , 197, g grandfa , 197
  William, md , 97
ROBSON, Benjamin R , wit , 239
ROCHEAD, James, res , 226, convey , 226; propri , 226
ROCKAWAY (see FAR ROCKAWAY), Indians, set , 299
ROCKAWAY NECK, ment , 74
ROCKBRIDGE, ment , 245, 251
ROCKHILL, Ann, wid , 183, md , 183
ROCKY BROOK, ment , 114, bndry , 115
ROCKY HILL, ment , 37
RODMAN, Dr John, friend, 175, leg , 175
RODNEY, Admiral, capture by, 371
ROE, Miss M J , res , 187, geneal , 187
  Francis, wid , 153, leg , 153
ROGERS, burying-ground, ment , 319
  Mr , md , 286
  Amelia, dau , 255, res , 255
  Anna, w , 378, leg , 378, dau , 378
  Ann Seabrook, w , 255, mo , 255**
  Benjamin, convey , 319, decd , 319, bur , 319
  Catharine, dau , 255, res , 255
  David I C (D I C†), md , 325, as Judge, author , 325†, letter of, 325†
  Emilius, s , 255, res , 255
  Hannah Shepherd, w , 286
  Hannah Stout, w , 325, 363
  John, fa , 140*, grandfa , 140**
  Josiah, md , 255, decd , 255, fa,, 255**
  Mary J , w , 344
  Phebe, md , 142
  Ruth, dau , 140, sis , 140
  Sarah Cravel, w , 325
  Theodosia, md , 140, dau , 140, sis , 140, b , 140, mo , 140**, wid , 140, d , 140, will, 140
  Wesley M , md , 344
  William, md , 325, 363
  William, Jr , husb , 378

ROMAIN (ROMAINE, ROMINE†), Abigail Stout (Abby Stout†), w , 344†
  Christopher (Stophelt), his wid., 180†, decd , 180†, res , 180†
  Ghertie, wid , 180, prchs , 180, res , 180
  Stophel (see Christopher)
  William P , md , 344
ROMANIS RIVER, alias Hope, 326
ROMBOUTS, Francis, appr , 17
ROSE, his Majesty's Ship, 263
  Miss, md , 98, mo , 98
  J L , md , 275, living, 275
  Mrs J L , w , 275, living, 275, re coat of arms, 275, Bible, 275
  Martha Mary, age, 275
ROSEMARY LANE, ment , 152**
ROSENDALE, ment , 207
ROSENKRANS (ROSENKRANZ†), Alexander, s , 333†
  Catharine, dau , 333†
  Harmon, md , 333†, fa , 333**†, 340, husb , 340, grandfa , 340**
  John, s , 333†
  Joseph, s , 333†
  Mary, dau , 333†
  Mary Stout, w , 333†, 340, mo , 333**†, 340, grandmo , 340**
  Rachel, dau , 333†, 340, md , 340, mo , 340**
ROSS, John, physician, 379, prchs , 379, survey , 379
ROSS HALL, ment , 33
ROUNSWELL, Freegift, s , 349
  Isaac, s , 349
  Rachel Stout, w , 349, mo , 349*
  Richard, md , 349, fa , 349*
ROYAL, Elizabeth, md , 270, living, 270, mo , 271**
ROYALISTS, Morris of Mon Co , 44*, Seabrooks, 276, Stouts, 313
RUBY, Mr , md , 214
  Elizabeth, dau , 214, leg , 214
  Elizabeth Salter, w , 214
RUCKMAN, John, Jr , prchs , 224
RUDYARD, Gov Thomas, his Council, 18
RUE, Mr , md , 143, fa , 143
  Mrs , w , 119**
  Ann, dau , 119*, b , 119*, d , 119*, md , 119, w , 119**, mo , 119**
  Catherine, w , 119
  Eleanor (Ellent, Nelliett), dau , 119*†, md , 119†, w , 119†, 143†
  Elizabeth, w , 119**, mo , 119**, g - grandparent, 119
  Enoch, s , 119, b , 119, md , 119
  Hannah, dau , 119, b , 119, d , 119
  Harriet Mount (Hatty Mount†), w , 143†, mo , 143†
  James, s , 119*, md , 119, b , 119, d , 119
  Jean, dau , 119, bp , 119
  John, s , 119**, 143, b , 119**, md , 119**, 143, d , 119*, fa , 119**, husb , 119, his guard , 137
  Joseph, s , 119**, b , 119, md , 119**, m l , 119, res , 119
  Joshua, s , 119, d , 119
  Lewis, s , 119, b , 119, d , 119
  Lydia, w , 119
  Margaret, dau , 119*, 134, b , 119, 134, bp , 119, d , 119, 134, md , 119, 134

INDEX

RUE, *Continued*
Margaret Mount, w., 119*, mo, 119**, wid, 119, md, 119, grandmo, 119**
Martha, her guard, 137
Mary, dau, 119*, b, 119*, d, 119*, md, 119*, w, 119**, mo, 119**
Mrs. Mary Holmes, dau law, 119, res, 119
Matthew, s, 119*, b, 119, d, 119*, md, 119**, fa, 119**, husb, 119*, bur, 119, g grandparents, 119, exr, 142*
Matthew W, s, 119*, md, 119, husb, 119, fa, 119*
Matthias (Mathias), signed bond, 4, res, 4, prchs, 117 s, 119**, b, 119**, d, 119*, age, 119, md, 119** fa, 119**, 134, husb, 119*, 134, grandfa, 119**, his guard, 137
Nathaniel S, Esq, fa law, 119
Peter, s, 119, b, 119
Phebe, dau, 119*, b, 119, d, 119, md, 119*, w, 119*, 134, mo, 119**, 134, grandmo, 119**
Rebecca, dau, 119, md, 119, 138, res 119, 138, w, 119**, mo, 119*
Samuel, s, 119*, md, 119, fa, 119, d, 119
William, s, 119, md, 119
RUMSON (see NARUMSUNK, see NORRASONT), land at, 381
RUMSON NECK, ment, 34, 39, 381
RUNKLE, Abraham, md, 352, m 1, 352, fa, 352
Sarah Stout, w, 352, mo, 352
RUNS (see BROOKS, CREEKS, RIVERS), Long Meadow, 185*, Mill, hndry, 113
RUNYON, Miss, md, 338, 340, remov, 338
Clarissa, md, 148, res, 148, mo, 148**, b, 148, d, 148
Maria, w, 340, mo, 340
Naomi, md, 340, dau, 340
Reuben, husb, 340, fa, 340
RUSSELL (RUSSEL), Joseph, tombs, 265, donor, 265
Mary, tombs, 265, donor, 265
Mary Ann, md, 137, English beauty, 137
RUTHERFORD, Helen, w, 43
Helen Morris (see Magdelena Morris), w, 43
John, md, 43
Magdelena Morris (see Helen Morris), w, 43
Robert, md, 51
Sabina Morris, w, 51
RUTTER, Thomas, res, 209, his wid, 209
RYAN, John, m 1, 110°
RYDER, John, trust, 73
RYE, Church, Vestrym of, 75
RYER, Mary Morris, w, 54
William, md, 54
RYERSON, Churchyard, bur, 195
RYERTZ, A, wit, 196
RYNDERS, Johanna, w, 36, mo, 36, grandmo, 36**

S

SACHEMS (see INDIANS), of Raritan River, re lands, 302

SADLER, Col, md, 42, res, 42
Dorothy, md, 42, mo, 42**
Dorothy Morris, w, 42
Jane, wid, 307, leg, 307
Richard, husb, 307, res, 307, will, 307
SAGAMORE, pet. for bridge, 216
SAINT (SAYNTE, ST), Andrew's Church, bur, 177, Parish of, 177, Yard, bur, 377, do, tombs, 377
ST BARTHOLOMEIS, the Less ment, 256
ST BUTTOLPH, Parish of, 178
SAYNTE DE'NIS, Backchurch, parishe, Rejester Booke, 256
ST ETHELRED Church, bur, 177
ST GEORGE'S, bp, 87, 88, 110°, Church, bp, 97, 110**, 110a**, do, md, 83, 86, 87, 97, 98, 110**, 110b**, 110a**, do, Rec, 110**, 110a**, 110b**, do, Vestrym, 76; Parish of, 177, do, Church, md at, 96
ST GILES, Church, 257
ST JAMES, Parish of, ment, 72
ST JOHN'S, Church bur, 251, do, tombs, 246, Churchyard, tombs, 251
ST JOHN'S ISLAND, Parish Church, ment, 265
ST JONE'S NECK, ment, 107
ST MARY Barquentine, ment, 380
ST MARY, Parish of, ment, 95, 152, Aldermary, Parish Regist, 257, Church, Burlington Rec, 189, Churchyard, Burlington, bur, 190
ST MICHAEL'S, Parish of b, 25*
ST NICHOLAS ACKONS, church, 257
ST PAUL, Parish Church, bur, 260, Parish, ment, 260, 271, 274, 275**
ST PETER, ment, 256, do, church, 257, Parish Regist, 257
ST THOMAS, the Apostle, Regist, 256, do, Hospital, leg, 152*
ST VEDAST, ment, 256
SALEE, Anthony Jansen of, robbed, 301, farm, 301
SALEM TOWN, ment, 22
SALT PETRE, kittles, ment, 101
SALT WORKS, order to destroy, 44
SALTER (PSALTER, SALTAIRE, SALTER, SOLTFR†), in Civil War, 205, 206, geneal, 185, re house building, 192, in King Philip's War, 178, orig papers, 196, in Rev War, 195*, 215, 216, spelling of name, 196, Tories, 195, in U S Navy, 203, 206, 211, Whigs, 195, of Monmouth County, 176-213, arms, 179, Descendants of Ebenezer, 209-213, English family, 176, 177, 179, hist, 176, 177, 179, homestead, 187, manor house 176, in Militia, 180, Miscellaneous Notes, 208-213, negroes, 184, 210, Quakers, 191, ref, 176*, 177*, 178*, 180*, 182, 183*, 184, 185*, 187, 188, 189*, 190, 191, 192, 193, 194, 203, 208*, 209, 212, 213, res, 188, in Rev War, 178*, 180, 191, silver, 210, re spellings, 177, 196, of England, 176, 177, of Illinois, 206, 207, of New Hampshire 213-218, English orig, 213, ment, 177, ref, 218*, in Rev War, 215, 216, of

SALTER, *Continued*
New York, 197, of North Carolina, ment, 177, in Rev War, 177, of Pennsylvania, ment, 178, 179, 190, 191, 192, 193, 194, 196, 197, 199, 209 210, 211, 212, 213, of Rhode Island, ment, 177, of Virginia, 191, 201, 202
Abigail, w, 361
Charity Stout, w, 353†
David, md, 361
Edwin, letter to, 324, 325
Eliza, dau, 99
Miss Frances, granddau, 188, author, 188, letter of, 194
Henry, md, 353†, m 1, 353†
Hannah, dau, 99
Huldah Mott, w, 90, 99, mo, 99**, 100**, grandmo, 99**
James, s, 100, neph, 102, letter of, 102, bro, 102, sig, 102
Joseph, md, 90, 99, res, 90, 99, m 1, 99, fa, 99**, 100**, grandfa, 99**
Margaret, dau, 100
Mary, coi, 382, md, 382
Rachel, dau, 99, md, 99, 102, mo, 99**, sis, 102, w, 197
Richard (Rich⁴), ment, 37, s, 100, arb, 226
Sarah, dau, 100, w, 197, 382, mo, 197*, 198*, grandmo, 197, cor, 382, md, 382*, wid, 382
Smith, Esq, res, 196, orig papers, 196
Thomas, his wid, 382, uncle, 382
SALTAR'S DAM, ment, 180
SALTER'S ISLAND, ment, 213 214
SAMMIS, Martha, md, 110°
SAMMONS, Martha, m 1, 110°
SAMPSON, East India's Co ship, 3/1
SANBORN, Ebenezer, md, 214, b, 214
Martha, dau, 214, leg, 214
Martha Salter, w, 214
SANDERSON, Thomas (Thoˢ), deft, 290
SANDFORD, William, memb council, 28, address, 28
SANDS, Catharine, md, 92, dau, 92, b, 92, mo, 92**
Deborah, md, 92, s, p, 92, dau, 110ᵃ,granddau, 110ᵃ,g granddau, 110ᵃ, w, 110ᵃ, d, 110ᵃ, m 1, 110ᵃ, age, 110ᵃ, cor, 376
Edward, fa, 110ᵃ, s, 110ᵃ, grands, 110ᵃ
James, fa, 110ᵃ, grandfa, 110ᵃ, g-grandfa, 110ᵃ
John, s, 110ᵃ, husb, 110ᵃ, fa, 110ᵃ, grandfa, 110ᵃ, as Capt, fa, 92, husb, 92, grandfa, 92**
Richard, kinsman, 92, exr, 92
Sybil (Sybyl), w, 92, 110ᵃ, mo, 92, 110ᵃ, grandmo, 92**, 110ᵃ
SANDY HOOK, coroner's inquest at, 2, shipwreck, 373
SARAH, Nicholas, re striking, 34, res, 34, abused just, 34
SAVAGE, Robert, convey, 174
SAXBY, Elizabeth, sis, 264, w, 264, leg, 264
George (Geo), husb, 264, res, 264*, gent, 264**, prchs, 264**
SAXTON (see SEXTON), Arlissa, md, 337, dau, 337, mo, 337
Jared, md, 334, fa, 337, grandfa, 337**

INDEX

SAXTON, *Continued*
  Mabel, md, 337, mo, 337**, 340, grandmo, 337, 340**, w, 340, g-grandmo, 340*
  Mary Stout, w, 334
SAY AND SEAL, Lord, ment, 243
SAYBROOK, re its name, 243
SCATTERGOOD, Hannah, w, 377, mo, 377
  Thomasin, w, 377, mo, 377
SCHENCK (SCHANCK†), Mr, md, 121, author, 145, 146, as Rev, author, 323
  Ann, granddau, 162†, leg, 162†
  Catharine (Catherine), w, 284, md, 363
  Eleanor (Nellie†), md, 284†, nickname, 284†, mo, 284†
  Elisha, s, 284, md, 284*
  Elizabeth Mount (Betsy Mount), w, 121†
  Rev G C, author, 373
  Gertrude, dau, 284, b, 284, md, 284
  Hendrick V B, md, 284
  Henry, md, 139, 284, b, 139, 284, d, 139, s, 284
  Ida, md 284, w, 284
  John, md, 254, 355, fa, 355**, as Capt, md, 161†, remov, 161†
  John P, s, 165, d, 165, age, 165
  Prof John Stillwell, ment, 153; res, 153
  Kourtenous (Koert†), prchs, 121, fa, 284†, husb, 284†, grandfa, 284**†
  Maria, w, 9, mo, 9, grandmo, 9*, 10*
  Martha, md, 107
  Martha Washington, w, 254
  Mary Ann, w, 139, 284
  Mary D, md, 285
  Peter, wit, 5*, s law, 162, exr, 162, md, 165†, fa, 165**†, d, 165†, age, 165†
  Peter Voorhees, md, 284, s, 284, fa, 284**
  Rebecca, md, 51
  Rhoda, w, 161†, remov, 161†, dau, 165, d, 165, age, 165
  Rhoda Ogborne, w, 165†, d, 165†, age, 165†, mo, 165**†
  Roelef, arb, 226
  S M, Esq, g grandfa, 282†, res, 282†
  Samuel Mount, Esq, author, 122, 145, late, 145
  Sarah, md, 142, 284, dau, 165, 284, d, 165, age, 165, w, 284*, mo, 284, grandmo, 284**
  Sarah Shepherd, w, 284, d, 284, bur, 284, mo, 284**
  Theodosia Stout, w, 355, mo, 355**
SCHMIDT (see SMITH, SMYTH), Claes, murdered, 300
SCHUYLER, in Rev War, 104
  General, ment, 104
  Elizabeth, god-mo, 37
  Ruth Ann, md, 97, mo, 97
SCOLLAY, Mrs, author, 212, 382*
  Anne Lane, res, 211, author, 211
  Mrs John, res, 211, author, 211
SCOTCH PARTY, ment, 28
SCOTS CHISTLR BURG, alias Edinburg, 104

SCOTT, Ann (Anne), md, 137, dau, 195
  Catharine, w, 65, mo, 65
  Charles, s, 195
  Eliza, dau, 195
  Henry, s, 195, md, 195, fa, 195**
  Jacob, deft, 89
  Miriam, md, 202, dau, 202
  Mc Samuel, appr, 3
  Susan Saltar, w, 195, mo, 195**
  Thomas, fa, 202, res, 202
SCROGGY, Sarah, w, 166, 167, mo, 166, 167, grandmo, 167**
SCUDDER, family hist, 107
  Dorothy, md, 98
  Hon Edward, Supreme Court, 153, res, 153
  Dr Nathaniel, guard, 4, res, 4
  Phebe Rose, md, 107, mo, 107**, 108*
SCULL, Mary, md, 320
  Peter, m 1, 84, 110⁶, res, 84, 110⁶
SEA ISLAND, re planters, 275, Seabrooks of, 270, set of, 263
SEABROOK (SEABOROUGH, SEABRA, SEABROKE, SEABROOCK, SEA BROOK, SEABROOKE, SEABROOKES, SEABROOKS, SEBRA, SEBRAK, SEBROOKE), arms, 273, crest, 273, -Hendrickson, controversy, 238, in Militia, 236, 237, negroes, 238, a place, 277, in Rev War, 236, 237, 276, Royalists, 276, of Monmouth County, 219-260, arms, 219, 246, 251*, Bible, 246, 251*, do, rec, 233, family Bible, 225, do, rec, 225, 276, do, regist, 243-245, Book of afairs, 230, re cannon shot, 237, cemetery, 238, in Connecticut, 259, crest, 219, English family, 219, in England 257, 258, 259*, do, characteristics, 257 family rec, 241, 255, farm, a battlefield, 248, hist of family, 219, do, re Conn, 243, homestead, 220, 223, 235, 237*, 238, House, ment, 257, miniatures 243, 251, Miscellaneous Notes, 256-260, negroes, 228*, 237, 243, 244**, 245, notes, 233, orig papers, 247, Plantation, 243, ports, 243, Shoal Harbor plantation, 224, rec lost, 253, ref, 219, 220, 223, 224, 225, 226, 227, 233, 234*, 235, 237*, 239, 255, 256, 257, 258*, 259*, 260, relics, 248, res, "old ship," 245, in Rev War, 247*, 252, sketches, 248, do, pencil, 248, silver, 237, 238, 239, 246, 248*, slaves, 245, -Taylor controversy, 232, of Baltimore, 277, of Bedfordshire, 258, of Colerain, 277, of Edisto Island, 264-276, anecdote, 265, 266, 276, arms, 273, 275, Bible, 275, homestead, 266*, 267, 269*, miniature, 274, miscellaneous notes, 275*-276*, newspaper items, 271, nicknames, 270, photos, 267, re War Rebellion, 267, 271, 275, ref, 268, 271, tombs, 265, 266, traditions, 276, in Eng land, 219, of Kent, 258, of Long Island, 219, in Maryland, 250, 276 277, miscellaneous notes, 277, ref, 277, in New York, 219-223, 276, of North Carolina, 240-242, of

SEABROOK, *Continued*
  Pennsylvania, 255, 277, ref, 277; of Philadelphia, 277, Sea Island families, 270, of South Carolina, 258, 259, 260-264, 275, 276, ancestry, 257, arms, 219, Bibles, 260, in Civil War, 275, English family, 260, re geneal lost, 261, homestead, 263, negroes, 263, orig, 260, in Rebellion, 260, in Rev, 260, ref, 260, 261*, 264, 275, 276, Royalists, 276, slaves, 263, 264, do, Indian, 262, do, negro, 262, tombs, 261, Tories, 260, of Virginia, 243-246, 250*, 251, 276, negroes, 246, ports, 243, ref, 246, family regist, 243-245, silver, 246, of Yorkshire, 258, of Westchester, 219, of Wickhambrook, 258
  Mrs author, 296, 301*, 307, granddau, 362*, inform, 362*
  Ann (Anna†), cor, 382*†, md, 382*†
  Catharine, w, 382
  Daniel, appr, 3
  Elias, cor, 382, md, 382
  Elizabeth, md, 115, b, 115, d, 115, will, 115, mo, 115**, 123, w, 123, grandmo, 123**
  Mrs, Henry, ment, 260, res, 261, 271, 298, author, 271, 298
  James, cor, 382, fa, 382**
  John, cor, 382, md, 382
  Rev Joseph B, author, 260
  Mrs Joseph B, author, 271, 298
  Lydia, cor, 382, md, 382
  Maria, cor, 382
  Martha, cor, 382, md, 382
  Mrs Martha C, author, 271
  Mary, cor, 382*, md, 382*, w, 382
  Robert E, letter of, 275
  Sarah, w, 382
  Stephen, cor, 382, md, 382
  Mrs T W, author, 253, 254, 255*, 296, 298, 301*, 307, 309, 362, granddau, 362*, inform, 362*
SEABROOK ISLAND, ment, 263**, 266
SEABURY, Mr, md, 145
  John S, md, 358
  Margaret Stout, w, 358
  Ruth Mount, w, 145
SEAMAN (see SIMMONS), article, ment, 75, in militia, 75, Quakers, 85, 96, ref, 85, will, 76*
  Adam, s, 85
  Benjamin, md, 76, husb, 76*, 85*, fa, 76*, 85
  Benjamin, Jr, wit, 85
  Elizabeth, dau, 85**, granddau, 85, leg, 85*, w, 85, mo, 85
  Elizabeth Mott, w, 85, 96
  Hester, md, 131, mo, 131
  James V, fa, 109, res, 109, grandfa, 109**
  Jane, dau, 76, w, 76, mo, 76*
  Jane Mott, w, 76, 85**, mo, 85**, cousin, 85
  John, will, 76, fa, 76, res, 76, 219*, convey, 76, 219*, as Capt, fa, 75, 85*, res, 75, 85*, grandfa, 85**
  Kesia, md, 87, 376, dau, 87, 376, b, 376
  Marianna, dau, 109, md, 109, mo, 109**
  Mary, md, 95, dau, 95, 96, leg, 96*, mo, 96**

SEAMAN, *Continued*
  Nathaniel, fa , 87, 376, b , 87, husb,
    87, 376
  Richard, will, 76, 85*, 86, 95, uncle,
    75, 85, 86, s , 85*, fa , 85**, 95, 96,
    husb , 85**, b , 85*, cousin, 85*,
    bro , 85, md , 85, Friend, 85,
    grands, 85, exr , 85, d , 85, his
    exr , 86, 95, testa , 95, 96, grandfa , 96**
  Sarah, dau , 75, md , 75, sis , 85, w ,
    85, 87, 376, mo , 376
  Solomon, s , 85, fa , 85, grands , 85,
    re m l , 85*, husb, 96, res , 96
SEARLES, leg , 152
SEEBOHM, Jacob, md , 132, res , 132
  Margaret Woodward, w , 132
SEELLY, Phebe, md , 167, mo , 167
SEEMUR (see SEYMOUR), George, wit , 383
SEMINOLE INDIAN WAR, ment , 98
SERVANTS (see NEGROES, SLAVES),
  Irish boy, David, 80
SERVIS, Ann Stout, w , 337
  Catharine, md , 355, dau , 355, mo , 355**
  Catharine Stout, w , 345
  Garret, md , 357
  Philip, md , 337 fa , 355, grandfa , 355**
  Richard, md , 345
  Susan Stout, w , 357
SEVEN STARS, theft by crew of, 301
SEWANT, sale pd in , 259
SEXTON (see SAXTON), Mr , s , 125*,
  re name, 125*
  Ann (Anna†, Anne), w , 124, 339,
    358, mo , 124*, 339, 341**†, 358,
    grandmo , 124**, 125*, 341**†,
    dau , 125, md , 341†
  Daniel, s , 125, md , 125, b , 125, fa , 125, husb , 125
  Deborah, w , 125
  Elizabeth, w , 48, 124, 125, mo , 48,
    125*, leg , 48, dau , 48, 125, granddau , 48, md , 125, d , 125
  Elizabeth Mount, w , 140
  Ezekiel, s , 124, b , 124, d , 124, md , 124*
  Gertrude, md , 140, dau , 140
  Henrietta, w , 124
  Jacob W , s , 124, grands , 124
  James , s , 124*, 125, d , 124, fa , 124,
    125**, bro , 124, md , 124, 125*,
    b , 125*, will, 125
  Joseph, s , 125, b , 125, d , 125, md , 125
  Mary, w , 140, mo , 140
  Mercy, w , 125
  Patience, dau , 125*, will, 125, d , 125
  Peter, md , 124, 125, 140, b , 124, d ,
    124, age, 124, bro , 124, s , 124*,
    125, will, 124, fa , 124**, 125**,
    grandfa , 124, 125*, grands , 124,
    friend, 124, exr , 124*, convey, as
    do , 124, res , 124
  Phebe, w , 124
  Rachel, dau , 125*, md , 125*, b , 125
  Rachel Mount, w , 124, sis , 124,
    mo , 124**, 125**, grandmo , 124**
    125**, d , 124
  Rebecca, dau , 125

SEXTON, *Continued*
  Rebecca Mount, w , 124, 125, will,
    125, mo , 125**
  Richard, s , 124, md , 124
  Samuel, s , 124*, d , 124, md , 124,
    fa , 124*, grands , 124
  Sarah, w , 124, 125*, d , 124, mo , 124**, 125
  Thomas, s , 125, b , 125, d , 125,
    md , 125, fa , 140, husb , 140
  William, fa , 48, 124**, husb, 48,
    124, s 124, grandfa , 124**, 125**
SEYMOUR (see SEEMUR), Frances,
  md , 317, dau , 317, mo , 317, 319,
  320**, grandmo , 320**, g grandmo , 320*
SHACKERLY, William (Wm), letter by , 15
SHACKFORD, Samuel, res , 185, author, 185, descendant, 185
SHARK RIVER, ment , 23, 320, 321,
  bndry , 226, Presbyterian Church, ment , 232
SHARP (SHARPE), Elisha, md , 353*
  Elizabeth, dau , 159, leg , 159
  Jane (Jean†), w , 156†, 158, 159,
    leg , 158, mark, 159, aunt, 159,
    in t , 159, will, 159, res , 159, wid , 159, mo , 159**, testa , 159, molaw, 159*, grandmo , 159**
  John, md , 156, 158, res , 156, 158**,
    s , 158, leg , 158, will, 158, husb ,
    158, 159, fa , 158*, 159**, cor , 380, d , 380
  Mary Stout, w , 353
  Samuel, s , 158, leg , 158
  Sarah, dau , 159, leg , 159
  Sarah Stout, w , 353
  Thomas, s , 158, leg , 158
  William, agrmt , 72, ies , 72, mer , 72, s , 158, leg , 158
SHATTOCK, William, hay stolen, 34; sell , 38
SHAW, Ann, dau , 190, md , 190
  Elizabeth, w , 377, mo , 377
  Elizabeth Saltar, w , 190, d , 190, bur , 190
  John, s , 190, admr , 190, md , 190,
    m l , 190, res , 190*, bondsm , 190, gent , 190, "Inn holder," 190,
    fa , 190**, d , 190, intest , 190, re
    admn est , 190
  Mary, dau , 190, md , 190, d , 190, bur , 190, age, 190
SHEPHERD (SHEPARD, SHEPHARD, SHEPPARD†, see McLFAN), Bible, ment , 279, 283,
  family, re relation, 288, do ,
  \arious, 288, Miscellaneous Notes,
  287, 288, Irish orig , 287, ref , 288,
  in Rev War , 282*, spelling of
  name, 287, traditions, 287, of
  Monmouth County, 278–288, Bible, 279, 283, homestead, 281, negroes, 278, 279, in Rev War.
  282, ref , 281, 282, 288, silver, 279,
  tradition re emigration, 287, of
  Boston, 288, of Halifax, 288, of
  Jersey City, 287, in New England,
  287, of New Orleans, 281, of Salem
  County, 288, of Saratoga Springs,
  287, of Penn Yan, 287, of West
  Jersey, 287
  Mrs, author , 4, 6, author, 287
  Catharine, w , 130, mo , 130

SHEPHERD, *Continued*
  Mrs E N , author , 287, 288
  Helena Stout, w , 313, living, 313
  Jef , md , 315
  John Mickleberry (John M), md ,
    244†, 251†, fa , 245†, 251†, res , 251†, d , 251†
  Joseph, cooper, 39, bondsm , 39
  Mrs Mary E , author , 287, res , 287
  Moses, Jr , bndry , 121
  Rhoda Stout, w , 345
  Sarah Ann (Sally Ann), w , 244†,
    251†, sis law, 244†, d , 244†, age, 245†, mo , 245†, 251†
  Seabrook, s , 245†, 251†, b , 245†, 251†
  Mrs Silas, author , 6
  Thomas, Esq , md , 313
SHEPHERDSTOWN (SHEPHERD'S
  TOWN†), ment , 281**, founder
  of, 279†, 281†
SHERMAN, Catherine Maria, w , 60
  Georgeanna, dau , 344
  Capt Henry B , md , 60, b , 60, d , 60
  James B , md , 344, fa , 344**
  Mary Arline dau , 344
  Rebecca Stout, w , 344, mo , 344**
  Stout, s , 344
SHEWELL, Miss, cousin, 193, md , 193, mo , 193
SHINN, John, res , 155, convey , 155
  Joseph B , husb , 198*, md , 199, remov , 199
  Rebecca, niece, 198, 199, w , 198,
    199, leg , 198, 199, remov , 199
  Rebecca S , niece, 198, w , 198, leg , 198
  Thomas admr , 378, guard , 378
SHIPS (BARKS*, BARQUENTINES*,
  BRIGANTINES*, BRIGS*,
  SCHOONERS†, SLOOPS††, PRIVATEERS**), attack on Haiti,
  14, bark attached, 280*, British
  fleet, 242, capture of, 178, crew
  massacred, 290, death on, 2, to be
  disposed of, 103††, drowned from,
  201, re imports, 16, sloop, letter
  written aboard, 101*††, orphan's
  boat, 17, owned, 214, prison, 12,
  do , death on, 12, sailboat, 265,
  re sailing, 102, sloop, ment , 17††,
  do , sailed to explore, 302††, do ,
  wrecked, 103††, vessel willed, 238,
  re voyage, 37, 103, war, 298, do ,
  frigate, 215, do , schooner, 258,
  wrecked, 21, 23, 234, 296, 297,
  298, 305, 314, 372, 373, Catharine,
  cleared, 18††, Cedar, 178, "ye
  Privateer," 178**, Content, 366††,
  Fortune 95†, Francis, 222, Friends'
  Adventure, 20, 380, General Sullivan, 216**, Harlequin, 368††,
  Hopewell, 73, Johanna, 234*, Mermaid, 44*, Orange, 233*, Rose,
  263*, St Mary, 380*, Sampson,
  ment , 371, Scorpion, 216*, do ,
  Letter of Marque, 216*, Seven
  Stars, 301
SHIPLEY, Ann (Nancy†), md , 197†,
  dau 197†, sis , 197†, mo , 197†
  Mary, md , 197, dau , 197, sis , 197,
  mo , 197**, grandmo , 197
  Rachael, w , 197, mo , 197*, grandmo , 197**, g grandmo , 197

SHIPLEY, Continued
Robert, fa , 197*, husb , 197, grandfa , 197**, g grandfa , 197
Sarah, w , 197, mo , 197*, grandmo , 197**, g grandmo , 197
SHIRLEY, Hon Washington, Esq , commander, 44
SHOAL HARBOR (SHOLE HARBOR, SHOLE HARBOR, SHOULHARBUR), lands at, 2
SHREWSBURY (SHREWSBERRY†, SHREWBURY), bp , 310, Barrens, ment , 226, b , 172, 173, Christ Church, bp , 2*, 3**, 4*, 23, 24, 39, 44*, 45, 49*, 69, 122**, 133, 283, 365, do , bur and d , 24, do , md , 24, do , Rec , 54, do , Regist , 4*, do , Churchyard, bur , 198*, Court, 22, 25, do , Common Pleas, 26, do , Quarter Sessions 159 do , County, Sessions, 173*, Episcopal Church, Rec , 362, do , Churchyard, bur , 198*, Friends', leg , 19, do , Meetings, 15, md , 23, 24, Meeting House, 154, Co of Militia, 34, Monthly Meeting, Rec , 158, Patriotic Comtee , 5, Plantation, 243, Poor, fine imposed for, 22, do , Book, 175, do , Rate, 240, Quaker Rec 171, 175, rum at Grave, 230, Stouts of, 320, Tinton Manor, 33, town, highway, 232, do , Book, ment , 363, do , Poor Book, 3, 39, 46, 47, 50, do , do , Rec , 12, 187, 191, Township of, 103, 114
SHREWSBURY RIVER, ment ,33, 140, bndry , 121*, North, Ice Yacht Club, 10
SHRIEVE (SCHRIEVE, SHREVE), Caleb, fa , 155, grandfa , 155**
Catharine Ashfield, w , 38
Sarah, md , 155, 351, dau , 155, mo , 155**
Rev Thomas, md , 38, res , 38*
SHULTZ, Susan, md , 344, s p , 344
SIBLY, Catharine, m l , 110e
SICKELS, Mr , md , 369
Helen Stout, w , 369
SILL, Lyban, md , 344
Melvina Stout, w , 344
SILVA, Josephine A , md , 149, b , 149, res , 149
SILVESTER'S ISLAND, ment , 17
SIMMONS (see SEAMAN), Benjamin (Ben), farmer, 266†, negro, 266†
Hannah, md , 110b
Solomon, m l, 85
SIMPSON (see TIMPSON), Catharine, md , 335, 348*, wid , 335, 348, cousin, mo , 335, 348**, leg , 348, w , 348, 365, grandmo , 348, line of, 365
William, m 1 , 110b
SINGER, Agnes res , 202, md , 202
SINGLETON, William, neph , 152, leg , 152, res , 152
SIX MILE STONE, ment , 368*
SKELTON, family, md , 297
Alice, dau , 328, 329*, sig , 329*, grandmo, 329
Alice Stout, w , 328**, 329*, res , 328, mo , 328*, 329, wid , 328, grandmo., 329*
Robert, md , 328, m l 328, fa ,

SKELTON, Continued
328*, 329*, jur , 328, husb , 328*, 329*, res , 328, mvt , 328, 383, est , 328, do , admr , 383, grandfa , 329, res , 383, decd , 383*, his wid , 383, wit , 383*, appr , 383
Susanna, dau , 328, 329, md , 328, 329, sis , 329, mo , 329, living, 329
SKILLMAN, Abraham, md , 334, 339
Henrietta Stout, w , 339
Sarah Stout, w , 334
SKYHAWK (SCHIHOK†), Martha (Marthew†), md ,333†, m 1 , 333†, mo , 333**†
SLACK, Dr , md , 143
Ann Mount. w , 143
Ann Stout, w , 353
Cyrus, md , 353
SLAUGHTER, H , oath before, 20, sig , 20
SLAVES (see NEGROES, SERVANTS), Mott, 87
SLEEPER, family, ref , 378, of Massachusetts, 378, of New Hampshire, 377, 378, of Otsego Co , 378, Lion's House, ment , 378, Quakers, 378
Aaron, fa , 377, husb , 377
Anna M , granddau , 378, has manuscript, 378, res , 378
Benjamin, author, 378, s , 378*, grandfa , 378
Elizabeth, w , 377, mo , 377
Hannah, cousin, 377, w , 377, 378**, mo , 378**, admrx , 378, d , 378, will, 378
John, s , 378**, b , 378, res , 378, carpenter, 378, his guard , 378, bro , 378, leg , 378, Quaker, 378, md , 378, fa , 378**, husb , 378, remov , 378, g grandfa , 378
Jonathan, md , 377, 378, s , 377, 378†, res , 377, 378, set , 377, fa , 378**, bro , 378, leg , 378, husb , 378**, miller, 378, est admn , 378, decd , 378
Leah, dau , 378*, md , 378*, mo , 378**
Mary, dau , 378, mo , 378, w , 378, g grandmo , 378, unmd , 378, res , 378, d , 378, sis., 378*, testa , 378, will, 378
SLIGH HEDGE, alias dirty lane, 259
SLOCUM (SLOKOM†), Catharine, w , 24†
Edward Randolph, Jr , md , 66, b , 66
Jonathan, m 1 , 24, res , 24
Lillie Adams, w , 66
Peter, m 1 , 24*†, res , 24*†, md , 24†
SLOPFR, Mr , md , 214
Sarah, dau , 214, leg , 214
Sarah Salter, w , 214
SMART, D , md , 108
Mary, w , 108
SMILEY, Ann, md , 273, mo , 273**
SMITH (see SCHMIDT, SMYTH), in Rev War, 105
Leiut , res , 222, oath before, 222
Miss, md , 119, 164; dau , 164
Mr , md , 157*, 164, s , 164, fa , 164, lawyer, 266
Widow, md , 333, s p , 333
Abigail Baylis, w , 143, d , 143
Abraham, wit , 162

SMITH, Continued
Alexander, fa , 131, husb , 131, grandfa , 131
Amy Mott, w , 110b
Andrew, husb , 332, exr , 332, s , 333, md , 333*, fa , 333**
Mrs Andrew, w , 333
Ann (Anne), w , 164, mo , 164**, grandmo , 164, dau , 333, md , 333
Anthony, md , 70, res , 70
Catharine Stout, w , 338
Charles, s , 333, md , 333
Crawford C , md , 148, res , 148
Daniel, md , 164, fa , 164**, grandfa , 164
Deborah, w , 164, mo , 164
Edward, tinman, 369, his est , 369; ovsr , 372
Dr Edward Sutton, md , 286, res , 286
Eleanor Morris, w , 70, res , 70
Elizabeth, md , 69, 94, 107, 109, 131; b , 131, d , 107, 131, dau , 131, mo , 94**, 109, 131, m 1 , 110e, w , 157, 380
Elizabeth Mott, dau , 87, w , 87, 110e, leg , 87
Ezekiel G , md , 98
George, s , 333, md , 333, fa , 333*
Mrs George, w , 333, mo , 333*, w , 333
Grace Mott, w , 72
Jacob, friend, 80, exr , 80, 87, res , 80
John, bndry , 113, convey , 159, res , 159
Jonathan, s , 333, md , 333
Mrs Jonathan, w , 333
Jonathan, Jr , md , 72
Jone Mott, dau , 87, w , 87, leg , 87
Josephine, md , 61, 62, b , 61, 62, mo , 62
Margaret, w , 92, niece, 92, leg , 92
Margaret Mott, w , 105, mo , 105, grandfa , 105
Martha, md , 87
Mary, md , 61, 62, mo , 62
Mary Elizabeth, w , 286
Mary Green, md , b , 89, 97, d , 97, age, 97, mo , 97, 98**, grandmo., 97, 98
Mary Mott, w , 98
Mary W , md , 107, b , 107, d , 107; mo , 107*
Melancthon, husb , 92, md , 105, fa., 105, grandfa , 105, as Admiral, s , 105, grands , 105, as Col , s , 105, fa , 105
Penelope, res , 145, set , 145, w., 145, mo , 145*
Peter, md , 338, minister, 338
Philip, bndry , 183
Rebecca, md , 69
Rebecca Ingraham, w , 148
Col Rescarrick Moore, treas , 143, md , 143
Samuel (Sam¹¹), husb , 87, appli of, 89, md , 110e, author, 295, 296, 207, 301*, 302
Sarah, w , 131, 157, 380, mo , 131, grandmo , 131, as Mrs , md , 255, living, 255, mo , 255*, grandmo , 255**
Sarah Ann, md , 202, res , 202, mo., 202*, grandmo , 202**
Sarah Stout, w , 332, 333, mo., 333**

INDEX   429

SMITH, Continued
  Solomon, friend, 55, exr, 55
  Susan, md, 369
  Thomas (Tho⁸), wit, 46, 183, md, 380
  Timothy, husb, 87, md, 333
  Mrs Timothy, w, 333
  Timothy, Jr, md, 380
  William, m 1, 24, pltf, 225
  Zebulon, md, 110ᵇ
SMITH'S CREEK, ment, 240**
SMITH'S FLY, ment, 369
SMITH'S LANDING, ment, 166
SMOCK, in Rev War, 163
  Alletta, md, 283, b, 283, dau, 283, mo, 283**
  Anna V, md, 62, dau, 62
  Lieut Barnes, his Troop, 163
  Cornelia, md, 357, remov, 357, mo, 357
  Elizabeth, w, 283, mo, 283, grandmo, 283**
  Garret, fa, 62, husb, 62
  Hannah Shepherd, w, 279
  Johannas (see John), dispute, 226, release to, 226
  John (see Johannas), fa, 283, husb, 283, grandfa, 283**, as Col, md, 279, res, 279
  Mary Ann, w, 357
  Susan J, w, 62, mo, 62
  William H, md, 357
SMYTH (see SCHMIDT, SMITH),
  Joseph (Jo⁸), land pd, 231, his atty, 231
  Lawrence (Lawr), depy secry, 78, s, 313, engaged, 313, shipwrecked, 314
SNAPE, John, convey, 154
SNEDEKER (SNEDECKER), Ann Salter, w, 208, mo, 208**, grandmo, 208
  Garret I, s, 208
  Gertrude, dau, 208
  Harriet, md, 364
  Isaac G, md, 208, fa, 208**, grandfa, 208
  Margaret Chambers, dau, 208, md, 208, mo, 208*
  Thomas Salter, s, 208
SNOWHILL, George, prchs, 130
SNOWSELL, Thomas, Sr, prchs, 305
SNYDER (SNYDOR†), Althea, md, 280
  Ann, md, 243†, 250†, dau, 243†, b, 243†, 250†, w, 243†, mo, 243†, 244*†, 250**†, 251**†, res, 243†, 244†, d, 244†, bur, 244†, grandmo, 250†, 251**†
  Ann Ogborne, w, 149
  Edward G, s, 244†, farm, 244†
  Emma, md, 207, mo, 207*
  Rev Garner, md, 149, b, 149
  William, fa, 243†, res, 243†, husb, 243†
SOMERENDIKE, Ann, m 1, 110ᵇ
SOPER, Ann, w, 175, leg, 175
  John, husb, 175
SORTER, Widow, md, 333, age, 333, s p, 333
  Esther Stout, w, 336
  Henry, md, 335
  Peter, md, 336
  Rebecca Stout, w, 335
SOULE, Julia M, md, 97, s p, 97
SOUTH RIVER, ment, 119

SOUTHAMPTON, Church, Rec, ment, 365, England, ment, 72*, rec, 73
SOUTHARD, Lydia Stout, w, 364, res, 364
  Wesley, md, 364, res, 364
  Mary (Polly†), md, 110ᵇ†, md, 110ᵉ
SOUTHWICK, Josiah, prchs, 378
SPADER, Mr, md, 8
  Adelaide Morford, w, 8
  Anne, md, 8, 11, b, 8, d, 8, mo, 11
SPICER (SPYCER), burying-ground, 383, & Learning's Collection, 383, in Rev War, 294, tombs, 383, of New York and New Jersey, 289-294, bur, 293, homestead, 293, miscellaneous notes, 294, Quakers, 291*, 292, 293, do, ref, 293, ref, 289 290, 291, 293**†, 294*, tombs, 293, tradition, 293, of Cape May, ref, 294, of Connecticut, 294, of Rhode Island, 289
  Mr, re mines, 18
  Deborah, w, 382, 383, mo, 382**
  Jacob, husb, 382, as Col, cor, 382, surro, 382, just, 382, d, 382, age, 382, remov, 382, memb Legislature, 382, fa, 383**, tombs, 383, as Esq, will, 382, fa, 382**†, 383**, husb, 382, 383*, est, 382, bur, 382, eminent, 383, s, 383, prchs, 383, mer, 383, md, 383, revised laws, 383, memb Legislature, 383, grandfa, 383**, tombs, 383, as 3ʳᵈ, s, 383, mcr, 383, res, 383, d, 383, fa, 383*
  Judith, bur, 382, d, 382, dau, 383*, md, 383, mo, 383**, age, 383, w, 383*, tombs, 383
  Rachel, w, 383, s p, 383, d, 383*, bur, 383, age, 383
  Sarah, cor, 382, w, 382, d, 382, age, 382, monument, 382, dau, 383, md, 383, mo, 383**
  Sylvia, dau, 383, md, 383*
  Walter, educated, 383, md, 383, school-teacher, 383, s p, 383, last male, 383, res, 383, d, 383*, age, 383, bur, 383
SPICER'S FERRY, ment, 292
SPICER'S NECK, ment, 291, 292*
SPRING, Rev Dr, res, 367, officiating clergyman, 367
SPRINGER, Addie, md, 167, mo, 167
SPROWL (SPROULS†), Oliver, md, 165†
  Sarah Ann, md, 315, w, 315
  Sarah Ogborne (Sally Ogborne†), w, 165†, d, 165†, age, 165†
SQUANKUM (SQUAN, SQUANCOM, SQUANCOME, SQUANCUM), called Farmingdale, ment, 41
SQUIRES, Louisa Morris, w, 53
STAATS, Bible rec, 36
  Johanna, w, 36, mo, 36, grandmo, 36**
  Dr Samuel, fa, 36, husb, 36, grandfa, 36**, res, 36
  Trintie, md, 36, dau, 36, b, 36, d, 36, age, 36, mo, 36**, aunt, 36
STACY, Daniel, leg, 222, res, 222, bro, 222
  William, leg, 222, res, 222, bro, 222
STANLEY, Frances, w, 41, mo, 41, grandmo, 41*, 42**

STANSBURY, Lydia, md, 110ᵇ
STANTON, Abigail Spicer, w, 293, 294, mo, 294
  Daniel, md, 293, 294*, s, 294*, fa, 294*, husb, 294, b, 294*, d, 294*, grandfa, 294
  Elizabeth, w, 294, mo, 294, grandmo, 294
  Sarah, w, 294
STARKEY (STARKEE†, see TUCKER), John, res, 170†, husb, 170†, convey by proxy, 170†, 171, mark, 170†
  Mary, w, 170†, convey by proxy, 170†, res, 170†, mark, 170†
STARKIN (STARKINS), Joseph, md, 83, husb, 83, grandfa, 83, s, 83, leg, 83, 95, neph, 95
  Mariana Mott, w, 83, wid, 83
  Mary Ann, dau, 83, mo, 83, wid, 83
STARR, Mr, md, 62
  Mrs A M, author, 62, res, 62
  Agnes Morris, w, 62
STATEN ISLAND, Black Horse, 195, re British, 195, Coll of, 195, Dutch Church, 81, first Court, 195, ref, 110, rec, 205
STEELE (see STELLE), Dr, res, 279, descendant, 279
  Mr, md, 279, his descendant, 279, as Rev, ment, 271
  Gabriel, took invt, 172
  Hannah Shepherd, w, 279, her descendant, 279
STEEN, James, Esq, author, 65, 70, 179, 236, res, 179, 236
STEENDAM, Jacob, prchs, 71
STEENWYCK (STEENWYCH†), Mr, guard, 16
  Capt Cornelius, admr, 25†
STELLE (STILL†, see STEELE), Elizabeth, w, 319, prchs, 319
  Gabriel, prchs, 319, husb, 319, re deed, 319
  Hannah, dau, 278†, leg, 278*†, sis, 278
  Mary, md, 145†
  Pontius, pltf, 233
STEPHENS (see STEVENS)
STEPHENSON (see STEVENSON)
STERLING, James, md, 190
  Mary, w, 190, d, 190, age, 190, bur, 190
STERNS, Chauncey, md, 343
  Katurah R, w, 343
STEVENS (STEPHENS†, see STEVENSON, STEVESANT, STUYVESANT), Directory, ment, 213†
  Benjamin, fa, 283
  Benoni, fa, 283
  Catharine Morris, w, 53
  Goesen, fa, 259, deed, 259
  H H, M D, md, 53
  Hannah, md, 194
  James, convey, 107, res, 107
  Janneckey (Janitie, see Judith), dau, 259*, m 1, 259
  John L, s, 283, traveler, 283
  Judith (see Janneckey), leg, 259*, re name, 259, sis, 259
  Shore, md, 90, husb, 90
  Mrs Shore, w, 90
  Thomas, pltf, 240
STEVENSON (STEPHENSON†, STEPHENSZEN††, STEPHENS-

INDEX

STEVENSON, *Continued*
    ZENS, see GOOSEN, STEVENS, STEVESANT, STUYVESANT), ment in will, 259††
    Mr, guard of, 101*, 102
    Benjamin, s, 283, res, 283
    Benoni, s, 283, bp, 283
    Catharine (Katharine), convey, 84†, w, 84†
    Daniel, husb, 81
    Edward, fa, 132, husb, 132, grandfa, 132*
    Elizabeth, md, 130†, 144†, b, 130†, 144†, d, 130†, 144†, mo, 144**†, 145**†
    Enoch, convey, 84†, husb, 84†
    Hannah, granddau, 81, w, 81, leg, Sr
    Jan, md, 259††, fa, 259**††
    Mary, w, 259††, mo, 259**††
    Peter, s, 259
    Rebecca, md, 121, 132, b, 121, 132, d, 121, 132, dau, 132, w, 132, mo, 132**, grandmo, 132**
    Shore, fa, 283
    Thomas, prchs, 125, res, 125
STEVESANT (see STEVENS, STEVENSON, STUYVESANT), Isaac, step-s, 250
    Peter, step-s, 259
STEWARD (STEWARDS†, see STEWART), Aaron, husb, 155*, s, 155, his wid, 155†
    John, fa, 155, husb, 155
    Letitia, wid, 155†, d, 155†, age, 155†, w, 155†
    Letitia Ogborne, w, 155†, bur, 155†
    Martha, w, 155, mo, 155
STEWART (see STEWARD), Agnes, md, 59
    Charles, s, 211, leg, 211, step-s, 211
    Helen, dau, 211, leg, 211, step-dau, 211
    John, s, 211, leg, 211, step-s, 211
    Margaret, md, 234
    Sarah, md, 209, 211**, wid, 209, 211, mo, 209**, 211**, dau, 211, leg, 211*, step-dau, 211, w, 211
STILL (see STELLE)
STILLINGIS, his accts, ment, 100
STILLWAGON, Benjamin, fa, 65
    Daniel B, md, 65, s, 65, b, 65
    Jane Elizabeth, w, 65
STILLWELL (STILLWEL, STILWELL), Bible, ment, 236, family, ment, 74, 280, do, names, 85, farm, ment, 282, geneal, ment, 164, graveyard, ment, 282, Hist Miscell, ment, 72
    Dr, ment, 153*, 241, res, 153*, fa, 241
    Miss, dau, 164, md, 164
    Mrs, w, 164
    Widow, ment, 104, bndry, 121
    Alice, w, 163, 284, 328, mo, 163, 284, grandmo, 163, 284, dau, 329
    Alice Throckmorton, w, 329, mo, 329*
    Ann (Anne, Nancy†), m l, 118, 125, res, 125, dau, 163, 284†, b, 163, md, 282†, 284†, granddau, 284†, mo, 284†, as Mistress, mo, 74, res, 74
    Asher, md, 164, fa, 164

STILLWELL, *Continued*
    B M, Memoirs, 74, 234
    Charlotte, md, 57, dau, 57, mo, 57**
    Daniel, husb, 74, s, 329
    Deborah, md, 164, dau, 164, mo, 164
    Delia Ann, dau, 239, 249, leg, 239*, granddau, 239, md, 249
    Elizabeth, dau, 120, 121, md, 121, w, 160, mo, 160, grandmo, 161**
    Frances Amelia, w, 149, d, 149
    Frances Morris (Fanny Morris†), w, 67†
    Gershom, fa, 160, husb, 160, grandfa, 161**
    Hannah (Hanah), dau, 238, leg, 238, sis, 238, mo, 239, 241, w, 241
    Hannah Seabrook, w, 243, 249, b, 249, d, 249, mo, 249**
    James, fa, 57, grandfa, 57**
    Jane, w, 164, mo, 164
    Jeremiah, took invt, 172, his corner, bndry, 213, as Esq, fa, 2, res, 2, grandfa, 2*
    John, cred, 40, wit, 116, fa, 102, 163, 164, 189, 234, 282, 284, grandfa, 102*, 163**, 189**, 282**, 284, husb, 163, 189, 282, res, 163, 164, 189, 234, re sent admn, 189, s, 234, 284, 328, 329, deft, 247, admr, 247, exr, 247, grands, 284, b, 320, as Esq, md, 163, 328*, m l, 163, s, 163, b, 163, d, 163, fa, 163**, 328**, 329**, res, 328*, as Major, s, 163, b, 163, md, 164, husb, 164, 165, fa, 164*, grandfa, 164
    John, Jr, bondsm, 160, yeom, 160, res, 160
    John E (J E†), author, 243† as Dr, owns Bible, 225†, owns miniatures, 243†, 274, orig papers, 74†, 160†, 220†, 247†, res, 160†, 240†, 249, s, 249, b, 249, letter to, 383†
    John S, md, 149, d, 149
    Joseph (Jos), s, 163, 164, 328, b, 163, his home, 164, friend, 227, 232, admr, 227, 229*, 230, 231*, admn granted to, 227, detr as admr, 229, sig, 229, 230, exr, 227, 231, 232*, decd, 232, 247, res, 232*, 279, 280, his admr, 247, md, 279, 280, fa, 280**, bro, 282, memb Legislature, 282
    Julia, leg, 230**, granddau, 239*, dau, 249, md, 249
    Lydia, md, 139
    Martha, md, 120, 121, 164, dau, 121, 164
    Mary, md, 74, 85, 120, 160, dau, 74, 160, 163, 234, 329, orig m l, 74, w, 85, 120, 234, wid, 120, 234, d, 120, 160, mo, 120*, 121**, 161**, b, 160, decd, est admn, 160, res, 160, deed, 232, bndry, 232, granddau, 234, single, 234, sis, 234, leg, 234
    Mary Ogborne (Polly Ogborne), w, 163, 164†, b, 163, d, 163, 164†, 165†, mo, 163**, age, 164†, bur, 164†, 165†, res, 165†, cousin, 165†
    Mercy, w, 163, 282, mo, 163, 282,

STILLWELL, *Continued*
    grandmo, 163**, 282**, re will, 227, res, 227
    Nicholls, cred, 40, in cen, 74, detr, 84, his admr, 84, Life and Times of, 300, as Lieut, sol, 300
    Obadiah, his wid, 120, d, 120, fa, 120*, farm, 362
    Rebecca, md, 55, 120, 189, 282, mo, 55**, 189**, 212, 282**, dau, 120, 189, 282*, 329, remov, 120, w, 189, 212, 282, 328, grandmo, 189**, 212**, 282*, res, 189, quitclaim, 189, heir, 189, ch memb, 212, re home, 282, m l, 282, age, 282*, d, 282, bur, 282, sis, 282, will, 282
    Rebecca Throckmorton, w, 328, mo, 328**, 329†
    Rhoda, dau, 164, md, 164
    Richard (Rich^d), re will, 227, res, 227, fa, 234, grandfa, 234, bro, 234, will, 234, s, 328, as Dr, bill pd, 231
    Samuel, bonds, 84, cousin, 84, mer, 84, res, 84
    Sarah, dau, 2, 164, 278, md, 2, 164, mo, 2*, 164**, leg, 278*, sis, 278
    Sarah Ogborne, w, 163, d, 163, age, 163, res, 163, mo, 164**, grandmo, 164**
    Sarah Shepherd, w, 279, 280, mo, 280**
    Thomas, wit, 2, cred, 40, fa, 163*, 284*, s, 163, 164, 284, 328, 329, grandfa, 163, 164**, 284*, 329**, husb, 163, 284, convey, 224; grands, 284, md, 328, 329, res, 329
    William (Lame Billy†), md, 163, 164†, s, 163, 164†, grands, 163, res, 163, fa, 164**, grandfa, 164**, bond, 190, m l, 190, as Dr, s, 163, b, 163, 249, husb, 243, md, 249, d, 249, fa, 249**
    Dr William E, s, 249, res, 249
    William I, md, 67
STOCK, Susannah, w, 223, mo, 223*
STOCKTON (STOCTON†, see HOCTON), township, ment, 292
    Mr, atty, 3†, md, 333, fa, 333*, d, 333
    Abigail, w, 376, mo, 376
    Ann (Anna†), w, 153†, 376**, dau-law, 153, leg, 153, s p, 376, dau, 377, md, 377
    Daniel, s, 376, leg, 376, exr, 376, fa, 377, husb, 377
    David, s, 376**, leg, 376, exr, 376, d, 376, age, 376, b, 376
    Elias Boudinot (L Boudinot†), as Rev, author, 376, 380†, res, 380†
    Hannah, w, 377, mo, 377
    John, husb, 153, 376**, md, 154, 376, s, 376, b, 376, fa, 376**, testa, 376, 379, s p, 376, will, 376, 379*, step-fa, 376, 379, fa-law, 376, d, 376, step-grandfa, 379
    Joseph, s, 333
    Mary, w, 376, mo, 376
    Rachel Stout, w, 333, mo, 333*, wid, 333, md, 333
    Richard, s, 333, fa, 376, husb, 376
    Samuel, sell, 378, prchs, 378, bro, 378*

INDEX 431

STOCKTON, Continued
Sarah, sis, 378*, d, 378, age, 378, granddau, 378, leg, 378
William, comm, 197, bro, 378*, leg, 378, sell, 378
STOGDALE, Elizabeth, leg, 37, mo, 37, 44, will, 44, mo law, 44, grandmo, 44**
Mary, dau, 44
STOKES, Mr, md, 157
James, md, 380
Mary, w, 157, 380
STONE MILLS, old, ment, 371
STONO RIVER, ment, 260, 264, bndry, 263
STOOTHOOF, Elbert Elbertse, p r c h s, 291
STORMES, Miss, md, 201, mo, 201
STORY, Catharine Morford (Kate Morfordt), w, 8†
William, md, 8
STOUCE (see STOUT)
STOUT (STOUCE, STOUTE, STOUTT, STOUTTE), Bible, ment, 325, 344, -Bryant-Lanning, item, 349, burying-ground, bur, 365, farm, ment, 315, in French war, 371, graveyard, bur, 312, hist of, 371, 372, in Militia, 307, Oath of Alleg, 360**, in Rebellion, 359, in Rev War, 316, 325*, 368, Royalists, 313, Tories, 310, unattached lines, 367-374, in Union army, 359, re in War 1812, 324, of Monmouth County, 295-374, anecdote, 299, 301, 318, 362**, 372, 373, article on, 296, bp, 332, 365, Bible, 320, burying-ground, ment, 319, 347*, 362*, characteristics, 362, re geneal, 295, 296, Grants and Concessions, 302, 303, hist of, 295, 296, homestead, 347*, 362, house, 305, manuscript, 301*, 354, md rec, 363, 364, in Militia, 300, 339, miscellaneous items, 360-366, negroes, 332, ref, 295*, 296*, 297, 299, 300, 301*, 302*, 303, 318, 319, 321, 322, 326*, 328, 331, 349, 350, 360, 362*, 365, 366, 373, in Rev War, 338, sol, 299, 301, tombs, 323, Tories, 321, traditions, 296, in Union army, 343, of Canada, ment, 313, do, ref, 313, of Connecticut, ment, 367, of Delaware ment, 346* deeds lost, 346, Quakers, 347, of England, ment, 295, 365, hist of, 298, of Illinois, ment, 356, of Indiana, ment, 341, 350, of Iowa, ment, 357, 359, of Kentucky, ment, 332, 359, 371, in Maryland, ment, 346, of New York, ment, 357, 369, anecdote, 368, bp, 367, bur 366, 369*, 370, 372, in Directories, 373-374, house searched, 368, in Militia, 368, 369, Loyalists, 368, 369, negroes, 369, ref, 367, 369, 372, in Rev War, 370, unplaced, 366-367, of N Y and N J, anecdote re Indians, 296, 297*, anecdote, 298*, 309, Baptists, 297, Bible, 309, Grants and Concessions, 304, 306*, graveyard, 308, hist of, 298, house, 306, negroes, 308, property confiscated, 313, ref, 296, 297, 298, 306, 307,

STOUT, Continued
set, 298, traditions, 298, warrants, surveys, etc, 304, 307, of Ohio, ment, 351, 353, 355, 358, of Pennsylvania, ment, 332, 357, 360, of Shrewsbury, ment, 320, of Virginia, 351, 355, 359
Mr, md, 59
A G, md, 52
Abraham, fa, 283, husb, 283, grandfa, 283*, 284**
Adelaide Morris, w, 61
Alice, cor, 383
Ann (Annet), md, 60†, dau, 60†
Anne Morris, w, 52
Caroline, w, 148, d, 148
David, md, 118, d, 118, husb, 124
Eleanor Gertrude, w, 59
Elijah, md, 148
Esther Morris (see Hester Morris), w, 63
Hannah, mo, 60, w, 60
Hannah Mount, w, 118
Helena, md, 283, dau, 283, b, 283, mo, 283*, 284**
Henrietta Morris, w, 61
Hester Morris (see Esther Morris), w, 69
James Hervey (J Hervey†), author, 306, as Mr, res, 299†, s, 299†, orig papers, 299†
James W, md, 61*, b, 61, d, 61
Jediah, m 1, 42
Jonathan, md, 63, 69, land ment, 238
John, his Br dge, ment, 1, husb, 6
Lucy, w, 188, mo, 188, grandmo, 188**
Lydia, md, 6, b, 6, dau, 6, half-sis, 6
Lydia Tilton, w, 64
Mary (Molly†), b, 6, w, 6, 283, mo, 6, 283, wid, 6, d, 6, will, 6, half-sis, 6†, grandmo, 283*, 284**
Mary A, dau, 356, author, 356, res, 356
Mercy (Marcy†), res, 124†, convey, 124†, w, 124†
Mercy Mount, w, 124
Nathan, author, 298, 332*, 350, 354, author, 332*, as Capt, author, 299
Philena Chamberlain, w, 42
Richard, took in v t, 112
Mr S H, author, 365, letter of, 365
Seymour, cor, 383
Thomas, wit, 247
William, fa, 60, husb, 60, md, 64
STOUT'S CREEK, bndry, 325
STRATFORD, alias Cupheage, 259, set of, 259
STREBECK, Rev George, md, 98, fa, 98
Jerusha Mott, w, 98, mo, 98
Lavinia, md, 97, s p, 97
STREETS, Dr Thomas Hale, author, 346
STRICKLAND (STRICKLANDS, STRICKLIN†), Hannah, md, 364
Thomas (Thom*), surety, 126†
STRINGHAM, Anne, w, 124, mo, 124*, grandmo, 121**, 125**
STROBART, Miss, md, 272
STRONG, Emily, md, 108
STRYKER (STRICKER†, STRIKER), Miss, md, 62

STRYKER, Continued
Catharine, md, 315†, w, 315†
Catharine Stout, w, 364, res, 364
Daniel, md, 364, res, 364
Gerrit D, md, 131, res, 131
Lavinia, md, 97, b, 97, d, 97, mo, 97**
Mary, md, 206, mo, 206*
Sarah Mount, w, 131, d, 131
William S, Esq, author, 44
STUDDIFORD, Mrs Dr, res, 243, has ports, 243
STULTS, Charity Salter, w, 208, mo, 208
Peter, md, 208, res, 208, fa, 208
STUYVESANT (see STEVENS, STEVENSON, STEVESANT), and Council, ment, 73, in will, 259
Governor, his successor, 302
Gosen, s, 259
Isaac, s, 259
John, s, 259
Peter, gives pat, 289
SUGAR HOUSE, death in, 120, Prison, ment, 281
SULLIVAN, in Rev War, 98
General, guide to, 98
SUTPHEN (SUTPHIN), Widow, née Demott, 337, md, 337, mo, 337
Col Abram, s, 327
Adaline, dau, 61, b, 61
Albert, md, 341
Catharine Ann, dau, 61, b, 61
Clark, s, 61, b, 61
Content Morris, w, 58, 60, mo, 61**
Derick (see Richard), s, 323
Elizabeth Morris, w, 70
James, s, 327
Jane, md, 208, mo, 208**, grandmo, 208
Jane Elizabeth, dau, 61, b, 61
Joanna Stout, w, 327, mo, 327**
John (Jan†), s, 323*†, bp, 323†, md, 323, remov, 323, fa, 323**
John, Jr, husb, 323, fa, 323
John Wesley, s, 61, b, 61
Joseph D, md, 70
Mary Emily, dau, 61, b, 61
Melville S, s, 61, b, 61
Penelope Stout, w, 323, mo, 323**
Pieternella Stout, w, 323, mo, 323
Rachel Stout, w, 341
Richard (see Derick)
Rulif, md, 327, fa, 327**
Samuel, s, 61, b, 61
Sarah, dau, 323
Sarah Emily, dau, 61, b, 61
Sarah W, md, 70
Stout, s, 323
Thomas, md, 58, 60, fa, 61**
William Henry, s, 61, b, 61
SUTTON, Freelove, md, 88
John, his exrs, 92, res, 92, 335, md, 335, minister, 335, as Rev, b, 335, md, 335, descendant, 335
Martha, m 1, 110°
Mary (Polly†), md, 88†
Ruth Stout, w, 335, descendant, 335
William, descendants, 335, res, 335
SUYDAM (SUIDAM, SYDAM), Jacob, guard, 119
Jane, md, 120
Mary (Polly†), md, 54, 69†
SWAN, Mary Elizabeth, md, 131
SWAT, Elizabeth, w, 226, mo, 226

INDEX

SWAT, *Continued*
  Godfrey, fa, 226, husb, 226
  Sarah dau, 226, b, 226
SWEET, Godfrey, mate, 234, drowned, 234
SWIFT, Dane, ment, 240
  Lydia, md, 99
SWIMMING (SWIMING) RIVER, ment, 18, 19, 23, 318*, Bridge, 20
SWINDLE, Ann, w, 241, mo, 241**
  William, md, 241, fa, 241**
SWINDLER, Jonathan, md, 130
  Letitia Mount, w, 130
SWINEY, Taerlaugh, prchs, 170, res, 170
SWYM, Miss, md, 335, mo, 335**

T

TABER, Daniel, m 1, 24, res, 24
TAGGART, James md, 368
  Sarah Stout, w, 368
TALLMAN (TALMAN, TOLMON), family ment, 187
  Abigail, w, 90, mo, 90, grandmo, 90**
  Ann, w, 186, mo, 186
  Benjamin, s, 186*, b, 186, md, 186, fa, 186, husb, 186, grandfa, 186, descendant, 187
  Deborah, md, 90, dau, 90, mo, 90**
  James, husb, 90, fa, 90, grandfa, 90**
  Jeremiah (Jerimiah), award agnst, 3
  Joseph, md, 65
  Margaret A, w, 65
  Martha, md, 236, d, 236, mo, 239**
  Patience, w, 186, mo, 186, grandmo, 186
  Peter, fa, 186, res, 186, grandfa, 186
  Stephen (Stephan, Steven), as Dr, bndry, 121, bill pd, 229, 231*, re silver, 237
  William, descendants, 185, md, 186, s 186, grands, 186, b, 186, d, 186, fa, 186
TAPPIN, Abraham, husb, 331
  Ruth, w, 331
TAPSCOTT, James, wit, 184, 235, bndry, 187
TASTOLF, Hudson, wit, 152
TASTOTF, Hudson, wit, 152
TATE, Mr, ment, 104
TAYLOR, house, ment, 237, of Middletown, ment, 153, Seabrook controversy, 232, Tories, ment, 237
  Mr, *B rascall*, 242
  Abigail Ogborne, w, 161, d, s p, 161
  Amelia, md, 97, mo, 97
  Asher, author, 90, 332, as Esq, 76, 164 283, 310, 332*, 347, geneal, 332
  Catharine Morford, w, 3
  Edward, md, 3, 160, 161*, 188*, 349, fa, 3*, 160**, 349*, emig, 3, appr, 118, land owner, 160, mcr, 160, res, 160*, 161, 232*, s, 3, 160, 161*, grands, 160, 161, 188, b, 160, d, 160, admr, 160, 227, 229*, 230, 231*, sig, 160, 229, 230, m 1, 161, s p, 161, nickname, 161, friend, 227, 232, exr, 227, 231, 232**, 243, admn granted to, 227, detr as ad-

TAYLOR, *Continued*
  mr, 229, cred, 230, bill pd, 231, release by, 232, d, 232, his exrs, 232, 247, re fence cutting, 238**, dispute, 238, ment, 243, decd, 247, bndry, 310, as the Emigrant, fa, 160, 161, grandfa, 160, 161
  Edward, Jr, prchs, 188, yeom, 188, s, 188
  Eleanor, dau, 160, b, 160
  Ella Wolcott, w, 66
  Essie, error, 10
  Fanny, dau, 9, md, 9, b 9, d, 9, mo, 9**
  Frank Mulgrave, md, 66, b, 66, d, 66
  George (Geo), wit, 3*, error, 10, fa, 160, s, 160, grandfa, 160**, deft, 225, re arrest, 225, bill pd, 229, bond do, 231*, bndry, 308, md, 309, earmark, 309, as Col, s, 160, b, 160, robbery, 237, as Mr, order to pay, 224
  George, Jr, cattle-mark, 309, earmark, 311
  Grover, fa, 9, grandfa, 9**
  Hannah, mo, 161, w, 161, dau, 164, md, 164
  Squire Henry, house site, 304
  Hester Stout, w, 310
  James, s, 6, md, 6
  James Grover, md, 6
  Joanna Morris, w, 45
  John, wit, 40, sig, 100, letter of, 100, s, 160, 188, b, 160, prchs, 188, yeom, 188, his est, 224, bro, 224, res, 224, decd, 224, deft, 247, exr, 247*, md, 327, fa, 327
  John G, md, 6, fa, 6
  Joseph (Joe†), fa, 5, grandfa, 5, md, 64, 310†, wit, 83, s, 160, b, 160, boatman, 310†
  Leah Stout, w, 311
  Louvinna, md, 363
  Lucy Ann, w, 6
  Lucy Ann Morford, w, 6, b, 6
  Lydia Morford, w, 6
  Margaret, md, 309, dau, 309, d, 309, will, 309, mo, 309*, 310**, grandmo, 309, 310**
  Mary, b, 6, w, 164, mo, 164, md, 375, m 1, 375
  Mary Ogborne, w, 160, mo, 160**
  Nathaniel, wit, 3
  Peter, s, 327
  Rebecca, md, 3, dau, 3, mo, 3*, bp, 3
  Rebecca Stout, w, 309, 349, mo, 349*
  Samuel, s, 160, b, 160, d, 160, md, 311, m 1, 311
  Sarah, dau, 5, md, 5, mo, 5
  Sarah Morford, w, 6
  Sarah Stout, w, 327, mo, 327
  Susan Morris, w, 64
  Thomas (Tho*), re trust, 182, debt discharged, 182, plantation, 209, decd, 209, fa, 309, grandfa, 309, 310**
  W, letter of, 102, sig, 102, guard, 102
  William, md, 45, 164, 310, res, 45, fa, 161, 164, s, 161, error, 310, as M*, res, 224, bro, 224, leg, 224
TENBROOK (TEN BROECK), Widow,

TENBROOK, *Continued*
  md, 335, mo, 335**, grandmo, 335**
  Ann (Anna†, Nancy††), ment, 312†, granddau, 312†, w, 312*†–††, leg, 312*†, md, 312†–††, m 1, 312††, b, 312††, tombs, 312††, d, 312††, age, 312††, mo, 312**†, 313**†
  Dirck† (Richard), s, 312†, grands, 312†, leg, 312†
  Elizabeth, dau, 312, granddau, 312, leg, 312
  Jacob, s, 312, grands, 312, leg, 312
  Neeltie, w, 312*, dau, 312, mo, 312**, leg, 312
  Richard (see Dirck)
  Wessell Jacobson, fa 312**, husb, 312*
TENNENT CHURCH, bp, 117**, 118, 126**, bur, 130*, Churchyard, ment, 4, bur, 119, 247, Old, bp, 126, 127, do, hist of, 126, do, Churchyard, bur, 252
TERRY, Rev Dr Roderick, md by, 281, res, 281
THACHER, Miss, md, 349
THAIN (see THEARN), Chloe, sis, 140, res, 140
THEARN (see THAIN), Chloe Mount, w, 125
  James, md, 125
THOMAS (see ELLIOTT), Jane Salter, w, 217
  John, fa, 260, husb, 260, res, 260, prchs tobacco, 301
  Mary, w, 260, mo, 260
  Samuel W, md, 217
THOMPSON (THOMSON†, TOMSON††), Mr, gardener, 267
  Ada L, md, 360†
  Cornelia, md, 134, b, 134, d, 134, age, 134, bur, 134
  Cornelius, res, 35††, yeom 35††, will, 35††, fa, 35††
  John, exr, 126††
  Joseph, surety, 68††
  Lewis, s, 35††, leg, 35††
THORN (THORNE), Caroline Amelia, w, 149
  Elizabeth, dau, 80, m 1, 80
  Phebe, cousin, 81, dau, 81, leg, 81
  Richard, fa, 81, kinsman, 92, exr, 92, 96, res, 92, uncle, 96
  Thomas, land ment, 238
  William, husb, 80, fa, 80, grandfa, 81**, g grandfa, 81
  William S, md, 149
  Winifred, w, 80, mo, 80, grandmo, 81**, g grandmo, 81
THORNWELL, President, of college, 268
THORP, Miss, dau, 164, md, 164
  Benjamin, wit, 40, mark, 40
  David, md, 164, fa, 164*, grandfa, 164
  Hannah Ogborne, w, 164, mo, 164*, grandmo, 164
  Jane, dau, 164, md, 164, mo, 164
  Mary, dau, 164, md, 164, mo, 164
THROCKMORTON (THROGMORTON†, THROCK MORTON), family, md, 297†, do, ment, 4
  Mr, bark attached, 289
  Alice, w, 163, 284, mo, 163, 284, 329*, grandmo, 163, 284, dau, 328, 329, md, 328, 329

INDEX

THROCKMORTON, *Continued*
  Alice Stout, w , 303, 328**, 329, land grant, 303, mo , 328**, 329*, grandmo , 328**, 329**, wid, 328, md , 328, m 1 , 328, line of, 328, 329
  Deliverance, dau , 328, d , 328
  Elizabeth Morris, w , 69
  Forman, md , 69
  Frances, w , 320*, b , 320
  Jane, cousin, 235, md , 235, b , 235, remov , 235, mo , 235*, grandmo , 235
  Job, bro , 3, exr , 3**, res , 3, 320*, s , 4, 320*, m 1 , 4, b , 4, 320, d , 4, bur , 4, bndry , 209, fa , 320*, husb , 320*, md , 320*
  John, re set, 289, 300, his associates, 291, husb , 303, 328**, 329*, land grant, 303, md , 328, s , 328, fa , 328**, 329*, d , 328, grandfa , 328**, 329**
  Joseph, fa , 4, heirs of, 189, decd 189, arb , 247, s , 328*, decd , 328, intest , 328, bro , 329
  Mary Morford, w , 4, b , 4, d , 4, age, 4, bur , 4
  Patience, dau , 328, md , 328*, m 1 , 328
  Rebecca, w , 189, mo , 189, grandmo , 189**, 328**, 329** res , 189, dau , 328*, md , 328*
  Sarah, w , 320*, mo , 320*, 329**, dau , 328, 329, md , 329, step-fa , 222
THROCKMORTON'S NECK (THROGMORTON'S NECK), ment , 291*, 292**
THROG'S NECK, ment , 289
THURSTON, geneal , ref , 110
TIBBITS (TIBBIT), family, hist of. 218
  Harriet Chase, md , 217, d , 217, mo , 217**
  Israel, md , 214
  Mehitable Salter, w , 214
  Sarah, md , 217
TIBLITS, Mr , ment , 103
TIBOUT, Jan, wit , 20
TICE (TISE†), Ann (Nancy†), md , 248†, mo , 248**†
  Obediah hired, 102†
TILFORD, Mrs Frank, her parents, 286, res , 286
TILTON, tombs , 323
  Captain, wit , 140
  Abigail, md , 56, 173, dau , 56, 173, mo , 56, 57**, d , 56, b , 173
  Amor (see Amos)
  Amos, md , 56, s , 56, b , 56, d , 56
  Ann, mo , 8, w , 8, grandmo , 8**
  Benjamin M , s , 64, b , 64, d , 64, md , 64
  Catharine (Catherine), mo , 56, w , 56, 249, grandmo , 56, 57**
  Catharine Mount (Katherine Mount†), w , 116†
  Edward, md , 132, d , 132
  Elizabeth H , w , 60
  Elizabeth White, w , 56
  Esther (see Hester), md , 308, sis , 308, dau , 308, b , 308, mo , 308*, 320, d , 308, w , 320, grand-mo , 320
  Ezekiel, md , 63, 64, s , 63, 64, fa , 64**
  George, md , 249, res , 249

TILTON, *Continued*
  George Morris, s , 64, b , 64, d , 64, md , 64
  Hester (see Esther), mo , 56, 293**, w , 56, md , 293, dau , 293, b , 293
  Jeremiah, fa , 60**, husb , 60*, grandfa , 60*
  John, wit , 23, bndry , 33, will, 292, fa , 293, husb , 293, res , 293*, grandfa , 293**, pat , 293, house, 364
  John H , md , 60, s , 60, b , 60
  Jonathan, fa , 63, 64, husb , 63, 64, grandfa , 64**
  Joseph, md , 116, m 1 , 116
  Lydia, md , 8, 64, dau , 8, 64, mo , 8**, 173, d , 8, age, 8, w , 173
  Lydia Morris, w , 63, 64, mo , 64**
  Margaret Hogarth, w , 64
  Maria A , w , 64
  Mary, w , 63, 64, 293, 308**, 335, mo , 63, 64, 293, 335, grandmo , 64**, 293**, 309**, 335**, sis , 308, dau , 308, b , 308, sig md cert , 308, cousin, 308, g grandmo , 335
  Mary Elizabeth, md , 60, mo , 60, sis , 60
  Peter, md by , 24, just , 24, 34, abused, 34, fa , 173, 308*, husb , 173, 308, re land, 305, grandfa , 308*, 309**
  Phebe Mount, w , 116
  Rebecca (Rebekeh), w , 308, mo , 308*, grandmo ,308*, 309**, house, 308, wit , 330
  Rebecca S, w , 132, wid , 132
  Samuel, fa , 8, husb , 8, grandfa , 8**, ptchs , 33, res , 33, 365, md , 309; sig , 365, cred , 365, admr bond, 365, yeom , 365, affirm , 365, Quaker, 365, appr , 365
  Mrs Samuel, w , 309
  Sarah, w , 60*, mo , 60**, grandmo 60*, dau , 64, d , 64, md , 64, do , cert , 308, cousin, 308
  Sarah A , md , 60, dau , 60, mo , 60, sis , 60
  Silas, md , 116, m 1 , 116
  Thomas, fa , 56, husb , 56, grandfa , 56, 57**
  William, fa , 56, husb , 56
TIMPSON (see SIMPSON), Rebecca Mott, w , 110b, res , 110b
  William, md , 110b, res , 110b
TINGEY, Mrs , mo , 255
TINTON (TINTERN†), ment , 14**†, 15, 18†, 22, 25†, 30*, 37, 38†, 45, 162, iron works, 19*, 20
TINTON FALLS, ment , 26, 163
TINTON MANOR, ment , 18, 25, 26, 33**, 34**†
TITUS, Miss, md , 349
  Ann, w , 333
  Anna Stout, w , 337
  Edward, convey , 73
  John, res , will, 110, fa , 110, his exrs , 110, md , 333
  Johnson, md , 337, m 1 , 337
  Margaret, md , 359, mo , 359**
  Mary Mott, leg , 110
  Sarah Mott, w , 110°
  Stephen, md , 110°
TODD, Anna M , w , 371, mo , 371*
  Charles S , res , 371, md , 371, fa , 371*

TOMS, Anne, md , 127, b , 127, mo , 128**
TOM'S RIVER, ment , 103, 167, 198, 317, Cemetery, Old, bur , 366, md , rec , 363
TOM'S RIVER BRIDGE, salt works, 44
TOPANEMUS, bur , 119*, buryingground, ment , 4
TOPPAN, Ann Salter, w , 216
  C S , md , 216
TORIES, ment , 321, Stouts, 310, Taylors, 237
TOTTENGEN, church of, 176
TOWN BOOK, Westchester, entries, 73
TOWNLEY, Richard, memb council, 28, address, 28, as Coll , res , 27, *cryed out*, 27
TOWNSEND, Ann Mott, w , 81
  John, bro law , 75, exr , 75, res , 75
  Jonathan, md , 81, as Esq , s law, 80, exr , 80, res , 80
  Lydia, md , 106, dau , 106, as Miss niece, 103, cousin, 103
  Mary, w , 221, 222, convey , 221, mark, 221, res , 221, wid , 222, leg , 222
  Mary Seabrook, 270
  Obadiah, fa , 106
  Richard, md , 270
  Roger, sell , 220, ment , 220, bill of sale, 221, res , 221, 222, husb , 221, convey , 221, mark, 221, md , 222, will, 222, testa , 222, step-fa , 222**, 95, exr , 95
  Sylvanus (Silvanus), neph , 95, leg , 95, exr , 95
TOY, James, bill pd , 230
TRAFFORD, Mehitable White, w , 130
  Samuel, md , 130, d , 130
  Samuel W , admr , 130
TREADWELL (TREDWELL), John, md , 81, bro law, 87, his exr , 87, fa , 96, res , 96
  Mary, granddau , 81, leg , 81, dau , 96, md , 96
  Mary Mott, w , 81
TREAT, Susan, md , 194
TREDICK, J M , md , 216
  Mary Salter, w , 216
TREMAINE, Abigail, md , 195
  Mary, md , 194
TRENTON, ment , 98, 99, 102**, Academy, ment , 109, Admn , ment , 194, attack on, 98, bur , 131, Coll of Port, 107, Convey , ment , 307, Deeds, 172, 188, do , ref , 376, First Baptist Church, 107, Greenwood Cemetery, bur , 137, m 1 , 68 69, Quaker Bur Ground, 99, Rec , ment , 158, 179, 187, 365, State House, re will, 349, Supreme Court Files, 226, 233, Wills, ment , 183, 184, 190, 235
TRINITY CHURCH, Rector of, 370, Vestry of, 32, Churchyard, bur , 366*, 370, 372, do , New York, bur , 369*, do , tombs , 368, House, poor of, leg , 152
TRIUMPH Privateer, ment , 370
TROOP OF HORSE, Col Lewis Morris raised, 14
TROTTER, Elizabeth, ment , 349, res , 349
TROUGHTON, Sam'l, wit , 152
TROUT, Ann, dau , 46*, leg , 46

U

TRUAX (TRUEX), family, ment , 346,
  do , md , 297
  Miss, md , 346
  Mr , md , 280, fa , 280**
  Mrs , w , 280*, mo , 280**, s p , 280
  Agnes, w , 346, b , 346
  Althea, w , 280
  Emily Morford, w , 8
  Getty, md , 364, res , 364
  James, s , 280, md , 280, s p , 280
  John, s , 280, md , 280
  Rebecca (Becky), dau , 280†, md , 280†
  W A , md , 8
TRUEHEART (TRUESHEART), Ann Maria (Anna Maria), dau , 244, 251
  Bartholomew, md , 243, 251, husb , 243
  Daniel, md , 244, 250, fa , 244**, 250, 251*, bro law, 244, husb , 251
  Elizabeth Seabrook (Betsy Seabrook†) w , 244†, 250†, mo , 244**†, 250†, 251*†
  Gilbert La Fayette, s , 244, 251, b , 244, 251
  John Seabrook, s , 244, 250, b , 244, 250
  Mary, w , 251, has Bible, 251
  Mary Duchess, consort, 251, d , 251, age, 251, bur , 251
  Mary Seabrook (Polly Seabrook†) w , 243†, 251†, d , 243†, sis , 243†, d , 243†, 251†
TRUESDALL, Elizabeth, md , 214, 216, d , 216, dgd , 216, mo , 216**
TUCKER (see STARKEY), Ann Mount, w , 122
  Daniel, md , 353
  Ebenezer Allen, md , 122, b , 122, d , 122
  Elizabeth, ment , 349, res , 349
  John, res , 170, husb , 170, convey by proxy, 170, mark, 170, pd quitrent, 170
  Martha Stout, w , 353
  Mary, w , 170, convey by proxy, 170, res , 170, mark, 170
TULLIS, Mr , md , 59, res , 59
  Matilda Morris, w , 59
TULLY, Robert, monk, 256
TUNIS, family, res., 167, author , 167
  Miss, dau , 163
  Abraham, md , 163, res , 163, fa , 163*
  John s , 163
  Lydia Ogborne, w , 163, mo , 163*, d , 163
TURNER, Mr , md , 156, propri , 224
  Jane, w , 156, 379
  John, md , 379
  Robert, convey , 227
TURNIPSEED, Dr , fa , 269, grandfa , 269
  Miss, md , 269, mo , 269, dau , 269
TUTTLE (TOTHILL, TUTTHULL††), Daniel, appli of, 89
  Jeremiah, took invt , 383†
  Sarah M , md , 341
  Samuel (Sam'l), appli of, 89††
  Timothy, appli of, 89
TYE, Capt , takes prison , 282
TYLER, Miss Odette, md , 281, acct of do , 281

U

ULRICH (see BUTLER), Caspar, fa , 209**, husb , 209*, res , 209*, deed, 209, decd , 209, will, 209
  Eve, mo , 209**, w , 209*, deed, 209, res , 209, wid , 209, relict, 209
  Philip, bro , 209, s , 209, res , 209, baker, 209, deed, 209
  Susannah, md , 209, dau , 209*, w , 209, sis , 209, d , 209
UMBAUGH, Charles W , md , 359
  Mary C , w , 359
UNDERHILL (VNDERHILL†), in Militia, 71
  Ann, w , 92, mo , 92
  David, husb , 92, s law, 92, exr , 92, md , 93
  Elizabeth, w , 92, dau , 92, leg, 92
  Elizabeth Mott, w , 93
  Capt John, agrmt , 71
  Mary, dau , 92, md , 92, 105, mo , 105**, d , 105
  Nathaniel (Nathaniell), wit , 222†
  Samuel, husb , 92, fa , 92, res , 92
  Sarah, w , 92, mo , 92, grandmo , 92
UNION ARMY, Stouts in, 343, 359, Williams in, 108*
U S ARMY, Brooks in, 52, McComb in, 108, McIntosh in, 358, Morris in, 53*, Prince in, 204, Wallace in, 204
U S NAVY, Hamilton in, 272, McKinstry in, 108, Saltar in, 203, 206, 216
UPDYKE, Edward, md , 345
  Jesse, fa , 334, s , 334
  John I , md , 334, res , 334, s , 334, grands , 334
  Laurence (Laurence), fa , 334, grandfa , 334
  Mary, w , 334
  Mary Titus, w , 345
UPPER FREEHOLD (see FREEHOLD and LOWER FREEHOLD), Baptist Church, ment , 46, township, 115
URQUART, Jane, md , 43, b , 43, d , 43
USTICK, E , md , 195
  Elizabeth Saltar, w , 194
  Hannah, w , 194, d , 194
  Jane, md , 194
  Sarah (Sally†), w , 194†
  Susan, md , 194
  Thomas, md , 194*
  William, md , 194

V

VACANT RIGHT, prchs of, 383
VAIL, Laura, md , 202, res , 202
  Rachel, md cert , 330
VALENTINE, Elizabeth, md , 92
  Jacob, convey , 242
  James, husb , 87
  Martha Mott, dau , 87, w , 87, leg , 87
VALLEY FORGE, ment , 98*
VAMOY, Abraham, Jr , prchs , 107
VAN, Mrs William, author , 167
VAN ANTWERP, Catharine, md , 50
VAN BRAEME, Catalina, md , 43, 53, mo , 53**
VAN BRACKLE (VANBOCKEL, VAN BRACKEL, VANBRACKLE, VANBRAKLE, VAN BROCLE,

VAN BRACKLE, *Continued*
  VAN BROCKEL, VANBROCLE, VAN BROCKLE), Ann (Anne), md , 161, m l , 161, dau , 161, 162, b , 161, d , 161, age, 161, res , 161, bur , 161, mo , 161, 162**, grandmo , 161, 162, will, 161, 162; w , 162, bond, 162
  Guisbert (Gifbert, Gifebert), fa , 161, 162, 163, husb , 161, 162, grandfa , 161**, 162**, sig , 162, guard bond, 162, decd , 162*, his exrs , 162*, 163, est div , 163
  Rachel, w , 161, 162*, mo , 161, 162*, grandmo , 161**, 162**, bond, 162, res , 162, sig , 163; dau , 163, recd money, 163
  Stephen (Steven), bondsm , 162*, 163, exr , 162*, 163
VAN CLEVE (see VAN CLYFF), Ann Jane, w , 145
  Benjamin, md , 144
  Hugh, md , 145
  Mary, md , 70
  Mary Stephenson, w , 144
VAN CLYFF (VAN CLYFF, see VAN CLEVE), Dirck†(Richard),comm , 17†
  Richard (see Dirck)
VAN CORLER (VAN CURLER, VAN CURLER, VAN CURLES), case postponed, 291
  Mr , invt , 289
  Arent, secry , 289, lessor, 289, pltf by atty , 290, gives power atty , 290, deft , 291†
VAN COURTLANDT (VAN CORTLANT) Eve, w , 72, release, 72, dau , 72
  Helena, w , 43, md , 53, mo , 53**
  Jacobus, husb , 72
  Olof Stephenszen, wit , 73
  Stephanus, guard , 17*, resgn as do , 17
VAN DAM, Rip, claims of, 30, Pres , 30
VANDERBEAK, Paul, pltf , 89*
VANDERHOOF (VANDER HOEF), Mrs , ill, 102, w , 102
  Elijah, md , 364, res , 364
  Elizabeth Stout, w , 364, res , 364
  Mary, wit , 163
VANDERHORST, Ann Morris, w , 51
  Elias, md , 51
VANDERVERE (VANDEVEER, VANDEVERE), Miss, dau , 249
  Mr , s , 249
  Abraham, md , 320
  Abraham 1 , md , 9
  Arthur, s , 249, md , 249, remov , 249, fa , 249
  Elizabeth, dau , 250, md , 250, d , 250, mo , 250
  Hannah, w , 320
  Helen, dau , 250
  Jacob, s , 250
  Jane, dau , 249, md , 249, mo , 249*
  John, s , 249*, 250, md , 249, fa , 249**, grandfa , 249*, b , 250, res , 250, living, 250
  Maria N , w , 9
  Martha (Patty†), dau , 237†, 238, 249†, 250, anecdote, 237†, leg , 238, sis , 238, md , 249†, mo , 249**†, res , 250, d , 250
  Martha Seabrook, w , 249, mo , 249**,

INDEX 435

VANDERVERE, Continued
　250, grandmo, 249**, 250**, g grandmo, 249*
　Newton, s, 250
　Ruth, dau, 250, md, 250
　Sarah, md, 136, b, 136, d, 136
　Seabrook, s, 250
　Thomas, s, 250, md, 250, fa, 250**, grandfa, 250
　Tunis, s, 249, res, 249**, living, 249, md, 249, d, 249, age, 249, fa, 249**, 250, grandfa, 249**, 250**, g grandfa, 249*
　William, s, 249, fa, 249*
VANDEVANTER (VANDEVANDETER, VANDEVANDETERE),
　Hannah, bill pd, 230, nurse, 230
　Peter, wit, 305, 306, sig, 305
VANDEWAL, Mr, excluded exr, 245
　Daniel, exr, 245
VAN DORAN, Mary J Mott, w, 107
　Matthew D, md, 107
VAN DORN, Jacob, prchs, 180
　Jane, md, 6 9, mo, 9**
VAN DUYN, Olivia, md, 167, mo, 167*
VAN DYKE (VAN DIKE, VANDYK, VANDYKE), Adelaide, md, 339, mo, 339
　Anne, md, 337, b, 337, d, 337, bur, 337, mo, 338**, grandmo, 338**
　Cessie, dau, 253
　Eliza A, w, 358
　Garret, md, 352, fa, 352
　George, md, 358
　James, md, 253, fa, 253
　Jane, md, 339
　John, fa, 337, grandfa, 338**, g grandfa, 338**
　Martin (Martain†), sig, 3†, res, 3†, as Mr, appr, 3, res, 3
　Mary Ann, w, 253, mo, 253
　Mary Stout, w, 352, mo, 352
　Peter, md, 352, fa, 352*
　Rachel Stout, w, 352, mo, 352*
VAN GIFSON, Francis, md, 315
　Mrs Francis, w, 315, dau, 366
VAN HOOK, Mary, dau, 117, leg, 117, granddau, 117
VAN HORN (VAN HORNE), family Bible, 233, do, geneal of, 233
　Abraham, s, 233, b, 233, md, 233, remov, 233, bro, 233**, emig, 233, res, 233, half-bro, 233
　Anna, w, 233, remov, 233
　Burt, res, 233, his Bible, 233, grands, 233, letter of, 233
　Catharine, convey, 213, w, 213
　Cornelius, pltf, 183, md, 225, bro, 232, bro law, 232, exr, 232, s, 233, b, 233, as Capt, md, 232, m l, 232, fa, 233**, bro, 233**, remov, 233, emig, 233, res, 233, half bro, 233
　Daniel, s, 233, b, 233
　Hannah, mo, 233, w, 233
　Hannah Seabrook, w, 225, 232, mo, 233**
　James, s, 233*, b, 233, his Bible, 233, grandfa, 233
　John, detr, 100, s, 233, b, 233
　Lena, half-sis, 233, emig, 233, res, 233
　Mr M A De L, atty, 233, res, 233, author, 233

VAN HORN, Continued
　Mary, dau, 233, b, 233
　Matthias, convey, 213, husb, 213
VAN HOUTON, Mrs, wid, 196, sis, 196, md, 196
VAN KIRK (VANCURCK†, VAN KIRK, VANKIRK), Alice, md, 55, wid, 55
　Edna, md, 59, b, 59, d, 59
　Eleanor (Nelly†), md, 285†, mo, 285*†
　Elizabeth Brewer, w, 51
　Elizabeth Stout, w, 352, mo, 352*
　James, md, 51
　John, exr, 5†, qual as do, 5, bndry, 180*, md, 352, fa, 352*
　Mary, md, 55
　Sarah, dau, 4, md, 4, m l, 4
　William, fa, 4, fa law, 5†, res, 49, bondsm, 49
VAN KLEEK, Elizabeth, md, 124
VAN LIEW, Frederick, md, 338, res, 338
　John, md, 338, res, 338
　Penelope Stout, w, 338
　Sarah Stout, w, 338
VAN MATER (VAN MARTER†, VANMATR), Mrs, d, 102†, dau, 102†
　Chryneonce (Chrineyonce), md, 161, fa, 161, wit, 278
　Cyrenius, wit, 278
　Elizabeth Morris, w, 56
　Huldah, mo, 102†, 161, w, 161
　Johnson, md, 56
　Lloyd, s, 161, md, 161
　Mrs Lloyd, w, 161
　Rhoda C, md, 59, b, 59, d, 59, mo, 60**
VAN MEUL, Dr, md, 283
　Mary, w, 283
VAN NEST, Mr, md, 138, fa, 139
　Harriet Chamberlain, w, 138, mo, 139
　Sarah, md, 142
　Vincent D, s, 139, grands, 139
VAN NORT, Mary, md, 55, 59, mo, 59**
VAN NOTE, Alexander, md, 344
　Lydia Stout, w, 344
　Orphau Stout, w, 364
　William, md, 364
VAN PRINCIS (VAN PRINCE†, VANPRINCES, VANPRINCIS), Miss, dau, 373, mo, 373, md, 373, emig, 373
　Mr, fa, 297
　Penelope, md, 295, 297, 298†, 305**, 362†, 373, dau, 297, saved, 297, w, 297, 373, age, 297, 305**, 373†, mo, 297**, 299†, 301*, 305**, 306**, 373**†, wounded, 297, 299†, wounds, 298, narrative, 298, emig, 298†, 301, 305, husb killed, 299†, 373, saved, 299†, ransomed, 299†, wid, 299†, 305, anecdote, 301, 373*†, b, 305**, wrecked, 305, d, 305**, 373, re name, 362*†, descendants, 373, lived, 373†, posterity, 373†
VAN RIPER, Christopher, md, 206
　Elizabeth Salter, w, 206
VAN SCHELLUYNE, Dirck, notary, 290, recd power atty, 290, atty, 290, compt, 290

VAN SCHOICK, Hannah Morris, w, 69, res, 69
　William, md, 69, res, 69
VANTASSEL, Barney, md, 70, res, 70
　Deboran Morris, w, 70, res, 70
VAN TWILLER, Johannes, res, 291, mer, 291, gives bond 291
VAN URDEN, Temperance, w, 236
　William (Wm), husb, 236
VAN VARCK (see VARICK)
VAN VOORHIES (VANVORUS†, see VOORHEES) Johannus Corten (Johanus Courten), bndry, 180†, his line, 180†
　John, prchs, 189
VAN WICKELL, Nicholas, sell, 130
VAN WICKLEY, Alice, md, 119, m l, 119, mo, 119*, 120*
　Nicholas, guard, 119
　Simon (Symen), surety, 119
VAN WINKLE, Antoinette Morris, w, 63
　Asa T, md, 63
　Jacob, md, 7, b, 7, d, 7
　Meribah West, w, 7, b, 7, d, 7
　Meribah West Morford, b, 7, d, 7, w, 7
VAN ZANDT, Miss, md, 338, mo, 339*
VANZEE, Ann Eliza, w, 202
　Anthony, md, 202
VARICK (VAN VARCK†), Andrew, fa, 369, hatter, 369, grandfa, 369**, g grandfa, 369**, 370**
　Effie (Effee), md, 367*†, 369, dau, 369, d, 369, age, 369, res, 369, seamstress, 369, mo, 369**, grandmo, 369**, 370**
VATAUGA RIVER, ment, 191
VAUGHAN (VAUHAN, VAHAN†, VAHNE, VAUGHN, see WAIN), Asher, md, 313, 364
　Charity Stout, w, 313, 364, living, 313
　John, wit, 306
　Martha, m l, 55, w, 55, leg, 55, exrx, 55, md, 55, mo, 55**
　Mercy (Marcy†, Massey††) w, 115*†, 123, 124†, convey, 115†, 123, 124*†, 363††, md, 115†, 139, res, 124†, 363, sell, 124†, re md, 124†, leg, 124††, cxrx, 124††, 363, b, 139, d, 139, age, 139, bur, 139, mo, 140*
　Mercy Mount, w, 124, mo, 124
　Permelia, dau, 123, leg, 123
　Permelia Mount, w, 123, d, 123
　Samuel, md, 123, 124, b, 123, 124, d, 123, 124, s, 124, grands, 124
　William, ch memb, 46, prchs, 115, 123, 124, gent, 115, 123, will, 115, 124, husb, 115†, 123, 124, convey, 115†, 123, res, 115, 123, 124**, 363, d, 123, 124, md, 124, fa, 124, sell, 124, ycom, 124, wealthy, 124, his exrx, 363
VEGHTE, Matilda, md, 143
VENABLE Admiral, ment, 14
VENICOMB (VINICOMB), Elizabeth, md, 379, dau, 379
　Francis, fa, 379, husb 379
　Rachel, md, 379
　Zilpha, w, 379, mo, 379
VERA CRUZ, Battle of, 109
VERBRUGGE, Carel, wit, 74
VERMILJE, Johannis wit, 20

INDEX

VERNER, Mr, in care of, 101
  Mr James, in care of, 101, res, 101
VINING, John, prchs, 95
VIRGIN HALL, township, 367*
VOORHEES (see VAN VOORHIES),
  Catherine, md, 119
  Charity, md, 134, b, 134, d, 134
  Hannah, md, 9, b, 9, d, 9, mo, 9**
  John D, fa, 249, res, 249, grandfa, 249**, 250*, g grandfa, 249*
  Mrs John D, w, 249, mo, 249**, grandmo, 249*, 250*, g grandmo, 249*
  Sarah, md, 129, mo, 120*, 284, w, 284, g grandmo, 284**
VREELAND, George, md, 206
  Rachel Salter, w, 206, d, 206, mo, 207**

W

WADDLE (see WARDELL), in Militia, 237, in Rev War, 237
  Captain Henry, his Co, 237
WADMALOW (WADMELAW†) ISLAND, ment, 263**†
WADY, Humphrey, bill pd, 230
WAEIR, Timothy, res, 308, prchs, 308, yeom, 308
WAILIS (see WALLACE), Mr, tombs, 265, donor, 265
WAINWRIGHT (WAINRIGHT), Frances, mo, 59, w, 59
  Hannah E, md, 59, dau, 59
  Josiah, fa, 59, husb, 59
  Mary, w, 171, convey, 171
  Nicholas, convey, 171, 321, res, 171, husb, 171, prchs, 171
  Rebecca Mount, w, 124, mo, 124**
  Vincent, md, 124, fa, 124**
WAKEFIELD (see WEAKFIELD)
WALKER, Miss, md, 202, s p, 202
  Abraham, res, 366, his atty, 366, cred, 366
WALL, Burying-ground, bur, 161, claims of, 318, family, ment, 113, graveyard, bur, 312
  Elijah, md, 137*
  Elizabeth Ogborne, w, 161, d, 161, age, 161, tombs, 161
  Garret (Garrat, Gerrit, see Jarat), test, 113, bro, 113, s, 161, fa, 161, convey, 223, bndry, 224, as the Emigrant, ia, 161, grandfa, 161
  Humphrey, md, 161, m l, 161, s, 161, murdered, 161, d, 161, age, 161, husb, 161, grands, 161, tombs, 161
  Jarat (Jarrat, see Garret), fa, 2, husb, 2, will, 2, grandfa, 2, took invt, 112
  John, wit, 162, bill pd, 230
  Lydia, mo, 2, w, 2, grandmo, 2
  Mary, dau, 2, md, 2, mo, 2, 41, w, 41
  Mary Mount, w, 137
  Rebecca, md, 112, 113, mo, 113**, 114**, gift to, 113, sis, 113
  Rebecca Mount, w, 137
WALLABOUT BAY, ment, 12
WALLACE (see WAILIS), in U S A, 204
  Mrs, res, 204

WALLACE, Continued
  Elizabeth (Lizzie†), dau, 204†
  Col George W, md, 204, fa, 204**
  Grizzle, md, 35, res, 35, mo, 35**
  Jane A, md, 63, d, 63, mo, 63**
  Susan Henrietta, w, 204, mo, 204**
  Thomas, s, 204
  William, s, 204
WALLEN, in Rev War, 101
  James, re exch, 101
  John (Jn°), re exch, 101
WALLING, family, ment, 148
  Mr, md, 253, bro, 253
  Alida Morris, w, 63
  Ann (Annie†), dau, 252†, w, 382
  Ann Eliza, w, 253, mo, 253, grandmo 253
  Ann Seabrook, w, 255
  Bishop, s, 252, md, 252
  Mrs Bishop, w, 252
  Catharine, w, 254, mo, 254, grandmo, 254**
  Cornelius, md, 148, b, 148, d, 148, fa, 148*
  Deborah, w, 312
  Elijah, md, 252, dec d, 252, fa, 252**, bro, 253
  Elizabeth, w, 252, 253, 315, mo, 253, grandmo, 253**, g grandmo, 253**, md, 315
  Elizabeth Murphy, w, 148, mo, 148*
  Fitzroy, s, 252, md, 252
  Isadore, dau, 252
  James, bndry, 88
  John, ment, 298
  Joseph (Joe†), ment, 298†
  Leonard, husb, 254, fa, 254, grandfa, 254**, md, 312
  Lucinda, w, 253
  Maria A, md, 64, b, 64
  Mary, md, 255, 382, mo, 255*
  Mary Ann, w, 252, mo, 252**, 253, dau, 253, md, 253
  Mary Elizabeth, md, 252
  Parmela, sis, 252, md, 252
  Richard Poole, md, 253, fa, 253, grandfa, 253
  Samuel, md, 255, 382
  Sarah, md, 255, 382, mo, 256**
  Theresa (Therese†), dau, 252, 254, md, 254, b, 254, mo, 254**, author, 298†
  Thomas, md, 63, bndry, 88, ment, 298
  William, wit, 78
WALT, Mr, md, 59
  Catharine Morris, w, 59
WALTERS (WALTER†), bond pd, 231†
  Charity Stout, w, 339
  Edward, wit, 221
  John, md, 21, d, 21, s p, 21, s. law, 21, est, 21
  Mrs John, w, 21, d, 21, s p, 21
  Jonathan, md, 339
  Samuel, pltf, 178†
WALTON, in Rev War, 12*
  Mrs, bond pd, 234
  Widow, bond pd, 230
  Alice, md, 201, res, 201, mo, 201**, 202**
  Ann, md, 43, 53, mo, 53**
  Jacob, fa, 43, husb, 43, grandfa, 43**
  John, made invt, 159, author, 167, res, 167, as Capt, his troop, 12

WALTON, Continued
  Maria, w, 43, mo, 43; grandmo, 43**
  Mary, md, 43, dau, 43, b, 43, d, 43, mo, 43**, grandmo, 43**, as Mrs, bond pd, 229, 231*, res, 231
WAMPUM, ment, 291, tribute of, 299
WAR OF 1812, Chadwick in, 324, Morris in, 63*, re Stout in, 324
WARD, Carrie, md, 149, res, 149, b, 149, d, 149
  Mary Mount, w, 122
  Nathaniel, md, 122
WARDELL (see WADDLE), Mr, md, 130
  Abigail, md, 344
  Benjamin, bro, 6*, res, 6
  Ebenezer, bndry, 121
  Elizabeth, m l, 24, res, 24
  Mrs Hannah, md, 60, d, 60
  John, bill pd, 230
  Joseph, wit, 319
  Margaret White, w, 130
  Maria, md, 6, 66, sis, 6*, b, 6, d, 6, mo, 6**, 66**
  Phebe, md, 124
  Robert, bro, 6*, res, 6
  Samuel, bndry, 121
WARDEN, John, md, 46
  Julia Salter, w, 202
  Lydia Morris, w, 46, d, 46
  Washington, md, 202, res, 202
WARFORD, Mr, md, 327
  Elizabeth Stout, w, 327
  John (Jno), prchs, 326, yeom, 326, res, 326, bndry, 326
WARM SPRINGS, ment, 243
WARNE, Stephen, prchs, 114, yeom, 114, wit, 117
WARNER, Mr, md, 327, fa, 327**
  Hannah, m l, 155, md, 155, mo, 155, bur, 155
  John, md, 155, m l, 155, res, 155
  Mercy Stout, w, 327, mo, 327**
  Sarah Ogborne, w, 155
WARREN, Mr, md, 127
  Jacob, m l, 127, res, 127
  Rebecca Mount, w, 127
WASHINGTON, in Rev War, 98
  General (Gen, Genl), ment, 44, guide to, 98, his trusted agent, 132; his aide, 145*, 288
  President, his bro, 268
  Martha, engaged, 268, descent, 268
WASSE, James, res, 22, chyrurgeon, 22, convey by atty, 22
WATERMAN, James, pet, 367
WATERS, Ann, w, 212, mo, 212, grandmo, 213**
  David W, md, 287, fa, 287
  Eleanor, md, 212, dau, 212, b, 212, mo, 213**
  Hannah, md, 342, mo, 342**
  Louisa, dau, 287, md, 287
  Louisa Shepherd, w, 287, mo, 287, living, 287
  Thomas, fa, 212, husb, 212, grandfa, 213**
WATHEMS, Susannah Spicer, w, 292
  William, md, 292
WATSON, Isaac, line, bndry, 187
WAY, Mr, md, 166
  Jane, md, 106, dau, 106, d, 106, mo, 106**
  Lydia Ogborne, w, 166

INDEX 437

WAY, Continued
　Samuel, fa , 106, grandfa , 106**
WAYCAKE, ment , 113
WAYNE (WAIN, see VAUGHAN),
　Martha, w , 55, leg , 55, exrx , 55,
　md , 55, mo , 55**
　Mary Morris, w , 51
　W C , md , 51
WEAKFIELD, William (Wm), nurse,
　229, 230, 231, bill pd , 229, 230, 231
WEART, Catharine Stout (Kitty Stout†),
　w , 339†
　Jacob, md , 339
　John, Jr , md , 339
　Kitty (see Catharine)
　Lois, md , 328, m l , 328, mo , 328*
　Margaret (Margaretta†), md , 339,
　　age, 339†, d , 339†, bur , 339†,
　　mo , 339**, grandmo , 339
　Mary, md , 342, mo , 342**
　Susan Stout, w , 339
WEATHERBY, Mrs A H , res , 65,
　author , 65
　Mrs Isaac, res , 236, g granddau ,
　236
WEATHERILL (WETHERELL,
　WETHERILL), Christopher
　(Christoff), bndry , 156†
　Hannah Mount (Nanny Mountt),
　　w , 116†, d , 116†
　John. md , 116, banns, 116
　Mary, dau , 376, leg , 376
　Sarah, md , 135, wid , 135
　Vincent, his wid , 135
WEBB, Ann (Nancy), md , 141, grand-
　mo , 141, b , 141, d , 141, age, 141,
　mo , 141**
　John (Jno), sig , 233, capt , 233,
　detr , 233
WEBLEY (WEBLY), bp , 23, 24, bur
　and d , 24, est , 23, md , 24, m l ,
　24, negroes, 23, relationship, 23
　Mrs , w , 24, bur , 24
　Ann, dau , 22, 23, leg , 22, md , 23,
　　bp , 23, age, 23, 24, b , 23, 24, d ,
　　24
　Audrey (Audna†), w , 22†, 23*†, leg ,
　　22†, mo , 22**†, 23**, bp , 23, 24,
　　age, 23, 24, b , 23 24, wit , 23**,
　　24, dau, 251, m l , 24, res , 24
　Catharine, dau , 22, 23, 24, leg , 22,
　　md , 23, 24, bp , 23, 24, age, 23, 24,
　　b , 23, 24, m l , 24*, res , 24*
　Edward, uncle, 23**, testa , 23, prchs ,
　　23, convey , 23, res , 23, d s p , 23
　Elizabeth, w , 23, 24, mo , 24, d , 24,
　　age, 24, b , 24
　John, s , 22, 23**, leg , 22, 23, md ,
　　23, neph , 23, res , 23, 24, wit ,
　　23**, d , 24, age, 24, b , 24, m l ,
　　24, fa , 24**, bill pd , 230, grave-
　　digger, 230 his daus pd , 230
　Margaret, wit , 24, m l , 24, bp , 24,
　　dau , 24
　Mary, dau , 22, 23, 24*, leg , 22, bp ,
　　24*, age, 24, b , 24, m l , 24, res ,
　　24, md , 24, 317
　Mary Morris, w [?], 21, 23, mo ,
　　23*
　Sarah, dau , 24, bp , 24, age, 24,
　　m l , 24, res , 24
　Thomas (Thos), res , 19, 22**, 23,
　　leg , 19, 22, 23*, bro , 22, 23, will,
　　22*, 23*, kinsman, 22, 23**, detr ,
　　22, wit , 22**, 24, bondsm , 22,

WEBLEY, Continued
　sentenced, 22, fined, 22, pd do ,
　22, s , 22, 23*, appr , 22, clk and
　rec , 22, yeom , 22, husb , 22, 23,
　24*, fa , 22**, 23**, 24, depn , 22,
　age, 22, jur , 22, gent , 22, atty ,
　22, convey as do , 22, md , 23,
　drowned, 23, neph , 23*, prchs, 23,
　invt , 23, clk , 77
　Walter, relative, 15, re secreted
　goods, 15†, 19, 21*, 22*, re do ,
　16*, 17, summons, 16, pass, 16, 21,
　kinsman, 16, comm , 17, guard ,
　17, md , 21, facts about, 21, res ,
　21**, oath of alleg , 21, violated
　parole, 21, fined, 21, deft , 21, kin,
　21*, neph , 21*, 22**, 23, error, 21,
　cousin, 22, plantation, 22, atty , 22,
　agent, 22, trust , 22, wit , 22, liv-
　ing, 22, bro , 22, 23, s , 23, fa , 23*
WEBSTER, Amy Mount, w , 131, mo ,
　131*
　Frederick, s . 131
　James, s , 131
　Mrs Sidney, re miniatures, 52, dau ,
　52
　William, md , 131, remov , 131, fa ,
　131*
WEEKHAM, John, wit , 305, 306, sig ,
　305
WEEKS, Edwin Lassee, md , 11, b , 11
　Francis, pltf , 289
　Jane Osborn, w , 11
　Jane Osborn Morford, b . 11, w , 11
WELLS, Mr , md , 325, fa , 325
　Mrs , w , 325, mo , 325
　Caroline, md , 203, wid , 203, mo ,
　203**, 204**, grandmo , 203*
　James (Jeams†) wit 324†, math,
　324†, grands , 324, leg , 324, md ,
　325, fa , 325, s , 325
　Mrs James, w , 325, mo , 325
　Richard, prchs , 96
WELCH (WELSH†), Rev Mr , ment ,
　271†
　Ashbel, md , 254, engineer, 254, s ,
　254*, b , 254*, res , 254, fa , 254**,
　256, d , 254, grandfa , 254**, 256,
　husb , 254 256, remov 254
　Mrs Ashbel, has miniatures, 251
　Ashbel, Jr , s , 256, b , 256, md , 256,
　manager, 256, res , 256, fa , 256
　Ashbel Russell, s , 256, b , 256
　Caroline Corsen, dau , 254, md ,
　254
　Elizabeth Seabrook, dau , 254, md ,
　254, d , 254
　Margaret dau , 254*, b , 254*, d ,
　254*, w , 254, mo , 254, grandmo ,
　254**, remov , 254
　Marie, mo , 254, w , 254
　Mary Hannah, w , 254, 256, b , 254,
　d , 254, mo , 254**, 256, grand-
　mo , 254, 256
　Mary Merriam, dau , 254, unmd ,
　254, res , 254
　Olivia, dau , 254
　William, s , 254, md , 254, fa , 254
WELSH TRACT, Baptist Church, ment ,
　330*
WENHAM, Thomas (Tho*), res , 366,
　admr , 366, trust , 366
WEST, Ann (Anne), w , 42, mo , 42,
　grandmo , 42**, convey , 310, sis ,
　310, leg , 310, dau , 317, md , 317

WEST, Continued
　Anne Stout, w , 310
　Audrey, md , 23, dau , 23, mo , 23**,
　w , 23
　Bartholomew, fa , 23, husb , 23,
　grandfa , 23**
　Benjamin, wife's cousin, 193
　Catharine, w , 23, mo , 23, grand-
　mo , 23**, md , 309
　Elizabeth, dau . 317, error, 317, w ,
　317*, deed, 317, res , 317, mo ,
　mo , 317**
　Frances, w , 317*, mo , 317**, dau ,
　317, wid , 317*, md , 317
　John, wit , 24, jur , 41, husb 317,
　error, 317, s , 317, bndry, 320,
　md , 358
　Joseph, m 1 , 24, res , 24, md , 24,
　317, will, 120, s , 317
　Joseph H , Esq , author , 142
　Margaret, wit , 170, w , 321, con-
　vey , 321
　Mary, w , 24, 317, dau . 317, md ,
　317
　Rebecca, md , 7, b , 7, d , 7, mo , 7**
　Robert, md , 317, fa , 317, d , 317*,
　husb , 317, deed, 317, res , 317
　Robert, Jr , s , 317, oath of alleg , 317
　Robert, Sr , oath of alleg , 317, res ,
　317*, md . 317*, fa , 317**
　Sarah Stout, w , 358
　Stephen, res , 226, re his land, 226,
　bndry , 320
　Thomas, prchs , 310, bro , 310*
　William (Wm), res , 22, bro , 22,
　took invt , 23, wit , 170, re mow-
　ing, 226, md , 310, m 1 , 310, sig ,
　310, husb , 321, convey , 321
WEST CREEK ment 383*
WEST FREEHOLD (see FREEHOLD,
　LOWER AND UPPER), Mount's
　Corner, hotel at, 145
WEST JERSEY, affairs of, 293, re arb
　div line 112, laws of, 293, Prov-
　ince of, ment , 332 Soc , sold, 383
WEST KEYPORT (see KEYPORT)
WEST NECK, ment , 72
WEST WINDSOR (see WINDSOR,
　EAST WINDSOR), ment , 126,
　142*
WESTBURY, Friends' Meeting, leg ,
　107, do , Rec , ref , 92, Monthly
　Meeting, leg , 96, Rec , ment ,
　93**
WESTCHESTER (WEST-CHESTER),
　Cen of, 75, county, just of, 74, hist
　of, ref , 70, 109, 110, Indians, re
　surrender murderer 300, Militia,
　ment , 43, plantation, 33, Town
　Book, entries, 73, Town Rec ,
　ment , 75, 110, 223
WESTCHESTER TOWN, ment , 81
WESTERVELT, Sheriff, ment , 196
WHALE POND BROOK, bndry , 319
WHALES, re wounded, 84
WHALEY, Miss, md , 267, 270, mo ,
　270
　Mr his wid , 271, as Rev , ment ,
　271
　Lydia, wid , 271, md , 271
WHARTON (see BICKLEY), family,
　hist of, 199
　Charles, friend, 210, exr , 210
　Elizabeth, dau , 199, 202, md , 202,
　mo , 202*, d , 202

WHARTON, *Continued*
  Fanny, dau , 202, md , 202, d , 202
  George, s , 199, d , 199, unmd , 199
  James, s , 199, res , 199
  John, s , 199, d , 199, unmd , 199
  Kearney, md , 199, res , 199, b , 199, d , 199, fa , 199**
  Lloyd, s , 199, 202, leg , 202, changed name, 202, md , 202, fa , 202**
  Lucy, dau , 202, md , 202, mo , 202**
  Maria Saltar, w , 199, mo , 199**, 202**, grandmo , 202**, g grandmo , 202**
  Sarah Ann, w , 202, mo , 202*, grandmo , 202**
  Thomas L , s , 199, 202, b , 199, md , 202, fa , 202*, grandfa , 202**
WHEELER, Charity, w , 88
  David, md , 88, exrs of, 89, decd , 89, m 1 , 110°, res , 110°
  Francis, md , 363, res , 363
  Rachel Stout, w , 363, res , 363
WHIGS, Mott, 98
WHIPPO, James, m 1 , 110°
WHIPPY, William, tombs , 265, donor, 265
WHITAKER, Martha, md , 274, res , 274, mo , 274*
WHITE, Col , fa , 35
  "The Miss," dau , 371
  Agnes, dau , 56, b , 56, d , 56
  Amanda Morris, w , 61
  Amos, fa , 47, 310, 311**, husb, 47, 310, res , 47, fa law, 47, 310, 311, exr ,47, grandfa ,47**,310*,311**, will, 310, 311, g grandfa , 311**, md , 311
  Andrew, s , 311*
  Ann (Anne, Annie†, Nancy††), dau , 54††, 56†, bp , 54††, b , 56†, d , 56†, w , 56, mo , 56, grandmo , 56**
  Anna Shepherd, w , 286
  Col Anthony, md , 33, 35, b , 35, d , 35, will, 35, fa , 35
  Anthony W, fa ,35, s , 35, will, 35
  Augustus J , fa , 61, husb , 61
  Avis, dau , 311, md , 311
  Benjamin, md, 49, 56, m 1 , 49, 56, 69, s , 56, b , 56, d , 56, fa , 56**
  Benjamin Morris, s , 56, b , 56, d , 56
  Benjamin Theodore, md , 61, s , 61
  Caroline, dau , 56, b , 56, d , 56
  Catharine C , md , 7, dau , 7, b , 7, d , 7, mo , 7**, granddau , 7
  Dr Charles II , md , 286, res , 286
  Charlotte Morris, w , 61
  Deborah, dau , 51, b , 51
  Elizabeth, dau , 56, 118, b , 56, d , 56, md , 56, 118, mo , 118**, grandmo , 118**
  Elizabeth Morris, w , 33, 35, b , 35, will, 35
  Frances, mo , 41, w , 41, grandmo , 41*, 42**
  Garret, fa , 344, husb , 344, grandfa , 344**, g grandfa , 344**
  George, fa , 56, husb , 56, grandfa , 56**
  Gertrude, md , 61, dau , 61
  Hannah, w , 7, 130, 310, 311, mo , 7, 310, 311**, grandmo , 310*, 311**, g grandmo , 311**, dau , 311, md , 311

WHITE, *Continued*
  Hannah Morris, w , 54
  Harrison D , md , 61, b , 61
  Henry, mer , 371, fa , 371*, named for, 371
  Jacomyntie, md , 41, dau , 41, b , 41, d , 41, mo , 41*, 42**
  James William, M D , ancestry of chn of, 323
  Jane, w , 56
  Jane Borden, w , 47, mo , 47, grandmo , 47**
  Jemima Mount, w , 118, 130, mo , 130**
  Joanna, dau , 56*, b , 56*, d , 56*
  Joanna Morris, w , 54, mo , 54*
  John, s , 56, md , 56, b , 56
  Joseph Embree, s , 56, b , 56, d , 56, md 56
  Joseph T , fa , 61, husb , 61
  Josiah, sell , 378, prchs , 378
  Leah, m 1 , 47, res , 47, dau , 47, 310, 311, mo , 47**, 310**, 311**, md , 310, 311, bp , 310, w , 310**, b , 310, living, 310, grandmo , 311**
  Lucy G , w , 61, mo , 61
  Lydia, w , 48, mo , 48
  Margaret, mo , 65, 130, w , 65, 130, grandmo , 65*, 66, 130**, name, 130, dau , 130, md , 130*
  Mary, dau , 56, 344, b , 56, 65, d , 56, 65, md , 56, 65*, w , 61, mo , 61, 65**, 66, 344**, grandmo , 65, 344**
  Mary Jane, w , 358, mo , 358
  Mary Morris, b , 49, d , 49, w , 49, 56, 60, mo , 56**
  Mehitable, dau , 130, b , 130, d , 130, md , 130
  Morris, s , 56, b , 56, d , 56
  Rachel, w , 56, mo , 56
  Rebecca, w , 344, mo , 344, grandmo , 344**, g grandmo , 344**
  Robert, fa , 41, 130, husb, 41, 130, grandfa , 41*, 42**, 130**, md , 60, name, 130, s , 130, admn on est , 130
  Samuel, md , 118, 130, s , 130, fa , 130**
  Sarah W , w , 56
  Susannah (Susan†), dau , 56*†, b , 56*†, d , 56*†
  Thomas, s , 54, bp , 54, md , 54, fa , 54*, husb , 54, his invt 170, carpenter, 170, res , 170, prchs , 171, 381, singleman, 381
  Timothy, fa , 7, husb , 7, name, 130, s , 130, md , 130, admn on est , 130
  William, fa , 65, husb , 65, grandfa , 65*, 66
  Zephaniah, wit , 306, will, 309, 311**, testa , 309, 311**, 314, s , 311, d , 311**, uncle, 311**, 314
WHITE HILL, ment , 132*
WHITE OAK SPRINGS, ment , 365
WHITE PLAINS, Rec at, 110
WHITE RIVER, ment , 73
WHITEHEAD, Daniel, magist , 72
  Elizabeth Stout, w , 351, mo , 351**
  John, m 1 , 110°, md , 351, fa , 351**
  Richard, friend, 210*, leg , 210, exr , 210
  William, note, 229
WHITENACK, Isaac, md , 338

WHITLOCK (WITTCLOCK†), family, emig , 298, do , set , 298, set , 301*
  Gertrude, w , 284
  Hezekiah, fa , 56, husb , 56
  Mary, w , 56, 223*, mo , 56, 223*, remov , 223
  Mary White, w , 56
  Roger Haddock, md , 284
  Susannah, w , 223, mo , 223*
  Thaddeus, md , 56, s , 56, b , 56
  Thomas, md , 221, 223, res , 222, 223**, 224, pat , 222, prospector, 222, deft , 222, husb , 222, 223, release, 222†, propn , 223, prchs , 223**, mark, 223, convey , 223*, 224*, fa , 223*, career, 223, remov , 223*, house, 223, 227, step-fa , 223, carpenter, 223, 224, fa law, 223, 224, controversy, 223, land, dispute, 223
  William (W^m), pd on acct , 230
WHITMIEL, Mr , md , 65
  Mrs , w , 65
WHITSON (see WILSON), Rachel, m 1 , 110°
WICKATUNCK (WICKATUNK), ment , 179, 191, 192
WICKLOW, Mary C , md , 359
WICKOFF (see WYCKOFF)
WILBUR, Anna Stout, w , 363
  Edward, md , 363
  Elizabeth C , md , 10, b , 10, mo , 10**
  Hannah, w , 320, mo , 320, grandmo , 320**, g grandmo , 320*
WILCOCKS, Elizabeth Ashfield, w , 38
  William, md , 38, res , 38
WILD (WILDE), Henrietta, md , 60
  James, prchs , 155
  John, convey , 154, res , 154
WILD GOOSE FARM, ment , 281**, 282
WILDMAN, Ann, md , 380
WILDERNESS, Battle of the, 275, 276
WILEY, Miss, aunt, 103
  Mr , md , 62
  Amanda Morris, w , 62
WILKINS, line, bndry , 213
  Elizabeth Salter, w , 215, d , 215
  Isaac, md , 36, d , 36
  Isabella Morris, w , 36
  William Henry, md , 215
WILLARD, Abigail, md , 294, m 1 , 294, d , 294
WILLETTS (WILLET†, WILLETT††, WILLITS, see WILLIS), silver, 93, 94
  Abigail, w , 82, mo , 82, res , 82, grandmo , 82**, 93*, 94, will, 93*, 94, g grandmo , 93**
  Elizabeth, md , 8††, b , 8††, d , 8††, mo , 8**††
  Isaac, md , 33, d , 33
  Margaret Morris, w , 33
  Mary, w , 283††, 313†, mo , 283††, 313**†, grandmo , 283*††, 284**††, md , 313†, b , 313†, d , 313†; leg , 313†
  Phebe, md , 82, dau , 82, b , 82, d , 82, *minister*, 82, wid, 82, leg , 82, mo , 82**
  Richard, husb , 82, fa , 82, res , 82, grandfa , 82**
  Samuel, re trust, 182†, debt discharged, 182†

INDEX 439

WILLIAMS, leg , 152, in Union Army, 108*
　Bishop, author , 108
　Lieut , author , 108
　Cecelia, dau , 108, b , 108
　Charity, md , 313, m 1, 313, mo , 313**
　Edmund T , exr , 199
　Elizabeth, md , 103, 108, mo , 105*, dau , 108, w , 194
　Elizabeth Salter, w , 205, mo , 205**, living, 205
　Ferdinand, s , 108, b , 108
　George, exr , 174, res , 174
　Gershom Mott, s , 108*, b , 108, md , 108, Bishop, 108, res , 108, grands , 108
　Capt Jacob Conover, res , 205, md , 205, fa , 205**
　James Mott, s , 108, b , 108
　John, appr , 3, age, 171, res , 171, 364, test , 171, took invt., 171, 174, Cordwinder, 174, md , 325, 364
　John Constantine, s , 108, b , 108
　John C Devereux, s , 108, md , 108
　John R , md , 108, res , 108, fa , 108**, grandfa , 108**, as Lieut , s , 108, grands , 108, as Mr , md , 105
　Margaret, md , 359, mo , 359**
　Mary, wit , 24, granddau , 73*, leg , 73, dau , 108, b , 108, md , 108*
　Mary Josepha, dau , 108, granddau , 108
　Mary Mott, w , 105
　Obadiah, wit , 321
　Rachel Stout, w , 325, 364, res , 364
　Theodore, s , 108, b , 108, md , 108
　Thomas, bndry , 49, s , 108, b , 108, d , 108, fa , 108**, prchs , 185, 326, res , 326, yeom 326, as Gen , a major, 108, killed, 108, fa , 108**
　Tylee, md , 194
WILLIAMSON, Charlotte Dayton, dau , 203, decd , 203, w , 203, mo , 203**
　Henrietta Louise, dau , 203, decd , 203
　Jane, w , 65, mo , 65
　Jesse md , 212
　Matthias, lawyer, 200, fa , 200, grandfa , 200**
　Sarah, sis , 210**, leg , 210**, niece, 210*, mo , 210, w , 212
　Susan Henrietta, md , 200, dau , 200, mo , 200**, d , 200, age, 200
　William D , md , 203, fa , 203**
　William Saltar, s , 203, decd , 203
WILLINGBROOK (WILLINBROOK), ment , 106, 107, est at, 95, farm named, 84
WILLIS (see WILLETTS), Friends, 93
　Adam, s , 93, b , 93, d , 93
　Amy, dau , 93, md , 93, b , 93, d , 93
　Ann Maria Mott, w , 97
　Caleb, md , 97
　Clementina Mott, w , 97
　Elizabeth Mott, w , 93, b , 93, d , 93, mo , 93**, leg , 93, granddau , 93
　John, exr , 82, res , 82, 93, md , 93, s , 93, minister, 93, b , 93, d , 93, fa , 93**
　Mary, w , 93**, mo , 93**, 106**, grandmo , 93**, 106, dau 106 md , 106, d , 106

WILLIS, Continued
　Nathaniel, md 97
　Phebe, dau , 93, b , 93
　Samuel, s , 93, b , 93, husb , 93**, fa , 93**, grandfa , 93**
　Sarah, md , 93, dau , 93, b , 93, d , 93, mo , 93**
　William, fa , 106, grandfa , 106**, g -grandfa , 106
WILLOCKS, Mr , re disputes, 29*, gains liberty, 29, nonjur , 29, journey, 29
　Mrs , carries letter, 27, 29
　George (Geo), letter of, 27*, sig , 27, re recognizance, 27, rescue of, 27, sell , 38, husb , 38, res , 38, convey, 180, 326*
　Margaret, sell , 38, w , 38, res , 38
WILMOT, Elizabeth, md , 42, mo , 42**
WILSON (WILLSON, see WHITSON), burying ground, bndry , 240
　Mr , md , 157 as Rev , has family silver, etc , 248
　Abigail Mott, w , 90
　Asia, md , 70, res , 70
　Elizabeth Morris, w , 70, res , 70
　Elizabeth Seabrook, w , 273
　Euphemia C , md , 248, dau , 248, b , 248, living, 248, s p , 248
　George, Quaker, 291, entertained, 291
　Isaac, md , 380
　James, deft , 226
　John, gent , 2, prchs , 2
　Lydia, granddau , 121, statement, 121, w , 382
　Lydia H , w , 248, d , 248, age, 248
　Lydia Seabrook, w , 254, b , 254, d , 254, age, 254, mo , 254*
　Martha (Matt), md , 254†, s p , 254†
　Martha Seabrook, w , 254, s p , 254
　Mary, md , 70
　Mary Anna, dau , 254, md , 254, s p , 254
　Nicholas, wit , 239
　Rachel, md , 110*
　Rebecca, w , 248, mo , 248, md , 364
　Rebecca Layton, w , 131
　Sarah, w , 157, 380, md , 375, m 1, 375, mo , 375*
　Thomas, md , 273, res , 273
　William, md , 90, 131, b , 131, d , 131, bur , 131, fa , 248, husb , 248
　Rev William V , husb , 248, md , 254*, 382*, res , 254, 382, fa , 254*, s p , 254
WINANS, Cornelius, his exr , 84
WINDER, Elizabeth, w , 108
　John, md , 108
WINDSOR (see EAST WINDSOR, WEST WINDSOR), township, 117, 122, 128
WINSLOW, Susan, md , 343, s p , 343
WINSON, ment , 348
WINTER (WINTERS†), family, ment , 120, in Rev War, 281
　Miss, md , 67, dau , 281
　Mr , md , 283
　Andrew, took invt , 279, s , 281, md , 281
　Deborah, md , 120*, 281, mo , 120, dau , 281
　Deborah Golden, w , 67
　James, md , 279, 281, d , 281, fa , 281**

WINTER, Continued
　Joseph, md , 67
　Mary Shepherd, w , 279, 281, mo , 281**
　Rachel, w , 281
　Rebecca Shepherd, b , 283, w , 283
　Sarah, dau 281
WIRTZ, Commission, ment , 109
WISE, Joshua, wit , 246
WITCH HOLLOW, alias Highlands, 4, or Navesink, ment , 4
WOBURN burying-ground, bur , 178
WOLCOTT, Ann (Anne), md , 65*, dau , 65, b , 65, d , 65, age, 65, mo , 65**, w , 65, grandmo , 65**
　Benjamin, fa , 65, husb , 65, grandfa , 65**
　Mary, mo , 48
WOLFE, Miss, md , 252
WOLSEY, Lucretia, md , 42
WOOD (WOODS†), Consider, ment , 220†
　Dolly, md , 235, mo , 235
　Hannah, md , 110°
　Jemima, granddau , 80, leg , 80
　Jemima Mott, w , 81, mo , 81
　Lockie, md , 60
　Phebe, granddau , 80, dau , 80, leg , 80
　Rebecca (see Lockie)
　Richard, s , 81, bp , 81
　Stephen, fa , 80, 81, leg , 80, detr , 80, md , 81
WOODBRIDGE (WOODBRIDE†, WOOD BRIDGE††), bur , 331, jail, ment , 27, do , attack on, 27, 29, land at, 158†, Monthly Meeting, Minutes of, 158**, Presbyterian Cemetery, bur , 331, tavern at, 236*
WOODBURY, Alice, md , 206, mo , 206
WOODHOUSE, Lydia Woodward, w , 132
　William, md , 132, res , 132
WOODMANSEE (WOODMANSIL), lands in New England, 174
　Miss, md , 173
　Abigail, dau , 174, leg , 174
　Ann, dau , 174, leg , 174
　David, s , 173, leg , 173, wit , 174
　Elizabeth, dau , 174, leg , 174
　Gabriel, s , 173, leg , 173
　Hannah, dau , 174, leg , 174
　John, s , 173, leg , 173, wit , 174
　Lydia (Leadea), dau , 174, leg , 174
　Margaret, dau , 174, leg , 174
　Sarah, dau , 174, leg 174
　Thomas, s , 173, leg , 173, will, 173, res , 173, 3 eom , 173, husb , 173, 174, fa , 173**, 174**, sig , 174
WOODRUFF (WOODRUF), Eliza, md , 358, mo , 358**, grandmo , 358**
　Elizabeth, m 1 47, res , 47
　Jane, md , 358, mo , 358**
WOODWARD, Adelina, w , 252
　Anthony, fa , 121, s , 121, 133, grandfa , 121, d , 133, age, 133, as the Second, fa , 132, grandfa , 132**, 133*
　E M , author, 132
　George, s , 132*, md , 132*, remov , 132, b , 132, d , 132, age, 132, re md , 132, fa , 132**, 133*
　George S , md , 121, m 1, 121, s , 121, grands , 121
　J K , md , 252

INDEX

WOODWARD, Continued
  Jesse, s , 132, d , s p , 132
  Lydia, dau , 132, md , 132
  Margaret, dau. 132, md , 132
  Margaret Mount, w , 121, 132, d ,
    121, age 121, mo , 132**, 133*
  Margaret Wynkoop, w , 132, remov ,
    132
  Martha, dau , 133, md , 133
  Rebecca, dau , 132, md , 132
  Thomas will, 168, res 168
WOOLLEY (WOOLEY), family, ment ,
    309
  Abigail, w , 234, mo , 234, grandmo ,
    234
  Adam, wit 321, pr will, 321
  Adria (see Audrey), md , 120*, dau ,
    120, res , 120
  Annie Forsyth, w , 60
  Audrey (Ordery†, see Adria), md ,
    120*, m 1 , 120*, w , 120*†, mo ,
    120**†
  Bartholomew, md , 120, wit , 120,
    d , 120
  Benjamin, md , 308*, 309**, fa , 308,
    b . 309, s , 309, husb , 309, fa ,
    309*
  Mr Brittain, age, 10
  Catharine, md , 69, w , 309
  Catharine Hatfield (Katie Hatfield†),
    w , 60†
  Catherine Maria, b , 60, dau , 60,
    md , 60
  Charles Henry, s , 60, b , 60, md ,
    60*
  Daniel, md , 60, s , 60, b , 60, d , 60,
    fa , 60**
  Dr Daniel Morris, s , 60, b , 60, md ,
    60
  Edith, w , 60
  Edward, convey , 171
  Elizabeth, md , 23, w , 294, 325,
    mo , 294, 325, grandmo , 294, 325
  Elizabeth Mason, w , 60
  Emeline, w , 66, mo , 66, grandmo ,
    66**
  Esther, decd , 308, mo , 308**, dau ,
    308
  Esther Stout, w , 308*, 309*, b , 308,
    309, dau , 308, 309, mo , 308, d ,
    309*
  George W , s , 60, b , 60, md , 60*
  Hannah, w , 120, wit , 120, wid 120,
    md , 120, grandmo , 120**
  Mrs Hannah Wardell, w , 60, d , 60
  Henrietta Wilde, w , 60
  Jane Pierce, w , 60
  Janie Bush, w , 60
  John, md , 171*, 329, 380, do , cert ,
    308, 329, agent, 171, s law, 171,
    friend, 171, yeom , 171, fa , 172,
    309, husb , 309, 380
  John, Jr , prchs , 308, 321
  John Wesley, s , 60, b , 60, d , 60,
    md , 60
  Joseph Addison, s , 60, b , 60, md ,
    60*
  Julia A , w , 60, d , 60
  Lockie Wood, w , 60
  Louis F , s , 60, b , 60, d , 60, md , 60
  Lydia, w , 60, mo , 60, grandmo ,
    60**
  Mary, dau , 171, leg , 171
  Mary A , md , 66, dau , 66, b , 66,
    d , 66, mo , 66**

WOOLEY, Continued
  Mary Finnegan, w , 60
  Mary Potter (see Mercy Potter),
    w , 171
  Mercy, dau , 171, leg , 171*, affi ,
    171, w , 309, 380, mo , 309
  Mercy Potter (see Mary Potter), w ,
    171
  Montillon, fa , 60, 66, husb , 60,
    66, grandfa , 60**, 66**
  Patience, w , 308, 329
  Phebe, w , 309
  Rachel, w , 380
  Rebecca (see Lockie Wood)
  Sarah Morris, w , 70
  William (Wm), wit , 23, md , 70,
    exr , 172, s , 172, 320, res , 172,
    320, prchs , 172, 320*, re mowing,
    227, bill pd , 230, fa , 320, yeom ,
    320
WOOLMAN, Asher, husb , 210
  Rachel, niece, 210, w , 210, leg , 210
WOOLSTON, gravestones, 377
  Ann, w , 377, mo , 377
  Barzillai, d , 377, age, 377, tombs ,
    377
  Jacob, fa , 124, grandfa , 124*
  Job, d , 377, age, 377, tombs , 377
  John, fa , 377, husb , 377, grandfa ,
    377**
  Joseph, d , 377, age, 377, tombs , 377
  Joshua, d , 377, age, 377, tombs , 377
  Lettice, w , 377, mo , 377, grandmo ,
    377
  Michael md , 376, 377, husb , 376*,
    convey , 376, b , 377, d , 377, age,
    377, will, 377, fa , 377**, s , 377,
    step-fa , 377*
  Sarah, md , 124, dau , 124, mo ,
    124**, 377**, dau law, 376, step-
    dau , 376, leg , 376, w , 376*, 377**,
    convey , 376, will, 377*, grandmo ,
    377**, invt , 377, mo law, 377, g -
    grandmo , 377**
WORTH, Mr , md , 333, fa , 333*
  Ann Stout, w , 333, mo , 333*
  William, friend, 175, leg , 175, 381,
    res , 175, 381
WORTHLEY, Laura M , md , 9, 11,
    mo , 11
WORTMAN, Clementina Stout, w , 357
  John, md , 357
WRIGHT, Ann (Anne), md , 138, b ,
    138, d , 138, bur , 138, mo , 138*,
    w , 190
  Catharine, md , 195, prchs , 195,
    mo , 195**, m 1 , 195, grandmo ,
    195,
  Daniel, husb , 86*
  Ellis, md , 190, admr , 190
  Jane, md , 56
  Jonathan, res , 376, convey , 376,
    exrs advertise, 379, farm, 379
  Maria, md , 70, res , 70
  Phebe Mott, dau , 86, w , 86*, leg ,
    86
  Thomas, res , 318, husb , 318, offer
    to , 318, re deed, 318, his descend-
    ants, 318, re set , 318, div land,
    318
WRIGHTON, Henry, wit , 262, just ,
    262
WURDEMANN, Caroline Morford, b ,
    9, d , 9, w , 9
  William, md , 9

**WYCKOFF (WIKOFF, WYCOFF,
    WYKOFF)**, Miss, md , 236, 316,
    340, mo , 316*, grandmo , 316**
  Almira Morford, w , 9
  David S , md , 9
  Frederick D , md , 10
  Garret P (Garrit P), buy, 136;
    admr , 136
  Hannah Stout, w , 334, mo , 334,
    grandmo , 334
  Jacob, resgn , 237, sig , 237
  James, md , 334, m 1 , 334, fa , 334,
    grandfa , 334
  John, md , 338, 357
  Laura M , w , 10
  Laura M Morford, b , 10, w , 10
  Lydia, w , 165
  Mary, w , 140, mo , 140, dau , 334,
    md , 334
  Mercy, md , 125, d , 125
  Peter, s , 334, fa , 334
  Sarah Stout, w , 338, 357
  Susan J , w , 62, mo , 62
  William, appr , 5, md , 165, res , 165
  Williampe, md , 351, mo , 351**
WYNKOOP, Margaret, md , 132

Y

YALE COLLEGE, ment , 42
YARD, Catharine (Cataline†, Cateline†),
    sig , 310†, convey , 310†, sis , 310†,
    leg , 310†
  Catharine Stout, w , 310, living, 310,
    age, 310
  George, md , 310
YARDS (see BURYING-GROUNDS,
    CEMETERIES, CHURCH-
    YARDS), Baptist Meeting, ment ,
    376, Cranbury, bur , 117, do ,
    graves in, 126, Hightstown, bur ,
    138*, St Andrew's, bur , 377, do ,
    tombs , 377
YARNELL, Mary, w , 186*, living, 186
  Francis, husb , 186, living, 186, bro -
    law, 186
  Francis, Jr , md , 186
YARROW, Thomas (Thos), exr , 58
YATES, Hannah, md , 380
YELLOW MEETING HOUSE, ment ,
    13, graveyard, 183, memb , of, 123
YONGE'S ISLAND, ment , 266
YORK, ment , 106, 107*, alias Little
    Creek Hundred, 96
  Duke of, his commrs , 73
YORKSHIRE, North Riding of, ment ,
    219*, West Riding of, Court of, 291
YOUMANS, Hannah, md , 70, 341, 344,
    res , 70, mo , 344**
  Rebecca, md , 57, 60, mo , 60*,
    grandmo , 60*
YOUNG (YOUNGS†), family, ment , 84
  Archilus, pltf , 89
  Hannah, mo , 110†
  Henry, depn , 84
YOUNGHUSBAND, Isaac, wit , 245
  Isaac, Junr, wit , 245
  Pleasant, his Corner, 245, wit , 245

Z

ZACHES, Lamuecrt, wit , 20
ZANKIN, cousins, ment , 103, girls,
    ment , 104
ZENGER, case, re liberty of press, 30
ZIMMERMAN, Mr , md , 277*, res , 277
  Elizabeth Seabrook, w , 277
  Florence Seabrook, 277

CPSIA information can be obtained
at www.ICGtesting.com
Printed in the USA
BVOW06*0233130217
476020BV00007B/29/P